D1061304

THE MAJOR
SEAPORTS OF THE
UNITED KINGDOM

QUEENHITHE, LONDON, AT LOW TIDE

Looking north-west. Formerly *Ripa Reginae quae appelatur Athereshethe* (*temp*. Henry II, twelfth century)
and Æderedys Hyde (A.D. 899). Located on Fig. 85.

THE MAJOR SEAPORTS OF THE UNITED KINGDOM

JAMES BIRD
B.A., PH.D.

Lecturer in Geography
University of London King's College

HUTCHINSON OF LONDON

HUTCHINSON & CO. (Publishers) LTD
178–202 Great Portland Street, London, W.1

London Melbourne Sydney
Auckland Bombay Toronto
Johannesburg New York

First published 1963

*This book has been set in Bembo type face. It has
been printed in Great Britain by The Anchor Press,
Ltd., in Tiptree, Essex, on Smooth Wove paper.*

To my wife

CONTENTS

CONTENTS

CONTENTS

ILLUSTRATIONS

PLATES

MAPS AND DIAGRAMS

ACKNOWLEDGEMENTS

Acknowledgements are made beneath plates and figures. Many of the line drawings in this book are based upon Ordnance Survey maps which are Crown Copyright protected, and such drawings have been inserted by permission of the Controller of H.M. Stationery Office. Figs. 26 and 27 are based, by permission, on the Crown Copyright maps of the Ordnance Survey of Northern Ireland.

PREFACE

THIS BOOK would have been impossible without the full co-operation of all the port and conservancy authorities concerned who allowed visits to their installations and in many a friendly interview presented the viewpoint of those responsible for port administration and operation day by day. I am also very sensible of my debt to many writers on special topics. On the other hand, I have tried to maximize a possible advantage of a one-man attack on a wide subject—by instituting comparisons between ports wherever that seemed to throw more light upon them. The references are arranged at the end of each chapter to give a bibliography port by port. No such general bibliography of British ports has hitherto been compiled, and I hope that those who wish to carry some aspect of port study further than has been possible here will find some signposts among the references. It has proved impossible to study at first hand all port books, company minutes, and the MS. sources inherited by port authorities. When these have been thoroughly examined no doubt my tables of 'eras of development' will need amendment. But my principal objective has been to attempt an explanation of the ports as they are today, emphasizing only those events of the past throwing the greatest light upon the present scene.

In order to concentrate on port installations, the material on shipping and port labour has been curtailed. Hitherto the studies of ships and shipping lines have been more numerous than discussions of their terminals. Port labour is a complicated subject. On the goodwill of dock workers all ports depend, but apart from describing some features of the present labour position, there has been space only to direct readers to the specialist literature cited.

As this study was drawing to a close the Minister of Transport announced the setting up of a comprehensive Committee of Inquiry into the Major Ports of Great Britain. This text has been submitted as evidence to that Committee which has the responsibility of making recommendations about the future of British ports. Thus I have felt free in the last chapter to put forward some propositions together with the evidence that seemed to call them into existence. Even if the propositions meet with disagreement, the evidence might be of interest. The proposition that I would most strongly urge is one that the Rochdale Committee might make with diffidence —that such a committee, or a port research organization, should be a permanency.*

It is a pleasure to acknowledge much assistance in the preparation of this book. Professor R. Ogilvie Buchanan, M.A.N.Z., B.SC. (ECON.), PH.D., most kindly read through the whole text, and his advice has been of the greatest value. Miss E. M.

---

* This proved to be one of the principal conclusions in the *Report* of the Rochdale Committee; these conclusions are summarized in the Appendix to this book.

Horsley of Messrs. Hutchinson & Co. (Publishers) Ltd. was always patient with my demands for complicated lay-outs. Miss J. Chaundy drew most of the maps with help from Miss E. Woodhams. Both are cartographers in the Joint School of Geography, University of London King's College—London School of Economics and Political Science. Mrs. M. E. Sinclair also performed equal wonders with some of my queer pencil drafts; and Mr. C. R. Polglaze, Chief Technician of the Department of Geography, University of London King's College, patiently carried out the required miracles with his photographic equipment. Grants from the Central Research Fund of the University of London and from the University of London King's College have assisted me in meeting the fieldwork and cartographic expenses encountered.

I should also like to thank my fellow-geographers, members of the Institute of British Geographers, many of whom gave freely of their expert advice on aspects of British ports with which they are familiar as local objects of study. My wife, who is also a geographer, became secretary to the whole project and helped to compile many of the statistical tables. Without her encouragement I never should have started; without her aid, I never should have finished.

JAMES BIRD

Department of Geography,
  University of London King's College, 1962

THE MAJOR
SEAPORTS OF THE
UNITED KINGDOM

INTRODUCTION

Chapter 1

METHOD OF ATTACK:
THE DEVELOPMENT OF *ANYPORT*

OF THE 112 British seaports recognized by Her Majesty's Customs for statistical purposes, only about a dozen deserve the adjective 'major', dealing as they do with nine-tenths of the total foreign trade by value. Whatever method is used to choose the major seaports of the United Kingdom, based on whatever lower limit is chosen, some large ports will fall just below a line rigidly drawn. Port statistics must be handled with great care if they are to give valid comparisons of the size of port functions, and some of the statistical pitfalls are summarized below.[1]

TABLE I

Criteria for Assessing Comparative Sizes of Ports

Criteria	Main Disadvantage
Berthing accommodation for ships Capacity for cargo handling	} May not be fully used by vessels trading regularly
Depth of port approaches Depth of accommodation for ships	} Ports which can accommodate the largest ships are not necessarily the largest ports
Weight of cargoes landed and shipped	Raw material and fuel-handling ports over-'weighted'
Value of cargoes landed and shipped	Fluctuates with rise and fall of prices
Net registered tonnage of shipping entering	Vessels may arrive with partly-loaded cargoes or in ballast

This analysis shows that the disadvantages of two of the criteria cancel each other out to some extent; value of cargoes landed and shipped; and net registered tonnage of shipping entering.

The value of overseas cargo dealt with at British ports is accurately known for H.M. Customs purposes, although the value of coastwise cargoes carried between British ports are not classified and published. Variations in monetary values are obviously not a difficulty in this study since the ports in question are all in the same country. If the criterion of value is used, ports handling highly priced foods and manufactured goods will certainly appear at an advantage over those handling bulky raw materials and fuels. So they should. As cargoes increase in value per unit of weight, so increases the complexity of their handling within the port area. This generalization is modified in practice by the actual volume of cargoes; for example, the most valuable cargoes, like jewellery, bullion, and *objets d'art*, may occupy very little space. The coastwise trade of the port, mainly dealing with cargoes of low value per unit of weight, the passenger trade, and any distortions due to very small cargoes of very high value are taken into account by considering the net registered tonnage of shipping foreign and coastwise entering the port. In return, the disadvantage of this criterion, which is that the ships entering may not be fully loaded, is countered by the first criterion—the value of goods actually dealt with by the port. By using these two sets of figures in conjunction, the major ports of the United Kingdom may be found.[2]

If the ports of the United Kingdom are arranged in two lists, in descending order of magnitude, according to the net registered tonnage of all ships entering, and secondly according to values of overseas cargoes landed and shipped, the major ports are those that appear among the first ten in either of the two lists. There is a similarity between the two lists, though Belfast, Harwich, Newcastle, and Swansea

TABLE 2

Ports of the United Kingdom Arranged in Order of Net Registered Tonnage of Ships Arriving with Cargo and in Ballast, Foreign and Coastwise, Annual Average, 1958–60 inclusive

Thousand Tons

1	LONDON	42,279
2	SOUTHAMPTON	24,816
3	LIVERPOOL	19,743
4	GLASGOW (including Greenock)	9,499
5	MANCHESTER	8,118
6	NEWCASTLE	7,555
7	BELFAST	7,448
8	BRISTOL	6,017
9	HULL	5,919
10	DOVER	5,694
11	Middlesbrough	5,090
12	SWANSEA	4,977
13	HARWICH	3,736
14	Cardiff	3,336
15	Grimsby (including Immingham)	3,008

Total (all ports) ... 210,314

Of which total, percentage entering London and Liverpool 30
Of which total, percentage entering Major Ports in
capitals above 70

Source: *Board of Trade Journal, 1958–61*

TABLE 3

Ports of the United Kingdom Arranged in Order of the Value of Their
Foreign Trade, Imports, Exports, and Exports of Imported
Merchandise, 1958–60 inclusive

£ *Thousand*

1	LONDON	2,605,555
2	LIVERPOOL	1,656,475
3	HULL	411,045
4	MANCHESTER	386,564
5	SOUTHAMPTON	310,458
6	GLASGOW (including Greenock)	295,244
7	BRISTOL	194,463
8	HARWICH	124,683
9	SWANSEA	112,114
10	DOVER	109,813
11	NEWCASTLE	106,624
12	Middlesbrough	83,832
13	Grimsby (including Immingham)	71,160
14	BELFAST	66,716
15	Goole	66,522
	Total (all ports)	7,192,463

Of which total, percentage entering London and Liverpool 59
Of which total, percentage entering Major Ports in capitals
above ... 89
Source: *Annual Statement of the Trade of the United Kingdom,*
Volume IV: Supplement, 1962.

appear within the first ten ports in only one list. If these are added to the eight ports that appear in both lists, this may give a reasonable assurance of having separated out all the ports that may safely be classified as 'major'. These twelve ports of the United Kingdom dealt with nine-tenths of the foreign trade of the country 1958–60 inclusive. It may appear unfair to leave out ports just below a line arbitrarily drawn. There is the opposite danger of including too many ports, some of which are so small that they are really not to be compared with the major ports. There is not a rapid fluctuation in the relative status of these major ports, as can be seen from similar data compiled for the years 1936–8. Other ports in the vicinity of each major port, or very like it in function, are studied where useful comparisons can be made. In the following chapter on Newcastle the ports of Sunderland and Middlesbrough are also discussed, and there are other combinations: Hull and other Humber ports; Swansea with other South Wales ports, Dover with Harwich and Holyhead; and Glasgow includes Greenock. The largest ports not dealt with at all are Blyth, East Coast Scottish ports, Fishguard, Folkestone, Hartlepools, Lancaster, Newhaven,

Plymouth, Portsmouth, and Preston. These are large ports, and larger than some of the ports included here for the sake of comparison. But none of the smaller ports omitted can be described as a major port of the country.

Even so the subject matter appears quite wide enough. Indeed, the major British seaports are extremely complex organizations, in some cases spread over tens of miles. Although they discharge the same basic function—the two-way exchange of traffic between land and water, at first sight they seem rather dissimilar in lay-out. Closer investigation reveals a number of basic similarities; and one becomes intrigued by the different combination of these similarities and tempted to present the story of the 'highest common factor' of port development. This common theme is presented below as the development of a hypothetical port—*Anyport*. In this account *Anyport* is taken as being sited at an estuary head, like London or Bristol, although the information may be found applicable in large measure to other ports with different land and water sites. Estuary head sites were usually chosen because water transport was the cheapest form of transport absolutely, and rivers were therefore

TABLE 4

Ports of the United Kingdom Arranged in Order of Net Registered Tonnage of Ships Arriving with Cargo and in Ballast, Foreign and Coastwise, Annual Average, 1936–8 inclusive

Thousand Tons

1	LONDON	30,965
2	LIVERPOOL	17,467
3	SOUTHAMPTON	13,366
4	GLASGOW (including Greenock)	9,899
5	NEWCASTLE	9,066*
6	BELFAST	7,561
7	Cardiff	7,269*
8	HULL	6,178
9	Plymouth	5,908**
10	MANCHESTER	3,941
11	BRISTOL	3,782
12	SWANSEA	3,464
13	Middlesbrough	3,135
14	Newport	2,344*
15	Grimsby (including Immingham)	1,969
	Total (all ports) ...	184,900

* Lower relative position at present because of greater coal export trade pre-war.
** Lower relative position at present because of pre-war practice of more frequent calls by liners.

Source: *Board of Trade Journal, 1938–9*

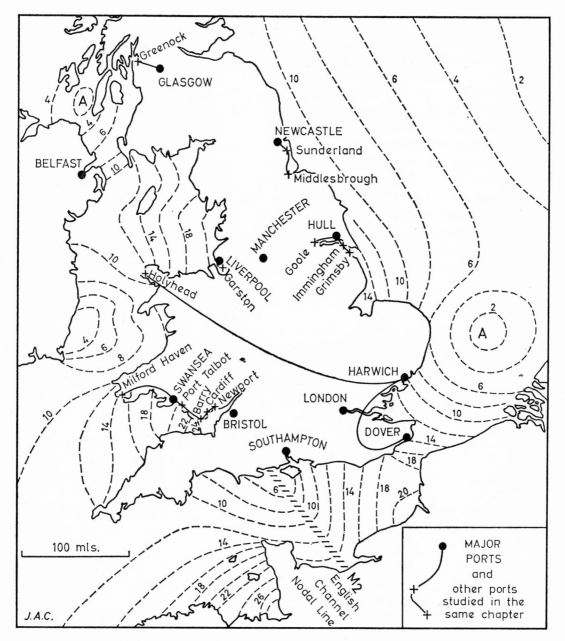

FIG. 1 Location of Major Ports and Other Ports Studied; and Co-Range Lines for Tides in British Waters

The average tidal range is given in feet for M_2, the semi-diurnal lunar constituent. A, represents an amphidromic (or non-tidal) point. There is a nodal line of low values for M_2 in the English Channel. Co-range lines from Admiralty Chart No. 5058 with the permission of the Controller of H.M. Stationery Office and of the Hydrographer of the Navy.

TABLE 5

Ports of the United Kingdom Arranged in Order of the Value of Their Foreign Trade, Imports, Exports, and Exports of Imported Merchandise, 1936–8 inclusive

£ Thousand

1	LONDON	556,217
2	LIVERPOOL	320,074
3	HULL	89,059
4	SOUTHAMPTON	66,728
5	MANCHESTER	62,870
6	GLASGOW (including Greenock)	60,279
7	BRISTOL	31,534
8	NEWCASTLE	28,569
9	HARWICH	27,422
10	SWANSEA	21,348
11	Grimsby (including Immingham)	18,997
12	Leith	16,694
13	Cardiff	15,646
14	Goole	14,376
15	BELFAST	13,888
16	DOVER	12,475
	Total (all ports) ...	1,469,949

Source: *Annual Statement of the Trade of the United Kingdom, Volume IV: Supplement 1938*

used as far inland as possible. In early days the further inland ships penetrated, the further they were away from the marauders of the open sea and the navigational dangers of the estuary when performing the delicate operations of unloading and loading. Around British coasts the tide furnished free motive power for sailing vessels up and down estuaries. Of course, if the estuary were shallow, a site nearer the sea would have been preferred, which explains Liverpool's growth compared with the Runcorn-Widnes site and Greenock's superiority to Glasgow until the deepening of the Clyde. The purpose of using the hypothetical *Anyport* is not to display a pattern into which all ports must be forced, but to provide a standard with which to compare the development of actual ports. Actual lay-outs that differ markedly from the generalized scheme will provide the greatest interest for the student of port development. *Anyport* has been designed as *Any [British] port* for the purpose of this study. Students of ports in other countries may find the concept useful, if only for the contrasts revealed between British and other ports as six eras of development unfold. It looks as though the histories of ports are going to be compared. In fact, as will be seen, each new step in the story of *Anyport* involves an addition to or a change in the physical lay-out of the port, helping to build up to the complex pattern of a modern major port.

The Development of Anyport

Anyport's story begins when the two-way exchange between land and water transport is regularly performed at a place, even if there are no port installations of any kind upon the shore. It would be unusual if the place had no physical advantages for a harbour,[3] or if some assistance for handling cargoes, however crude, were not

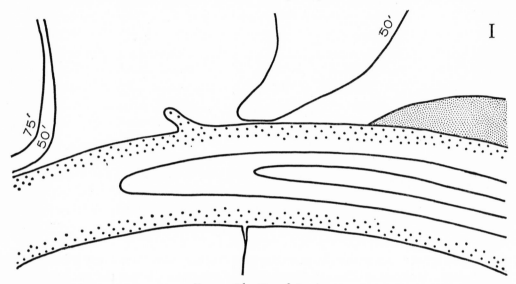

FIG. 2   The Site of *Anyport*

A left bank tributary of an estuary has caused an embayment, largely dry at low tide (coarse stipple in the estuary) and flanked by slightly higher land, before estuarine marshes begin downstream (fine stipple on the right of the diagram). North points, scales, and diagram borders have been omitted on purpose from the illustrations in this chapter of the hypothetical *Anyport*.

soon provided on shore. Four aspects of the port's location must be borne in mind: the actual area chosen for the installations on land and their immediate physical surroundings (land site); the position with relation to the physical geography of the hinterland the port is designed to serve (land situation); the harbour (water site); and the nature of the water approaches from the nearest sea lanes (water situation). As a port grows bigger these four locational aspects will have to be studied over larger areas. At some point along *Anyport*'s estuary an easier, and therefore busier, place for a harbour may be found, perhaps where a tributary enters, with slightly higher land giving protection on either side before the estuarine marshes begin downstream.

In the first or *primitive* era of *Anyport* the port nucleus appears as the inhabitants find it best to use a road running inland at right-angles to the waterfront if possible —the quickest route for sending goods to inland markets. The most logical place for a port nucleus is where this transverse track departs from the river bank. Other inland routes may also be necessary, perhaps parallel to the major estuary upstream, even making use of the estuary itself by means of inland waterway navigation. Ships have always been larger carriers than land vehicles, and sailings bound by wind or tide cannot be matched exactly with what land transport can perform. So a store is erected where some goods can remain under cover while in transit, and this is best provided near the nucleus, where the port authority and houses for merchants are found, including banks, taverns, and, most important, the Custom House. As the trade of the port increases (and if *Anyport* is to be the exemplar of a modern major port, its trade must go on increasing all the time), not every ship will be able to anchor near the nucleus. At the same time not every transit shed, or warehouse for longer storage, will find a site at the nucleus since room is limited. Along the waterfront, a line of quays extends on both flanks of the original port nucleus. Quays, sheds, and warehouses are served by a longitudinal road parallel to the waterfront behind the quayside buildings and connected to the quay by narrow lanes.

A line of quays may be limited upstream or downstream by some natural feature or defence work of the port, for example the town wall. A bridge is also a limitation upon port expansion, because early bridges had wide piers and narrow arches so that even small vessels could scarcely sail upstream. The logical site for a bridge is at the point where the early transverse road inland meets the waterfront. While the opposite shore is no longer inaccessible, port expansion there is only half-hearted because it is too far away from all the advantages of the port nucleus, with its military protection and customs privileges. The quays provided are designed to steepen the gradient between water and land, and though a modern quay makes a vertical junction with deep water, the small vessels at *Anyport*'s *primitive* quayside find no difficulty in sitting on the layer[4]—a bank of mud exposed at low tide alongside the strand. But after the fifteenth century this grounding at every tide becomes a hazard as ships grow bigger with two or more masts.[5] The modern charterparty usually stipulates that the hired vessels must never go aground. Larger ships, or a larger number of small ships, cause the port nucleus to be extended, usually seawards: or, if this is impossible, the port may begin again in another part of the town altogether. The most common significant occurrence is the extension of the quays beyond the limit of the medieval town walls or town gates. Such an overflowing of the port function from the *primitive* nucleus, or a change in port location, can usually be dated, and the event marks the end of the port's *primitive* era.

The second era of *marginal quay extension* in *Anyport* is a *lineal* extension which soon outstrips the *areal* expansion of the town. A separate port district of the town is encouraged to grow up at this stage, with a distinctive atmosphere, its buildings facing and serving the waterfront. If the port is compelled to start up again on a new site, the formation of a separate port district is accelerated. A principle of urban geography is that as a town grows larger so grow more distinct and separate its many

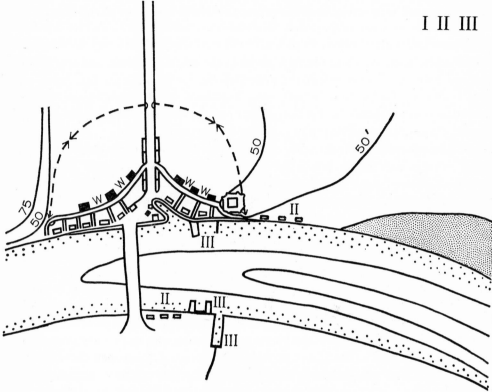

FIG. 3   *Anyport* After Three Eras of Development

I—The *Primitive Port*.
II—*Marginal Quay Extension*.
III—*Marginal Quay Elaboration*.
W—Warehouses; Quayside buildings, warehouses or transit sheds; Semi-circular town wall, with
        stronghold where the wall meets the estuary downstream.

functions and the areas, or precincts, of the town that they occupy. Meanwhile, there is a limit to the feasibility of *Anyport*'s expansion in one line from the *primitive* nucleus. Apart from physical obstacles, distance from the town's centre may cause difficulties for the distribution and collection of cargoes. There is the heavy hand of customs authorities, who preferred at one time to have compact landing places for easier surveillance of dutiable cargoes.

A solution is found in the third era when a change from the continuous line of quays marks an era of *marginal quay elaboration* where large cuts are made in the river bank or jetties extended into the water. *Anyport* may find it difficult to provide empty sites where large cuts can be made; if the river is narrow or deposits silt, jetty berths may not be possible. Should quay elaboration prove difficult, congestion of shipping results as *Anyport*'s trade further increases. Large vessels become embarrassed by the rise and fall of *Anyport*'s fifteen-foot tide which they have to ride out, sheering and ranging together. This third era of port development is ended by some event which expands the area of safe water for vessels—the physical expansion of the harbour or the opening of the first commercial dock.

The fourth era is one of *dock elaboration*. A site for the first commercial dock may well be found by demolishing an outdated part of the port nucleus. If this is impracticable, it is necessary for *Anyport* to break new ground, preferably downstream by excavations in the river's flood-plain. If the river is sufficiently wide, an alternative is to build a dock on land more palpably reclaimed from the river—a water-encroaching site. *Anyport*'s dock is equipped with a tidal basin to lock in a number of sailing vessels at one time. This may not be *Anyport*'s first dock, but previous docks were used for shipbuilding and shiprepairing. In Britain this era usually occurs in the first half of the nineteenth century, with further docks provided as trade increases, each larger than the previous and built progressively downstream and further from the nucleus. Lengthening landward communications back to the port distribution centre are later dealt with by the railway. These earlier docks have elaborate outlines, either by means of branch docks or jetties within one dock.[6] Dock engineers wished to have the maximum convenient length of quay for a given water area. Such docks are equipped with transit sheds and warehouses if their trade is predominantly of general cargo.

Defects of the dock with elaborate outline first become apparent at the end of the nineteenth century. As ships grow longer and wider, it is not easy to alter the inflexible dimensions of the berths in branch docks or at included jetties. The complex quay perimeter proves awkward when rail access to quays is required. Even worse is the difficulty of making approach roads for quay areas designed for horse and cart transport. Every peninsula within a dock proves a dead-end for access and incapable of being widened without great expense. Such docks cannot berth large modern passenger-cargo liners. The problem for marginal quays along *Anyport*'s river is not so acute because of the inherent lineal nature of their lay-out. There is thus an important role for them in the port for the berthing of smaller vessels whose shallow draught prevents them grounding on the ebb of the tide.

In this century the increasing length of ships has required *simple lineal quayage*, if the port is to berth the largest vessels efficiently. The provision of such berths marks the fifth era at *Anyport*. The minimum requirements of *simple lineal quayage* may be defined as 1,500 feet of quay in one uninterrupted line and 26 feet of water alongside; if this quay is in an impounded dock, the lock entrances should be at least 750 feet long. It must be emphasized that these are minimum requirements, for the largest liners would need at least 10 feet more water alongside and a much longer entrance lock. But since a port can have a large liner traffic without having facilities for the largest vessels, the requirements have been kept at a moderate standard. They are, in any case, sufficient to eliminate practically all unamended dock lay-outs of the nineteenth century; and while the extended marginal quays along *Anyport's* river may be longer than 1,500 feet in one line, it is unlikely that there will be as

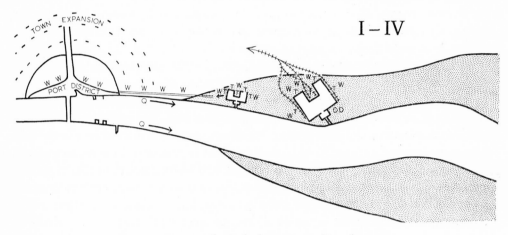

FIG. 4 *Anyport* at the End of Four Eras of Development

I–III as Fig. 3.
IV—*Dock Elaboration.*
DD—Dry dock associated with later docks; Q, Continuing *marginal quay extension*, T and W, Transit sheds and warehouses.

much as 26 feet L.W.O.S.T. alongside.[7] The advantages of *simple lineal quayage* are the flexibility for the berthing of ships: a 1,500-foot length of quay can take two vessels up to 750 feet long, or three vessels up to 500 feet long, or accommodate all these classes, or even the very longest vessel if other dimensions permit. Only one swinging ground would be necessary for manœuvring on to the quay, compared with a number of swinging grounds for each jetty or the provision of a vestibule dock for branch docks. On the land there need be no dead-ends for road and rail transport, and transit sheds arranged in one line alongside berths are not impeded by the working of other transit sheds arranged back-to-back across a narrow peninsula.

The story of *Anyport* would end with the provision of *simple lineal quayage* if all the cargoes received were general packaged goods, or goods in small lots in the holds of cargo liners. But side by side with the increase of general trade there grows up a trade in goods specifically destined for waterside factories and other processing plants. Perhaps the first industries to make that distinctive mark on the waterfront are shipbuilding and shiprepairing, and fishing. But during this century *Anyport* finds it necessary to provide additional specialized quayage for large-scale industry and bulk cargoes. Ships have become in some instances more specialized carriers of cargoes—the bulk carriers. The first important classes of such vessels were colliers, grain clippers, and oil tankers.[8] Since oil requires distinctive port handling techniques, provision by *Anyport* of berths for oil tankers in deep water may be taken as opening up a sixth era of *specialized quayage*. It must be admitted that conversion of quays from general cargo to specialization on single cargo has gone on since the nineteenth century, but the term *specialized quayage* may be reserved for berths dealing with really large amounts of one cargo.

Although there are oil tanker docks at Eastham on the Manchester Ship Canal and at Avonmouth because of the difficulties of berthing in the upper Mersey and Severn estuaries, oil tankers are not ideally accommodated in docks.[9] The fire hazard is increased in an enclosed dock or confined port area. The great size of super-tankers has overriden the dimensions of all dock entrances and all but the deepest of approaches to the hearts of ports. Since even the largest tanker can be emptied in twenty-four hours, the time taken in docking and undocking or sailing up a long approach channel adds unduly to the cost of turn-round. The unloading of oil needs no complicated handling techniques, merely a pipe and a pump. Because of all this, *Anyport* finds it cheaper to construct a berth in deep water, rather than dredge a channel to an existing quay. If possible, the berth is close to the open sea in the estuary away from existing port installations, as is explicitly required by *Anyport*'s bye-laws.[10] This berth may be in the form of a simple T-head jetty connected to the land by a fragile stem carrying the discharging pipes. Sometimes the stem has to be fairly long to reach deep water. The trend towards special cargo liners has extended to bulk grain- ore- and sugar-carriers, even bulk wine-carriers. They carry goods more cheaply per ton-mile because of a reduction in the proportion of motive power to carrying capacity and the saving of individual packaging. The speed of handling cargo is increased perhaps by suction from the huge hatches of simple clear holds. Such special carriers, in which may be included the modern collier, must however have special shore-based appliances for discharging and loading. The vessel travels to the same berth each time, and this is best provided away from the press of the general cargo vessels. Practically all imported grain, sugar, and oilseeds are milled, refined, and crushed in premises adjacent to tide-water, and *Anyport*'s estuary sites are in demand by manufacturers for modern large-scale plants served direct by ship. Between the original port nucleus and the deep-water oil berths near the sea, a series of specialized berths is constructed directly serving public utilities, gas works and generating stations, and those industries of *Anyport* that vitally depend on the import or export of goods via tide-water. As already indicated, the tendency is for berths in docks also to become specialized either from the point of view of cargo, or of class of vessel, or by being appropriated by one liner company. In the present era of *specialized quayage* the development of the waterfront between the port nucleus and open water proceeds, and vestiges of former eras are adapted to present-day requirements.

Anyport's development has been analysed into six eras terminated by events

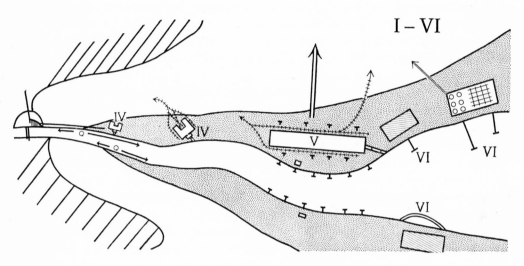

FIG. 5   *Anyport* Complete

I–IV as Fig. 4.
V—*Simple Lineal Quayage*, over 1,500 feet uninterrupted in one line, 26 feet of water L.W.O.S.T. alongside, with, if necessary, an entrance lock 750 feet long.
VI—*Specialized Quayage*, notable at T-head jetties and at large wharves in the river.
Q—Continuing *marginal quay extension*.
T—Transit sheds, or, in the river, jetties serving a continuous frontage of industry.

which can be dated. Each of these eras was called into being by increased trade and technical advance in the design of ships. The ship designer has always been the pacemaker in shipping transport innovations since his creation has merely to float and sail economically per ton mile; whereas the port engineer has to cope not only with the demands of ship designers, but also with the physical difficulties of the port's land and water sites. Despite these extra problems the port engineer must provide his new facilities before the ship that has made them necessary comes into service, or trade may be lost. One era supersedes another, but the installations remain. Stress must be given to the fact that though an era of port development is recognized as having come to an end, the installations built during that era will probably have a long working life before them for the following reason. Because of the great capital cost of port installations, it is often cheaper progressively to downgrade a dock or quay in traffic importance rather than scrap it altogether. Many docks and quays actively in use today were laid out perhaps 150 years ago; then they served the largest vessels using the port, but later only medium-sized vessels could approach their berths, and today you may find only coasters tied up alongside. The adaptation of old installations to modern use poses great problems, often ingeniously solved. One of the most fascinating aspects of port study is that the various eras of port development can be seen co-existing in present port lay-outs. So it is worth while paying attention to the way in which the organization of a major port has grown in area. Understanding of the present scene is impossible without reference to the past, but only cross-sections of the ports' development in time are given in this study rather than detailed continuous histories since the main theme is the recognition of significant developments in area.

In the detailed accounts of the ports which follow an attempt will be made to point out individual characteristics of lay-out as revealed by a comparison with *Anyport*. If the story of *Anyport* is remembered, one is kept alert for any unusual features of lay-out. At the same time such an account, though hypothetical, may have the effect of giving some hope of understanding the rather complex pattern presented by a modern major port, perhaps spread over many miles of an estuary. The usefulness of *Anyport* as a vade-mecum derives from the fact that, with many different combinations, a number of features recur in the lay-outs of major British seaports. It is to be hoped that this comparative approach will be helpful in gaining an understanding of the development of each of the seaports as they are studied successively in the chapters which follow.

TABLE 6

Summary of the General Theme of the Development of a Major Port

	Era	*Terminated by the Epoch of . . .*
I	Primitive	the overflowing of the port function from the *primitive* nucleus of the port or the change in location of the dominant port function
II	Marginal Quay Extension	the change from a simple continuous line of quays
III	Marginal Quay Elaboration	the opening of a dock or the expansion of the harbour
IV	Dock Elaboration	the opening of a dock with *simple lineal quayage*
V	Simple Lineal Quayage	the provision of oil berths in deep water
VI	Specialized Quayage	the occupation of all waterside sites between the port nucleus and the open sea

34

TABLE 7

Comparison of Dates of the Termination of Port Development Eras at Major and Other Ports

Ports with MAJOR PORTS in Capitals	End of Primitive Era	End of Marginal Quay Extension Era	End of Marginal Quay Elaboration Era	End of Dock Elaboration Era
NEWCASTLE	1707	1857	—	1924
Sunderland	1822	1837	1850	1909
Middlesbrough	1769	1830	1842	1962
GLASGOW	1792	1867	—	1931
Greenock	1809	1809	1878	—
BELFAST	1714	1849	1849	1963
HULL	1778	1778	—	1962
Grimsby	1801	1852	—	—
SOUTHAMPTON	1411	1803	1842	1895
BRISTOL	1248	1809	1877	1894
SWANSEA	1597	1852	—	—
Port Talbot	1839	1837	1898	—
Cardiff	1794	1839	—	1907
Newport	1842	1842	—	1914
DOVER	1495	1583	1844	1909*
HARWICH	1863	1883	—	—
MANCHESTER	—	—	—	1905
LIVERPOOL	1561	1635	1715	1927
LONDON	200	899	1802	1921
Anyport (median dates of the twelve major ports)	1597	1809	1842–4	1921

★ *Simple lineal quayage* as incidental to the Government decision to complete the Admiralty Harbour

REFERENCES

1. F. W. Morgan, *Ports and Harbours* (Hutchinson University Library, 2nd edition, 1958), 14 *et seq.*
2. U.K. port statistics have been analysed by J. Bellamy and M. Webb, *The Foreign Trade of Humberside: a Study of Post-war Trends*, Hull: University College, 1952; *ibid.*, 'Some Post-war Aspects of Humberside Foreign Trade', *Yorkshire Bulletin of Economic and Social Research*, 5 (1953), 199–213; and J. Bellamy, *Trends in the Foreign Trade of United Kingdom Ports*, including 'The Foreign Trade of Humberside: a Comparative Analysis', Hull: *Port of Hull Journal*, Newham, 1954.
3. R. S. MacElwee, *Encyclopaedia of the Social Sciences*, London: Macmillan, 1934, Vol. 12, 255, defines a port as a harbour with terminal facilities, and a harbour is 'a body of water protected from wind and wave action with water of sufficient depth and with bottom of good holding ground so that vessels may find haven in it and anchor safely.' p. 184.
4. A term used in a Swansea record of 1555, and referred to in an Act of 1796 when the Glamorganshire Canal was to be extended to the 'Lower Layer' south of Cardiff.
5. A very early reference to these difficulties for the year 1464 is to be found in J. Stow, *A Survey of London 1603*, 2 vols., ed. C. L. Kingsford, Oxford: Clarendon, 1908, 362, original pagination.
6. '. . . the greatest facilities for the trade that can be desired', A. Giles, in discussion upon the original jetties of the Royal Victoria Dock, London, W. J. Kingsbury, 'Description . . . of the Victoria (London) Docks *etc.*', *Minutes of the Proceedings of the Institution of Civil Engineers*, 18 (1858–9), 445–89, 470.

7. Only at Southampton and Newcastle has it been possible to provide such *simple lineal quayage* at riverside berths.
8. An early work was A. C. Hardy, *Bulk Cargoes: a Treatise on their Carriage by Sea and Consequent Effect on the Design and Construction of Merchant Ships*, London: Chapman and Hall, 1926. Recently, A. R. M. Graham has considered 'The Implications of the Bulk Carrier', *The Dock and Harbour Authority*, 43 (1962), 87–9.
9. See a section on the siting of oil refineries in Britain with reference to deep water in J. R. James, S. F. Scott, and E. C. Willatts, 'Land Use and the Changing Power Industry in England and Wales', *Geographical Journal*, 127 (1961), 287–309, 304–7; also H. Rees, 'The Shipment of Petroleum to and from Ports of the United Kingdom', *Scottish Geographical Magazine*, 72 (1956), 109–12.
10. The harbour authority must regulate the places at which ships are to load and discharge petroleum and where tankers are to be moored, *Petroleum (Consolidation) Act*, 18 & 19 Geo. 5 c. 32, 1928, Section 7 (I).

FURTHER GENERAL WORKS ON BRITISH PORTS

Chambers, F. T. *English Port Facilities*. Report to U.S. Shipping Board Port Facilities Commission. Washington: U.S. Government Printing Office, 1919.

Cole, S. *Our Home Ports*. Effingham: Wilson, 1923.

Commercial Ports of the United Kingdom. Central Office of Information Pamphlet, 1960.

Cornick, H. F. *Dock and Harbour Engineering*. London: Griffin, 1957, Vol. 1, The Design of Docks; 2, The Design of Harbours; 3, Buildings and Equipment; 4, Dock and Harbour Construction.

[The] *Dock and Harbour Authority*. Monthly, 1920 to date.

Owen, Sir David. *The Origin and Development of the Ports of the United Kingdom*. London: Allman, 1948.

Rees, H. *British Ports and Shipping*. London: Harrap, 1957.

Report by Docks and Inland Waterway Executive on Review of Trade Harbours 1948–50. British Transport Commission, 1951.

Report of the Committee of Inquiry into the Major ports of Great Britain. [Rochdale Committee] London: H.M.S.O., Cmnd. 1824, 1962.

[Third] *Report of the Ports Efficiency Committee to the Ministry of Transport and Civil Aviation*. H.M.S.O., 1956.

[Final] *Report of the Royal Commission on Transport*. London: H.M.S.O., Cmd. 3751, 1931, 125–39.

Schultze, J. H. *Die Häfen Englands*. Leipzig: Wissenschaftliche Buchandlung, 1930.

U.K. Shipping and Ports. A Financial Times Survey, June 24, 1957.

Walmsley, L. *British Ports and Harbours*. London: Collins, 1942.

INDUSTRIAL AND COMMERCIAL ESTUARIES—I

Chapter 2

NEWCASTLE AND TYNESIDE
WITH WEARSIDE AND TEES-SIDE

THERE are three large estuaries in north-eastern England. A glance at a simple solid geological map shows that the River Tyne flows entirely across Carboniferous rocks *due east* to the sea. But the River Wear reaches post-Carboniferous rocks $1\frac{3}{4}$ miles in a direct line from the coast; and the River Tees reaches the same boundary 25 miles inland. These last two rivers change direction over the last 20–25 miles of their courses to flow *north-east* to the coast. Though each river has been interrupted by glacial boulder clay or drift, the fundamentally different relationships between the present rivers and the actual build of the country rock has caused the major differences in the physical framework of their estuaries. The Tyne has the greatest catchment area and has been made into the deepest estuary. Its port nucleus is ten miles from the sea, whereas Sunderland and Middlesbrough first grew up at sites within only two miles of the original coastline. Each of the three estuaries now has one conservancy authority: the Tyne Improvement Commission (established 1850); the River Wear Commission (1859, succeeding the first 'Commissioners of the River Wear', 1717); and the Tees Conservancy Commission (1852, succeeding the Tees Navigation Company, 1808).

The Port of Newcastle becomes Tyneside

In the first two eras of port development on the Tyne it is correct to write of the Port of Newcastle, physically separate from any other use of the river downstream. In 1723 the *primitive* port extended from the port nucleus at Sandhill (formerly the estuary of the Lort Burn) to the thirteenth-century town wall at Sandgate (Fig. 6). *Marginal quay extension* beyond the town wall could not be established permanently until the Act of Union with Scotland in 1707. For example, in 1644 the Marquess of Newcastle, confronted by the invading Scots army,

'for the better Guard of the Town, set the Sandgate, a Street without the Walls, and other Suburbs, on fire . . .'[1]

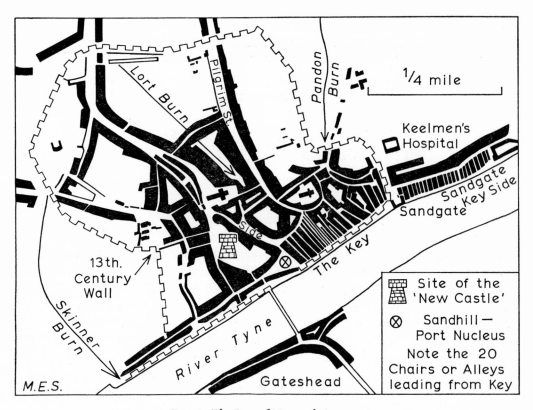

FIG. 6 The Port of Newcastle in 1723

The *primitive* port has been enlarged by the *marginal quay extension* of Sandgate Key Side. Solid black represents built-up areas shown on J. Corbridge's original engraving reproduced in T. Oliver, *The Topographical Conductor or Descriptive Guide to Newcastle and Gateshead*, Newcastle, 1851, facing page 73.

By 1723 the *marginal quay extension* of Sandgate Key was one of the bases of the keelmen who transferred coal from the staiths on the shallower reaches of the river upstream to colliers waiting downstream. Sandgate, the first suburb of Newcastle, was occupied largely by keelmen.

> 'As I came thro' Sandgate,
> I heard a lassie sing:
> "Oh, weel may the keel row,
> That my laddie's in." '
> [Northumbrian tune, 18th century]

Gateshead was hardly more than a symbol of the Bishop of Durham's sway over the south bank of the Tyne, because the bishop had ports elsewhere. Its name recalls

38

London's Southwark (south-work of the bridge). Like London also, Newcastle spanned one tributary, its town walls reaching to two others. On the 1723 map the port area immediately downstream of the bridge is indicated by the numerous narrow streets (chairs or chares) leading back from the riverside. But a great contrast to the land site of London is the steep ascent of 100 feet from the river to the easily

TABLE 8

Eras and Epochs in the Development of the Port of Newcastle and Tyneside

Eras and Chief Areal Characteristics		*Present-day Symbols*
I	*Primitive:* port immediately downstream of bridge, town side of river	Newcastle Corporation Quays, Nos. 8 and 9
Permanent extension beyond town wall possible after Act of Union with Scotland, 1707		
II	*Marginal Quay Extension:* eastward extension of town quays serving keelmen's suburb of Sandgate	Newcastle Corporation Quays, Nos. 10–20
Necessity for deeper-draught vessels to anchor downstream, before the effective deepening of the River Tyne, up to 1862		
IV	*Dock Elaboration:* docks at least seven miles downstream of *primitive* port	Oil storage and tanker berths; on site of Northumberland Dock (1857), partially filled in 1958–60; Tyne Dock, 1859; Albert Edward Dock, 1884
Other developments upstream possible after Tyne dredging, *post* 1863		
V	*Simple Lineal Quayage:* marginal quay extension on deepened river	Newcastle Corporation Quays, Nos. 22–29, progressively 1924–63

VI *Specialized Quayage:* large-scale installations for:

Shipyards, since 1883	when	{ Extension of Swan, Hunter & Co's Wallsend Yard	6
grain, since 1891	*i.e.*	C.W.S. Flour Mill, Dunston	3
coal shipment on the riverside (not simple gravity), since 1932	*i.e.*	Harton Staiths	18
oil storage, since 1922	*i.e.*	Jarrow Oil Wharf	4
iron ore discharge, since 1953	*i.e.*	Iron Ore Quay, Tyne Dock	1

N.B. The figures at the extreme right are the present total number of such shipyards, mills, or berths on Tyneside. Shiprepairing berths are omitted.

fortified plateau upon which the rest of the medieval city was laid out. At Newcastle the Tyne encounters a resistant rock, the Gateshead Fell Sandstones,[2] the highest series of the Coal Measures in Northumberland and Durham, with a west-facing scarp. This together with the deep denes of small streams cutting into the sandstones on the north bank gave a natural defensive rampart to the site of the town. The very name[3] of Newcastle shows this to have been more important than any question of 'lowest crossing-point', for the Tyne could have been bridged further downstream.

The land situation of Newcastle was in a frontier zone in Roman times; Hadrian's Wall runs right across the site of the medieval city to reach the Tyne at Wallsend.[4] After the Act of Union, 1707, the Tyne Gap route to the Solway Firth and the east coast road to Scotland, using the scarp-top route along the Gateshead Fell Sandstones, gave the town a crossroads land situation.[5] But the eastern limb of the cross 'roads', the Tyne estuary itself, was shallow in its natural state.

In mid-Tertiary times, some 35 million years ago, the North Pennine Massif was tilted eastward, and streams consequent upon the slope drained eastward or south-eastward to the sea.[6] At this time the ancestor of the present South Tyne—lower Tyne river was aided by a faulted trough between the North Pennine Massif and the Cheviots, now known as the Tyne Gap.[7] The line of drainage eastward from this gap is thus very ancient, and the river once carved a wide valley, except where it encountered the Gateshead Fell Sandstones, only to open downstream to nearly as much as four miles wide. But all pre-glacial river valleys in this area were filled with glacial boulder clay or 'wash' as it is locally termed. For the most part the post-glacial Tyne, unlike the Wear, has re-established itself along the line of its wide pre-glacial wash-filled valley.

> 'Especially is this so in the higher reaches where the courses of the two water-ways are almost identical [certainly where they both cross the resistant Gateshead Fell Sandstones at Newcastle in a narrow water gap]; but in its lower parts, east of Newcastle, the rock is cut into at many places, as, for instance at Felling Shore [2], Bill Quay [3], and St. Anthony's [3½], and therefore . . . the course of the present river [differs] considerably from that of the former river in this region.'[8] [Figures represent mileage downstream of Tyne Bridge.]

This non-concordance, as it may be termed, between post-glacial and pre-glacial courses of the Tyne, causing valley sides to have the solid rock closely subjacent, is to be contrasted with the river further downstream. Two miles from the sea the present valley is a notch with gentler slopes cut into a soft fill of wash, some 150 feet deep occupying a buried pre-glacial valley nearly four miles wide.[9] These profound changes in the cross-profile of the river are easily observed in the riverside scene today, heightened by the contrasts in riverside activity they help to bring about (see Table 12). The soft wash material in the river valley, easily eroded, helped to choke its lower course, and form a bar at the river's mouth. The post-glacial rise in sea-level while reducing the gradient and velocity of the river did not supply enough erosive power in the ebbing and flooding streams to remove these obstacles.

Nothing very significant was done to improve the river until 1838. Even then there was only one dredger at work, and such minor improvement works as were carried out, erecting jetties here, cutting away a high bank there, 'were of a fitful and partial character'.[10] As in the early history of so many British ports, municipal control caused the diversion of port revenues into the town's coffers. In the period 1809–49 the sum received as port dues *etc.* was £957,973; the total sum laid out upon the river during that time was only £397,719. The balance went to the Corporation of Newcastle. Captain [later Admiral] Washington, quoting these figures in his *Report* in an Admiralty inquiry on the Tyne Conservancy Bill, 1849, went on to deliver a stinging attack on the municipal port control.

'It must be manifest that the several duties usually attached to the conservancy of a harbour have not been attended to on the Tyne; that the most ordinary duties of river engineering—such as regulating and deepening the channel, cutting off projecting points, dredging away or otherwise removing the shoals so as to produce a uniform bed of the river, registering the tides and freshets, and occasionally taking soundings and cross-sections—have been all but entirely omitted; . . . [and] no attempt has been made to improve the bar. . . .'[11]

The result was the setting up of a Tyneside port authority in 1850—the Tyne Improvement Commissioners.[12] Following recommendations by a Royal Commission in 1855, a policy was begun of constructing full tide-walls to narrow the cross-section of the river. This confirmed a plan, suggested by John Rennie in 1816, for making the Tyne more uniform in width, by removing some points projecting on the inside of meanders and constructing transverse jetties to be linked by longitudinal walls.[13] Seventeen years previously, in 1799, Rennie had made a similar recommendation about the Clyde (see below, p. 80). The lower Clyde like the lower Tyne flows across a pre-glacial valley course choked with glacial drift. Depths had been increased by fifteen feet over the shallowest part of the Clyde as early as 1824, whereas J. Guthrie noted the much later date of 1860–1 as marking the Tyne at its worst (see Table 9).[14]

When the Corporation of Newcastle was the conservator of the river

'the capabilities of the river in its unimproved state—a "Natural Dock", as it was called—were great for the class of vessels then in use . . .'[15]

On the other hand, Glasgow could not become a seaport at all, until the river had been improved. This explains the later date of Tyne deepening. As on the Clyde, a narrower and more uniform channel would increase the velocity of the river and help it to maintain by natural scour the increased depth given by steam dredging. This was the burden of J. F. Ure's *Report to the Tyne Improvement Commissioners*, October 13, 1859, with a subsequent *Report*, October 29, 1860.[16] Ure was appointed engineer to the Commissioners in 1859, having been previously, and most appropriately in view of the comparison instituted above, engineer to the Trustees of the Clyde Navigation. His recommendations were embodied in an Act of 1861. The effects were soon seen after October 15, 1863. On that date a 55 horse-power dredger was added to another 55 h.p. vessel introduced just two months earlier, both recommended by Ure. Within that space of time the total steam dredging power had been increased from 145 to 255 h.p. Before 1860 the total material dredged had never exceeded half a million tons per annum; from 1864 to 1870 inclusive, at least four million tons were raised every year. In 1863 dredging began on the bar, for by this time the piers begun in 1854 had penetrated far enough into deep water to prevent waves re-piling material upon the shoal (although the piers were not finally completed in their present form until 1909).

TABLE 9

Some Depths at Low Water Ordinary Spring Tides in the River Tyne circa 1720,[17] 1860,[18] 1875,[19] and 1960[20]

Miles Downstream of Newcastle Bridge or Swing Bridge	Opposite	Circa 1720	1860	1875	1960
$\frac{3}{8}$	Newcastle Quay	7	5	20	25
$1\frac{3}{4}$	St. Peter's	6	1	25	25
$2\frac{1}{4}$	St. Anthony's Point	9	3	24	25
$3\frac{3}{4}$	Walker	6	2	20	25
$6\frac{3}{4}$	Howdon	7	4	25	25
$10\frac{1}{2}$	Tynemouth (the Bar)	7	6	23[21]	30

The *dock elaboration* era was marked by the opening of two docks, Northumberland Dock (1857) and Tyne Dock (1859). They were designed to assist rail shipment of coal to colliers waiting in the river. Northumberland Dock was made as a by-product of river improvement, when a river wall cut off an embayment of the riverside. Upon this embayment were some of the busiest coal-shipping staiths. The cost of bringing them forward to the line of the river wall would have had to be defrayed from the Tyne Improvement Fund, so a full-tide dock was made in which entrance dues were levied to defray its cost. South of the river the Tyne Dock was opened in the semi-tidal Jarrow Slake[22] by the North Eastern Railway Company, and remained a railway-operated dock until purchased by the Tyne Improvement Commission in 1937. The sites of these docks can be understood as chosen best to serve the 'sea-sale' collieries of the middle of the nineteenth century. A line joining the most easterly of these collieries north and south of the Tyne in 1850[23] crossed the river close to the entrances of these docks. It must be remembered that to the east the riverfronts of North and South Shields were already largely built over by glass and chemical industries with their associated slag heaps. The riverside was also encumbered by colliery tips and ballast hills built by returning colliers. But there was room between the Northumberland Dock and North Shields, and here the Commissioners erected their own staiths at Whitehill Point (Act of 1867) and opened the Albert Edward Dock 1884, accommodating vessels drawing 26 feet at a time when Newcastle Quay had only 20 feet minimum alongside.

Compared with *Anyport*, Newcastle is seen to be a port which had difficulty in expanding immediately downstream in the *dock elaboration* era because of the lack of available land, especially in the non-concordant section of the valley with its steep valley sides. For some time, too, in the middle of the nineteenth century the Newcastle Quay was handicapped by the shallowness of the river. For these reasons, and also because after about 1770 more coal was produced from the area to the east of Newcastle, the docks were all sited at least seven miles downstream. Once the Tyne improvement scheme had been able to bring deep water alongside estuary head sites, however, *simple lineal quayage* was easily provided by extending the Newcastle Quay downstream. This indicates the success of the plans of J. F. Ure, for only at Southampton with its magnificent water site is there a parallel case of the *simple lineal quayage* well upstream of the total *dock elaboration* pattern.

So the Port of Newcastle became Tyneside for three chief reasons. The very shallowness of the river in its natural state caused the river to be looked at as a whole from 1850. Secondly, the difficulties of the river and the riverside caused docks to be built at least seven miles downstream from 1857. Lastly, ribbon patterns of industry along the banks: glass-works east from Newcastle; wooden shipbuilding and glass and salt works at South Shields; collieries, and the chemical industry formed almost a continuous thread between the Tyneside settlements by the middle of the nineteenth century.

Shipbuilding[24]

Though South Shields was an important centre in the era of wooden shipbuilding, the industry on the Tyne is perhaps more conveniently dated from 1842, when the first iron ship was launched from a slip at Walker. At this time the river bank was occupied by staiths, ballast hills (largely built by colliers returning to the Tyne in ballast), and the glass and chemical industries. After 1870 these industries declined[25] as other inland areas went ahead, helped by the railway or by the adoption of new processes. On the other hand, the shipbuilders successfully working with iron often expanded their works over the former premises of these dying industries. With the exception of the smallest shipyard, shipbuilding on the Tyne is concentrated in a five-mile stretch of riverfront from Bill Point to the Albert Edward Dock Entrance and downstream of the river's gorge-like passage through the Gateshead Fell Sand-stones. Shiprepairers, who are not also shipbuilders, are particularly to be found downstream of the docks in North and South Shields. Shipbuilding in Britain is a large subject, which diverges considerably from the main theme of this book. Only the basic features of the modern shipbuilding industry can be given here to show how it fits in with other activities at ports.

Since the Second World War a revolution in shipbuilding has taken place as great as the change from wood to iron.[26] Electric welding has taken the place of riveting for joining the structural parts of ships. This has many advantages. Welding gives a decrease in the weight of the hull (through the elimination of angle-connec-tions, plate overlaps, and butt-straps), saving up to 20 per cent in cost and 12 per cent in steel.[27] A flush-welded hull has 15 per cent less resistance to motion than a riveted hull, and the welded ship is lighter; her engines require a smaller horse-power to drive a given capacity at a given speed. Another advantage is the ability to prefabricate large sections of the welded hull away from the building berths.

It is in mould lofts or rooms that drawing office designs are rendered into actual shapes, i.e. copies on scrieve boards or wooden templates for the guidance of workers in platers' shops and on hulls.[28] Such rooms are often conveniently sited on first floors because they are dealing with shapes rather than with any heavy raw material. A joiners' shop is necessary for all the ships' furniture, decking, and lifeboats. The remaining installations should be ideally in one line from inland to the berth along-side deep water. First comes a storage area for the reception of steel. Smaller welded structural units may be made in the platers' shops. A much larger central welding shop is where prefabricated assemblies of the largest size are constructed. Cranes of fifteen to twenty tons are common in such shops, with some yards able to move 50- and 100-ton prefabricated sections. This explains why the simple pole-derricks on shipbuilding berths with only 5-ton capacity have been replaced by hammerhead cranes of large capacity, changing the skyline of shipbuilding rivers.

Electric welding is most efficiently carried out under cover, with the members that are to be welded together laid out horizontally. This has led to the erection of very large covered sheds, with large storage areas adjacent. Longer berths are necessary if the yard is to be able to build tankers of 60,000 tons deadweight and upwards. Such modernization has proved very difficult in old-established shipyards on cramped sites often hemmed in by houses outside their landward walls or other port installations upstream and downstream.

'In some cases, it has even been found necessary to reduce the number of building berths in order to find the required space, but this reduction has been more than compensated for by the increased efficiency and speed with which ships can be built at the remaining berths.'[29]

On the Tyne several ballast hills have been removed to give room; and at the ship-yard of Joseph L. Thomson & Co., Ltd. on the Wear several hundred houses have been demolished in the past decade and a neighbouring shipyard purchased to provide room for a new long berth and new methods of prefabrication. The large prefabricated units are generally moved to the building berths on rail-track bogies, but at the yard of Charles Connell & Co., Ltd. on the Clyde the assemblies are actually lifted through the roof of the welding shop.

On the building berth itself access is required to all parts of the hull. Hammerhead cranes lift the prefabricated units into position, and the old pattern of wooden scaffolding to support riveters and other workers has given way to light portable steel structures. The main machinery (and guns and mountings for warships) is generally placed in position at fitting-out wharves after launching. Some shipyards have their own fitting-out crane, such as the 250-ton crane at Vickers-Armstrongs (Tyne) with an outreach over two vessels. Floating cranes are also available, while on the Clyde the port authority has established heavy-lift cranes for common use on the quaysides (see Fig. 17).

For the future, the most desirable development would be higher productivity based on good organization, specialization, and standardization of orders, with fewer 'bespoke tailor-made' ships.[30] In Norway, standard-type ships are produced stern first from long prefabrication sheds transverse to the water;[31] but in Britain generally, and certainly on the Tyne and Wear, yards have little space available back from the river (see also Fig. 19).

TABLE 10

Shipbuilding in the United Kingdom

Locality	Annual Average of Gross Registered Tonnage of Ships Launched 1958, 1959, & 1960 (Thousand Tons)		Percentage of Total
North-east Coast:	645		46
Tyne		259	19
Wear		243	17
Tees (including West Hartlepool) ...		144	10
Clyde	406		29
Belfast	138		10
Birkenhead	55		4
Forth	34		2
Barrow	25		2
Tay	22		2
Dee and North-east Scotland	21		2
Humber	19		1
Others	30		2
Total (U.K.)	1,394 (16 per cent of world launching)[32]		

Shipbuilding is primarily an assembly industry, though shipbuilders may also be marine engineers.[33] In the United Kingdom it is a little difficult to generalize about the distribution of the industry, but something may be attempted. The site must obviously be close to deep water, with sufficient flat land adjacent, but the situation is not so circumscribed. Fuel and steel can be delivered, if necessary, by water, and the ship sails away under her own power to the buyer. The foci of the industry on the Clyde and the North-east Coast, accounting for three-quarters of the present output, developed from a wooden shipbuilding industry, especially at South Shields, on the Wear, and at Greenock. There are several important outposts with one notable omission—the Thames. Near London the high cost of labour, driven up by competition from other industries, distance from fuel and raw materials, and competition from other users of the river for upstream sites would seem to be obvious disadvantages. But it was all this *added* to the fact that managerial initiative was to be found more in evidence elsewhere that assisted in the complete decline of the Thames as a shipbuilding centre.[34]

The last factor seems to be the most potent today, for there is a national wage agreement for shipbuilding labour. The progressive establishment also of a uniform delivered price for steel sheets and plates would seem to suggest that the industry could be carried on at any physically suitable site. But in the United Kingdom between the two world wars there were too many shipyards and since then there have been steel and labour shortages. More recently, the labour techniques have become increasingly complicated, making it more costly if labour is to be trained from scratch. The remarks about shortages do not of course apply to shiprepair, which every major port must supply as part of its service to maintain the turn-round of shipping. It is thus more widespread in location than shipbuilding; and it is an industry with a much steadier load factor. In this connection it is significant that in the only new location for a major shipbuilding industry established in this century, the Atlantic Shipbuilding Co. at Newport build ships not on a slipway but in a dry dock that can also be used for shiprepair. The shipbuilding dock may well replace conventional slipways in large shipyard lay-outs of the future.

Coal Export (see also pp. 222–3)

The export of coal from Tyneside dates from as early as the thirteenth century.[35] 'Sea-coal' from the north-east coast has been brought to London for some 600 years, the early stimulus being the short-distance from 'sea-sale' colliery to a navigable waterway, the Tyne or Wear. In 1600 the Hostmen[36] of Newcastle were confirmed by charter as the monopolists of coal export on the Tyne, and they were the employers of the keelmen who plied their shallow-draught boats to the coal staiths

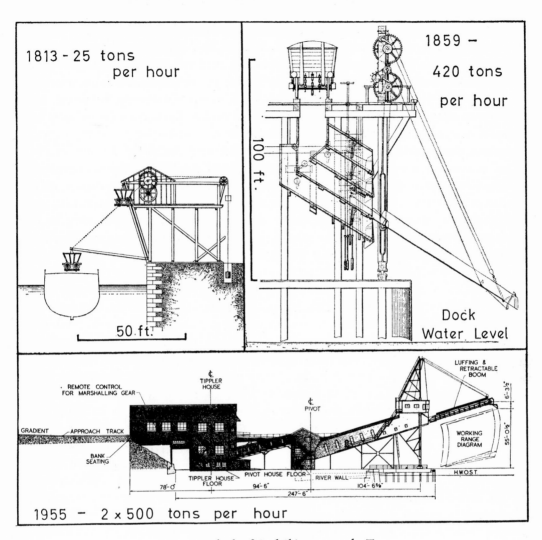

FIG. 7   Methods of Coal Shipment on the Tyne

Top Left: Pelaw Main Spout in 1813.
              Chaldron wagon lowered in cradle to deck level to avoid coal breakage.
Top Right: Improved Gravity Staiths in Tyne Dock with hoppers to prevent coal breakage and chutes
              adjustable through 20 feet to deal with different heights of vessels in the dock.
Bottom: Whitehill Point Coal Shipping Plant.
              There are two shipping-out gantries served by two rotary wagon tipplers in the tippler
              house.
Profiles after T. E. Harrison, 'On the Tyne Dock at South Shields: and the Mode Adopted for Shipping
Coals', *Minutes of the Proceedings of the Institution of Civil Engineers*, 18 (1858–9), 490–524, parts of
Plate 8 [for 1813 and 1859] and R. Hammond, *loc. cit.* [for 1955].

D

on the upper reaches of the Tyne. Higher prices resulting from this monopoly encouraged the rise of a similar trade by keels upon the Wear, a river outside the influence of the Newcastle Hostmen. From 1671 collieries were linked to the river by horse traction upon wagonways.[37] When, at the beginning of the nineteenth century, iron plates were nailed upon the wooden rails to give greater durability, the 'platelayer' began his work, forerunner of the worker upon the modern railway which was born on the banks of the Tyne.[38] As the focus of coal mining shifted eastward at the end of the eighteenth century, working down the geological dip into the Wallsend Basin, there was progressively less work for the keels to do. They were finally defeated by the extension of the wagonway (or rail) network to staiths serving ships direct, and the deepening of the Tyne even upstream of the bridges. A measure of this change and of the increase of coal exports can be gleaned by a consideration, if only in elevation, of the changes in coal-shipping equipment (Fig. 7) and of the amounts exported in selected years (Table 11).

TABLE 11

Coal Export from the Tyne

Year	Coastwise	Total
	Thousand Tons	
1600	?	190
1710	?	475
1776	?	680
1820	?	3,200
1880	2,972	8,131
1923	3,315	21,554 (peak year)
1952	7,416 (peak year)	9,251
1961	5,203	6,144

The Modern Port of Newcastle

Some modern features of the port will now be described in a downstream direction, to differentiate various reaches of the Tyne.[39] Although the port limits are eighteen miles upstream from the mouth, the upper three miles are scarcely used by port traffic, the low water depth of the river being only twelve feet or less; and Scotswood Suspension Bridge ($3\frac{3}{4}$ miles upstream of Tyne Bridge) gives only $17\frac{1}{2}$ feet of clearance at high water. Before beginning the survey, a word of caution is necessary. The industrial area along Tyneside contains many works close to the river that do not have berths on the riverside and do not make use of the river. In many cases they are sited on artificial terraces some distance above the water. Other works actually on the riverside may have used water transport at one time, but now make use of road transport exclusively; alternatively, such works may have taken over sites left vacant by the abandonment of glass and chemical works in the nineteenth century. Today there is little internal river traffic from one part of the river to another. This account confines itself to those premises making direct use of the river (in solid black on Fig. 8), and reference will be made to north and south banks (N or S), with mileage upstream and downstream of Tyne Bridge.

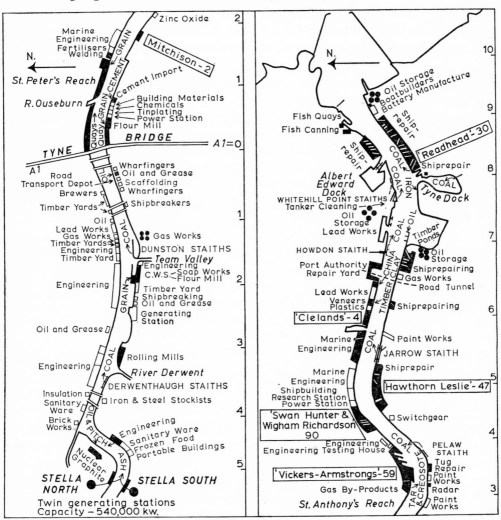

FIG. 8   Tyneside Premises: Annotated Diagram

Riverside premises making use of the river are shown in solid black. Notable exports and imports are shown with appropriate arrows. Short names of shipbuilding firms are within rectangles, followed by a figure representing the annual average gross tonnage (in thousands) launched 1958–60 inclusive. The outline of the river is schematic, with mileage upstream and downstream of Tyne Bridge shown in the right-hand margin of each half of the diagram.

TABLE 12

Patterns of Port Activity on the River Tyne

		Location
		Miles upstream of Tyne Bridge
I	*Upper Tidal Tyne:* grain import, coal export; Tyne Haughs	8–0
		Miles downstream of Tyne Bridge
II	*St. Peter's and St. Anthony's Reaches:* commercial quays dominant, with grain import; steep banks of the Tyne	0 –3¼
III	*Mid Tidal Tyne:* shipbuilding dominant, with coal export and oil import	3¼–7½
IV	*The Docks*	7½–8¼
V	*The Tyne at North and South Shields:* coal export, shiprepair, shipbuilding, and fishing harbour	8¼–9½

The *Upper Tidal Tyne* is flanked by several *haughs*, the local name for alluvial flats of the flood-plain of the Tyne contained within meanders. On Newburn and Ryton Haughs (5¼ N and S) are sited twin power stations—Stella North and Stella South—the largest serving the Tyneside conurbation with a combined capacity of 540,000 kw, which is one and two-thirds times the capacity of the five pre-1939 power stations serving Tyneside. Generating stations are also found on the *Upper Tidal Thames,* but on Tyneside, all the coal is of course brought by rail from the coalfield, the river merely providing flat land, water for cooling, and a means of ash disposal. Perhaps a more startling contrast is found by comparing the inland sites of these twin power stations with the sites of the twin power stations *seaward* of the commercial port of Belfast. A factory adjacent to Stella North has a large consumption of electric power to make graphite, for use in nuclear power stations, from imported raw material. Coal from the western part of the Durham coalfield is exported via Dunston Staiths (1½S). The chief import traffic, upstream of the Tyne Bridge, is grain to the C.W.S. Flour Mill at Dunston (1¾S), the oldest of the three grain mills on the river, developed from a mill first established here in 1891. (The nation-wide Co-operative Wholesale Society began in Newcastle in 1871.) Whole cargoes can be received ex ship because the only low-level bridge downstream is the Swing Bridge, and there is 23 feet L.W.O.S.T. in the river opposite the mill. Towards Tyne Bridge the riverside premises are less continuous because the river is entering its narrow water-gap as it cuts through the Gateshead Fell Sandstones, east of the Team Valley (1¾S); and four high-level bridges span the river across the defile (Fig. 8).

The Tyne Bridge itself dates from 1928 and is the largest arch in the country, 531 feet, with a rise of 170 feet, giving a clear headway for shipping of 84 feet at H.W.O.S.T.[40]

St. Peter's and St. Anthony's Reaches are dominated by the Newcastle Corporation Quays which extend for a mile and a quarter immediately downstream of and literally below Tyne Bridge, extending eastward from the *primitive* site of the port.

As Fig. 9 shows, the *simple lineal quayage* of deep-water quays is to be found east of the Ouseburn, a tributary of the Tyne which has cut a dene, or post-glacial notch, in the steep valley side of the Tyne. At these Corporation Quays most of the general dry cargo trade of the port is focused, a traffic which has expanded so much in recent years that the quays have been extended east of the second grain mill on Tyneside—Spillers, dating from 1938. This consists of a flour and provender mill and dog biscuit factory all under one roof. While Spillers have priority at the berth opposite

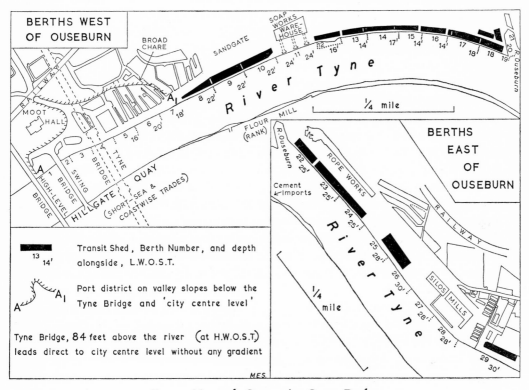

FIG. 9   Newcastle Corporation Quays, Berths 1–29

the mill, it is on this open quay that more bulky cargoes can, if necessary, be handled, and the quay is equipped with a 30-ton crane.

With the exception of the two Norwegian Mail Lines operating from the Tyne Commission Quay and Extension, adjacent to the Albert Edward Dock, North Shields, all cargo lines have their berths at Newcastle Quay, in certain cases at particular berths: for example, Danish traffic at Sheds 9, 11, 16, and 17; Swedish cargo at No. 8; and Dutch, German, and coastwise traders at No. 10. Deep-sea general cargo vessels trading to Atlantic ports of Canada (Berth No. 25) and the

U.S.A., and to Australia normally berth east of the Ouseburn, where eighteen electric cranes are to be found from 3- to 30-ton capacity. Thos. Hedley and Co., Ltd. (soapworks, etc.), back from the river, can receive oil and tallow from a pipeline at No. 10 Berth. While some bulk exports are handled by a small mobile loading appliance, the quays act principally as a larder door for the Tyneside conurbation. But little warehousing takes place near the quay for the hinterland is hardly large enough to warrant centralized warehousing depots.

On the south bank, Hillgate Quay is used by Coast Lines Ltd. for coastwise and near continental traffic; but the quays on this bank, still with timber decking, have never been as important as those on the north bank. The road access is just a little more awkward, and being on the inside of a meander it is a little more difficult than on the north bank to get a deep-water berth. The flatter land parallel to the Tyne at the Ouseburn confluence is an added advantage to the north bank. But south bank development is certainly possible; the third great grain mill, Rank's Baltic Mill (1949), is on the Gateshead Bank. A little to the north of this mill an interesting change of function can be observed. Cement is regularly imported from the Thames to a wharf just downstream of a derelict riverside cement works.

St. Anthony's Reach ($1\frac{1}{2}$–$3\frac{1}{4}$) is the non-concordant section of the River Tyne (see p. 40 above). Just as there is calm in the centre or 'eye' of a hurricane, so St. Anthony's Reach may be called the 'eye' of the conurbation, where the river seems deserted. Here the Tyne is confined between steep sides with the solid rock out-cropping at one or two points on the bank, so that riverside sites are cramped. There is little in the way of port activity to be observed for a mile and a half from the very small shipbuilding yard of T. Mitchison Ltd. ($1\frac{3}{4}$S) to the gas by-products works at St. Anthony's on the north bank ($3\frac{1}{4}$N). For example, though the marine engineering works of R. W. Hawthorn Leslie & Co., Ltd. are sited here ($1\frac{1}{2}$N), cut into the bank, the link with the Hebburn Shipyard (5S) is maintained by road.

The Mid Tidal Tyne ($3\frac{1}{4}$–$7\frac{1}{2}$) accommodates four of the five large Tyneside shipbuilders.[41] Plate I gives an idea of this pattern. Vickers-Armstrongs are furthest upstream, just at the end of the non-concordant valley pattern, their slips sited on a reclaimed strand originally deposited by the river on the inside of a sharp meander. There are also two modern coal shipment plants on this stretch of the river operated by the Tyne Improvement Commissioners, at Jarrow (1936) and at Whitehill Point (1955),[42] where ships can be loaded with coal at the rate of 500 tons per hour (Fig. 7). The largest dry dock has been provided at the Palmers Hebburn Works of Vickers-Armstrongs (Shipbuilders) Ltd., 850 feet long (for tankers of 80,000 deadweight tons), capable of being lengthened to 1,000 feet (for tankers up to 120,000 deadweight tons).

The modern functions of *The Docks* area are summarized on the annotated diagram (Fig. 10). The Northumberland Dock has been partially filled in, and the coal shipping staiths removed, with imported oil actually flowing across the site—a vivid change of function. The Iron Ore Quay (36 feet L.W.O.S.T.) was opened in 1953 for the import of iron ore to the Consett steel works, the only one remaining in west Durham. After being unloaded from ore carriers of up to 40,000 tons dead-weight by 5 10-ton unloader cranes, the ore travels an average of 750 feet on conveyors and is raised to a height of 80 feet. It then drops into 10 storage bunkers from

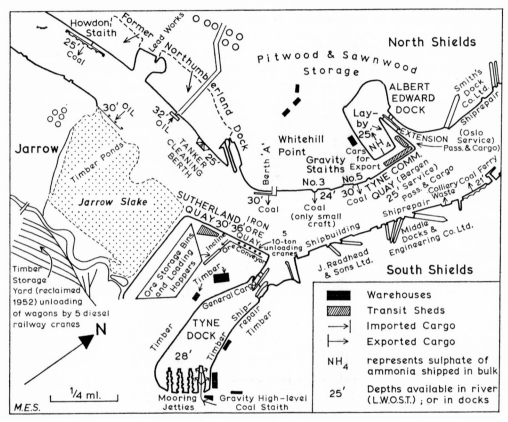

FIG. 10 Tyneside Docks, and Tyneside from Jarrow to North Shields

which it can be measured out by two travelling scale cars into loading-out bunkers. The reason for raising the ore to a height in the storage bunkers is to speed railway-wagon loading and to provide an ore reservoir, with the minimum number of wagons to provide the service. From the loading-out bunkers a train of nine 56-ton wagons can be loaded in less than a minute.[43] The train loaded with 500 tons of ore, one of three trains used exclusively on this route, then has to make a 900-foot ascent in its journey of 24 miles to Consett steel works, the steepest gradient being 1:35.

53

Sutherland Quay, opened in 1942 for use by Liberty Ships, is a general cargo quay which suffers from a poorer land site than the general cargo quays upstream for distribution to the Tyneside conurbation.

The industries of South Shields are closely linked to the port: shiprepairing, shipbuilding, marine engineering, boiler scaling, iron founding, timber-handling, and coal export. It has been suggested that the reason why shiprepairing is more prominent than shipbuilding (an industry not represented at all in North Shields) is that in the third quarter of the nineteenth century the sites on the narrow strip of land bordering the river were occupied by the then declining glass and chemical industries. This was at a time when the shipbuilding industry was growing fast on the slightly wider and certainly less encumbered sites of the *Mid Tyne* area in Wallsend, and Hebburn.[44]

Finally, trawlers alongside the Tynemouth Corporation Fish Quays (9N) signify that the Port of Newcastle, in its widest sense, embracing North Shields[45] in the Borough of Tynemouth, is one of the important fishing ports of the country, specializing in prime North Sea fish (see Table 49). There is also a considerable import of Norwegian fish by Bergen Line Steamers to the Tyne Commission Quay adjacent to Albert Edward Dock.

TABLE 13

Fifteen Most Valuable Foreign Trade Imports into Newcastle
(incl. North Shields and South Shields), 1960

	Value £ Million
Iron Ore	5·6
Wheat	5·3
Sawn Softwood	4·0
Fresh and Frozen Fish (not of British Taking)	1·6
Sisal	1·4
Organic Chemicals	1·2
Paper and Paperboard	1·0
Maize	1·0
Antimony	1·0
Metal Manufactures	·9
Mining Timber	·9
Canned Fish	·8
Canned Fruit	·8
Pulp	·8
Plywood	·7

Total of all Imports ... 63·9 (1·5 per cent of total U.K. imports by value)

TABLE 14

*Fifteen Most Valuable Foreign Trade Exports from Newcastle
(incl. North Shields and South Shields), 1960*

	Value £ Million
Steam Turbines	3·9
Ships and Boats	3·8
Road Vehicles	2·9
Coke	2·8
Tractors	2·8
Internal Combustion Engines	2·2
Coal	1·6
Arms and Ammunition	1·2
Dyeing Chemicals	1·1
Plastics	1·1
Cotton Thread	·9
Wool Tops	·9
Mechanical Handling Equipment	·8
Electric Generators	·8
Chemical Elements and Compounds	·7
Total of all Exports ...	47·6

(1·4 per cent of total U.K. exports by value)

The table of imports reveals the importance of the Corporation Quays at Newcastle as 'larder doors' to feed north-east England, while the imports to the grain mills emphasize this characteristic of the port. Many of the other imports are dealt with at the installations of the Tyne Improvement Commissioners in the docks or on the riverside, with the work of the Iron Ore Quay showing up strongly in the latter category. The wide range of the table of exports may cause surprise. Certain commodities are obviously locally produced: among which may be included the arms and ammunition, largely from the two Vickers-Armstrong Works on the *Upper Tidal Tyne*; and the sulphate of ammonia, from the I.C.I. works in the Tyne Corridor. But the exports of textiles indicate the influence of the port's foreland in Scandinavia, to which there are several cargo liner services. So exports are drawn from a much wider hinterland of northern Britain, betrayed by the presence in the table of both woollen and cotton textiles.

The Port of Sunderland and Wearside

The River Wear in pre-glacial times took a course northwards, now occupied by the diminutive River Team, to join the River Tyne close to Gateshead. When this valley was blocked by glaciers, the waters of the Wear were trapped to form a lake between the Pennines and the west-facing escarpment of the Magnesian Limestone of east Durham. Eventually,[46] the River Wear escaped eastward to the sea by cutting a gorge, now between 120 and 250 feet deep, across the drift-covered limestone plateau. From this may be derived two interlocking facts about the physical framework of the Wear estuary, both vital to an understanding of the present lay-out of the Port of Sunderland: the river bed is solid limestone rock; and there is little flat

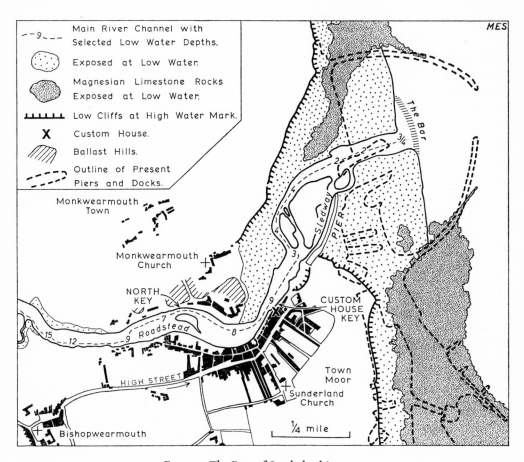

FIG. 11   The Port of Sunderland in 1737

The *primitive* port, where colliers awaited loading from keels, is within a mile of the Bar and is served by the longitudinal street of Sunderland High Street. After part of *A Plan of the River Wear from Newbridge to Sunderland Barr as it Appeared at Low Water*, by Burleigh and Thompson, 1737, where the most easterly coal staith is shown to be seven miles upstream, and where the three 'Wearmouth' settlements are clearly shown as separate from each other. H. D. Longstaffe, 'Unused Evidence Relating to SS. Cuthbert and Bede', *Archaeologia Aeliana*, 13, second series (1889), makes the reasonable suggestion that when Wearmouth port was first considered separately from Bishopwearmouth in the twelfth century it was called 'Sunder[ded]land'.

land bordering the river, although the limestone slopes are less steep on the inside of meanders. Because of the difficulty of dredging a long deep-water channel through solid rock, all the port activity is confined within the lower three and a half miles of the river, with dock development on land won from the sea along the coast.

The first improvement to the river was the construction of a South Pier (1726), with foundations on Magnesian Limestone rock, aligned to direct the land flow on to the bar.[47]

'... the lengthening of the south pier into the estuary was the principal object of each successive engineer. Now the effect of the south pier was, in stormy weather, to check the flood tide passing southward, and consequently to send it up the river loaded with sand, and acting like a groyne, it had a tendency to cause a deposit of silty matter beside it.[48]

From 1752 it was decided to concentrate on the Sledway, the south channel of the river's bifurcation before the bar. Though a North Pier was completed by 1802, the bar still existed. In 1847 there was only four feet above it at L.W.O.S.T.[49] As the Commissioners of the River Wear were at that time a 'rather retrograde body'[50] and controlled the river entrance, the Sunderland Dock Company, which had opened the Hudson Dock in 1850, decided to make an independent communication to the sea. This was the South Outlet of 1856, a very unsatisfactory port entrance.

'In bad weather the sea ran athwart the entrance and it was impossible to keep the channel open unless dredging was carried out 500 feet seaward of the pier-heads. ... [It was] recognized by mariners to be a foul passage, as the sea approach to the channel was studded with [Magnesian Limestone] reefs.'[51]

In the early part of this century it was considered that both the *outer* piers should be completed before any dredging of the river was begun, as it was believed that a deepened approach would cause an increased swell in the new harbour, so that the inner piers would be jeopardized. But by 1909 the entrance channel was successfully dredged to 15 feet L.W.O.S.T., and the river was deepened for a mile to 21 feet 3 inches L.W.O.S.T., all through solid limestone. This caused the south outlet to be entirely superseded as a direct entrance from the sea to the docks. The South Docks were transferred from railway ownership to the River Wear Commissioners in 1859, and the North Dock was similarly transferred in 1922.

'... in the course of deepening operations [it was found] that the site of the old bar was largely occupied by reefs and pinnacles of magnesian limestone which combined to present a natural barrier on which loose materials accumulated.'[52]

The river is now dredged to the depth of 21 feet 3 inches L.W.O.S.T. for $2\frac{1}{2}$ miles upstream of the entrance between the outer piers, the depth decreasing to 12 feet 9 inches L.W.O.S.T. at Pallion, $3\frac{1}{2}$ miles upstream. These dimensions of $2\frac{1}{2}$ miles by 21 feet 3 inches contrast greatly with the Tyne, $11\frac{3}{4}$ miles by 25 feet, or the Clyde, 19 miles by 25 feet. They indicate the difficulties in deepening a glacial spillway across solid rock compared with digging out valleys merely choked with their own deposits eroded from a fill of glacial drift. In 1960–1 while deepening the approach channel to the repair berth of T. W. Greenwell & Co., Ltd., across the site of the North Dock, the rock dredger encountered the 'cannon-ball'[53] layer of Magnesian Limestone as it cut its way to 23 feet L.W.O.S.T., and even the specially toughened steel lips of the dredger's buckets were severely buckled by this very hard stratum.

TABLE 15

Eras and Epochs in the Development of the Port of Sunderland

	Eras and Chief Areal Characteristics	Present-day Symbols
I	*Primitive*[54]: port in river, where colliers loaded from keels, especially from the mid-seventeenth century[55]	Lower mile of the River Wear
	Era ended [56] by gravity-loading staiths from 1822	
II	*Marginal Quay Extension:* gravity coal-exporting staiths on narrowest part of the river	Hetton Staiths, 1822, Wearmouth Staiths, 1835
	Era ended by the opening of the North Dock, 1837 (by Wearmouth Dock Company)	
III	*Marginal Quay Elaboration:* on north shore near river mouth	Site of North Dock, tidal since 1935
	Era ended by opening of Hudson Dock, 1850 (by Sunderland Dock Company)	
IV	*Dock Elaboration:* on land reclaimed along the coast	Hudson Dock, 1850, with extension, 1855; Hendon Dock, 1868
	Larger-scale developments possible on narrow sites after dredging of the River Wear, 1909	
VI	*Specialized Quayage:* 7 shipyards and 2 shiprepairing yards Corporation Quay 1934 (raw materials for Sunderland's industries especially silver sand (glass), sisal (ropemaking), and pulp (paper)) Hetton Staiths Wearmouth Staiths (See II above, but now with 20 feet L.W.O.S.T. alongside)	 18 shipbuilding berths 5 berths 1 berth

Coal-export was certainly the stimulus for the rise and development of the port. As on the Tyne, the early method was to use a wagonway to a staith on the river at least seven miles upstream, and thence keels of shallow draught took the coal to colliers waiting inside the rivermouth bar. The collieries were within three miles of the river, though all collieries north of the latitude of the Wear's mouth exported via the Tyne, with easy down gradients along the Team and Derwent valleys.[57] This capture by the Tyne of the hinterland of the Durham coalfield north of the latitude of the mouth of the Wear was repeated in the railway era with the opening in 1834 of the Pontop and South Shields Branch of the Stanhope and Tyne Railway which runs to the Tyne, within half a mile of the north bank of the Wear.[58] This lop-sided coalfield hinterland explains the port lay-out with the docks all south of the river mouth. Hetton and Lambton Staiths began as the terminus of a wagonway from the first shaft sunk in 1822 through the limestone to reach the Coal Measures, at Hetton six miles south-west of Sunderland. Despite competition from Newcastle to the north, and later from Seaham and the Hartlepools to the south-east, Sunderland has always been well situated to export from the zone of coals extending for some seven miles east of Durham City, an area which was gradually extended eastwards after 1822. Monkwearmouth Colliery sited actually within the borough of Sunderland was opened in 1834.[59] The historical pattern of coal and coke export from Sunderland is remarkably similar to that of the Tyne: the peak year for total shipments is almost the same (1927, 5,498,179 tons), with the peak year for coastwise shipments likewise delayed, until 1951 (2,504,534 tons)

TABLE 16

Coal Exports from Sunderland 1960
(Thousand Tons)

Coastwise	...	...	1,858	From River Wear Staiths	...	1,095
Foreign ...	...	...	343	From South Docks	...	...	1,106
	Total ...		2,201		Total ...	2,201

While there was insufficient flat land for docks along the river, the shipyards are hampered not so much by narrow land sites as by the narrowness of the river, the maximum width being but 400 feet. For this reason the modern shipyards are sited where the river changes direction, so that the berths, at a narrow angle to the shore, can face a longer stretch of water diagonally across the river, or in some cases actually pointing down a reach. This is graphically illustrated by the reorganization of the Southwick Shipyard of Austin & Pickersgill Ltd. Three short berths merely facing a short stretch of water diagonally across the river were scrapped in 1954 in favour of three berths *upstream* but facing a much wider stretch of water on a meander corner

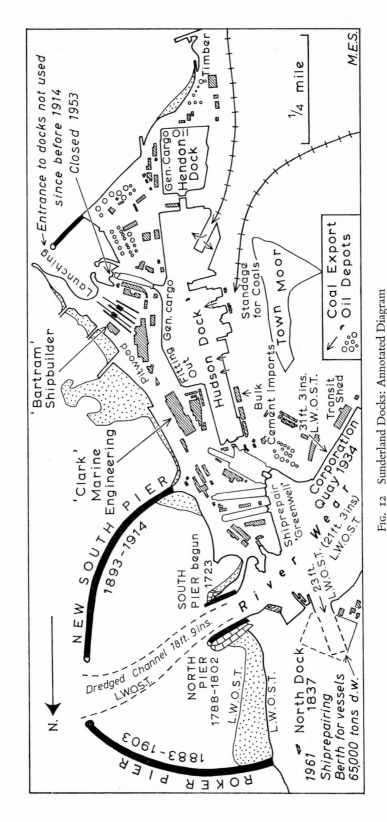

FIG. 12   Sunderland Docks: Annotated Diagram

Hulls are actually launched into the sea from the shipbuilding berths of Bartram & Sons (annual average launch in gross tons, 1958–60, 39,000), via the old 1856 docks outlet, thence between the piers and into the river, and finally to the fitting-out quay in Hudson Dock, only a thousand feet from the point of launch.

(see Fig. 13). On the inside shoulders of meanders shipbuilders have found sites a little less steep for the erection of platers' and welders' shops. In contrast, the high-level coal-shipping staiths are found where the river is narrowest with steep banks; and the three bridges span the river where it is straight, the symmetrically steep sides there reducing the gradients to high-level crossings and also the length of approach abutments. The clear height of the lowest of these bridges is the same as the high-level bridges spanning the gorge-like reach of the Tyne at Newcastle (82½ feet H.W.O.S.T.)

If Sunderland is compared with *Anyport*, the difficulties of the river, in part expressed by the absence of *simple lineal quayage*, are easily seen. There is no flood-plain to a glacial spillway, and sites have either been carved out of rather steep valley sides or made seaward of the docks by thrusting excavated material out to sea. A. E. Smailes has compared Wearside to the Shields component of Tyneside, although the mid-Tyne pattern of shipbuilding certainly also has its counterpart in the shipbuilding along three miles of the lower Wear. The first bridge, built in 1796, had the effect of welding settlement together on both sides of the Wear and confirming the town centre at the cross-roads south of the bridge. The High Street of old Wearmouth, combining the longitudinal and transverse routes of *Anyport*, now becomes progressively less important east of the bridge. The lack of general cargo imports for wide inland distribution is revealed in Table 17. Imports generally outweigh the

TABLE 17

Seven Most Important Imports and Three Most Important
Exports (Foreign and Coastwise), excluding Coal Dealt with at
the Port of Sunderland, 1960
(Thousand Tons)

Petroleum	275
Cement	57
Iron and Steel Scrap	40
Pitwood	10
Esparto	9
Timber	9
Wood Pulp	8
Total of Imports ...	450
Petroleum and Benzole	23
Limestone	16
Machinery	12
Total of Exports ...	55

exports, excluding coal, by eight to one. The terse title over an article by the Chairman of the River Wear Commissioners may be borrowed. 'Bulk Cargoes Predominate',[60] with coal exports forming 82 per cent of all Sunderland's trade by weight in and out during 1960. The iron ore imports for the Consett Iron Company Limited were lost after 1953 to the Iron Ore Quay at Newcastle, where there is 36 feet of water always available for ever larger ore carriers.

All appears to return to the difficulties of the river, but ships drawing up to 30 feet can now use the Wear. Large vessels and even super-tankers are built, launched,

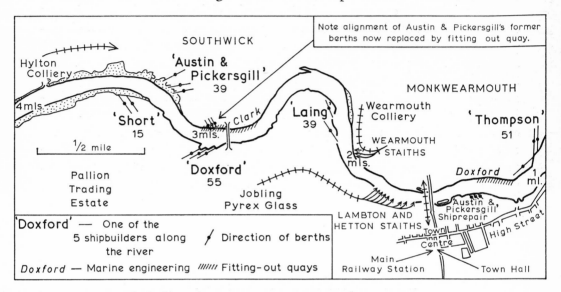

FIG. 13   Shipbuilders, Shiprepairers, and Staiths along the River Wear, Sunderland
Mileage along the river is measured from a point between the outer piers.

repaired, and moved light on the top of the tide. While Sunderland appears well down the list of commercial ports of the country, due to its proximity to the Tyne with its greater general cargo trade, it is the largest town on the east coast of England astride the country's third most important shipbuilding estuary, meriting more than anywhere else the title of the 'town of shipbuilders', since all the yards are within the borough boundary.

The Port of Middlesbrough and Tees-side

To reach the sea the River Tees crosses a low-lying area of Triassic rocks between the Magnesian Limestone to the north and the Liassic rocks outcropping on Eston Moor, a mere three miles to the south. This Triassic saddle was covered by glacial

PLATE I THE TYNE

Above: Looking east, downstream across central Newcastle, *cf.* Fig. 9.

Below: Looking north-east, five miles downstream of Tyne Bridge, see Fig. 8.

PLATE II TWO CONTRASTING RIVERS: THE WEAR AND TEES

Above: Looking north-west up the Wear from central Sunderland, *cf.* Fig. 13.

Below: The Tees, looking north-east, downstream, from the Ironmasters' District, *cf.* Fig. 15.

boulder clay, by deposits impounded in a glacial lake, and by the alluvial fill caused by a continuous rise in sea-level from about 8,000 to 2,000 B.C. Although the present sea-level has dropped about thirty feet from this maximum, the estuary in its natural state was still subject to flooding and floored by unconsolidated deposits except where Keuper Marl protruded at one or two 'scarps' in the river ('ninth-buoy scarp' and 'fifth-buoy scarp'), notably forming the site of Redcar Wharf, and along the coast.[61]

Compared with Tyneside and Wearside, the Port of Middlesbrough was a late starter. The meandering and shallow course of the lower River Tees in its natural state was, however, not the cause. Before 1825 the coalfield south of Durham City was not exploited, and the nearest coal mine was more than fifteen miles from the site of Middlesbrough and well within the orbit of the Wear trade. In the next twenty-five years not only was the coalfield opened up to within ten miles of the Tees, but the railway made light of the long haul. The *primitive* port of the unimproved Tees was at Yarm, seven miles south-west of Middlesbrough, but the rising market-town of Stockton, only three miles away, took over the river trade when a stone bridge was erected there over the Tees in 1769. Gradually, coal exports from Stockton and other trade increased, but it took a vessel six days to navigate the estuary of the Tees, and even when the river had been straightened between Stockton and Middlesbrough by cuts across meanders in 1808–10 and 1831, it still took two tides for a vessel to reach Stockton.[62]

Meanwhile, in 1825 the world's first public railway, the Stockton and Darlington, delivered coal to Stockton staiths more efficiently than it could be exported, and Joseph Pease, a director of the railway company, led a group of Darlington Quakers determined not to wait for the second cut by-passing a river meander, but to by-pass it instead by extending the railway three and a half miles to 'Port Darlington' *i.e.* Middlesbrough. Here in 1830 eight coal drops were erected, with the wagons raised by two steam engines, and then the wagon descended to the deck level of colliers at the ends of the jetties. Unfortunately for Port Darlington, in that same year of 1830 the Tees Navigation Company began to erect a series of transverse groynes from Stockton downstream to bring the river to a uniform width. While the groynes performed this task effectively,[63] and also deepened the river in mid-channel abreast of the groynes by increasing the velocity and scour in a narrower channel, shoals persisted downstream of the last groyne where the river suddenly widened. The transverse jetties of Port Darlington also acted as breakwaters, the silt piling against their stems and reducing the amount of water at their heads so that vessels of only 150 tons burden could use them. A wet dock was resolved upon to aid coaling, for two reasons: the progressive shoaling at Port Darlington; and the desire to be able to load colliers cheaply by gravity, by running railway tracks on to a raised platform and eliminating the expense of lifting engines. The entrance to the dock was by means of a channel a quarter of a mile long cut through alluvium to the river, and

E

when other traffic increased, the triangular area of the raised platform was used as the site of *dock elaboration* by making included peninsulas where more vessels could lie. Meanwhile, the shoaling downstream continued.

> 'One day during the present week the pilots report, you could walk across the bed of the river near the ninth buoy [three miles downstream of the dock] dry shod, with the exception of one part, about 8 yards wide, which was ankle deep.' [December 18, 1849][64]

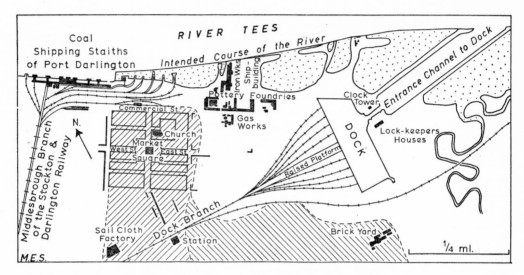

FIG. 14 Port Darlington, and Middlesbrough Town and Dock, 1846

Stipple indicates tidal mud about to be reclaimed; diagonal ruling indicates drift-covered Keuper Sandstone to the west, Keuper Marl to the east, and elsewhere is alluvium. After G. Turnbull, 'Account of the Drops Used for the Shipment of Coals at Middlesbro' on Tees, with a Short Description of the Town and Port of Middlesbro'', *Proceedings of the Institution of Civil Engineers*, 5 (1846), 248–54, Plate 17. Geological detail based in part on Crown Copyright Geological Survey maps by permission of the Controller of H.M. Stationery Office.

From 1852, with the establishment of the Tees Conservancy Commissioners it was decided to build longitudinal training walls[65] using slag from the iron works and support their effect by steam dredging. The first task was to block off the middle channel, in the vicinity of the present I.C.I. refinery site, and the river was trained in the most southerly of its three natural estuarine channels. The slag was also used in the construction of the South Gare Breakwater from 1863, where it was deposited at the rate of 600–700 tons per day in blocks of 3 tons, occasionally tipped into the sea red-hot. The iron masters paid the Commissioners 1½d. per ton for its removal (later increased to 4d.); the railway charged ¼d. per ton mile; and the maximum distance the material was hauled was five miles. So the breakwaters and twenty-five miles of training walls were built cheaply, the main cost being the facing walls. Some of the foundations for training walls and breakwaters were deposited by barges (training walls and South Gare Breakwater finished 1888; North Gare Breakwater, 1891). The only place where rock boring machinery was necessary was in the vicinity of the present Redcar Wharf—the 'eighth-buoy scarp' of Keuper Sandstone.

So far the port development is easy to understand: migration downstream for ever more efficient methods of coal export, the river aided by being the first in the Durham coalfield with a rail link. After 1850 the Tees coal exports declined as other ports nearer to the mines were linked by rail with their hinterland. But in 1850 the main seam of the Cleveland ironstone was discovered on the northern face of the Eston Hills just five miles from Middlesbrough. The discoverer was John Vaughan who with Henry Bolckow had set up a foundry, rolling mill, and puddling furnaces just west of Port Darlington in 1841, using pig iron from their iron works on the Durham coalfield at Witton Park. Henceforward, Tees-side was to be the great meeting-place of Durham coke and Cleveland ore, with wide sites available on

TABLE 18

Eras and Epochs in the Development of the Port of Middlesbrough

	Eras and Chief Areal Characteristics	Present-day Symbol
I	*Primitive:* Yarm	nil
	Era ended by erection of Stockton Bridge, 1769	
II	*Marginal Quay Extension:* terminus of Stockton and Darlington Railway, 1825	Stockton Corporation Quay 970 ft. × 14½–16 ft. L.W.O.S.T.
	Era ended by railway extension to 'Port Darlington', 1830	
III	*Marginal Quay Elaboration:* terminus of Stockton and Darlington Railway in eight coal shipping jetties at 'Port Darlington', 1830	Site of Dent's Wharf, Middlesbrough
	Era ended by opening of Middlesbrough Dock, 1842	
IV	*Dock Elaboration:* rectangular dock, with outline progressively elaborated in 1869, 1885, and 1898	Middlesbrough Dock
VI	*Specialized Quayage:* marginal quays on trained river frontage; oil jetties	18 private wharves, Teesport 1950–4
V	*Simple Lineal Quayage:* quay 3,000 feet long, dredged to 32 feet L.W.O.S.T.	Tees Dock—No. 1 Quay, 1962

either side of the Tees as the river was progressively confined between training walls. When it became necessary to import non-phosphoric foreign ores to feed a Bessemer steel plant in 1875, the Tees was available to become the great ore-importing port that it is today, as Cleveland supplies dwindled to about only seven per cent of current Tees-side demands.

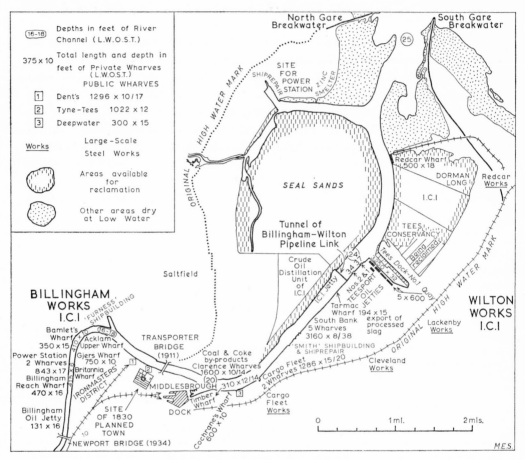

FIG. 15   Tees-side: Annotated Diagram

With reference to the two shipbuilding yards: the average annual gross tonnage launched 1958-60 was: The Furness Shipbuilding Co. Ltd., 73,340; and Smiths Dock Co. Ltd. 42,424.

Fig. 15 shows how much land has been made available for industrial development by reclamation up to the line of the training walls. Since 1931 the Tees Conservancy Commissioners have pumped on to reclamation grounds the material dredged from the river.[66] Two hundred and fifty acres of the Seal Sands have been reclaimed in this way. Altogether, since land reclamation began, nearly 3½ thousand acres have been made available for industry. Almost as much awaits reclamation, and indicates the great areas available for the growth of Tees-side industry and of its servant, the port.

In a comparison of Middlesbrough with *Anyport*, the progressive development downstream is the same, but on the Tees the estuary head sites with only 16 feet L.W.O.S.T. have become overshadowed by downstream industrial development. With iron ore imports becoming so important after 1875, the port development from that date diverges from that of *Anyport*. Docks of progressively simpler outline were not excavated since the traffic was carried in colliers and tramps of a smaller size than the general dry cargo liners of the twentieth century. But for many years Middlesbrough has attracted large vessels loading heavy bottom cargo, and also large bulk carriers of oil and ore. Furthermore, the *simple lineal deep-water quayage* of Tees Dock, Lackenby, has become necessary. This provides the expanding Tees-side industrial complex with a modern berthing lay-out, with no limitations on access by road and rail. The result is that eras V and VI are in reverse order from that of *Anyport*.

Space does not permit an account of Tees-side industry, though it has had a profound influence on the port's trade; fortunately, a recent comprehensive survey[67] is available. Instead, two tables are provided giving a selection of significant dates in the development of two of the largest companies, Imperial Chemical Industries Ltd. and Dorman Long & Co. Ltd., which between them employ one-fifth of Tees-side's quarter of a million workers.

TABLE 19

A Few Significant Dates in the History of Dorman Long[68] vis-à-vis Port Development on Tees-side

1842	Iron rolling mill and puddling furnaces established in the Iron Masters' District by Bolckow and Vaughan
1850	Discovery of Cleveland ironstone on Eston Moor
1851	First blast furnace at Middlesbrough
1854	Cleveland Works begun
1875	Bessemer Steel Plant, necessitating imports of non-phosphoric iron ore
	Dorman & Long commence an iron works in Iron Masters' District taking over the Britannia Works
1899	Amalgamation of Dorman Long with Bell Brothers at Port Clarence
1916	Steel works and Plate Mills at Redcar
1917	Dorman Long acquire all works but one in Iron Masters' District
1934	Beginnings of rationalization (*i.e.* specialization[69] by each works)

Post Second World War
- Cleveland Works—unloading and preparation of ore, iron-making, rail mill
- Redcar Works—steel plate
- Lackenby (1953)—steel ingots, universal beam mill, steel wire
- Iron Masters' District—bridge and constructional works
- Port Clarence—coke oven by-products, refining of crude tar and crude benzole

TABLE 20

A Few Significant Dates in the Development of Imperial Chemical Industries Ltd. vis-à-vis Port Development on Tees-side[70]

1918	Billingham site chosen by Government
1920	Manufacture of ammonium sulphate by Brunner Mond & Co., buyer of the site from the Government
1926	Formation of I.C.I. Ltd.
1927	First mining of anhydrite under the site
1930	Manufacture of sodium and cyanides
1936	First production of *Perspex*
1946	Construction begins at Wilton on 2,000 acres of land with all divisions of I.C.I. Ltd. represented on the site
1949	Plastics Division (*Perspex*)
1951	Heavy Chemicals Division—oil cracking plant fed from Teesport
	General Chemicals Division (Chlorine) from Durham saltfields
	Development at Billingham and Wilton linked by a pipeline under the Tees ten miles long, nine feet in diameter
1954	Plastics Division (*Polythene*)
	Fibres Division (*Terylene*)
1956	Dyestuffs Division (*Nylon*)
1963	Heavy Chemicals Division—first distillation of *crude* oil on reclaimed area north of the Tees

From the footbridge west of Middlesbrough Dock one can see the commodities in railway sidings; steel tubes, plates, beams, and sections. Such cargo attracts a considerable liner traffic to the port and is first stowage in freight liners to all parts of the world. Many ships start loading this ideal heavy and stable bottom cargo in Middlesbrough before completing loading at other ports on either side of the North Sea. This characteristic of steel in attracting trade to Middlesbrough may be compared to the tinplate attraction for liners at Swansea. Another attraction of the Port of Middlesbrough is that men engaged on dock or riverside work have two shifts, beginning at 6 a.m. and 2 p.m.—a most rare state of affairs in British ports.

Reference to the following tables of imports and exports shows the overwhelming importance of ores, oils, chemicals, and steel manufactures in the trade of the port. This is heavy 'unhandable' cargo. Most berths are therefore equipped with multiple rail tracks, and the shape of the Middlesbrough Dock is so designed that rail lines diverging from access tracks to the west can serve both the jetties and the quays. Because the new Tees Dock, No. 1 Quay is at right-angles to the river, and rail tracks can approach only from the landward end, the original idea of having the whole quay in one line was modified. The innermost berth of the five has been constructed at an angle of 24° to the other four, so as to enable separate rail access to be provided for it and also to facilitate the rail working of the other berths.[71]

Ore import and steel export deserve special mention. Iron ore is received on the Tees at Dorman Long's South Bank Wharf and for the South Durham Steel and

Iron Co., Ltd., at the Cargo Fleet Wharf. The South Bank Wharf is divided into four berths, and up to 85 per cent is grabbed out by the two 19-ton unloaders at No. 5 Berth, the ship being moved to other berths for finishing off. Special ore carriers can be wholly unloaded at No. 5. The purpose of the finishing-off berths is to ensure that the maximum amount of ore shall be unloaded at No. 5 which has the deepest water (33 feet L.W.O.S.T.) and the fastest unloading performance, up to 850 tons per hour. Immediately downstream is a lay-by dolphin berth, 750 feet by 38 feet L.W.O.S.T., where deep-laden ore carriers can lie, to be moved to No. 5 Berth at

TABLE 21

Ten Most Valuable Foreign Trade Imports into Middlesbrough, 1960

	Value £ Million	
Iron Ore	18·5	
Manufactured Fertilizers	2·0	
Crude Petroleum	1·9	
Manganese Ore	1·8	
Organic Chemicals	1·5	
Fuel Oil	1·5	
Refined Spirit Oils	1·5	
Phosphate of Lime	1·2	
Calcium Carbide	1·2	
Iron and Steel Scrap	·9	
Total of all Imports ...	38·7	(0·9 per cent of total U.K. imports by value)

TABLE 22

Ten Most Valuable Foreign Trade Exports from Middlesbrough, 1960

	Value £ Million	
Iron and Steel Tubes and Pipes	7·4	
Uncoated Iron and Steel Plates and Sheets ...	4·8	
Iron and Steel Girders and Beams	4·1	
Plastics	3·7	
Railway Construction Materials	2·9	
Alcohols	2·3	
Iron and Steel Angles, Shapes, and Sections ...	2·3	
Finished Metal Structural Parts	2·0	
Ammonium Sulphate	1·9	
Ships and Boats	1·8	
Total of all Exports ...	49·2	(1·5 per cent of total U.K. exports by value)

any state of the tide. The Cargo Fleet Wharf is equipped with two 12-ton ore unloaders serving its two berths. The ore is stacked adjacent to the wharf, but for Dorman Long it has to be hauled a short distance by rail to the foot of an ore-stacking gantry (see also p. 230).

Tees-side could hardly form a greater contrast with Tyneside and Wearside. Contrasts in the transverse profiles of the rivers are summed up by Middlesbrough's Transporter Bridge (1911) and Vertical Lift Bridge (1934) compared with the high-level bridges across the other rivers. Contrasts in plan reveal the great flat areas available for future development on Tees-side compared with the slope constrictions at least in St. Peter's and St. Anthony's Reaches on the Tyne and all along the Wear. Upon these three estuaries the ports now have very differently balanced functions. These differences have increased during this century as a result of: (i) the growth of general cargo trade to Newcastle Corporation Quays from 1923; (ii) the transfer of the last chemical works on Tyneside to Tees-side in 1926; (iii) the relative loss of shipbuilding on the Tees compared with the Wear, owing to the rationalization schemes of the 1930's (*cf.* Tees 6 of 8 yards closed; Wear 4 out of 11); (iv) the movement of the most important *extra*-Sunderland import (iron ore for Consett) from the Wear to the Tyne after 1953; and (v) the import of feedstock oil and *crude* oil for distillation at Middlesbrough from 1951 and 1963 respectively, for cracking and distillation on Tees-side. These are five examples of this diversification. Unfortunately, the Tyne and Wear lack extensive flat land close to the water available for industry. Such a feature formerly easily provided is now becoming increasingly difficult to find in Britain. This fact will ensure industrial tenants for the great areas being reclaimed on Tees-side and will cause the Tees further to outdistance the Wear and even make it a rival of the Tyne, as far as the total volume of its trade is concerned. But the growth is likely to be in the 'unhandable' heavy cargoes. The Tees-side steel worker will still receive much of his food through Newcastle and other general cargo ports; and the contrasts in these three estuaries within thirty miles of each other on the north-east coast will become even more obvious as time goes on.

REFERENCES

1. J. Rushworth, *Historical Collections*, 1692, Vol. 2, Part 3, 614.
2. These overlie the High Main Coal in three distinct 'posts' or sandstones, the upper sometimes known as the Grindstone Post.
3. 'The early castle from which the town is called was that built by Robert Curthose, eldest son of William the Norman, in the autumn of 1080, when he returned from his futile expedition of that year, against King Malcolm of Scotland . . .' C. H. Hunter Blair, Editor, *Archaeologia Aeliana*, Letter to *The Times*, April 19, 1960. See also J. H. Hinde, 'On the Original Site and Progressive Extensions of Newcastle-upon-Tyne; with an Estimate of Its Population at Various Periods', *Archaeologia Aeliana*, 3, new series (1859), 53–64, 54.

4. A. E. Smailes, *North England*, London: Nelson, 1960, has a map of medieval Newcastle's site and lay-out, Fig. 25, and a panorama of sixteenth-century Newcastle, Plate 43. The Romans erected a bridge and a fort at Pons Aelius (Newcastle), but their main road crossed the Tyne to Corstopitum (Corbridge), sixteen miles to the west.

5. M. R. G. Conzen, 'Geographical Setting of Newcastle', *Scientific Survey of North-eastern England*, Newcastle: British Association, 1949, 191–6.

6. J. B. Sissons, 'Erosion Surfaces, Cyclic Slopes and Drainage Systems in Southern Scotland and Northern England', *Transactions and Papers*, 28 (1960), Institute of British Geographers, 23–38, has attempted to reconstruct this eastward slope in map form, Fig. 2.

7. The Tyne Gap to Carlisle, originally a structurally faulted trough, was glacially modified by ice moving eastward. The maximum height in the gap is only 500 feet, and it has been an important route since General Wade's eighteenth-century military road.

8. D. Woolacott, 'The Superficial Deposits and Pre-glacial Valleys of the Northumberland and Durham Coalfield', *Quarterly Journal of the Geological Society*, 61 (1905), 64–96, 79. Bill Point, 72 feet high, projected 150 feet into the channel until 2 million tons of sandstone were cut away, P. J. Messent, 'Description of the Improvements of the River Tyne', *Transactions of the Institution of Naval Architects*, 22 (1888), 122–35, 128; and 36,000 tons of sandstone were removed from Felling Point in 1938–9 in a similar endeavour to widen the channel and improve navigation and visibility around a meander bend.

9. D. Woolacott, 'The Origin and Influence of the Chief Physical Features of Northumberland and Durham', *Geographical Journal*, 30 (1907), 36–60, 46, Section 1. Borings in connection with the construction of the Tyne Commission Quay indicated solid rock at 70–82 feet below low water, R. F. Hindmarsh, 'Tyne Commission Quay, North Shields', *Proceedings of the Institution of Civil Engineers*, 230 (1931), 25–39, 72–98, 26.

10. J. Guthrie, *The River Tyne: Its History and Resources*, Newcastle: Reid, 1880, 67. The author was secretary to the Tyne Improvement Commissioners from 1861–80 and cites the most important documents concerning the history of the port and river up to that time.

11. *Ibid.*, quoting the *Report*, 78.

12. There was some wrangling between Newcastle and the estuary mouth towns (North and South Shields and Tynemouth) over the numbers of their representatives on the Commission. All was resolved by compromise, *Ibid.*, 71–111.

13. *Ibid.*, 59–60.

14. *Ibid.*, 122.

15. *Ibid.*, 62.

16. *Ibid.*, 125–33.

17. From a chart by G. Collins, published in 1723, though probably referring to a survey carried out much earlier, *ibid.*, facing p. 56.

18. Calculated from depths on a *Chart of the River Tyne from the Sea to Wylam* (from surveys made under the direction of J. F. Ure in 1860), *ibid.*, facing p. 122.

19. *Ibid.*, from a survey made by P. J. Messent, 1875.

20. The present dredged maintenance level is 30 feet (L.W.O.S.T.) from pier heads to Jarrow Oil Jetty (7 miles downstream of Tyne Bridge); thence 25 feet to Elswick ($1\frac{1}{4}$ miles upstream of Tyne Bridge); thence 23 feet to Derwenthaugh Staiths ($3\frac{1}{4}$ miles upstream of Tyne Bridge); thence shoaling to 12 feet to the harbour limit, $8\frac{1}{4}$ miles upstream of Tyne Bridge.

21. In 1879.

22. Eroded by tributaries (River Don etc.) working northwards along the strike in front of the Magnesian Limestone scarp which is now largely buried by drift in the Shields area. The Slake is the low-lying area at the confluence of these tributaries with the Tyne and is now partially drowned by the tide.

23. A. E. Smailes, *op. cit.*, Fig. 38.

24. Valuable works for British shipbuilding with many references are: S. Pollard, *The Economic History of British Shipbuilding, 1870–1914*, unpublished Ph.D. thesis, University of London, 1951; L. Jones,

Shipbuilding in Britain Mainly Between Two World Wars, Cardiff: University of Wales Press, 1957; and J. R. Parkinson, *The Economics of Shipbuilding in the United Kingdom*, Cambridge: University Press, 1960. See also A. K. Cairncross and J. R. Parkinson, 'The Shipbuilding Industry', *The Structure of British Industry*, edited by D. Burn, Vol. 2, Cambridge: University Press, 1958, 93–129; and 'Report on Shipbuilding', *The Economist Supplement*, June 2, 1956. Further references are given below and also at the end of the chapters in this book on the Ports of Newcastle, Sunderland, Glasgow, Belfast, and Liverpool (Birkenhead).

25. P. Pilbin, 'External Relations of the Tyneside Glass Industry', *Economic Geography*, 13 (1937), 301–14, 314; and B. P. Hill and G. R. Clemo, 'Chemicals', *Scientific Survey, op. cit.*, 161–70, 162.

26. H. B. R. Powell, 'Shipbuilding', *Scientific Survey, op. cit.*, 112–19, 113. The first large all-welded vessel was launched in 1920 at Birkenhead, but before the large-scale developments of welding during the Second World War in the construction of Liberty and Victory Ships, an all-welded ship could not receive an A1 classification in Lloyd's Register, J. R. Parkinson, *op. cit.*, 112ff.

27. L. Redshaw, 'Welding as Applied to Shipbuilding', *Welding Research*, 3 (1949), 36–46.

28. Mould lofts may well be superseded by fully automatic photo-electrically controlled flame-cutting machines which work from process-drawings made at one-tenth scale. In this operation a drawing office, already necessary for prefabrication processes, totally replaces the mould loft. Messrs Bartram & Sons Ltd., Sunderland were the first to use this method in the United Kingdom.

29. H. B. R. Powell, *loc. cit.*, 116.

30. R. Atkinson, 'British Shipbuilding: the Way Ahead', *The Times*, January 3 and 4, 1961; see also *Research and Development Requirements of the Shipbuilding and Marine Engineering Industries*, Department of Scientific and Industrial Research: H.M.S.O., 1960; and J. R. Parkinson, *op. cit.*, 213–17.

31. At the yard of A/B Gotaverken, Arendal.

32. Reasons given for the decline to this proportion from before the Second World War, when the United Kingdom launched a third of the world's total shipping, have been given by a shipbuilder. '. . . the resurgence of Continental countries with their devastated establishments rebuilt with the most modern equipment and their employees only too eager to make the fullest and best use of it; the building up of the Japanese industry with American backing and a labour force more numerous than that available in any comparable plants, and, more recently, the apparently inescapable surge of national feeling in many countries undergoing industrial development, involving in some cases an attempt to set up a shipbuilding industry.' J. Brown, 'The End of an Era', *The Glasgow Herald 1960 Trade Review*, 1961, 27. For a *Report to the Ministry of Transport* [from outside the industry] *by Messrs. Peat, Marwick, Mitchell and Company* [see] *Shipbuilding Orders Placed Abroad by British Shipowners*, October 10, 1961, H.M.S.O.

33. See J. R. Parkinson, *op. cit.*, Table 1.

34. S. Pollard, 'The Decline of Shipbuilding on the Thames', *Economic History Review*, 3 (1950), 72–89,

35. A. E. Smailes, *op. cit.*, 115; and R. L. Galloway, 'An Account of Some of the Earliest Records Connected with the Working of Coal on the Banks of the River Tyne', *Archaeologia Aeliana*, 8 (1880). 167–97.

36. An Act of 1529 gave exclusive privileges to the Merchant Adventurers' Co. of Newcastle in respect of trade upon the Tyne. Members of this body dealing with coal export became known as the Company of Hostmen, since under their privileges they acted as 'hosts' to merchant strangers who had no power to trade under the 1529 Act. For a graphic description of keels at work on the Wear, see T. Potts, *Sunderland: A History of the Town, Port, Trade and Commerce*, Sunderland: Williams, 1892, 127–32. See also R. Smith, 'The Hostmen of Newcastle', *Sea-Coal For London*, London: Longmans, 1961, 7–14.

37. A. E. Smailes, *op. cit.*, Fig. 35 and Plate 32.

38. The early locomotives, *Puffing Billy* (1813) and *Blucher* (1814), were constructed by the engineers of Wylam Colliery (eight miles west of Newcastle) and of Killingworth Colliery (six miles northeast of Newcastle). The latter was George Stephenson.

39. This survey, and the accompanying map of the river, might usefully be compared with a survey by B. Plummer, *Newcastle-upon-Tyne: Its Trade and Manufactures*, Newcastle: Reid, 1874, 63–87.

40. D. Anderson, 'Tyne Bridge, Newcastle', *Proceedings of the Institution of Civil Engineers*, 230 (1931), 167–88.

41. On the loss of shipbuilding (Palmer's) and steel-making at Jarrow, see E. Wilkinson, *The Town that was Murdered: the Life-Story of Jarrow*, London: Gollancz, 1939; and for a picture of inter-war years, G. H. J. Daysh, 'A Distressed Region—Tyneside', *Economic Geography*, 11 (1935), 159–66; and *ibid.*, 'Economic Problems of the North East Coast', *Geography*, 22 (1937), 105–15.

42. R. Hammond, 'New Coal-Shipping Plant on the Tyne' [Whitehill Point Staiths], *Mechanical Handling*, 42 (1955), 272–8; G. B. Marriott, 'A Modern Coal-Loading Plant on the River Tyne', *Proceedings of the Institution of Civil Engineers*, 5, Part 2 (1956), 432–46. Howdon Staiths were closed in 1961.

43. 'Discharging Iron Ore from Ship to Wagon', *Engineering*, 178 (1954), 207–11.

44. G. H. J. Daysh and N. R. Elliott, 'The Location of Industry within the Port of South Shields', *Proceedings of the VIIIth General Assembly*, XVIIth Congress of the International Geographical Union, Washington, 1952, 148–51.

45. 'Shields' derived from 'Shiels'—*Scots*, 'huts', probably used by fishermen.

46. As long as the level of the lake was above 320 feet O.D. its waters appear to have escaped southward to cut the Ferryhill Gap, a convenient direct overflow channel across the Wear-Tees watershed followed by the main east coast railway. But when the glaciers retreated northward, a lower escape route across the Magnesian Limestone was uncovered, the present route of the lower ten miles of the Wear.

47. This section has been based on the following papers: J. Murray, 'An Account of the Progressive Improvement of Sunderland Harbour and the River Wear', *Proceedings of the Institution of Civil Engineers*, 6 (1847), 256–83—Plates 24–30 are a series of plans of the mouth of the River Wear 1719–1846; and 'On the Progressive Construction of the Sunderland Docks', *ibid.*, 15 (1855–6), 418–44; also W. Simpson, 'The Improvement of the Entrance to Sunderland with Reference to the Reduction of Wave Action', *ibid.*, 209 (1919–20), 198–250.

48. J. Murray (1847), *loc. cit.*, 268.

49. *Ibid.*, 279.

50. W. Simpson, *loc. cit.*, 211.

51. *Ibid.*, 225.

52. *Ibid.*, 203.

53. C. T. Trechmann, 'The Permian Formation in Durham', *Proceedings of the Geologists' Association*, 36 (1925), 135–45, 141–2.

54. For the early history of the 'three Wearmouths'—Monkwearmouth on the north side of the river; Bishop's Wearmouth, the parish on the south side of the river; and the port of Wearmouth at the mouth of the river on the south side, see M. H. Dodds, 'The Bishop's Boroughs', *Archaeologia Aeliana*, 12, third series (1915), 81–185, referring to the Bishop of Durham's lordship over the County Palatine of Durham.

55. A graphic description of keel traffic is to be found in T. Potts, *Sunderland: a History of the Town, Port, Trade and Commerce*, Sunderland: Williams, 1892, 127–32.

56. The end of the era rather than of the keels which lingered on until 1853, *ibid.*, 154.

57. A. E. Smailes, *op. cit.*, 147, Fig. 35.

58. W. W. Tomlinson, *The North Eastern Railway: Its Rise and Development*, London: Longmans, 1914, 217.

59. A new shaft penetrates 2,100 feet through the limestone to the Coal Measures and when fully modernized in 1966 it is estimated the colliery will produce 4,000 tons of coal per day.

60. S. J. Adamson, *The Times Review of Industry, Supplement on Sunderland*, January, 1961, 11–38, 15.

61. For the physical framework see R. Agar, 'Glacial and Post Glacial Geology of Middlesbrough and the Tees Estuary', *Proceedings of the Yorkshire Geological Society*, 29 (1953), 237–54; with a summary in J. W. House and B. Fullerton, *Tees-side at Mid-Century*, London: Macmillan, 1960, 24 *ff*.

62. Details of the early cuts are to be found in W. Fallows, *Fragments of the Early History of the Tees*, Middlesbrough, 1878, 7–15.

63. Contributions by Messrs. Simpson and Cubitt to a discussion on a paper entitled, 'The Engineering of the Rhine', *Minutes of the Proceedings of the Institution of Civil. Engineers*, 7 (1848), 246.

64. J. Taylor, 'Description of the River Tees and the Works upon It Connected with the Navigation', *Proceedings of the Institution of Civil Engineers*, 24 (1864–5), 62–103, 66, quoting a letter from a ship-owner.

65. The transverse groynes were removed from 1858 onwards.

66. There is a dredged depth at the river entrance of 26 feet L.W.O.S.T. with a mean range of 15 feet. It is not worth while deepening the river further until an area 4,000 feet long outside the entrance with 25 feet L.W.O.S.T., the Middle Ground, is dredged. This is being studied in a programme of hydraulics research, *Hydraulics Research: 1960*, published for the Department of Scientific and Industrial Research, H.M.S.O., 1961.

67. J. W. House and B. Fullerton, *op. cit.*

68. See C. Wilson, 'Dorman Long', *Steel Review*, 6 (1957), 11–23. The omissions in the table embrace the important part played by Lowthian Bell at Port Clarence.

69. There is a similar location specialization by the other great company in the Tees area—the South Durham Steel and Iron Company Ltd.: steel plates and slabs at Hartlepool; constructional steel at Cargo Fleet; and pipes, tanks and welded fabrications at Stockton.

70. Based on material in J. W. House and B. Fullerton, *op. cit.*, 153–94. See also *The Story of I.C.I. Ltd.*, London: The Times, 1962.

71. G. A. Wrigley, 'Further Developments at Teesport with Special Reference to the Construction of No. 1 Quay', *The Dock and Harbour Authority*, 43 (1962), 37–41.

FURTHER REFERENCES FOR NEWCASTLE AND TYNESIDE

Caesar, A. A. L. 'A Preliminary Note on the Major Exports of the North East Coast Ports during the Twentieth Century', *Journal of the Tyneside Geographical Society*, 1938/9, 145–52.

Charleton, R. J. *A History of Newcastle-on-Tyne*. Newcastle: Robinson, 1895.

Davies, J. C. 'Shipping and Trade in Newcastle-upon-Tyne 1294–6', *Archaeologia Aeliana*, 31, 4th Series (1953), 175–204.

Daysh, G. H. J. and E. Allen. 'Features of the Industrial Geography of the Tyne, Wear and Tees', *Scottish Geographical Magazine*, 1933 (49), 1–18.

Elliott, N. R. *Tyneside—A Study in the Development of an Industrial Seaport*. Unpublished Ph.D. thesis, University of Durham, 1955, published in an abridged form in *Tijdschrift voor economische en sociale geographie*, 53 (1962).

Garson, W. S. *The Origin of North Shields and Its Growth*. North Shields: Northern Press, 1926.

Gray, W. *Chorographia: or a Survey of Newcastle upon Tyne*. Newcastle, 1649.

Harvey, A. L. 'Two New Quays at Tyne Dock', *Journal of the Institution of Civil Engineers* [Maritime Engineering Division], 3 (1944–5), 1–38.

Hearnshaw, F. J. C. *Newcastle-upon-Tyne*. Newcastle: Sheldon, 1924.

Hodgson, G. B. *The Borough of South Shields*. Newcastle: Reid, 1903.

Johnson, R. W. *The Making of the Tyne*. London: Scott, 1895.

Lyall, A. C. *Old Gateshead*. Gateshead: Keely, 1920.

Macgregor, J. *Observations on the River Tyne with a View to the Improvement of Its Navigation*. Newcastle, 1832.

Middlebrook, S. *Newcastle-upon-Tyne: Its Growth and Achievement*. Newcastle Journal, 1950.

Pilbin, P. *Geographical Studies of the Development of Certain Industries of Tyneside and North-east England*. Unpublished Ph.D. thesis, University of Durham, 1935.

Rendel, G. D. *Newcastle: Its Municipal Origin and Growth*. London: Arnold, 1898.

Richardson, W. *History of the Parish of Wallsend*. Newcastle: Northumberland Press, 1923.

Sargent, A. J. 'The Tyne', *Geographical Journal*, 40 (1912), 469–86.

Scott, A. 'Deep Water Quays, Newcastle-on-Tyne', *Minutes and Proceedings of the Institution of Civil Engineers*, 119 (1895), 291–7.

Welford, R. *History of Newcastle and Gateshead*. 3 vols. London: Scott, 1884–7.

AND NOTABLY

Donkin, W. C. and E. F. Patterson. *Northumberland and Durham: a Bibliography*. London: H.M.S.O., 1946.

Donkin, W. C. *Outline Bibliography of the Northern Region*, University of Durham, King's College, Newcastle; the North East Industrial and Development Association; and the Cumberland Development Council, 1956.

FURTHER REFERENCES FOR SUNDERLAND

Burnett, J. *The History of the Town and Port of Sunderland and the Parishes of Bishopwearmouth and Monkwearmouth*. 1830.

Corder, J. W. *Miscellaneous Manuscript Historical Notes on Sunderland, Monkwearmouth, Bishopwearmouth, and Wearside Shipbuilding*. In Sunderland Central Library, 1947.

Garbutt, G. *A Historical and Descriptive View of the Parishes of Monkwearmouth, Bishopwearmouth, and the Port and Borough of Sunderland*. 1819.

Mitchell, W. C. *History of Sunderland*. Sunderland: Hill Press, 1919.

Summers, J. W. *The History and Antiquities of Sunderland*. Vols. 1 and 2 [incomplete]. Sunderland: Tate, 1858.

FOR SUNDERLAND SHIPBUILDING

Smith, J. W. and T. S. Holden. *Where Ships are Born: Sunderland 1346–1946 (and Later Years)*. Sunderland: Reed, 1949; supplemented by R. S. Cogdon, 'Civil Engineering in the Development of Shipyards, Marine Engine Works and Shiprepair Yards in the Port of Sunderland', *Institution of Civil Engineers Northern Counties Association*, Chairman's Address, 1960–1, containing an extensive account of the optical marking and automatic flame-cutting installation at Messrs. Bartram & Sons Yard, 36–45.

FURTHER REFERENCES FOR MIDDLESBROUGH

Lillie, W. *Middlesbrough 1853–1953*. Middlesbrough: Jordison, 1953.

Lock, M. [Director] *Middlesbrough Survey and Plan*. Middlesbrough Corporation, 1948.

Chapter 3

GLASGOW AND CLYDESIDE

THE lay-out of the modern Port of Glasgow reveals three contrasting areas: the *canalized Clyde* from Glasgow Bridge to Bowling, eleven miles downstream; the *Clyde estuary* with included banks, from Bowling to Greenock, twenty miles downstream from Glasgow Bridge; and thence the estuary forms a node with the *sea lochs*, Gare Loch, Loch Long, Holy Loch, and also with the Firth of Clyde. The *primitive* Port of Glasgow was the Broomielaw Quay, sited as might be expected, immediately downstream of the first bridge on the town side of the river. Until the river improvements of the second half of the eighteenth century, Glasgow and its *primitive* port were

> 'checqued and kept under by the shallowness of her river, every day more and more increasing and filling up, soe that noe vessells of any burden [greater than six tons] can come neerer up then within fourteene miles . . .' (1656)[1]

In 1755 John Smeaton reported that there were twelve shoals in the first five miles below Glasgow Bridge, four with only 18 inches at low water, and one, 400 yards below the bridge, with only 15 inches.[2] Until such conditions were remedied, no quay extensions were called for at the *primitive* port. This meant that vessels were discharged downstream of the worst shoal[3] (Dumbuck Shoal, thirteen miles below Glasgow Bridge), in the river area here termed the *Clyde Estuary* at Port Glasgow and Greenock.

In 1668 Glasgow City Council had purchased fourteen acres adjacent to Newark Bay, downstream of the Dumbuck Shoal and eighteen miles from the parent city.[4] Until 1774 the town and harbour built there by Glasgow were known as Newport, and after that date, Port Glasgow. Until the deepening of the Clyde between it and Glasgow, Port Glasgow was very busy. But despite its excellent water site, the land site is poor, a

> 'level strip . . . in places only 130 yards wide, . . . backed by the fault-riven edge of the hard basaltic plateau-lavas.'[5]

TABLE 23

Eras and Epochs in the Development of the Port of Glasgow

Eras and Chief Areal Characteristics	Present-day Symbols
I *Primitive:* quay on north side of Clyde downstream of bridge	Broomielaw Quay

Overshadowed by Port Glasgow, 1677–1815: Era ended by effective deepening of Clyde after 1792

II *Marginal Quay Extension*	Lancefield Quay

Era ended by the opening of Kingston Dock, 1867

IV *Dock Elaboration:* three docks in sites behind river quays	Kingston Dock, 1867; Queen's Dock, 1877–80; and Prince's Dock, 1892–7

Era ended by the opening of King George V Dock, 1931

V *Simple Lineal Quayage*	King George V Dock, 1931; Shieldhall Riverside Quay, 1958
VI *Specialized Quayage:* bulk handling (with iron ore imports replacing coal exports) alternate with shipyards on the *canalized Clyde*	Merklands, Meadowside, Shieldhall, and General Terminus Quays; Rothesay Dock, 1907; Shipyards; Bowling and Finnart Oil Terminals on *Clyde Estuary* and Loch Long respectively

Port Glasgow is no longer a port (see Table 25). Greenock with a similar water site, had a land site on a wider raised beach,[6] with the steep edge of the Carboniferous plateau lavas further to the south. Here industries developed after 1750 so that Greenock is now the chief port on the *Clyde Estuary*.

Glasgow, in contrast, grew up at a favourable land site, where the Clyde could be forded at all states of the tide, and in a favourable land situation which R. Miller has called the Howe of Glasgow—'Howe—a hollow place—ringed around by bleak plateaus.'[7]

TABLE 24

Particular and Relatively Favourable Factors in Clyde Ports' Location
(checked below)

	Water Site	Water Situation	Land Site	Land Situation
Greenock	✓	✓	✓	
Port Glasgow	✓	✓		
Dumbarton			✓	
Glasgow (before Clyde improvement)			✓	✓
Glasgow (after Clyde improvement)	✓	✓	✓	✓

TABLE 25

Some Facts about Greenock and Port Glasgow vis-à-vis Glasgow

Year		Greenock	Port Glasgow		Glasgow
1667 ↑	Checked by opposition of Royal Burghs	Glasgow attempts to buy land here for a port: thwarted		Checked by shallowness of Clyde	
1668			Port initiated by Glasgow Council		
1677			Declared to be the only port on the Clyde for customs purposes		
1710 ↓		Completion of harbour based on designs of that at Port Glasgow			
1714		Member port of Port Glasgow			
1780					Member port of Port Glasgow
1792					First recorded extension or Broomielaw Quay
1812		Declared an independent port			Declared an independen port
1833			Completely independent of Glasgow governmentally	Deepening of Clyde	
1840			Railway hastens decline as a port		
1845			Trading virtually at an end		

The nodality of Glasgow's land site and situation, enhanced by the establishment of a bishopric, cathedral, and permanent market by the end of the twelfth century, at first far outweighed the usefulness of the unimproved Clyde as a routeway. As late as 1782 (Fig. 16) the dominance of the 'cross of Lorraine' pattern[8] can still be discerned extending north-east from the ford. The double-barred cross reflected separate religious and market quarters, with only a very small built-up river frontage at the *primitive* port of the Broomielaw Quay. Indeed, because of its shallowness the river was liable to flood, and except at the bridge and the Broomielaw, buildings were confined to higher ground[9]

The shallowness of the Clyde in its natural state is derived partly from the fact that it flows north-west, a unique direction for a large river in Scotland. That part of its course in the Glasgow region below Lanark is subsequent, bearing a general longitudinal alignment with the strike of the underlying rocks.[10] It is hard to tell what this valley was like before glaciation. Boreholes indicate a deep valley trending westwards north of Glasgow, with a subsidiary valley (pre-glacial Clyde?) meeting it near Clydebank (west Glasgow). It is a fair guess that from this point the valley did not widen progressively downstream, but like the present Clyde was hemmed in

Airviews (M/c)

PLATE III THE LOWER CANALIZED CLYDE

Looking north-west, downstream. Part of Rothesay Dock, and the shipbuilding yard of John Brown & Co., Ltd., Clydebank, are in the foreground. Note the river training walls and the Long Dyke, located on Fig. 20.

Airviews (M/c

PLATE IV GLASGOW AND BELFAST

Above: Looking north-east up the Clyde across Glasgow's inner harbour, *cf.* Fig. 17.

Below: Looking south, upstream across Belfast's harbour and shipyard, *cf.* Fig. 26.

Aerofilm

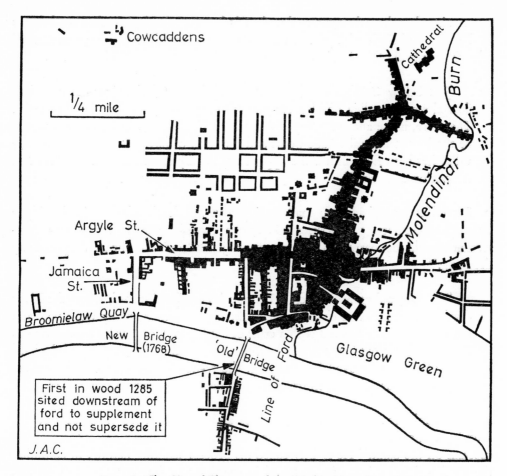

FIG. 16 The City of Glasgow and the *Primitive* Port, *circa* 1782

The buildings shown appear on James Barry's map of Glasgow. Certain streets have been 'filled in' to emphasize the original double 'Cross of Lorraine' pattern, here becoming soldered to the port at the Broomielaw via the developing Argyle and Jamaica Streets.

between Bowling and Erskine (ten miles downstream of Glasgow Bridge) by hard Carboniferous lavas. These set a limit to the lateral widening of the valley. Imagine then a deep valley, eroded far below present sea-level, trending west-north-west to near the present site of Greenock. Such a gutter was filled with debris deposited by glaciers, moving down from the highlands in the north-west, and by material derived from glacially impounded lakes. Closer to their source of origin these glaciers had greater erosive power, gouging out fiords represented by Holy Loch, Gareloch, and Loch Long and the Upper Firth of Clyde. Thus the pre-glacial valley filled with loose material, through which the Clyde flowed so sluggishly in its estuary, is rather abruptly connected to the Clyde sea area with more than ten fathoms in the lochs and Firth of Clyde. In the Glasgow area itself the Clyde, re-established after the removal of the ice, has attempted to exhume its pre-glacial valley.

'Just below Cambuslang [East Glasgow], however, the river has ceased to flow along this valley, and has cut into solid rock as well as into loose material. Therefore, if the ancient valley had not been filled in . . . , Cambuslang would be the lowest natural bridge point and the head of navigation; while since the valley has been filled in it is the upper limit of easy canalization of the river and excavation of docks.'[11]

Several attempts had been made to improve the depth of water in the Clyde before John Golborne gained success. In 1768 he recommended that the river's cross-section should be narrowed by transverse jetties and the shoals deepened by dredging.[12]

'The first and grand obstacle is Dumbuck Ford [see Fig. 20], where the River dividing itself into two channels the re-flowing current is greatly weakened, and the bottom, being covered with a crust of hard gravel, cannot be worn down to a proper depth; but if a jetty . . . [were] . . . to confine the current, and the hard crust of gravel removed by dredging, the re-flowing current would then act with greater force, and soon grind down a deep and capacious channel;'[13]

By 1773 Golborne had erected 117 jetties and completed his work of scouring Dumbuck Shoal by scraping the bottom with iron cases drawn across the river by capstans on the bank.[14] He rightly called his process 'assisting nature'. In confining the Clyde's flow by jetties he increased its speed. Since the power of river erosion increases approximately as the square of the velocity, the river was able to maintain the increased depth given by dredging.

Low Water Depths at Former Dumbuck Ford

1759 & 1769	2 ft.	1824	17 ft.
1774	7 ft.	1871	21 ft.
1781	14 ft.	present	29 ft.

In 1799 John Rennie[15] recommended that low walls of rubble ('wing-dams'), parallel to the river, should be made joining the transverse jetties, and in 1806 Thomas Telford[16] suggested that these should be extended, concurring in the use of dykes parallel to the river to bring it to a more uniform width. Material dredged from the river was used behind the dykes to consolidate the riparian lands, reclaimed from the river's flood-plain, which were to become valuable riverfront industrial sites. The whole process was accelerated with the introduction of steam dredging in 1824. All this was possible because the valley was filled with loose material; the increased depths were achieved not by increasing high waters but by removing material from the river bed. Only once, in 1854, was solid rock encountered. At Elderslie, just over 4½ miles downstream of Glasgow Bridge, a volcanic dyke (dolerite), associated with very hard boulder clay, 925 feet long and 320 feet wide, lay menacingly only eight feet below low water. It took fifty-three years to overcome this obstacle completely by underwater dynamiting.[17] J. B. S. Gilfillan and H. A. Moisley reflected how fortunate it has been for Glasgow that this was the only serious obstacle ever encountered on the canalized Clyde.

> 'Had the natural channel been floored by solid rock, like that of the Wear, for example, improvement would have been prohibitively expensive; Greenock might have become another Liverpool and Glasgow its Manchester.'[18]

Later engineers of the canalized Clyde, following Golborne, Rennie, and Telford, had to think in terms of a 300-foot wide channel, and therefore many of the original parallel dykes had to be set back to give the line of the present riverfront. The low water depth off the Broomielaw is now 25 feet. To achieve it the Clyde has been dug out like any canal.

From 1770 the Glasgow Town Council were trustees of the river. Since 1825 their representatives have been gradually added to by representatives of other riparian town councils, trading interests, and ratepayers, constituted since 1858 as the Clyde Navigation Trust, the Port of Glasgow authority.

Development beyond the *primitive* port came late as compared with *Anyport*. Glasgow possesses the land site of an estuary head favourable in this country to the early development of a port; but at Glasgow the water site was originally very poor. When the Act of Union, 1707, allowed Scotland to trade with the transatlantic English colonies, the Clyde ports had a magnificent water situation on the north Atlantic approaches. This no doubt stimulated efforts to deepen the Clyde in the eighteenth century. *Marginal quay extension* could not take place at Glasgow until this was achieved. *Marginal quay elaboration* into the river never occurred because, like the Rivers Tyne, Hull, and Avon, the canalized Clyde was so narrow, not even permitting the use of any lighters in the modern port.

Dock elaboration behind the riverfront is well represented, though it might be permissible to dub this *marginal quay elaboration* since the Prince's and Queen's Docks are really tidal basins, the average tidal range at Glasgow being only thirteen feet, about the same as at Southampton. *Simple lineal quayage* is represented downstream by the Shieldhall Riverside Quay (1958), and by the King George V Dock (1931), with a possibility of further similar docks to the west, which would make a lay-out similar in plan to another dock system opening on to a canal—that of the Manchester Terminal Docks. But on the Clyde each dock would be comparable to the largest dock at Manchester, meriting the term *simple lineal quayage*.

	Length	*Width*
Glasgow King George V Dock	2,483 ft.	350 ft.
Manchester No. 9 Dock	2,700 ft.	250 ft.

Specialized quayage is rather widely dispersed, though more dominant downstream of the commercial quays. Since 1951 it also occurs in the sea lochs area, in Loch Long, where no regular commercial port functions had ever been previously performed.

Modern Functions of the Port of Glasgow

The description will proceed from Glasgow Bridge (successor to the Broomielaw New Bridge of 1768, see Fig. 16) to Loch Long, twenty-six miles to the west. Reference to location is by means of mileage downstream of the bridge and to north and south banks (N or S).[19]

TABLE 26

Patterns of Port Activity on Clydeside
(Mileage below Glasgow Bridge)

		Location	
	Nature of Pattern	*North Bank*	*South Bank*
I	Continuous marginal commercial quayage, with *dock elaboration* behind	0–2	0–1¾
II	Commercial quays and docks, and ship-building yards alternating on opposite sides of the river	2–6¼	1¾–6¼
III	Widely spaced shipbuilding yards, with one oil depot	6¼–19	6¼–19
IV	Port of Greenock		
V	Sea Lochs Area		

Since these patterns are quite clearly separated, it is possible to name the first three after the areas of waterway where they occur:

    I *The Canalized Clyde* from Glasgow Bridge to River Kelvin (2N);
   II *The Canalized Clyde* from River Kelvin to River Cart (6¼S);
 III *The Lower Canalized Clyde* and *the Clyde Estuary.*

The *Canalized Clyde* from Glasgow Bridge to River Kelvin is lined by commercial quays. A few of the smallest vessels serving the Western Isles (up to 150 n.r.t.) penetrate four bridges to the Custom House[20] Quay, where sand and gravel are also discharged from barges. But coastwise traffic is mostly accommodated in the Kingston Dock (1867, rebuilt 1917; $\frac{1}{2}$S), the first of the Glasgow tidal docks, for Scottish Isles services; or at the Anderston and Lancefield Quays (0–1N), rebuilt extensions of the Broomielaw, and Windmillcroft Quay ($\frac{1}{4}$–$\frac{1}{2}$S), all for the Irish ferry traffic. The original trading stimulus for the extension of the *primitive* Broomlie-law is seen in the names of the first transverse route inland, Jamaica Street, Plantation Quay (1840–60; 1$\frac{1}{4}$S), and Kingston Dock itself. The longitudinal road on the

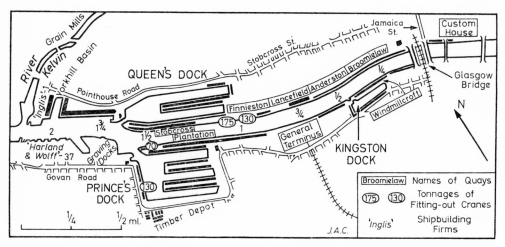

FIG. 17   The Canalized Clyde, from Glasgow Bridge to the River Kelvin

The figures after shipbuilding firms represent the average annual gross tonnage (in thousands) launched 1958–60. Figures in the river are miles downstream of Glasgow Bridge.

south, serving the riverside, is Govan Road until cut off by the King George V Dock (4S). Stobcross Street (formerly Finnieston Street) and Pointhouse Road have a similar function, but they in their turn are cut off by the River Kelvin (2N). Because of such obstacles the main Renfrew and Dumbarton Roads run a little further inland.

The Queen's Dock (1877–80, 1$\frac{1}{2}$N) and Prince's Dock (1892–7, 1$\frac{1}{2}$S) are both located on the sites of former shipyards which have been moved downstream to more extensive land sites and a slightly wider river. By means of their included peninsulas the tidal docks provide ten extra quays, parallel to the river, eight equipped with transit sheds, but the innermost landward quays are used for mineral handling. Yorkhill Basin (1908, 2N) has links with North America, with whisky consignments an important feature, since this is Glasgow's most valuable export.

Two notable rail lay-outs transverse to the river are seen. The first serves General Terminus Quay ($\frac{3}{4}$S), designed originally for the export of coal brought by rail from the Lanarkshire coalfield, without crossing any main railway line. With the decline of coal exports, and the exhaustion of the blackband iron ore interbedded with the coal, the traffic of this quay has been altered and reversed. Since 1958 it has been an iron ore importing berth. Three grabbing appliances can unload up to 1,800 tons of ore an hour, discharging on to a conveyor system to fill whole trains (30 × 34-ton wagons) bound for the steel works at Ravenscraig (Motherwell), eleven miles away. Two 16,000-ton deadweight ore carriers can be discharged simultaneously; and when the water level falls 12 feet to a 23- or 25-foot depth at low water the

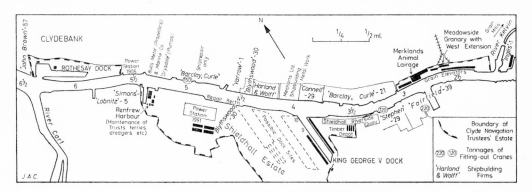

FIG. 18   The Canalized Clyde, from the River Kelvin to the River Cart

The figures after shipbuilding firms represent the average annual gross tonnage (in thousands) launched 1958–60. Figures in the river are miles downstream of Glasgow Bridge.

vessels have a reduced draught, so quickly is their cargo removed (see also p. 230). When this quay opened, the saving in unloading and freight charges to Ravenscraig compared with Rothesay Dock was ninepence per ton. Another rail lay-out transverse to the river is observed in the second pattern of port activity beyond the River Kelvin, serving the Meadowside Quay (2,500 ft.; $2\frac{1}{2}$N). This is the principal grain berth in the port. A 1914 granary, enlarged in 1937, was doubled in capacity in 1959–60. There is a short road haul to millers along the River Kelvin. Adjacent is the Merklands Quay (1,350 ft.) with a lairage for live cattle imported from Ireland and a transit shed for fruit. For four miles (2–6 approx.) commercial functions now alternate with shipbuilding yards, with their cranes and slipways dominating the river scene. From this group of shipbuilders[21] it is possible here to select only one firm for brief mention as a typical case.

In 1818 John Barclay commenced shipbuilding at Stobcross (1N), where there was a pool of deep water in the river. Robert Curle, the manager of the shipyard, was taken into partnership in 1845, and in 1855 the Whiteinch Yard was opened (3¼N). By 1861 the firm was producing engines in the Finnieston district behind the original shipyard. This Stobcross site had to be given up in 1874 to make room for the port extensions in the Queen's Dock area, so further development was concentrated at Whiteinch and at Elderslie (5N) where there are two dry docks. The engine works are adjacent to the Whiteinch Shipyard (and also still in Finnieston), and a 150-ton crane is maintained on the fitting-out wharf. From 1955–61 an extensive £3 million reconstruction of this yard has been carried out to provide a straight-line production system. Steel is delivered at the western end to storage areas where overhead cranes serve motorized conveyers feeding the platers' sheds and assembly sheds. Thence welded sub-assemblies emerge on to the building berths (Fig. 19). The average yearly output of this firm is 21,000 gross registered tons of all types of vessel, and repair work is undertaken at Elderslie.[22] Some general considerations about shipbuilding and ports have been dealt with above (pp. 43–6). A significant point in connection with Glasgow shipbuilding is that it became a major industry after the tobacco and the cotton textile industries had suffered setbacks in turn.[23] Undoubtedly, the change in shipbuilding from wood to iron and steel gave at least an initial advantage to shipbuilders with yards near Glasgow over those having *Clyde Estuary* sites, further from the iron ore interbedded with the coal seams of the Lanarkshire coalfield. However, very important shipbuilding yards are to be found today on *Clyde Estuary* sites near Dumbarton, Port Glasgow, and Greenock. The historical change in the 'balance of power' is baldly illustrated by four sets of figures in Table 27.

TABLE 27

Clyde Shipbuilding: Comparative Launching Data
(Tons)

Year(s)[24]	Clyde Estuary Yards		Canalized Clyde
1786–7	6,190	(all wooden)	169
1847–51 {	4,110	(wooden ships)	860
	1,290	(iron ships)	1,920
1958–60	153,100		249,782

Shieldhall Riverside Quay (3½S), 1,700 feet long, with 32 feet L.W.O.S.T. is the most recent provision of *simple lineal quayage*. Since 1958 it has been the main timber berth, although the open berths 9 and 10 in the King George V Dock (4S) still deal with timber in addition to shipping manufactured steel goods. This dock, opened in 1931, is the principal commercial dock of the port. There is room for two other docks of similar size to the west on the Shieldhall Estate owned by the Clyde Navigation Trust. Transit sheds line this dock, some 55 feet back from the quay, compared with the mere 15 feet of space between quay wall and sheds regularly

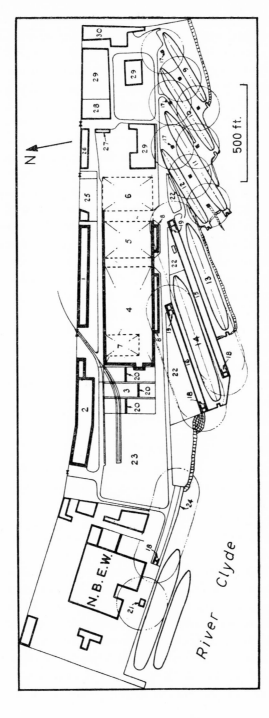

Fig. 19 A Reconstructed Shipyard on the Clyde: Clydeholm Shipyard and North British Engine Works

The yard is sited 3½ miles downstream of Glasgow Bridge. 1. Workshops, Power House, Canteens, etc.; 2. Joiners' Shop and Boiler House; 3. Steel Stockyard; 4. Platers' Shed; 5. Assembly Shed; 6. Unit Storage Area; 7. Mould Loft over Platers' Shed; 8. Offices and Stores; 9. No. 1 Berth; 10. No. 2 Berth; 11. No. 3 Berth; 12. No. 4 Berth; 13. No. 5 Berth; 14. No. 6 Berth; 15. No. 4 Trackway; 16. No. 5 Trackway; 17. 10-ton Cranes; Berths 1–4; 18. 10-ton Travelling Cranes; 19. 60-ton Travelling Cranes; 20. 10-ton Electric Overhead Cranes; 21. 150-ton Crane; 22. Storage Areas; 23. Area for Future Development; 24. Extension to Fitting-Out Wharf; 25. Car Park; 26. Main Office; 27. Managers' Offices; 28. General Store and Riggers' Loft; 29. Covered Storage; 30. Plumbers' Shop and Paint Shop.

found in the Queen's and Prince's Docks. The western part of the Shieldhall Estate is occupied by the Braehead Power Station (1951, $4\frac{3}{4}$S) which uses the river only for cooling water. The Rothesay[25] Dock (6N), 1907, completes the pattern of riverside activity between the Rivers Kelvin and Cart. It was designed for coal export, but its pattern of trade has changed and been reversed in direction, as at the General Terminus Quay; limestone from North Wales (Llanddulas), for steel-makers' flux, pig-iron, and iron ore imports are its chief cargoes today. The lay-out of the Rothesay Dock indicates its role as a handler of bulk raw materials and fuel—the absence of quayside sheds, the open rail lay-out along the quays, and the coaling appliances fed by transverse rail tracks on the north quay.

Beyond the River Cart ($6\frac{1}{4}$S), the pattern of port activity is much less continuous. The south bank has no port function until the shipyards of Port Glasgow (18S) are reached, for the navigable channel has been trained closer to the north shore. Opposite the River Cart on the north bank is perhaps the most famous shipyard on the Clyde. John Brown & Company, a large Sheffield steel firm, bought the Clydebank[26] Engineering and Shipbuilding Works ($6\frac{1}{2}$N) in 1899, as 'it was desired to find some automatic outlet in the shipbuilding trade'[27] for their heavy forgings. The opportunity to launch very large vessels is given by the increased water area available through the confluence of the Cart with the Clyde opposite the shipyard. The eight berths are arranged to converge on this water site—two groups of four with a fitting-out basin in the centre. It was in No. 4 Berth of the eastern group, 1,100 feet by 135 feet wide, that the *Queen Mary* and the *Queen Elizabeth* were built. The light draught of the *Queen Mary* was 35 feet. Before safe deep water could be reached, she had to travel $15\frac{1}{4}$ miles downstream on one tide where the channel was 25–26 feet deep L.W.O.S.T. with a 12-foot range. The keel of the newly-launched vessel passed 33 feet below the point where the bed of the river had been at Dumbuck Shoal two centuries before. In addition the bed of the Clyde had to be widened by 100 feet for three-quarters of a mile west of the River Cart ($6\frac{1}{2}$–$7\frac{1}{4}$S) and again by 100 feet for one mile on the north bank at Dalmuir (8N).[28]

The Forth and Clyde Canal enters the *Clyde Estuary* at Bowling ($10\frac{1}{2}$N). This canal, opened in 1775, contributed to weakening Glasgow's links with the timber ports of northern Europe by putting the Clyde in water communication with Grangemouth and other ports of eastern Scotland. A branch to Glasgow (Port Dundas) was opened in 1790. But very little traffic had been carried on the canal since the coming of the railway, and in 1961 it was decided to close the canal altogether. Since 1920 the Bowling Oil Depot ($11\frac{1}{2}$N) has developed, at the point where the navigable channel swings closest to the north shore, and now receives refined oil from Fawley (Southampton). Dumbarton's river, the Leven (14N), is dominated by the famous shipyard of William Denny & Bros. Ltd., where the *Rotomahana* was launched in 1879, the first ocean-going vessel to be built of mild

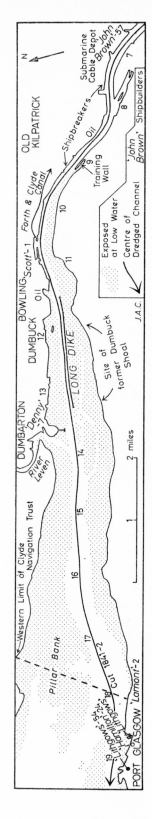

FIG. 20   The Lower Canalized Clyde and the Clyde Estuary

The figures after shipbuilding firms represent the average annual gross tonnage (in thousands) launched 1958–60. In 1961 Lithgow's amalgamated their east yard with that of their subsidiary, Hamilton's. Figures in the river are miles downstream of Glasgow Bridge.

steel, and epitomizing William Denny's pioneering championship of steel in the construction of ships. The Long Dike, completed in the early nineteenth century, prevents the ebb channel wandering as the estuary widens. Diagonally opposite the Leven (16–17S) are the derelict timber ponds east of Port Glasgow, reminders of the days when Greenock and Port Glasgow far outdid the *Canalized Clyde* in the building of wooden ships. Port Glasgow's only connection with the river is its shipbuilding, but at Greenock (20S) the dredged ebb–channel swings amazingly

TABLE 28

Eras and Epochs in the Development of the Port of Greenock[29]

Eras and Chief Areal Characteristics	Present-day Symbols
I *Primitive:* small piers, followed by construction of the original harbour	Filled-in West Harbour of 1707
II *Marginal Quay Extension:* within original harbour, *circa* 1750	nil
Era ended by opening of physically separate harbour, 1809	
III *Marginal Quay Extension:* further harbours and a pier on reclaimed land	East India (1809), Victoria (1850), and Albert Harbour (1867): Princes Pier (1870)
Era ended by opening of a wet dock, 1878	
IV *Dock Elaboration:* major commercial dock	James Watt Dock, 1878 (the only impounded and therefore true dock on the Clyde)
V *Simple Lineal Quayage:* never completed because of lack of finance and competition from Glasgow	Great Harbour, 1878
VI *Specialized Quayage:* taking advantage of deep-water sites	Graving Docks; and Tanker de-sludging berth, Great Harbour

close to the southern shore. The flood–channel, interlocking with the dredged channel, is to the north of the banks. There is a notable import of raw sugar for Greenock's sugar refining industry, established in the eighteenth century during the early trading with the transatlantic English colonies. The Port of Greenock (Fig. 21) has its own harbour trust, dating from the thrusting days of the early eighteenth century, when the magnificent natural water site enabled it to compete with Glasgow's outport of Port Glasgow immediately upstream. And the Port of Greenock certainly outstripped the Port of Glasgow in the early nineteenth century.

In 1945 the Clyde Estuary Committee proposed one port authority for the whole of the Clyde instead of the seven existing undertakings of which the Clyde Navigation Trust and Greenock Harbour Trust are overwhelmingly the most important.[30] This will have added weight when the Clyde's largest graving dock (1,000 × 150 × 45

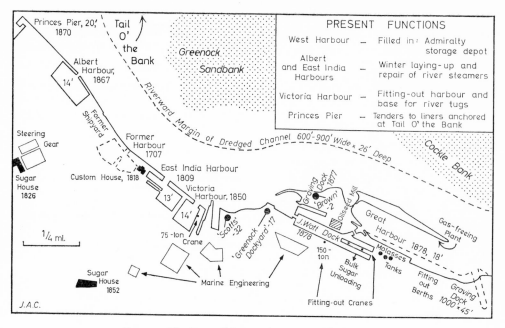

FIG. 21 The Port of Greenock: Annotated Diagram

The names within single inverted commas are shipbuilding firms with a figure representing the average annual gross tonnage (in thousands) launched 1958–60. Depths in feet are L.W.O.S.T. The new graving dock is due to be completed in 1964. After I. A. G. Kinniburgh (1960), *loc. cit.*

feet deep) is finished at Inchgreen in 1964.[31] No doubt Greenock is proud of its port's history, which is longer than that of Glasgow, but it would certainly seem most desirable to have one river conservancy authority from Glasgow Bridge to the seaward termination of the sea lochs.

At Finnart, on Loch Long, *Anyport's* 'oil berths in deep water' find dramatic illustration. Oil was first discharged here in February, 1951,[32] and pumped through a 57 mile-long pipeline across Scotland to the refinery at Grangemouth. The Port of Grangemouth can receive tankers up to only 14,000 tons deadweight, and even if a very long jetty had been built in the Firth of Forth it would still have had a limit of about 32,000 tons. A fiord like Loch Long, with steeply-plunging banks gouged by ice, provides magnificent deep-water sites. Jetty No. 2 at Finnart, opened in 1959, has a stem extending only 200 feet from the edge of the loch, yet the jetty head has a low-water depth of 55 feet (12 feet is the average tidal range) and is capable of receiving oil tankers of 100,000 tons deadweight at all states of the tide. The steep banks of the sea lochs of course provide no large flat site suitable for an oil refinery. This is the effect of the Clyde's debouching into an area radically altered by mountain glaciation rather than having eroded its own valley continuously down to the sea.

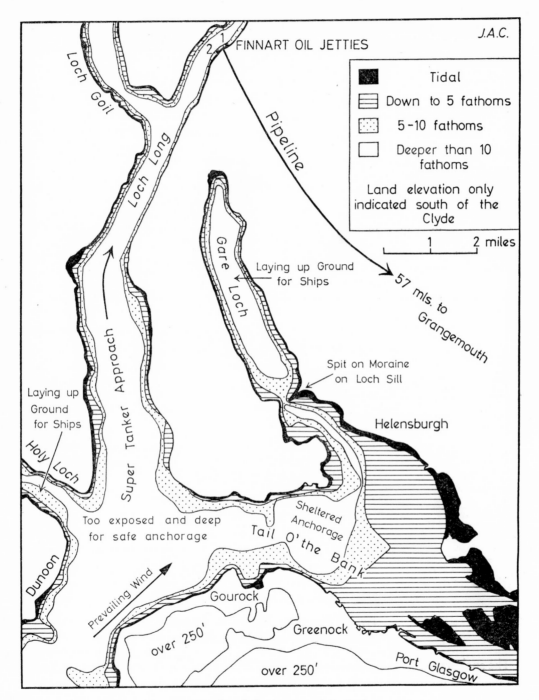

FIG. 22   The Clyde Estuary and Sea Lochs

Finnart was the first terminal in Europe to be capable of taking tankers of 100,000 tons deadweight. The following table gives the present capacities of other British oil terminals:

TABLE 29

Major Oil Terminals of the United Kingdom

Oil Terminal	Maximum Deadweight Tonnage Capacity	Oil Terminal	Maximum Deadweight Tonnage Capacity
Ardrossan	14,000	London (Canvey Island)	21,000
Belfast	32,000	London (Coryton)	45,000
Finnart	100,000	London (Shellhaven)	18,000
Glasgow (Bowling)	16,000	London (Thameshaven)	60,000
Grangemouth	14,000	London (Thames, Long Reach) ...	32,000
Heysham	18,000	Manchester (Eastham)	32,000
Hull (Salt End)	27,500	Manchester (Stanlow)	16,000
Isle of Grain	50,000	Milford Haven	100,000
Liverpool (Tranmere)	65,000	Southampton (Fawley)	65,000
Swansea	25,000		

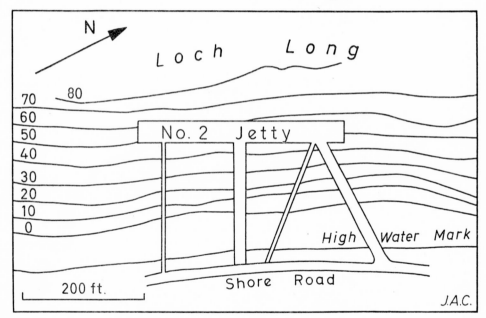

Fig. 23 No. 2 Jetty, Finnart Oil Terminal
The contours refer to depths at L.W.O.S.T.

The anchorage for vessels awaiting berths at Finnart and for those awaiting the tide to proceed up river is the Tail o' the Bank, a graphic name coined when the banks gave notoriously shallow water before the nineteenth century. Perversely, the haven is limited to the west by water which is too deep for safe anchorage, but nevertheless the Tail o' the Bank area is the safest, largest, and most sheltered anchorage on Britain's west coast.

TABLE 30

Fifteen Most Valuable Foreign Trade Imports into the Port of Glasgow (incl. Bowling), 1960

	Value £ Million
Crude Petroleum (via Finnart)	23·9
Iron Ore	11·4
Maize	5·9
Wheat	5·3
Butter	4·3
Unmanufactured Tobacco	4·0
Live Cattle	4·0
Wood (Simply Worked)	3·6
Fuel Oil	3·0
Oilseed Cake	2·9
Raw Rubber	2·8
Office Machinery	2·5
Raw Cotton	2·3
Newsprint	2·1
Raw Wool	1·9
Total of all Imports ...	137·0

(3·2 per cent of total U.K. imports by value)

TABLE 31

Fifteen Most Valuable Foreign Trade Exports from Glasgow (incl. Bowling), 1960

	Value £ Million
Scotch Whisky	37·4
Iron and Steel Tubes and Pipes	8·4
Ships and Boats	7·1
Sewing Machines	6·8
Boilers and Boiler-house Plant	4·5
Uncoated Iron and Steel Plates and Sheets ...	3·7
Road Vehicles	3·7
Office Machinery	3·3
Tractors	2·6
Aircraft Engines	2·4
Woven Fabrics Containing Man-made Fibres ...	2·3
Finished Metal Structural Parts	2·1
Carpets	2·0
Metal Working Machinery	2·0
Woven Woollen Fabrics	1·9
Total of all Exports ...	154·9

(4·7 per cent of total U.K. exports by value)

TABLE 32

Most Valuable Imports into Greenock (incl. Islay, Oban, Port Glasgow, and Tobermory), 1960

Imports	Value £ Million	
Sugar	7·5	
Oil Seeds	2·2	
Tobacco	1·8	
	——	(0·3 per cent of total
Total of all Imports ...	13·0	U.K. imports by
	——	value)

TABLE 33

Most Valuable Exports from Greenock (incl. Islay, Oban, Port Glasgow, and Tobermory), 1960

Exports	Value £ Million	
Ships and Boats	10·3	
Explosives	·3	
Refined Sugar	·1	
	——	(0·3 per cent of total
Total of all Exports ...	10·9	U.K. exports by
	——	value)

Because of a location on the west coast of Scotland, Glasgow has relatively little short-sea traffic to the continent of Europe. The value of exports is, surprisingly, higher than that of imports. This is because many of the imports after manufacture (and value added) find their way back to the same port for export, and this emphasizes the concentration of Scottish industry within the Central Valley of Scotland and Glasgow's immediate hinterland. The port hardly competes at all for the traffic of England and Wales. All railway stations operating Export Express Services to Glasgow are in Scotland.

'. . . it is certainly true that Glasgow has something approaching a monopoly in many branches of Scottish overseas trade, particularly with more distant ports. No other Scottish port can rival the number of services to all parts of the world.'[33]

Glasgow is very often the end of a shipping route—vessels arrive with part cargoes, and sail for other European ports, Dublin, Birkenhead, or Bristol Channel ports before voyaging overseas. Imports may arrive later at Glasgow than at English ports for instance; and exports must be loaded earlier. This is a factor restricting Glasgow's hinterland to Scotland. But this 'last port of call' characteristic of trade often makes it convenient for vessels to be repaired at this terminal port.

'Summing up, it might be said that traffic responded well to expenditure on the Port until 1914, but since then it would appear as if the Trustees' New Works have only maintained traffic not increased it. Grain and ore should help to remedy this situation in the near future.'[34]

To these commodities might be added 'road vehicles' in view of the factories close to Clydeside at Bathgate (West Lothian) and Linwood (Renfrewshire).

This most northerly major British port—Glasgow Bridge lies closer to the Arctic Circle than the Kremlin[35]—is both Scotland's shipyard and her window on the west. But developing industries in east Scotland, and the short-sea continental and coastwise traffics, allow east coast Scottish ports to co-exist with this major port of Scotland.

REFERENCES

1. *Report by T. Tucker on the Condition of Towns in Scotland*, quoted by Sir James D. Marwick, *The River Clyde and Clyde Burghs*, Glasgow: Maclehose, 1909, 94–6.

2. 'Report by J. Smeaton, 3rd September, 1755', *Reports on the Improvement and Management of the River Clyde and Harbour of Glasgow from 1755 to 1853*, Glasgow: Hedderwick, 1854, 1–4.

3. Irvine, on the Ayrshire coast, was used as the Port of Glasgow until it silted up at the end of the sixteenth century. This landing-place necessitated a journey by pack-horse of twenty-three miles. Until Port Glasgow was founded vessels also anchored in the Clyde estuary off Greenock, and merchandise was transported upstream in shallow-draught boats.

4. W. F. Macarthur, *History of Port Glasgow*, Glasgow: Jackson, Wylie, 1932, 17, gives the wording of the contract of sale.

5. I. A. G. Kinniburgh, 'John Ainslie's Map of Port Glasgow in 1806', *Scottish Geographical Magazine*, 76 (1960), 23–4, 23. There is still a 'vertical break' between old and new Port Glasgow. The western harbour was filled in to form a park in 1937.

6. Raised beaches are due to isostatic recovery from the burden of ice in glacial times. At Greenock and Port Glasgow there are remnants of the '25-foot Neolithic' beach; elsewhere in the *Clyde Estuary* and *Canalized Clyde* a '100-foot' beach is represented.

7. R. Miller, 'The Geography of the Glasgow Region', *The Glasgow Region*, R. Miller and J. Tivy eds., prepared for the meeting of the British Association, Glasgow, 1958, 1–16, 1.

8. *Ibid.*, 5.

9. *Ibid.*, Fig. 3.

10. Originally pointed out by Sir Halford Mackinder, *Britain and the British Seas*, London: Heinemann, 1902, 132; D. L. Linton, 'On the Former Connection between the Clyde and the Tweed', *Scottish Geographical Magazine*, 50 (1934), 82–92, concurs, 87.

11. 'Studies of Glasgow', *Geography*, 15 (1929–30), 36–40; report of a paper read by J. S. Thoms to the British Association at Glasgow, 1928, 36.

12. 'Report of John Golborne, Relative to the Deepening of the River Clyde and Harbour of Port-Glasgow, 1768', *Reports etc., loc. cit.*, 4–9, 5.

13. *Ibid.*, 5–6.

14. Described by T. Pennant, *A Tour in Scotland and a Voyage to the Hebrides*, 1772, London: White, 1790, Vol. I, 158–9; and J. Deas, 'The River Clyde', *Minutes of Proceedings of the Institution of Civil Engineers*, 36 (1872–3), 124–52, 145–7.

15. 'Report, etc., 1807', *Reports, loc. cit.*, 22–7, 23, referring to oral part of 'Report, etc., 1799', *ibid.*, 14–18.

16. 'Mr. Telford's Report Respecting the River Clyde, 1806', *Reports, loc. cit.*, 18–21.

17. Sir Thomas Mason, 'The Improvement of the River Clyde and the Harbour of Glasgow, 1873–1914', *Minutes of Proceedings of the Institution of Civil Engineers*, 200 (1915), 101–75, 122, 173.

18. J. B. S. Gilfillan and H. A. Moisley, 'Industrial and Commercial Developments to 1914', *The Glasgow Region, op. cit.*, 150–89, 184.

19. For further details of the first eleven miles see H. A. Moisley and J. R. Parkinson, *Notes on the Port Installations and Industries along the Navigable Clyde, Glasgow—Bowling*, Pamphlet for river passengers, July, 1958.

20. Built in 1837 and much smaller than that at Greenock (1818), reflecting the relative sizes of the two ports at the beginning of the nineteenth century. The Upper Harbour, Broomielaw Quay, and Kingston Dock will be closed if and when the proposed Clyde Ferry Bridge ($\frac{1}{2}$) is built; the Clyde Navigation Trust have filed formal objection to the scheme and will seek compensation of 'several million pounds' if it is carried through.

21. For further details see A. M. Robb, 'Shipbuilding and Marine Engineering', *The Third Statistical Account of Scotland: Glasgow*, eds. J. Cunnison and J. B. S. Gilfillan, Glasgow: Collins, 1958, 171–208, with bibliography, 974.

22. *Ibid.*, 205; H. A. Moisley and J. R. Parkinson, *loc. cit.; Development of Shipbuilding on the Upper Reaches of the Clyde*, Glasgow: Barclay, Curle, 1911; and 'The Reconstruction of the Clydeholm Shipyard, Glasgow: a Modern Lay-out for Welded Sub-Assemblies', *The Dock and Harbour Authority*, 41 (1960–1), 351–4. The firm is now a subsidiary of Swan Hunter & Wigham Richardson Ltd., Wallsend, Newcastle-upon-Tyne.

23. J. B. S. Gilfillan and H. A. Moisley, *loc. cit., passim.*

24. Annual average, the ratios between the various years are approximate because the gross tons of 1958–60 are not the same as the 'tons' of previous years, though the ratios for each set of years are correct. For 1786–7 and 1846–51 see J. B. S. Gilfillan and H. A. Moisley, *loc. cit.*, 175–6. The 1958–60 figures add up to less than the figures quoted for the 'Clyde' in the national table, since Ardrossan and Clyde boat-builders have been omitted from this table.

25. Opened by the then Duke of Rothesay who was also Prince of Wales.

26. An unusual case of a shipyard giving its name to the burgh that developed close by.

27. Sir Allan Grant, *Steel and Ships: the History of John Brown's*, London: Joseph, 1950, 37.

28. A. C. Gardner, 'River Work for the *Queen Mary*', *The Dock and Harbour Authority*, 17 (1936–7), 51–5.

29. Based on I. A. G. Kinniburgh, 'Greenock: Growth and Change in the Harbours of the Town', *Scottish Geographical Magazine*, 76 (1960), 89–98.

30. *Report of the Clyde Estuary Committee*, London: H.M.S.O., 1945. There is a unified Clyde Pilotage Authority, established in 1920, and a Clyde Lighthouses Trust, established in 1755.

31. Called into being by the fact that previously the largest vessels built on the Clyde could not be maintained or repaired on Clydeside.

32. A wartime oil depot was established by the Admiralty at Faslane Port on the eastern side of the Gare Loch. The Gare Loch is used for the laying-up of medium-sized vessels and as a submarine base (as is Holy Loch). Largest vessels cannot navigate its entrance where depth is restricted by a sill, a possible moraine based on rock, close to the loch entrance, also encumbered by a spit at Rhu.

33. H. A. Moisley, 'Glasgow Spheres of Influence', *The Glasgow Region, op. cit.*, 293–7, 297.

34. 'The Port of Glasgow: Review of Developments over the Last 200 Years', *The Dock and Harbour Authority*, 40 (1959–60), 245–9.

35. A comparison made by J. B. S. Gilfillan, *The Third Statistical Account of Scotland: Glasgow, op. cit.*, 17.

FURTHER REFERENCES FOR GLASGOW

Abercrombie, Sir Patrick and R. H. Matthew. *The Clyde Valley Regional Plan.* 1946. Edinburgh: H.M.S.O. 1949, esp. 231–6.

Holmes, J. 'The Upper Clyde Estuary ("Tail o' the Bank") and Its Regional Development', *Scottish Geographical Magazine*, 43 (1927), 321–41.

Oakley, C. A. *The Second City.* Glasgow: Blackie, 1946.

Renwick, R., Sir John Lindsay, and J. Eyre-Todd. *History of Glasgow.* 3 vols. Glasgow: Maclehose, 1921, esp. vol. 3, Chap. 25.

Robertson, W. F. 'History of the River Clyde and Port of Glasgow', *The Dock and Harbour Authority*, 30 (1949), 148–52.

[A] *Shipbuilding History*, 1750–1932. Glasgow: Alexander Stephen & Sons Ltd., 1932.

Thom, A. S. 'Investigation of Tidal Phenomena in the Clyde Estuary, using a Scale Model', *Journal of the Institution of Civil Engineers*, 33 (1949–50), 100–25.

Walker, J. *The Influence of Geographical Factors on the Economic Evolution of Scotland to the Beginning of the Eighteenth Century, mainly as Revealed in the Development of Overseas Trade, especially that of the Clyde Ports.* Unpublished thesis, Ph.D., University of Edinburgh, 1927–8.

For further references see *Glasgow: The Third Statistical Account of Scotland*, 969 et. seq.

Minutes of Proceedings of the Institution of Civil Engineers, 121 (1895), 314–17.

FURTHER REFERENCES FOR GREENOCK

Campbell, D. *Historical Sketches of the Town and Harbours of Greenock.* 2 vols, 1879, 1881.

Hamilton, T. W. *How Greenock Grew.* Greenock: McKelvie, 1947, containing a bibliography, 103–6.

Kinipple, W. R. 'Greenock Harbour', *Minutes of Proceedings of the Institution of Civil Engineers*, 130 (1897), 276–97.

INDUSTRIAL AND COMMERCIAL ESTUARIES—III

Chapter 4

BELFAST ON THE LAGAN

THE Port of Belfast[1] began in the estuary of the River Farset, one of five rivers which combine to silt up the head of Belfast Lough, the largest of these rivers being the River Lagan. The advantage of the water situation at the head of Belfast Lough, twelve miles long and gradually opening to a width of five miles to face Britain, is not difficult to understand. The Lagan Valley provides a land situation with easy routes leading to the heart of Ulster and also to Dublin. Since the port first arose on the Farset rather than on the banks of the much bigger Lagan, a question arises as to the choice of site for the port's first era of development. The struggle to align the channel of the River Lagan, involving reclamation and excavation in its delta, is the background to port development ever since, and this struggle is still continuing.

In the modern plan, the Victoria Channel, completed as far as the Twin Islands in 1849, represents the re-aligned River Lagan estuary. Sited each side of this port approach are the Musgrave[2] Channel (1903) and the Herdman[3] Channel (1933), both in an area of deltaic tidal mud, called locally 'slobland' or 'sleech'. The material excavated in the construction of these channels has contributed to land reclamation not only between the channels, but also between the newer channels and the former shores of the lough.[4] The River Farset, now buried beneath Belfast High Street, was the origin of a major separation of functions within the port. In the River Lagan itself the more important commercial quays have always been on the town (or Farset) side of the river. Today, in plan, the three channels look like the prongs of a trident with the handle formed by the approach channel in Belfast Lough; but even along the central prong—the Victoria Channel—there is a neat separation of commercial and industrial quayage. Leaving the Abercorn Basin, as one sails down the Victoria Channel all the commercial quayage, with the exception of oil jetties, lies to port and all the shipbuilding to starboard.

The north-east to south-west direction of Belfast Lough is an expression of the geological structure disposed in Caledonian trends south-westward from Scotland. The Southern Boundary Fault of the Central Lowlands of Scotland is responsible for a zone of weakness upon which has been developed the southern shore of Belfast

TABLE 34

Eras and Epochs in the Development of the Port of Belfast

Eras and Chief Areal Characteristics	Present-day Symbols
I *Primitive:* quays in River Farset estuary	Site of Belfast High Street and Queen's Square; and unusually large width of the High Street

Era ended by first use of the River Lagan frontage on reclaimed ground, 1714[5]

II *Marginal Quay Extension:* on banks of River Lagan, firstly south and north of the Farset confluence	Donegall Quay *circa* 1800 and Queen's Quay (both later rebuilt on the re-aligned River Lagan, 1848–9)
III *Marginal Quay Elaboration:* transverse cuts in River Lagan's left bank to form so-called docks	Clarendon Nos. 1 (1800) and 2 (1826) Graving Docks; and York Branch Dock (originally Dunbar's Dock, *circa* 1800)

Era ended by straightening the River Lagan, 1839–49

IV *Dock Elaboration:* docks opening off Victoria Channel	Clarendon Dock, 1851, to York Dock, 1897
V *Simple Lineal Quayage*	Stormont Wharf (648 feet) being extended to 2,400 feet
VI *Specialized Quayage:* for shipbuilding	On right bank of Victoria Channel, *post* 1851; and on Musgrave Channel, *post* 1903
for grain;	*e.g.* Pollock Dock, 1933
for deep-sea vessels;	*e.g.* Sinclair Wharf, 1958
for industry;	*e.g.* Stormont Wharf, 1959
for ferry cargo services;	*e.g.* Herdman Channel West, 1962
deep-water oil berth, 1963	

Lough and a corridor stretching from Belfast south-westward to the Lough Neagh Lowlands.[6] Although the course of the River Lagan has been interrupted by glacial deposits,[7] it is this river that has been mainly responsible for the erosion of an area of low relief (*lagán*, Irish—a plain) stretching for some twenty miles south-west from Belfast. For this distance the river flows north-east, parallel to the basalt-crowned edge of the Antrim Plateau which forms a dramatic backdrop to Belfast Lough on the north-west. The Rivers Blackstaff, Farset, and Milewater are streams which flow swiftly down the face of this scarp, originally to join the lough close to the Lagan estuary, all contributing to the deposition of post-glacial sleech at the head of the lough.[8] Early Belfast was built entirely upon this slobland, which in places is fifty feet thick, and in particular upon the deposits of the Farset, Blackstaff, and Lagan. The estuaries of two other streams, the Milewater and Connswater north and east of early Belfast, have been overrun as the port expanded. There was some difficulty in crossing the estuarine Lagan at the confluence with the Farset, and this circumstance is preserved in the very name of the city—'Béal-fersat'—'the mouth of (= approach to) the sandbank (or crossing)'[9]

Belfast began as an English base. Its castle, probably dating from the thirteenth century, was for a long time less important than that of Carrickfergus, nine miles seaward on the western shore of the then *Carrickfergus* Lough. But, despite the difficulties of Belfast's deltaic site, the strategic nature of the land situation at the opening provided by the Lagan lowland was appreciated and marked by the building of an English town after 1603. The disadvantages of the land site were turned into an advantage once the River Lagan had been bridged in 1688. Only the handicap of a mud-encumbered water site in the Lagan remained, but by that time work had already begun on taming the Lagan shore.

The founding charter of the town, 1613, had explicitly required the freemen to choose a site for a wharf, and, owing to the difficulties in the Lagan, they picked the estuary of the River Farset to set up their *primitive* quay. Gradually, the banks of this river were faced and converted into permanent quays.

'. . . it is ordered that every person shall build up or cause to be builded up and topt ye bankes of ye River of this towne of Bellfast. . . .' [1663][10]

The first custom house was on the north side of the Farset.[11] The High Street ran along each side of the river which was not completely covered over until 1847. This street was not only the main transverse track inland, but its eastern extension formed the actual *primitive* quays of the port. A map of 1685 shows this lay-out and also 'improvements made out upon the strand' of the River Lagan. This inscription appears north of the Farset confluence. *Marginal quay extension* is represented by Hanover Quay shown on J. Maclanachan's Map of Belfast, 1715. A second transverse road serving Hanover Quay appears on this map, almost fully built up—the present-day Ann Street. Later *marginal quay extension* took place with the Merchant's Quay fronting the Lagan on the northern side of the 'Dock' served by the transverse street, Broad Street, now Waring Street. The port now presented in plan the shape of a letter **T**, the stem being the 'Dock' in the High Street, and the cross-piece represented by the quays facing the Lagan. If Hanover Quay was the first use of the Lagan by the port, Merchant's Quay represents the first move towards deeper water, probably soon after 1769, when Chichester Quay was built.

During the eighteenth century the garrison town was slowly changing into a market town as communications down the Lagan Valley improved. Woodland was cleared,[12] a turnpike road to Dublin established in 1733,[13] and a canal alongside the River Lagan completed in 1763,[14] both along a route 'pointing to the very heart of Ulster and also leading south towards Dublin.'[15] The pace increased with the introduction of cotton to the city in 1777 which, unlike flax, was at that time spun

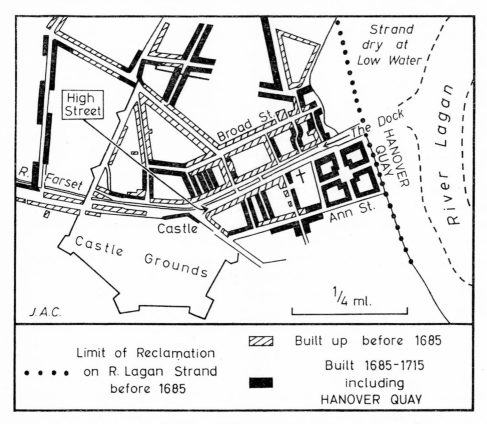

FIG. 24   The *Primitive* Port of Belfast and the First *Marginal Quay Extension*—Hanover Quay
(1714)

The *primitive* quays are the eastern extension of the High Street, each side of the so-called Dock, in the estuary of the River Farset where it joins the River Lagan. Based on maps by T. Phillips (1685) and J. Maclanachan (1715).

by machine and not by hand, with urban industrialization further encouraged by the introduction of the steam engine after 1790. But the cotton industry was dealt a severe blow by the financial collapse of 1825, and later its supplies were interrupted by the American Civil War.[16] After 1830 linen became the dominant textile industry, taking over the role of cotton which had:

'first brought masses of workers into the town, and was of equal importance with the commercial centralization of the linen industry there in founding the modern city.'[17]

To this might be added the role of the shipbuilding industry, which first assumed importance during the next port era of *marginal quay elaboration.*

This era embraces the five transverse cuts into the left bank of the Lagan, each involving further land reclamation north-east of the town. These so-called docks were really tidal inlets for shipbuilding and shiprepair. The commercial quays were the existing marginal quays, to which the original Donegall Quay was added during the first years of the nineteenth century. One of the cuts, Ritchie's Dock, was the nursery of the Belfast shipbuilding industry, while Clarendon Graving Dock No. 1 (1800) and No. 2 (1826), and Dunbar's Dock (reconstructed as York Branch Dock, 1897) can still be identified in the modern plan.

In the first half of the nineteenth century some ships could reach Donegall Quay, but the larger vessels, drawing more than ten feet at neaps, or more than fourteen feet at springs, were forced to anchor at Garmoyle Pool, three miles out in the lough, whence their goods were conveyed to the quays by lighters.[18] The Donegall family owned the land alongside, upon which improvement would have had to take place, and was not sympathetic to the development of the port. But the disentailing of the estate to help the second Marquess in financial difficulty removed the sting from that powerful opposition after 1822. The average size of vessel using the port rose from 44 tons in 1786 to 102 tons in 1830.[19] With the port being throttled by the silt in the Lagan, a debate on the way to improve the lay-out lasted from 1814 until 1837.[20] The alternatives were either the conversion of the Lagan into a floating dock by means of impounding gates or the straightening and dredging of the channel to give room for improved quayage on the reclaimed land on either side. The second proposal was first made by James Walker in 1830.[21] An Act was obtained for carrying out Walker's plan, including borrowing powers, in 1837.

That the decision was right is not now open to doubt. Firstly, the spring tidal range at Belfast is only ten feet, so that impounded water is not necessary. Dufferin Dock (1872) was originally fitted with lock gates, but these were found to be a hindrance and removed in 1922–3. A more serious objection to an impounded harbour was that it would have set a finite limit to the port's development seaward which would no doubt have had to be overcome at some later date. The plan adopted has allowed the port to develop seaward and in width *progressively*, by means of two processes: by excavation and reclamation; and by dredging and reclamation which have gone on continuously, except for the two World Wars.[22] James Walker foresaw this in 1830. His aim was:

'To make the design so that the improvements be such as may be carried into effect by degrees, each step or measure being quite complete in itself, but at the same time a part of a great and connected whole which may be extended, and the remaining parts executed as the trade of the port may require and the means of payment justify.' (1830)[23]

Fig. 25 shows that the channel excavated following Walker's recommendations was in a straight line from Dunbar's Dock (used as a small shipbuilding yard) to the natural deep water of the North Channel (with its tributary inlet the Old Seal

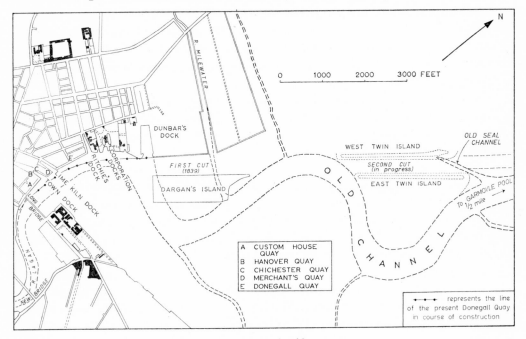

FIG. 25   The Port of Belfast in 1847

Channel), 8 feet L.W.O.S.T., followed for half a mile to the depth 18 feet L.W.O.S.T. at Garmoyle Pool. This involved two artificial cuts, the first opened in 1841, the second not being proceeded with until 1846-9, when the success of the first had been demonstrated. Two islands resulted *between* the cuts and the original channel: Dargan's Island and the East [originally, the South] Twin Island, occupied now by the Abercorn and Queen's Shipyard of Harland & Wolff Ltd. and the East Twin Power station respectively.

The marginal quays were altered. By 1849 the Town, Lime Kiln, and Ritchie's Docks had been filled in; and a new quay had been thrust forward 50-150 feet into the former river bed, receiving the name—Donegall Quay (reconstructed in 1879).

At the same time the Queen's Quay opposite was set back 250 feet[24] (reconstructed in 1877 and again in 1949–51). The original line of the left bank of the Lagan can be traced on the modern plan by joining the eastern end of Albert Square to the entrances of the Clarendon Graving Docks, which appear on the 1847 plan as the [Ballast] Corporation Docks (*cf.* Figs. 25 and 26). Dargan's Island was named after the contractor who carried out the channel excavation. After Queen Victoria had opened the completed channel in 1849, the name was changed to Queen's Island, fronting the Victoria Channel, and the island became for a short time a park and pleasure resort. But the Harbour Commissioners provided a patent slip for ship-repair in 1849 and fitted out part of the island as a shipbuilding yard in 1851 to make up for the loss of facilities on the left bank of the Lagan.[25] Queen's Island, now joined to the East Twin Island, forms a peninsula, a mile and a half long. This is the home of Harland & Wolff Ltd., who now have all the *specialized quayage* of ship-building (see below).

None of the openings out of the Victoria Channel in the *dock elaboration* era (1851–97) has *simple lineal quayage*, though a move in that direction came in 1922–3 when the Dufferin and Spencer west quays were joined in one line, 1,300 feet in length with 29½ feet L.W.O.S.T. alongside.

The magnificent straight approach to the Port of Belfast was not finally achieved from Garmoyle Pool until 1891. Reclamation has proceeded steadily. By 1939 firm ground was made not only between the channels themselves, but also between the channels and the shores of the lough up to a line joining the lough shores through the northern tips of the Twin 'Islands'. Since then an area of 315 acres, north-east of the airport, has been reclaimed, providing a site for the oil refinery with its *specialized quayage* at a jetty at the head of a causeway, 1,022 feet in length, projecting towards the Victoria Channel to a depth of 38¼ feet at L.W.O.S.T. The channel has been deepened from 12 feet L.W.O.S.T. to 27½ feet L.W.O.S.T., as far as the turning basin at the junction of the channels, and to 31¼ feet, to allow vessels of 32,000 tons deadweight to proceed to the refinery. It has also been widened by slicing 350 feet off the West Twin Island, and the channel has been deepened to 25½ feet as far as Stormont Wharf. This progressive deepening enables ships with draughts of up to 33 feet to use the port, and tankers of 65,000–80,000 deadweight tonnage to be catered for at the shipyard.

The first port authority was set up under an Act of 1729 as a 'Ballast Office' under the direction of the free burgesses of the town, having a monopoly of powers to supply vessels with ballast. This had to be taken out of the channels and not from any part of the strands or banks—the first regulation about dredging in the port. In 1785 an Act set up a body separate from the municipality, 'The Corporation for Preserving and Improving the Port of Belfast', but which was still referred to popularly as the 'Ballast Board'. In 1831 and 1837 the Board was twice reconstituted when major port improvements were in contemplation, finally emerging after an 1847 Act as the present Belfast Harbour Commissioners, an elected port trust.

In contrast to *Anyport*, it is seen that the early difficulties of the water site compelled the port of Belfast to begin upon a small tributary rather than upon the main river. This is very similar to early developments at Hull, except that the difficulty with the Lagan was its meandering channel and mudbanks rather than flooding difficulties, as on the Humber. The progressive development downstream of *marginal quay and dock elaboration* opening from the re-aligned Lagan is a good parallel with *Anyport*. But thereafter the *specialized quayage* of shipbuilding dominates the lay-out. It must be admitted that Belfast suffers from the arbitrary limits set for the category of *simple lineal quayage*: a continuous quay over 1,500 feet in length with 25 feet alongside L.W.O.S.T. For the Spencer-Dufferin western quay is 1,300 feet and the Sinclair Wharf is 1,240 feet long. The *marginal quays* on the Lagan are much longer than 1,500 feet, but they are not deep-water quays. This does bring out the fact that Belfast's trade has been in the main carried by small vessels in the ferry traffic to and from Britain rather than in the largest class of deep-sea vessel voyaging direct from overseas. This is corroborated by Belfast's position in the national table of ports arranged in order of tonnage of vessels arriving foreign and *coastwise* being higher than its position when the ports are arranged in order of the value of the cargo in the foreign trade only. However, the current extension of Stormont Wharf to a total length of 2,400 feet will equip Belfast with a fine length of *simple lineal quayage* on the Victoria Channel.

A recent dock—the Pollock Dock (1933)—contains *specialized quayage* for the grain trade, while the easternmost extension of Stormont Wharf, the power station coaling berths and the oil jetty are typical examples of recent developments on the deep-water approaches to a port to serve specific industries.

Shipbuilding at Belfast

Shipbuilding at Belfast is now carried on by one firm, Harland & Wolff Ltd. This is an industry which at Belfast is based on imported raw materials and fuel and which has to export to supply its market. The full history of this company is yet to be published, but many of the early details are known. As the story first develops, it is clear that there are subtle influences working from Britain—the export of ideas and experience, particularly from the Clyde. Belfast might well be regarded as an outpost of the Clyde shipbuilding area—a bridgehead established from Scottish and English bases. But in this campaign the perimeter of the bridgehead has been more easily expanded than those of the parent bases cramped along the Clyde, Tyne, and Mersey, with commercial docks and other riverside users attacking for position.

William Ritchie came to Belfast in 1792 from Saltcoats on the Firth of Clyde, bringing his own men and raw materials, and having to reclaim the ground on which he built his vessels at Ritchie's Dock.[26] Ritchie died in 1834, and his dock was filled in during 1848-9. There were other shipbuilders in the port, and many ships were built as a sideline to engineering work.[27] To compensate for the obliteration of the graving docks (dating from the *marginal quay elaboration* era) by the new Donegall Quay, in 1851 the Belfast Harbour Commissioners provided a patent slip and room for a yard on the newly-formed Queen's Island. This was taken over by Robert Hickson, the owner of the Belfast Iron Works, in order to find an outlet for his iron plates—a reason very similar to that behind John Brown & Company's take-over of the Clydebank Shipbuilding Works forty-six years later. At this point it is perhaps useful to make some general observations about shipbuilding in Northern Ireland (Table 35).

TABLE 35

Shipbuilding in Northern Ireland

Initiation in the Mid-nineteenth Century	*Expansion in the Twentieth Century*
Disadvantages	*Disadvantages*
Raw material to be imported	The same
Fuel to be imported	The same
Engines imported until 1880	
Wage rates as high or higher than those in Britain[28] (especially for imported skilled labour)	National shipbuilding wage agreement, 1936
Above form high proportion of costs of finished vessels	Proportion grows less as engines are built and vessels become more complicated to construct
Advantages	*Advantages*[30]
Excellent water site for launching and fitting out	The same, with no difficulty about expansion on reclaimed land and alongside deepened channels
Engine works close to yards	The same
Export transport costs negligible since finished ships sail under their own power[29]	The same

This attempts to show that economic factors were more difficult to overcome in the mid-nineteenth century than they are today. Manifestly, in order to develop, the Belfast shipyard in its early days had to offer something extra. At first, this was largely the experience and contacts gained by Edward Harland. These could scarcely

106

have been more fitting: five years' apprenticeship on the Tyne in a general engineering works; two years on the Clyde with a marine engineering firm, just starting their own shipyard; and then a managership of a shipyard on the Tyne owned by a Mr. Toward. But this last business was not an expanding one, and so Harland answered an advertisement for the managership of the Belfast yard. He was appointed there at Christmas, 1854. Harland himself takes up the story.

> '. . . I went repeatedly over to the Clyde for the purpose of enlisting fresh hands. . . . I obtained a considerable accession of strength from Newcastle. On the death of Mr. Toward, his head foreman, Mr. William Hanston, with a number of leading hands, joined me. [Hickson sold the yard to Harland in 1858.] The transfer and the purchase were soon completed, through the kind assistance of my old and esteemed friend Mr. G. C. Schwabe, of Liverpool; whose nephew, Mr. G. W. Wolff, had been with me for a few months as my private assistant. . . . While in Glasgow, I had endeavoured to assist the Messrs. Bibby in the purchase of a steamer; so I was now intrusted by them with the building of three screw steamers . . .; and contracted with Macnab and Co., Greenock, to supply the requisite steam-engines. . . . As I required frequently to go from home, and as the works must be carefully attended to during my absence, on the 1st of January, 1862, I took Mr. Wolff in as my partner . . .'[31]

Experience alone is not sufficient unless it leads to practical results. Harland suggested increasing the length of the ships called for by Bibby's second order without increasing their beam or power. The ships had sharp bows to go through the crest of waves rather than rising to every sea, taking the 'shortest road'. Furthermore, the 'Bibby's coffins' were given a flatness of bottom and squareness of bilge to increase the carrying capacity—the 'Belfast bottom'. The length-beam ratio was increased to the previously unheard-of figure 10 : 1[32] and even more,[33] and the success of the idea led to many orders for the lengthening of ships. It is natural that a major innovation should have been in the design of the hull, because Harland & Wolff made no engines until 1880. In 1869 the firm had received orders for the new fleet of the Oceanic Steam Navigation Company Ltd., because the speed of the 'Belfast bottom' was an advantage in competing with the Cunard and Inman Lines on the north Atlantic run.[34] Thus began a famous partnership. The line which became known as the White Star Line never possessed a ship (all their names ending in—*ic*) that had not been built at Belfast until the shipping company was merged with Cunard in 1934. By that time Harland & Wolff had become a staple part of the British shipbuilding industry, the firm's fortunes closely following the national fortunes of the industry. Since 1926 the Belfast 'employees in shipbuilding' curve has remained remarkably parallel to the national curve,[35] and this must be due to the firm's success, by skill in construction and by ability to offset the disadvantages of location, which are much less now than when Edward Harland successfully overcame them.

A second large shipbuilding firm arose at Belfast—Workman & Clark Ltd., first on the Antrim (western) side of the Victoria Channel in 1879, expanding on to the other shore opposite—the present Victoria Shipyard. After shipbuilding had suffered setbacks during the inter-war years, the Antrim Works of Workman & Clark were closed down and the rest of their installations acquired by Harland & Wolff in 1935, to form the present largest single shipbuilding lay-out in the world operated by one company, covering 300 acres and employing some 10,000 people.

The Modern Port of Belfast

If the modern port is described from the Musgrave Channel westward, the first part of the account will deal briefly with the present lay-out of the shipyards to be followed by some facts about the commercial quayage.

The Musgrave Channel, opened in 1903, is largely used for fitting-out and repair on the western side, though No. 4 Quay is a coal importing berth for the East Twin Power Station. Opposite this quay are oil berths for the oil depots established in 1923 a little way inland along the canalized River Connswater. A very important wharf for Harland & Wolff is adjacent to the Musgrave Shipyard (founded during the First World War) where the firm receives steel imports via Glasgow from Colville's steelworks at Ravenscraig, Scotland. The Musgrave Shipyard has a very rational lay-out: drawing office, mould loft, through the plater's shop to the slips. Here aircraft carriers, other naval vessels, oil tankers, and passenger vessels of the largest size are built.

The Abercorn Yard is on the site of the original shipyard, which was expanded to include the site of the present Queen's Works, where the original engine works was sited (1880), with the Hamilton Graving Dock built as early as 1867. The Alexandra Works and Victoria Yard were the eastern installations of Workman & Clark (1891). A few other characteristics of Queen's Island are most easily given in tabulated form.

TABLE 36

Yards and Works on Queen's Island[36]
Yards South to North

ABERCORN SHIPYARD

Moderate-sized passenger ships, cross-Channel ships, general cargo liners, oil tankers

QUEEN'S SHIPYARD

Large passenger vessels and oil tankers

VICTORIA SHIPYARD

Cargo vessels

THOMPSON SHIPYARD

Fitting-out and repair
[For Musgrave Shipyard see text above]

Works south to north

ABERCORN WORKS AND QUEEN'S WORKS

Fitting, erecting, and machine shops, boiler shop, iron and brass foundries; with railway lines to fitting-out wharves

VICTORIA WORKS

Marine and land engines, boiler installations and repair works; diesel engines for export; with railway lines to fitting-out wharves

SYDENHAM WORKS

Self-contained steel-construction works, all classes of structural steelwork undertaken

ALEXANDRA WORKS

Sawmill, timber-drying, joiner's shop, boat-building shop (lifeboats), decking and furniture

THOMPSON WORKS

Pipe work, smiths' work, and sheet-iron work

KING'S WORKS

All electrical work (except control-gear and switch-gear at Sydenham Road factory), including work for shore stations at home and abroad

Steel is also received at the wharf at Queen's Shipyard, while vessels are finished off after launching at Victoria Wharf close by. The Thompson Graving Dock, 850 × 100 × 26 feet is not able to accommodate the largest ships built in Belfast, and so there has been a proposal to construct a new graving dock, 1,250 × 150 × 45 feet. Lastly, the Abercorn Basin is the traditional landing-place for imported coal.

The remainder of the Abercorn Basin is also used for coal imports, almost exclusively by vessels of the Kelly fleet with the prefix *Bally-*. Since the Second World War the Queen's Quay has also been used by the larger vessels in this trade. Northern Ireland, being coal deficient, receives supplies from coalfields in western Britain: South Wales, Lancashire, Cumberland, and particularly from the Ayrshire coalfield of Scotland. K. S. Isles and N. Cuthbert estimated that the sea transport of

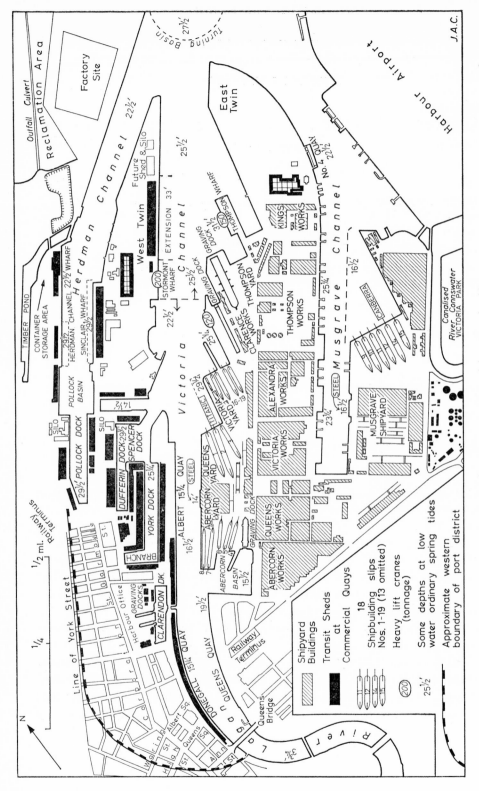

FIG. 26 The Present Lay-out of the Port of Belfast

Stormont Wharf, 648 feet long, is to be extended by 1,254 feet, for general cargo, and by another 500 feet, to serve a new grain silo at the extreme north end of West Twin, fronting the Victoria Channel. These developments will equip Belfast with *simple lineal quayage* for the first time.

coal raised the price in Belfast 16 per cent above the average price that an industrialist might pay in Britain.[37] From their investigation it appeared that transport costs diminished as coal was carried in bigger vessels up to 2,000 tons deadweight, which the port installations of Belfast can accommodate. The average deadweight tonnage of colliers is about 1,200, a figure that has doubled since 1953. But it must be remembered that many of the vessels also run to smaller Northern Ireland ports that could not accommodate the 2,000-ton class collier.

Donegall Quay, the ferry-boat terminus, is the busiest part of the commercial port, with one-storey transit sheds fairly close to the quay, and quayside cranes in the range one- to twelve-ton capacity. Indeed, it is necessary for ferry-boats to have adequate craneage at their berths, for many of them, running on a fixed route, are not equipped with ships' gear (cf. the Dublin-Bristol lines). From north to south the quay provides for the following services.

TABLE 37

Regular Passenger and Cargo Services from Donegall Quay, Belfast[38]

Berth No.	Destination	Type of Service	Sailings per Week
1 and 2	Liverpool and Manchester	General cargo and containers	3
3	Bristol	General cargo and containers	6
4		Reserve berth for special sailings	
5	Liverpool	Passenger, general cargo, and containers	6
6	Heysham	General cargo and containers	6
7	Heysham	Passenger, general cargo, and containers	6
8	Glasgow	*do.*	6
9	Preston	General cargo and containers	3
		Here is Queen's Bridge	

Much of the cargo carried by the ferry-boats is in ten-ton containers. The advantages of container traffic resemble those of a train ferry up to a point. (A train ferry is not possible at Belfast because of the different gauge of Northern Ireland railways). There is a reduction in pilferage, breakage, and also the cost of packing. A specific instance of delay and damage amounting to 10 per cent of the product being reduced to 0·5 per cent by the container-ferry service has been quoted.[39] Because standardized shapes are being loaded and unloaded, ships' turn-round is speeded. In the Belfast container-cargo services, ships normally turn round in a day. But the shipper must pay for the empty space if the container is not filled; while there is a great loss if the container travels empty one way. In addition, the question of ownership and size standardization of containers looms large if the trade is not balanced in both directions. So far it seems that as the length of voyage increases, these difficulties also increase. For coastwise traffic containers have already assumed great importance.

H

111

One effect that the regular transit of weatherproof containers may have on port lay-outs is the designing of berths with large open storage areas, the associated transit sheds for 'non-container' cargo being placed at right-angles to the quay, instead of parallel to the quay, as hitherto, so that containers can be moved more easily to and from vessels. For this reason the road behind the Donegall Quay transit sheds has been subject to some congestion. Although the purely cargo services of British Railways have been diverted to the western side of the Herdman Channel, many cargoes arrive in passenger-cargo ferry-boats, and passengers naturally prefer to arrive at terminals as close to the centre of Belfast as possible.

Donegall Quay is continued northwards by Albert Quay (1874), mainly used for coal imports. Behind these quays are the docks of the *dock elaboration* era. General cargo vessels are dealt with, including a liner service to the St. Lawrence Seaway ports by vessels specially designed with a 24-foot draught. A Clyde cargo service is maintained from York Dock. The Clarendon Dock is used mainly for laying-up and repairs. The largest vessels berth against the western quay of the combined Spencer-Dufferin Docks, but as there are no cranes, discharge is by ship's gear, with suction discharge of grain to a silo on the north-west of the quay. The Milewater Basin, with Admiralty vessels laid up as a depot, marks the original course of the River Mile-water before the 1849 channel straightening (Fig. 25). North of the Milewater Basin on the West Twin Island was the original shipyard of Workman & Clark Ltd., stretching westwards towards old timber ponds—an area now occupied by the Herdman Channel (1933). Another power station occupies most of the West Twin Island, but this part of the Victoria Channel is dominated by the 200-ton cantilever crane, centrally sited on the 650-foot long Stormont Wharf. This installation is certainly an example of *specialized quayage*, since it was provided specially to load the giant turbo-alternators made by the 1957 factory of the British Thomson-Houston Co., Ltd., at Larne.

The Pollock Dock is maintained at a greater depth (29 feet 6 inches L.W.O.S.T.) than the Herdman approach channel (22 feet 6 inches), and here are two grain silos with paper imports also received at the east quay. Open quayside areas deal with timber and building materials. The western side of the Herdman Channel is used for container cargo services of British Railways. A recent wharf (1961), Herdman Channel Wharf Extension, gives a total length of 1,083 feet for the expected devel-opment of the container cargo services. Opposite this wharf is the coaling berth, for the West Twin Power Station, itself a twin of No. 4 Quay on the Musgrave Channel. Two other installations on the Herdman Channel deserve special mention.

On the east quay of Pollock Basin is the quayside ramp for the roll-on roll-off 'transport ferry' service operated between Belfast and/or Larne and Preston (and also between Tilbury, London and Antwerp/Rotterdam). This service is especially useful for the carriage of up to seventy laden road vehicles, cutting out quayside handling altogether because the vehicle is driven straight on to the vessel—or a road trailer is left behind by a 'mechanical horse' (road tractor) to be met by another 'horse' on the other side. This is a development of the container traffic[40] offering in addition even speedier handling of cargo and turn-round of vessels.

The splendid quay (1,240 feet) and shed (1,100 feet) at Sinclair Wharf can certainly be used by deep-sea vessels trading direct to Belfast for there is 30 feet L.W.O.S.T. alongside. Imports direct from overseas are as cheap as those direct to British ports because the usual quoting is 'C.I.F. to any British port', whereas

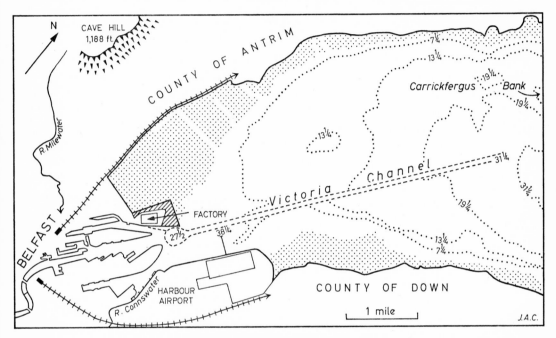

FIG. 27 Belfast Port Approaches

The railways were sited close to high water mark in 1848, and they show the area reclaimed since to make port sites. (In Antrim the railway itself reclaimed a strip 200 yards wide along the shore.) Figures represent low water depths in feet ordinary spring tides. The most recent area of reclamation is shaded and the tidal sleech is stippled.

imports into Northern Ireland transhipped from Britain must have their charges increased.[41] The construction of Sinclair Wharf shows some of the difficulties of working in the slobland. At the site stiff clay is not encountered until 40–45 feet below the sleech (30 feet) and fine red and grey sand (10–15 feet). Piles 56 feet long with a special blister shape are used to support the wharf. At Stormont Wharf the 200-ton crane is supported by 84 concrete piles in length up to 82 feet, surmounted by a reinforced concrete cap.

Along the west side of Herdman Channel there is a sulphuric acid and fertilizer factory on the most recently reclaimed land, with further reclamation proceeding west of the site. Opposite is the Belfast Harbour Airport with the aircraft factory of Short Bros. & Harland Ltd., famous for their seaplane construction. The airport, first opened in 1933, is very little used by civil traffic, having been superseded in 1947 by Nutts Corner, about ten miles west on the Antrim Plateau, because of the poor visibility aggravated by smog drifting over from the built-up area to the south-west. Adjacent to the airport is an oil refinery constructed during 1961–3 with a standard type of location, close in situation to a deep-water approach but with a rather isolated land site.[42]

The port district of Belfast is largely confined within an arc joining the Queen's Bridge to York Street, thence by a straight line to Pollock Dock (Fig. 26). This is the north-eastern section of the 'warehousing-manufacturing' pattern that surrounds the city centre.[43]

TABLE 38

Eight Most Valuable Foreign Trade Imports into Belfast (incl. Larne), 1960

	Value £ Million
Unmanufactured Tobacco	16·5
Maize	6·7
Wheat	5·1
Barley	4·9
Flax	3·8
Oilseed Cake	3·4
Timber (Simply Worked)	3·3
Cereal Feeding Stuffs	2·7
Total of all Imports ...	61·1

(1·4 per cent of total U.K. imports by value)

TABLE 39

Eight Most Valuable Foreign Trade Exports from Belfast (incl. Larne), 1960

	Value £ Million
Textile Machinery ... ...*	2·6
Ships and Boats	1·6
Flax Yarns	1·2
Seed Potatoes	·6
Implements and Tools	·5
Air and Gas Compressors	·3
Worsted Yarn	·2
Potatoes (not Seed)	·2
Total of all Exports ...	9·4

(0·3 per cent of total U.K. exports by value)

TABLE 40

*Eight Most Important Imports (Foreign and Coastwise) into Belfast
by Weight, 1960*

	Weight (Thousand Tons)
Coal	1,587
Fuel and Gas Oil	333
Maize	331
Barley	226
Feeding Stuffs	201
Wheat	184
Timber	152
Iron and Steel	150
Total of all Imports ...	4,588

TABLE 41

*Eight Most Important Exports (Foreign and Coastwise) from Belfast
by Weight, 1960*

	Weight (Thousand Tons)
Potatoes	159
Iron and Steel Products	75
Livestock	73
Textile Manufactures	49
Machinery	35
Bacon, Ham, and Pork	33
Eggs	20
Tobacco	20
Total of all Exports ...	734

It has been thought worth while to include tonnage figures of cargo, since the value figures of H.M. Customs concerning foreign cargo exclude the important 'coastwise' or ferry traffic to and from Britain.

To a large extent the Port of Belfast must act as a 'tradesmen's entrance' for Northern Ireland as far as consumer goods are concerned. Where goods are destined for industrial use or processing: coal, steel, grain, textiles, tobacco, and other raw materials, the most economic site is in the port area itself, since costs mount quickly inland, especially for goods with low value per unit of weight.[44] This helps to preserve Belfast's position as the dominant area for heavy industry in Northern Ireland. In the list of exports the presence of a largely agricultural hinterland is revealed, although the most important item, ships, is omitted from the tonnage table. The term 'tradesmen's entrance' of course excludes the importance of Belfast as a passenger ferry port, and as a shipbuilding and oil refinery centre, but it does serve to emphasize the dominance of import tonnages and the relatively few direct links with ports across deep seas. However, the entrance is magnificent, a straight approach to water and land sites respectively excavated and made by the ingenuity of the men who have followed the first correct step proposed by James Walker.

REFERENCES

1. Indispensable to any study of Belfast are the papers of E. Jones, from 1952, culminating in *A Social Geography of Belfast*, London: Oxford University Press, 1960.
2. Named after the then chairman of the Belfast Harbour Commissioners.
3. *Ibid.*
4. E. Jones, *op. cit.*, 8–16. See also, M. J. Watkins, *Developments in Belfast Harbour, 1920–33*, paper read to the Belfast Association of Engineers, 1934, 8–9.
5. Hanover Quay must be after 1713, Hanoverian succession 1714, and before 1715, the date of J. Maclanachan's map upon which it appears. At the same time, the south side of the River Farset was built up and called George Quay. This in turn became Hanover Quay when the second custom house was erected on the original Hanover Quay which became known eventually as Custom House Quay. In 1769 the north side of the Farset estuary was rebuilt as Chichester Quay.
6. *Belfast in Its Regional Setting: A Scientific Survey*, edited by E. Jones, published for the British Association at Belfast, 1952, Fig. 2.
7. J. K. Charlesworth, 'Geology', *ibid.*, 29–39, has a map of glacial 'Lake Lagan', Fig. 6.
8. E. E. Evans, 'The Site of Belfast', *Geography*, 22 (1937), 169–77; *ibid.*, *Belfast, the Site and the City*, 1944, reprinted from the *Ulster Journal of Archaeology* (3rd Series), 7 (1944); and *ibid.*, 'Block Diagram of the Site of Belfast Looking from Castlereagh', quoted as a frontispiece by E. Jones, *op. cit.*
9. J. B. Arthurs, 'Place Names and Dialects', *Belfast in Its Regional Setting*, *op. cit.*, 190–200, 193.
10. *The Town Book of the Corporation of Belfast, 1613–1816*, edited by R. M. Young, Belfast: Ward, 1892, 98, with a first reference to the port in 1672, p. 120. Documents relating to the port from 1675–1800 will be found assembled in G. Benn, *A History of the Town of Belfast*, London: Ward, 1877, 470–85.
11. *The Humble Petition of the Principal Merchants and Trading Inhabitants of the Town of Belfast*, 1740, quoted by G. Benn, *op. cit.*, 479.
12. E. R. R. Green, *The Lagan Valley 1800–50*, London: Faber, 1949, 26.
13. E. R. R. Green, 'Economic History', *Belfast in Its Regional Setting*, *op. cit.*, 119–26, 120.
14. E. R. R. Green (1949), *op. cit.*, 34.
15. E. Jones, *op. cit.*, 31.
16. J. J. Monaghan, 'The Rise and Fall of the Belfast Cotton Industry', *Irish Historical Studies*, 3 (1942), 1–17.
17. E. R. R. Green (1949), *op. cit.*, 111.
18. 'Report of John Rennie on Improving the Harbour of Belfast, April, 30, 1821', *History of the Harbours of the United Kingdom: Belfast*, Admiralty: Harbour Department, 1852, Appendix 5.
19. From figures quoted by D. J. Owen, *A Short History of the Port of Belfast*, Belfast: Mayne, Boyd 1917, 23.
20. *History of the Harbours of the United Kingdom: Belfast*, *op. cit.*, summarizes this debate, 11–21 and quotes the relevant reports as Appendices 2–24, with appropriate maps 2–11.

21. Even this plan (Plan A of 1830), upon which design the first cut was made, included impounded docks north of the town and opposite in County Down. These were abandoned in the Act passed in 1837.

22. E. Jones, *op. cit.*, 8–16.

23. *Report of Walker and Burges, Civil Engineers, on the Best Means of Improving the Harbour of Belfast*, July 10, 1830, quoted as Appendix 11 in *History of the Harbours of the United Kingdom: Belfast, op. cit.* The report appears to be largely the work of James Walker.

24. D. J. Owen, *op. cit.*, 39.

25. There appears to have been a political bias in favour of the County Down (or eastern) side of the channel at this time.

26. J. Dubourdieu, *Statistical Survey of the County of Antrim*, Part 2, Dublin, 1812, 521–4 quotes verbatim an account by W. Ritchie himself. See also D. Rebbeck, *The Belfast Shipyards 1791–1947*, Belfast Association of Engineers, Presidential Address, 1947, 5.

27. D. Rebbeck, *The History of the Iron Ship-building on the Queen's Island up till 1874*, Unpublished Ph.D. thesis, The Queen's University, Belfast, 1954, 49.

28. K. S. Isles and N. Cuthbert, *An Economic Survey of Northern Ireland*, Belfast: H.M.S.O., 1957, 217.

29. *Ibid.*, 102.

30. The advantages of good management are presumed constant throughout the firm's history. 'It is the skill of management, availability of labour and the application of technical progress that determine where shipbuilding can be carried on . . .' J. R. Parkinson, *The Economics of Shipbuilding in the United Kingdom*, Cambridge: University Press, 1960, 20. Belfast benefited greatly from the disappearance of shipbuilding at Liverpool in the nineteenth century, D. Rebbeck (1954), *op. cit.*, 127 *ff*; and C. N. Parkinson, *The Rise of Liverpool*, Liverpool: University Press, 1952, 143–5.

31. E. J. Harland, 'Shipbuilding in Belfast—Its Origin and Progress', S. Smiles, *Men of Invention and Industry*, London: Murray, 1884, 288–323, 303–5, summarized in J. G. Peirson, *Great Shipbuilders or the Rise of Harland and Wolff*, London: Stockwell, 1935.

32. D. Rebbeck (1954), *op. cit.*, 206.

33. On the opening of the Suez Canal, Bibby gave an order for three vessels: *Istrian, Iberian*, and *Illyrian*, 390 feet long and 37 feet beam. These were the ships, launched in 1868, that impressed the founders of the White Star Line (see below), E. J. Harland, *loc. cit.*, 311–2.

34. The White Star contract was received through the assistance of G. C. Schwabe who was associated with T. H. Ismay in founding the Oceanic Steam Navigation Company Ltd. It will be remembered that Schwabe had financed Harland eleven years before. N. R. P. Bonsor, *North Atlantic Seaway*, Prescot: Stephenson, 1955, 253–4; and S. C. Gilfillan, *Inventing the Ship*, Chicago: Follett, 1935, 154–5 point out that the new White Star ships embodied several important innovations in the realm of passenger accommodation.

35. K. S. Isles and N. Cuthbert, *op. cit.*, 102.

36. This information is derived from a personal visit and 'Shipbuilding and Engineering at Belfast: an Account of the Works of Messrs. Harland & Wolff Ltd.', *The Shipbuilder and Marine Engine-Builder*, 59 (1952), 14–22.

37. K. S. Isles and N. Cuthbert, *op. cit.*, 134–5.

38. For full details of all services from Belfast to Great Britain see *Freight Services to and from Northern Ireland*, Belfast: Northern Ireland Development Council, 1959 and later editions.

39. K. S. Isles and N. Cuthbert, *op. cit.*, 131.

40. Up to thirty containers can also be carried on the upper deck.

41. See remarks on the difficulty of ascertaining this increase, K. S. Isles and N. Cuthbert, *op. cit.*, 152–3.

42. A further recent industrial development on the shores of Belfast Lough is the 200-acre site of a man-made fibre factory, three miles north-east of Carrickfergus, a total of ten miles from Belfast. See also M. D. Thomas, 'Manufacturing Industries in Northern Ireland', *Annals of the Association of American Geographers*, 46 (1956), 177–96.

43. E. Jones, *op. cit.*, Fig. 27, 109.

44. K. S. Isles and N. Cuthbert, *op. cit.*, Chart i (x) and ii (x) 132.

FURTHER REFERENCES

Centenary 1847–1947. Belfast Harbour Commissioners, 1947.

Evans, E. and E. Jones, 'The Growth of Belfast', *Town Planning Review*, 26 (1955), 93–111.

Kelly, N. R. 'The Alexandra Graving-Dock, Belfast', *Minutes of the Proceedings of the Institution of Civil Engineers*, 111 (1893), 59–74.

Owen, D. J. *History of Belfast*. Belfast and London: Baird, 1921.

Salmond, T. R. 'The River Lagan and Harbour of Belfast', *Minutes of the Proceedings of the Institution of Civil Engineers*, 55 (1878–9), 22–35.

COMMERCIAL AND INDUSTRIAL ESTUARIES—I

Chapter 5

HULL AND OTHER HUMBER PORTS

The great Humber, an estuary draining one-sixth of the area of England and Wales, has set some difficulties before the builders of ports. It was not until 1852, with the opening of the Royal Dock, Grimsby, that the Humber foreshore was used as the site of a dock. Put shortly, the difficulties have been three in number: dangers from flooding; meandering of the deep-water channel within the estuary; and Humberside sands covered by a tide averaging 22 feet in range. Early-developed ports, like Hull and Grimsby (and Hedon), originated upon water sites of tiny Humber tributaries. Much later, two ports were founded *presto* by excavation of alluvium, to form a dock on the estuary shore at Immingham, or far upstream at Goole. Of these four ports, Hull is by far the largest and is described first. The other three will then be treated more briefly to complete a picture of port activity on Humberside.

Port development at Hull is simple to understand in broad outline. Before 1778

TABLE 42

Eras and Epochs in the Development of the Port of Hull

Eras and Chief Areal Characteristics	Present-day Symbols
I *Primitive:* port on western side of River Hull estuary	Wharves on east side of High Street, Hull
Era ended by the opening of the first dock at Hull, 1778	
II *Marginal Quay Extension:* after 1809 concomitant with	Wharves on east side of Hull estuary
IV *Dock Elaboration:* docks transverse to Humberside before 1846; parallel to Humberside after 1846	The Docks at Hull
No further elaborate quayage built after 1914	
V *Simple Lineal Quayage:* recent modernization of pre-First World War installations	New north quay, King George Dock, 1959–62
VI *Specialized Quayage:* oil berths, with specialized wharves	Salt End Jetties; Upper Hull Estuary (north of the old walls)

the port was almost entirely confined to the western side of the lower River Hull, a left bank tributary of the Humber. Thereafter, emphasis shifted to docks constructed upon the site of the old walls and moat to the north and west of the town, with layouts transverse to Humberside. After 1846 docks were constructed with sites parallel to Humberside flanking the Hull-Humber confluence, of progressively later date as one moves away from the confluence east and west. There were two very lengthy eras of port development at Hull: the *primitive* site sufficed alone until 1778; and the *dock elaboration* era lasted from then until the First World War. W. G. East, tracing the port's development up to 1840, recognized that there had been

> 'two distinct phases of development: in the first, it is a small medieval river port; in the second it has become a modern port, artificially extended in size . . .[1]

General considerations of Hull's land and water situations on the Humber and the local circumstances of the early land and water sites on the Hull are both linked to the effects of the glaciation of Yorkshire.

It is necessary to consider first the pre-glacial appearance of east Yorkshire. The Ouse and the Trent had eroded wide lowlands upon weak Triassic rocks to form the Vales of York and Trent. Their waters were taken eastwards across the chalk Wolds by the pre-glacial Humber via a water gap eroded along a line of faulting.[2] The pre-glacial picture is obscure, but in the last inter-glacial period the Humber certainly met the sea close to the western suburbs of Hull. This is indicated by a buried line of sea-cliffs revealed by borings.[3] The cliffs are buried because the last onset of the ice overwhelmed them with the glacial drift deposits extending from the area of Holderness. This ice sheet riding in from the sea not only plugged the Humber gap (to form Lake Humber[4] in the vales to the west), but as the ice front retreated east, a marginal stream ran curving to the south-east, ancestor of the present River Hull and of the Humber south-east of Hull. The resultant contrast between the channels of the upper and lower Humber west and east of Hull are very real for shipping today.

The modest River Hull has an origin linked to glacial diversion like the mighty lower Humber east of the Wolds. Here the underlying Chalk dips eastward. In the last inter-glacial period short eastward-flowing streams, consequent upon that dip-slope, probably ran independently to a sea that battered against the chalk cliffs. Such streams would later have been blocked by the same ice sheet that buried the cliffs and later diverted the lower Humber.[5] They would then have been diverted southward along the edge of the retreating ice until they joined the Humber. Thus was formed the Hull lowland. Support is given to this idea by the evidence of two parallel valleys in the south (represented by two lines of meres and carrs),[6] suggesting that as the ice retreated eastward a second line of drainage took over from the first.

The River Hull flows in the western channel, particularly fed by springs on the east side of the Wolds; it has noticeably fewer tributaries from the hummocky glacial drift of Holderness to the east. This curious geomorphological history explains why the River Hull is unique in being a large tributary of the Humber east of the Humber gap across the chalk Wolds. On this largest tributary has grown the largest Humber port.[7]

The earliest mention of the *primitive* port appears to be in connection with the wool contributed by Yorkshire Cistercian and Gilbertine monasteries towards the ransom of Richard I in 1193 (Pipe Roll 5 Ric. I Mich. 1193).[8] At this time the port was called Wyke (*vik.*, old Scandinavian; creek or inlet) after the name then applied to the Hull estuary.[9] In 1293 Edward I, realizing that the Hull estuary had strategic port qualities, gave the Abbot of Meaux (the abbey is sited seven miles due north of the Hull estuary) the lands he had in Wawne (East Riding) and Wilsby (Lincolnshire) in exchange for Wyke.

'he changed the name of the said villa of Wyke and caused that same villa to be called Kingston-upon-Hull.'[10]

Kingston grew up on the west bank of the Hull near the confluence with the Humber. Some historians[11] have inferred from documents that the estuary of the River Hull was once further to the west and was later diverted, but no dock excavation along Humberside ever revealed the filled-in course.[12]

The *primitive* port was simply the western bank of the River Hull, with a longitudinal street faithfully parallel to the curves of the river and first called, appropriately enough, Hull Street, now High Street. J. Bilson has produced a map of Wyke in 1293, the very year it became Kingston, by collating the record of the Valuation and Rental of that year with later rentals.

'The lay-out of the town proves conclusively that it was not developed from an agricultural hamlet but that it had its origin with the port and grew up with it. The most important streets were Hullstreet following the line of the river Hull, with Marketgate [now Lowgate] parallel to it and Monkgate [now Humber Street] parallel with the Humber . . .'[13]

Soon there were walls and a moat around Kingston defending the town against floods as well as enemies. The centre of the oldest part of Hull is today five or six feet below H.W.O.S.T., built on tidal silt. The walls cut the town off from the dangerous Humber, and the medieval port was concentrated on the Hull frontage with small alleys called staithes, many of which still exist, linking the waterfront

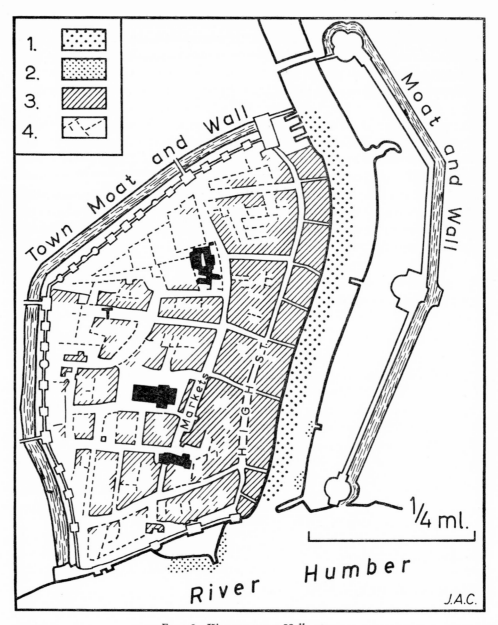

FIG. 28   Kingston-upon-Hull, 1640

This diagram has been adapted from an engraving by W. Hollar showing an oblique view, so that orientation and scale are not completely accurate.

1. Anchorage in the River Hull for larger vessels; 2. Anchorages for smaller vessels; 3. Built-up area; 4. Low walls and hedge boundaries; T. Main transverse route inland; Churches solid black. Note the eight 'staithes' leading to the River Hull.

with Hull Street. Little *marginal quay extension* took place before the first dock was built,[14] because the east side of the river was occupied by defence works of the Crown. No *marginal quay elaboration* was possible because of the narrowness of the Hull and the steepness of its banks laden with tide-driven silt. In the *primitive* era the chief transverse track inland departed via Whitefriargate and the Beverley gate, and thence along the causeway parallel to the River Hull to Beverley, capital of the East Riding. In the medieval period Kingston was primarily the port for the East Riding. But by the fourteenth century there is ample evidence of its exports of wool and grain from river ports on the Ouse, Don, and Trent, foreshadowing the trade of the last two hundred years in a reverse direction.[15]

Possibly because of the Crown's interest in Kingston, or the intercession of the Archbishop of York, or perhaps simply due to the fact that it was a compact port enclosed by walls, Hull was the only large port in the kingdom not to have legal quays appointed by a commission in 1558. (Act 1 Eliz. c. 11, II (5) specifically exempted Hull.) Smugglers were thus given great opportunities. Eventually, by an Act of 1774, the Commissioners of Customs forced a dock upon the port. They had threatened to establish a legal quay elsewhere on Humberside unless a dock with declared legal quays was excavated. The Customs contributed £15,000 to the expenses of the new Dock Company, and the Crown gave the buildings and ditches along the town walls from the River Hull on the east to the Humber on the south.[16] The long era of *dock elaboration* in Hull had begun. From soon after the opening of the first dock in 1779 is dated the decline of the High Street from its position as the city's main street.[17]

To gain the entrance of the first dock ships had to negotiate the crowded harbour, where small craft clustered to the wharves of the Hull estuary

> '. . . and the Entrance [to the River] is blocked up; it also frequently happens that the Baltic Ships get neaped in the Old Harbour and then it is also blocked up . . . there are frequent instances when Vessels are many days in passing from the Harbour's mouth to the Dock and *vice versa*.' (1793)[18]
>
> 'The increase of the trade of Hull having rendered the present Dock very inadequate . . .' (1787),[19]

the second dock, Humber Dock (1809), did have the advantage of opening direct from the Humber. Another subsidy was forthcoming in the grant of lands by the Crown to the Corporation of Hull and to the Corporation of Trinity House at Hull in return for their subscriptions to the capital of the Hull Dock Company. These lands consisted of the area on the east side of the Hull given up as military installations so that this riverside at last became available for *marginal quay extension*.[20] It is still known as Garrison Side. The subsidies were necessary because, as at

Southampton, local capital from a city with few industries was not of itself sufficient to meet the expense of providing the first two docks.

This was also the reason for the twenty-year delay, 1809–29, between the second and third docks. During this time Hull's hinterland was extending westward to embrace the West Riding, growing in industrial power. Yet the port changed little. Firstly, nothing was done to improve the harbour in the river.

> 'Commissioner.—(Addressing the Town's Husband [Treasurer])—You have not shown that anything material has been laid out for the improvement of the port or haven . . .' (1834)[21]
> . . . the old Harbour remains in nearly the same state as in 1774 . . .' (1835)[22]

Secondly, the Humber Dock Act, 1802, had stipulated precisely the conditions upon which the third dock might be excavated.[23] These conditions were certainly fulfilled by 1822–4. The difficulty was as usual financial. After the Humber Dock, the Dock Company had had to withhold payment of dividends for several years in order to liquidate its share of the capital cost.[24] The Dock Company and the Hull Ship-owners' Society reached an agreement in 1825 about financing the third dock by increasing dues. Opposition to the increases came from other ports, so Humber, Ouse, and Trent ports were promised exemption from the additional rate on goods.

> 'But when an exemption was carried in committee in favour of all seaport towns trading coastwise with Hull, the Dock Company abruptly withdrew their Bill.' (June 4th, 1825)[25]

The Prince's Dock, joining the first dock to the Humber Dock, was not finally opened until 1829.

The twenty-year gap between the second and third docks is important because it helps to explain the rise of Goole. An Act of 1820 empowered the Undertakers of the Rivers Aire and Calder to construct a canal from Knottingley to Goole, and this was completed in 1825. In the following year docks were provided at Goole where the canal joined the Ouse, near the canalized outfall of the River Don. Goole was appointed a port with legal quays in 1828, just one year before Hull resumed its port development by opening a third dock, and ever since Goole has always offered severe competition to Hull for coastwise trade on the Humber.

Seven further docks were constructed along Humberside, east and west of the Hull confluence, before the First World War. This growth was mainly to cater for the developments in the industrialized West Riding.

> 'In the fourteenth century the East Riding . . . was only a little less populated

than the much more extensive West Riding; by 1801, however, the West Riding had five times the population of the East Riding.'[26]

Hull could easily serve this area, first by its river craft penetrating the Ouse waterway system, and the railway made the links stronger after 1840. Hull's railway stations originated as termini of lines from the west.[27]

The water situation of Hull favoured links across the North Sea, the coastwise export of coal, a large share in the nation's trawler fishing after 1850, and raw material imports for the West Riding and the dispatch of its exported manufactures. From this generalization, one may safely deduce that Hull's trade was not predominantly carried in the largest class of dry cargo liner. The size of the largest vessels visiting the port in the nineteenth century was not as large as at London, Liverpool, or Southampton. And so, even in the last dock in 1914, *simple lineal quayage* was not provided. The lay-out was to have had four arms, only two of which were fully completed. Only one arm was equipped with transit sheds suitable for general cargo liners. But with the increase in Hull's dry general cargo trade since the Second World War, *simple lineal quayage* has been provided for deep-sea vessels in the King

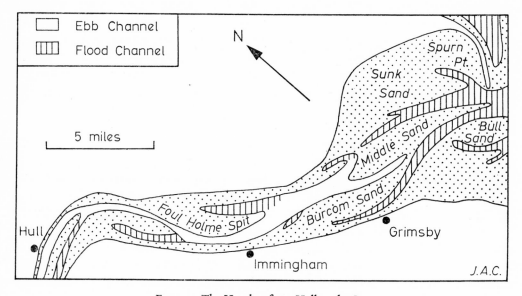

FIG. 29 The Humber from Hull to the Sea

Because of the amount of land water discharge the ebb-stream has scoured the main channel, minimum depth of 18 feet L.W.O.S.T. The narrow estuary allows little scope for flood streams west of Grimsby, with progressively shorter 'barbs' facing upstream at the meander bends of the ebb-channel. Compare the fundamentally different nature of the water approaches to Grimsby on the one hand, and to Immingham and Hull on the other. After A. H. W. Robinson, 'Ebb-Flood Channel Systems in Sandy Bays and Estuaries', *Geography*, 45 (1960), 183–99, Fig. 3.

George Dock. Apart from the fish quays, and wharves progressively modernized on the River Hull, *specialized quayage* is principally represented by the oil jetties at Salt End, most appropriately named, where an industrial estate has developed from an oil depot begun in 1914.

The port has ample depth in its water approaches as indicated by the 18-foot submarine contour L.W.O.S.T. (Fig. 29). As might be expected, this meanders more than the estuary shorelines would suggest, a self-maintaining ebb-channel. Depths are increased by a large tidal range, as much as 24 feet off the Hull estuary. Upstream of Hull Roads, as the geomorphological history has suggested, the estuary shoals considerably, and the channels have less stability. Discussion of these reaches may be postponed until the approaches to Goole are considered. The Corporation of the City of Hull is the conservator of the River Hull, deriving authority from a charter of 5 Richard II, 1382. But the authority for the Humber is the Humber Conservancy Board, set up in 1907.[28]

The Hull Dock Company, which had constructed and operated the first docks, suffered from a lack of working capital and was forced to sell out to the North Eastern Railway Company in 1893, the year following a similar docks purchase by the railway at Southampton for a similar reason. There had been, however, a determined local opposition to the North Eastern Company's monopoly of rail communications to the port. The Corporation received powers to assist the Hull and Barnsley Railway Company to build a line[29] to their Alexandra Dock of 1885. This company, maintaining a successful separate existence, opened the King George Dock in 1914 as a joint enterprise with the North Eastern Railway Company. All the docks have now been inherited by British Transport Docks.

Hull port development compares quite closely with that of *Anyport*, although the divergencies reveal certain important characteristics of the port. Firstly, as with all ports on the Humber except the relatively modern Immingham Dock, the port was forced to begin on a subsidiary waterway because of the danger of floods from the Humber and the width of its marginal sandbanks. The lay-out of the *primitive* port is very similar to that of *Anyport*. The narrowness of the River Hull prevented *marginal quay elaboration*, though of course Hull had an advantage of better water approaches than Beverley, connected to the River Hull by an artificial cut eight miles upstream. *Marginal quay extension* was blocked, until the *dock elaboration* era had begun, by the military installations east of the Hull. The long duration of this *dock elaboration* era has been explained by the lack of trading by really large liners. This is not to say that Hull is not a large port; but it is a large regional port, like Bristol, rather than having liner traffic some of which serves the whole country as at London, Liverpool, and Southampton. This point is illustrated by the longest quay provided at Hull, the north quay of the King George Dock, which up to 1960 was interrupted by coal hoists placed in echelon formation so that the line of the quay was interrupted by knuckles. This certainly helped Yorkshire coal exports but limited the quayage available for general cargo liners. A tendency towards a simpler dock lay-out may be discerned by comparing the Alexandra Dock (1885), 53¾ acres, total quayage 13,391 feet, with the King George Dock (1914) 53 acres, 9,774 feet. Hull has, however, recently acquired modern *simple lineal quayage* and the *specialized quayage* at Salt End. Here for the first time Humber depths have proved inadequate. The 36-foot depth off Salt End jetties allows regular access by tankers of up to only 27,500 tons deadweight. Larger tankers cannot be accommodated, and no oil refinery was possible on the Salt End industrial estate. But, as at London, lighter traffic enables *specialized quayage* with restricted water access to develop on the site of the *primitive* port in the River Hull.

Modern Functions of the Port of Hull

The River Hull can receive only vessels which are less than 200 feet in length. Scarcely one hundred yards wide at its mouth, the river flows through the city as in a canyon, the walls of which are the grain and oilseed mills, and the modern warehouses, successors of the merchants' stores of the *primitive* port. Like the Thames, the Hull is thronged by lighters, many of which are dumb (without an engine), all flat-bottomed, but none swim-ended as at London. The barges sit on the bottom at the side of the river at low tide. This forms beds or ledges, with a perilous slope down to the low water channel of the river. The craft are often moored three or four abreast, and then there is only very narrow passage room in this overworked waterway.

In contrast to the position in London, the 'free water' concession enabling lighters and river craft to enter the docks free of charge does not derive from a specific statement in the first Dock Act. Nevertheless, since it had theretofore been a custom not to charge tonnage dues upon lighters and river craft, these were allowed to enter the first dock free of charge. Indeed, lighters and river craft are able to enter the Port of Hull freely from any part of the Port of Hull as existing at 1774, *i.e.* from Humber, Ouse, or Trent ports, notwithstanding the separate ports that have been created since (*Hull Docks Act*, 1844, Sec. 196). Section 45 of the first Dock Act at Hull provided specifically that wharfage rates should be paid on goods landed *on the dock quays*. The effect of such provision, repeated in subsequent Hull Dock Acts,[30] was that no wharfage payments were or could be levied upon goods discharged or loaded overside to or from lighters or river craft. The advantages of overside working in the docks, which accounts for about one-third of the total trade at Hull (excluding coal, fish, oil, and spirits), are similar to those at London (p. 395). Nearly 1,000 river craft and lighters are involved.[31]

The River Hull is lined continuously by frontagers using the river up to two and a quarter miles north of the confluence with the Humber. Oilseed mills, which became a prominent industry after 1840 with the decline of whaling, and grain mills dominate the scene. Amid other properties, marine engineers, builders' merchants' yards, and paintworks, one might single out a shipyard as worthy of special note, since it builds ships in the reclaimed entrance[32] to the first dock.

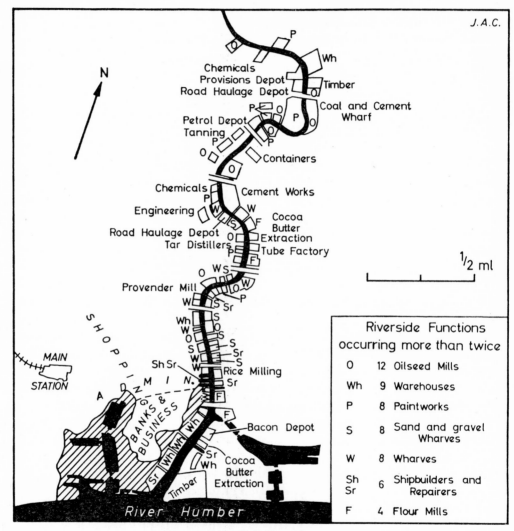

FIG. 30   River Hull Riverside Functions

This diagram, which slightly simplifies the pattern, also attempts to show the separate functional areas of central Kingston-upon-Hull, with diagonal ruling covering the area where port functions are dominant.

TABLE 43

River Craft Registered by the Humber Conservancy Board, 1960

Where Owned	Mechanically Propelled	Others
Hull and East Riding	313	259
Grimsby, Barton, and South Humber Shore	38	7
Goole and Lower Ouse	31	13
Upper Ouse	112	21
Trent	80	23
Total ...	574	323

The first dock, Queen's Dock,[33] was purchased by the City Corporation in 1933, filled in, and laid out as a public open space, Queen's Gardens, remodelled in 1960 with the construction of a technical college at the eastern end. The other three docks, built on the site of the old moat and walls, have been downgraded in traffic since their entrance via Humber Dock is only 158 feet long and 41½ feet wide. They are used mainly by coastwise traffic and lighters. If for some reason Goole had not arisen, these docks would now be much busier, and indeed the Queen's Dock might still be functioning. Yet Paris and Brussels services are still maintained from Humber Dock; a group of six-storey warehouses, south of the Railway Dock, interrupts the general arrangement of one-storey wooden transit sheds and store sugar and grain from lighters; and there is a tobacco bonded store south of Prince's Dock.[34]

The docks on Humberside west of the Hull differ from those on the east in that they had to encroach on the Humber as the built-up land and the railway allowed little room for inland excavation. Land east of the River Hull could be excavated further back from the Humber, and the contrast may easily be seen in observing the difference in the position of the line of the Humber waterfront east and west of the Hull. The lay-out of the western docks, long and narrow, was thus conditioned by the available site. As a generalization it may be said that the Albert and William Wright Docks receive vessels predominantly in the Scandinavian and West German trades for import and export traffic, except at berths equipped with coal hoists. Both St. Andrew's Docks are fish docks, and the fishing activities of the port will be described concurrently with those at Grimsby. The new Riverside Quay, on reinforced concrete piles, 1,000 feet long, was re-opened in 1959, after wartime destruction of the original wooden quayage. The principal advantage of a tidal quay is the quickness of turn-round offered, especially for the Hull–Rotterdam service. This may save up to nine hours waiting for a tide, but is possible only for vessels drawing less than 19 feet. As part of the Riverside Quay scheme, a 1,065-foot quay with three new sheds for a similar class of traffic was opened on the south side of the

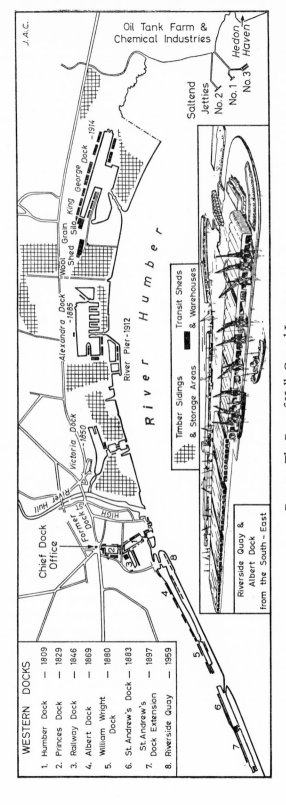

WESTERN DOCKS

1. Humber Dock — 1809
2. Princes Dock — 1829
3. Railway Dock — 1846
4. Albert Dock — 1869
5. William Wright Dock — 1880
6. St. Andrew's Dock — 1883
7. St. Andrew's Dock Extension — 1897
8. Riverside Quay — 1959

J.A.C.

Oil Tank Farm & Chemical Industries

Hedon Haven

Saltend Jetties
No. 2
No. 1
No. 3

King George Dock — 1914

Grain Silo

Wool Shed

Alexandra Dock — 1885

River Pier — 1912

Victoria Dock — 1850

Former No. 1 Dock — 15

Chief Dock Office

River Hull

HIGH

River Humber

Timber Sidings & Storage Areas

Transit Sheds

Warehouses

Riverside Quay & Albert Dock from the South-East

FIG. 31 The Port of Hull: General Lay-out

The original Riverside Quay, 1906, was destroyed by enemy action in 1941.

Albert Dock. Much fruit is unloaded, and the sheds have an interior clear height of 20 feet for high piling by mechanical appliances.

The Victoria Dock (1850) was laid out on the old military estate. Indeed, though nothing remains of the original garrison, the triangular pattern of both roads and railways west of the dock reflects the former garrison lay-out. The original basin of the dock and the entrance via the River Hull were previously timber ponds constructed from the moat. Timber is the principal cargo dealt with at this dock. Here is displayed an unusual method of removing timber to stacking yards—on bogies with small diameter wheels running on standard gauge rails, each carrying up to $2\frac{1}{2}$ standards[35] of timber.

The Alexandra Dock is also dominated by timber discharge particularly from those ships (often from Russia) too big to enter the Victoria Dock. There are coal hoists on the north-eastern part of the north quay, and the triangular eastern dock extension was probably designed for further coal export facilities. Despite many quayside cranes, vessels are berthed stern first to the north-west quay to assist discharge overside of all kinds of oilseeds to lighters. The River Pier, 1,300 feet long, is an older counterpart of the Riverside Quay and also with 19 feet of water minimum alongside, dealing with a similar class of traffic, especially fruit.

The King George Dock handled for many years a mixture of general cargo working on the north-west arm, with coal and timber discharge elsewhere. No. 12 Quay has been rebuilt in reinforced concrete, 1,356 feet in length (1954). No. 11 Quay provides facilities for ships undergoing wet dock repairs, and Nos. 8 and 7 Quays provide open berths for such cargoes as timber. Opposite No. 7 Quay in the south-west arm there is a depth of fifteen feet of water for the mooring of barges. Work began in 1960 on converting the north quay to one simple line, 3,700 feet long with a total of seven transit sheds for general cargo. This work epitomizes a change in the structure of the trade of the port. At a time of declining coal exports, the general cargo trade, particularly with Australia, New Zealand, and the Far East, has remained buoyant, so much so that the six pre-war transit sheds in the King George Dock proved insufficient. This will be apparent when it is realized that grain ships have priority at No. 1 Shed Berth, nearest the silo, and also make use of No. 4 Shed Berth, both berths being at the western end of the north-west arm. Here quayside grain elevators deliver the cargo to conveyor belts running to the silo beneath the quay, while floating elevators may discharge grain overside to lighters. This trade has also increased in recent years, and the capacity of the dock silo has been enlarged by half since 1960. The Wool Transit Shed is, oddly enough, not on the quayside. After the Second World War this large structure was inherited from the Admiralty, and since 1957 has been used for overflow wool imports when quayside transit sheds are fully occupied. The quayside sheds are single-storey (1, 2, and 3) and double-storey (4, 5, and 6), all except No. 3 being equipped with roof cranes to facilitate working inland of the shed. Like other docks east of the River Hull, King George Dock has many timber yards. The lay-out emphasizes the great areas required by timber storage. It has been found necessary to provide extra storage space north of the Hedon Road as there is no further room on the Humberside dock estate.

East of the King George Dock is the Salt End Industrial Estate which stretches across the lower reaches of Hedon Haven, where oil barges are loaded. How much anguish there would have been in medieval Hedon had it been realized that the rival Port of Hull would eventually expand to impress its seaward developments crushingly across Hedon Haven! The industrial estate is dominated by oil storage and an

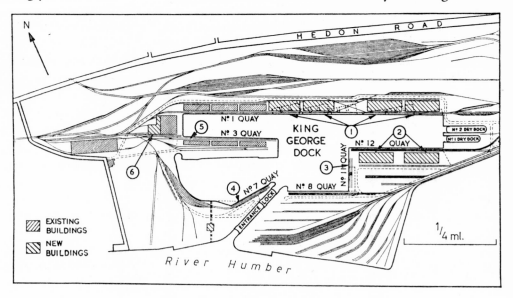

FIG. 32 Improvements at King George Dock, Hull, 1959–62

1. Extension of No. 1 Quay to 3,700 feet in one line with four new transit sheds; 2. Two new transit sheds on No. 12 Quay; 3. Extension of No. 11 Quay with a 10-ton crane; 4. Extension of No. 7 Quay with four 10-ton cranes; 5. Provision of grain elevators on No. 4 Quay; 6. Extension of grain silo.

Former quay outlines, including the *en echelon* plan of former coal hoists on No. 1 Quay, shown by pecked lines.

industry using oil as a raw material for industrial alcohol, solvents, plastics and paints, boot polish and pickles, textiles and lipstick.[36] Molasses is also stored, and another factory imports bauxite to make abrasive material for grinding wheels. Salt End Jetty No. 1 was constructed in 1914; No. 2 in 1928; No. 3 in 1960, with No. 1 reconstructed off No. 3 stem. All project about 1,500 feet into 36 feet minimum depth of water. From No. 3 the ebb-channel curves away from the left Humber bank, and one looks due south-east to Immingham on the opposite shore.

Until the Queen's [the first] Dock disappeared in 1934 the docks made 'down-town' Hull an island. But during this century the shopping centre of gravity has shifted decidedly westward towards the main railway station. This migration has sharpened the distinction between the port and the business districts. A line can be traced within which almost all the buildings connected with the port are to be found (Fig. 30). The whole of the original longitudinal street of the *primitive* port, the High Street, is in this zone. This is a curious High Street now, without a retail shop. To the south is Humber Street, the centre of the wholesale fruit trade. In the northern half of the medieval core is a 'city aura' of banks and offices, some in small alleys, one or two illuminated by hanging reflecting mirrors (as is common in the City of London), all deserted at night.[37] The functional areas have begun to crystallize out, including a 'west end', a 'city', and a separate port district.

If the pattern of port activity along the Humber and the Hull appears as an inverted **T**, this is reflected in a similar distribution of Hull's industry;[38] a survey in 1951[39] revealed that three-quarters of the area in industrial use was north of the Humberside Docks or along the Hull. Further land is available for industry at the northern and eastern arms of the inverted **T** at Stoneferry and Marfleet.

By value Hull's foreign trade exports were worth only two-thirds of the imports in 1960. Of the fifteen most valuable imports it is not difficult to assign some to one

TABLE 44

Fifteen Most Valuable Foreign Trade Imports into Hull (incl. Keadby), 1960

	Value £ Million	
Raw Wool ...	36·6	
Sawn Softwood ...	17·0	
Butter ...	13·8	
Wheat ...	12·6	
Bacon ...	12·0	
Unwrought Nickel ...	8·4	
Maize ...	6·9	
Ferro-chromium Alloys ...	4·4	
Aluminium ...	4·0	
Flax or Linseed ...	3·3	
Cocoa Butter ...	3·2	
Palm Kernels ...	3·0	
Soya Beans ...	2·9	
Wood Veneers ...	2·6	
Canned Bacon and Hams ...	2·6	
Total of all Imports ...	259·0	(6·0 per cent of total U.K. imports by value)

TABLE 45

Fifteen Most Valuable Foreign Trade Exports from Hull (incl. Keadby), 1960

	Value £ Million
Wool Tops	8·4
Textile Machinery	7·1
Woollen Yarns	5·4
Plastics and Rubber-working Machinery ...	4·9
Raw Wool	4·8
Dyeing Chemicals	4·5
Woven Woollen Fabrics	4·4
Manufactured Chemical Elements and Compounds	4·2
Plastics Materials	3·7
Man-made Fibres	3·2
Iron and Steel Tubes and Pipes	2·9
Uncoated Iron and Steel Plates and Sheets ...	2·2
Excavators	2·1
Mechanical Handling Equipment	1·9
Rubber Tyres and Tubes	1·9
Total of all Exports	182·3

(5·5 per cent of total U.K. exports by value)

of three areas as a dominant trade: West Riding (wool and cocoa), Scunthorpe-Frodingham iron and steel area (ferro-alloys), and Hull itself (linseed, palm kernels, cocoa butter). A striking feature of the export trade was that over 80 per cent of the total (foreign and coastwise), excluding fuel, was bound for Europe.[40]

Grimsby and Immingham

Like other medieval ports using Humber approaches, Grimsby was sited on a very small tributary estuary, Grimsby Haven. Nevertheless, this was the largest estuary in the area because it carried the united discharge of two or three small streams. There was another stream which was much larger than each of the Haven streams, because its upper course is fed by several springs in the Lincolnshire Wolds; but its estuary was smaller than the Haven. This was the River Freshney, with an estuary originally in the parish of Great Coates, about one mile west of the Haven. Though Grimsby was incorporated as a borough as early as 1201, its haven must have been difficult to navigate, with a danger of silting within intricate meanders in the one and a half mile passage from the sea.

At the end of the eighteenth century the *primitive* port was described as being 'the ground lying on the West and South Sides of the Two Branches of the said Haven, and next adjoining the Town . . .'[41]

In its natural state the haven was said to have been

'navigable for Sloops only, and at certain Times of the Tide [; and the] publick Quay . . . [was] very narrow and inconvenient . . . nor admit [ted] of Two Carriages to pass each other . . .'[42]

In 1696 an agreement was made between Grimsby and Sir Thomas Barnardiston, owner of the parishes to the west—Great and Little Coates, whereby the River Freshney could be used by the borough. As a result a 'New Cut' was made in 1698 between the River Freshney and Piper Creek, and extended eastwards to the haven in the following year. This cut became silted up within a few years, and it was not until one hundred years later that the work was thoroughly overhauled by the Grimsby Haven Company as part of a plan which inaugurated the era of *marginal quay extension*.[43] The haven was deepened by the increased flow provided by the newly-scoured diverted Freshney. It was also straightened and impounded to form a dock of fifteen acres (Fig. 33), forerunner of the present Alexandra Dock. Careful observation of the modern plan reveals that the curves in the quays of the South Arm of the Alexandra Dock have been superimposed upon the early nineteenth century quays.[44]

The *dock elaboration* era began with the opening of the Royal Dock in 1852 by the Manchester, Sheffield and Lincolnshire Railway Company, which had bought

TABLE 46

Eras and Epochs in the Development of the Ports of Grimsby and Immingham

Eras and Chief Areal Characteristics	Present-day Symbols
I *Primitive:* port near confluence of minor streams	West Haven, River Head
Era ended by successful diversion of River Freshney, 1801	
II *Marginal Quay Extension:* quays along straightened haven in 'Old Dock'	South Arm, Alexandra Dock
Era ended by opening of Royal Dock, 1852	
IV *Dock Elaboration:* encroachment on to former mudflats and salt marsh	Royal Dock, 1852; Junction Dock and Alexandra Dock, 1872–9; Immingham Dock, 1912
VI *Specialized Quayage:* Fish Docks	(see text pp. 141–3)

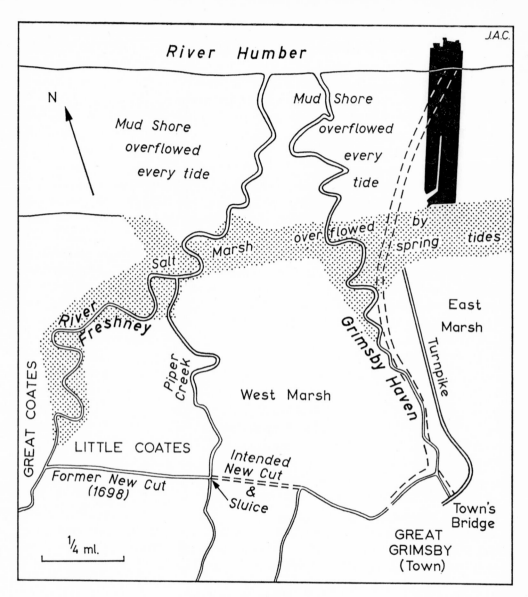

FIG. 33 Grimsby Haven, 1795

'Freshney water is intended to be taken into the former new Cut to be thence conveyed thro' a sluice into Piper Creek, and thence into the new Drain. . . .' *A Plan of the Haven of Great Grimsby in the County of Lincoln* (*with the Proposed Alterations*), 1795, Grimsby Corporation Library. The water area of the Royal Dock (1852), its walls founded on Chalk at 78 feet below the surface, has been inserted from the modern plan to show the amount of water encroachment by the present dock system.

out the Grimsby Haven Company in 1846. Fig. 33 shows that the site of this dock was entirely on former Humber tidal mudbanks like 'a large groyne thrown across the foreshore'.[45] Once the Royal Dock entrance in deep water had been provided it was possible to redevelop the old haven as the South Arm of the Alexandra Dock in 1872 and make an extension westwards in former saltings, the Alexandra Dock West Arm in 1879, with the narrow link in the system becoming known as Junction Dock.

The land situation of Grimsby was certainly isolated before the arrival of the railway from Sheffield in 1848. When *The Woman in White* of Wilkie Collins's novel wished to avoid discovery in 1850, she went to Grimsby, even at that late date 'one of the most out-of-the-way places in England'. Unlike Hull and Goole the port is far from the industrial area of the West Riding, but Grimsby's great asset is its water situation with short approaches to the North Sea. This was the advantage upon which the railway-owned docks relied after 1852.

In comparison with *Anyport* it is the early difficulties of the narrow water site of the haven that stand out. The diversion of the Freshney is like the use of the River Dour for harbour scour at Dover; whereas the impounding of the haven in 1801 is similar to that of the Avon carried out at Bristol only a few years later. Like the Floating Harbour at Bristol the impounded haven really forms part of a *marginal quay elaboration* era. It is quite distinct from the later *dock elaboration* that led on to the modern lay-out. River jetty construction was impossible, as at Hull, because of the narrowness of the water site. The depth of the water approaches has proved insufficient for the larger class of general cargo liner, and, consequently, there have been no developments of *simple lineal quayage*. The Fish Docks have of course a form of *specialized quayage* which will be discussed later.

The Alexandra Dock is not now intensively used. Indeed, the Corporation Tram Depot was established on a part of the eastern quay of the South Arm in 1925. Timber importers now prefer direct unloading to railway wagon, and all the timber yards of the Alexandra Dock receive Baltic timber from ships in the Royal Dock. This saves labour because a long manual carry is necessary from the older quays, many of timber staging, in the Alexandra Dock. North of the rolling bridge across the South Arm coasters deliver grain to the east quay; and cross-Humber traffic from Hull uses the River Head branch of the Alexandra Dock—the site of the *primitive* port, though the West Haven is unused.

The Royal Dock proved to be the last development possible for general cargo trade at Grimsby. The Great Central Railway erected a shed on the west quay, originally to deal with the passengers and freight from continental steamers.[46] In 1959 this same shed was set back and shortened, giving 66 feet between the shed and the quay wall to allow road access to a berth where previously the railway had been supreme. Norwegian traffic is dealt with. Scandinavian trade also predominates at the transit shed berths opposite. Danish dairy produce in particular is received; and there are cold stores available immediately behind the transit sheds. In the north-east part of the dock Scandinavian export traffic is handled, recalling the functions of the Albert Dock at Hull. Practically all Grimsby's non-fish trade is handled through the Royal Dock. Pulp and china clay, often unloaded in Junction Dock, are also imported for Grimsby's paper mill.

The older shopping centre at Grimsby ceases close to the River Head and Victoria Street (the 'Turnpike' on Fig. 33), which has been zoned for industry. Grimsby is rather cut in two by the railway leading to the docks,[47] and the port

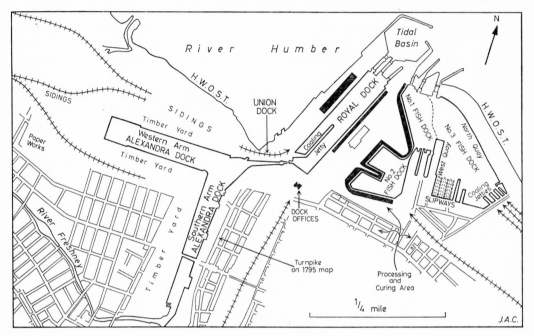

FIG. 34 Grimsby Docks

district is most noticeable close to the fish docks and in the streets immediately south of Fish Dock No. 2.

Unfortunately, the foreign trade of Grimsby is not distinguished from that of Immingham in H.M. Customs returns. In tonnage, if fish landings are excluded, the trade at Immingham is two and a half times that of Grimsby.

During a period of trade expansion, particularly of coal exports, the Great Central Railway built the separate and larger dock at Immingham, opened in 1912. The advantage of Immingham over Grimsby is that here the deep-water ebb-channel swings closer to the southern Humber shore whereas the Grimsby approach is a subsidiary flood-channel (Fig. 29). The dock was not provided with *simple lineal quayage* because the long quay was equipped with seven coal hoists, the eastern three of which have recently been removed. One of the most remarkable features of the lay-out of the dock is the 166 miles of sidings serving these coal hoists. Sidings for some 8,000 wagons were necessary because the journey from the Nottingham-Derby coal pits was much longer than from the Durham pits to tide-water. During the years of peak coal export these vast sidings were needed to ensure constant supply to the quayside hoists from the pits, after journeys which to this dock take as long as eight hours. From the storage sidings the movement of wagons to the hoists is by gravity, and after being tipped the wagons are released from the hoists at a high level to gravitate to the empty sidings. Much of the material forming the ramps on the flat alluvium south of Immingham Dock was derived from colliery waste. In 1959 two of the hoists were converted into electric radial arm conveyors, each capable of dealing with 55 wagons of 21-ton capacity every hour, the most modern coal shipping equipment in Britain.

The annotated diagram (Fig. 35) gives a summary of the functions of the various

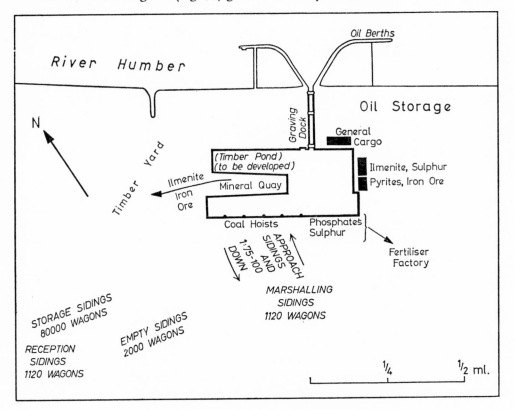

FIG. 35   Immingham Dock: Annotated Diagram

The commodities named are imports (coal excepted). There are only three quayside buildings, marked in solid black. All rail tracks are omitted.

TABLE 47

Fifteen Most Valuable Foreign Trade Imports into Grimsby (incl. Immingham), 1960

	Value £ Million
Bacon	12·9
Butter	9·3
Fresh and Frozen Fish (not of British taking) ...	7·5
Sawn Softwoods	5·1
Fuel Oil	4·8
Pulp	4·4
Motor Spirit	4·0
Iron Ore and Pyrites	3·2
Gas Oil	2·6
Phosphates of Lime	2·0
Titanium Ores (Ilmenite)	1·9
Sulphur	1·4
Cheese	1·3
Fruits and Vegetables	·9
Potassium Chloride (Prepared Fertilizer) ...	·7
Total of all Imports ...	69·7

(1·6 per cent of total U.K. imports by value)

TABLE 48

Fifteen Most Valuable Foreign Trade Exports from Grimsby (incl. Immingham), 1960

	Value £ Million
Coal	1·2
Uncoated Iron and Steel Plates and Sheets ...	·9
Coke	·8
Textile Machinery	·8
Tractors	·8
Paper and Paperboard	·7
Cereals	·7
Wool Yarns and Woven Fabrics	·6
Wool Tops	·4
Dyeing and Tanning Materials	·4
Malt	·4
Miscellaneous Textiles	·4
Iron and Steel Bars and Rods	·3
Iron and Steel Angles, Shapes, and Sections ...	·3
Creosote	·3
Total of all Exports ...	16·0

(0·5 per cent of total U.K. exports by value)

quays. Bulky cargoes predominate: iron ore is particularly consigned to the steel works at Scunthorpe and Frodingham, twenty-three miles away; and ilmenite, sulphur, and pyrites distributed by barge are used for titanium pigments in factories on Humberside between Immingham and Grimsby.[48] Because of the relatively isolated land site, Immingham Dock is one of the few places accepting traffic known as Shipping Category C—explosives with a 'mass explosion lift'. The contrast in the size of vessels entering this dock and the Grimsby Docks is summed up by the maximum permissible draught each can receive: Immingham 30 feet, Royal Dock, 21 feet, and Alexandra Dock, 16 feet 4 inches.

East and West Immingham have retained their village-like character in spite of some recent growth created by the Humberside factories (titanium, and viscose yarn from wood pulp) rather than by the dock. Until 1960 dock workers were able to commute from Grimsby on the light railway. Now a bus service links the dock with Grimsby by a roundabout road. Lack of urban growth at Immingham may well be due to the poorer social amenities (especially schools) than in the older established centre.

Fish Docks at Hull and Grimsby

Like shipbuilding, the fishing industry is a major topic in its own right and touches the main theme of this book only in its port aspect. The following summary account therefore concentrates on the fish docks rather than on the fishing industry as a whole.[49]

Hull and Grimsby emerged as large fishing ports after 1850 with the discovery of the Silver Pits, a prolific area of the Dogger Bank, and the ability of the railway to make trawler catches quickly available to inland urban markets. Indeed, the railway actively reintroduced the fishing industry to Grimsby. For a time the Manchester, Sheffield and Lincolnshire Railway quoted free landings in the Royal Dock, free transport to London, and promoted with two other rail companies the Deep Sea Fishing Company with nine vessels (1853–4) to encourage the fishing industry by example. Fishermen were attracted from other ports, Scarborough, Harwich,[50] and even from Hull. A fish dock was provided at Grimsby in 1856, equipped with a floating pontoon which rose and fell with the tide.[51] Here five sailing vessels could unload their catch. A short-term advantage was that River Freshney water was pure enough to keep cod alive in the free-flooding boxes of fishing smacks, which was impossible at Hull. The dock was doubled in size; a second dock was opened in 1886, eventually extended and thrown into the first in 1900.

Meanwhile, Hull fishermen had been removed from the Old Harbour to the tidal basin at Humber Dock in 1809. In 1869 a quay was provided on the south-east side of the Albert Dock. Finally, a special fish dock, the St. Andrew's, was opened in 1883 and doubled in area by the Extension in 1897. The dock developments at Hull and Grimsby in 1883 and 1886 were caused by the rise in the number and size of steam trawlers,[52] especially after 1895, which explains the dock extensions of 1897 (Hull) and 1900 (Grimsby).

By this time the general lines of the lay-out of a specialized fish dock had appeared. The area occupied by quayside buildings is almost as large as the water area of the docks where the fish is landed. The fish quays are narrow for quick delivery of the kits to a covered area for display. The quayside buildings also provide merchants' premises. The quays are always wet; delivery of ice and water is necessary to every part of the quay. Ancillary quays provide for fuel supply, outfitting, repair, refit, supply of ice (south quays of St. Andrew's Docks, Hull; Fish Dock No. 3, 1934, Grimsby), epitomized by the name of the Great Grimsby Coal, Salt, and Tanning Co. Ltd., founded in 1873. In both ports there is a very sharp separation between fish marketing and trawler refitting. Fish processing, including smoking and quick-freezing, also takes place in areas outside the dock estate, north and west of St. Andrew's Dock Extension in Hull and between Fish Dock No. 2 and Cleethorpes Road in Grimsby. Important by-products are fish meal, manure, and cod liver oil extraction.

The trawlers enter the docks in strict order—the deep-sea trawlers penetrate to the inner quays of the docks, so that the order is distant water, middle water, near water, and seine net vessels.[53] The fish docks are much smaller than those for general cargo. A fishing trawler is the smallest general type of vessel to go deep-sea voyaging regularly, though a limit is now put on trawler size (800 gross tons) by the size of the fish dock entrances.[54] The very specialized task of building modern trawlers, small by cargo liner standards, has been able to remain in shipyards with remarkably restricted water sites at Beverley, Grimsby, Goole (opposite the docks), and Selby.

Fish dock auctions contributed substantially to the concentration of fishing at the two ports:

'. . . small ports realize poorer prices for catchers and consequently lose their supply of fish progressively because there is an insufficient size of market.'[55]

But at the present time the fishing industry is going through a period of change created by the growth of quick-freezing processes and the twelve-mile sea limit international dispute. Since June 1960 the 'Outer Seven' European countries have been able to send fish to Britain with progressively lower import tariffs, limited by a quota until 1970.

'In many ways the industry appears to have reached the parting of the ways.

Large scale financial operations were unknown before the war; now large combines are a feature . . .'[56]

TABLE 49

Some Fish and Fishing Statistics, 1960[57]
(Bold face figures in brackets represent percentages of total figures for
Great Britain)

	Hull	Grimsby	North Shields	Total	
Value of Fish Landed Direct from Fishing Grounds (£ Thousand)	14,151 **(25)**	15,638 **(27)**	907 **(2)**	57,046	
No. of Fishing Vessels:				*England & Wales*	*Scotland*
Trawlers (over 140 ft. long) ...	139 **(46)**	105 **(35)**	—	301	} 160
„ (under 140 ft. long)	3	71	19	1,753	}
Seiners	8	98	15	215	?
Others	—	17	19	2,483	2,961
					Great Britain
Total ...	150	291	53	5,444	

Contract sales by trawler owners direct to processing firms for filleting, freezing, and packaging began in 1958 and are likely to be steadily extended as quick-frozen fish in supermarkets progressively replaces the wet fish on the fishmonger's slab. For the fish docks, this will tend to reduce the importance of dockside wet fish auctions which will be outflanked by fish that passes straight to processing factories erected on or close to the dock estate.

In a section on the fishing ports the Fleck Committee on the Fishing Industry (1961) was highly critical of conditions and practices obtaining at British fish docks, in particular the failure to make structural improvements, such as the strengthening and renovation of the market floors and the lack of mechanical handling equipment.[58] The Committee, however, recognized that the fish docks (on which heavy financial losses occur) benefit from being run in financial conjunction with commercial docks. But they observed that certain German fish docks rebuilt since the war had a larger lay-out in relation to catch than British fish docks. One recommendation was that a port-by-port investigation should take place, and if the pace of improvement in fresh fish handling is seen still to be slow by about 1965, the Committee recommended the establishment of port fish market authorities separate from the authorities responsible for the fish docks.[59]

Goole

The opportunity for Goole to arise as a port during a pause in the development of Hull has been discussed. The canal links with the West Riding have been all-important, underlined by the fact that the port was administered by the Aire and Calder Navigation Company until nationalization in 1947.[60]

Fifty miles from the open sea, Goole seems to have a water situation close to the estuary head where so many north-west European ports have originated and flourished. The great defect here is the shifting, shallow nature of the Humber channel upstream of Hull. The Humber, it will be remembered, cuts through both Oolite and Chalk strata. The Oolite outcrops on Humberside at Winteringham and at Brough Scalp (Fig. 36); although the Chalk does not appear in the Humber bed of the river,

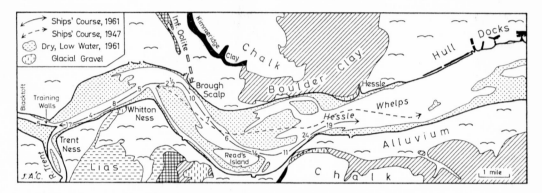

Fig. 36 The Humber from the Trent Confluence to Hull Docks

Figures are depths in feet at low water (ordinary spring tides, to which can be added 23 feet at spring high waters, 16 feet at neaps, Hessle Whelps; decreasing upstream to 18 and 11 feet respectively opposite Blacktoft). Based on part of a chart, *River Humber: Barton Haven to Burton Stather*, corrected to March 31, 1961, with floating marks [by which the channel is significantly indicated], corrected to April 27, 1961, issued by the Humber Conservancy Board, with the warning that, 'thereafter, on account of the quickly shifting character of the bed no warranty is afforded that such data can be relied on. . . .' Geological material based on Crown Copyright Geological Survey Maps by permission of the Controller of H.M. Stationery Office.

the Boulder Clay on its flanks certainly constricts the cross-section of the river between Hessle and Barton. This helps to explain the sandbanks upstream of the constriction of Hessle Whelps, similar to the shoals of the Upper Basin upstream of the Narrows in the Mersey. These upstream sandbanks are scoured by ebb-channels made more complicated by the fact that the Trent, Don,[61] and Ouse river systems may flood at different times. Training walls, built between 1934 and 1937, of fish-tail pattern in plan, help to stabilize the Ouse and Trent outfalls. But between Trent Falls and Hull Roads instability reigns. Two examples may be quoted. During dry weather material is deposited on Whitton Ness which grows to the north-west, and the channel is deflected northwards in a meander bend. After the 1947 flood, the great land discharge caused the ebb to cut a channel, north of Read's Island, much straighter than the previous meandering channel south of the island. No wonder that daily sounding surveys of these reaches are carried out, and printed supplements to the charts have to be issued every month.

Vessels up to 1,000 gross tons trade regularly to Goole, and the port shares in the short-sea and coastwise trades of the Humber as well as relying on its canal communications to the West Riding and Doncaster. The dock lay-out is all of the *dock elaboration* type, showing an exceedingly complex lay-out. The dates of construction of the separate dock components of the system help to sort out the pattern (Fig. 37). Before the canal to the West Riding (1825) and the first docks (1826), Goole was nothing.[62] The town arose to serve the port. Two main factors

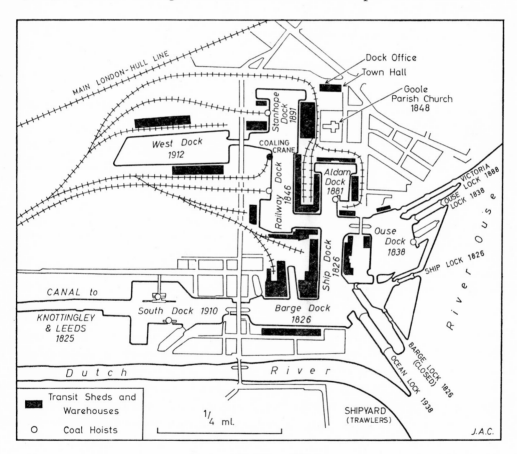

FIG. 37   The Port of Goole

in the port's development must be seized on, the coming of the railway and the limits to port expansion set by the built-up area of the town itself.

The railway and the canal companies had a working agreement that resulted in the Railway Dock of 1846. Thus two transverse tracks ran inland, the railway, and the canal leading to the Ship and Barge Docks, which were older by twenty years. By 1848 the parish church of St. John the Evangelist had been built. Hence after the Aldam Dock (1881) and Stanhope Dock (1891) had been built it was impossible to expand the port to the north-east. Indeed, the Stanhope Dock wall and church wall are the same. Thus two westward wings had to be built if the system were to expand: South Dock (1910) and West Dock (1912). This results in the major dis-

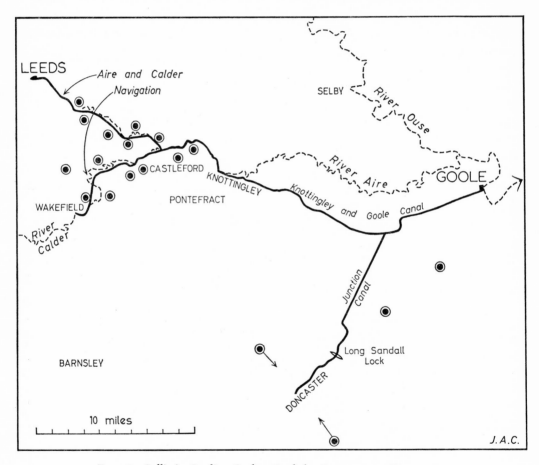

Fig. 38 Collieries Sending Coal to Goole by Compartment Boat, 1960
The two southernmost collieries (with arrows) have exported coal via Doncaster, the Junction Canal, and Goole since the enlargement of Long Sandall Lock in 1959.

146

advantage of the system: ships bound for the largest dock in the system, West Dock, have to make three right-angle turns after entering from the River Ouse.

The most important single commodity at Goole is coal, and Goole's exports have dropped less than those of other Humber ports because of a unique system of coal transport from the collieries. Steel compartments of 40-ton capacity (called locally 'Tom Puddings') are used to transport coal from several collieries in the West Riding and near Doncaster. Up to nineteen of these boats, with a special 'headpiece', form a 'train' to be hauled by the tug. At Goole the compartments are lifted and tipped by coal hoists in the South, Aldam, and Ouse Docks. There are 680 of these compartments, and they account for one-quarter of the coal tonnage exported from Goole.

Practically all Goole's foreign trade is with north-west Europe, and the list of chief articles exported reveals the very great importance of textile products from the West Riding. Goole's foreign trade is overshadowed by coastwise traffic, particularly wool imports (from London) and coal exports. And everywhere in the system the putt-putt-putt of self-propelled barges is heard, evidence of the importance of canal and Humber traffic, with some exports carried to ships in glass fibre containers.

That the town of Goole is very much dependent on the fortunes of the port is summed up by the fact that the Dock Offices and Town Hall are adjacent.[63] The Custom House is opposite, with the main shopping centre between it and the station.

TABLE 50

Fifteen Most Valuable Foreign Trade Imports into Goole
(incl. Blacktoft), 1960

	Value £ Million	
Canned Pig Products	9·2	
Bacon	8·0	
Raw Wool	3·4	
Paper and Paperboard	1·3	
Textile Machinery	1·1	
Steel Wire Rods	·9	
Petroleum Coke	·8	
Carpets	·8	
Synthetic Organic Dye-stuffs	·7	
Potassium Chloride	·7	
Uncoated Iron and Steel Plates and Sheets ...	·7	
Cheese	·6	
Ball Bearings	·5	
Beer	·5	
Non-metallic Mineral Manufactures	·5	
	———	(0·8 per cent of total
Total of all Imports ...	36·2	U.K. imports by
	———	value)

TABLE 51

Fifteen Most Valuable Foreign Trade Exports from Goole
(incl. Blacktoft), 1960

	Value £ Million
Wool Tops	2·9
Raw Wool	2·6
Textile Machinery	2·4
Tractors	2·3
Wool Yarns	1·8
Woven Cotton Fabrics	1·3
Woven Woollen Fabrics	1·2
Wool Waste	1·0
Copper and Copper Alloys	·9
Rags	·8
Hair Yarns	·8
Road Vehicles	·7
Iron and Steel Tubes and Pipes	·7
Agricultural Machinery	·7
Organic Chemicals	·6

Total of all Exports ... 36·7   (1·1 per cent of total U.K. exports by value)

Summary on Humber Ports' Location

Four separate ports on the Humber imply that no one site and situation could supply all the locational advantages for traffic on this estuary. In fact each of the ports suffers from some relative locational defect that has allowed other ports to co-exist with it. It must be assumed that the water site of each is favourable or capable of being made favourable—otherwise a port would never have arisen in the first place. It is then possible to see limitations in other directions.

TABLE 52

Particular and Relative Defects in Each Humber Port's Location
(crossed below)

	Water Situation	Land Situation	Land Site
Hull		X	
Grimsby		X	X
Immingham		X	
Goole	X		

If Hull had been situated near Goole it would have been better placed to serve the West Riding. The slight disadvantage allowed Goole to develop. The poor water approaches to Goole ensured that it could never become the port dominating the estuary. Grimsby's distance from the main ebb-channel gave Immingham its chance to arise. But both ports on the south side of the Humber have much longer land communications than Hull except for a limited hinterland, which includes Scunthorpe and East Anglia.[64] The position, however, is complicated by the different classes of traffic. For instance, Grimsby's water approaches are poor for the larger general cargo vessels (Fig. 29); but its situation closer to the open sea is an advantage Grimsby seine net vessels possess in particular over Hull. Again with reference to the fishing fleet it has been remarked that

'Grimsby and Hull are much farther apart than appears at first sight, as the Humber is not bridged below Goole. Thus there is less overlap of hinterland than there seems. North of the Humber, Hull has a marked advantage over Grimsby, and vice versa.'[65]

Lest the table of relative defects in each Humber port's location appear somewhat fanciful, it is well to remember that if one port had been able to develop continuously in area to overcome all the problems of location, there would now be one continuous port on the Humber today, as on Thameside or Tyneside. There would not be the present pattern on the Humber: one major port and three others, all separated by several miles.

REFERENCES

1. W. G. East, 'The Port of Kingston-upon-Hull during the Industrial Revolution', *Economica*, 11 (1931), 190–212, 191. In contrast L. R. Jones, 'Kingston-upon-Hull: a Study in Port Development', *Scottish Geographical Magazine*, 35 (1919), 161–74, recognizes four phases of port development before dock construction began. These are based largely on developments within Hull's hinterland. They appear to be more difficult to date precisely than the scheme of 'eras and epochs' herein adopted.

2. H. C. Versey, 'The Structure of East Yorkshire and North Lincs.', *Proceedings of the Yorkshire Geological Society*, 27 (1947–9), 173–91, and 'The Hydrology of the East Riding', *Ibid.*, 231–46; and *Ibid.*, 'The Humber Gap', *Transactions of the Leeds Geological Association*, 6 (1946), 26, for evidence of a fault through the Humber Gap.

3. See map in P. F. Kendall and H. E. Wroot, *The Geology of Yorkshire*, Vol. 1, Printed for the Authors, 1924, 452 and 453–60. The complications of multiple glaciation are here omitted. See A. Raistrick, 'The Correlation of Glacial Retreat Stages across the Pennines', *Proceedings of the Yorkshire Geological Society*, 22 (1931–4), 199–214; Fig. 1 gives a map of the glaciation at the Hessle Clay stage, and stages are discussed on pp. 212–13 with a summary in Fig. 3. See also H. Valentin, *Glazialmorphologische Untersuchungen in Ostengland*, Berlin: Reimel, 1957; Map 3 shows the former 'steep cliff' of the Wolds. For an appraisal of the changes in the Lower Humber since glaciation, with maps, see W. G. East, 'The Humber and Humberside in Historical Times', *The Dock and Harbour Authority*, 19 (1938–9), 88–9.

4. A. C. Dalton, 'Lake Humber as Interpreted by the Glaciation of England and Wales', *North Western Naturalist*, 16 (1941), 256–65; J. S. Gayner and S. Melmore, 'The Pleistocene Geology of the Area between the Tees and the Trent', *Quarterly Journal of the Geological Society*, 92 (1936), 362–4 [Abstract

and Discussion]. V. Wilson, *British Regional Geology: East Yorkshire and Lincolnshire*, Geological Survey: H.M.S.O., 1958, includes a useful summary of the glaciation of the Humber drainage area, 71–82.

5. G. de Boer, 'A System of Glacier Lakes in the Yorkshire Wolds', *Proceedings of the Yorkshire Geological Society*, 172 (1953), 223–33. This whole section on drainage evolution has been written in the light of comments kindly supplied by G. de Boer.

6. J. A. Sheppard, 'The Hull Valley: the Evolution of a Pattern of Artificial Drainage', *Geographical Studies*, 5 (1958), 33–44, Fig. 2.

7. The Port of Hedon, five and a half miles east of Hull, declined after the rise of Hull because its haven, in contrast to the Hull estuary, was flushed less efficiently by a minor Holderness stream, the Humbleton Beck. J. R. Boyle, *The Early History of the Town and Port of Hedon*, Hull: Brown, 1895; M. W. Beresford, *History on the Ground*, London: Lutterworth, 1957, 137–49; and *ibid.*, and J. K. S. St. Joseph, *Medieval England*, Cambridge: University Press, 1958, 200–1. There is the terrifying example of Ravenser Odd, sited on a small north Humber sandbank, which had a brief span of a somewhat piratical character. In the middle of the fourteenth century it disappeared so completely beneath the Humber flood that no one is now quite sure where it was. J. R. Boyle, *The Lost Towns of the Humber*, Hull: Brown, 1889, Frontispiece; and L. F. Salzmann, *English Trade in the Middle Ages*. Oxford: Clarendon, 1931, 222–3.

8. J. Bilson, 'Wyke-upon-Hull in 1293', *Transactions of the East Riding Antiquarian Society*, 26 (1926–8), 37–105, 105.

9. 'Hull' is also probably Scandinavian in origin meaning 'deep', A. H. Smith, *The Place-Names of the East Riding of Yorkshire and York*, English Place Name Society, Cambridge: University Press, 1937, 7.

10. *Ibid.*, 210.

11. G. Hadley, *A New and Complete History of the Town and County of the Town of Kingston-upon-Hull*, 1788, 3–4; and C. Frost, *Notices Relative to the Early History of the Town and Port of Hull*, London, 1827, Chapter III.

12. J. Travis-Cook, *Notes on the Origin of Kingston-upon-Hull*, London: Brown, 1909, 44–9 points out there was no disturbance of strata found in the excavations for the City Hall, across which site the former Hull was supposed to have run, nor in the Albert Dock excavations close to the supposed confluence. Sir William Wright, 'The Hull Docks' and J. C. Hawkshaw, 'The Albert Dock Hull,' *Proceedings of the Institution of Civil Engineers*, 41 (1874–5), 3–44, Plate 8 clearly shows, in an east–west geological section along the north quay of the Albert Dock to the Humber Dock Basin, no interruption to a 10-foot thick clay stratum, only some 17 feet below L.W.O.S.T., resting on a lower clay likewise continuous.

13. J. Bilson, *loc. cit.*, 81.

14. R. Thew's map of 1784 clearly shows no port development on the east side of the Hull and little development north of the walls, see T. Sheppard, *The Evolution of Kingston-upon-Hull as Shewn by Its Plans*, Hull: Brown, 1911, facing page 88.

15. R. A. Pelham, 'Fourteenth-Century England', *An Historical Geography of England before A.D. 1800*, ed. H. C. Darby, Cambridge: University Press, 1951, Figs. 46 and 47.

16. A little extra land had to be bought for the four docks on the site of the walls and moat—some twenty acres altogether, B. B. Mason, *A Brief History of the Origin and Progress of the Dock Company at Kingston-upon-Hull*, Hull: Kirk, 1885.

17. C. Frost, *op. cit.*, 75; J. J. Sheahan, *History of the Town and Port of Hull*, Beverley: Green, 1866, 391; and J. Symons, *High-Street Hull Some Years Since*, 1862.

18. *Report by W. Jessop Relative to the Making of a New Dock at Hull*, 1793.

19. *Report* by H. Etherington, 1787. Hull City Reference Library L387·1/7621.

20. 'Trinity-House and the Corporation erected jetties and staithes made roads and prepared the land on the east side of the Hull in consequence of the land granted to them there as a result of their contributions towards the expense of making Humber Dock.' *The Evidence Taken before a Committee of the House of Commons on the Hull Dock Bill*, 1825, Evidence of W. Bunney, 86–7.

21. *Report of the Inquiry into the Existing State of the Corporation of Hull*, 1834, 263.

22. *Report of the Proceedings of the Committee of Owners of Property on both Banks of the River Hull*, 1835.
23. When the average tonnage of vessels for any three successive years should bear the same proportion to the area of the two docks as that of the years 1791–3 bore to the area of the first dock. This section is based on W. G. East (1931), *loc. cit.*, 197–9, who provides detailed references.
24. J. Hill, *A Letter to the Merchants, Ship-owners and Other Inhabitants of the Port of Hull on the Subject of a Junction-Dock Hull* [eventually Prince's Dock, 1829], November 21, 1818.
25. W. G. East (1931), *loc. cit.*, 199.
26. *Ibid.*, 207.
27. G. G. MacTurk, *A History of the Hull Railways*, Hull: Packet Office, 1880; G. de Boer, 'The Evolution of Kingston-upon-Hull', *Geography*, 31 (1946), 139–46, Fig. 3; and J. H. Appleton, 'The Railway Network of Southern Yorkshire', *Transactions and Papers*, 22 (1956), Institute of British Geographers, 159–69, Fig. 9.
28. Jurisdiction—Spurn Lightship to Trent Falls, up the Trent to Gainsborough, and Trent Falls to Goole for pilotage.
29. Because of the difficulties caused by the North Eastern Railway's level crossings within the city, the new line was made to run on a viaduct. Across the Wolds its route was circuitous, and via a tunnel, because the North Eastern Railway controlled the low-level route along the Humber, J. H. Appleton, *loc. cit.*, 168 points out that the Hull and Barnsley Railway Company was able to maintain a separate existence until within eight months of the 1923 railway grouping. 'It is perhaps the supreme irony of railway history that the Hull and Barnsley . . . was acquired by the company whose monopoly it had been designed to smash.'
30. The 'free water' clause first appears specifically in the *Hull, Barnsley and West Riding Junction Railway and Dock Act*, 1880, sec. 112.
31. This paragraph is based on information kindly supplied by the Hull Incorporated Chamber of Commerce and Shipping.
32. The long-established Drypool Engineering and Dry Dock Company Ltd., with the splendid address of No. 1 High Street, Hull, built its first ship here, a tanker of 1,100 tons deadweight in 1958. The entrance had been allowed to silt up after the closure of the dock, but the silt was removed in 1956–7.
33. It had received only river craft and trawlers fitting out between 1918 and the time when it was filled in.
34. Add a cold store, north-western corner of the William Wright Dock; a warehouse, south-west of Alexandra Dock; and the upper storey of the No. 4 Transit Shed, King George Dock. This is the dock estate total; the rest of the port's warehouses line the River Hull.
35. A standard is 165 cubic feet, about two and a half tons of timber.
36. A prophetic survey by A. R. Tankard, *Survey of Imports . . . Synthetic Products and Their Relationships to the Old and Newer Industries . . . in the Humber Area*, Hull: Development Committee, 1936, linked the already established paint industry to the very wide range of derivatives possible from the distillation industry. For a general survey of Hull's industry see J. M. Bellamy, 'Augmenting a Maritime Economy', *The Times Review of Industry* [Kingston-upon-Hull and Its Hinterland Special Inset], October, 1958, 15–17.
37. The southward prolongation of Lowgate, Queen Street, is 'kept alive' in the evening by its function as an approach road to the New Holland (trans-Humber) ferry.
38. G. de Boer (1946), *loc. cit.*, 145–6.
39. H. F. Alston, *The Times Review of Industry*, *vide supra*, 40.
40. British Transport Commission statistics. For further details see J. Bellamy and M. Webb, *The Foreign Trade of Humberside: a Study of Post-war Trends*, Hull: University College, 1952; *ibid.*, 'Some Post-war Aspects of Humberside Foreign Trade', *Yorkshire Bulletin of Economic and Social Research*, 5 (1953), 199–213; and J. Bellamy, *Trends in the Foreign Trade of United Kingdom Ports*, including 'The Foreign Trade of Humberside: a Comparative Analysis', Hull: Port of Hull Journal, Newham, 1954.
41. *An Act for Widening, Deepening, Enlarging, Altering and Improving the Haven of the Town and Port of Great Grimsby in the County of Lincoln*, 36 Geo. III, c. 98, 1796, sec. xix.
42. *Ibid.*, preamble and sec. xix.

43. E. Gillett, 'Grimsby and the Haven Company, 1787–1825', *Lincolnshire Historian*, 10 (1952), 359–74. See also *Ibid.*, 'The History of Grimsby', *Grimsby Official Guide*, London: Batiste, 1959, 38–52.

44. The Alexandra Dock, with its two arms, of 49 acres was really a new dock, rather than a mere re-modelling of the impounded haven of only fifteen acres.

45. E. H. Clark, 'Description of the Great Grimsby (Royal) Docks', *Minutes of the Proceedings of the Institution of Civil Engineers*, 24 (1864–5), 38–61, 58. The most notable architectural feature in all Grimsby is the original hydraulic water tower at the Royal Dock lockhead, 309 feet high, and built in the style of the campanile at Venice. Its 26,000-gallon tank is now used to supply water to the fish markets.

46. G. Dow, *Great Central*, 2 vols., London: Locomotive Publishing, 1959, and in press.

47. There is a sharp division between shopping centre and industry west and north-east of the River Head, the site of the *primitive* port. In 1960 a model gown shop was observed sited opposite a brewery. There are in fact two shopping areas of equal status entirely separated by the Victoria Street industrial area and the railway.

48. For location of the factories, their main products, and raw materials, see O. S. Hiner, 'Industrial Development on South Humberside', *Geography*, 46 (1961), 354–7.

49. A selection of material for a study of the U.K. fishing industry: *Sea Fisheries Statistical Tables*, Ministry of Agriculture and Fisheries and Food, and *Scottish Sea Fisheries Statistical Tables*, Scottish Home Department, both annually; *Reports of the White Fish Authority*, London: H.M.S.O., annually; E. W. White, *British Fishing Boats and Coastal Craft: A Historical Survey*, London: Science Museum, 1950; R. Morgan, *World Sea Fisheries*, London: Methuen, 1956; *The Economics of Fisheries*, edited by R. Turvey and J. Wiseman, Rome: F. A. O., United Nations, 1957; G. S. Clark, *The Location and Development of the Hull Fishing Industry*, Unpublished thesis, M.Sc., University of Hull, 1957; J. Bird, 'Billingsgate: A Central Metropolitan Market', *Geographical Journal*, 124 (1958), 464–75; *Report on the British Fishing Industry* [Distant Waters], British Trawlers' Federation, 1956 and 1958; *Grimsby: The World's Premier Fishing Port* [Grimsby Fishing Vessel Owners' Association], London: Burrow, 1959; and C. L. Cutting, 'The Fishing Industry of Great Britain: Handling and Marketing', *Atlantic Ocean Fisheries*, London: Fishing News, 1961, 122–37.

50. 'Mr. John Howard of Manningtree had been induced to settle at Grimsby with his eight sailing liners in 1855.' *Grimsby: the World's Premier Fishing Port*, op. cit., 19. Here is a specific example of Grimsby supplanting the fishing functions of Harwich.

51. The fish market at Grimsby is still called the 'pontoon' locally.

52. Now diesel-driven (or diesel electric) vessels have lower fuel consumption which causes them to displace as much as 400 tons less than a corresponding oil-fired steam unit.

53. Vessels up to 65 feet in length responsible for a large amount of the prime fish landed from the North Sea, for which Grimsby has long been famous, though after the depression of the 1930's Grimsby was forced to concentrate on the coarser types of distant water fishing as Hull had done for some time.

54. A. Hunter, 'Trawler Design', *The Times Review of Industry*, vide supra, 31. A much larger trawler, the 1,200 tons net *Lord Nelson* designed to freeze part of her catch at sea sailed on her maiden voyage from Hull in July 1961.

55. I. Bowen, 'Port Markets', *The Economics of Fisheries*, op. cit., 149, fn. 21.

56. I. Class, 'Fish Marketing and Distribution', *The Times Review of Industry*, vide supra, 27. The factory trawler *Fairtry I* (2,605 gross tons) is compelled to dock at Immingham while *Fairtry II* and *III* (2,857 gross tons) used the Royal Dock, Grimsby.

57. Based on *Sea Fisheries Statistical Tables*, 1960, Ministry of Agriculture and Fisheries and Food: H.M.S.O., 1961; and *Scottish Sea Fisheries Statistical Tables*, 1960, Scottish Home Department, H.M.S.O., 1961.

58. *Report of the Committee of Inquiry into the Fishing Industry*, Cmnd. 1266, H.M.S.O., 1961, 53–67, para. 138, with graphic descriptions of fish landings and auctions at Grimsby, paras. 117–27.

59. There are separate harbour and market authorities already at North Shields and Aberdeen.

60. The conservator of the Ouse, from $1\frac{1}{4}$ miles upstream of the docks to the confluence with the Trent,

is British Transport Docks, an unusual state of affairs, but part of the legacy from the Aire and Calder Navigation Company.

61. The canalized Don, made by Cornelius Vermuyden in 1633 and known as the Dutch River, close to the Goole Docks, is not used by canal traffic.

62. Airmyn, one mile north-west of Goole, is quoted as an example of a medieval river port now defunct in M. W. Beresford and J. K. S. St. Joseph, *op. cit.*, 195–6.

63. Other industries, dependent on the port, are tar distilling and paint and fertilizer manufacture. A 150-acre industrial estate west of the town has been developed since 1949, mostly using female labour.

64. See remarks of K. C. Edwards, 'Grimsby and Immingham: a Port Study', *Preliminary Report of the Commission on Industrial Ports*, International Geographical Union Congress, 1952, 40–4, 43.

65. R. Morgan, *op. cit.*, 143.

FURTHER REFERENCES FOR HULL

Bates, E. P. *A Note on the History of Queen's Dock Hull*. Hull: Printed for Private Circulation, 1931.

Davies, W. J. *The Town and Trade of Hull, 1600–1700*. Unpublished thesis, M.A. University of Wales, 1937.

Gent, T. *History of Hull*. 1735.

Harris, A. 'The Humber Ferries and the Rise of New Holland, 1800–1860', *East Midland Geographer*, 15 (1961), 11–19.

Hurtzig, A. C. 'The Alexandra Dock, Hull', *Minutes of Proceedings of the Institution of Civil Engineers*, 92 (1888), 144–86.

Jones, W. R. *The History of the Port of Hull to the End of the Fourteenth Century*. Unpublished thesis, M.A., University of Wales, 1944.

[The] *Port of Hull Journal*, monthly.

Tickell, J. *History of the Town and County of Kingston-upon-Hull*. 1796.

Timperley, J. 'An Account of the Harbour and Docks at Kingston-upon-Hull'. *Transactions of the Institution of Civil Engineers*, I (1842), 1–51. [The first paper ever presented to the Institution.]

FURTHER REFERENCES FOR GRIMSBY

Bates, A. *A Gossip about Old Grimsby*. 1893.

Davies, M. *The History of Grimsby*. Grimsby: Barnetts, 1942.

[A] *Description of the New Docks at Great Grimsby*. Manchester, Sheffield and Lincolnshire Railway Company, 1852.

Lincoln, B. *The Rise of Grimsby*. 2 vols. London: Farnol, Eades, Irvine, 1913.

Chapter 6

SOUTHAMPTON AND SOUTHAMPTON WATER

SITED on a peninsula between two rivers, Southampton has the good fortune to possess capacious water approaches, rendered even more useful by a double-crested tide, with, until quite recently, wide, flat land sites along Southampton Water, all undisputedly available for port development. The spacious land site has allowed every new era of port development to be started in a new place. Despite the antiquity of the port and its present great size, the symbols representing each era of development can be identified quite separate from each other on the ground. For something like three hundred years until the mid-nineteenth century the port stagnated. Before 1833 the land site occupied by the port was hardly more extensive than it is known to have been in 1411. While the land situation of Southampton vis-à-vis the English possessions in France gave it a precocious start, the Industrial Revolution had at first hardly any repercussions on Wessex. Even today the lack of a compact immediate industrial hinterland has an adverse effect on the cargo trade of the port.

The basic features of Southampton's land and water sites are best understood in the light of their geological (and geomorphological) development. Before the Ice Ages the Chalk of the Isle of Purbeck in Dorset was continuous with the east-west ridge of chalk across the Isle of Wight. This was certainly the case in Early Pleistocene (Calabrian) times when the Hampshire Basin with an almost complete rim of chalk was submerged below the very high sea-levels then obtaining. Apart from minor east-west folds in the basin itself, the Chalk dips south more gently from Salisbury Plain than its steep plunge northwards from the Isle of Wight. It is not hard to imagine how, on the withdrawal of the Calabrian sea, a trunk river became established flowing west to east close to the southern Chalk. This 'Solent River'[1] has left behind a record of its former courses in a series of river terraces in the New Forest area and south-east Hampshire, just like the staircase of terraces left by the Thames in the London Basin. The Test and Itchen were two southward flowing streams whose combined course was a tributary of the Solent River. This conjoint tributary was aligned north-west to south-east because the Solent River itself flowed eastward. Came the post-glacial world-wide rise in sea-level: the Isle of Wight was

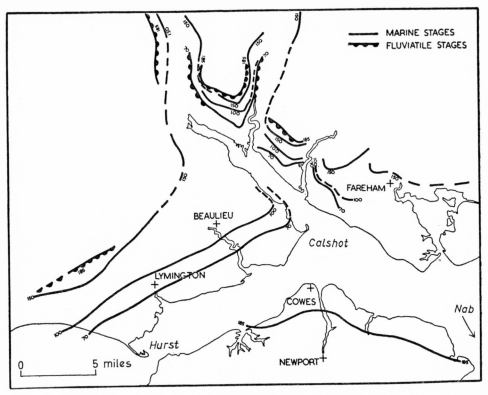

FIG. 39   Changes in the Position of the Strand-line in the Hampshire Basin as the Sea-level Fell after Early Pleistocene (Calabrian) Times

Heights are in feet. After C. E. Everard (1954), *op. cit.*, Fig. 4. Reproduced by permission of the Institute of British Geographers.

finally severed from Dorset; and the lower courses of the rivers were drowned.[2] The combined Test–Itchen became Southampton Water; and the former Solent River is now represented on land by the River Frome in Dorset, while its lower drowned course is represented by the straits of the Solent and Spithead.

Knowledge of the evolution of the Hampshire Basin explains the origin of the following features about Southampton's land and water sites. The Isle of Wight provides a natural breakwater for the immediate port approaches. Southampton Water, the Solent, and Spithead are floored by the submerged gravels and clays of former river terraces and flood-plains. The higher remnants of the terrace series are now seen on the borders of Southampton Water, nowhere presenting long steep slopes and often consisting of almost flat gravel over distances of one or two miles. All these features have been of great importance as the port developed.

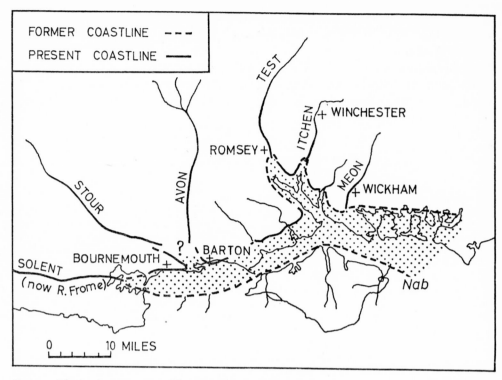

FIG. 40   The Drainage Pattern of the Hampshire Basin Preceding the Low Sea-levels of the Ice Ages
In the above diagram the sea-level is 100 feet higher than the mean sea-level obtaining at present.
After C. E. Everard (1954), *op. cit.*, Fig. 5. Redrawn from a diagram originally published by the
Institute of British Geographers, by permission.

The modern plan of the port reveals a glimpse of the *primitive* port fossilized by
later developments. After the Norman Conquest the Port of Southampton was
initiated on the western side of a peninsula formed within the angle of the Test-Itchen
confluence.[3] This area, still often called the 'Western Shore', was left high and dry
by the reclamation of the West Bay, attendant on the construction of the New Docks
after 1927. The eastern side of the peninsula was encumbered by a lagoon and a spit,
but on the western river bluff the Normans built a castle. The *primitive* port developed
around the West Quay, opposite the West Gate of the town, and the Castle Quay,
both in the shadow of the castle's protection. The West Gate, rebuilt in the mid-
fourteenth century, is still to be seen flush with the general line of the present Town
Walls. Until the mid-sixteenth century the port flourished, deriving benefit from its
general situation in relation to the English possessions in France and the trading cities
of Venice and Genoa. Wine from south-west France,[4] wool from England,[5] and
goods from the Mediterranean and Levant were the chief articles of commerce.

Marginal quay extension became necessary at the beginning of the fifteenth century. A patent of 12 Edward IV, 1411 states that the burgesses had constructed a 'wharf and a crane upon it at Watergate [or the South Gate] and the King authorized them to take toll of those who used it.' The port had begun to make use of the southern tip of the peninsula, which remains the nucleus of the port to this day. An incentive for building the Watergate Quay was the protection given by the early fifteenth

TABLE 53

Eras and Epochs in the Development of the Port of Southampton

Eras and Chief Areal Characteristics	Present-day Symbols
I *Primitive:* quays opposite the West Gate and the Castle	West Gate
Era ended by construction of separate quay opposite South Gate, some time preceding 1411	
II *Marginal Quay Extension:* two quays, with some small wharves between, on western side of peninsula	Site of Town Quay and direction of High Street, Southampton
Era ended by Southampton Harbour Commissioners' quayside improvements after 1803	
III *Marginal Quay Elaboration:* a second jetty from the Town Quay	Royal Pier of 1833
Era ended by opening of Outer Dock, 1842	
IV *Dock Elaboration:* docks built on artificial southward prolongation of peninsula	Outer Dock (1842), Inner Dock (1851), Empress Dock (1890)
Era ended by completion of Itchen Quays, 1895	
V *Simple Lineal Quayage:* straight quays with direct access from Southampton Water	Itchen Quays (1895), Test Quays (1899–1902), Ocean Dock (1911), New Docks (1934)
VI *Specialized Quayage:* terminals independent of docks on water approaches	Fawley Oil Jetties, 1951

century God's House Tower at the vulnerable point where the walls meet the shore downstream—a site similar to that of the Tower of London. There is evidence that the Watergate Quay soon became the most important quay because a Steward's Book of 1468 mentions the 'Kynges custum hows dore by ye Water gate'.[6] By this time the most important street in the town was the transverse route inland from the Watergate Quay. This High Street leading from the tip of the peninsula northwards via the Bargate (or north gate) retains its dominance in the street pattern today, so that the town appears based on the axis of one street, the old High Street and its extra-mural northward extension, though dock traffic makes use of the ring road completed in 1961.

These two quays, with about 120 feet added during the eighteenth century, sufficed for about three hundred years.[7] No port expansion beyond the medieval town walls took place until 1842, so little did the trade of the port develop until that time. Firstly, the loss of the English possessions in France reduced French wine imports. Later the trade of Southampton fell into the hands of London capitalists, through the lack of local sources of finance. The Londoners abandoned Southampton when its value as an outport to the Thames decreased. One reason appears to have been the better design of ships, making the voyage round the North Foreland of Kent and up the Thames much easier.[8] After the middle of the sixteenth century the Port of Southampton vegetated.

Marginal quay elaboration was the work of the Southampton Harbour Commissioners set up in 1803. They built a new breast-wall in front of the Town Quay, provided warehouses, and added the Royal [originally the Victoria] Pier 1833. Until then Southampton had had no berths which were not dry at low water. This new pier accommodated steam packets operating to the Isle of Wight, as it still does, the Channel Islands, and France—a humble beginning of the port's great passenger traffic to come.

Dock elaboration became necessary with increasing packet-boat activity. If docks had been built near the silted lagoon on the eastern side of the peninsula, much dredging would have been necessary for ship access. The tidal marsh south of the peninsula was preferred to the existing port installations on the western shore. John Rennie reported to the Harbour Board in 1805:

'In the constructing of a Wet Dock west of the Town the whole must be taken from the Tideway . . . [and this] . . . would be very expensive, not to mention the purchase of the Baths [a relic of eighteenth-century spa activity] and other Houses which lye in the way of the Docks. Whereas Docks in . . . the Marsh will be attended with no such Expense, for altho' there will be much Earth to excavate, yet it can be conveniently deposited round the Dock.'[9]

At the south-eastern tip of the peninsula a bank was built between tides, enclosing twenty acres, and coffer dams were erected north-south along the line of the Outer Dock's eastern quays. Banks and coffer dams were then joined together and the tide shut out in 1841. Excavation then proceeded within the banks and coffer

---

FIG. 41 Southampton, *circa* 1611, with Its Two Legal Quays

A. Watergate and Watergate Quay; B. The Custom House; P. The West Quay; L. The Westgate. Their respective proximate strongholds are God's House Tower, D, and the Castle, Z. Although the width of the streets is much exaggerated, the High Street, B, is patently the most important transverse route inland. Part of a map quoted as Sheet III in *Maps and Plans of Southampton*, W. H. Rogers, editor and annotator, Southampton Record Society: Cox and Sharland, 1907.

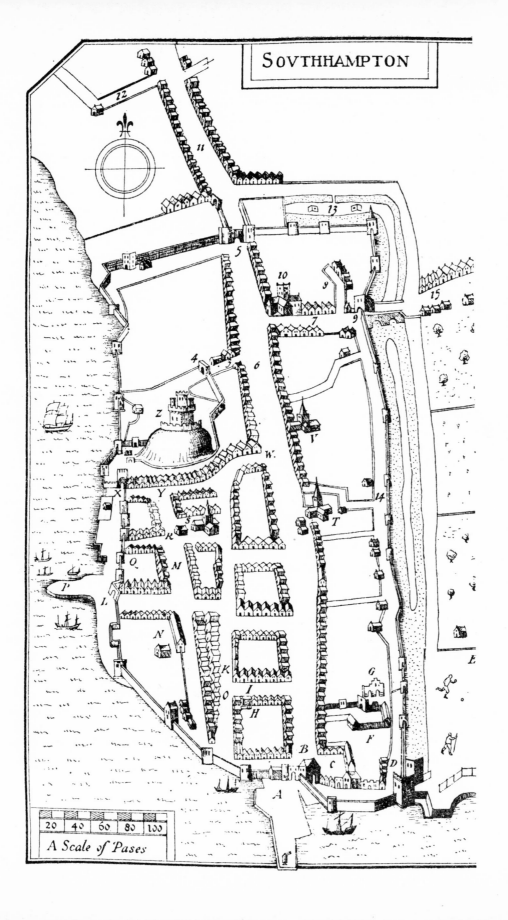

SOVTHHAMPTON

A Scale of Pases

20 40 60 80 100

dams, with the spoil used to reclaim further areas around the first two docks.[10] Such was the principle of construction of what are now called the Old Docks, all built before the First World War as an artificial prolongation of the peninsula. During the era of *dock elaboration* two important features of the port appeared: the close association with the railway; and the growth of liner traffic, including transatlantic services.

An Act in 1803 set up the Harbour Commissioners (reconstituted in 1913 as the present Southampton Harbour Board). It specified the one objective as the 'making of a convenient Dock', but restricted the Commissioners in their borrowing powers. Eventually, in 1836 a group of local men and a London capitalist formed the Southampton Dock Company. An element of weakness, as in the sixteenth century, was the lack of local capital from a moribund spa without industrial development. The Corporation allowed the Company to purchase the required mudlands at a low price—216 acres of mudland adjoining the Town Quay were sold for £5,000.[11] At this time the London and Southampton Railway Company was constructing its line. It seemed natural to employ the railway engineers, Francis and Alfred Giles, father and son, as designers of the proposed dock.

From this decision flowed two important results. The railway was from the beginning linked to the Dock Company and aided it when lack of working capital became an embarrassment. The London and South Western Railway Company finally purchased the docks in 1892, when it was obvious that there was simply no other source of capital for dock expansion. Secondly, there was early realization of the advantage of having deep-water quays closely connected to a rail network. Southampton's land situation was brought within ninety minutes of London. The original railway station (1839) is closer to the docks than to the town, built outside the walls on what was meadow land. The railway to London became the dominant transverse route from the port inland. The port nucleus accordingly migrated five hundred yards eastwards from the bottom of the High Street to a location near the railway station, now called the Terminus Station. This move was recognized when a new Custom House was erected near the railway station in 1847.

The growth of liner traffic called for further docks after the opening of the Outer Dock in 1842. In 1843 the Post Office transferred its mail packet establishment from Falmouth to Southampton. Services were started to the Middle and Far East, and the continents of the southern hemisphere by forerunners of the present P. & O. Steam Navigation Company, the Royal Mail Steam Packet Company from 1845, and the Union-Castle Line from 1854. By 1855 Southampton could be called 'a mail packet town'.[12] In 1856 the Union Steamship Company, which later became amalgamated with the Castle Line (the present Union Castle Mail Steamship Co. Ltd.), made Southampton its home port for all steamers engaged in the South, African trade.

The development of Southampton into the major north Atlantic passenger port of Britain was not due solely to the ability of its water approaches to accommodate large ships. An equally important consideration has been the water situation of Southampton close to the shipping route of the English Channel and to the French ports of Cherbourg and Le Havre. In the nineteenth century Southampton developed as a *port of call* for liners using continental ports as European terminals for the north Atlantic route. After short-lived American services, the north Atlantic liner traffic from Southampton was German until 1893. The Hamburg–American Line based on Hamburg and the Norddeutscher–Lloyd Line based on Bremen naturally used the English Channel route from their European terminals. A shipping route is often more profitable if before crossing a wide ocean a group of ports with traffic 'in line of route' can be called at. After the American Civil War there grew up a vast traffic in emigrants from continental Europe, and developing trade across the Atlantic

TABLE 54

The Growth of Southampton's North Atlantic Services[13]

	Some Developments at Southampton	Operators of Service	European Terminal
1842	Outer Dock		
1847–57		OCEAN STEAM NAVIGATION Line (U.S.A.)	Bremen
1851	Inner Dock		
1857–61		VANDERBILT Line (U.S.A.)	Le Havre
1858–69		HAMBURG-AMERICAN Line	Hamburg
1859		NORDDEUTSCHER-LLOYD Line	Bremen
1876	First Itchen Quays		
1889	First channel deepening to 26 ft. L.W.O.S.T.	HAMBURG-AMERICAN Line (service resumed)	Hamburg
1890	Empress Dock opened		
1893	Channel 30 ft. L.W.O.S.T.	AMERICAN Line (from Liverpool)	Southampton
1899	First Test Quays		
1907		WHITE STAR Line (from Liverpool)	Southampton
1907–9	Channel 32 ft. L.W.O.S.T.	for *Oceanic, Majestic, Teutonic, Adriatic*, etc.	
1911	Ocean Dock opened		
1910–13	Channel 35 ft. L.W.O.S.T.	for *Olympic, Titanic*, etc.	
1914	Widen swinging ground off Ocean Dock		
1919		CUNARD Line (from Liverpool)	Southampton
1921		UNITED STATES Line	Bremen
1926–36	King George V Graving Dock; further widening of swinging ground; channel 1,000 ft. wide, and 38 ft. L.W.O.S.T. below Calshot	for *Queen Mary*	
1962	Further widening of swinging ground	for *France*	

161

fostered other passenger voyages. This traffic, swelled by the considerable 'southern hemisphere' liner services, stimulated the opening of the Empress Dock in 1890. The American Line started north Atlantic voyages in 1893, the first time Southampton was used as the regular terminal. The White Star services were transferred from Liverpool in 1907, and the Cunard Line was weaned from Merseyside in 1919, replacing the German services. In 1921 the United States Line inaugurated a New York service using Bremen as a terminal and Southampton as a port of call, like the pioneer services of the mid-nineteenth century. During this time the facilities of the port and approach channel depths had been steadily increased to cope with and attract the ever larger vessels on the north Atlantic run.

By 1911 the Old Docks system was complete. Because the spring tidal range is only thirteen feet the docks are open. They are really tidal basins (only the Inner Dock of 1851 is impounded), and the marginal quays along the Itchen and Test are fully tidal. The site of the system was originally 'a spit of mud, extending for more than half a mile from the beach covered at high tide by 12 feet to 16 feet of water, but uncovered at low water.'[14] The entrance to the Empress Dock is near to the original junction of the two river channels. The era of *simple lineal quayage* begins with the completion of the Itchen Quays in 1895 and confirmed by the completion of the Test Quays in 1902 and the opening of the Ocean (originally the White Star) Dock in 1911. It may seem perverse to split the berths of the Old Docks in this way in order to fit them into different eras. But the contrast in development within the Old Docks is real, as the following facts show: Empress Dock (*dock elaboration* era), longest quay is 850 feet; Itchen Quays (*simple lineal quayage* era), greatest uninterrupted length is 1,590 feet. There is an even more striking contrast between the Empress Dock and Ocean Dock. The total quayage of the two docks is not dissimilar (3,880 feet compared with 3,807 feet). But because the Ocean Dock has a simpler shape, it has two long quays of 1,595 feet and 1,592 feet, compared with the two longest quays of the Empress Dock of only 850 feet each. The width of the entrance to the Ocean Dock is 400 feet, allowing direct access to berths compared with an entrance width of only 165 feet to the Empress Dock, with indirect access to berths. These contrasts between the two docks were immediately seized on by F. Palmer (later Sir Frederick Palmer, first Chief Engineer to the Port of London Authority) in 1913, during a discussion on the Ocean Dock.

'Probably reasons of a financial nature had prevented the construction of a large dock when the Empress Dock was under consideration. [He suggests that a dock with a 500 ft.-wide opening from the Test and including the old Inner Dock would have been better.] The value of long straight quays, or of quays susceptible of development in straight lines would be apparent from a brief study of the enormous growth in the size of steamers.'[15]

This is the first explicit recognition by a British engineer of the value of *simple lineal quayage*.

The above statement is of the greatest interest and importance in view of the next major development in the *simple lineal quayage* era. The Ocean Dock was the last possible large-scale work on the peninsular site. When further large liner berths were required after the First World War, the Southern Railway Company, which then owned the docks, was forced to build upstream on the River Test. The River Itchen is narrower and its riverfront was already built up; downstream, in Southampton Water the navigable channel is nearly three-quarters of a mile from the shore. The upstream drowned section of the River Test remained. From a seaman's point of view the western side of the Test might have been preferred to the actual site of the New Docks, a lee-shore to the prevailing south-westerlies;[16] but the two dock systems would then have been separated on each side of the River Test, making the rail network very complicated.

Since the New Docks were the largest civil engineering construction at British ports between the wars, advice was sought in 1926 of Sir Frederick Palmer, who had drawn up a master plan for the Port of London in 1910, and he again advocated the idea of *simple lineal quayage* that he had made à propos of the Ocean Dock thirteen years before.

> 'The proposal which has already been made consists of a series of jetties, five in number, each 1,000 feet long, affording accommodation for two vessels (one on each side), and this provision of 10,000 lineal feet of quay giving ten berths, for vessels over 500 feet in length, represents the total capacity of the site on this method of lay-out . . . It has . . . the disadvantage of a very large waste of quay space in all cases, excepting in the case of three or four of the largest vessels. For instance, the *Leviathan*, 950 feet in length, fills a berth with no waste of quay space, but vessels of the Union-Castle Line, 550–600 feet in length, would leave useless 450–400 feet of each quay.
>
> . . . The great advantage of long quays as compared with quays 1,000 feet in length is the flexibility of utilization.'[17]

There are no 'dead ends' for rail or road transport in the New Docks estate; no train need be reversed. Jetties would also have necessitated dredged swinging grounds for each berth or pair of berths, instead of only two swinging grounds now maintained, one at each end of the quay line. Part of the area behind the quay wall became a proposed industrial estate, and another area was given to Southampton Corporation in compensation for depriving the western side of the peninsula, including the old West Quay riverfront, of its water frontage.

The sixth era of *specialized quayage* is represented by the independent deep-water jetties of Fawley Oil Refinery on the western side of the Southampton Water approach to the docks.

Southampton's development provides justification for recognizing the same six eras as at *Anyport*. But the slow development of trade after 1550 resulted in the fact that the port did not expand beyond the medieval walls at the end of the *primitive* era as at *Anyport*, but nearly three hundred years later, when the Outer Dock initiated the era of *dock and marginal quay elaboration*. Thereafter, Southampton closely resembles *Anyport*, except that the great expanse of drowned river valleys allowed *simple lineal quayage* to take place upstream of the *primitive* port, a feature very similar to the Parkeston Quay development upstream of the Harwich peninsula. Since the giant King George V Graving Dock is at the upstream end of the New Docks, there is the bizarre circumstance at Southampton that the very largest vessels in the world proceed to near the head of navigation. (Coasters with timber cargoes regularly berth at Eling Quay one mile further upstream.)

Already in the era of *specialized quayage* the 1936 view of the 'possibilities of indefinite extension'[18] have come up against the competing claims for land use of the estuarine sites. This refers to the proposal for a second oil refinery opposite Fawley and a little downstream. A tidal model covering both the east and west entrances of the Solent satisfied the Harbour Board that the proposed oil jetties would not interfere with the dredged channel. But the Hampshire County Council, among other objectors, wish to establish a coastal green belt, and the scheme was opposed. The project was eventually abandoned in 1961, since the oil company (Caltex) decided to confine its north-west European activities to refineries in Eire and at Rotterdam.

The Water Approaches to Southampton

For the captain of a large vessel there are the following four helpful features of the tidal regime of Southampton Water;

(1) double high waters (meaning a double crest at high tide);

(2) the halt in the tidal rise, known as 'the young flood', occurring two to four hours after low water;

(3) the fact that the tidal streams are in phase with vertical rises and falls (*i.e.* the stands are periods of slack water); and

(4) the short duration of the ebb, occupying only $3\frac{3}{4}$ hours of the $12\frac{1}{2}$-hour tidal cycle, during the remainder of which the water is either rising or, for all practical purposes, standing.

The latter two circumstances are of course valuable for manœuvring large ships in and out of berths.

Double high waters are not caused by the Isle of Wight. Le Havre and Honfleur also have a double-crested tide. Most tides can be successfully predicted by harmonic analysis—the chief constituent around the shores of the British Isles is the principal lunar semi-diurnal constituent known as M_2. The amplitude of M_2 alone at Southampton is only 4·46 feet, which would give a tidal range of 8·92 feet. Now the average range of tide at Southampton is 10·675 feet. Around Britain, in deep water, M_2 nearly always accounts for about 98 per cent of the average tidal range. A glance at Fig. 1 shows that the co-range lines of M_2 are so distributed in the English Channel that a nodal line of low results for M_2 runs from the Orne estuary (20 miles west of Le Havre) to about Christchurch (20 miles west of Calshot at the entrance to Southampton Water). The low value of M_2 in the Southampton (and Le Havre) tides allows additional (and normally small) tidal constituents to contribute in adjusting the predicted curves to a closer likeness to their actual appearance in nature. In addition,

'In shallow waters . . . oscillations are often set up which have periods which are submultiples of the major diurnal or semi-diurnal lengths.'[19]

These are M_4 M_6 . . . *etc.* In Fig. 42 a semi-diurnal tide, M_2, is combined with a quarter-diurnal tide, M_4, to give a resultant tide, X, with double high waters. Two conditions are necessary for this: the amplitude of M_4 must be at least equal to one-quarter of M_2 (possible only where M_2 values are low), and the trough of M_4 must occur near the crest of M_2 (*i.e.* the phase relationship must be suitable). But suppose, as at Southampton, M_4 has insufficient amplitude, it then produces merely a marked flattening of the crest at high water (curve X on Fig. 42). This will allow higher species of shallow-water tides to have further retouching effects, provided again that their phase relationships are suitable. In the case of Southampton the high water stand and young flood halt

'can be reproduced roughly by including M_6 among the constituents for harmonic prediction [pecked line on Fig. 42 bottom], but perfect correspondence between predicted curve and actuality cannot be achieved even by 30 constituents.'[20]

With a spring range of only 13·1 feet no impounded docks are necessary.

South of Calshot the tidal regime is not so favourable to shipping. Fig. 43 shows that the ranges of tide at each end of the Solent-Spithead duct are not the same, but 7 feet (at Hurst Castle Spit, or the Needles, western entrance) and 12 feet (at the Nab, eastern entrance). Low waters occur at the same time so that there are tidal

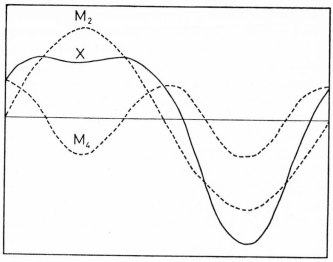

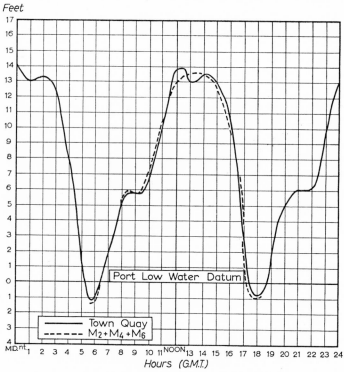

Feet

FIG. 42 Tidal Curves at Southampton
Top: Theoretical double high waters (X) produced by a suitable combination of semi-diurnal and
quarter-diurnal curves
Bottom: An actual spring curve almost reproduced by a combination of $M_2 + M_4 + M_6$.

streams set up, going east, until the height at the Nab overtakes that at the Needles, and then reversing to the west. Though in Southampton Water (north of Calshot)

'the vertical stands of tide fortunately correspond with small stream rates for docking, . . . outside Calshot the strongest tidal rates occur when vertical levels are near high-water values . . .'[21]

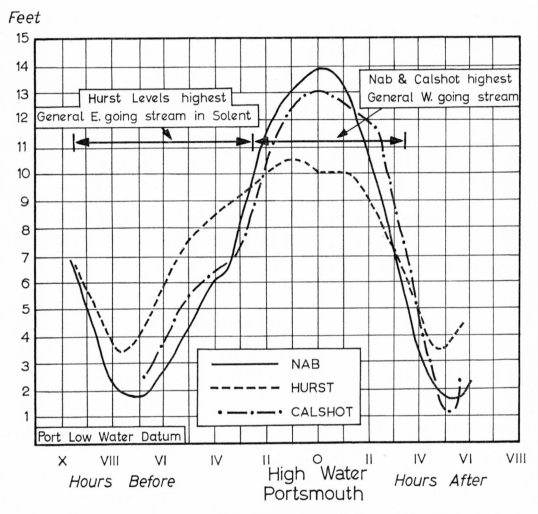

FIG. 43 Reciprocating Movement of Solent Tidal Streams According to Relative Heights of the Tide at Hurst Castle and the Nab

Hurst Castle is at the western entrance to the Solent, and the Nab is at the eastern entrance (see Fig. 39).
After D. H. T. Macmillan, *op. cit.* (1952).

Calshot is also the place where the physical configuration of the bed changes. To the north, the channel, cut in the submerged gravel terraces and flood-plain clays, is kept scoured by the ebb. The channel is stable because the prevailing south-westerlies have little fetch to affect tidal streams in a channel aligned north-west to south-east. But south of Calshot the reciprocating action of tidal streams has precluded the removal of the Bramble Bank, probably a surviving submarine meander of the Solent River.

In 1961 the first of five supertankers was launched, of 77,000 tons deadweight. Such vessels trading to Fawley draw 47 feet when fully laden. By comparison the *Queen Elizabeth* has a loaded draught of 39½ feet. The safe passage of such tankers requires an approach of 55 feet; but due to the tidal conditions a dredged channel of 45 feet permits the vessel to enter Spithead and proceed to Fawley, for high water is progressively later up the channel. Dredging to 45 feet in the inner approach channel presents no problem: the waters are sheltered, the soil is removable by conventional bucket dredger, and past experience has shown that little maintenance will be required. To attain 45 feet minimum throughout the whole approach, however, it has been necessary to dredge the bottom of the open sea across Nab Shoal, five miles due east of the eastern extremity of the Isle of Wight.

Large vessels generally enter the port from the east of the Isle of Wight and travel up Spithead because the Needles entrance to the Solent (30 ft. L.W.O.S.T.) is much narrower allowing less room for manoeuvre. Liners must next navigate round the Bramble Bank, a 110° starboard turn.[22] Before the port-hand margins of the approach channel were removed by dredging in 1951 this turn was difficult, complicated by west-going tidal streams near high water (Fig. 43). A further 75° turn to port is necessary round Calshot Spit.

Calshot Spit is the point where both the tide and the approach channels change for the better. Henry VIII recognized its quality as a belvedere by building there a castle to watch for invading ships in 1538. A similar function is discharged today by the Calshot Signal Station built atop the Tudor castle, where movements of shipping to and from the port are observed. The Station obtains excellent radar displays of all Southampton Water and the West Solent. Passenger liner schedules are known for long periods ahead, but tanker movements are dictated to a large extent by the operation of the oil jetty terminal and may not be known twenty-four hours ahead. The co-ordination of these two different classes of traffic on a narrow approach is

---

FIG. 44   Port Approaches in Southampton Water and the Solent

The North Channel has not been dredged to provide a straight approach because, lying at right-angles to Solent-Spithead currents, it might be unstable and expensive to maintain. In addition, the lie of the channel would oblige ships to 'slew' to make allowance for the cross-tidal effect; and also in the case of long (1,000 feet) ships, the velocity of the tidal stream when entering such a channel from the south would vary along their length in an embarrassing manner.

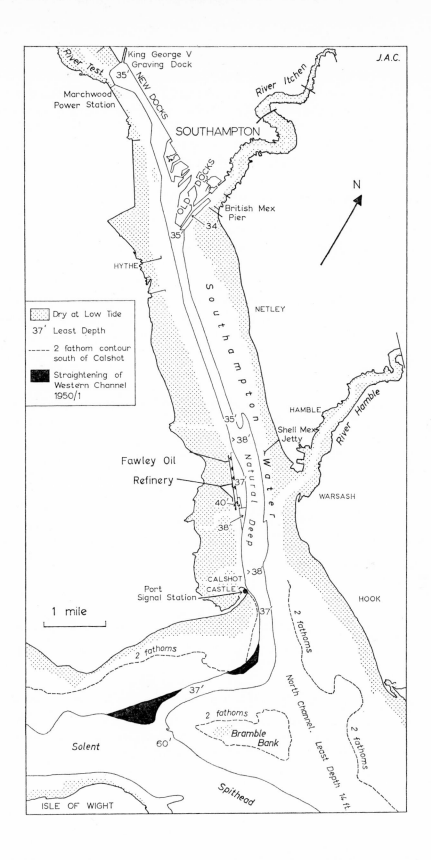

J.A.C.

King George V
Graving Dock

River Test

NEW DOCKS

35'

Marchwood
Power Station

River Itchen

SOUTHAMPTON

N

OLD DOCKS

British Mex
Pier

35' 34

HYTHE

Dry at Low Tide

37' Least Depth

———— 2 fathom contour
south of Calshot

▪ Straightening of
Western Channel
1950/1

NETLEY

Southampton   Water

35'
>38'

HAMBLE

Shell Mex
Jetty

Natural Deep

River Hamble

Fawley Oil
Refinery

37'

40'

WARSASH

38'

>38'

CALSHOT
CASTLE

HOOK

Port
Signal Station

37'

1 mile

37'

2 fathoms

North Channel. Least Depth 14 ft.

Solent

60'

2 fathoms

Bramble
Bank

2 fathoms

2 fathoms

Spithead

ISLE OF WIGHT

carried out from Calshot Signal Station. Vessels like the *United States*, drawing 30 feet of water could be scheduled 'round the clock' irrespective of the tidal depths. In practice the *United States* uses slack tidal periods (at 'young flood', high and low waters) when docking. Since the minimum depths in the approach channels at springs and neaps are 35 feet and 38 feet respectively, only the *Queen Mary* and *Queen Elizabeth* and the largest tankers drawing up to 45 feet are tied to the famous prolonged high water features when for nearly two hours the depth in the approach channels north of Calshot is 45 feet at small neaps, and 48 feet at ordinary springs.

Modern Functions of the Port of Southampton

The berths at Southampton have been numbered approximately in order of their construction 1–51 in the Old Docks and 101–110 in the New Docks. Surveying them in numerical order, a few of their more important modern functions will now be described.

The Outer Dock (the first dock) is typical of berths still functioning after more than a century because they have been downgraded in use. Since it has a minimum depth of only 18 feet, it is not used by ocean-going vessels, but is a base for cross-Channel services to St. Malo (during the season), Le Havre, and some cargo services to the Channel Islands. Since May 1961 the British Railway passenger services to the Channel Islands have been concentrated at Weymouth. The Inner Dock, the only impounded dock, is used for laying up small craft and cross-Channel steamers for which Southampton is the main British Railways depot. Shiprepairing workshops are sited on the peninsula west and south of this dock. It seems that the Inner Dock is nearing the end of its career. Many of its sheds and warehouses were bombed during the last war, and its quays are in need of renewal. However, between these two docks, opposite 1, 10, and 18 Berths, are the only warehouses in a port where the cargoes are predominantly in transit. A trade in sherry has developed, and raw tobacco is stored for manufacture in Southampton.

Empress Dock has traffic transitional between these oldest docks and the later quays. Channel Islands cargo traffic is handled particularly at 22–23 Berths, while since 1959 a modern banana berth has been operated at 24–25 for cargoes from the West Indies and West Africa. This berth is of course equipped with the usual endless belt overhead conveyors, but, unlike other ports, has also been equipped as a passenger terminal, since banana boats to Southampton may carry up to 110 passengers. In 1961 a single-storey cargo shed was opened to deal with fruit and vegetables from the Mediterranean.

The North Itchen Quays, Berths 30–33, with a passenger hall completed in 1959, are used mainly by liners on the Canadian and United States services. Generally,

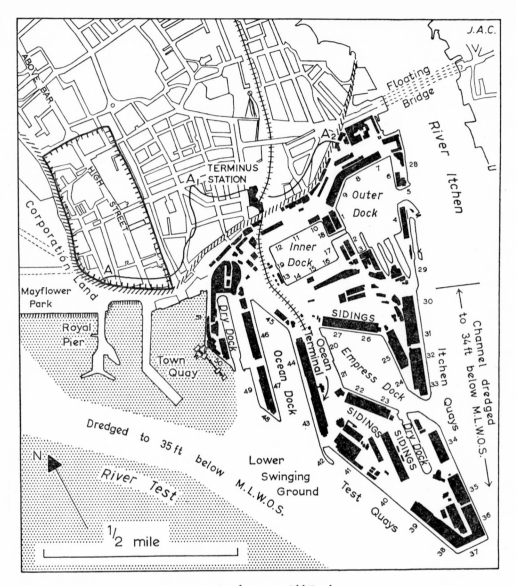

FIG. 45 Southampton Old Docks

Short diagonal ruling represents the original southern limit of the peninsula, with the medieval town walls enclosing the western corner. All berths have rail access, though only the general direction of the track to the Ocean Terminal is shown. A — A_1 — A_2 is a line enclosing an area with a predominant port function.

it is a case of one ship, up to 15,000 (n.r.t.), to two berths at these quays, so much has the length of vessel increased since the quay was laid out at the end of the nineteenth century. The South Itchen Quays, Berths 34–36 are used for imported cargoes, particularly Australian and South African fruit, and U.S. Government traffic. The Test Quays are available to troopships or other vessels without an allocated berth. Southampton is the home port of troopships making long voyages.

The Ocean Dock is the European terminal of the weekly north Atlantic ferry service maintained by the *Queen Elizabeth* and *Queen Mary*, and these vessels have priority at Berths 43–4. Alongside is the Ocean Terminal, a worthy complement to mammoth ships. On arrival up to 1,700 passengers must be dealt with and the following main facilities must be provided: customs and immigration examination, waiting lounge with full passenger services, cargo working area, platform for two boat trains, and a car park for those leaving by road. In the Ocean Terminal, opened 1950, these functions are separated in a two-storied building 1,300 feet long (the *Queen Elizabeth* is 1,031 feet in length), so that they are kept within a short horizontal distance of the quayside (see section Fig. 46). The terminal is one of the very few large exclusively ocean passenger terminals built since the Second World War. Its great size is justified by the large numbers of passengers involved. But, like all seaport passenger terminals, after short periods of full-scale activity it must lie idle between voyages. The *Queens* have priority at the Terminal, but as many other large vessels as possible are fitted into the berthing schedule. Opposite at 47 and 48 Berths are the old-style single-storey sheds where passengers and cargo are separated off at the same level on the ground floor. This results in a lower standard of passenger accommodation than at the Ocean Terminal.

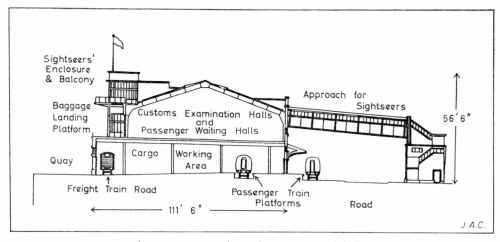

FIG. 46   The Ocean Terminal, Southampton: Simplified Cross-section

Between the so-called Old and New Docks lie the Town Quay and the Royal Pier, owned, managed, and operated by the Southampton Harbour Board. The Town Quay is a jetty, the basic structure dating from the late nineteenth century, with four berths on each side. The two berths nearest the shore are used exclusively by coastwise traffic. The seaward end of the Quay is used for assembling export cargoes, for stocking imports of timber, and for standing ground for vehicles receiving cargoes direct ex ship. Three double-storied transit sheds and a bonded warehouse are used for moving foreign cargoes en route between the Quay and Sweden, Portugal, and Canada on regular shipping routes. In addition stores are sent from the Town Quay to the oil tankers at Fawley and general cargo to the Isle of Wight. Passengers for the Isle of Wight, and their vehicles, are dealt with from the floating pontoons of the Royal Pier, where a considerable traffic in heavy vehicular goods has grown up in recent years.

How fortunate for Southampton that nowhere in the Old and New Docks estates is the solid rock more than 35 feet beneath the mudlands, providing good foundations beneath easily dug material. The quay area of the New Docks is based on 146 concrete monoliths, 45 feet square, sunk to a depth of between 70 and 100 feet, but through only about 20 feet of mud and peat.[23] The general arrangement from quayside landwards is: a depth of water alongside of 45 feet L.W.O.S.T., and a quay about 50 feet wide with 3- and 6-ton travelling cranes. Their jibs tend to be longer than those in some impounded docks, because they serve high-decked passenger vessels rising and falling at tidal berths. There are usually two railway tracks between the quayside and the shed wall. The transit sheds, 150 feet wide, have floors which rise up gently until they are at railway platform level (3 feet 3 inches) at the rear for easy entraining of passengers and loading of wagons inside the shed (see a similar arrangement at the Ocean Terminal, Fig. 46). This arrangement is ideal for quick delivery to wagon by electric truck, and the gentle cant of the floor does not prevent the piling on pallets where storing of goods may be required; but very high piling would be difficult. The slope of transit shed floors thus sums up the quick movement of most cargoes characteristic of Southampton. Behind the sheds there may be as many as four railway tracks, and then the main dock road. Much of the reclaimed land is still available for development. There is a motor assembly works at the northern end, several small private warehouses and distribution depots, and some light industrial development on the Corporation land. But only two installations make direct use of the quays, by overhead conveyor: the Solent Flour and Grain Mills via 103 Berth and the marine cable factory via 109 Berth. It is likely that light rather than heavy industries will be built on the remaining sites, since those heavy industries that vitally require waterside sites now prefer to have their own quayage.[24]

Three other berths deserve more extended mention: 102, 105–6, and 108 Berths. Eight Union-Castle Line vessels maintain a weekly service to South Africa. In 1956 a new passenger-cargo terminal was provided at 102 Berth for inward liners of this service which arrive every Friday morning at 5.45. But compared with the *Queens* the number of passengers is about 750 per vessel and there is much more cargo. The passenger hall, therefore, occupies only the eastern 200 feet of the 932-foot long two-storied building. Here the major portion of the South African imported cargo is received; the upper floor is used mainly for baled cargo—wool, hides, and skins—and the ground floor for fruit and wine. The famous sailing time to South Africa ('every Thursday at 4 p.m.!') takes place from 104 Berth. This is unusual; at Southampton liners generally remain at one berth. In 1960 a Reception Hall was opened, centrally situated between 105 and 106 Sheds, for the Australian and trans-Pacific service of the P. & O.—Orient Lines fleet, including the new vessels *Oriana* and *Canberra*. Thirdly, at 108 Berth is the four-storied Cold Store opened in 1958. As this is the only cold store in the port its interior chambers are at various temperatures to cope with the wide range of products now received chilled or frozen. The critical temperatures depend on water content, and since they are so close to storage temperatures very careful refrigeration control is necessary.

TABLE 55

Cold Storage Temperatures for Various Foodstuffs[25]

				Storage Temp. °C.	Critical Temp. °C.	Storage Period
MEAT	Chilled	...	...	−1·0	−2·0	10–15 days
	Frozen	...	...	−9·5	−12·0	1–10 months
DAIRY PRODUCE	Butter...	...	...	−9·5	−15·0	1–6 months
	Frozen Eggs ...	...		−15·0	−17·5	1–2 years
	Shell Eggs	...	...	−0·5	−1·0	6–10 months
	Cheese	...	...	+4·5	+2·0	1–6 months
FISH				−17·5	−15·0	2–3 months
FRUIT	Apples	...	...	+2·0	−0·5	1–6 months
	Pears ...	...	...	0	−1·0	1–4 months
	Oranges	...	...	0	−0·5	1–4 months
VEGETABLES	Green ...	...	...	+2·0	0	10–20 days
	Root ...	...	...	+3·0	+1·0	1–3 months

At the western end of the docks is the King George V Graving Dock, the largest in the world, designed to take vessels of 100,000 gross tons. There is room for another large dry dock immediately to the west. While Southampton can maintain the largest vessels, shipbuilding, by a large yard on the east side of the Itchen, is confined to vessels of not more than about 4,000 gross tons.

With so many large liners using the port there were many pre-Second World War oil storage depots at Fawley, Hamble (opposite Fawley) and opposite the

PLATE V PORT OF HULL, CENTRAL LAY-OUT

Above and Below: Looking north-west, successive views from an aircraft flying down the River
Humber, *cf.* Figs. 30 and 31.

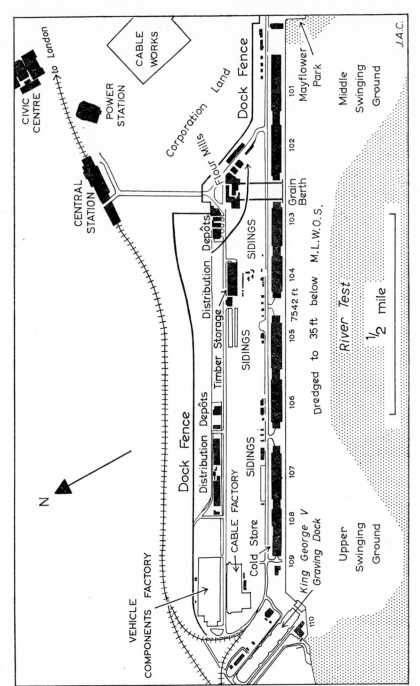

FIG. 47 Southampton New Docks

PLATE VI PORT OF SOUTHAMPTON

Looking north-west up the River Test, with the Old Docks in
the foreground, *cf.* Fig. 45, and the New Docks in the background,
cf. Fig. 47.

Test Quays on the Itchen. But the *specialized quayage*, as distinct from the docks, assumed significance only with the opening of Fawley Oil Refinery with its five tanker berths in deep water. Fawley's site advantages are very close to those described for *Anyport*, with the added merit of being built on terrace gravel rather than on estuarine marshes. The gravel is of course almost flat (see Fig. 39), has good bearing properties for buildings up to 250 feet high, and is easily excavated for underground pipe lines. Five berths for ocean-going tankers are provided on the mile-long jetty. Twenty-eight hours suffices for their turn-round. Four berths are provided for coastwise vessels on the inside of the jetty. Since it costs three times as much to distribute refined products by road and rail as by a 1,000-ton coastwise tanker, the end products have hitherto left almost entirely the same way they came —via Southampton Water. But a new development for coastal refineries in Britain is delivery by pipe-line. Like oil refineries on the Thames estuary, Fawley delivers refined oil by pipeline to a depot near London Airport. Fawley also has a pipeline supply to a power station opposite the New Docks at Marchwood and to synthetic rubber and petro-chemical plants, north of the refinery. General purpose synthetic rubber is manufactured from styrene and butadiene which are most economically made from by-products of oil refining. This plant has a capacity greater than the total synthetic rubber demands of the United Kingdom and when opened in 1958 saved 25 million dollars a year in imports. Oil refineries are truly nurseries for other industries.

TABLE 56

Sea Passenger Traffic to and from British Ports, 1960
(Leading ports in each class of traffic only, in thousands)

	Channel Islands	Irish Republic	European Continent	Non-European Countries
Dover			2,679	
Fishguard		270		
Folkestone			736	
Harwich			674	
Holyhead		893		
Liverpool		240		92
London				127
Newhaven			310	
Southampton	124*		124	340
Tyne Ports			134	
Weymouth	130			
Total (all ports) ...	254	1,460	4,772	594

*Traffic transferred to Weymouth, from 1961

Source: *Board of Trade Journal, 1961*

TABLE 57

Fifteen Most Valuable Foreign Trade Imports into Southampton
(incl. Lymington), 1960

	Value *£ Million*
Crude Petroleum	80·1
Fuel Oil	9·6
Cars	7·1
Unwrought Copper	6·6
Raw Wool	6·2
Undressed Fur Skins	4·7
Oranges	3·9
Bananas	3·5
Wheat	3·0
Grapes	2·9
Sawn Softwood	2·7
Apples	2·7
Ships and Boats	2·5
Unmanufactured Tobacco	2·4
Silver Bullion	2·3
	——
Total of all Imports ...	191·8

(4·4 per cent of total U.K. imports by value)

TABLE 58

Fifteen Most Valuable Foreign Trade Exports from Southampton
(incl. Lymington), 1960

	Value *£ Million*
Cars	7·5
Woven Woollen Fabrics	6·3
Woven Cotton Fabrics	3·2
Motor Spirit	3·2
Printed Matter	2·9
Gas Oil	2·6
Cigarettes	2·5
Aircraft Parts	2·0
Tractors	2·0
Fuel Oil	2·0
Musical Instruments (and Musical Reproduction)	2·0
Office Machinery	1·9
Electric Cables	1·8
Plastics	1·7
Kerosene	1·7
	——
Total of all Exports ...	123·5

(3·7 per cent of total U.K. exports by value)

Current trends are that sea passenger traffic is modestly increasing (with a marked increase in cruises), while air traffic is increasing greatly. Southampton, in particular, deals with three-quarters of the passenger traffic to South Africa and the U.S.A. On the north Atlantic route the idea of the 'travelling hotel' applies, as it does on the shorter ferries to Europe operating at night. Nearly three-quarters of the passengers on the *Queen* vessels are tourists.

The selected 'most valuable' import list clearly reveals the importance of Fawley Oil Refinery (and other oil depots receiving refined fuel) and the South African liner service. Southampton is the principal British port for South African wool, subsequently dispatched inland to the West Riding. Here is another demonstration that the regularity of a liner service to a port's 'foreland' overseas is a powerful routeing factor. It generally overrides questions of internal distance in the relatively small island of Britain or any question of competing port hinterlands.

Practically all South African deciduous fruit for Britain and three-quarters of South African citrus fruit imports are received by this one port. The exports present a cross-section of British manufacturing industry drawn from the whole country. Apart from refined petroleum and cigarettes very few exports are manufactured in the Southampton area.

Southampton is just large enough (population about 200,000) for its several functions to be separated out in precincts. There is certainly a recognizable port area distinct from the shopping and other 'regional centre' services that Southampton performs. This is epitomized by two of the railway stations: the Central (formerly the 'West'), for the modern town; and the original Terminus Station, for the port. Southampton might be called a '*ville double*'[26], with the medieval area of the town left apart by the port and the modern development alike. The New Docks certainly gave a new directional focus to the town. Until the First World War the general development of the town of Southampton was based on the chord of a circle lying east-west across the base of the original peninsula. Now the semicircular shape to which the town tends is based on a diameter running north-west to south-east along the northern shore of the River Test to where the River Itchen enters Southampton Water close to the southern tip of the Old Docks.[27]

REFERENCES

1. C. E. Everard, 'The Solent River: a Geomorphological Study', *Transactions and Papers*, 20, Institute of British Geographers (1954), 41–58, for further details, making clear the effects of *multiple* glaciation omitted here.
2. *Ibid.*, 'Submerged Gravel and Peat in Southampton Water', *Proceedings of the Hampshire Field Club and Archaeological Society*, 18 (1954), 263–85, provides details of the buried channels which the post-glacial rise in sea-level has flooded to give the present waterways.
3. Not the first settlement in the area, but forerunners have no influence on the port lay-out. See M. R.

Maitland Muller, 'Southampton before the Norman Conquest', *Collected Essays on Southampton*, edited by J. B. Morgan and P. Peberdy, Southampton Borough Council, 1958, 15–37. For graphic imaginative drawings of Southampton at this and later periods see L. A. Burgess and H. S. Faircloth, *Historical Perspectives of Southampton*, County Borough of Southampton Education Committee, 1954.

4. D. T. Williams, 'The Maritime Relations of Bordeaux and Southampton in the Thirteenth Century', *Scottish Geographical Magazine*, 47 (1931), 270–5, and *Ibid.*, 'Medieval Foreign Trade: Western Ports', *An Historical Geography of England*, edited by H. C. Darby', Cambridge University Press, 1951, 272 *et seq.* Many Norman and Early English wine vaults are to be found within walled Southampton, see *Historic Buildings of Southampton*, Southampton Museums Publication No. 5, 1959. '. . . a copy of the famous Rolls of Oléron, a code of sea law devised in Aquitaine primarily for the regulation of the wine trade, is entered in the *Oak Book of Southampton* side by side with the regulations of the merchant gild—clear indication of the importance of the Gascon trade to the Hampshire port.' A. A. Ruddock, 'Merchants and Shipping in Medieval Southampton', *Collected Essays, vide supra*, 48–57, 49–50.

5. The fourteenth-century Wool House, close to the Town Quay, still stands.

6. P. Studer, *The Port Books of Southampton 1427–30*, Southampton Record Society, 1913; and D. B. Quin and A. A. Ruddock, *The Port Books of Southampton for the Reign of Edward IV 1469–81*, 2 vols., Southampton Record Society, 1937–8, give the trade of the port in these years.

7. The Pilgrim Fathers sailed from the West Quay in 1620. One of the two ships, the *Speedwell*, later broke down, and the party put into Plymouth so that Southampton's role as an embarkation port has been overshadowed.

8. A. A. Ruddock, 'London Capitalists and the Decline of Southampton in the Early Tudor Period', *Economic History Review*, 2, second series (1949), 137–51, 149. See also *Ibid.*, *Italian Merchants and Shipping in Southampton 1270–1600*, Southampton: University College, 1951, with a full bibliography.

9. *Report by J. Rennie to Southampton Harbour Board, July 31, 1805*, MS, Southampton Corporation Archives, Ass. 223.

10. A. Giles, 'On the Construction of Southampton Docks', *Minutes of the Proceedings of the Institution of Civil Engineers*, 17 (1857–8), 540–54, 540–1, Figs. 2 and 10.

11. Because of the lack of local capital the control of the port passed away from the municipality, never to return, not without protests from a minority within the Town Council, see P. Ford, *Work and Wealth in a Modern Port*, London: Allen and Unwin, 1934, 11–20. However, Southampton Harbour Board still contributes one-fifth of the dues on shipping (less expenses) to the Corporation for relief of rates as laid down in the 1803 Act.

12. A vivid article under this title appeared in *Household Words*, January 6, 1855, the magazine edited by Charles Dickens.

13. There are of course many books on the histories of individual shipping companies. Three excellent general histories of the north Atlantic route are: H. P. Spratt, *Outline History of Transatlantic Steam Navigation*, London: H.M.S.O., 1950; C. R. V. Gibbs, *Passenger Liners of the Western Ocean*, London: Staples, 1952; and N. R. P. Bonsor, *North Atlantic Seaway*, Prescot: Stephenson, 1955.

14. T. W. Shore and J. W. Elwes, 'The New [Empress] Dock Extension at Southampton', *Proceedings of the Hampshire Field Club and Archaeological Society*, I (1899), 43–56, 43. See contoured maps of sub-surface gravel, Figs. 3 and 4 in C. E. Everard, *vide supra*, footnote 2. Also W. R. Galbraith on the Empress Dock, *Minutes of the Proceedings of the Institution of Civil Engineers* [in discussion on a paper on the Kidderpur Docks], 124–9.

15. F. E. Wentworth-Shields, 'The Construction of the White Star [now Ocean] Dock and Adjoining Quays at Southampton', *Proceedings of the Institution of Civil Engineers*, 195 (1913–14), 1–108, 34.

16. See Discussion in M. G. J. McHaffie, 'Southampton Docks Extension', *Journal of the Institution of Civil Engineers*, 9 (1937–8), 184–236, 224, 234, and 558.

17. *Report [by Sir Frederick Palmer] on the Proposed Dock Extension (Western Shore) at Southampton Docks, June 19, 1926* (by courtesy of Messrs. Rendel, Palmer & Tritton), 2 and 3. The *Queen Mary* and *Queen Elizabeth*, and the *France* launched in 1960 (1,035 feet long), would have projected some 50 feet beyond a 1,000-foot long jetty.

18. J. Cottier, 'Le port de Southampton', *Annales de Géographie*, 45 (1936), 240–56, 242.

19. F. H. W. Green, 'Tidal Phenomena with Special Reference to Southampton and Poole', *The Dock and Harbour Authority*, 32 (1951–2), 143–8 and 154, 148.

20. D. H. T. Macmillan, 'The Approach Channels to Southampton', *Journal of the Institute of Navigation* 5 (1952), 178–94, 180. A nearly complete bridge between harmonic analysis and Southampton's observed tidal curve is to be found in A. T. Doodson and H. D. Warburg, *Admiralty Manual of Tides*, H.M.S.O., 1941, Chapter XXVI, where the necessary amplitude-ratios and phase-relationships between M_2, M_4, and M_6, are explained. See also D. H. T. Macmillan, 'Tidal Features of Southampton Water', *The Dock and Harbour Authority*, 29 (1948–9), 259–64; and, with R. C. H. Russell, *Waves and Tides*, London: Hutchinson, 1952, which contains a general account of tidal theory.

21. D. H. T. Macmillan (1952), *loc. cit.*, 183.

22. For some years a straighter shipping lane across the Bramble Bank has been talked of. N. B. Webber and T. L. Shaw, 'A Model Investigation into the Possibility of a New Approach Channel to Southampton Water', *The Dock and Harbour Authority*, 41 (1960–1), 127–9. As yet there is no conclusive evidence that such a channel would be self-maintaining or not cause shoaling in the existing channel. See also W. Wright and R. D. Leonard, 'An Investigation of the Effects of a Proposed Dredging Scheme in Southampton Water by Means of a Hydraulic Model', *Proceedings of the Institution of Civil Engineers*, 14 (1959), 1–18, 16 (1960), 194–208.

23. M. G. J. McHaffie, *loc. cit.*, 193 *et seq.*

24. This probably fits in with Southampton's requirements. 'The Southampton region needs greater diversification of industry to give it stability.' P. Ford and C. J. Thomas, *A Survey of the Industrial Prospects of the Southampton Region*, Oxford: Blackwell, 1950, 49.

25. After H. W. Evans, 'New Cold Store at Southampton Docks', *The Dock and Harbour Authority*, 39 (1958–9), 157–62, 162.

26. A term which describes several continental towns with a constricted medieval core and a modern town outside the old walls.

27. This was first hinted at by O. H. T. Rishbeth in *Southampton: A Civic Survey*, ed. P. Ford. London: Oxford University Press, 1931, 31, even before the New Docks were opened.

FURTHER REFERENCES FOR SOUTHAMPTON

Cobb, H. S. *The Port Book of Southampton for 1439–40, edited with an Introduction Relating to Local Port Dues and the Coastal Trade of Southampton.* Unpublished thesis, M.A., University of London, 1957. [Published by Southampton University Press, 1961]

Daysh, G. H. J. 'The Future of the Port of Southampton', *Scottish Geographical Magazine*, 45 (1929), 211–9.

Dredging: Port of Southampton 1950–51. King's Lynn: The Dredging and Construction Company Ltd., 1951.

Morris, P. H. *Southampton in the Early Dock and Railway Age, 1830–60.* Unpublished thesis, M.A. University of Southampton, 1957.

[The] *Port of Southampton 150th Anniversary Publication.* Southampton Harbour Board, 1953.

Shillington, E. P. *The Story of Southampton Harbour.* Southampton: Wilson, 1947.

Speed, J. *The History and Antiquity of Southampton.* circa 1770.

Tavener, L. E. 'The Port of Southampton', *Economic Geography*, 26 (1950), 260–73.

Wentworth-Shields, F. E. 'The Port of Southampton', *Scottish Geographical Magazine*, 42 (1926), 1–11.

Wiggs, J. L. *The Seaborne Trade of Southampton in the Second Half of the Nineteenth Century.* Unpublished thesis, M.A., University of Southampton, 1954.

COMMERCIAL AND INDUSTRIAL ESTUARIES—III

Chapter 7

BRISTOL, THE AVON, AND AVONMOUTH

DOMINATING the development of the present lay-out of the Port of Bristol has been the great tidal range in the progressively narrowing Bristol Channel and Severn Estuary. Here are the largest tidal ranges off the British Isles, exceeded in the world only by the tides of the Bay of Fundy, Nova Scotia. The tidal range at Avonmouth is sometimes as much as 48 feet, and it has always been difficult to establish tidal berths along the Severn itself. Ports on tributaries have been preferred: the Wye (Chepstow), the Usk (Newport), and the Avon. Before coal-mining rose to importance, the land situations of any port on the western side of the Severn estuary were inferior to those on the eastern shore; a detour was necessary to reach any part of England south of Gloucester before 1886, and thereafter south of the Severn Railway tunnel. The Port of Chepstow, on the 'wrong' side of the estuary, never had much besides a coasting trade and passed out of existence with the coming of railways and the disadvantage of a non-industrial hinterland.[1] Even Newport and Cardiff at first had localized hinterlands upon the coalfield to the north-west.

Only Bristol has remained as a major port since the Middle Ages. Only the Avon enters the Severn estuary as a major stream from the east between Gloucester and the Bristol Channel. This river provided Bristol with its *primitive* harbour, an artery to the sea, and its City Docks, but later proved insufficient for all the needs of a modern major port.

Two criss-crossing structural trends are found in the Bristol area. The first lies just east of and parallel to the Severn Estuary (Lower Severn Axis, NE–SW). The limestone of the Failand Hills and Durdham Down just west of Bristol follow this trend as does the vale of Keuper Marl and New Red Sandstone in which Bristol is situated. Further east the structural trend line slightly changes direction in the southern Cotswolds (Bath Axis, N–S) and the Vale of Malmesbury. Upland alternates with vale, yet, remarkably, the Avon drains all of these, cutting gorges where necessary, and having a surprisingly wide catchment area considering the present compartment-like nature of the relief. The Lower Severn and the Bath Axes have been compared[2] to two promontories upon which younger E–W folds, well represented in the Mendips, broke as storm waves in the Broadfield Down and Kingswood anticlines. Because the promontories were struck head-on, the E–W waves were violently checked and even diverted to follow the lines of the older folds, as in the Westbury-on-Trym anticline. All this complicated structure was buried by later **X** rocks, and an early Avon could flow unhindered across these **X** rocks to the sea, perhaps even guided by folds or faults in them from re-activated E–W folds. The Avon, aided by its tributaries, removes the **X** rocks and exhumes older rocks beneath, folded NE–SW across its path. Such is a classic example of drainage superimposed across buried folded rocks—in this case the Avon Gorge cut across the

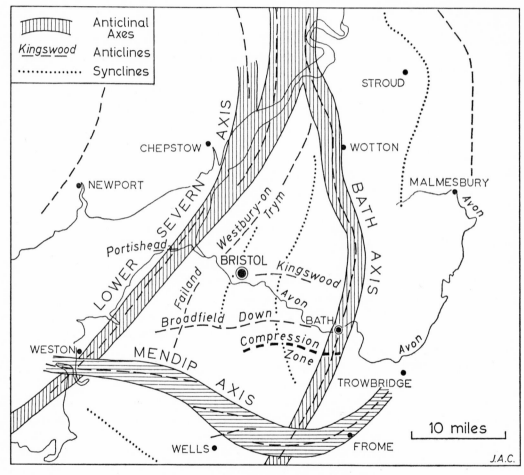

FIG. 48 Structural Trends in the Bristol Area

After G. A. Kellaway and F. B. A. Welch, *op. cit.*, 2nd edition, by permission of the Controller of H.M. Stationery Office.

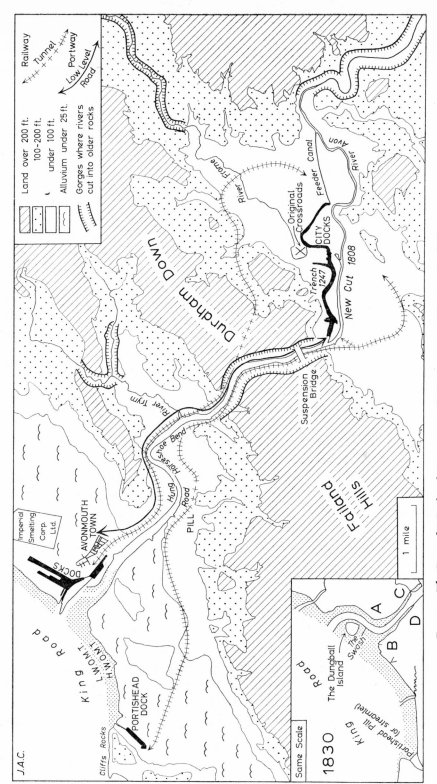

FIG. 49   The Port of Bristol and Lower Avon Drainage: Inset—The Mouth of the Avon in 1830

Westbury-on-Trym anticline, of Carboniferous Limestone (like the Limpley Stoke Gorge across the Bath Axis). Much support is lent to this theory by the fact that close to Bristol the Avon tributaries are also in process of discovering, as they cut down, the older resistant rocks formerly buried beneath their courses.

Upstream of its gorge, the Avon is joined by a right-bank tributary, the Frome, with the confluence at one time encompassed by marsh over which the Avon and Frome flooded before uniting to enter the gorge. Close to the confluence were a few sandstone islands in the marsh, and on one of these islands Bristol was sited. The narrow Avon Gorge was a defensive feature for the port while the relatively wide bed of the Avon, reflecting its surprisingly large catchment area, is a receptacle for the mighty Severn tide. This helped ships to penetrate eight miles inland.[3] Early Bristol was bounded on three sides by rivers. An appreciation of these features can be found in an account of Bristol in the mid-twelfth century:

> '. . . by the very situation of the place the best defended of all the cities of England. . . . Moreover a quick and strong tide ebbing and flowing abundantly night and day, causes the rivers on both sides of the city to run back upon themselves into a wide and deep sea; and forming a port very fit and very safe . . .'[4]

E. M. Carus-Wilson has contrasted this easily defended site with the more exposed sites of Hull and Southampton.[5] The confluence was the exclusive water site of the Port of Bristol until 1877. The modern plan of the Bristol City Docks shows the result of two major modifications to the *primitive* site: the diversion of the River Frome to begin the era of *marginal quay extension*; and the diversion of the Avon, which made *marginal quay elaboration* possible in a so-called Floating Harbour.

Welsh Back represents the *primitive* site of the Port of Bristol, immediately downstream of the Bristol Bridge on the town side of the Avon meander.[6] The *primitive* port grew up in the vicinity of the bridge, which was no doubt very early an important feature of the town known as Brycgstowe—the place at the bridge. High Street, Bristol, leads north-westwards from the bridge, and was also the original transverse route inland to the town centre from the *primitive* port.

Although the Avon was an advantage to the site of the town, providing a natural moat on the south-east, the very nature of its meander bend at the bridge made Welsh Back an awkward site for ships. Rivers cut steep banks on the outside of a meander, and this would have caused ships to roll uncomfortably when the tidal range left them high, precariously poised, and dry. Where the river straightened south of the town there was a rival quayside on the opposite bank—Redcliffe Back operated by men from this first suburb of Bristol. To improve the Bristol harbour a wonderfully bold scheme for the thirteenth century was decided upon. Part of St. Augustine's Marsh south-west of the town was purchased in 1239, and a straight

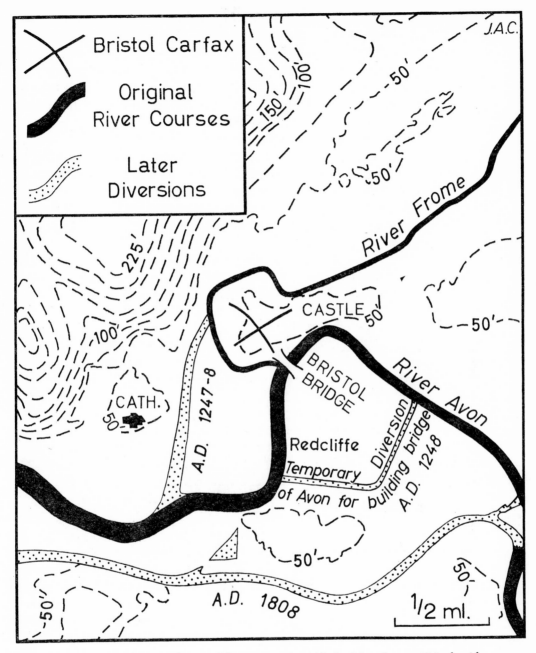

FIG. 50 Original Confluence of the River Frome with the River Avon at Bristol, with
Later Diversions

cut was made to divert the Frome. The men of Redcliffe were compelled to assist the work by royal order in 1240.

> '. . . to all worthy men of Redcliffe . . . whereas our beloved burgesses of Bristol . . . have begun a certain trench in the Marsh of St. Augustine that ships coming to our port of Bristol may be able to enter or leave more freely and without impediment . . . you shall give like efficacious aid as they themselves do . . .'[7]

The Key on the diverted Frome was prolonged south of the walls and completed by 1248.[8] Larger vessels berthed here than at the site of the *primitive* port, as they do today. Welsh and Redcliffe Backs were relegated to the coasting trade. Corn Street, the south-west arm of the original Bristol carfax pattern, now became the principal

TABLE 59

Eras and Epochs in the Development of the Port of Bristol

Eras and Chief Areal Characteristics	Present-day Symbols
I *Primitive:* port immediately downstream of wooden bridge	Welsh Back
Era ended by the completion of the trench in St. Augustine's Marsh, 1247–8	
II *Marginal Quay Extension:* quays on town side of the trench and Avon	Welsh Back, The Grove, Broad and Narrow Quays
Era ended by the completion of the Floating Harbour, 1809	
III *Marginal Quay Elaboration:* quays along impounded Frome Cut and Avon	Princes and Bathurst Wharves, 1866
Opening of Avonmouth Dock, 1877	
IV *Dock Elaboration:* Severn-side docks	Original area of Avonmouth Dock, and Portishead Dock
Era ended by Avonmouth Docks extensions beginning 1894	
V *Simple Lineal Quayage:* provision of longer quayage at Avonmouth	Avonmouth Dock North Quay (extended 1894); Eastern Arm, Royal Edward Dock, 1922–8, 1940
VI *Specialized Quayage:* oil berths, grain berths, and bulk-handling berths in the impounded docks	Oil Basin, 1914–23; Grain berths, Avonmouth Docks; Phosphate berths, Eastern Arm and Portishead

route inland from the port area. This era of *marginal quay extension* until the beginning of the nineteenth century was the time of Bristol's highest relative position among British ports, second only to the Port of London. E. M. Carus-Wilson[9] has traced the expansion of Bristol's trade[10] during the later Middle Ages showing how Bristol ships then sailed not only to ports of eastern, southern, and western Ireland,[11] but also to the whole western seaboard of Europe, and even as far away as Iceland[12] and the Mediterranean.

The Bristol Channel is an annexe to the Atlantic, and Bristol was in the van of transatlantic exploration at the end of the fifteenth century with the famous voyages of John Cabot from Bristol to Newfoundland and the American coast in 1497 and 1498.[13] The Society of Merchant Venturers of Bristol was incorporated in 1552. Henceforth, capital could be mobilized for westward voyages. But transatlantic trade did not flourish until the seventeenth century[14] when Bristol's water situation close to Atlantic western approaches was a helpful factor. Two important events stimulating trade in the second half of that century were the capture of Jamaica in 1655, which helped to give rise to sugar refining and later to the chocolate industry in Bristol;[15] and in 1698 the African trade was declared open. The slave trade and imports from the American colonies were founders of the tobacco trade in general and of many a Bristol private fortune in particular.

Towards the end of the eighteenth century certain general circumstances began to operate against an expansion of these trading successes. 'Bristol lost ground . . .'[16] The American trade did not recover after the Revolution (1783); England's trade with other continents expanded, thereby lessening the value of the forward nature of Bristol's situation when the westward trade was dominant; Bristol's interest in the slave trade declined against the growing competition of Liverpool,[17] with its lower costs;[18] and Bristol's hinterland was not in the forefront of the invigorating Industrial Revolution sweeping over the foothills of Lancashire. Lastly, engineering achievements in the building of larger ships revealed the inadequacies of the tidal berths in St. Augustine's Marsh.

During the seventeenth century the Society of Merchant Venturers took over from the Corporation many of the functions of a port authority.[19] They extended the quay in 1691,[20] and when vessels of over 150 tons burden had difficulty in ascending the Avon, they provided in 1728 additional moorings in Hung Road (seaward of the Avon Gorge).[21] In 1758 and 1765 ways were considered of improving the berthing of ships; in the latter year J. Smeaton proposed the conversion of the original St. Augustine's trench into a wet dock, but the expense was thought to be too great. Other plans were considered for keeping vessels always afloat. Merchants had complained at a meeting in 1764 that laden vessels grounded at each tide for several hours, and the strain involved 'wrought frequent damage to vessels'.[22] Two further disadvantages of the port were mentioned in the preamble to an Act in

1803: at neap tides vessels were unable to navigate the Avon to and from the sea; and when the harbour was dry a vessel could not be towed away if it caught fire, and there would be a lack of water for fire-fighting to the danger of houses in the city.[23] The early plans[24] were put aside on grounds of expense, and there were delays because of the conflicting advice of engineers. In 1793 the tidal quays of the port remained confined to the city side of the Avon and the Frome cut, with some ship-building yards opposite the quay and down river. But the commercial quayage had extended little beyond the sites used in medieval times.[25]

The modern plan of the City Docks shows what was done in 1804–9, following William Jessop's fourth amended plan to initiate an era of *marginal quay elaboration*. The whole pre-existing port, and much more of the River Avon, were included in the Floating Harbour. The Avon was diverted into a new cut to the south, while its old bed and the Frome cut were impounded just upstream of the Avon Gorge. Water is maintained in the tideless harbour by flow from the Frome under Broad Quay, and via the Feeder Canal, from the Avon, which also allows river craft to enter the harbour. Some of the main retouches to the original lay-out may be briefly indicated:

> 1865—present lock at Cumberland Basin 350 ft. by 62 ft. (originally only 189 ft. by 45 ft.);
> 1866—construction of Princes and Bathurst Wharves with railway connection;
> 1895—northern half of original St. Augustine's trench covered over to make Colston Avenue;
> 1906–8—A and B tobacco warehouses (C, 1920);
> 1907—Canon's Marsh Wharf

The original trench was further filled in to its present position, and Broad Quay became known as 'Tramways Centre', now a dual carriage-way with a wide island known locally as the 'Centre', despite the fact that the medieval centre is four hundred yards to the north-east and that the modern shopping centre is even further north-east of this old core.

The Floating Harbour of 1808 has proved to be the limit of port development on the Avon itself. A problem that bedevilled the next sixty-three years was the choice of site for *dock elaboration*. The port undoubtedly declined relatively to other ports, particularly Liverpool and those in South Wales. During this time many steamship companies were being founded, and Bristol's difficulties in the nineteenth century have resulted in only two steamship companies today having their line headquarters at Bristol.[26] The capital cost of the Floating Harbour had been nearly double the estimate, and one of the reasons for high port dues was the necessity for amortizing the capital within an acceptable time. The most spectacular loss of trade is exemplified by Brunel's *Great Western*. Launched into the Floating Harbour in 1837, this vessel of 1,340 gross tons was the second steamship to cross the north Atlantic. Yet the vessel had to lie at King Road in the Severn estuary because of difficulties in negotiating the harbour entrance and river approaches. The Bristol Dock Company nevertheless demanded full dues. Realizing that no pier was to be available near King Road, the owners of the *Great Western* decided to sail her alternately from Liverpool and Bristol after 1842. Port dues at Liverpool were found to be £200 less per voyage, and this port was used exclusively from 1843 onwards. From 1844–54 the port also suffered from being in the broad gauge railway area. Rail-borne goods from the Midlands had to be reloaded at Gloucester, and no doubt Liverpool and other ports profited from this at Bristol's expense.

TABLE 60

Port Charges (on Goods and Vessels) in the First Half of the Nineteenth Century

1824 Average Charges on 44 Articles[27] Bristol = 100		1847 Average Charges on 49 Articles[28] Bristol = 100	
Liverpool	45	London (including mercantile charges)	84
London	41	Liverpool	58
Hull	29	Hull	51
		London (wharfage alone)	31
		Cardiff	22
		Newport	10
		Southampton	4

The decline of trade was not absolute; foreign tonnage increased by a third in the period 1828–48,[29] and each decade of the nineteenth century showed a steady absolute advance.

A proposal to combat the relative decline of the port was the impounding of the entire Avon by a barrage at Avonmouth. This would have been a practical plan only between 1843 and 1860. In 1843 the Floating Harbour was proved to be inadequate for the largest class of vessel by the difficulties in getting the *Great Britain*[30] out of the harbour after her launching. In 1860 a report demonstrated that, among other considerations, deep-sea vessels were already being built too big to use the Avon.[31] The alternative was docks with direct access to the Severn with links back to the city made possible by the railway, the Great Western route having been completed to Bristol in 1841. The land sites of these docks are in Gordano,[32] a triangular area of alluvium covering the low ground between two anticlinal ridges associated with the Lower Severn Axis. A bigger problem was that of the water approaches.

Five miles north-north-east of the mouth of the Avon the deep water within the wide Severn estuary is confined in a V-shaped bottleneck about 450 yards wide and eighty feet deep which the river has eroded in Pennant Sandstone. The surface expression of this bottleneck is revealed at low tide as the Lady and Lower Bench on the Welsh side and by the English Stones.[33] This constriction is aptly named the Shoots since it directs the deep-water channel almost due south close to the English shore. Opposite Avonmouth the deep channel is known as King Road with a minimum of 34 feet and is the chief channel within the wide estuary. From here the approach to shore is made difficult by shallow water over the Severn mudflats, 400 yards wide at low water. These might be unstable if a channel, costly to maintain, were to be cut across their full width. Two sites appeared possible, first suggested in 1852 and 1853: north of the mouth of the Avon and at Portishead. Both sites have short approaches to the deep water of King Road for entirely different reasons.

Although charts show that the mouth of the Avon migrated southwards between 1865 and 1871[34] to the present Swash Channel, the river still bends northward in a considerable curve. A dock entrance on the north side could be placed landward of the Swash Channel with a straight approach (point A, inset map, Fig. 49). But any dock entrance on the south side of the Avon would either have Severn mudbanks to the north-west and mudbanks of the shallower part of the mouth of the Avon to the north (point B); or if placed further inland, a very curving approach channel within the Avon (points C and D).

To find a site for a dock entrance south of the Avon, it was necessary to go one and three-quarter miles along the coast to Portishead (*Portesheved*, Saxon). Here an east–west anticlinal complication of the Lower Severn Axis causes rocks to dip steeply offshore reducing the width of the Severn mudflats. This is where the Portishead Pier was built with easy access to King Road; here later Portishead Dock was sited with its entrance in the inlet of a small stream, Portishead Pill, later diverted.

After the 1860 *Report* docks independent of the River Avon had to be the next development. Bristol Corporation, operators of the City Docks after 1848, opposed this. Other delays were caused by the financial panic of 1866 and rivalry between private dock promoters. There were also constructional difficulties in the alluvial sites, and it was not until 1877 and 1879 that Avonmouth and Portishead Docks were opened and inaugurated the era of *dock elaboration*. Bristol is today the only major port of Britain municipally controlled, and the reason lies amid complicated developments in the nineteenth century,[35] of which the chief events are summarized below:

1803   Bristol Dock Company founded and later builds the Floating Harbour

1848   Corporation of the City of Bristol takes over the port estate, with the objective of reducing dues

1862   Act for a pier at Avonmouth and a railway, along the right bank of the Avon, completed 1864

1864   Act for a dock at Avonmouth

PLATE VII DEEP-WATER OIL TERMINALS

Above: Fawley Marine Terminal, looking west, located on Fig. 44.

Below: Milford Haven, looking south-east into the haven, *cf.* Fig. 55.

PLATE VIII PORT OF BRISTOL

Above: Looking north across the City Docks, *cf.* Fig. 51.

Below: Looking north across Avonmouth Docks, *cf.* Fig. 52.

1866   Bristol and Portishead Pier and Railway Company receive an Act conferring some of the powers of a dock company. Railway and pier completed 1867–70

1871   Acts for docks by rival companies at Avonmouth and Portishead

1877   Bristol Port and Channel Dock Company open Avonmouth Dock

1879   Portishead opens, having been delayed by collapse of west quay wall

1880   Docks Committee of Bristol Corporation proposes retaliatory measures against Severn-side docks because of competition with City Docks

1882–3 Agreement on dues between three separate dock authorities. City Docks compete well with rivals

1884   Corporation takes over Avonmouth and Portishead Docks

The main reasons, on both sides, for amalgamation were as follows. The hand of the Corporation *vis-à-vis* the dock companies was strengthened by the fact that the percentage of shipping using the port and entering the City Docks actually increased until a maximum of 73·9 per cent in 1895, with Avonmouth, 21·1 per cent and Portishead 5·0 per cent.[36] On the other hand, the Corporation began to lose money on the City Docks, the year after Avonmouth Dock was opened, a loss which rose to £17,000 in 1882.[37] The net loss after dock amalgamation was put at £3,000 per annum, although the city would, of course, benefit from any trade expansion.

In theory major disadvantages of municipal port control compared with a public trust are as follows: the docks committee of a corporation may be councillors drawn from non-maritime backgrounds with little experience of dock operation; they may retire just as they are becoming experienced; the port revenue may be regarded as a means of reducing town rates; and, if the port has to expand, this may well be outside the municipal boundary, in which case the attitude of a corporation may be a bar to port development. Such circumstances arose in acute form at both London and Liverpool. In Bristol the story was very different in practice. The twelve members of the Dock Committee of the Corporation of Bristol (The Port of Bristol Authority) have had a reputation for continuity of service.[38] Although the chairmen are elected annually, there were only four chairmen between 1893 and 1937, and the present chairman was first a member of the Committee in 1922. One disadvantage of municipal control is that of an extra sinking fund burden. A shorter period is allowed to local authorities for the redemption of debt than to other statutory bodies, such as a public trust. For this reason in some years the municipality has provided a rate-in-aid to the port to meet sinking fund charges. On the other hand, the Docks Committee can borrow capital at low rates, using the credit of the city finances as security. Expansion of the city boundary to the Severn was achieved in 1895 in order that the newly acquired Severn-side docks should be within the city limits. Municipal control first arose in 1848 with the idea of reducing rates, and in

1884 comprehensive control seemed better than the competition of three rival dock authorities. One spur towards efficiency of municipal control is that the port users have always the remedy of applying to the national government for another type of control if the case for this could be made good.

There are several differences between Bristol's development and that of *Anyport*. Examination of these differences supports a thesis that they arise in large measure from the difficulties of the water site, particularly the narrowness of the Avon in its gorge between Bristol and the sea, and the great range of tide. These were the very physical *advantages* of the port in the Middle Ages. The first simple *marginal quay extension* of the Port of Bristol entailed a prodigious trench cut by hand in the thirteenth century that can unhesitatingly be called a major piece of medieval engineering. With few further harbour developments, the port rose to be second in England. But *marginal quay elaboration* was very difficult. The narrowness of the waterways and the great tidal range prevented the more simple expedients of jetties or cuts in the river banks, or even of simple extension along the steep banks of the Avon. Before the Avon could be used commercially downstream from the medieval trench, it had to be impounded. The impounded section of the Avon is now called the City *Docks*. In the scheme of eras and epochs it has been called *marginal quay elaboration*; because the prime purpose of the impounding was to render existing quays and the adjacent river shore (potential quays) more safe by floating vessels at all states of the tide. Hence the first name—the Floating Harbour. Small docks had been built in the eighteenth century at Sea Mills (1712?–61?);[39] at the confluence of the River Trym with the Avon; and at Rownham (1762) near the later entrance to the Floating Harbour. The latter still exists as the Merchants' Dock. But both were acknowledged in the eighteenth century to be too far from the port nucleus. And the Floating Harbour has never become so congested that dock annexes in the banks have been necessary.

The reasons for the sites of docks in the *dock elaboration* era have been given; and at the Avonmouth site extensions of *simple lineal quayage* have been made as trade increased. Portishead Dock has been handicapped by the small size of its dock entrance which has not been extended. A clear example of the cramping effect of the great tidal range is seen when the *specialized quayage* is sought in the modern plan. All the oil berths are in the Royal Edward Dock, a most unusual juxtaposition of oil tanker and dry cargo liner traffics. Since the size of tankers is limited by the dimensions of the dock entrance, there has been no suggestion of an oil refinery at Avonmouth although the land site was available. There was no possibility of berthing tankers against T-head jetties in the Severn, as at *Anyport*, though tanker discharge is not altogether impossible. During the Second World War tankers did berth in a specially excavated deep-water basin on Severn-side. Ships could not come alongside the 1943 oil jetty but were moored to six floating barges fifty feet from the jetty head. Because of the great tidal rise and fall, the pipe couplings were complicated; connecting links had to be slung out to the ship by a large derrick crane. A more modern method under difficult tidal conditions is to berth vessels against buoys whence oil pipelines run along the sea bed to the shore. But this needs a large water area if ships swing through 360° or are moored fore and aft to buoys, and other tidal water sites have fewer difficulties for regular oil discharge. *Specialized quayage* must, therefore, be sought within the dock development of previous eras. At Bristol once Severn-side docks had been built the eras of *simple lineal quayage* and *specialized quayage* had to be superimposed on the same sites. This helps to explain much of the recent developments within the Severn-side docks. Because of the great tidal range, a 1924 statement,

> 'I still visualize the day when the right bank of the Avon, from the Avon-mouth Dock entrance will be a line of private wharves . . . serving factories immediately behind them',[40]

remains unfulfilled.

The port area of the City of Bristol is distinct, south of the medieval core between the two arms of the Floating Harbour. Conversely, one of the charms of Bristol is the seeming penetration of the harbour and its ships right into the heart of a modern city.

Modern Functions of the Port of Bristol

The Floating Harbour, or City Docks, retains the general pattern of the early nineteenth century. The 'trench' in the marsh, with Princes and Bathurst Wharves opposite, is more active in the foreign trade than Welsh and Redcliffe Backs. This contrast has been the same since the thirteenth century. In the western part of the docks the quayside installations are used for more bulky goods such as more extensive storage of timber in privately owned yards, and of tobacco in port authority warehouses. Just as in the eighteenth century when this western area was too far away from the city centre to become the nucleus of an expanding port, so in this century it has not developed an intensive dry cargo traffic with quayside transit sheds. Liners longer than 330 feet cannot ascend the Avon because of the difficulties in navigating the Horseshoe Bend. Larger liner traffic is of course catered for at Avonmouth. The shipbuilding yard of Charles Hill & Sons Ltd. is active in the building of the smaller class of merchant vessel.[41] A tanker of 4,300 deadweight tonnage (gross, 3,644) and length 330 feet launched in 1959, is likely to remain the biggest vessel ever built at Bristol because of the limitation mentioned above.

More goods are transported to and from the City Docks by coastwise vessels and barges than by vessels in the foreign trade. Some transhipment takes place for the City Docks at Avonmouth. Upstream of the fixed Bristol Bridge about twenty-five barges a week, towed by tugs with retractable funnels, supply paper mills and a tar works. Welsh Back has developed as a wholesale fruiterers' area. There is a sherry bonded store in the Back and another near Midland Wharf. Redcliffe Backs have a brewery, a steel store, and a grain mill (1898) served by coasters and barges. At Narrow Quay and Canon's Marsh, berths are not reserved for any particular dry cargo trade, except that a regular link is maintained between A Shed, Canon's Marsh, and the Low Countries, the vessels not being equipped with ships' loading gear because of the provision of quay cranes at the constantly used terminal ports. V and U Sheds in Dean's Marsh are usually reserved for wine. At the southern end of Narrow Quay is a small tobacco warehouse, with the most modern tobacco warehouses (1921, 1931, and 1935) sited behind the transit sheds in Canon's Marsh. Opposite are Princes and Bathurst Wharves, where the Irish trade is well represented, as in the early medieval Port of Bristol. Chilled meat and Guinness stout are imported from Eire; and timber and wood pulp come from Scandinavia. Farm machinery and crated cars for assembly in Ireland are exported.

If you stand on any narrow peninsula between the Floating Harbour and the New Cut, the contrast is striking between the placid water of the commercial harbour and the steep mud banks of the New Cut exposed at low tide and devoid of any port installations whatsoever.

At Avonmouth the position of the first dock entrance has already been discussed (page 190). Though Avonmouth Dock has a narrow south-eastern prolongation (1894), it was not possible to make a major extension in the narrow site between the river and the buildings of Avonmouth 'town'. Accordingly, the Royal Edward Dock was sited between the town and the coast and parallel with the Severn; its entrance lock is across the pre-1865 line of the Dungball Island in the mouth of the Avon (see inset map, Fig. 49). Avonmouth Dock began life as a general dock for liners which were too big for the Avon. It has very little general cargo today. Everywhere in this dock the air is permeated by the smell of grain and molasses. Since the 1930's, flour and provender mills have been built around the dock, having their usual modern location adjacent to deep water. Bananas were first received at Avonmouth Dock in 1901. In addition to the usual covered overhead endless conveyors, with a canvas bag for each stem, the loop railway lay-out provides ready marshalling of steam-heated wagons. Incidentally, the banana vessels provide the only ocean passenger service from Bristol.

In the Royal Edward Dock grain is delivered to the equivalent of a transit shed in the general cargo trade—a transit granary or silo (dating from 1928). Suction equipment draws the grain to the silos, whence it is transferred to mills, or to road

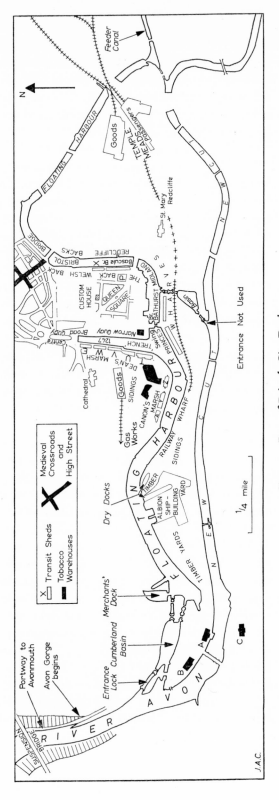

FIG. 51   Port of Bristol: City Docks

On the east side of Queen Square, laid out on the former marsh from 1701, are the head offices of the port authority, P, only 300 yards from the *primitive* port of Welsh Back.

and rail for milling elsewhere. At the rate of 150–200 tons an hour, travelling plants on the quayside deliver the grain on to high-speed conveyors running at the same speed as the conveying air, all enclosed in airtight trunking. All bulky machinery, including the vacuum pumps, are housed in the silo so that the movable quayside installations are quite light. The berth between U and P Sheds, Granary 3 Berth, is the only completely specialized berth in the dock and is devoted solely to grain handling. Otherwise, the dock is dominated by general cargo berths, of which a number can perform specialized functions. At Q, R, S, and T, general cargo berths, there are single-storey transit sheds. The last has six rail tracks on the quay and is frequently used for export cargoes. At U and V (general cargo plus grain) and W (general cargo only) there are multi-storey transit sheds, the upper floors of which are warehouses. The chief warehousing area of the port for dry cargo like cocoa, tea, tobacco, and wines is immediately behind these sheds. Similar to them are O and P, with their ground floor transit sheds, though here the first floor receives frozen meat for transmission to a cold store at the rear, or for immediate delivery to waiting lorries behind and below. X Berth has a paved concrete area, often used for assembling and loading motor vehicle exports. The qualifying use of the adverb 'often' with regard to export berths should be noted. Bristol's export trade is not of sufficient quantity or regularity to admit of berths used exclusively for exports. The eastern arm was made as wide as possible at 425 feet because of the necessity of providing room for overside working to barge. This was achieved at the expense of making the peninsula between the Eastern Arm and the Oil Basin rather too narrow, choosing 'the lesser evil'.[42]

Berth 5 is equipped with an aerial ropeway 1,500 yards long for unloading zinc concentrate, and, in smaller quantities, sulphate of ammonia and potash. An aerial ropeway is one method of carrying heavy material economically some distance to and from a deep-water berth. Here the ropeway takes the shortest distance to the raw material dump across railway sidings. By road the distance would be two miles, with an estimated 30 per cent increase of cost. There is no room on the dock estate for the factory; and no factory can have its private jetties on the Severn because of the great tidal range. The zinc plant, the first part of which was built by the Government in the First World War to combat a German and Belgian monopoly, now employs about 2,000 people, producing zinc and sulphuric acid from blende (zinc sulphide). The sulphuric acid is pumped to a neighbouring fertilizer factory on the Avonmouth Docks Estate north of Avonmouth Docks, where it is combined with phosphate imports to make superphosphate fertilizer.

The peninsula between the Eastern Arm and the Oil Basin graphically illustrates the ease of discharging oil compared with a more bulky cargo like timber. Cranes of 3-ton capacity, rail tracks (with inconvenient dead-ends on the peninsula), mobile cranes to move and sort the lumber, and a 50-foot high shed for sawn lumber are all

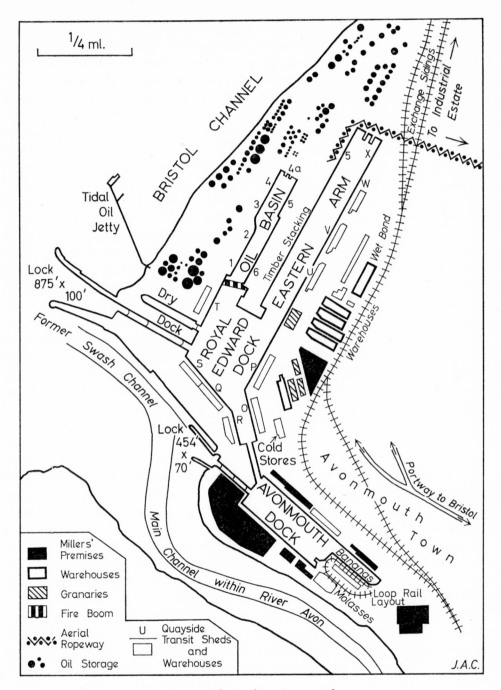

FIG. 52 The Docks at Avonmouth

necessary for timber discharge by the port authority. The transit storage area spreads two-thirds of the way across the width of the peninsula. Pipes running parallel with the quay occupying about twenty-five feet of quay width are all that are necessary for oil discharge; the tanks can be sited where convenient away from the quayside. The Oil Basin is sealed off from the rest of the dock by an electrically operated steel boom designed to prevent the risks to dry cargo ships presented by floating oil in an impounded dock. The inner berths are allocated for coastwise export, while between Oil Berths 5 and 6 there is a new deep-water tanker berth. Carbon black used in the rubber industry is also made from imported oil delivered via a 4-mile long pipeline to a factory on the industrial estate north of the dock.

Avonmouth Town appears to have developed hardly at all during this century. Municipal housing has expanded its area but little, since there were many other sites closer to the city. It has only a skeletal shopping centre for short-term items and only one commercial hotel, small branches of banks, and special port services like Missions to Seamen and the British Sailors Society. An inhabitant of Tilbury would feel at home here, except that his 'Gravesend' would be missing and his 'London' would be nearer. Avonmouth is linked to Bristol by a double-track railway and the fine low level road built in 1926 through the Avon Gorge—the Portway.

Of Portishead perhaps the most surprising feature is that its landward link is still via a single-track railway; no direct road has ever been constructed. The water area at Portishead has not been expanded since it was opened. For many years the dock was treated as a reserve while capital developments were concentrated at Avonmouth. Portishead is further from the city centre and is hemmed in by high land on one side. The tendency in recent years has been for the dock to become more self-contained. Soon after the First World War a power station, burning imported Welsh coal, was erected near the north quay; a post-Second World War power station sited alongside the north quay is designed in three units. One of these burns pulverized coal brought in by rail from the Somerset coalfield—here the only function of the water site is to provide cooling water; the second unit burns pulverized coal or oil; and the third burns oil exclusively. The fuel oil is brought in by coastwise tanker from Fawley. On the south quay Albright & Wilson (Mfg.) have been tenants of the port authority since 1954. The large amount of electricity available and the deep-water berths for the imports of phosphates were original attracitons for a fertilizer factory. Timber is dealt with at an adjacent berth, the only one that now resembles Portishead's early days. Timber is discharged here by travelling steam cranes on tracks running at right-angles to the quay. These, of course, are forerunners of the modern diesel-electric mobile crane, and although they appear somewhat historic today, the principle upon which they operate is sound. Nothing clutters up a quayside so quickly as timber discharge. A method of removing timber rapidly to a stacking ground is needed; the curiosities dating from

1905 at Portishead Dock have been doing this useful work for over half a century.[43] All the landward traffic, including power station coal, is carried on the Portishead–Bristol railway, which is perhaps one of the busiest single tracks in the country, with 1,000 wagons passing over it every day.

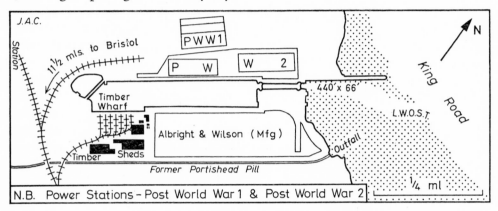

FIG. 53   Portishead Dock: Annotated Diagram

In commenting on Bristol's trade a table of tonnages imported and exported helps to sum up the current picture:

TABLE 61

Tonnages Handled at Bristol, 1960

	City	Avonmouth	Portishead
Imports			
Foreign	301,668	3,543,527	162,098
Coastwise	564,964	1,562,506	458,445
Exports			
Foreign	56,082	108,238	—
Coastwise	67,581	862,476	—

The dominance of imports over exports and of Avonmouth in the foreign trade is quite marked: total imports to exports 5·5 : 1 (by weight); and the share of Avonmouth in foreign trade 90 per cent (by weight).

In the foreign trade the dominance of imports over exports is even more striking. This has been a characteristic of the port for a long time.[44] A large proportion of the liners which arrive at Bristol only discharge a part cargo, the remainder at other British or Continental ports, returning particularly to a port that offers bottom cargo to begin loading exports. Shipowners have looked askance at the high cargo-space balance for ships at Bristol, the departing ship having to return in ballast or look for heavy bottom cargo and other exports elsewhere. The resulting scarcity of liner services has in turn driven exports elsewhere, particularly those from the West Midlands, where Bristol comes into competition with larger ports. British Railways

TABLE 62

Fifteen Most Valuable Foreign Trade Imports into Bristol (incl. Avonmouth, Portishead, and Weston-super-mare), 1960

	Value £ Million
Unmanufactured Tobacco	18·7
Aluminium	13·6
Wheat	9·6
Maize	8·9
Cocoa Beans	6·4
Butter	5·9
Iron and Steel Plates and Sheets	5·6
Unwrought Copper	4·6
Ground Nut Cake	4·5
Motor Spirit	4·5
Tea	4·3
Chilled or Frozen Lamb	4·2
Zinc Alloys	3·7
Gas Oil	3·7
Sorghums	3·0
Total of all Imports	179·8

(4·2 per cent of total U.K. imports by value)

TABLE 63

Fifteen Most Valuable Foreign Trade Exports from Bristol (incl. Avonmouth, Portishead, and Weston-super-mare), 1960

	Value £ Million
Cars	12·3
Carbon Blacks	1·3
Copper and Copper Alloys	·8
Tractors	·8
Lead and Lead Alloys	·6
Steel Wire Rods	·6
Paper Mill Machinery	·5
Power Generating Machinery	·5
Iron and Steel Tubes and Pipes	·4
Tractor Parts	·4
Drugs	·3
Scientific Instruments	·3
Nails and Bolts	·3
Aluminium	·3
Printed Matter	·3
Total of all Exports	32·1

(1·0 per cent of total U.K. exports by value)

Export Express Service even operates a 'concentration' depot in Bristol, cargoes in less than wagon-load quantities being guaranteed next-morning arrival at London and Southampton. Bristol, however, is helped by the growth of trade in specialized bulk carriers with such economical operating costs that a return in ballast has to be tolerated. The oil tanker and the grain ships are good examples. It so happens that staples of Bristol's trade are bulk imports: grain, especially to Avonmouth Dock; oil to the Oil Basin; and raw food especially to the Eastern Arm, Royal Edward Dock.

One way of attempting to understand this trade pattern is to consider Bristol's land situation. At first sight Bristol may appear as the major port in the south-west quadrant of England and Wales. Two areas where the port is likely to suffer competition from other ports are in South Wales and the Midlands. Undoubtedly, Bristol serves these areas by transhipment to the coastwise trade. But the area where Bristol is likely to be supreme, between the triangle of structural axes, and the agricultural counties of the south-west peninsula of England, is very much less than a quadrant either in area or in production—a 'south-western *octant* of England and Wales'. Bristol acts as a reception depot for this small area. This is well illustrated by the oil received from the refineries of various companies at home and overseas. The refined petroleum is then redistributed up the Severn navigation, to the south-western peninsula by coastal tanker or by road, and even to South Wales and southern Ireland. This redistribution area overlaps that of Milford Haven, Swansea (Llandarcy Refinery), and Southampton (Fawley Refinery) because of the various different companies involved. Grain is also redistributed coastwise. Some of the grain that enters the Royal Edward Dock is 'merchant grain' destined to be milled outside the Avonmouth dock area. Fruit and meat are also redistributed to feed the population of the south-west. The climate and dominant agricultural activity of the south-west also condition the character of the port. On this wetter side of Britain the area is cereal deficient, more particularly there is a need for wheat, most particularly there is a lack of barley. The great numbers of cattle need overseas supplies of feeding stuffs. Here are reasons for a marked dominance in Bristol's trade of oil, food, and feed. One food industry in Bristol reflects the old trading connections with Africa (cocoa for chocolate). The import of wines (notably sherry and port) is still an important traffic (*Bristol Cream, Bristol Milk*), and wine bonds are found both at Avonmouth and at the City Docks. The great tobacco industry of Bristol is inherited from the days of the triangular traffic across the Atlantic. Today the leaf is first imported to Avonmouth and thence taken by barge or lorry to the great warehouses near the Floating Harbour. About 60 per cent of the Avonmouth imports are processed at Bristol.[45] But the aluminium imports are largely for West Midlands industries upon whose growth the port has had no direct influence.[46]

The port authority's development programme announced in 1959 increases the emphasis on specialized handling, particularly of grain and oil. The granary capacity of Avonmouth is increased by half with the construction of a 30,000-ton granary behind the U and V Sheds in the Royal Edward Dock. Increases in home-produced beef and the broiler fowl industry will, it is believed, keep the coarse grain import trade buoyant. In the Oil Basin besides the new deep-water tanker berth a 'common user' pipeline system enables any oil company to discharge oil to its own storage tanks from any berth in the Oil Basin, reducing the number of discharge pipes, previously one for each company. One new general cargo berth is planned for the Avonmouth Dock, but three-quarters of the cost of the improvement programme is devoted to the grain and oil berths.

Imperial Chemical Industries began in 1960 the construction of their Severn-side Works, sister plant to that at Billingham, on a 1,000-acre site north of the Avon-mouth Docks. Much of the raw material, ethylene, will be supplied by pipeline from Fawley, but the Oil Basin will deal with extra petroleum imports. Other large plants to make ammonia, urea, and fertilizers will be erected. Though some 5,000 employees will be at work, capital investment will have run as high as £25,000 per man. Bristol's *specialized quayage* will be the scene of the port's greatest developments, and F. Walker, considering the trade of Bristol in 1939, made the discerning comment that its composition was

'a refutation of any idea that a port cannot prosper unless its trade is balanced and the basis of its commerce is varied.'[47]

Despite the great tidal range and narrowness of the Avon, goods still travel up the eight miles to be distributed from an inland port. But for the master of a deep-sea vessel Avonmouth is at present the Port of Bristol. Significantly, in 1959 the port authority acquired 700 acres of flat riverside land between the mouth of the Avon and Portishead. Should this be developed for port expansion, the dock systems on either side of the Avon estuary would at last be comparable in size.

REFERENCES

1. J. H. Andrews, 'Chepstow: a Defunct Seaport of the Severn Estuary', *Geography*, 40 (1955), 97–107; D. T. Williams, 'Medieval Foreign Trade: Western Ports', *An Historical Geography of England before A.D. 1800*, edited by H. C. Darby, Cambridge: University Press, 1951, 266–98, 282 *et. seq.*
2. F. B. A. Welch and R. Crookall, revised by G. A. Kellaway and F. B. A. Welch, *British Regional Geology: Bristol and Gloucester District*, Geological Survey: H.M.S.O., 1948, Fig. 3 and 38–42.
3. The velocity of the tidal stream is graphically illustrated today by the track of the Pill-Shirehampton ferry at the seaward end of the Avon Gorge: a sharp V, pointing upstream during the ebb, downstream during the flood.

4. From a chronicle of the reign of Stephen, translated by S. Seyer, *Memoirs, Historical and Topographical of Bristol and Its Neighbourhood*, 2 vols., 1821–3, Vol. 1, 409. See also *The Great Red Book of Bristol*, edited by E. W. W. Veale, Bristol Record Society, Vol. 2, 1931, 6.

5. E. M. Carus-Wilson (1933), *vide infra*, 183–4.

6. The *primitive* port became concentrated at Welsh Back after the building of the Bristol Bridge in stone (1248) which necessitated the temporary diversion of the Avon, see S. Seyer *op. cit.* Vol. 2, 28–44. 'Back' seems to derive from 'bakke', a pool of deeper water scoured out by the current flowing faster on the outside bend of a meander, E. W. Williams, 'The Bakke of Bristowe', *Transactions of the Bristol and Gloucestershire Archaeological Society*, 79 (1960), 287–92.

7. 27th April, 24 Henry II, 1240 translated in *Bristol Charters 1155–1373*, edited by N. D. Harding, Bristol Record Society, Vol. 1, 1930, 19. See also H. A. Cronne, *Bristol Charters 1378–1499*, edited by H. A. Cronne, Bristol Record Society, Vol. 11, 1946, 37–9.

8. Estimation of the dimensions of the trench at 2,400 ft., by an average of 120 ft. wide by 18 ft. deep at high water was made by S. Seyer, *op. cit.*, Vol. 2, 27.

9. E. M. Carus-Wilson, 'The Overseas Trade of Bristol', *Studies in English Trade in the Fifteenth Century*, Chap. V, edited by E. Power and M. M. Postan, Routledge, 1933; *ibid.* (selected and edited by), *The Overseas Trade of Bristol in the Later Middle Ages*, Bristol Record Society, Vol. 7, 1937.

10. E. M. Carus-Wilson, *Medieval Merchant Venturers*, London: Methuen, 1954.

11. E. M. Carus-Wilson (1937), map ii.

12. E. M. Carus-Wilson (1954), 98–142.

13. J. A. Williamson, *The Voyages of the Cabots*, London: Argonaut, 1929, 196–7 for the author's conclusions on the voyages.

14. P. McGrath, 'Bristol Since 1497', *Bristol and Its Adjoining Counties*, edited by C. M. MacInnes and W. F. Whittard, Bristol: British Association for the Advancement of Science, 1951, 207–17, 212–13. This volume contains several other chapters on Bristol's physical geography and history. See also *Merchants and Merchandise in Seventeenth-century Bristol*, edited by P. McGrath, Bristol Record Society, Vol. 19, xxi.

15. S. J. Jones, 'The Growth of Bristol', *Transactions and Papers*, 11, Institute of British Geographers (1946), 57–83, 71; and 'The Historical Geography of Bristol', *Geography*, 16 (1931), 175–86, both concise accounts of the development of Bristol.

16. *The Trade of Bristol in the Eighteenth Century*, edited by W. E. Minchington, Bristol Record Society, Vol. 20, 1957, xv. See also *ibid.*, 'Bristol—Metropolis of the West in the Eighteenth Century', *Transactions of the Royal Historical Society*, 5th Series, 4 (1954), 69–89.

17. C. M. MacInnes, 'Bristol and Overseas Expansion', *Bristol and Its Adjoining Counties*, *op. cit.*, 219–30, 228.

18. *Ibid.*, *A Gateway of Empire*, Bristol: Arrowsmith, 1939, 189–92; and C. N. Parkinson, *The Rise of the Port of Liverpool*, Liverpool: University Press, 91–6.

19. *Records Relating to the Society of Merchant Venturers of the City of Bristol in the Seventeenth Century*, edited by P. McGrath, Bristol Record Society, Vol. 17, 1952, 135 *ff.*

20. *Ibid.*, 152.

21. J. Latimer, *The History of the Society of Merchants of the City of Bristol*, Bristol: Arrowsmith, 1903, 206–7.

22. C. Wells, *A Short History of the Port of Bristol*, Bristol: Arrowsmith, 1909, 24.

23. *An Act for Improving and Rendering more Commodious the Port and Harbour of Bristol*, 43 Geo. III, c. 140, 1803.

24. By among others W. Champion (1767), J. Nickalls (1787), W. Jessop (1788), and Nickalls (1790). J. Latimer *op. cit.*, 208–14, and C. Wells, *op. cit.*, 24–30. Full details of these plans and their fates will be found in A. F. Williams, 'Bristol Port Plans and Improvement Schemes of the Eighteenth Century', *Transactions of the Bristol and Gloucestershire Archaeological Society*, in press.

25. E. Shiercliff, *Bristol and Hotwell Guide*, 1793, 60–1, quoted by C. Wells, *op. cit.*, 31–2.

26. Bristol Steam Navigation Company (1836); and Bristol City Line (1851)—Charles Hill & Sons pre 1879, see J. C. G. Hill, *Shipshape and Bristol Fashion*, Liverpool: Journal of Commerce and Shipping Telegraph, 1951.

27. Based on a *Report by the Bristol Chamber of Commerce, 1824.*

28. Based on a *Report by a Committee of the Corporation of the City of Bristol, 1847.*

29. L. Bruton, *Trade and Commerce of the City and Port of Bristol,* paper read to the British Association for the Advancement of Science, Bristol, 1875.

30. 3,270 tons gross, Brunel's iron ship which never returned to Bristol after once 'escaping', see N. R. P. Bonsor, *North Atlantic Seaway,* Prescot: Stephenson, 1955, 9–10.

31. T. Page and J. Hawkshaw, *Report on Whether the Plan for Converting the Bed of the Avon into a Floating Harbour would be Practicable . . . ,* July 26, 1860. For fuller details on this period see A. F. Williams, 'Bristol Port Plans and Improvement Schemes of the Nineteenth Century', *loc. cit., vide supra.*

32. From *gar,* a triangular spearhead, and *dene,* a valley (both Saxon), one of the rare *nom de pays* that has survived in England. See E. Wigan, *Portishead Parish History,* Taunton: Barnicott and Pearce, 1932.

33. Much is known of the sub-estuarine geology of the Shoots because this is the line of the Severn Railway Tunnel, see E. O. Jones, 'Description of a Section across the River Severn Based upon the Borings and Excavations Made for the Severn Tunnel', *Proceedings of the Geologists' Association,* 7 (1881–2), 339–51. See also J. Allen, *Scale Models in Hydraulic Engineering,* London: Longmans, 1947, Plate XVII.

34. J. Latimer, *The Annals of Bristol in the Nineteenth Century,* 1887, 386–7.

35. C. Wells, *op. cit.,* Chapter IX, 164–208.

36. The Severn-side docks did not catch up until 1913. In 1960 the percentages of net registered tonnage entering the port were: Avonmouth, 83; City, 12; and Portishead, 5.

37. *Bristol Port and Dock Commission Bill,* 1883, contains a useful diagram of trade in the critical period 1873–82. This Bill, which would have set up a port commission, was opposed by the Corporation and withdrawn.

38. R. H. Jones, 'The Administration of the Port of Bristol', *Public Administration,* 16 (1938), 314–23. Channel pilotage is the responsibility of a separate committee of the city council.

39. Notable as the third wet dock in Britain after those at Rotherhithe and Liverpool. The Romans, who ignored the site of Bristol, had a port at Sea Mills called Abona.

40. D. Ross-Johnson, 'The Port of Bristol in the Past and Present', *The Dock and Harbour Authority,* 4 (1923–4), 299–303, 303. This article includes many details of early port authority improvements.

41. A history of the firm of Charles Hill & Sons Ltd., owners of Albion Dockyard, has been published, J. C. G. Hill, *op. cit.*

42. D. Ross-Johnson, *op. cit.,* 303.

43. J. W. Kitchin, 'Notes on the Arrangements for Receiving Importations of Timber at Portishead Dock, Bristol', *Minutes of the Proceedings of the Institution of Civil Engineers,* 169 (1907), 337–48.

44. An analysis of the trade of Bristol before the Second World War is to be found in F. Walker, 'The Port of Bristol', *Economic Geography,* 15 (1939), 109–24; and up to 1951 in F. E. Cooke, *The Economic Development of the Port of Bristol 1900–1945,* Unpublished dissertation, M.Sc.(Econ.), University of London, 1953.

45. F. E. Cooke, *op. cit.,* 71.

46. Details on Bristol's industry are found in B. Little, *The City and County of Bristol,* London: Werner Laurie, Chaps. XIV and XV; A. G. Pugsley, 'Engineering in Bristol', *Bristol and Its Adjoining Counties, op. cit.,* 269–79; S. J. Jones (1946), *op. cit.,* 71 *et seq.;* and F. E. Cooke, Chapters 3 and 4, with remarks on the hinterland of the port, Chapter 6.

47. F. Walker, *op. cit.,* 124.

FURTHER REFERENCES FOR BRISTOL

Farr, G. E. 'Sea Mills Dock', *The Mariner's Mirror,* 25 (1939), 349–50.
——. 'Bristol Channel Pilotage', *The Mariner's Mirror,* 39 (1953), 27–44.
Harrison, G. *Bristol Cream* [a history of John Harvey & Sons Ltd.]. London: Batsford, 1955.

Lennard, E. W. 'Some Intimate Bristol Connections with the Overseas Empire', *Geography*, 16 (1931), 111–21.

Mackenzie, J. B. 'The Avonmouth Dock', *Minutes of the Proceedings of the Institution of Civil Engineers*, 55 (1878–9), 3–21.

Pugsley, A. G. *Some Contributions towards the Economic Development of Some Bristol Industries and of the Coalfield*. Unpublished M.A. Thesis, Bristol, 1929.

Rees, H. 'The Growth of Bristol', *Economic Geography*, 21 (1945), 269–75.

Walker, F. 'The Industries of Bristol', *Economic Geography*, 22 (1946), 174–92.

SOUTH WALES PORTS

Chapter 8

SWANSEA: WITH MILFORD HAVEN, PORT TALBOT, CARDIFF AND BARRY, AND NEWPORT

SOUTH WALES is well endowed with ports because the long axis of the rather elliptically shaped coalfield, extending for some sixty miles, happens to lie parallel to the coast.[1] Several sites on this coast have exclusive short hauls from separate parts of the coalfield, a centrifugal route pattern based on the diverging valleys of several separate river systems: the Tawe and Neath (Swansea); Avon (Port Talbot); Ely, Taff, and Rhymney (Cardiff); and Ebbw and Usk (Newport). This divergence[2] was accentuated by the rivalries of separate railway companies, one of which gave rise to the railway port of Barry, and another assisted the growth of Port Talbot.

Sand dune areas, or burrows, and marshes along the coasts have provided sites not only for port expansion, but also for the very large-scale industries of recent times. Such sites are not equally available everywhere along the coast, but, like the coalfield, they obviously lie parallel to it, again contributing to great contrasts in development among the ports.

On current trade figures Swansea is the only port of South Wales to qualify as a major port of Britain. Recent industrial developments will, however, increase further the trade of Milford Haven, Port Talbot, and Newport. This chapter is therefore not confined to Swansea. All the South Wales ports will be treated, from west to east; Swansea will, however, be given pride of place, and in discussing its oil trade, recent developments at Milford Haven will naturally arise.

Swansea[3]

The modern plan of the Port of Swansea is dominated by the eras of *dock elaboration* and *specialized quayage*, although the sites of the *primitive* port and its *marginal quay extension* can be made out, fossilized by later developments.

TABLE 64

Eras and Epochs in the Development of the Port of Swansea

Eras and Chief Areal Characteristics	Present-day Symbols
I *Primitive:* quay on west bank of the River Tawe	Street name of Quay Parade

Era ended by provision of a second quay, 1597	

| II *Marginal Quay Extension:* along west bank of River Tawe | Street name of Strand, and west side of abandoned site of old North Dock |

Era ended by opening of North Dock, 1852	

| IV *Dock Elaboration:* impounding of harbour and docks on reclaimed land below high tide level | Swansea Docks |
| V *Specialized Quayage:* coal shipment lay-out, oil jetties | Coal hoists; and oil jetties, Queen's Dock |

One of the earliest references to the *primitive* port has been traced in the borough papers for 1583 as

'. . . the perroge by the pill . . . nowe called the newe Key place . . .'[4]

The pill was a little creek (*cf.* Portishead Pill, p. 190) which entered the river where is now the inner wall of the half-tide basin to the old North Dock. The site of the sixteenth-century 'newe key place' is still called Quay Parade in modern Swansea. A very fine map (1771) by B. Jones[5] of the Tawe estuary (used as a basis for Fig. 54 inset) indicates the extent of *marginal quay extension.* By this time another quay had been erected just downstream of the *primitive* quay, and use of the river extended to a pottery 1,000 yards upstream (now Swansea High Street Station), including two other quays and three coal-shipping banks. On the east side of the river only one coal bank appears on the map.

At first, Swansea's hinterland was the agricultural land of the Gower Peninsula and west Glamorgan, but coal had been dug for domestic use at least as early as the fourteenth century; by the sixteenth century several thousand tons of coal, brought down in panniers on the backs of mules and horses, were being shipped from Swansea every year.[6] The second industry to have a major influence on the port's growth was copper smelting, begun in 1717 one and a half miles to the north, at Landore. Further copper works were established in the Swansea neighbourhood during the eighteenth century,[7] contributing to the growth of the port, where the increasing size of vessels progressively drew attention to the shoals in the river and its approaches. Eventually, the first Swansea Harbour Act of 1791 (31 Geo III c. 83) set up the Harbour Trustees.

> '. . . if there is one outstanding feature of the Trustees' earliest proceedings it is the dilatoriness, approaching indolence, which characterized their movements . . . our harbour lay from 1791 for more than sixty years in a mud-bound condition . . .'[8]

The Trustees did, however, build two piers to protect the mouth of the Tawe in 1809.

The Swansea Canal, 1798, penetrating seventeen miles up the Tawe valley, and the Tennant Canal, 1824, a junction canal to the Vale of Neath,[9] enabled the products of the hinterland to be brought more easily to the Tawe estuary. But the facilities of the port were not much improved until the New Cut of 1844, diverting the Tawe, allowed the former harbour in the bed of that river to be impounded as a floating harbour, a lay-out first suggested by T. Telford.[10] This was the North Dock of 1852, of which only the half-tide entrance now remains.

The physical expansion of the harbour began in 1859 with the opening of the South Dock and Basin on the burrows west of the Tawe estuary. Soon afterwards, the character of the metal-working in the district underwent a change with the decline of the copper industry.

> 'On returning to Swansea after an absence of some months, I am sorry to notice that the copper trade, hitherto the staple manufacture, is in a state of change and decadence. It is now admitted . . . that Australians and Chilians are able to produce and send home to England, and therefore to Europe, rough or bar copper at prices that, if continued, will probably beat the English makers out of the market. In the meantime *zinc* is taking the place of copper here, and not only are large quantities made, but some of the old copper works are being converted into zinc manufactories.' (1869)[11]

From being the chief copper smelting area of Great Britain Swansea became one of the chief zinc smelting areas. Copper manufacture is still carried on under the aegis of I.C.I. Metals at Landore where one thousand employees produce copper sheets and other metal goods incorporating copper. At Landore, too, in 1867 the Siemens process was first used to produce Siemens steel, the raw material for tin-plate, and this in turn provided the demand for iron ore and tin imported via the port. Sulphuric acid to clean the plates was obtained as a by-product from the then still extant copper industry.

A comparison of the modern plan of Swansea Docks with the original Tawe estuary shows that the port has been developed out into the sea, similar to developments at Cardiff and Newport. The King's Dock (1909), for example, which followed the Prince of Wales Dock (1881), was constructed on a site formerly well below high water of spring tides. First, a sea embankment was constructed and now forms part of the south quay of the dock. This was sited just seaward of half-way between the high and low water marks of spring tides and constructed 30 feet high for 1¾ miles to reclaim 393 acres. The dock was then excavated behind the reclaiming embankment.[12]

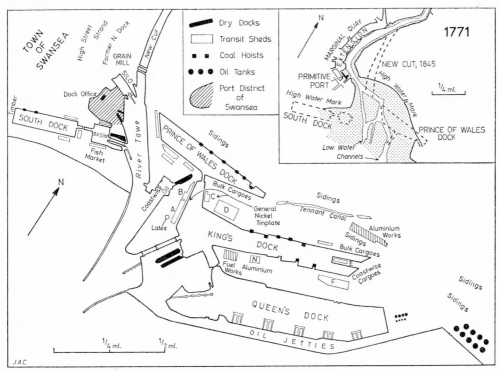

FIG. 54   The Port of Swansea: Inset—The Same in 1771
The inset map is based on that of B. Jones, *loc. cit.*, with details added for comparison.

Five miles north of Swansea in the Tawe Valley at Clydach, Dr. Ludwig Mond established the first nickel refinery in 1900. It is easy to see that such developments in industry would have repercussions on the port's trade. This was most clearly shown when the first major oil refinery to be built in the United Kingdom was opened in 1922 near Skewen, five miles north-east of Swansea. From the first it drew all supplies via the Queen's Dock (1920), which became an oil dock exclusively.[13]

Although the port approaches are well protected from the south-west by Mumbles Head, the River Tawe brings down much sediment, and the entrance channel has to be dredged right up to the North Dock Basin. Because of the great tidal range of twenty-eight feet, dredging is carried on day and night, as at other South Wales ports.

Swansea compares quite well with *Anyport*, despite the impossibility of *marginal quay elaboration* in the narrow River Tawe and the late date of the beginning of the *dock elaboration* era (1852). If the arbitrary rule for *simple lineal quayage* is strictly applied—an entrance of 750 feet to a quay 1,500 feet long—the era is not represented in Swansea. This may seem a rather too strict application of a subjective scheme. The South Dock has a quay 1,538 feet long, but its entrance is only 370 feet in length. The eastern docks have an entrance of 875 feet, but the longest straight quay usable throughout its length is only 1,207 feet. Nevertheless, this does emphasize the port's development as the servant not of a general cargo trade for a wide sector of the country, but for the rather specialized imports and exports of a restricted yet busy industrial hinterland. The decisive moment came when the port was able to throw off its dependence on the natural estuary site. This occurred rather late, in 1852, with the opening of the North Dock. Comparable emancipation from a tidal estuary had occurred at Cardiff in 1798, at Newport in 1842, and even at the much smaller Port Talbot in 1837.

The principal function of the North Dock Basin is to supply a berth on the north side for grain discharge by travelling suction plant to the Weavers Mills of J. Rank Ltd. The southern quay, called Corporation Quay because it belongs to the Corporation of Swansea, is used to discharge sand and gravel. All South Wales ports receive sand from small vessels called 'sand suckers', pumping river-washed sand with a very low saline content from the Flat Holm and Steep Holme area of the Bristol Channel (just east of the longitude of Cardiff).

A fish market is located on the south quay of the South Dock Basin, but the fishing trade is now restricted to inshore fishing with the withdrawal of steam trawling from Swansea in 1956. The small fishing vessels berth in the eastern arm of this basin. The South Dock itself is confined to use by sand suckers, small continental and coastal liners, and small vessels bringing Irish potatoes, since the entrance is only 370 feet long. There are two coal hoists on the north quay and a timber yard at the western end of the dock.

The Prince of Wales Dock has a sand and gravel berth and six coal hoists on its north quay, facing an open berth on the south-east where bulk cargoes are unloaded: pig iron, scrap iron, and pitwood. The south and south-west quays deal with coastal and continental liners, like the South Dock, via four transit sheds. The Tennant Canal, east of the dock, is now used only for industrial water supply.

The King's Dock also has five coal hoists on its north quay with an open quay for the bulk grabbing of ores and scrap iron to the east. E and F Sheds deal respectively with continental liners loading and discharging, and with vessels loading for

South America. N Shed deals with aluminium imports and exports,[14] while the Graigola Works is an experimental works of the National Coal Board. Perhaps the busiest berths in the port are those opposite A, B, and D Sheds, with C Shed Berth as a convenient standby. That most useful cargo tinplate is the most important commodity. A 'parcel' of 1,350 sheets of tinplate, measuring only 3 × 2 × 1½ feet, may yet weigh nearly a ton. So neat to handle and store and yet so heavy, tinplate is much sought after by steamship owners as bottom cargo. This is undoubtedly an attraction contributing to Swansea's extensive liner traffic. Two-thirds of Britain's tinplate is made by one company alone—the Steel Company of Wales Ltd.—which between 1947 and 1951 constructed modern tinplate works at Trostre (two miles east of Llanelly) and Velindre (four miles north of Swansea) within ten miles of the docks.[15]

Another manufactured export cargo is galvanized plates (the raw material for the galvanizing, zinc concentrate, having been grabbed out of ships' holds at one of the bulk-handling berths). Nickel copper matte is a regular import at these berths for the nickel refining industry. Other exports from D Shed Berth are cars (from the Midlands) and other manufactured goods, largely from one of the trading estates set up in South Wales just before and just after the Second World War.[16] Such exports may catch a cargo liner attracted in the first place by the tinplate as a bottom cargo. In addition, liquid latex can be discharged at A and B Sheds for feeding by pipeline to a latex depot to the south.[17] The peninsula between the main entrance lock and the river is fully occupied right to the tip, with a riverside oil wharf for discharge of refined petroleum (Regent Oil Co.).

Then Queen's Dock is a discharge terminal for the Llandarcy[18] Oil Refinery, Skewen, five miles to the east, served by pipeline. If *Anyport* had jetties in deep water, the Queen's Dock would provide the nearest analogy, five jetties as isolated as possible in a dock system, impounded because of the average tidal range of twenty-eight feet. The size of tanker is restricted by the entrance lock to about 25,000 deadweight tons. The approach channel in Swansea Bay could not in any case be deepened to take super-tankers, and this caused the operators of Llandarcy, the British Petroleum Oil Company Ltd. to seek a tanker terminal in Milford Haven on the Pembroke peninsula.

Milford Haven's relationship with the Port of Swansea might seem at first sight very much like the relationship of Finnart (on Loch Long) with the Port of Glasgow. The same company, British Petroleum, sought a deep-water site on the south side of the Haven to allow tankers of the 65,000 deadweight tons class and upward to supply the Llandarcy refinery. Two points of physical geography, however, show great contrast. Whereas Loch Long joins the Clyde estuary in the sea lochs area, Milford Haven is an estuary entirely divorced from the river systems of South Wales. Secondly, while Loch Long is a glacially eroded fiord, Milford Haven is a ria, an estuary eroded by a river, the conjoint East and West Cleddau, and then drowned by the rise in sea-level since glacial times. This is an important contrast. The sides of a fiord rise steeply to highland country with no extensive flat slopes close to water. A ria may have flat plateau surfaces close at hand which the rivers forming the estuary have not had time to destroy. The shores of Milford Haven rise up gently to a surface at about 200 feet, and these gentle slopes have provided a site for an Esso Oil Refinery north of the Haven, with its jetty almost opposite the jetty serving the Llandarcy refinery by pipeline. The Esso Company Ltd. developed the Fawley refinery on Southampton Water first because it had a land situation close to markets. With the Suez crisis came the concept of the super-tanker in 1956. It was impossible to increase the berthing facilities at Fawley, so that a favourable water site for a deep-water marine terminal became of more consequence than a favourable land situation. Milford Haven is a sheltered harbour, with a minimum depth in the approaches of as much as 54 feet. An oil port has been formed. Since 1960 oil has been transmitted via the 62-mile pipeline to Llandarcy, beginning only six weeks after the first tanker berthed at the Esso Refinery terminal opposite. The numbers of people employed are small because of the high degree of automation at the oil refinery—about 50 at

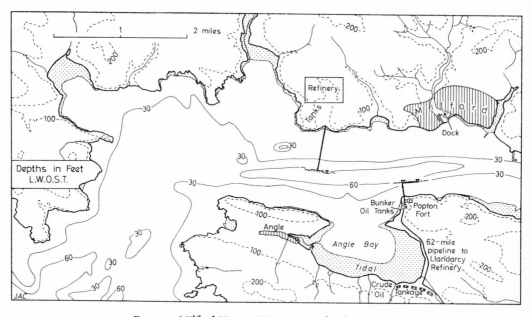

FIG. 55   Milford Haven: Water Sites of Oil Terminals

The minimum depth in the approaches is 46 feet, with 54 feet available at the jetty heads. The berths are protected from the prevailing south-westerly winds by the Angle Peninsula where another jetty could be sited. But this area, like the rest of the shores of the Haven, west of Milford, is within the Pembrokeshire Coast National Park where industrial developments provoke strong opposition.

the terminals and 600 at the refinery—though a petro-chemical industry may develop alongside the refinery. All this development has been permitted in a National Park, and careful landscaping and adaptation of installations has been carried out,[19] with the port itself regulated by the Milford Haven Conservancy Board set up in 1958. A project for a second oil refinery (Regent Refining Company) and a third oil terminal on the south shore, south-east of Milford town, to begin operations in 1964, might make Milford Haven the largest oil port in Europe. These Milford Haven developments and the water site restrictions at Swansea have prevented any spectacular developments at the Queen's Dock which has a shelving bank on the north side, though no doubt with the refinery's increased through-put, export of refined products via the dock will increase. After 1961 some of these will be petro-chemicals from the plant constructed alongside the Llandarcy Refinery.

In Swansea itself, commencing at the site of the 'newe Key place' of 1583, now Quay Parade, there is a small but easily traced port district between the half-tide—basins of the North and South Docks. The North Dock was filled in during 1930, and the southern portion is used as a road transport depot and car park. It seems likely that future use of the remainder of this central site, embracing an area which once comprised the whole of the port before 1850, will be for warehousing and light industry.

TABLE 65

Fifteen Most Valuable Foreign Trade Imports into Swansea, 1960

	Value £ Million
Crude Petroleum	23·0
Nickel and Nickel Alloys	15·4
Unwrought Aluminium	7·6
Strip Mill Coils for Re-rolling	2·0
Rubber Latex	1·5
Refined Petroleum	1·3
Pig-iron	1·2
Sawn Timber	·9
Ferro-alloys	·9
Zinc Ore	·9
Cobalt Oxides	·6
Iron and Steel Ingots	·6
Uncoated Iron and Steel Billets, Slabs, Plates, and Sheets	·5
Nickel Oxide	·3
Selenium	·3
Total of all Imports ...	61·1

(1·4 per cent of total U.K. imports by value)

TABLE 66

Fifteen Most Valuable Foreign Trade Exports from Swansea, 1960

	Value £ Million
Tinplate	25·1
Coal	5·1
Terneplates and Galvanized Sheets	2·7
Uncoated Iron and Steel Plates and Sheets ...	2·2
Metalliferous Ores and Scrap	1·3
Inorganic Chemicals	1·2
Laundering Machinery	1·1
Lubricating Oil	1·0
Gas Oil	·9
Diesel Oil	·5
Electrical Machinery	·4
Kerosene	·4
Road Vehicles	·4
Iron and Steel Hoop and Strip	·4
Lead and Lead Alloy	·3
Total of all Exports ...	57·7

(1·7 per cent of total U.K. exports by value)

The two lists of most valuable commodities in Swansea's trade show the importance of the immediate hinterland. Coal exports appear quite important because the western part of the coalfield producing anthracite—a premium fuel still in great overseas demand for central heating—has recently been subject to some of the largest capital developments by the National Coal Board.

Port Talbot

If the hinterland for Swansea's heavy, bulk cargoes was small, this applies even more completely to all cargoes at Port Talbot, which has a very restricted hinterland, and deals with hardly any general packaged goods at all. From the Rhondda watershed the River Avon, twelve miles long, drains south-westward to the coast. The valley is narrow and steep-sided, and at first pack-horses were used to move coal from the coalfield to the coast near the present site of the so-called Llewellyn's Quay. A tram line was constructed along the route in 1757, and in 1811 iron was first imported for newly-established iron works in the Avon valley. By 1839 copper was being landed at Copper Works Wharf, close to the site of the present Margam Wharf, for works in the Avon valley at Cwmavon. As at Swansea, coal export and copper import led to the growth of the port.

TABLE 67

Eras and Epochs in the Development of Port Talbot

Eras and Chief Areal Characteristics	Present-day Symbols
I *Primitive:* simple quay in a lagoon	Llewellyn's Quay

Era ended by construction of separate quay for copper works by 1839

II *Marginal Quay Extension:* Copper Works Wharf	Nil: the wharf was close to the site of the present Margam Wharf

Era ended by converting the lagoon into a Floating Harbour, 1837

III *Marginal Quay Elaboration:* quay development on edges of impounded lagoon	Site of Old Lock; Crown and Talbot Wharves; present course of Avon estuary

Era ended by extending the harbour towards Avon estuary, 1898

IV *Dock Elaboration:* south-westward extension of water area	More rational shape of south-westward extension compared with the rest of the water area
VI *Specialized Quayage:* quays lengthened and straightened in former lagoon	Steel Works Wharf and Margam Wharf

The estuary of the Avon entered a lagoon, and had to break through the barrier of sand-dunes to reach the sea, along a line south-east of its present course. These dunes are still visible near the present dock entrance. By an Act of 1836, the Aberavon Harbour Company, which had received powers to improve the lagoon as a harbour, became styled the Port Talbot Company, because of the financial interest of C. R. M. Talbot M.P. of Margam Castle, who owned part of the land around the site.[20] The company provided the present exit of the Avon[21] to the west of the lagoon which in 1837 was converted into a Floating Harbour by means of a lock, 150 × 50 × 26 feet. This was doubled in length in 1874. The influence of the copper industry and of the Talbot family in the nineteenth-century development of the port is seen in the distribution of the £129,000 shares value of the Port Talbot Company in 1876: Trustees of the Company of English Copper Miners,[22] £66,000; C. R. M. Talbot, £63,000. No further major improvements were considered until after the death of C. R. M. Talbot in 1890.[23]

By an Act of 1894 the port became the property of the Port Talbot Railway and Dock Company (a Miss Emily Talbot holding many of the shares) with two objectives: to make railway connection between port and coalfield, and to get bigger vessels into the port. A railway thirty-three miles long was built via the Dyffryn

Valley, the water area was extended to the south-west, and the present lock constructed in 1898 (450 × 60 × 33¾ feet). After this *dock elaboration, specialized quayage* was foreshadowed with the establishment of the Port Talbot Steel Works, 1901, and the Margam Iron and Steel Works, 1916. Besides contributing to the further trade of the port for iron ore import, these two works, among others, were incorporated in 1947 to form the Steel Company of Wales Ltd., which in 1951 opened the Abbey Works, along four miles of the coastlands east of Port Talbot, and improved the Margam Works. Such great developments have called for the *specialized quayage* of

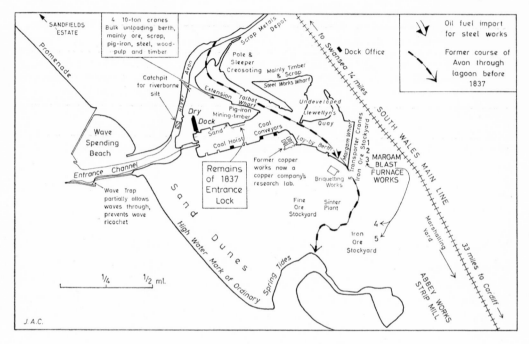

FIG. 56   Port Talbot: Annotated Diagram

Margam Wharf, 1,236 feet long, leased to the steel company, which can deal simultaneously with any two of the largest vessels to use the dock. This is one of the few quays in the country with twenty-four hours a day availability for working. Five transporter cranes unload to a stockyard serving three blast furnaces direct and two more by overhead conveyor. Other modern functions are indicated on the annotated diagram (Fig. 56).

The entrance channel and lock at present limit the size of iron ore carriers to an overall length of 427 feet and 58 feet beam, carrying 8,000–10,000 tons of ore. The normal depth of water in the dock is 27 feet 6 inches. For flotation clearance 1 foot 6 inches are allowed; and as the dock water is practically fresh, a further 8 inches must be allowed against a vessel's salt-water draught. This reduces the maximum permissible loaded draught to 25 feet 4 inches. Twenty-three ore carriers have been built to this limit, with, in addition, a beam clearance within the lock of only 1 foot. The entrance channel is maintained to a level of 3 feet above the dock cill. For flotation clearance 1 foot 6 inches are also allowed in the channel, and on occasions a further allowance must be made for swell, so that it is usually considered that only tides of 31 feet and upwards are practicable for the acceptance of maximum-size vessels. Constant dredging operations maintain the entrance channel, and with the provision of a diesel-electric suction dredger it is the intention to maintain the level to 1 foot above cill and thus enable the ore carriers to dock on 70 per cent of the tides.

The chairman of the Steel Company of Wales Ltd. estimated in January, 1961, that the annual consumption by the firm of imported ore would rise to 4¼ million tons and perhaps beyond. In order that Port Talbot may be able to deal with ore carriers of greater than 10,000 tons burden, a plan has been prepared to provide, adjacent to Port Talbot Dock a tidal basin, in which the largest ore carriers at present envisaged would be able to discharge at all states of the tide. An Act of Parliament would be necessary to set the plan in motion. Table 68 shows the dominance of iron ore imports in the trade of Port Talbot.

TABLE 68

The Major Items of the Foreign Trade of Port Talbot
(incl. Briton Ferry, Neath Abbey, and Porthcawl), 1960

Imports	Value £ Million	
Iron Ore	15·2	
Pig-iron	1·8	
Pulp	·6	
Calcium Carbide	·4	
Magnesite	·3	
Mining Timber	·1	
Total of all Imports ...	18·9	(0·4 per cent of total U.K. imports by value)

Exports	Value £ Million	
Uncoated Iron and Steel Plates and Sheets ...	5·1	
Tinplate	·5	
Coal	·2	
Non-ferrous Base Metals	·1	
Total of all Exports ...	6·4	(0·2 per cent of total U.K. exports by value)

The hills rise very steeply behind the port. This presented great difficulty in expanding the town and at the same time reserving adequate areas for coal mining. So Port Talbot was eventually forced to expand on to the sand dunes west of the river, with houses for 20,000 people provided on the Sandfields Estate.

Cardiff and Barry

Like Swansea, the Port of Cardiff began as a *primitive* quay on an outside bend of a meander of its river. In the early nineteenth century the 'Old Quay' on the River Taff occupied the same site on the east bank as the key shown on John Speed's map of Cardiff in 1610. The *primitive* quay site has now been left high and dry, indicated today only by the name of Quay Street, the first transverse route inland. The meander was cut off when the River Taff was straightened in 1850 to allow the Great Western Railway to build its General Station in the bed of the river.[24] By 1794, four years before the Swansea Canal was opened, the Glamorganshire Canal had penetrated 25 miles up the valley of the Taff, necessitating a rise through 49 locks of 543 feet, and linked Cardiff with its hinterland as far as Merthyr. Canal barges carrying twenty-five tons of iron soon replaced the road wagons which could carry only two tons of iron ore even on the turnpike completed about 1780.[25] Canal wharves became more important than the Town Quay, particularly when the canal had been extended seawards in 1798 and a 'sea lock' provided for sea-going vessels to lie in the widened canal near its entrance (103 feet × 27 feet, the first dock in South Wales). But the sea approach was winding, two miles long, and completely dry for three hours each tide. Only those vessels of less than 200 tons could enter the canal.

During the nineteenth century the local iron ore resources around Merthyr declined, but coal exports rose dramatically, about seven per cent every year. Cardiff had an advantage for coal export over the rest of the South Wales ports. The River Taff is the master stream of the central part of the South Wales coalfield, uniting five other streams, near Pontypridd, with easy communication to the River Rhymney system via an elbow in this river six miles north of Cardiff. From these deep, narrow valleys the mines reached the coal seams beneath the bleak sandstone plateaus. In this area are found all types of coal, except anthracite, ironically enough the type for which there has been the steadiest overseas demand. Another transverse track to the port was provided in 1841, the Taff Vale Railway, and thereafter railways became the dominant arteries along the mining valleys.[26]

To deal with the rising trade, the Bute West Dock had been opened in 1839, at the sole expense of one individual, the second Marquess of Bute, who wished to develop his mineral workings and make an outlet to the sea for his estates.[27] The site chosen was on the East Moors alluvium, south-east of the town alongside the canal.[28]

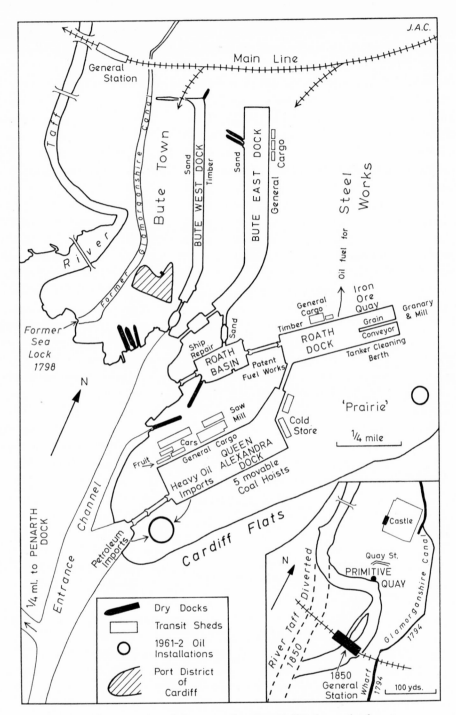

FIG. 57   The Port of Cardiff: Inset—The River Taff Before and After 1850

Further docks were provided during the nineteenth century, culminating in the Queen Alexandra Dock, 1907, on a site between high and low water with a further wide peninsula to the south, built out almost to the pre-existing low water mark on Cardiff Flats. The quays and entrance lock were founded on Keuper Marl, fifty feet below the mud surface. Coal exports called all the Bute Docks at Cardiff into being, a trade built upon the reputation of Welsh Steam [Raising] Coal, first exploited from the famous 'four-foot' seam near Merthyr in 1824 and first sent to Cardiff for export to London the same year. The bald facts of Tables 69 and 70 are the headlines of the port's development and that of its annexes, Penarth and Barry.

TABLE 69

Eras and Epochs in the Development of the Port of Cardiff

	Eras and Chief Areal Characteristics	*Present-day Symbols*
I	*Primitive:* quay on east bank of the River Taff	Street name of Quay Street

Era ended by provision of canal wharves, 1794 and after 1798

II	*Marginal Quay Extension:* canal-side wharves	Names of East and West Canal Wharves

Era ended by opening of Bute West Dock, 1839

IV	*Dock Elaboration:* on marshes and below high tide level	Bute Docks
V	*Simple Lineal Quayage:* straight quays with adjacent transit shed	General cargo quays, Roath and Queen Alexandra Docks
VI	*Specialized Quayage:* coal shipment lay-out, iron ore handling lay-out; oil traffic	Coal hoists; Iron Ore Quay, Roath Dock; Oil Terminal Berths

TABLE 70

Coal Exports and Port Developments:
Cardiff, Penarth, and Barry
(Total coal exports in thousand tons in bold face type)

1824	First substantial coal exports
1839	West Bute Dock, Cardiff, opened
1840	**166**
1850	**731**
1856	Bute Tidal Harbour (now part of Roath Basin)
1858	East Bute Dock
1859	Ely Tidal Harbour
1860	**1,915**
1865	Penarth Dock
1870	Coal staiths erected on east bank of River Taff
1870	**3,111**
1874	Roath Basin

1880	**5,861**
1887	Roath Dock
1889	Barry Dock No. 1
1890	**13,903**
1898	Barry Dock No. 2
1900	**23,129**
1907	Queen Alexandra Dock
1910	**29,471**
1913	**34,213** (peak year)
1920	**14,633**
1930	**16,161**
1936	Penarth Dock closed
1938	**10,807**
1960	**996** of which Cardiff, **373**; Barry, **623**

Following dissatisfaction with the Bute Dock facilities, a group of industrialists under the style of the Penarth Harbour, Dock, & Railway Company began construction of Penarth Dock, one and a quarter miles south-west of Bute West Dock, immediately south of the River Ely estuary, which the company converted into a tidal harbour for coal shipment in 1859. A railway six miles in length connected the installations with the Taff Vale Rail Company's main line, to which the whole undertaking was leased in 1865. Coal was overwhelmingly the dominant trade at Penarth, where quicker transhipment was claimed because dock and railway were in one hand.[29] With the decline of coal shipments, Penarth Dock has been closed to commercial shipping since 1936, for only colliers used its quayage; although there is coastwise import of oil at Ely Tidal Harbour. Both the Penarth and the Cardiff water sites are sheltered by the Liassic limestone promontory of Penarth Head. This is the first solid rock encountered on the northern shore of the Bristol Channel west of the Severn tunnel.

Barry developed a little later, also as a coal shipping outport to Cardiff, and also because of dissatisfaction with the Bute Docks when an additional penny a ton levy was made in 1882 to raise finance for the construction of the Roath Dock. The site chosen for the new port was in the lee (*i.e.* to the north-east) of Barry Island, which in fact had become partially linked to the shore by the deltaic deposits of a small stream, the Cadoxton River. David Davies of Cwmparc Colliery, Rhondda Valley, was one of the leaders of the Cardiff coal freighters, angered by the delays at Cardiff Docks, who saw advantages in an independent port with shorter approaches to deep water, even if the rail haul from the Rhondda Valleys were to be a little longer.

'We have five million tons of coal, and we can fill a thundering good dock the first day we open it.' [David Davies, 1882][30]

'It has been said that our railroad to the dock is very much longer than the road to the new Roath Dock [from the Rhondda] . . . our road to Barry is a mile and a half longer . . .' [David Davies, 1889][31]

The railway built to serve the first dock runs parallel to the inner edge of the former Barry Sound. Here the first dock was sited and made rather wide so that its quays could have foundations on solid ground on each side of the former delta or lagoon. The southern quay has its foundations on Lias shales on the downthrow side of the fault that forms the steep northern slopes to Barry Island.[32] The curious curved outline of the first dock represents the extent of the original marsh silt of a lagoon, with solid rock 55–60 feet below the original surface.[33]

Methods of coal shipment have developed according to the steepness of the land immediately behind the shipping point or the amount of relatively flat land transverse to the shoot.[34] An early method on the Tyne was to suspend a coal wagon in a

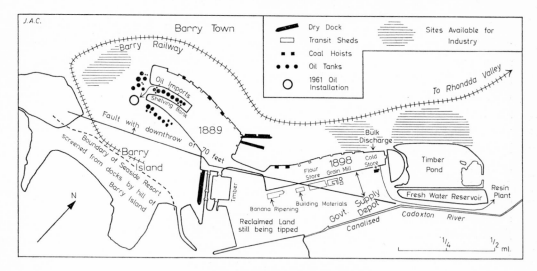

FIG. 58   Barry Docks: Annotated Diagram

cradle, counterbalanced by a heavy weight or suspended from sheerlegs, and lower it to deck level where coal was discharged into ships' holds by bottom doors in the wagon (Fig. 7). Where a river like the Tyne is deeply incised, elevated jetties (or staiths) could be built up over the river to deliver the coal by bottom-discharging wagons indirectly into holds by means of a hopper which feeds (perhaps by conveyor) inclined chutes or spouts. This method is economical, because no hoisting is necessary, the staiths can be made self-acting by gravity. It became customary at north-east ports where rivers have steep banks, even being adopted at Blyth where timber staging provides the height over the flat land adjacent to the tidal basin. Hard north-east coal will tolerate rough handling. The modern variant of this gravity method is illustrated at Whitehill Point Coal Staiths (opened in 1955) where the wagons are rotated in a cradle through 170° at high level with the coal travelling

222

British Transport Commission
PLATE IX   PORT OF SWANSEA
Looking north-east, with docks on reclaimed land either side
of the estuary of the River Tawe, *cf.* Fig. 54.

British Transport Commission

PLATE X TWO SOUTH WALES PORTS

Above: Port Talbot, looking east, *cf.* Fig. 56.

Below: Newport, looking north, *cf.* Fig. 59.

British Transport Commission

on a conveyor to a pivot-house, thence to a radial shipping gantry with a shipping boom which can be moved vertically or laterally on a semicircular track (Fig. 7). At South Wales ports special anti-breakage appliances are used to protect the more friable coal (except anthracite).

With shipment points on flat dock quaysides some form of hoist, up to seventy feet, is necessary, with the coal then tipped through end-doors. At Goole compartment boats are hoisted, and at Queen Alexandra Dock, Cardiff and North Dock, Newport movable coal hoists give greater flexibility of working, moving the hoist along the quay rather than the vessel. The next method also overcomes the lack of natural relief adjacent to the shipping point. At Port Talbot, Grimsby, and Jarrow Staiths on the Tyne, the wagons are tipped some distance back from the quay with the coal transported to the ship and raised above the hatches by an inclined conveyor belt to a quayside tower. This method was first used in Britain at Victoria Dock, Hull, just before the First World War. With modern equipment using any of the last three methods about 600 tons can be shipped per hour, while two radial conveyors installed at Immingham Dock in 1959 have the fastest discharge in Britain; each is able to dispatch up to 1,350 tons of coal per hour.

The decline in British coal exports after the First World War has been ascribed to competition from the U.S.A., development of hydro-electricity on the continent of Europe, the change-over to oil in ships' bunkers, and France's dependence on German reparations coal all contributing to a contracting market in the 1920's,

TABLE 71

Shipments of Coal, Coke, and Patent Fuel from South Wales Ports

				1938	1960
Aggregate shipments		...	...	19,562,000 tons	2,638,000 tons
				100%	100%
Barry	...	...	...	29%	24%
Cardiff	...	...	...	27%	20%
Newport	...	...	...	16%	13%
Port Talbot	...	...	...	8%	2%
Swansea	...	...	...	19%	41%

aggravated by the General Strike of 1926 and the world financial crisis in 1931. At Cardiff in 1936, for example, $97\frac{1}{2}$ per cent of the port's exports by weight was still coal, coke, or patent fuel, with imports accounting for only 15 per cent of the total trade, and general cargo forming only 8 per cent of the total trade.[35] The position at Barry became even more difficult, because Cardiff has a better land situation to deal with imports for central South Wales.

The first example of the move of the iron and steel industry to the coast occurred at Cardiff in 1891, when the Dowlais[36] Works moved to a site east of Bute East Dock.

'The decision to erect new works on the seaboard was a new departure, decided upon by Mr. G. T. Clark in consequence of the fact that the iron ores now used [rich non-argillaceous, and non-phosphoric required for the Bessemer process, not available from the then declining South Wales iron resources] are chiefly imported from Spain, and by having the works near the sea, inland carriage is saved on the raw material, and also on the manufactured iron and steel.' (1896)[37]

In addition to the advantage of having an iron and steel works adjoining the dock estate, Cardiff is nearer to the West Midlands industrial area than Barry and might expect to share a little more in any rise of general cargo exports. Both ports have recently-completed oil installations that will add to their trade, and each has several sites available to industry near the dockside, notably the 130-acre site at Cardiff, the centre of which is known at present by the significant name of 'The Prairie'. The absence of labour troubles has encouraged some trade, notably that of banana imports into Barry No. 2 Dock.[38]

The port business district of Cardiff is very compact near the pierhead, between the original dock and the abandoned Glamorganshire Canal. Immediately to the north is Bute Town, a narrow rectangle three blocks wide and half a mile long, with the axis along the once-fashionable Bute Street. The area developed as a mariners' and port workers' district, later becoming notorious as Tiger Bay, and now showing remarkable examples of urban renewal.

TABLE 72

Ten Most Valuable Foreign Trade Imports into Cardiff (incl. Barry Dock and Penarth), 1960

	Value £ Million	
Iron Ore and Concentrates	5·2	
Bananas	4·6	
Butter	4·3	
Wheat	3·9	
Sawn Softwood	3·2	
Fuel Oil	1·2	
Polyvinyl Chloride	1·1	
Cheese	1·0	
Mining Timber	·8	
Canned Pig Products	·7	
Total of all Imports ...	37·5	(0·9 per cent of total U.K. imports by value)

TABLE 73

Ten Most Valuable Foreign Trade Exports from Cardiff (incl.
Barry Dock and Penarth), 1960

	Value £ Million
Cars	4·3
Coal	1·3
Ships and Boats	·6
Manufactured Fuel	·6
Coated Iron and Steel Plates and Sheets ...	·4
Coke	·4
Chemicals	·3
Tractors	·2
Petroleum	·2
Steel Wire Rods	·2
Total of all Exports ...	10·5

(0·3 per cent of total U.K. exports by value)

Newport[39]

The development of Newport is remarkably similar to that of Swansea and Cardiff. Instead of the usual table of 'Eras and Epochs', it is perhaps useful to pick out some of the points of similarity in the three ports.

TABLE 74

Some Developments at Newport vis-à-vis Swansea and Cardiff

	Swansea	Cardiff	Newport
Canal Link	Swansea Canal (1798)	Glamorganshire Canal (1794)	Monmouthshire and Brecon Canal (1796)
Primitive Port on Banks of ...	Tawe	Taff	Usk
Secondary River Estuary not Used	Neath[40]	Rhymney	Ebbw
First Dock of Dock Elaboration	North Dock,	Bute West Dock,	Town Dock,
Era	1852	1839	1842
First Expansion on to Tidal	1859,	1856,	1875,
Mudflat	South Dock	Bute Tidal Harbour	Alexandra North Dock
Simple Lineal Quayage ...		Queen Alexandra Dock, 1907	Alexandra South Dock, 1914

The above table shows that Newport developed as fast as Cardiff in the first half of the nineteenth century. Indeed, its coal exports increased much faster than those of Swansea, faster even at first than those of Cardiff, which might seem surprising in that Newport, eccentric to the coalfield, has only two valley routes and rather longer hauls from pithead. Two factors at first favoured Newport. The eastern part of the coalfield extending into Monmouthshire had fewer iron resources, so that the coal instead of being entirely used in local smelting was available for export.

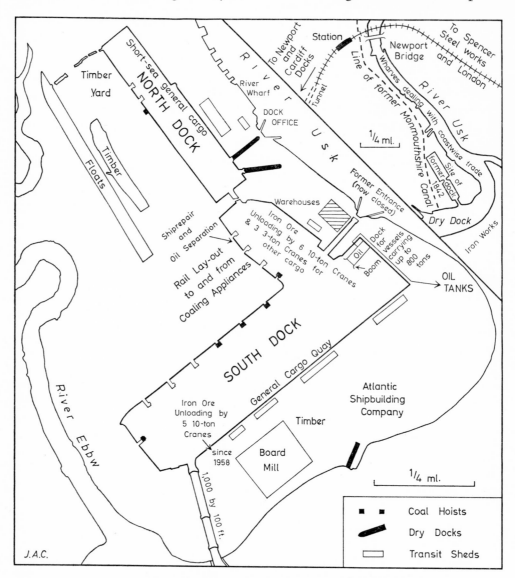

FIG. 59 Newport Docks: Inset—River Usk Wharves

The wharves occupy the original *primitive* site and *marginal quay extension* at Newport. The main entrance to the docks is 2·8 miles due south of Newport Bridge (shown on the inset).

Secondly, a provision in the second Monmouthshire Canal Act of 1792 stated that coal shipped at Newport could be delivered *duty free* to all ports eastward of the Holms (islands in the Bristol Channel, just east of the longitude of Cardiff).[41] This privilege lasted until 1831 when coastwise duties were repealed. During this time of privilege and of canal connections with the coalfield hinterlands, Newport more than held its own, since many tramways were linked to the canal in the eastern valleys. For example, in the 1819–30 period the coal exports from Swansea, Cardiff, and Newport were (in thousand tons): 2,508; 650; and 3,033, respectively. By 1850 with the decline of the use of local iron ore and the coming of the railway, which tied many valleys closely to Cardiff, the stage was set for Cardiff to overhaul Newport in coal exports.[42]

Here coal shipments proceeded from wharves on the west bank of the Usk, until the Town Dock was provided just east of the exit of the canal into the Severn, a parallel site to that of the first dock at Cardiff in relation to the Glamorganshire Canal. Like the first dock at Swansea, this dock has been filled in (1930), but its entrance lock is still discernible. The site of the dock is now partially used for pit-wood storage. From the southern end near the river looking north, there is a vivid impression of what Newport must have looked like one hundred years ago; for the modern town is foreshortened between the viewpoint and the Black Mountains and Brecon Beacons to the north. Between these hills ran the Monmouthshire and Brecon Canal, with connecting tramways, once the chief artery for coal exports from the valleys.[43]

The increasing coal exports, supplemented by iron ore for the furnaces of the eastern part of the coalfield, called forth the progressive development at the Alexandra Dock site: North Dock, 1875, most northerly 20 acres of South Dock, 1893; 48 acres of Southern Extension, 1907; and the remaining 28 acres and entrance lock, 1914. This dock, L-shaped to a 1,000-foot long entrance, is remarkably like the enlargement of Tilbury Docks; but at Newport the south quay is even longer, and a magnificent example of *simple lineal quayage*, 3,580 feet in one line. This is the longest example of *simple lineal quayage* in South Wales, and the entrance lock was the longest in the world when it was opened in 1914. The great foresight of this design appears to be due to John Macaulay, the General Manager of the Alexandra Dock and Railway Company at the time of construction. In 1914 he wrote:

'Perhaps the most convenient form for a dock is the rectangular; and there is no doubt that continuous quays in docks of this kind are preferable and more efficient in every way than those with breaks in them; since, in the former case, advantage can be taken of the whole of the quay space, whatever the size of the vessel may be that requires a berth. . . . The deepening of the Suez Canal to 10 metres, and the projected depth of the Panama Canal, being constructed by the United States Government, of 35 to 40 feet, with locks from 800 to 1,000 feet, are sufficient indications as to what is considered necessary in the present and future great trade routes. . . . Flights of imagination today may be sober facts tomorrow, and while there may be some reluctance to provide for more than the needs of the immediate future . . . reconstruction [is] the more expensive alternative.'[44]

The development of Newport is comparable with that of *Anyport*, except that the *specialized quayage* has had to be compressed within an existing dock system, as at other South Wales ports, because of the great tidal range. How Newport grew is a similar story to that of Swansea and Cardiff, but its import/export pattern of trade is now in opposite proportions to that of other South Wales ports.

TABLE 75

Foreign Trade at Newport and other South Wales Ports, 1960
(Value £ Million)

	Swansea, Port Talbot, and Cardiff (incl. Barry and Penarth) Together	Newport
Imports	117·5	28·3
Exports	74·6	34·3

If the land situation of Cardiff is central for distribution of imports to South Wales, Newport is nearer the industrial Midlands for exported cargoes.

TABLE 76

Ten Most Valuable Foreign Trade Imports into Newport, 1960

	Value £ Million	
Unwrought Aluminium[45]	9·9	
Iron Ore	4·2	
Strip Mill Coils for Re-rolling	2·8	
Unwrought Aluminium Alloys	2·6	
Iron and Steel Blooms, Billets, and Sheet Bars	2·4	
Plastics	1·1	
Sawn Softwood	·7	
Mining Timber	·4	
Bauxite	·4	
Steel Wire Rods	·3	
Total of all Imports ...	28·3	(0·7 per cent of total U.K. imports by value)

228

TABLE 77

Ten Most Valuable Foreign Trade Exports from Newport, 1960

	Value £ Million
Tinplate	9·5
Uncoated Iron and Steel Plates and Sheets ...	4·7
Cars	4·1
Iron and Steel Tubes and Pipes	2·4
Iron and Steel Hoop and Strip	1·4
Plastics	·7
Complete Tractors	·7
Ships and Boats	·6
Steel Wire Rods	·5
Metal-working Machinery	·4
Total of all Exports ...	34·3

(1·4 per cent of total U.K. exports by value)

These figures refer to the end of an era with iron as the leading import by weight in the trade of Newport. Henceforward, 'overwhelming' rather than 'leading' will be a more appropriate adjective. Through the South Dock overseas imports of iron ore will increase for the developing Spencer Works of Richard Thomas & Baldwins Ltd. (a nationalized undertaking). The imports of iron ore before 1961 were destined almost entirely for the Ebbw Vale works of this company which was rebuilt there in 1936 with State aid. In 1958 the Government announced two major semi-continuous strip mill projects, each to produce initially 500,000 tons a year, one in Scotland at the Ravenscraig Works, Motherwell, the other in South Wales. Here the site is actually in Monmouthshire, east of Newport, just south of the London–Newport railway line and extending for five miles along the estuarine alluvial levels. The works is the first in Britain to be built on a new site (no part of which had hitherto been used for steel-making) since the war.[46]

'Stage 1' of this project calls for a continuous hot strip mill with a capacity of finished strip of up to 4·5 million tons a year. There is room on the site for a doubling of the plant as at present planned. From Fig. 60 it is seen that in 1960 Newport was nearing the limit of the economic capacity of one ore-unloading berth. Since 1958 the port has in fact been equipped with a second iron ore discharging berth at the west end of the southern quay. The diagram shows that the berths will be intensively used to cope with Stage 1,[47] which calls for imports of $3\frac{1}{2}$ million tons of ore. The land haul of ore to the Spencer Works at Newport, though short, is forced to run parallel to the main South Wales passenger line through Newport Station, because of a tunnel only four tracks wide west of the station and because of the railway bridge across the River Usk immediately to the east. Every hour a train with 1,000 tons of ore (30 × hopper wagons carrying $33\frac{1}{2}$ tons) must leave the dock

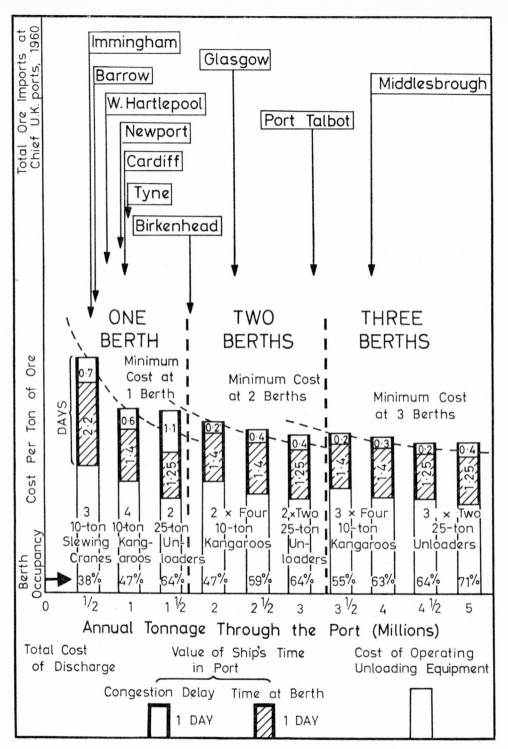

FIG. 60 Port Installations for Various Tonnages of Iron Ore Imports
The examples are of equipment (continuously manned) giving the lowest total cost of discharging ore from tramp ships. These costs can be much reduced, even below low tramp charter rates, by using specialized ore carriers, above 14,000 tons deadweight, operating between ports that are more than 2,000 miles apart. After R. T. Eddison and D. T. Owen, 'Discharging Iron Ore', *Operational Research Society*, 4 (1953), 39–51, Fig. 3.

throughout a 16-hour day. 16,000 tons a day for 250 working days a year gives a transit of 4 million tons per annum.

In South Wales each port (excepting Milford Haven) began where a river estuary gave some haven-like quality to a dune- or marsh-encumbered coast. The decisive moment in the development of each came when, like the era of *dock elaboration* at *Anyport*, the river in its natural state no longer sufficed, and a port had either to be carved out of dunes or marshes or to be embedded in a tidal mudflat formerly swept by a high-ranging tide. The impulse to develop further was provided by the coal export trade for which Cardiff, Penarth, and Barry were best situated in the railway era. Not only have these ports suffered most from the decline of this trade, but Milford Haven, Swansea, Port Talbot, and Newport have profited most from the recent growth in the oil and steel industries. Newport looks at present particularly ripe for a further increase of traffic. Where ports are so close together, each primarily dependent on a rather limited hinterland, itself subject to rapid industrial change, it must be expected that their relative importance may vary rapidly and widely.

REFERENCES

1. See L. R. Moore, 'The South Wales Coalfield', *The Coalfields of Great Britain*, edited by Sir Arthur Trueman, London: Arnold, 1954, Chapter 6, 92–125; and J. Pringle and T. N. George, *British Regional Geology: South Wales*, London: H.M.S.O., 1948.

2. In geomorphological terms the divergence is between south-east trending consequent streams superimposed from a vanished cover of Upper Cretaceous rocks and south-westward flowing subsequent streams. E. H. Brown, *The Relief and Drainage of Wales*, Cardiff: University of Wales Press, 1960, 123–57, 136, Fig. 43; and R. A. Yates, 'Physiographical Evolution', *Wales*, edited by E. G. Bowen, London: Methuen, 1957, 19–52, 30–2, Fig. 5.

3. 'Sweyn's eie' (the viking Sweyn Forkbeard's island—a record of Danish invasion in the early eleventh century) probably refers to a temporary islet between two arms of the Tawe, still discernible on a map of 1771 (Fig. 54, inset). M. Davies, *Wales in Maps*, Cardiff: University of Wales Press, 1958, for maps of Swansea at various dates, and also of Newport and Cardiff, Figs. 75–86.

4. W. H. Jones, *History of the Port of Swansea*, Carmarthen: Spurrell, 1922, 25.

5. *Ibid.*, quotes a facsimile as Map I.

6. M. Davies, *op. cit.*, has a map based on the earliest Welsh Port Books, Fig. 59. See also E. A. Lewis, *The Welsh Port Books 1550–1603*, London: Cymmrodorion Record Series No. 12, 1927; D. T. Williams, 'The Port Books of Swansea and Neath', *Archaeologia Cambrensis*, 95 (1940), 192–209 and *ibid.*, 'Medieval Foreign Trade: Western Ports', *An Historical Geography of England before A.D. 1800*, edited by H. C. Darby, Cambridge: University Press, 1951, 266–97, 288–9.

7. W. H. Jones, *op. cit.*, 299–316; G. Grant-Francis. *The Smelting of Copper in the Swansea District of South Wales*, London: Sotheran, 1881; and A. H. John, *The Industrial Development of South Wales, 1750–1850*, Cardiff: University of Wales Press, 1950, 28–30.

8. W. H. Jones, *op. cit.*, xiv.

9. C. Hadfield, *The Canals of South Wales and the Border*, Cardiff: University of Wales Press, 1960, 47–60, for the Swansea Canal, and 78–88 for the Tennant Canal. The latter terminated alongside a tidal harbour which could take vessels up to about only 80 tons. This 'Port Tennant' was obliterated

by the impounded docks of the modern port. See also H. Pollins, 'The Swansea Canal', *Journal of Transport History*, 1 (1953–4), 135–54.

10. *Report*, February 5, 1827, though he proposed making both the New Cut and the Old Harbour into floats, see J. Abernethy, 'Description of the Works at the Ports of Swansea, Blyth, and Silloth, *Minutes of the Proceedings of the Institution of Civil Engineers*, 21 (1861–2), 309–44, 310.

11. G. Grant-Francis, a MS. note recorded by W. H. Jones, *op. cit.*, 315. See also H. Carter, 'The Growth of Industry, 1750–1850', *Wales*, *op. cit.*, 204–19, 213.

12. P. W. Meik and A. O. Schenk, 'Description of Swansea Harbour and of King's Dock, Swansea', *Proceedings of the South Wales Institute of Engineers*, 25 (1906–7), 53–8, 54, 57.

13. The Swansea Harbour Trustees were denied Government adjustment of their financial deficiencies arising from the First World War trade depression (unlike the treatment of other South Wales ports, then railway owned). The Great Western Railway, which had by amalgamation under the Railways Act of 1921 absorbed all the competing ports on the north side of the Bristol Channel, purchased the Port of Swansea in 1923. All the docks have now been inherited by British Transport Docks.

14. There are large rolling mills in west South Wales using aluminium at Waunarlwydd, Resolven, and Port Tennant adjacent to King's Dock, Swansea.

15. G. M. Howe, 'The South Wales Coalfield', *Wales*, *op. cit.*, 353–400, 392; W. E. Minchinton, *The British Tinplate Industry*, Oxford: Clarendon, 1957, 236–8; and G. Manners, 'The Tinplate and Steel Industries in West South Wales', *Geography*, 44 (1959), 38–40.

16. J. F. Rees, 'The Industrial Revolution and After', *The Cardiff Region: a Survey*, edited by Sir Frederick Rees, Cardiff: University of Wales Press, 1960.

17. Processed at the Dunlopillo factory at Hirwaun, twenty miles inland.

18. A hybrid name derived from W. K. D'Arcy, one of the founders of the company.

19. For example, the offices of the British Petroleum Oil Terminal on the south side of the haven are in Popton Fort, built by the War Office in 1863. See also Lord Dynevor, 'Milford Haven', *British Shipping*, 17 (1961), 16–19.

20. Much information about Port Talbot has been supplied by E. A. C. Howells, including the MS. of a paper given to the Port Talbot Forum on October 21, 1959. *Port Talbot: Its History and Development*.

21. To save expense a trench only twenty feet wide and ten feet deep was cut through to the sea; and when the river was in flood it soon widened this channel to the present dimensions by erosion. H. R. Palmer, 'Description of the Harbour of Port Talbot (Glamorganshire)', *Minutes of the Proceedings of the Institution of Civil Engineers*, 2 (1842), 188–9.

22. A. H. John, *op. cit.*, 30.

23. W. Cleaver, 'Alterations and Improvements of the Port Talbot Docks and Railways during the Last Decade', *Minutes of the Proceedings of the Institution of Civil Engineers*, 191 (1913), 103–18.

24. In December 1960 the River Taff flooded and partially reoccupied its old bed, flooding Cardiff Arms Park.

25. C. Hadfield, *op. cit.*, 90–117, 94.

26. The Glamorganshire Canal was used to supply water to the docks after 1890. Since 1928 it has scarcely been used at all and is now mostly filled in. See also C. Hadfield, *op. cit.*, 117.

27. W. Turner, 'The Creator of Modern Cardiff', *Cardiff: an Illustrated Handbook*, edited by J. Ballinger, Cardiff: Western Mail, 1896, 36–9, 36. All the docks at Cardiff are known as the Bute Docks in honour of the second Marquess, who received powers to build his dock in 1830 but did not exercise them until 1836 when the Taff Vale Railway was authorized. D. S. Barrie, *The Taff Vale Railway*, Sidcup: Oakwood, 1939, 5. See also T. M. Hodges, *History of the Port of Cardiff in Relation to Its Hinterland, 1830–1914*, Unpublished thesis, M.Sc. (Econ.), University of London, 1946.

28. Captain W. H. Smyth advised against a dock near Penarth on the River Ely because of tidal currents and the difficulties when onshore easterly winds prevailed (both of which were to be overcome by vessels *steaming* to and from Penarth Dock opened in 1865), *Nautical Observations on the Port and Maritime Vicinity of Cardiff*, Cardiff: Bird, 1840, 13–14.

29. S. Thomas, 'Penarth Dock', *Cardiff: an Illustrated Handbook*, *op. cit.*, 237–40. A conflict between the Taff Vale Railway Company and the Bute Trustees arose from the Company, which had to maintain

its own coaling appliances in the first (West) dock, being denied access to the second (East) dock without payment of toll to the Rhymney Railway Company, granted exclusive use of the dock equipped with coaling appliances by the Trustees, D. S. Barrie, *op. cit.*, 13–14.

30. R. J. Rimell, J. Davies, and Hailey [*sic*], *History of the Barry Railway Company 1884–1921*, Cardiff: Western Mail, 1923, 15; and I. Thomas, *Top Sawyer: a Biography of David Davies of Llandinam*, London: Longmans, 1938, 278. See also L. N. A. Davies, *The Development of the Port of Barry in Relation to the South Wales Coalfield*, Unpublished thesis, M.A., University of Wales, 1938.

31. I. Thomas, *vide supra*, 304; and 270–311 for greater detail about the establishment of Barry Dock.

32. J. Robinson, 'The Barry Dock Works, including the Hydraulic Machinery and the Mode of Tipping Coal', *Minutes of the Proceedings of the Institution of Civil Engineers*, 101 (1890), 129–85, 152–3, 170.

33. J. Pringle and T. N. George, *op. cit.*, Fig. 29, Section 10.

34. For principles governing railway approach lay-outs see H. H. Bird, 'The Shipment of Coal with Reference to the Lay-out of Approach Roads and Sidings', *The Dock and Harbour Authority*, 8 (1927–8), 3–10. A general summary is given by N. G. Gedye, *The Mechanical Handling of Coal at Ports*, London: Institution of Civil Engineers [Vernon-Harcourt Lecture 1931–2], 1932.

35. E. L. Chappell, *History of the Port of Cardiff*, Cardiff: Priory, 1939, 120; and M. Crubellier, 'Le développement de Cardiff au cours du XIXe siècle et jusqu'à la crise actuelle', *Annales de Géographie*, 45 (1936), 469–85, discusses the then 'present crisis' in the coal trade, 481–5.

36. One of the first large ironworks in South Wales established near Merthyr in 1759 as the Dowlais Co-partnership.

37. A. A. Read, 'The Dowlais Works', *Cardiff: An Illustrated Handbook*, *op. cit.*, 175–8. For a brief summary of the change of the siting of the South Wales iron and steel industry see P. Massey, *Industrial South Wales*, London: Gollancz, 1940, 14–26.

38. Unfortunately, the splendid cold store at Queen Alexandra Dock, Cardiff, erected by the Government during the Second World War, is not fully used, as a result of an undertaking that it should not be employed to the detriment of commercial cold stores elsewhere.

39. Strictly, this port is not in South Wales but in Monmouthshire, though it is conventional to include it with other ports on the north side of the Bristol Channel. The name 'Newport' probably results from the supplantation of the older Roman port of Caerleon on the Usk, two miles to the north-east.

40. For a discussion of the disadvantages of the Neath estuary for a port see T. N. George, *The Geology, Physical Features and Natural Resources of the Swansea District*, Swansea: University College; 1939, 32; and D. T. Williams, 'The Port Books of Swansea and Neath', *Archaeologia Cambrensis*, 95 (1940), 192–209, 208–9.

41. J. W. Dawson, *Commerce and Customs: A History of the Ports of Newport and Caerleon*, Newport: Johns, 1932, 54 and C. Hadfield, *op. cit.*, 127–59, 132. By Section 50 of the third Monmouthshire Canal Act of 1802, this exemption was extended to coal shipped to Bridgewater.

42. A. H. John, *op. cit.*, 122 and 191, Appendix E. See also E. M. E. Davies, *Port Development and Commerce at Newport, Mon. 1835–1935*, Unpublished thesis, M.A., University of Wales, 1938.

43. For a map of the tramroads extending as far to the north-west as the Sirhowy Valley, see C. Hadfield, *op. cit.*, Fig. 7.

44. J. Macaulay, 'The Economics of Dock Administration', *Modern Railway Working*, Vol. 8, London: Gresham, 1914, 1–55, 9–12.

45. For a rolling mill at Rogerstone, the largest in Europe, just outside Newport, and another factory in Ebbw Vale.

46. Recent strictures, with evidence, on British ore-unloading ports are to be found in the *Report of the Committee of Inquiry into the Major Ports of Great Britain*, London, H.M.S.O., Cmnd., 1824, 1962, paras. 450–2; and 'Handling Bulk Cargoes of Iron Ore', *The Dock and Harbour Authority*, 43 (1962), 159–61.

47. R. T. Eddison and D. T. Owen, 'Discharging Iron Ore', *Operational Research Society*, 4 (1953), 39–51, Fig. 3. See also J. S. Terrington, 'Iron Ore Ports in Britain: A Method of Size Analysis', *Bulletin of the Permanent Association of Navigation Congresses*, 45 (1957, Vol. 1), 87–94.

FURTHER REFERENCES FOR SOUTH WALES PORTS

[Anon] 'The Alexandra Dock Extension at Newport', *Engineering*, 98 (1914), 33–7, 111–7, 177–80, 217–21.

Capper, R. 'Development of the Port of Swansea and Dredging a Deep Entrance Channel to Swansea Harbour', *Minutes of the Proceedings of the Institution of Civil Engineers*, 103 (1891), 352–9.

Hauck, H. 'Swansea, port et centre industriel', *Annales de Géographie*, 34 (1925), 46–52.

Massey, P. 'Shipping: The Coastal Towns', *Industrial South Wales*. London: Gollancz, 1940, 116–30.

Matthews, J. *Historic Newport*. Newport: Williams, 1910.

Paterson, D. R. *Early Cardiff*. Exeter: Townsend, 1926.

Reports of the Commissioner for the Special Areas (England and Wales), London: H.M.S.O., 1935–8.

Williams, D. T. 'The Economic Geography of the Western Half of the South Wales Coalfield', *Scottish Geographical Magazine*, 49 (1933), 274–89.

PACKET PORTS

Chapter 9

DOVER AND HARWICH, WITH HOLYHEAD

In a packet[1] port considerations of general situation, shortest distances across dividing
seas and between areas of densest populations, may call a port into being even where
local difficulties of a site are very great. This has certainly happened at Dover, where
physical difficulties of beach drifting beset the port and could not be overcome
merely by applying remedies which local revenue could reasonably afford. The
port was not rescued until by good fortune it was decided on national strategic
grounds to use public funds for the construction of a deep-water harbour. The date
of this happy event may be taken as 1850, when the Admiralty Pier penetrated
into deep water from Archcliff Point.

The oblique air view (Plate XI) illustrates what the modern plan suggests—that
Dover is a sea-encroaching port *par excellence*, because of the constriction of the land
site upon which writers far apart in time have commented:

'. . . the sea was confined by mountains so close to it that a spear could be
thrown from their summit upon the shore.' (55 BC)[2]
'. . . Dover is hampered by lack of space on account of the narrowness of its
valley and the cliffs at the eastern and western ends of the harbour . . . and this
will be one of the greatest limitations on the future growth of the port.' (1934)[3]

As a consequence, the port has been forced out to sea. Near the shore, successive
developments have been superimposed on preceding lay-outs. One result has been
the obliteration long ago of the *primitive* port in the estuary of the Dour.[4] The River
Dour cut a valley 275 feet deep between the Western Heights and Castle Hill at
Dover. Aid in the cutting of its deep valley has probably come from a north-west
trending joint system of the Chalk in this area.[5] This would provide weaker resistance
to river erosion operating in that direction. The master[6] stream of the area, the Dour,
was unable to keep its estuary free of shingle, partly because of the low gradient
of its bed near the coast,[7] but principally because of the beach drifting across Dover

235

Bay, impelled by south-westerly gales of long fetch. The river's ability to keep its estuary clear was further reduced by the dams that the early inhabitants of Dover erected,[8] so that the *primitive* port in the original mouth of the river became moribund.

Today the Western Docks and Inner Harbour, sheltering in the lee of the Admiralty Pier, form the most important area of the Port of Dover. This is the chief legacy of the *second* era of port development which took place to the west of the town within the shelter of successive piers built out from Archcliff Point. W. Minet has traced these unsuccessful forerunners of Admiralty Pier.[9] A transverse pier can arrest the movement of shingle caused by longshore beach drifting. This takes place when *waves of translation*, physically moving the water and the transported shingle, break with a swash upon the shore. But the supply of beach shingle will be cut off altogether only if the pier penetrates into water so deep that the waves off the pierhead are merely *waves of oscillation*, without the ability to move water and material along the shore. Until the nineteenth century it was beyond the capacity of the port to build a pier long enough to achieve this result.

TABLE 78

Eras and Epochs in the Development of the Port of Dover

	Eras and Chief Areal Characteristics	Present-day Symbols
I	*Primitive:* port in Dour estuary	Nil
	Era ended by construction of western pier, 1495	
II	*Marginal Quay Extension:* Paradise Harbour in lee of piers	Western part of harbour is the most important
	Era ended by construction of Great Pent in estuary of Dour, 1583	
III	*Marginal Quay Elaboration:* enlargement of Paradise Harbour	Sites of Wellington and Granville Docks, and Tidal Basin
	Era ended by construction of Wellington Dock, 1844	
IV	*Dock Elaboration:* superimposition of new docks and quays on former installations	Wellington Dock, Tidal Basin, and, later, Granville Dock (1874)
	Era ended when Admiralty Pier reached deep water, 1850	
V	*Simple Lineal Quayage:* Admiralty Pier wards off shingle and provides deep-water berths in its lee	Importance of Admiralty Pier to cross-Channel traffic, Eastern Arm Berths
VI	*Specialized Quayage:* 660 acres enclosed from open sea	Train Ferry Dock (1936); Car Ferry Terminal (1953)

236

As a report of 1581 succinctly put it:

> 'By experience it hath been always found that as the peere was built out, so the bankes of beache allso beganne to grow and lay farder out as the peere was farder built . . .'[10]

Although the first pier of 1495 initiated a westward movement of the port nucleus the relief from beach drifting was only temporary. Fig. 61 shows that during the sixteenth century the Paradise Harbour, in the lee of the first piers, remained completely separate from the town of Dover. Paradise may certainly be taken as an example of *marginal quay extension*. But *marginal quay elaboration* could take place only back towards the town; for the harbour could not, and still cannot, be developed westward of any protective mole from Archcliff Point.

The present sites of Wellington and Granville Docks, and the Tidal Basin are due to the epoch-making work which initiated the era of *marginal quay elaboration*,

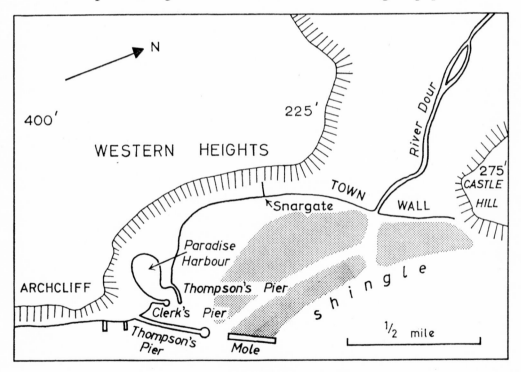

FIG. 61   Port of Dover *circa* 1550

Clerk's Pier, 1495; Thompson's Pier (with Mole), 1540, is the work on which Henry VIII is reputed to have spent £50,000–£63,000, and it ended at the root of the present Admiralty Pier. After W. Minet, *loc. cit.*

during which beach drifting was combated by another method. Water brought down by the Dour was impounded and then directed on to the bar across the harbour mouth at low tide. This was the plan of Thomas Digges. He aimed to profit from the fact that by the end of the sixteenth century the Dour oozed its sluggish way westward through a lagoon, lying between the western shore of Dover Bay and a shingle spit formed across the bay despite the piers. His Long Wall ran along the line of the shingle bar, and a Cross Wall formed the Great Pent in the lagoon. Sluices were so arranged that land water discharged into the harbour mouth and into the harbour itself.[11] This sluice method was used in the period 1581–1836 because it was inferred, correctly, that the short early piers had led to the formation of shingle bars. Though longer piers had been recommended in reports,[12] the harbour commissioners looked on the suggested remedies as possible causes of worse evils, and relied on the scouring effect of pent-up water. The fundamental defect of this method may be illustrated by the answer to a crucial question made by the harbour-master in 1836.

'Will you state in which way they [the new sluices then being constructed to direct pent-up water on to the shingle] prevent the formation of the bank [*i.e.* the harbour bar]?' 'They will not prevent the formation, but they are the most expeditious way of getting it away.'[13]

The certain inference is that if the method could only be used *after* the bar had been formed at high tide, the bar must have blocked the port at least from high to low tide on some occasions. In fact, the port had been completely blockaded for whole tides several times in the years preceding 1836.

Wellington Dock is the present-day descendant of the Great Pent of 1581, the Long Wall of which first reclaimed the peninsula to the south of Wellington Dock. This area is still the property of the harbour authorities where, appropriately enough, their headquarters are sited. A later Cross Wall, of 1660, is represented by the modern peninsula between Wellington and Granville Docks. The 1581 work made the road from town to harbour, Snargate Street, safe from storms and led to the rapid development of port installations south-westward from the south-western town gate, Snargate. This was demolished in 1683 because it was inadequate to deal with the increased traffic to and from the port area, which henceforth became known as the Pier District. Modern Snargate Street, the important artery from town to the Western Docks, has no room for large buildings back from the road because the chalk cliffs rise so close behind.

The *dock elaboration* era opened with the strengthening of the walls of the Pent and the provision of lock gates to make the present Wellington Dock in 1844. Following inquiries by a Royal Commission in 1840, and a House of Commons

Dover Harbour Board
PLATE XI PORT OF DOVER
Looking north-east, *cf.* Fig. 63.

PLATE XII TWO CONTRASTING ESTUARIES:
ORWELL HAVEN AND THE MERSEY

Above: Looking west-north-west across the Harwich Peninsula to Parkeston Quay, *cf.* Fig. 64.
Below: Looking north-west down the Manchester Ship Canal from Stanlow Oil Docks, *cf.* Figs. 68 and 70.

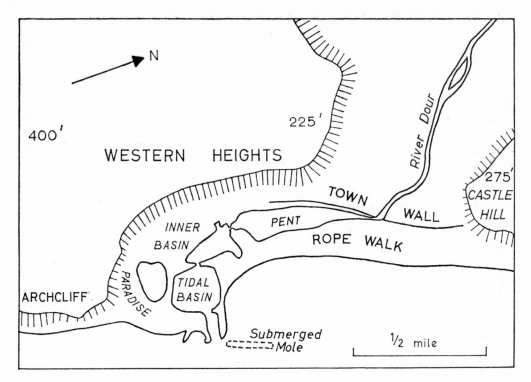

FIG. 62   Port of Dover *circa* 1740

The Pent, 1583, was not used by small craft and fishing vessels until 1734. It became Wellington Dock in 1844, and the Inner Basin became Granville Dock in 1874. The Mole Rocks are still features of the modern harbour (see Fig. 63). After W. Minet, *loc. cit.*

Select Committee in 1844, a report in 1845 recommended the construction of a harbour of refuge at Dover. A start was made on enclosing the whole bay beginning with the most vulnerable south-western quarter. Admiralty Pier was begun with public funds in 1848, and by 1850 it had reached 650 feet from the shore, ending the menace of shingle drift for ever.

For a further twenty-one years the Pier was extended into the sea, eventually providing berths of *simple lineal quayage* in its lee. The cross-Channel packets were allowed the use of these berths, and the railway arrived on the pier in 1854. By 1871 Parliament had realized the cost of the total undertaking, interest had been lost in the harbour of refuge, and work was stopped. The Dover Harbour Board decided to complete the harbour by its own efforts and began the Prince of Wales Pier in 1892. When this was three-quarters complete, the present plan of the Outer Harbour was decided upon by the Admiralty on strategic grounds. So the Prince of Wales Pier was completed in a straight line, instead of curving towards the Admiralty Pier;

the Admiralty Harbour had rendered it of limited use. It stands as evidence today of how small the harbour would have been, even with the western arm 'given', if public funds had not been made available for harbour development.

The present Outer Harbour is the Admiralty Harbour opened in 1909.[14] It will be noticed that the Admiralty Pier overlaps the western entrance—a device to throw off the flood or east-going tidal stream which would otherwise sweep across the entrance (see Plate XI). Unlike the original design of 1844 the eastern entrance was placed seaward of the limit of water charged with solid matter during stormy weather. Apart from being of use to vessels proceeding eastwards, this entrance is useful if the western entrance is made difficult by south-westerly gales, and it allows a circular flush of water in the harbour from the ebb or west-going tidal stream which reduces silting. In the period 1909–13 the root of the Admiralty Pier was widened by the Harbour Board and Dover Marine Station built on it almost complete by 1914, the railway company having, since 1906, a 999 years' lease on the area from the Harbour Board. The blocks for the construction of the Outer Harbour Piers were made in a 'block yard', a level piece of land of twenty acres, reclaimed at the base of the Castle [eastern] Cliffs which were blasted away. This area is now used by the factories of a miniature industrial estate and for approaches to the Car Ferry Terminal (1953). This and the Train Ferry (1936) have been the most noticeable *specialized quayage* constructed since the Admiralty Harbour was handed over to the Harbour Board in 1923. The Eastern Docks were handed over in 1929. All foreseeable port developments could easily be contained in the vast harbour, originally designed to shelter twenty large naval vessels. Though it was the base for the Atlantic Fleet from 1909–13, it can be a very uncomfortable anchorage; even large destroyers rolled as much as 25 degrees when it was a base for the Dover Patrol from 1914–19.[15]

The Port of Dover is the only functioning survivor of the original Cinque Ports (Dover, Sandwich, Romney, Hythe, and Hastings).[16] This confederation, which supplied the King with ships and men in return for certain rights, privileges, and immunities, reached its zenith about the end of the thirteenth century and thereafter declined. If Hastings claims leadership among these ports in precedence, the Lord Warden of the Cinque Ports has long had his headquarters at Dover, and he was included among the 'eleven discreet men' who became the port authority under Royal Charter in 1606. In the reconstituted Harbour Board of 1861 the Lord Warden remained as chairman until the Prince of Wales (and subsequent Lord Wardens) was relieved of the burden of chairmanship by Act of Parliament in 1905. The Harbour Board remains the port authority, but it now affords preferential facilities at certain berths for the ship/shore operations of the cross-Channel traffic of the British, French, and Belgian Railways.

As compared with *Anyport* the constriction of the land site and the difficulties of the water site are emphasized. Fortunately for Dover other ports on this coast have also been subject to beach drifting (the other Cinque Ports); or equally exposed to south-westerly gales (Folkestone); or, if provided with a naturally protected harbour, too far off the line of short-sea passage (Ramsgate). Unlike *Anyport*, town and port became physically separated during the *marginal quay extension* of Paradise Harbour; and then the port developed eastwards back towards the town. Yet the port nucleus has always remained close to the western pier, even though the main

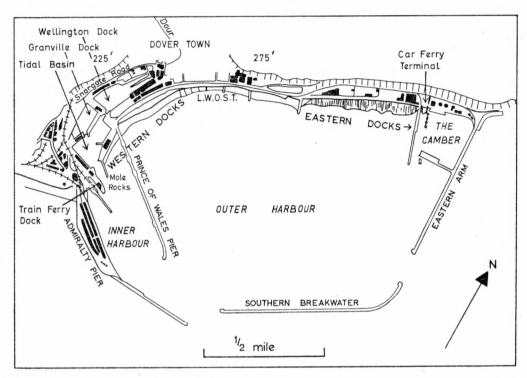

FIG. 63   The Present Lay-out of the Port of Dover

transverse track inland was Roman Watling Street (the present A2), aligned along the Dour Valley. The importance of this alignment was later modified when the South Eastern Railway Company reached the former Dover Harbour station, near the Pier, in 1844. Trains were allowed to run on to the Admiralty Pier itself in 1859. To achieve this it was necessary to build a track along the coast from the west and overcome the unstable Gault Clay in Folkestone Warren and tunnel through the Chalk.[17] There are no large docks of simple outline dating from the port's *simple lineal quayage* era because the quick turn-round of relatively small Channel packets did not imperatively demand them. The berths in the lee of the Admiralty

Pier are perhaps more indicative of simple *marginal quay* extension, since the depths alongside range from 26 feet to only 16 feet L.W.O.S.T.; but the Eastern Pier certainly affords *simple lineal quayage* of 1,700 feet with 27 feet L.W.O.S.T. alongside. Dover could have had little further development without some form of expensive 'sea-encroaching' harbour, which was, in fact, provided by circumstances quite apart from the commercial functions of the port. Although there are small depots in the Eastern Docks, there is no room for large oil berths, and the small amount of *specialized quayage* has been mainly an elaboration of Dover's overwhelmingly dominant function—the handling of cross-Channel passengers.

Modern Functions of the Port of Dover

Four separate areas of the modern port may be recognized: the Wellington and Granville Docks; the Admiralty Pier; the Train Ferry Dock; and the Eastern Docks, including the Car Ferry Terminal.

The spring tidal range at Dover is eighteen feet six inches. Yet there has been no great need for docks because passenger packet-boats which dominate the traffic require quick turn-rounds. The time taken locking in and out is to be avoided if possible. But there is some cargo trade at Dover, and the cross-Channel ships need refit bases. These are the functions of the two docks and the Tidal Basin:

> Wellington Dock—timber, ballast, and the laying-up of steamers;
> Granville Dock—coal (from the Kent Coalfield), fruit, road stone, timber, wood pulp (for the Kent paper mills), also a Trinity House Depot
> Tidal Basin—granite chippings, coal, and coke

The coastal and short-sea vessels that visit Dover mainly carry cargoes of low value per ton which have much smaller economic hinterlands than higher-priced goods, which can be supplied to south-east England from London. There is no dry dock at Dover, another legacy of the constricted land site, and dry-docking is carried out at Southampton. Three bonded warehouses are maintained at the Western Docks for the storage of wine, principally champagne, imported in large quantities by the Train Ferry service.

Towards the Admiralty Pier two railway lines from London converge. In the angle of their junction stands the former Lord Warden Hotel. Like many hotels in packet ports the building is now used for other purposes, most passengers travelling via 'through' connections. This building is now the local headquarters of British Railways (Southern Region) cross-Channel services and H.M. Customs and Excise.

The second line from London, via Canterbury and the Dour Valley, was constructed as a rival to the South Eastern Company's line which reached Dover along the coast from the west. This line, operated by the London, Chatham and Dover Railway Company, reached Dover Harbour Station in 1861 and received permission to run on to the Admiralty Pier in the following year. The difficulties of the Dour Valley–Canterbury route are well exemplified by the need for a tunnel nearly $1\frac{1}{2}$ miles long. The rivalry with the South Eastern Company's route via Folkestone was intense for many years before amalgamation in 1899. There is now great advantage in having two separate rail routes to London, and with electrification of both by 1962 faster schedules than the ninety-two minutes by steam train are possible. Both tracks terminate in Dover Marine Station, on the Admiralty Pier, with a passenger terminal serving the four packet-boat berths. Although these berths, east of the pier, are in the lee of the prevailing south-westerly winds, they are exposed to any easterly gale. One disadvantage of a very large harbour is that winds from certain directions may have a long fetch generating a swell within the harbour. Occasionally vessels are forced to stand off from the pier for this reason.

The Train Ferry was decided upon when it became clear that the Channel Tunnel was not to be built, defeated by a vote at Westminster in 1930. To operate a train ferry it was necessary to provide a dock at Dover. With an extreme tidal range of twenty-two feet even a 220-foot long variably inclined connecting bridge would sometimes have an impracticable rail gradient of 1 : 20. Because quick matching of rail lines between shore and vessel is necessary to provide punctual services round the clock, an impounded dock was constructed. Great difficulty was encountered because of fissures in the Chalk beneath the harbour. The dock could not be excavated 'dry' because the pressure of harbour water outside forced water up faster than the excavation could be pumped dry. This was the first dock to be constructed *under water*.[18] The ferry began operating in 1936, and its chief advantage is the through service it provides—for 8 sleeping coaches at night and 26 wagons during the day. In addition to this train deck there is room for 30 vehicles on the covered top deck. As many as five cargo services per day may be operated. The usefulness of this ferry for the import and export trade via through wagons explains why there is little container traffic at Dover. Fruit and vegetables are the chief imported cargoes. Before the war this was the simplest method of transporting a car to France. The great growth in this traffic has resulted in the Car Ferry Terminal of the Eastern Docks.

The Eastern Docks were once a base for submarines and motor torpedo boats. Another feature that has disappeared is the $7\frac{1}{2}$-mile aerial ropeway for coal exports from Tilmanstone Colliery. Today there are small oil depots served coastwise from Fawley (Southampton) and Thameshaven. The herring fleet land a catch here in winter, but the Car Ferry Terminal is the chief feature. The first car ferry from

Dover was operated by Townsend Brothers Ferries Ltd. in 1928, when 6,000 vehicles were handled. Cranes were needed for each vehicle, until the train ferry began to carry vehicles on its top deck in 1936. The number of accompanied vehicles rose to 31,000 in 1939 and to 373,000 in 1961 when the present Terminal had been open for eight years. Features of this Terminal (where the spring tidal range is 18½ feet) are

> '. . . two spacious loading berths, each 400 feet long, designed for stern-loading vessels of up to 65 feet beam, the twin towers or portals, suspending the loading bridges; and the spacious Customs building with its herring-bone layout, making possible the examination of 240 cars an hour.'[19]

The ferry services make Dover a major port. About five British Railway vessels and eleven owned by the French railways (S.N.C.F.), a separate French company, and the Belgian Marine maintain the services to Boulogne (B.R.); to Calais (B.R. and S.N.C.F.); the train ferry service to Dunkirk (B.R. and S.N.C.F. jointly); and to Ostend (Belgian Marine). Another vessel is operated by Messrs. Townsend Ferries. They range from 1,215 to 4,191 gross tons, and the largest carries 1,700 passengers; sometimes as many as thirty sailings are made from the port in a day. These short-sea ferry services are vital to Dover. Most of its foreign trade would vanish if these services were to be withdrawn. Only a small traffic, consisting mainly of the import of heavy goods brought coastwise for East Kent, would remain. And there is a threat to the ferry services. The Channel Tunnel project has been revived. The Report of the Government-appointed Channel Tunnel Committee in 1930 estimated the following diversions to a twin-track rail tunnel:[20]

	Per cent				Per cent
Short sea (Dover–Calais,			Newhaven–Dieppe	... ...	45
Dover–Boulogne,			Harwich–Hook ...	... ...	21
Folkestone–Boulogne) ...	...	100	Southampton–St. Malo	... ...	15
Dover–Ostend	...	26	Southampton–Havre	... ...	43

This was before the competition from air traffic. Obviously, ports closest to the line of the tunnel would suffer most. Dover lies in the centre of all possible sites for a Channel tunnel, within a zone running south-eastward between Folkestone and the North Foreland of Kent.[21] This emphasizes once again the importance of the situation of the Dour Valley in spite of the constriction of its site. Dover is one of Britain's major ports, yet it has a most uncertain future. If the tunnel is built, Dover may yet share the fate of other Cinque Ports.[22]

Harwich

Harwich, another large packet port, with ferry services across the North Sea, presents an interesting contrast with Dover.

TABLE 79

Eras and Epochs in the Development of the Port of Harwich

	Eras and Chief Areal Characteristics	*Present-day Symbols*
I	*Primitive:* quay at north-east end of peninsula[23]	Harbour east of the New Pier
	Era ended by transference of ferry services to the Continental Pier, 1863	
II	*Marginal Quay Extension:* Continental Pier at north-west end of peninsula	Continental Pier
	Era ended by transference of ferry services to Parkeston Quay, 1883	
III	*Marginal Quay Elaboration:* development upstream	Parkeston Quay
IV	*Specialized Quayage:* redevelopment of original peninsular site	Train Ferry Pier, 1924

Like Dover, but for a different reason, the port has a very restricted land site; the town is located on a peninsula, 750 yards wide at its maximum. The peninsula, which sufficed for all port functions up to 1883, projects into the excellent harbour (water site) of Orwell Haven, the combined drowned estuaries of the Suffolk Stour and Orwell rivers, which is more than a mile across in the latitude of Harwich. There is a minimum depth of nineteen feet in the navigable channel. Here is the greatest natural harbour on the east coast of England, a major contrast with the entirely artificial harbour of Dover. For some time the immediate excellence of the harbour overshadowed the advantage of the general water situation of the Harwich peninsula vis-à-vis the Low Countries and the Rhine-mouth line of communications. S. W. E. Vince[24] has summarized the contrasting functions of Harwich throughout the centuries, contrasts that have resulted from varied appraisals of the land and water sites and situations of the port.

The amplitude and depth of water in Orwell Haven made it a naval centre from Elizabethan times to the end of the Napoleonic Wars, the greatest development coinciding with the time when Holland was Britain's chief maritime rival. Ship-building depended on the same physical advantages of the harbour until the nearness to iron and steel centres became a factor of greater importance. General commercial traffic for the local region of southern East Anglia was almost entirely taken over by the Port of Ipswich, with its better inland situation, after the construction of Ipswich

Docks in 1842. Fishing declined with the coming of the railway; ports like Hull and Grimsby are twelve hours' sea journey nearer to North Sea fishing grounds. In this last respect the water situation of Harwich relative to the North Sea was disadvantageous.

With the precedent functions for one reason or another stripped away, Harwich was left with the ferry service across the North Sea. As early as the seventeenth century there was a service of coaches to London and packets to Hellevoetsluis. The service began to grow to its present dimensions only after 1850 following the economic development of Germany. In this respect the water situation of Harwich relative to the short-sea crossing to the Rhine-mouth is very advantageous.

In 1854 Harwich had been linked by rail with London, and from 1863 the Great Eastern Railway began a passenger and freight service to Rotterdam. The first vessels were of 600 gross tons. In the 1870's the vessels in service were nearly double the size, and the railway was becoming embarrassed by lack of room on the Harwich peninsula. The railway company

'became involved in a series of differences with Harwich Town Council, one dispute being over the supply of water to the continental quay. The quay already was too small to accommodate properly the increasing traffic . . . and, for some time, the railway company had been considering a move to a new quay, which actions the quarrels precipitated.'[25]

But in any case there was little space on the peninsula. Even if the required length of quay could have been provided, room could not be found for the sidings necessary to a railway port. The move could not be seaward, nor to the other side of the estuary if fast land communication with London was desired.

Upstream of Harwich the Stour once meandered over a flood-plain about a mile wide as it eroded the loam plateau of the Tendring Hundred, made of London Clay bestrewn by glacial gravels. The Harwich peninsula is the north-eastern extremity of this plateau. With the post-glacial rise of sea-level the lower Stour was drowned, and its former meander pattern is now represented by a series of promontories and tidal mudflat embayments, alternating on either side of the estuary. Retreating from Harwich the railway repaired to the first ness[26] upstream, the so-called Isle of Ray, isolated from the Harwich peninsula by a tidal mudflat embayment. Though cut off from the Tendring Hundred by the valley of the small Ramsey Creek, the Isle of Ray comes under the rating authority for the Hundred. This must have been additional attraction to the railway company in dispute with the Harwich authorities. The new quay was named after the then railway chairman, C. H. Parkes, and to the south a grid-iron pattern of houses was laid out for the port workers in a 'new town' of Parkeston.

The major contrast with *Anyport* is that Harwich itself has remained a small town (population 14,000). With the removal of the port nucleus one mile westward a vitalizing influence left Harwich. The economic and social centre of gravity moved south-westwards and the adjoining village of [lower] Dovercourt grew into the main shopping centre of the Borough of Harwich, with an important resort and holiday function.[27] Parkeston remains a physically separate area to this day. *Anyport's* fourth and fifth eras of *dock elaboration and extension* are not to be found here. As was discovered at Dover, ferry services are best operated at tidal quays if the tidal range permits. The extreme range in Orwell Haven is fifteen feet. There is no cargo which takes a long time to discharge passing through Parkeston and no coastwise traffic.

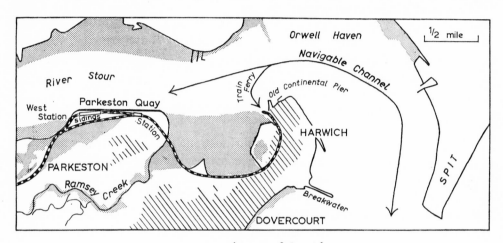

FIG. 64   The Port of Harwich

Stipple represents areas of tidal mudflat below high water and areas liable to flood. Diagonal ruling represents built-up areas.

One area of *specialized quayage*, however, is to be found. The train ferry to Zeed brugge began in 1924 from a site close to the old continental pier on the Harwic-peninsula. The restricted site does not inconvenience a train ferry, which neehs little siding space. With its special loading requirements it is best kept separate from the normal packet berths, as at Dover.

The port authority is the Harwich Conservancy Board, set up in 1863 to end disputes between Harwich and Ipswich. While the southward growth of spits must be guarded against near the harbour entrance, little dredging is necessary. In the three-mile twisting channel to open water, fogs are rare and the Hook ferry has been delayed only once in the last fifteen years—when the 1953 floods overtopped Parkeston Quay.

The quay rests on piles in the Stour alluvium. As this is considered to be a transit port, there is very little warehousing. The buildings are of comparatively light construction. Originally only 1,850 feet long with a timber deck surface, the present middle stone section of the quay was added in 1911. A further extension in 1934, Parkeston Quay West, brought the total length up to nearly 4,000 feet, providing eight rail-served berths with twenty feet minimum depth alongside. There are four transit sheds and two stations for passengers with the usual H.M. Customs and Immigration facilities. The eastern terminal is used by the 'Night Hook', the Danish passenger and cargo services, and the cargo service to Antwerp; the 'Day Hook' service and the Rotterdam cargo service use the western extension.

A glance at the relative passenger figures on the various routes (1960) provides a first key to the port's modern functions:

	Percentage of Total passengers
'Night Hook'	54
'Day Hook'	32·5
Parkeston Quay–Esbjerg	11
Harwich–Zeebrugge (train ferry)	2·5

The Rhine-mouth ferry route is still the basic function. The great numbers travelling at night show how short-sea ferry services may still compete with air services. Many travellers prefer overnight travel with sleeping facilities to finding accommodation at their destination after a quick flight. This idea of the 'travelling hotel' is now a basic advantage in the operation of sea ferry services.

Cargo Trade of Dover and Harwich—a Comparison

The most valuable imports and exports from Dover and Harwich are either perishable or have high value per unit of weight. Much of the cargo of both ports is transported in through-wagons on train ferries. The Harwich–Zeebrugge service now carries twice as much cargo as before 1939. Train ferries are literally extensions of the rail network across the sea and must operate to a time schedule. 'Roll-on, roll-off' loading is essential for speedy turn-round. The bulkhead deck on which the wagons run must be kept as low as possible to make an easy match with the quayside. A considerable sacrifice is made in carrying inert wagons across the sea. Pay-load may occupy as little as one-quarter of the volume between bulkhead and upper decks. The compensating advantages must be considerable. These are: speed in transit, since there is no handling of individual lots; no pilferage; and no packaging or labour for packaging required. This last point particularly applies to awkward shapes of machinery. In addition, refrigerated vans are available for food cargoes;

TABLE 80

Fifteen Most Valuable Foreign Trade Imports into Dover[28] (incl. Deal and Sandwich), 1960

	Value £ Million
Motor Bicycles	4·7
Cars	3·5
Tomatoes	2·2
Pulp	1·8
Grapes	1·7
Cotton Yarns and Woven Fabrics	1·4
Wine	1·4
Oranges	1·3
Textile Machinery	1·3
Refrigerators	1·3
Metal-working Machinery	1·2
Organic Chemicals	1·1
Cherries	1·1
Works of Art	1·0
Meat	·9
Total of all Imports ...	54·3

(1·3 per cent of total U.K. imports by value)

TABLE 81

Fifteen Most Valuable Foreign Trade Exports from Dover (incl. Deal and Sandwich), 1960

	Value £ Million
Road Vehicles	8·0
Woven Woollen Fabrics	3·6
Internal Combustion Engines	1·5
Safety Razors	1·4
Dyeing and Tanning Chemicals	1·4
Dressed Leather	1·3
Plastics	1·2
Aircraft Engines	1·1
Wool Tops	1·1
Laundering Machinery	1·1
Drugs	·8
Tractors	·8
Silver Bullion	·8
Paper and Paperboard	·8
Man-made Fibre Yarns and Woven Fabrics ...	·7
Total of all Exports ...	64·4

(1·9 per cent of total U.K. exports by value)

TABLE 82

Fifteen Most Valuable Foreign Trade Imports into Harwich (incl. Parkeston Quay), 1960

	Value £ Million
Bacon	9·1
Organic Chemicals	3·6
Refrigerators	2·9
Road Vehicles	2·2
Metal-working Machinery	2·2
Office Machinery	2·1
Internal Combustion Engines	2·1
Fresh and Frozen Fish (not of British taking) ...	2·0
Footwear	2·0
Butter	1·9
Photographic Apparatus	1·6
Textile Machinery	1·5
Musical Instruments (incl. Musical Reproduction)	1·5
Apples	1·4
Woven Man-made Fibre Fabrics	1·4
Total of all Imports ...	84·1

(1·9 per cent of total U.K. imports by value)

TABLE 83

Fifteen Most Valuable Foreign Trade Exports from Harwich (incl. Parkeston Quay), 1960

	Value £ Million
Road Vehicle Internal Combustion Engines ...	3·9
Road Vehicles	3·9
Woven Woollen Fabrics	3·9
Organic Chemicals	2·3
Tetra-ethyl Lead Anti-knock Compound ...	1·9
Leather	1·4
Textile Machinery	1·3
Radio Apparatus	1·2
Barley	1·1
Excavators	1·0
Tractors	1·0
Laundering Machinery	·9
Clothing (incl. Footwear)	·9
Refrigerators	·9
Dyeing Chemicals	·8
Total of all Exports ...	60·2

(1·8 per cent of total U.K. exports by value)

and tanker wagons for many liquids save enormous expenditure for barrels and the labour of filling them. Train ferries are especially useful for fragile material and for cargoes requiring quick transit. Perishable imports brought by the Dover train ferry are handled at a special continental depot at Hither Green, south-east London.

Dover for France and Ostend; Harwich for the Low Countries and beyond, and Esbjerg, Zeebrugge, and Antwerp. These routes are the compromise between the shortest direct line of movement from Britain to the destination on the one hand and the shortest sea passage on the other. Following a direct line in every case would require too many packet ports; taking the shortest sea passage would require ports where sites are too difficult and where too much land diversion is unavoidable. Even so, as has been shown, a compromise calls for large ports in quite difficult land sites.

Holyhead

As a pendant to Dover and Harwich, Holyhead may be briefly cited as an example of a very simple packet port on the west coast of Britain. Traffic to Eire and Northern Ireland is dealt with by many ports on the British side: either as a subsidiary to major port activity at Glasgow, Liverpool (including Garston), and Bristol; or from peninsular situations on the British coast at Stranraer, Heysham, Holyhead, and Fishguard.

The Holyhead route to Ireland has been used regularly since the end of the sixteenth century. The advantage lies in Holyhead's peninsular situation for fast road and rail traffic giving a short sea crossing to Dublin (now Dun Laoghaire) of only sixty-two miles, with a site protected from south-westerly gales in the lee of Holy Island. In 1756 the Royal Mail service was instituted, carried by Admiralty ships until 1849.[29] Thomas Telford's great road to Holyhead branching from Watling Street was completed in 1826 via the Menai Suspension Bridge. But the railway became the dominant artery for the port when Robert Stephenson completed the Chester and Holyhead line in 1848.[30]

The lay-out of the present harbour reveals this dominance. The railway provides not only the chief transverse route inland but for all longitudinal movement along the quays. There is no road access to berths. Import and export functions are neatly separated on either side of the harbour. The tidal range is only thirteen feet, and locks are not necessary. As in other packet ports, the hotel (built in 1880) has been closed; it is now used by British Railways, Midland Region, operators of the port. Except in the peak summer season, night passenger traffic is dominant for the same reasons as at Harwich. On this route most of the passengers are Irish who have found work in industrial Britain. No train ferry is possible here because Irish railways have a different gauge. Possibilities of future developments, making use of the excellent

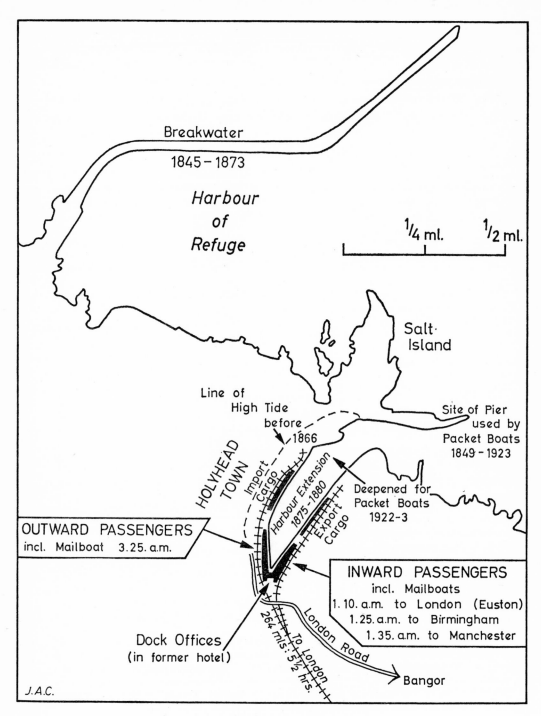

Breakwater
1845 – 1873

*Harbour
of
Refuge*

¼ ml.   ½ ml.

Salt·
Island

Line of
High Tide
before
1866

HOLYHEAD
TOWN

Import
Cargo

Harbour Extension
1875 – 1880

Export
Cargo

Site of Pier
used by
Packet Boats
1849 – 1923

Deepened for
Packet Boats
1922-3

OUTWARD PASSENGERS
incl. Mailboat   3.25. a.m.

INWARD PASSENGERS
incl. Mailboats
1. 10. a.m. to London (Euston)
1. 25. a.m. to Birmingham
1. 35. a.m. to Manchester

Dock Offices
(in former hotel)

To London
264 mls: 5½ hrs.

London Road

Bangor

J.A.C.

Fig. 65   Port of Holyhead: Annotated Diagram

water site of the old harbour of refuge, are indicated by the fact that two oil companies have purchased land, which continues to be farmed, close to the nineteenth-century breakwater.

Holyhead is an interesting example of a small port with a simple lay-out. There is, as yet, no industry requiring *specialized quayage*, yet the port itself provides practically the only form of industrial employment in Anglesey.

REFERENCES

1. Originally, the boat maintained for carrying the 'packet' of State papers and shortened to packet-boat early in the seventeenth century, see J. Evelyn's *Diary*, 'packet-boate', October 11, 1641.
2. Caesar, *De Bello Gallico*, IV, 23. For an account of the Roman pharos *vide infra* R. E. M. Wheeler (1930).
3. I. E. Muddle, 'The Suitability of the Port of Dover as an Outlet for Its Developing Hinterland', *Geographical Journal*, 83 (1934), 503–12, 507.
4. Similarly, because of the narrow valley site, modern and medieval Dover have been superimposed upon the Roman settlement. See E. C. J. Amos and R. E. M. Wheeler, 'The Saxon Shore Fortress at Dover', *Archaeological Journal*, 86 (1930), 47–58. R. E. M. Wheeler, *loc. cit.*, gives an account of 'The Roman Lighthouses at Dover', 29–46.
5. H. J. O. White, *The Geology of the Country near Ramsgate and Dover*, H.M.S.O., 1928, 7.
6. In geomorphological terms, the master subsequent stream; compare Dover Bay with the much smaller St. Margaret's Bay, three miles north-east (Plate XI), a result of a small consequent stream making a narrower angle with a retreating coast.
7. Gravel of marine origin has been traced one mile inland at Charlton. J. B. Jones, *Annals of Dover*, Dover: Express, 1938, 87.
8. Sir T. Hyde Page, *Considerations on the State of Dover Harbour*, 1784, 3–4.
9. W. Minet, 'Some Unpublished Plans of Dover Harbour', *Archaeologia*, 72 (1922), 185–224. See also A. Macdonald, 'Plans of Dover Harbour in the Sixteenth Century', *Archaeologia Cantiana*, 49 (1938), 108–26.
10. *Articles* [and other documents] *of the True Estate of Dover Haven both Before and Since the Building of the Peere*, 1581. Quoted in *Archaeologia*, 11 (1794), 212–54, 241.
11. An account of this work appears in *Holinshed's Chronicles of England, Scotland, and Ireland*, IV (1808), 845–68.
12. By J. Perry (1718), J. Smeaton (1769), J. Nickalls (1783), J. Rennie and J. Walker (1802), and J. Walker (1812).
13. *Report from the Select Committee on Dover Harbour*, July 1, 1836, para. 471.
14. M. F. Wilson, 'Admiralty Harbour, Dover', *Proceedings of the Institution of Civil Engineers*, 209 (1919–20), 31–112. The epic nature of the harbour walls is revealed by the following: the total length of masonry is nearly $2\frac{1}{4}$ miles; and the height of the walls is nearly 80 feet with about 50 feet permanently under water.
15. Sir Reginald Bacon, *The Dover Patrol 1915–17*, 2 vols., London: Hutchinson, 1919, I, 127.
16. For a brief account of the Cinque Ports (with further references) see J. A. Williamson, *The English Channel: a History*, London: Collins, 1959, Chapter 5.
17. The reason for this coastal approach is that between 1836–8 Parliament considered that there should be only one railway exit from London to the south. Under 1 *Vic.*, *c.* 93, 1837, sec. 135, the Dover line was permitted to branch from this single exit at Redhill. Since Redhill Junction is only six miles north of due west from Admiralty Pier, the coastal route, Folkestone–Dover is explained, despite great difficulties of construction in the Gault Clay of Folkestone Warren. See C. F. D. Marshall, *A History of the Southern Railway*, London: Southern Railway Co., 1936, 379–84.

18. C. Ellson, 'Dover Train-Ferry Dock', *Journal of the Institution of Civil Engineers*, 2 (1937), 223–60.
19. R. Scott, *The Gateway of England*, Dover Harbour Board, 1956, 33–4.
20. H. Slater and C. Barnett, *The Channel Tunnel*, London: Wingate, 1958, 139 *et seq.*
21. *Ibid.*, endpaper maps.
22. For similar conclusions based on more recent data see *Report of the Committee of Inquiry into the Major Ports of Great Britain*, London, H.M.S.O., Cmnd. 1824, 1962, para. 32.
23. B. C. Hughes, *The History of Harwich Harbour*, Harwich Harbour Conservancy Board, 1939, 22.
24. S. W. E. Vince, 'The Evolution of the Port of Harwich', *Geography*, 26 (1941), 178–86.
25. K. W. Jones, 'Parkeston Quay and the Antwerp Continental Service', *Railway Magazine*, 97 (1951), 759–62 and 776, 760.
26. Similar nesses upstream on the Essex shore are Wrabness and the promontory between Mistley and Manningtree.
27. Harwich and Dovercourt are administered from a gigantic town hall, the former Great Eastern Hotel in Harwich, which became a stranded white elephant to the railway, *cf.* the Lord Warden Hotel at Dover nearer the port nucleus which could be turned into a building for port administration.
28. Notice the absence of industrial raw materials in the trade of Dover.
29. E. Watson, *The Royal Mail to Ireland*, London: Arnold, 1917. Chapter XI explains how it was that the City of Dublin Steam Packet Co. operated the mailboat service from 1850–1920.
30. J. M. Dunn, *The Chester and Holyhead Railway*, Godstone: Oakwood, 1948.

FURTHER REFERENCES FOR DOVER

Bucknall, R. *Boat Trains and Channel Packets*. London: Stuart, 1957.
Jones, J. B. *The History of Dover Harbour*. Dover: Express, 1892.
Lyon, J. *The History of the Town and Port of Dover*. 2 vols. 1813.

FURTHER REFERENCES FOR HARWICH

Arnott, W. G. *Orwell Estuary*. Ipswich: Adlard, 1954.
Taylor, S. (*circa* 1676). *The History and Antiquities of Harwich and Dovercourt*, ed. by S. Dale. 1730.
Wilson, C. *Harwich and the Continent*. London and North Eastern Railway, 1947.

FURTHER REFERENCES FOR HOLYHEAD

Hayter, H. 'Holyhead New Harbour', *Minutes of the Proceedings of the Institution of Civil Engineers*, 94 (1875–6), 95–130.
Williams, L. 'The Development of Holyhead', *Transactions*, 38 (1950), Anglesey Antiquarian Society and Field Club, 51–70.

THE INLAND PORT[1]

Chapter 10

THE PORT OF MANCHESTER

LIKE Minerva who sprang fully armed from the brow of Jupiter, Manchester emerged all at once as a major port when the big ships sailed the whole length of the Ship Canal on January 1, 1894. The Port of Manchester consists of the thirty-six miles of the Ship Canal and the berths and docks that have access from it. There are no relics of a *primitive* port of Manchester. Manchester entered straightway into a *dock elaboration* era, with seven terminal docks constructed at the same time as the canal. It is worth while considering the circumstances leading up to the construction and opening of the port, for they help to explain the present lay-out and are well documented.

TABLE 84

Precedent Circumstances, Eras, and Epochs in the Development of the Port of Manchester

Precedent Circumstances

1.	1876–82	Conception of the idea that Manchester could be a deep-sea port
2.	1882	Engineers' plans
3.	1883–5	Parliamentary struggle to obtain permissive Acts, and modifications to the engineer's original plan
4.	1885–7	Raising of capital
5.	1887–94	Construction of the canal

Eras and Chief Areal Characteristics	*Present-day Symbols*
IV *Dock Elaboration:* terminal facilities provided concomitant with opening of canal	Manchester Docks 1–8 (less No. 5 not constructed)
V *Simple Lineal Quayage:*	Trafford Wharf, Manchester Dock No. 9 (1905)
VI *Specialized Quayage:* lower six miles of canal and elsewhere at favourable land sites	*e.g.* Stanlow Oil Docks (1922 and 1933); Ellesmere Port Wharf (1928); Irlam Wharf (1932); Ince Oil Berth (1941); Queen Elizabeth II Oil Dock (1954); Associated Ethyl Wharf (1955); Ince Coaster Berth (1957)

R

255

During the first half of the nineteenth century there were several attempts to raise public interest in the idea of a ship canal to Manchester.[2] None gained sufficient impetus. By 1850 it was plain that Manchester suffered from poor communications. The Port of Liverpool exacted heavy dues on inland cities importing and exporting goods, and only a small part of the dues was used to improve the port's facilities. The Bridgewater Canal connecting Manchester with the lower Mersey could not take barges of more than eighty tons; and the Mersey and Irwell Navigation was completely silted up. The coming of the railways did not emancipate the city, because their charges were much higher than the water transport by the inland navigation that they were intent on throttling. Yet if anyone thought of bringing sea transport to Manchester there was no sustained movement to produce a practical plan and secure the massive support necessary for Parliamentary approval. After an abortive scheme in 1845 the idea died for thirty years. It is therefore appropriate to give full credit to George Hicks, insurance agent and auditor, for being first author of an idea which, carefully publicized over many years, caught the attention of influential men, and brought eventual success after eighteen years.

The conception of the idea has fortunately been told by Hicks in his own words:

'I came to Manchester in 1875. I am a Scotsman, having been born and spent the first seventeen years on the Clyde. I lived at Bowdon upon coming to Manchester, and amongst the walks I had in various directions I visited Lymm. Seeing the river there I wondered why it was doing nothing. I had often heard ship canal schemes talked about, and *I thought something might be done in this case.* Accordingly, on October 11, 1876, I wrote a letter to the Manchester press urging upon the citizens the desirability of improving the navigation of the river.' [Italics added][3]

After reading this letter, Hamilton H. Fulton, a civil engineer, wrote to Hicks about the scheme on October 19, 1876. On December 16, Hicks wrote an article in *The Manchester Guardian*, entitled 'The Clyde and the Irwell', in which he drew a parallel between the Irwell and the Clyde made navigable for ocean-going steamers. In the same month Hicks commissioned a geological report, met Fulton in London, and asked him for an engineering report. After the Manchester Chamber of Commerce had passed a resolution favourable to the scheme in April 1877, a model of a proposed tidal navigation and docks by Fulton was put on display at the Royal Exchange, Manchester, and later at Salford Town Hall. Hicks continues:

'For the next three years efforts were made to induce men of capital in the city to take up the question. In 1881, Mr. J. W. Harvey, then head clerk in my office, began to write, under various *noms-de-plume*, a number of letters to the local press.'[4]

Harvey's letters and an address by Sir William Harcourt in October, 1881, praising the energy of Glasgow merchants and crying 'Heaven helps those who help themselves', brought the scheme to the attention of Daniel Adamson, an engineer and boiler manufacturer of Hyde. In November, 1881, Hicks and Adamson were introduced, and they determined to start an energetic campaign and that Harvey should write another pamphlet. In this he first argued that water transport was the cheapest form of inland transport and that Manchester suffered because the waterways (Mersey and Irwell Navigation and the Bridgewater Canal) were controlled by the railway.[5] The advantages of a ship canal were a saving in dock dues, carriage, and forwarding and terminal charges; and the founding of new industries, with a stimulation of coasting traffic.[6] Among examples drawn were those from the Clyde, Tyne, Suez Canal, and the North Sea Ship Canal, Holland of 1877.[7]

The next important move was an historic invitation which speaks for itself.

'The Towers, Didsbury,
Manchester.
June 8, 1882.

Dear Sir,

It has been arranged that on the 27th inst., at 7.30 p.m., a Meeting will be held at my house, at which it is expected there will be present several of the Mayors of the most important manufacturing towns of Lancashire and Cheshire and the West Riding of Yorkshire, as well as a number of gentlemen representing the great trades of these districts.

The object of the Meeting will be, to consider the practicability of a tidal waterway to Manchester, and to take such action thereon as shall be determined upon, after a full discussion of the subject. Several gentlemen favourable to this scheme, will lay their views before the Meeting.

The Pamphlet [by J. W. Harvey, see above] enclosed herewith, to which I beg to call your attention deals exhaustively with the great advantages to the Lancashire industries, which will result from the construction of the proposed Ship Canal.

Your presence is specially requested
I am, yours respectfully,
[Signed] Daniel Adamson.

At this meeting a Provisional Committee was empowered to obtain engineers' plans. Up to this time only a *tidal* navigation had been considered. Two plans came before the Provisional Committee on September 26, 1882: the tidal navigation of Fulton; and a proposed canal at different levels maintained by locks proposed by E. [later Sir Edward] Leader Williams, formerly engineer to the Bridgewater Navigation Company and with considerable local experience. Leader Williams dealt cogently with the necessity for a non-tidal canal.

'The length of the River Tyne, from Newcastle to the Sea, is 11 miles, and the low water line at Newcastle has been lowered by dredging, three feet six inches.

The distance from Port Glasgow to Glasgow is 18 miles and the Clyde low water level has been lowered eight feet at Glasgow. From Manchester to Garston by the proposed Tidal Navigation [Hamilton H. Fulton's Plan] would be 34 miles, and the natural low water level of the Irwell, at the site of the proposed docks in Manchester, *would be lowered no less than 71 feet.*

The Clyde and Tyne were always rivers of considerable width, and being already tidal, and the fall moderate, there was no difficulty in giving increased depth. The amount of hard material removed, in each case, bore but a small proportion to the whole; but the bed of the Irwell at the requisite depth for a Tidal Navigation is sandstone rock, and there would be *for a distance of 10 miles, an average depth of rock to be removed of over 40 feet . . .*' [Italics added][8]

These points were endorsed by J. Abernethy, a past-president of the Institution of Civil Engineers, and Leader Williams's plan was adopted by the subscribers to the guarantee fund on September 26, 1882.[9]

The Parliamentary struggle next ensued and the bare record is given in Table 85.

The principal opponents of the scheme were Liverpool Corporation, Liverpool Chamber of Commerce, the Mersey Docks and Harbour Board, and the Railway Companies. From the mass of statement and evidence in one of the longest-ever Parliamentary battles over a Private Bill only those points bearing vitally on the reasons for the present lay-out have been selected below.

In the Bill of 1884 the proposed canal was designed to enter the Mersey estuary between training walls terminating opposite Garston (Fig. 70). To combat the canal and the proposed training walls in particular, which the Mersey Docks and Harbour Board believed would be detrimental to the regime of the Mersey, Captain J. B. Eads was retained by the Board at the then very large fee of £4,000. He was an American who had been connected with the Mississippi for forty years and had deepened a mouth of that river from eight to thirty feet. Captain Eads stated that the proposed trained tidal channel would prevent erosion of the banks in the Upper Basin of the Mersey, and that the volume of the tidal flow would be reduced because of the

TABLE 85

Record of Parliamentary Discussion upon Ship Canal Proposals[10]
(Alleged non-compliance with Standing Orders of
Parliament, January 19, 1883; Standing Orders
suspended, March 5, 1883)

Session	House	Commenced	Finished	Result	No. of Days
1883	Commons	May 1	July 6	Agreed to	39
1883	Lords	July 30	August 9	Not passed[A]	10
1884	Lords	March 11	May 24	Agreed to	41
1884	Commons	July 7	August 1	Not passed[B]	20
1885	Lords	March 12	May 7	Agreed to	30
1885	Commons	June 15	August 3	Agreed to	35
					175

A Reason: The House of Commons had saddled the Bill with conditions entailing a further application to Parliament (the necessity of buying the Bridgewater Canal to obtain the rights to the Mersey and Irwell Navigation which went with it); and the Lords declined to allow a Bill which would in part depend upon a second Bill yet in the future.

B Reason: '. . . opponents attributed their success largely to the bait thrown out by Liverpool and the Dock Board to the Committee, that if the Ship Canal would avoid the estuary in a subsequent Bill their opposition should cease.'[11]

lesser volume of water able to flow into the Upper Basin. The bar outside Liverpool would accordingly increase. He pointed out that between 1825 and 1880 every part of the Upper Basin above Garston had been occupied by the channel eroding the banks (Fig. 70), which would be prevented if the channel were trained.

'Question 14131 [for the promoters]: I should like to know, if you had your free will what would you do, supposing you had to make Manchester a port? [Capt. Eads]: I should bring the canal down through the land to Garston.'[12]

Here was the first glint of an alternative lay-out, proposed by a hostile witness!

Sir Bosdin Leech relates that G. F. Lyster, engineer to the Mersey Docks and Harbour Board,

'. . . in the Session of 1884 placed on the walls of the Committee room a plan prepared by himself for construction of a canal along the Cheshire shore, by adopting which (he said) the promoters would be able to avoid injury to the estuary and not imperil Liverpool. The promoters, before the plan was removed from the wall, took a careful copy, and it was fortunate they did so, as evidently the opponents regretted the exhibit, and did not afterwards allow the identical plan to appear in the room.'[13]

'Question 7250: In your opinion is it at all necessary if they want to get from Manchester to Liverpool to construct the works by means of training walls through the estuary? [Capt. Eads]: I do not think it is. I think the works could be constructed along the Cheshire shore and the canal brought along there with decided benefit to many interests, and at quite as little cost as through where it is located.'[14]

In 1884 Sir William Forwood, on behalf of Liverpool Corporation, promised in evidence not to oppose the scheme if the canal skirted the Upper Basin. But when in 1885 Leader Williams, engineer of the canal, produced such a plan following precisely the suggestion of the opponents, Lyster, Eads, and Forwood, the promoters were still confronted by bitter opposition. This was defeated, and the Bill received the Royal Assent on August 6, 1885. There remains the bizarre circumstance that the general lay-out of the lower twelve miles of the canal west of Runcorn was first proposed by the opponents of the scheme. The actual lay-out is based on the general lines of a design by the then engineer of the Mersey Docks and Harbour Board, one of the most unrelenting opponents of the Ship Canal.

Raising the capital was the next important task. Daniel Adamson remained leader of the scheme and chairman of the newly-established company, but financial difficulties were encountered mainly through his insistence that the aid of capitalists was not essential and that small contributions from masses of people would suffice. In 1887 he resigned. A reorganized Board of Directors obtained the finance, let the contract, and work was begun in November, 1887. Financial troubles were not yet over. The Latchford section was flooded in January, 1890. In the following November two storms flooded the workings for a dozen miles in the Latchford to Manchester section. Such setbacks meant that more capital would have to be raised. The source was Manchester Corporation which eventually gave £5 million on the understanding that it should have a majority on the Board of Directors, eleven out of twenty-one. Hence the Manchester Ship Canal Company, the proprietor of the canal and docks and port authority, is a diarchy of municipal and private interests.[15] Before it became a port, Manchester was already a great manufacturing city. When the Ship Canal Company was in difficulties, local capital resources were available to see the job through. This is in great contrast to the story at Hull and Southampton where local resources were insufficient to retain control even of a developing port and could not possibly have undertaken the gigantic effort to cut a way through to sea approaches thirty-six miles distant.

That the Ship Canal achieved the objective of reducing freight rates between the sea and Manchester was obvious even a decade before it opened. In 1883 after the commencement of the canal agitation, Liverpool charges were reduced £112,000 per annum.[16] The *Manchester Ship Canal Act*, 1885 fixed the maximum port charges at half those of Liverpool plus half the railway rates from Liverpool to Manchester. The following table shows some of the actual savings on charges, once the Ship Canal had been opened.

TABLE 86

Some Cargo Rates at Manchester via Port of Manchester Expressed as a Percentage of Those via the Port of Liverpool and Thence Overland, 1899–1912[17]

Year	Commodity			Year	Commodity		
1896	Canned Meat	...	32	1899	Lumber	... ...	49
	Cotton	... ...	46		Starch	... ...	27
1899	Bacon	... ...	34	1901	Cotton	... ...	49
	Butter	... ...	42		Grain	... ...	41
	Cheese	... ...	34		Lumber	... ...	49
	Flour	... ...	33				
	Hay ...	... ...	40	1912	Cotton	... ...	49
					Grain and Flour	...	44

Comparison with *Anyport* emphasizes the Minerva-like quality of the Port of Manchester, beginning at once with the fourth era of *dock elaboration*. The docks designed in 1888 were all branch docks entering the canal at less than ninety degrees, with included peninsulas, in two series: docks 6, 7, and 8 on a triangular site between the Manchester racecourse on the north, the built-up Trafford Road on the east, and the Trafford Park estate on the west;[18] and Pomona Docks on a narrow site (Pomona Botanical Gardens) between the original course of the Irwell and the Bridgewater Canal. For some time in the early years of the port, traffic was disappointing, because Manchester industrialists had close ties with Liverpool importers, and shipping companies were chary of risking large vessels in the canal. Two highly successful enterprises were launched to overcome these handicaps: the Trafford Park Industrial Estate opened in 1897 (see below, p. 264); and the registration of Manchester Liners Ltd., Manchester's own shipping line, in 1898. These developments called forth the *simple lineal quayage* of No. 9 Dock (1905) and Trafford Wharf, on the eastern side of the industrial estate. Opportunities for *specialized quayage* have been quite considerable along the canal. But a port with water sites confined to a canal has had difficulties in dealing with the modern requirements of oil traffic.

The complete elision of three eras of normal major British port development during the mere six years' excavation of the Ship Canal is a striking testimony to a great civil engineering achievement. Further details of this achievement may be conveniently dealt with in describing the modern functions of the port.[19]

Modern Functions of the Port of Manchester

The description will proceed from Manchester westward to Eastham Locks, which are six miles south-south-east of Liverpool.

One result of Manchester's sudden advent as a major port is the lack of a distinct port area in Manchester or Salford. Indeed, opposite the main dock gates is the 14-acre Ordsall Park. Offices connected with the port have remained in the centre of Manchester, one-and-three-quarter miles away, where the transport and forwarding agents had their premises before the opening of the Ship Canal. As might be expected, in such a large city there has been a functional grouping. Two-thirds of the steamship and forwarding agents and trade organizations connected with the port have premises within a circle of diameter 500 yards with a circumference passing through the Royal Exchange, General Post Office, and Town Hall. But this area, like the City of London, also contains many buildings having functions unconnected with the port.

The port limits are actually at Hunt's Bank,[20] close to Victoria Station, but for one-and-a-half miles westward the narrow Irwell is navigated only by barges serving riverside premises. The Ship Canal begins half a mile above Pomona Docks, with only that first half-mile of its course actually within the city boundary of Manchester. These docks, with only 16-foot depths, were designed for use by coastwise shipping. Guinness (Shed No. 1), other Dublin services (No. 4), Belfast services (Nos. 3 and 4), and sailings to Portugal (No. 2) are the trades dealt with, on the principle of one shed per dock.

Manchester deep-water Terminal Docks, actually sited in the City of Salford, can accept vessels drawing up to 26 feet 6 inches, and vessels up to 12,500 tons deadweight regularly navigate the canal to these docks. In addition to Pomona Docks the original docks dating from 1894 are Nos. 6, 7, and 8. A planned No. 5 Dock south of No. 6 was partially excavated, abandoned, and filled in. The length of the docks and the angle of the eastern quays of Nos. 6 and 7 were dictated by the alignment of the pre-existing Trafford Road. No. 8 Dock has an eastern quay at right-angles to the long quays to provide room for the rail link to the main exchange sidings. These sidings account for the great width of the peninsula between No. 8 Dock and the longest dock No. 9, opened in 1905 on the site of the Manchester racecourse. Its two quays, each 2,700 feet in length, merit the term *simple lineal quayage*.

'The promoters could not at the outset rely upon wharves and docks being provided by separate interests, so a large dock scheme for Manchester formed part of the Company's original undertaking and has since been added to.'[21]

The Ship Canal Company undertakes all quayside services and has a statutory monopoly of warehousing. This is the only major British port where the conservancy, estate, commercial, and operating activities are vested in one authority. The fundamental traffic operation for imports is direct delivery. Two-thirds of the imports never touch the quay. The Ship Canal Company is also a railway company, and from 1897–1950 it had statutory duty to deliver cargo by rail to factories and tenants of the port estate or in Trafford Park at a cost of 6d. per ton. In 1950 an amending Act succeeded in raising the rate only to 1s. 3d. a ton, because factory owners protested that they chose their sites in the first place because of the facilities provided by the port authority. A successful *Quay Delivery Bureau* for road transport was instituted in April, 1957; and since January, 1959, preference has been given to 'pre-advised'[22] road vehicles applying for discharged import cargo between specified hours.

From south to north the docks become capable of receiving larger vessels, epitomized by 2-ton cranes in Nos. 6 and 7 Docks and 3-ton cranes in Nos. 8 and 9. The sheds are five-storey south of No. 6 (the 'South Six Warehouses') and three-storey south of No. 7, rather narrow because there is little room for expansion. The continental and short-sea trades, dealt with particularly at Nos. 6 and 7, are in very small lots. The low lifting-capacity cranes, narrow loopholes, and small compartments of the sheds are really no disadvantage. All the docks were designed for rail

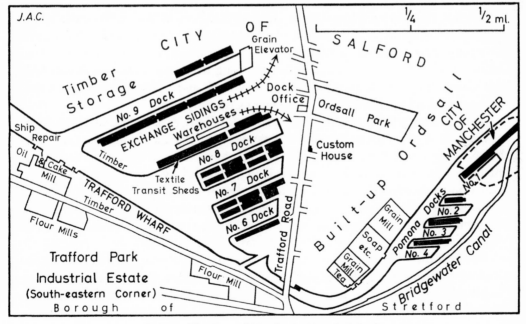

FIG. 66 The Port of Manchester Terminal Docks

working exclusively, and there has been some difficulty in providing adequate road access. On the peninsula between Nos. 7 and 8 Docks, for example, there are four rails between the sheds with only ten feet between adjacent pairs of tracks. To allow road access, the two inner rails cannot be used together because there is no room, even for pedestrians, between the outer rails and the walls of the sheds. Particularly noticeable are Sheds 1, 3, and 5 north of No. 8 Dock, built only nine feet from the edge of the quay. This type of design, usually avoided for general cargo since the early nineteenth century, is particularly suitable for unloading light cargoes direct to upper floors. These were the famous cotton-unloading berths of the port; and cotton and wool are still worked through these sheds and the warehouses behind. In the 1959–60 season 408,000 bales were imported from fifteen different cotton-producing areas, compared with 514,000 in 1949–50, a remarkable achievement considering the reduction in spindleage that had taken place.

There are several other warehouses on the Trafford Park Industrial Estate (Fig. 67) but these are owned by private firms. Only in the larger *simple lineal quayage* of No. 9 Dock are import and export berths permanently separated, with the eastern inner berths used for exports. The grain elevator (1915) has a similar site to that adjacent to the King George Dock, Hull, and similarly receives grain from conveyor belts running to dock berths beneath the quays. Grain is the chief cargo distributed in the port by barge, particularly to Kellogg's Co., Ltd., on the Bridgewater Canal.

Further *simple lineal quayage* is provided by Trafford Wharf, half a mile long, opposite the deep-water Terminal Docks, and also the property of the Ship Canal Company. From south to north this gives deep-water frontage to C.W.S. Flour Mills, a timber storage ground; a cable-exporting overhead conveyor; British Oil and Cake Mills Ltd. (Unilever); and the dry dock and shiprepairing base of the port operated by the Manchester Dry Docks Company Ltd.

Behind these installations is the 1,200-acre Trafford Park Industrial Estate, one of the first of such estates, bought by a syndicate in 1897, and until that time the home of the de Trafford family since the Conquest. This is the largest industrial estate in the country, now a man-made island, bounded by three miles of the Ship Canal on the north and east, and by the Bridgewater Canal for a similar distance on the south and west. Indeed, on entering the estate from the south, one might be forgiven for imagining oneself to be in another insular industrial area near the heart of another major port—Queen's Island, Belfast. At Trafford Park, however, instead of one firm there are more than 200 factories, employing over 50,000 workers. In contrast to many other planned industrial estates, Trafford Park has some heavier large-scale industries. The largest is Associated Electrical Industries (Manchester) Ltd. (formerly Metropolitan-Vickers Ltd.). Geoffrey Westinghouse chose the site in 1899, and the principal advantages influencing this decision were good transport facilities by rail, road, and canal, the nearness of ocean port facilities, and the abundant supply of labour.[23]

An imaginary journey is now made down the canal, with reference to location by means of mileage from the Eastham entrance in the Mersey and to north or south banks (N or S).

The Mode Wheel Locks impound the water in the docks and upper two miles of the canal and like all the five lock systems are founded on New Red Sandstone (Fig. 69). In the first two miles from Mode Wheel are five oil berths, the wharf of

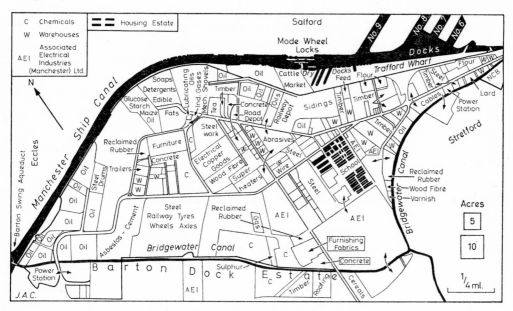

FIG. 67 The Trafford Park Industrial Estate

The diagram attempts to show only a selection of the type of goods handled and of the products manufactured. Railways have been omitted.

Brown & Polson Ltd. (33S), where whole cargoes of maize are received, while the adjacent soap works of Thos. Hedley & Co., Ltd. receive vegetable oils and whale oil from the oil wharf on the opposite bank by a pipeline ninety feet above the canal. Irwell Park Wharf (32½N) is the port's main bulk discharging berth for: sulphur, phosphates, manganese and chrome and iron ores.

Barton Swing Aqueduct (32) merits a digression. The Bridgewater Canal was England's first commercial canal dug independently of any river course. In 1759 the third Duke of Bridgewater had obtained an Act to make a canal from his collieries at Worsley to a terminus near Manchester, and this was opened in 1761 (additional branch to Runcorn on the Mersey estuary, 1776).[24] He employed as engineers his chief agent, John Gilbert, and James Brindley, who were faced with the problem of the canal's crossing of the River Irwell at Barton, to reach Cheshire markets and arrive in Manchester on the town side of the river.[25] If they made the canal with staircases of locks down to cross the river, much water would have been lost to the canal by vessels locking in and out, and there would have been delays. Their brilliant solution was an aqueduct carrying the water 39 feet above the Irwell. The canal prospered, and in 1845 the competitive but backward Mersey and Irwell Navigation was absorbed, finally forming the Bridgewater Navigation Company Ltd. in 1872, with conservancy rights over the Mersey and Irwell systems. It was for these rights that the Ship Canal Company had to purchase the Bridgewater undertaking for £1,710,000 in 1887 in order to be able to build the canal. Brindley's famous aqueduct was an obstruction to the building of the Ship Canal because it gave insufficient clearance for ocean-going ships sailing up the Ship Canal in the canalized Irwell. Sir Leader Williams matched the original engineers' daring by designing a swinging aqueduct, on an island, which can be aligned parallel with the Ship Canal, allowing vessels to pass. The aqueduct is swung *full of water*, retained in a 235-foot long trough by gates at each end. The Bridgewater Canal thus still carries an important traffic in barges of up to eighty tons burden, supervised by the Bridgewater Department of the Ship Canal Company. In view of the two remarkable aqueducts built for the Bridgewater Canal, the name is certainly apt—if coincidentally so.

TABLE 87

Water Sites of the Manchester Ship Canal

Location		Distance	Total Distance from Eastham	Water Site
Eastham–Runcorn ...	...	13	13	Mersey marshes, with about eight miles separated from Mersey only by embankments
Runcorn–Rixton ...	...	11	24	Virgin cutting in Mersey flood-plain
Rixton–Irlam ...	...	4	28	Canalized River Mersey
Irlam–Manchester ...	...	8	36	Canalized River Irwell

At this point (32) also the Ship Canal cut the old township of Barton-upon-Irwell in half, and thereafter separated the predominantly residential area of the Borough of Eccles (founded 1892) to the north from the industrialized Trafford Park and Barton Dock Estate to the south. The arrival of the Barton High Level Bridge carrying the M62 (Stretford and Eccles By-pass) assisted commuting between these two areas.[26]

Westward, the Ship Canal passes through several rural stretches, with occasional industrial development; wharves for a soap, candle, and margarine factory ($28\frac{1}{2}$N),

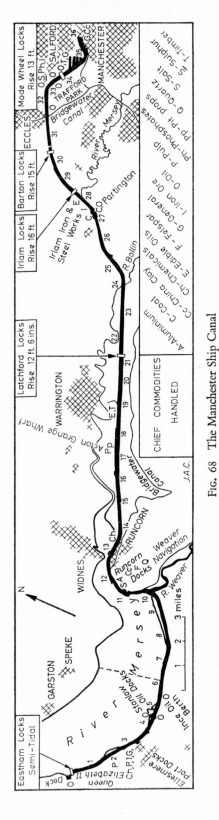

FIG. 68   The Manchester Ship Canal

Cross-hatching indicates built-up areas, and the pecked line in the Mersey estuary represents the boundary between the Ports of Manchester and Liverpool for customs purposes.

an iron and steel works (27½N), and the coal, oil, petro-chemicals (27S) and tar distilleries (27N) at Partington-Cadishead. Partington has a remarkable situation, for here the deep water of the Ship Canal is crossed by the railway[27] at the nearest point to the collieries of Lancashire and Staffordshire, with plenty of room for petro-carbon and petro-chemical installations on the former Carrington Moss. As chief coal exporting basin of the canal, Partington might be considered to be the western counterpart of Immingham on the Humber.

Where the canal closely follows the line of the Mersey, it often forms a short cut-off between original meander bends. Since the canal had to be excavated in the dry, these short sections of the canal had to be complete before the cross-banks of the river were cut through, leaving man-made ox-bow lakes, or the abandoned meander, filled with excavated material. The canal crosses the original course of the Mersey no less than thirty times.

TABLE 88

Some Dimensions of the Manchester Ship Canal

Excavated Depth:	Excavated water depth 26 ft.; water level raised 2 ft., 1904; lower 5 miles dredged to 30 ft., 1927; water level from Eastham to Latchford raised 2 ft. to 32 ft., 1956; lower 21 miles semi-tidal[28]
Width:	120 ft. generally at excavated depth; surface width varies with character of embankments
Locks:	Eastham $\begin{cases} 600 \text{ ft.} \times 80 \text{ ft.} \\ 350 \text{ ft.} \times 50 \text{ ft.} \end{cases}$

Latchford,	rise 12 ft. 6 in.	
Irlam,	rise 16 ft. 0 in.	600 ft. × 65 ft.
Barton,	rise 15 ft. 0 in.	350 ft. × 45 ft.
Mode Wheel,	rise 13 ft. 0 in.	
Total	rise 56 ft. 6 in.	
	(above mean sea level)	

Clearance beneath Bridges: 71½ ft.[29]

In the southern suburbs of Warrington (21–19), only two wharves are found before Runcorn: Warrington Laybye (19N), timber; and Acton Grange Wharf (18N), pitprops. East and west of Runcorn (13½N and 11¼S) are wharves for I.C.I. chemical works, and at Runcorn Docks (12¼S) china clay is an important cargo, brought coastwise from Cornwall for distribution up the River Weaver Navigation to the Potteries. The River Weaver, like other upstream tributaries of the Mersey, flows into the canal; but this river escapes into the Mersey estuary via the Weaver Sluices (10N),[30] though the River Gowy (5) actually passes under the canal through a siphon to reach the Mersey.

Runcorn and Widnes are not twin settlements. Runcorn has the advantage of deep-water berths for its industries and also the canal links of the Weaver Navigation and the Bridgewater Canal for the tanning industry. The railway at Runcorn is at a high level, over 150 feet, and so has had little locational influence on industry compared with the lineal arrangement east and west of Widnes of industries close to railways.[31] West of Runcorn, nearly eight miles of massive embankments are necessary for the Ship Canal to arrive at Eastham, while about five miles of its course are across the fringing marshlands of the Upper Basin of the Mersey estuary interrupted by a Bunter Sandstone promontory at Stanlow.[32]

At Ellesmere Port (35) the canal was constructed on the shore line of an embayment across an existing port, as a contemporary description shows:

'Here the Canal enters the river [Mersey] bed and for fully a mile retains that course across the Port . . . the bank [i.e. embankment] being tipped to the immense width of 70 feet giving a base 140 feet in thickness.' [1891][33]

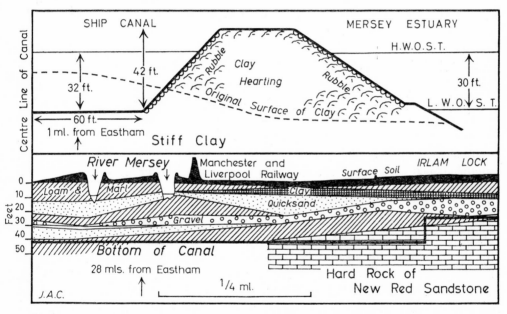

FIG. 69   Manchester Ship Canal: Transverse and Longitudinal Sections

Top: Transverse section, one mile from Eastham. After W. Elliot, 'The Manchester Ship Canal: Mersey Estuary Embankments—Eastham Division', *Minutes of the Proceedings of the Institution of Civil Engineers*, 131 (1898), 31–41, Fig. 10;

Bottom: Longitudinal section at Irlam Locks. Redrawn from a section in *Engineering*, 44 (1888), Fig. 23, between pp. 374–5, one of a series of 34 geological sections along the canal.

This port, now part of the Port of Manchester, is an example of port installations growing up at a favourable water site, with industrial development later because of a favourable water situation. The Shropshire Union Navigation (built in 1795 as the Dee–Mersey Branch of the Ellesmere Port and Chester Canal) entered the Mersey at this point because of difficult terrain for early canal-makers to north and south—the sandstone outcrops of Eastham to the north and the Ince marshland to the east.[34] The growth of the port was certainly stimulated by the improved water situation provided by the deep water of the Ship Canal.

'The most significant single factor in the markets served by the industries of Ellesmere Port (grain mills, dye works, galvanizing mill] is their wide dispersal.'[35]

A mile north of Ellesmere Port is Bowaters Wharf, serving a large paper mill, established in 1934.[36] It is a counterpart to the Northfleet mill on Thameside, with a land situation diagonally opposite, convenient to Manchester, the centre of the northern editions of national daily newspapers.

The last six miles of the canal are dominated by oil installations, just as at *Anyport*. Here the difficulty has been the impossibility of using T-head jetties in the Upper Basin of the Mersey opposite the canal.

'There had been berths already in use for tankers in the Mersey during the war and since the war. They were used for the T.2 class [about 16,000 tons deadweight] of tanker, and the greatest difficulty had been found in maintaining the berths at sufficient depths to accommodate even tankers of that size so that when considering the use of big ships, it had been decided that the tanker berths in the Mersey were totally unsuitable, in the first place because they could not be maintained at the requisite depth, and secondly, because they would be too exposed to the weather.[37]

These difficulties did not become acute until a Government decision in 1947 selected Stanlow as a site for an oil refinery (actually on the Ince Marshes). The first oil berths for the pre-existing depots had been provided in docks at Stanlow Point, the promontory of Bunter Pebble Beds (Stanlow Oil Dock No. 1, 1922; No. 2, 1933). These docks were connected to the oil depots on the Ince Marshes opposite by oil-pipe subways beneath the Ship Canal. In 1941 an oil berth was made in the canal itself at Ince (5S), and by 1949 the refinery was added to the oil depots on Ince Marshes.

By 1950 came the problem of catering for oil tankers of far greater size than the canal dimensions could tolerate (limit: 30,000 tons deadweight). Because of the above-mentioned difficulties of berthing in the Upper Basin of the Mersey, an

Airviews (M/c)

PLATE XIII MANCHESTER TERMINAL DOCKS
Looking west down the Ship Canal, with Trafford Park Industrial Estate to the left, *cf.* Figs. 66 and 67.

almost square enclosed dock with four berths was built. This Queen Elizabeth II Dock, opened in 1954, has a separate entrance from the Mersey, 807 ft. × 100 ft. (Fig. 70, inset map). The approach to Eastham has always been difficult to maintain. From 1954 to 1961 the channel shoaled by as much as seven feet, and the total dredging costs account for nearly half of the total expenditure of the Ship Canal Company.[38] Crude oil is delivered to the Stanlow Refinery from the oil dock by a 6-mile long pipe-line. From Stanlow another 23-mile pipe-line delivers refined oil to Partington, the first oil depot in Britain to be fed entirely by pipe-line.

'Unfortunately, very large tankers of the latest dimensions with their deeper draughts [*i.e.* up to 70,000 tons deadweight and drawing more than 35 feet] are not able to negotiate our approach channel to the Queen Elizabeth II Dock. It therefore became necessary for the Shell Company to secure alternative berths in the Mersey [at Tranmere] so as to be able to employ ships of the most economical size required for the importation, by means of connecting pipe-lines, of crude oil needed for their refinery at Stanlow.'—Chairman of the Manchester Ship Canal Company, 1957.[39]

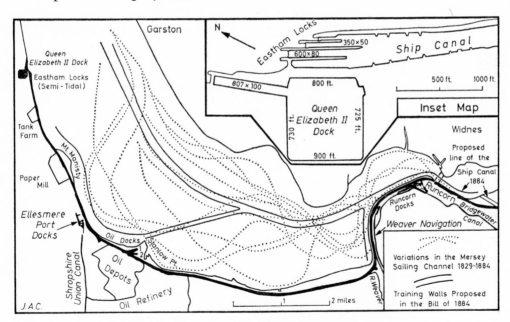

Fig. 70 Mersey Sailing Channel Variations 1829–84[a]; and the Lower Thirteen Miles of the Manchester Ship Canal: Inset—Queen Elizabeth II Oil Dock and Eastham Entrance Locks

[a]After Sir Thomas Bosdin Leech, *op. cit.*, Map No. 5. For discussion of more recent channel variations see p. 294; and J. A. Cashin, 'Engineering Works for the Improvement of the Estuary of the Mersey', *Journal of the Institution of Civil Engineers*, 32 (1949), 296–367, Figs. 8(a) to 8(e).

Airviews (M/c)
Plate XIV MANCHESTER SHIP CANAL,
NEAR WARRINGTON

Looking north-east up the canal, twenty-one miles from Manchester Terminal Docks. Latchford Locks, in the background, with a rise of 12 feet 6 inches, are located on Fig. 68.

For this reason the scheme for extending the Queen Elizabeth II Dock, envisaged in the design, is in abeyance.

There still remains much deep-water frontage along the canal. The slow development of such flanking wharves was once attributed

'mainly to the fact that, owing to the increase in size of oversea tonnage, the greater proportion of oversea traffic is now carried as part of general merchandise cargoes, although formerly it was imported in the much smaller vessels of the period.' (1920)[40]

Now that there is a trend towards specialized bulk-carrying vessels, this may no longer be a disadvantage.

In value of foreign trade handled, Manchester may be accounted the fourth port of the United Kingdom after London, Liverpool, and Hull. This is the measure of the achievement in making the canal.

'What the Ship Canal cost can be reckoned to a halfpenny. How much it has enriched the vast community it serves cannot be measured in millions.'[41]

TABLE 89

Fifteen Most Valuable Foreign Trade Imports into Manchester (incl. Ellesmere Port, Partington, Runcorn, and Warrington), 1960

	Value £ Million
Crude Oil ...	34·2
Unwrought Copper	29·5
Pulp	20·9
Tobacco	19·1
Raw Cotton	15·0
Newsprint ...	9·7
Wheat	7·4
Fuel Oil	7·2
Tea ...	7·1
Sawn Softwood	6·7
Raw Wool ...	5·9
Unwrought Aluminium ...	5·7
Lubricating Oil	5·6
Asbestos	5·5
Motor Spirit	4·3
Total of all Imports ...	285·2

(6·6 per cent of total U.K. imports by value)

TABLE 90

*Fifteen Most Valuable Foreign Trade Exports from Manchester
(incl. Ellesmere Port, Partington, Runcorn, and Warrington),
1960*

	Value *£ Million*
Road Vehicles	10·4
Woven Woollen Fabrics	6·1
Motor Spirit	5·8
Tractors and Tractor Parts	5·3
Wool Tops	4·1
Tetra-ethyl Lead Anti-Knock Compound ...	3·0
Internal Combustion Engines	3·0
Domestic Pottery	2·8
Textile Machinery	2·6
Woven Cotton Fabrics	2·5
Iron and Steel Tubes and Pipes	2·2
Wool Waste	2·0
Steel Wire	1·9
Organic Chemicals	1·6
Steam Coal	1·5

——

Total of all Exports ... 127·9

——

(3·9 per cent of total
U.K. exports by
value)

But the last word should remain with Daniel Adamson, in his hour of triumph, and the reader may judge if his assurance was justified.

'If the subscribers get no other reward we may be assured that we will receive the thanks and prayers of thousands who succeed us for the good work we have done in our day and generation.'[42]

REFERENCES

1. A title borrowed from a local publication, *The Inland Port of Manchester* (prepared by the Manchester Education Committee), Port of Manchester Committee of the Manchester Chamber of Commerce, 1938. This chapter has benefited from the comments of P. Reed whose help is gratefully acknowledged.
2. Mentioned in *Resolution and Achievement*, Manchester Ship Canal Company, 1956, 7–8; Sir Bosdin Leech [a member of the original Provisional Committee], *History of the Manchester Ship Canal from Its Inception to Its Completion*, 2 vols., Manchester: Sherratt and Hughes, 1907, Chapter V; Sir Edward Leader Williams, 'The Manchester Ship Canal', *Minutes of the Proceedings of the Institution of Civil Engineers*, 131 (1898), 14–30, 15–16.
3. Interview with George Hicks, *Manchester City News*, January 6, 1894.
4. *Ibid.*
5. Mancuniensis [pseudonym of J. W. Harvey], *Facts and Figures in Favour of the Proposed Manchester Ship Canal*, May, 1882, 9.

6. *Ibid.*, 12.

7. *Ibid.*, 23, 26.

8. Report of Mr. E. [later Sir Edward] Leader Williams [annexed to the] *Report of the Provisional Committee to the Subscribers to the Guarantee Fund of the Manchester Ship Canal, September 26th, 1882*, 13–15.

9. One dissentient was A. Provand, *The Manchester Ship Canal: a Criticism*, 1882, who advocated a small barge canal, and this stopped the flow of subscriptions to the Parliamentary fund. J. Lawrence, *The Manchester Ship Canal: A Reply to Mr. A. Provand's Adverse Criticism*, 1883, 162 pp., demy 8vo, written in four days, restored confidence.

10. W. B. Tracy, *et al., Port of Manchester*, Manchester: Hind, Hoyle, and Light, 1901, 18.

11. Sir Bosdin Leech, *op. cit.*, I, 249.

12. *Evidence and Proceedings on the Manchester Ship Canal Bill before a Select Committee of the House of Lords*, April 3, 1884.

13. Sir Bosdin Leech, *op. cit.*, I, 281.

14. *Evidence and Proceedings on the Manchester Ship Canal Bill before a Select Committee of the House of Commons*, July 24, 1884.

15. See also Anon., 'The City and Port of Manchester: Relation of the Municipality to the Port Authority', *The Municipal Review*, 2 (1931), 361–5.

16. Evidence of T. B. Hornby, Chairman of the Mersey Docks and Harbour Board, *Evidence . . . before . . . House of Lords*, 1884, *vide supra*.

17. Compiled from J. S. McConechy, 'The Economic Value of the Ship Canal to Manchester', *Transactions of the Manchester Statistical Society*, 1912–13, 1–126, Tables 1–4. Further early examples are given in W. B. Tracy, 'The Manchester Ship Canal: The Story in Brief from 1708–1896', *Journal of the Manchester Geographical Society*, 12 (1896–7), 205–36.

18. Originally, in 1885, on a smaller triangular site, one triangular dock with included peninsula, with another dock cutting across the peninsula towards the Pomona Docks. See Sir Bosdin Leech, *op. cit.*, I, plans facing p. 210. Sir Humphrey de Trafford who had been antagonistic to the Ship Canal died in 1886, and then more land was made available to port works on the Trafford Park side of the Irwell, so that the dock east of Trafford Road was not necessary.

19. See Sir Edward Leader Williams (1898), *loc. cit.*; followed by W. Elliot, 'The Manchester Ship Canal: Mersey Estuary Embankments—Eastham Division', 31–41; Sir Edward Leader Williams '[*ditto*]: Mersey Estuary Embankments and Other Works—Runcorn Division', 42–9; and W. O. E. Meade-King '[*ditto*]: Irlam Division', 50–60.

20. At the confluence with the Irk where Manchester was founded see G. H. Tupling, 'Old Manchester', *Journal of the Manchester Geographical Society*, 45 (1934–5), 5–23.

21. M. Stevens [a member of the Provisional Committee, 1882; general manager on the formation of the Ship Canal Company; and originator and first managing director, Trafford Park Estate Ltd.], 'The Manchester Ship Canal as a Factor in Transport', *The Dock and Harbour Authority*, I (1920–1), 158–61, 159.

22. *E.g.* vehicles applying at the quaysides between 8 a.m. and 10 a.m. or between 1 p.m. and 2 p.m. the arrival of which has been notified by telephone the previous day or morning receive preferential treatment over vehicles arriving without notice.

23. In the centre of the estate is a curious remnant of an Edwardian estate of some 600 houses, built at a time (from 1899) when it was thought an advantage to have workers close at hand. Laid out on a rectangular plan with three main 'avenues', twelve 'streets', and a skeletal shopping centre, it is now completely surrounded by industry. For further details on the history of the industrial estate see T. H. G. Stevens, *Some Notes on the Development of Trafford Park 1847–1947*, Trafford Park Estates Ltd., 1947.

24. H. Malet, *The Canal Duke: a Biography of Francis, Third Duke of Bridgewater*, London: Phoenix, 1961, explains that this was not the first canal in England—there was John Trew's small boat canal on the Exe 1562–6, and the Sankey Canal following the course of the Sankey Brook from St. Helens to the Mersey Estuary, 1756. But the project was the first in the world to link an underground mining canal to an open canal running across country, 55.

25. *Ibid.*, writes of the 'canal triumvirate', 68–80, and of the secret purchase of land at Liverpool for the eventual Mersey link, 55. V. I. Tomlinson, 'Salford Activities Connected with the Bridgewater Canal', *Transactions of the Lancashire and Cheshire Antiquarian Society*, 66 (1956), 51–86, 68–70, also suggests that the future link with the Mersey estuary was already envisaged; see also H. Clegg, 'The Third Duke of Bridgewater's Canal Works in Manchester', *Ibid.*, 65 (1955), 91–103.

26. A. E. Lumb, *Eccles: a Study in Town Development*, Unpublished thesis, M.A., Victoria University of Manchester (Geography Department), 1954, 156–7.

27. All the five main line railways which crossed the intended route of the canal had to be carried over it with a clearance of at least 73 feet above water level, with approach embankments 1¼ miles long made out of material excavated from the canal.

28. When the water level in the Mersey rises to the statutory water level of the Ship Canal, Eastham Lock Gates are opened, and the water level in the canal rises with the river. This is a safety factor for the eight miles of embankment between the Mersey and the canal, the hydraulic pressure on either side of the embankment being equal. At high water the sluices at Weaver Mouth and Randles are opened, and when the canal water descends to the statutory level the gates at Eastham and the sluices are closed, thus maintaining the level in the canal whilst the water in the Mersey descends to low water.

29. Equipment is available at Eastham for removing and replacing the tops of masts and funnels.

30. These sluices allow as much water from the River Weaver to enter the Mersey as before the construction of the Ship Canal, despite the fact that the canal runs right across the Weaver's mouth. This was done to appease interests in Garston and Widnes, who feared that their waterways in the Mersey estuary would be impaired if its catchment were reduced.

31. S. Gregory and A. T. A. Learmonth, 'The Middle Mersey and the Chemical Area', *A Scientific Study of Merseyside*, Liverpool: University Press, for the British Association, 1953, 251–67, Fig. 57, and 262.

32. It was impossible for the Ship Canal to go further inland because of a rise to 75 ft. at Ince Village (Bunter Pebble Beds) and 462 ft. at Helsby Hill (Bunter Pebble Beds capped by Keuper formations).

33. *The Ship Canal News*, 5 (1891), 38; see also W. Elliot, *loc. cit.*

34. M. Glazzard, *Ellesmere Port*, Unpublished thesis, B.A., Victoria University of Manchester (Geography Department), 1954, 12.

35. *Ibid.*, 71.

36. Opposite is Mt. Manisty, named after the engineer in charge of this section of the canal during construction, and consisting of excavated material dumped on the Bunter Pebble Beds of Pool Hall Rocks.

37. D. C. Milne, 'The Queen Elizabeth II Dock, Eastham', *Proceedings of the Institution of Civil Engineers*, 4 (Part II, 1955), 1–54, 43.

38. Sir Leslie Roberts, annual meeting of the Company, February 28, 1959. See also F. H. Allen and W. A. Price, 'Density Currents and Siltation in Docks and Tidal Basins', *The Dock and Harbour Authority*, 40 (1959–60), 72–6, for details of silting complicated by differences in salinity between estuary, oil dock, and the Ship Canal.

39. Sir Leslie Roberts, annual meeting of the Company, March 1, 1957.

40. M. Stevens, *loc. cit.*, 161.

41. *Resolution and Achievement*, *op. cit.*, 24.

42. Speech at the Free Trade Hall, Manchester, August 19, 1885, after the passing of the first *Manchester Ship Canal Act*.

FURTHER REFERENCES FOR THE PORT OF MANCHESTER

Baker, H. 'Manchester—Heart of Industrial England', *Canadian Geographical Journal*, 18 (1939), 346–57.

Barker, W. H. and W. H. Fitzgerald. 'The City and Port of Manchester', *Journal of the Manchester Geographical Society*, 41–2 (1925–6), 11–31.

Chaloner, W. H. 'Manchester in the Latter Half of the Eighteenth Century', *Bulletin of the John Rylands Library, Manchester*, 42, No. 1 (September, 1959).

Clay, H. and K. R. Brady. [eds.]. *Manchester at Work: a Survey*. Manchester: Sherratt and Hughes, 1929.

Cox, S. *The Growth and Development of the Port of Manchester*. Paper read to the Graduate and Student Society, Institute of Transport, Manchester, January 14, 1946.

Fairhall, D. 'The Manchester Ship Canal', *Geographical Magazine*, 35 (1962), 32–46.

Fitzgibbon, G. 'The Manchester Ship Canal', *The Great Ship Canals of the World*. London: Institution of Civil Engineers [Vernon-Harcourt Lectures], 1922, 28–38.

M'Farlane, J. 'The Port of Manchester: the Influence of a Great Canal', *Geographical Journal*, 32 (1908), 496–503.

Oldham, H. 'The Manchester Ship Canal', *Geographical Journal*, 3 (1894), 485–91.

Redford, A. 'The Dock Board [Liverpool] and the Ship Canal', *Manchester Merchants and Foreign Trade 1850–1939*, Vol. 2. Manchester: University Press, 174–85.

Rees, H. 'A Growth Map for the Manchester Region', *Economic Geography*, 23 (1947), 136–42.

[A] *Scientific and Historical Survey of Manchester*, edited by C. F. Carter. Manchester: British Association for the Advancement of Science, 1962.

Chapter 11

ERAS IN THE DEVELOPMENT OF THE PORT OF LIVERPOOL

An outstanding feature of the development of the Port of Liverpool is that the nucleus of the port has never migrated more than six hundred yards from the site it first occupied. There is little doubt that the focus of the port is at the three Pierhead buildings, the centre of the line of Liverpool Docks; and these offices stand on sites reclaimed in front of the medieval strand of the *primitive* port. Since the port hardly developed in area for five hundred years after receiving King John's Charter in 1207, it may first be encountered in 1699 when Liverpool was at last recognized as a parish. This was in answer to a successful petition which began thus:

'It was formerly a small Fishing Town; but many People coming from London in the time Of the Sickness, and after the Fire, several Ingenious Men settled in Leverpool; which encouraged them to Trade to the Plantations, and other Places; which occasioned sundry other Tradesmen to come and settle there . . .'[1]

Liverpool seems to have gained from the disasters that befell London in the seventeenth century when transatlantic trade was beginning to expand, though several other causes for Liverpool's rise at this time have been suggested.[2] The increasing importance of products of the hinterland is certainly in evidence. There is reference to a trade in Lancashire coal exports in 1611;[3] and there was the discovery of rock salt in Cheshire in 1670 which became a 'readily saleable back-cargo' for vessels making longer voyages.[4]

A salt-works was established south of the Pool in 1696. Cotton textiles certainly increased in importance.[5] From the beginning, trading connections with Ireland had been close. But in the 1660's several Acts had the effect of causing a serious decline in Irish trade, and this encouraged Liverpool ships to enter the transatlantic trade to the West Indies. The port benefited from the wider horizons. At the same time the rise of the French Navy caused Liverpool to be a safer port than any further south.[6] Finally, the lack of a parish church at Liverpool may well have encouraged the Dissenters to settle at the port, some of the 'Ingenious Men' of the above quotation.[7]

TABLE 91

Eras and Epochs in the Development of the Port of Liverpool

Eras and Chief Areal Characteristics	Present-day Symbols
I *Primitive:* port on waterfront between Chapel Street to the north and the north bank of the Pool to the south	Street-names, The Strand, Sea Brow, and Strand Street
II *Marginal Quay Extension:* 'Newe Havon' on north shore of the Pool, 1561, improved 1635 [possibly with a short jetty giving III *Marginal Quay Elaboration*]	
New Quay, north of Chapel Street, end of seventeenth century, abandoned 1802	Street-name, New Quay
Era ended by opening of Old Dock, 1715	
IV *Dock Elaboration:* on Mersey foreshore, north and south of Water Street port nucleus; with development at Birkenhead after 1847	Liverpool and Birkenhead Docks constructed before 1881; and Garston Docks
Era ended when Gladstone Entrance Lock opened (1,070 feet long) 1927	
V *Simple Lineal Quayage:* uninterrupted quayage of 1,500 feet in straight line giving berths for three deep-water vessels, all with post-Second World War transit sheds along their full length	Alexandra Dock, West Side; Alexandra Branch Dock No. 1, South Side; Alexandra Branch Dock No. 3 North Side (1881); Gladstone Branch Dock No. 1, South Side (1927); Canada West Side (1961); Vittoria Dock, North and South Sides (Birkenhead extended 1960)
VI *Specialized Quayage:* developed within the existing docks (earliest example Brunswick Dock originally for the timber trade, 1832); and extra-docks	Bromborough Dock, 1931: Extra-docks at Dingle Oil Jetties (1922); and Tranmere Oil Terminal (1960)

Little remains of the *primitive* port of Liverpool before the docks, except the alignment and names of certain streets, since the docks were superimposed on the original port sites obliterating them. But to understand the *dock elaboration* era one has to go back over 200 years, for the oldest surviving Liverpool dock, Salthouse Dock, admitted vessels as long ago as 1753; and it is necessary to go back even further to find out why the port nucleus was established where it has remained.

The Port Nucleus Established

Fig. 71 shows the *primitive* port on the Mersey waterfront, the nucleus being at the junction with Water Street forming with Dale Street the principal transverse route inland via the only bridge across the Pool valley. From north to south on the waterfront the principal buildings were the Church of St. Nicholas, with its Chapel of St. Mary del Quay, the Tower on the north side of Water Street, and the Custom House opposite, erected in 1680.[8] The Tower had been fortified by the Stanleys, one of two powerful Liverpool families, as early as 1406 and was used for direct

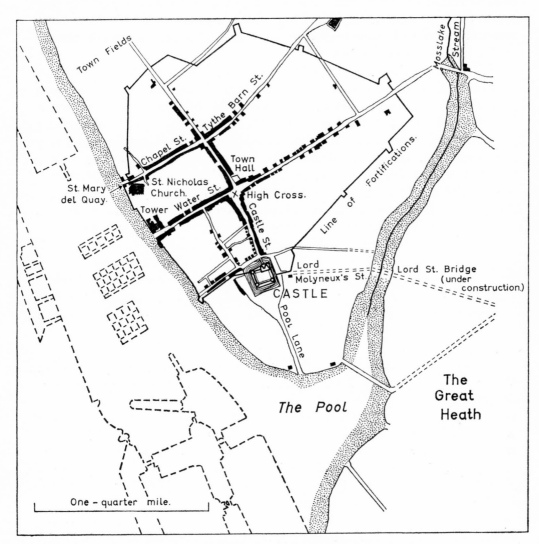

FIG. 71   The *Primitive* Port of Liverpool in 1668

The outlines of the present docks, Georges Pier, and the three Pierhead buildings have been inserted to show the amount of reclamation carried out upon the foreshore of the *primitive* port (*cf.* Plate XVI). The map is from Sir Edward Moore, *Liverpool in King Charles the Second's Time*, edited by W. F. Irvine [map compiled by the editor], Liverpool: Young, 1899, opposite page 1.

279

military embarkation to Ireland. A second transverse route was apparently necessary, giving Liverpool an **H** lay-out. This was Chapel Street, leading from the church of St. Nicholas, significantly the patron saint of seafarers. *Marginal quay extension* took place when a quay was erected on the north side of the Pool in 1561, but the Pool was shallow and only small craft used it. This silt-laden estuary probably gave rise to the name of the port (*O.E.* lifrig—thick or muddy pool).[9] A New Quay was added northwards from the Chapel about the end of the seventeenth century, and the site still bears that name.

The water situation was favourable, with Atlantic trade developing. The land situation in the north-west quadrant of England was favourable, the port developing as a counterpart to London, Bristol, and Newcastle–Hull. So much for the larger horizons of Liverpool in the late seventeenth century. The land site was upon a promontory of sandstone projecting southwards towards the Mersey shore at a very acute angle (Fig. 74), with possibilities for defence, since the sandstone rises some seventy feet above the floor of the Pool valley inland. Only the water site was defective. Not only is the range of tide as much as thirty feet, but the current is strong in the Narrows and the deep channel is on the far side of the waterway. The main anchorage therefore was not in front of the town.[10] According to the sailing directions of Greenville Collins in 1690:

> '. . . The ships lye aground before the town of Liverpool; 'tis bad riding afloat before the town by reason of the strong tydes that run there; therefore ships that ride afloat, ride up at the Sleyne, where is less tyde.'[11] [The Sloyne anchorage is off Tranmere, with present-day depths of up to 55 feet L.W.O.S.T.]

The difficulties of the water site will be dealt with more fully in the succeeding chapter, but at least it may be remarked that the swiftness of the current prevented the port from being choked with the silt of Liverpool Bay that killed the first major port in the north-west quadrant, the now totally defunct Port of Chester. If the water site of Liverpool is compared to that of Bristol, the advantage is with the southern port as long as ships lie aground. Both ports are afflicted with high tidal ranges, but the Port of Bristol could be extended over the marshes of a river flood-plain. In contrast, the Port of Liverpool waterfront was a rather steep foreshore which early became an embarrassment to ships. A graphic painting by J. McGahey,[12] based on an old print, shows a north-west gale lashing the Strand and the Tower as mariners struggle to haul a boat ashore at the foot of Water Street. As Daniel Defoe put it:

> 'for tho' the Mersey is a noble harbour, and is able to ride a thousand sail of ships at once, yet those ships that are to be laid up, or lye by the walls all winter,

or longer, as sometimes may be the case; must tide there, as in an open road, or (as the seamen call it) be haled a shore; neither of which would be practicable in a town of so much trade: And, in the time of the late great storm, they suffer'd very much on that account'.[13]

Liverpool had, however, in contrast to Bristol, a convenient inlet immediately south of the port, which gave prospect of calm water once it was cut off and impounded.

The famous Old Dock at Liverpool in the mouth of the Pool began the long *dock elaboration* era at the port. This was the first wet dock in Britain with legal quays, and there is an interesting link between it and an earlier dock on the Thames. In 1709 George Sococold, the probable engineer of the Howland Dock on the Thames, was invited[14] to Liverpool, though it was Thomas Steers,[15] probably his assistant, who in fact designed and completed the Old Dock authorized by an Act of 1709.[16] The really novel feature of Liverpool's first dock, as C. N. Parkinson has pointed out,[17] was its 'water-encroaching' site, since Steers's design (Fig. 72) placed the four-acre dock actually in the mouth of the Pool. This set the pattern for all the other docks at Liverpool—on sites reclaimed from the Mersey. The rest of the

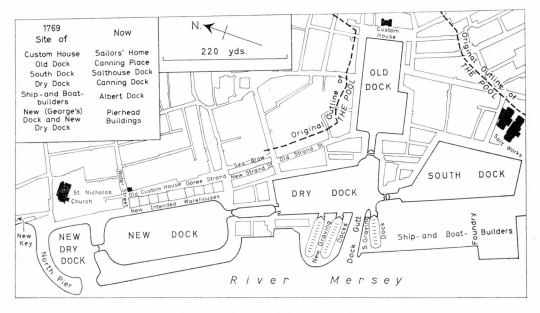

FIG. 72   The Port of Liverpool, 1769

Based on part of the map by George Perry. The 'new intended [Goree] warehouses' were built, but lost by fire in 1802. All the streets shown were entirely built-up. The original outline of the Pool is taken from H. Peet, 'Thomas Steers', *Transactions of the Historic Society of Lancashire and Cheshire*, 82 (1930), 163–242, 186

Pool was filled and levelled up all around the dock, and a new Custom House was erected on the east side of the dock (where the Sailors' Home stands today), thus symbolizing the slight southward migration of the port nucleus from the foot of Water Street. With the success of the Old Dock and increasing trade, Thomas Steers, who had been appointed first dockmaster, was on hand to design and lay the foundation stone of a second dock to the south—the Salthouse Dock, named after the 1696 salt-works. Financial and engineering difficulties delayed the opening of this dock for seventeen years until 1753, and, modified in form, it is the oldest surviving dock in the present lay-out of the port. Both these docks had single gates which kept back the water during the ebb of the tide. They were sited to the south of the *primitive* port on the Mersey foreshore, which had become the home of ship- and boat-builders, until in 1759 the dockmaster was ordered to keep the foreshore clear. The Corporation further authorized the deposition of rubbish north of the Old Dock entrance to begin the reclamation of the site of what became the third dock immediately to the west of Water Street obliterating the *primitive* port. This was George's Dock opened in 1762. Here is the first example of the priority given to docks over shipbuilding on the Liverpool foreshore. Some shipbuilders remained on the foreshore west of Salthouse Dock until they in turn were superseded by the foundations for the Albert Dock in 1840.[18]

The long *dock elaboration* era lasted until 1927, including developments at Birkenhead and Garston.

TABLE 92

Docks at Liverpool and Birkenhead in Order of Construction
(see Figs. 78–81; and Fig. 84)

N—north of Water Street port nucleus; S—south of port nucleus; B—Birkenhead

1715	S	Old Dock (closed 1826)
1718	S	Dry Basin (adjacent to Old Dock)
1753	S	Salthouse Dock
1762		Georges Dock (closed 1900), opposite nucleus
1776	S	Duke [of Bridgewater]'s Dock
1788	S	King's Dock
1796	S	Queen's Dock
1812	S	Union Dock
1821	N	Princes Dock
1829	S	Canning Dock (Old Dock Dry Basin remodelled)
1830	N	Clarence Dock (first dock for steamships—now occupied by Clarence Generating Station)
1832	S	Brunswick Dock (originally for timber)
1834	N	Waterloo Dock
1836	N	Victoria and Trafalgar Docks
1846	S	Albert Dock; Old Dock(Garston)

1847	B	Morpeth and Egerton Docks
1848	N	Salisbury, Collingwood, Stanley, Nelson, and Bramley-Moore Docks
1849	N	Wellington Dock
1851	N	Sandon Dock
1852	N	Huskisson Dock (for timber trade having outgrown Brunswick Dock)
1858	S	Coburg Dock (Union Dock and Basin remodelled)
1859	N	Canada Dock
1860	B	Great Float
1863	B	Low Water Basin
1864	S	Herculaneum[19] Dock
1866	B	Alfred Dock (formerly part of Low Water Basin)
1874		North Dock (Garston)
1881	N	Brocklebank, Langton, Alexandra, and Hornby Docks
1883	S	Harrington Dock
1884	B	Wallasey Dock (formerly part of Low Water Basin)
1888	S	Toxteth Dock
1909	B	Vittoria Dock; Stalbridge Dock (Garston)
1927	N	Gladstone Dock
1933	B	Bidston Dock

The docks of the late eighteenth century were brought into being by the development of the Atlantic trade ('triangular' trade with West Africa and America), particularly after the American War of Independence. Cotton was one of the most important cargoes, and Liverpool became an important cotton market as well as a cotton port. It might be thought that Manchester would have become the chief market, but the cotton broker needed experience of the raw material in order to be able to supply the varied specialized needs of the manufacturer.[20] More bulky cargoes were provided with a new transverse track inland, the Leeds and Liverpool Canal, begun in 1770, though not finished until 1816;[21] direct connection with the Mersey was not made until 1846. Meantime the corn traders of the port were becoming exasperated with the canal monopolists, and they were leaders in the struggle for the Liverpool and Manchester Railway, opened in 1830, the first railway in the world linking important towns.[22] In that year also was opened the Clarence Dock for steamships. It occupied an isolated position north of the other docks because steamships at that time were considered dangerous vessels. The site has now been used for the Clarence Generating Station; and this part of the dock estate can easily be identified from the river and on air photographs by the three tall chimneys of the power station. Cotton, coal, grain, timber, and West Indian produce (rum and sugar) all increased in the early nineteenth century, with the cotton textile manufacturers of Lancashire as pacemakers of Britain's Industrial Revolution. The corn trade particularly developed after the Repeal of the Corn Laws in 1846. The response of Liverpool to these developments matched the opportunity presented. Throughout the nineteenth century the longest interval between the opening of successive docks was only twelve years, at the beginning and end of the century. Whatever the other shortcomings of municipal administration of the port, the Corporation's Dock Committee was alive to the necessity of keeping up with the demand for dock accommodation.

'Hitherto we have always been in arrear. When the new works are completed which are now in progress [Salisbury to Bramley-Moore Docks] we shall still be in arrear. . . . in Hull the increase [of trade] for two years amounts to less than one-third, and that of Bristol to one-fifth of the increase in Liverpool for *the last six months.*' [*Report of the Speech of J. Bramley-Moore, Dock Committee Chairman, on the Subject of Dock Extension, January 19, 1846*]

Great warehouses were erected for all manner of general cargo at Albert Dock, for tobacco at Stanley Dock, for grain at Waterloo Dock, and specialized timber storage was provided on the dock estate.

In 1848 the line of docks creeping northwards reached the point where the shore receded in the former Bootle Bay. This can be identified in the modern plan by the oblique angle made by the south and east quays of the Bramley-Moore Dock. Thereafter, to the north, the quays transverse to the shore could be longer. While the river wall remained in almost a straight line, the shore trended further to the east. The Huskisson Dock, originally with three branch docks and a vestibule or turning dock, became the pattern for docks constructed later. This lay-out has been contrasted with the earlier lay-out of a small rectangular dock parallel to the shore.[23] But it must be pointed out that the Princes Dock is opposite the very narrowest part of the Narrows. Moreover, where site restrictions were imposed by the projection of sandstone south of Brunswick Dock, the docks had to revert to the longitudinal rectangular lay-out in Toxteth and Harrington Docks, as explicitly stated by the dock engineer who designed them.[24] Certainly, there is a narrow Branch Dock extending from Herculaneum Dock, but it had to be blasted out of solid sandston and is only 125 feet wide. All this nineteenth-century dock development was punctuated by two great interrelated crises, concerned, firstly, with the way in which the port was to expand on to the opposite shore; and, secondly, with the administration of the port.

The Mersey Docks and Harbour Board

King John's Charter of 1207 gave the Liverpool burgesses the right to collect 'Town Dues' on ships trading to the port under their control, specifically administered by the Town Council of the Corporation of Liverpool under an Act of 1762. A further

Act in 1811 reduced the administrative body to a committee of 21 drawn from the 41-strong Town Council known as the Trustees of the Dock Estate; in 1826 this committee was reconstituted to include 15 members with a further 8 to be elected by dock ratepayers (merchants and shipowners), users of the port, who until then had not been represented in the port's administration. There was still much dissatisfaction. The freemen of Liverpool paid no dues, although this was remedied by the Municipal Corporations Act of 1835. More serious, the Common Council could veto the Trustees' decisions, and much of the port's revenues was diverted into the Corporation's coffers through the imposition of Town Dues, a familiar weakness of municipal management of port affairs. The Dock Committee had borrowing powers of up to £1 million, and the record shows that it could not be accused of lethargy in dock construction at Liverpool. But the municipality could not regard development across the river with the same enthusiasm. Plans and counter-plans for the expansion of the port across the Mersey resulted in an entirely new port authority —the first docks public trust in England. The story is complicated, and here it is possible only to summarize the main events, adding the possible motives involved (in italics).[25]

1824   Francis Jordan proposes a ship canal along Wallasey Pool.

1828   *Report* on the ship canal scheme by T. Telford, R. Stevenson, and A. Nimmo [favourable].
Liverpool Corporation purchases all the property adjacent to Wallasey Pool it can lay hands on for £180,264. *To prevent ship canal project.*

1840   Railway reaches Birkenhead.

1844   Liverpool Corporation sells its Wallasey Pool land for £330,000. *One party, within the Corporation, believes that more docks by private promoters, led by William Jackson and William Laird, are necessary, with no chance of Liverpool Corporation agreeing to construct them at Birkenhead. Another party believes that there is no chance of Birkenhead Docks becoming a reality, so the Corporation should take its profit on the sale of the Wallasey Pool land.*

1847   Two docks, Morpeth and Egerton, and the Low Water Basin open at Birkenhead, all in unsatisfactory condition because of financial difficulties[26] and the unsoundness of the original plans of J. M. Rendel.

1853   Royal Commission recommends a new body to take charge of Mersey harbour, to whom all property and dues should be transferred.

1855   Parliamentary Committee refuses Liverpool Corporation's application to build further docks along the north shore at Liverpool and recommends that the next port expansion should be the completion of the Birkenhead Dock scheme. Repurchase of Birkenhead Dock Estate by Liverpool Corporation for £1,143,000 (*cf.* 1828 and 1844 above) *because of above Parliamentary ruling.*

1856   Liverpool Corporation promotes a Bill including new plans for Birkenhead. *J. Hartley, the Liverpool dock engineer, rejects Rendel's plans as unsound.*

1857   Alarm of Great Western Railway Company, *because railway facilities were well provided for in Rendel's plans.* Co-operation between railway company, Manchester Chamber of Commerce, and Manchester Commercial Association in promoting a Bill which became an Act constituting the Mersey Docks and Harbour Board. *The Manchester interests are chiefly concerned in abolishing the Liverpool Town Dues.*

Thus the new port authority for Liverpool was forced upon the town by outside interests, the management of the successful Bill before Parliament actually being undertaken by the Town Clerk of Manchester. There were twenty-eight members of the new Mersey Docks and Harbour Board (hereinafter called the Board), of which 24 are elected by ratepayers. Significantly, 'Liverpool' was omitted from the title. Under the 1857 Act, Birkenhead became legally a part of the Port of Liverpool. In the Liverpool County Court in 1884 Judge Collier held that Birkenhead was a part of the Port of Liverpool relying on the 1857 Act and a Consolidation Act of the following year. A similar decision was given at Liverpool Assizes on February 8, 1928. This unity of port control at Liverpool is by no means matched by unity of local government control in the Merseyside conurbation. The township of Bootle

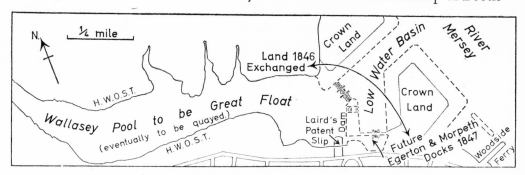

FIG. 73   The Birkenhead Project, 1843

Based on J. M. Rendel's *Report*, October 25, 1843. Sluices were to be provided within the dam through which water from the Great Float was to scour silt from the Low Water Basin. These proved a complete failure when finally operated, also seriously endangering vessels in the Great Float because of the rush of water. Parts of the Crown Lands were exchanged making room for Morpeth Dock, east of Egerton Dock, by 1847.

was incorporated as a separate borough in 1868; Birkenhead achieved similar status in 1877. When Liverpool Corporation advanced its case for annexation of Bootle in 1903 on the grounds of continuity of built-up area and common dependence on the docks, the fact that the docks were already under another comprehensive authority weakened the case for annexation, and to this day the 'Liverpool' Docks north of Canada Dock are within the Boroughs of Bootle and Crosby. Birkenhead was originally laid out on a grand scale, with a vast town square and a rectilinear street pattern, the longest streets two miles long in a straight line. As late as 1907 it was described as a town of 'unfulfilled promise',[27] an allegation being that the Board favoured 'their own side of the river',[28] so that the docks were under-employed. The last charge can no longer be sustained, but Birkenhead itself still lacks a city focus other than the crossing at Woodside, where ferries and tunnels speed traffic straight to the heart of Liverpool.

Mersey Docks and Harbour Board
PLATE XV LIVERPOOL SOUTHERN DOCKS
Looking south-east from the Pierhead as far as Toxteth Dock,
cf. Fig. 78.

In the criteria used hitherto for *simple lineal quayage*—1,500 feet of quay in one line for vessels of deep draught—it will be apparent that had such quays been provided parallel to the shore at Liverpool, the dock system there would have been unduly lengthened. It is six miles long from north to south as it is. If all the quays transverse to the shore had been made 1,500 feet long, or more, the river wall would have had to be further from the shore, so that longer ships could turn into the quays in impounded water. This would have put up costs of construction enormously. Instead, only four quays have been made of this length (see Table 91), each now able to take up to three deep-sea vessels, and one of these quays lies on the inner side of the river wall, Alexandra Dock, West Side. A fifth *simple lineal quay* has been added on the inner face of the river wall, Canada Dock, West Side, made possible by the reconstruction of the Langton–Canada entrance. Further quay development on these lines on the inner face of the river wall is restricted by the interruptions of dock entrances at an oblique angle within the wall itself; and there is the necessity for bridges between the wall and projecting dock peninsulas. Another long quay might, however, be possible at Gladstone Dock, West Side, if the river wall were widened immediately north of Gladstone Entrance Lock. There appears more room for larger vessels at Birkenhead in the Great Float, but here there is physical restriction in developing the entrance locks. Nevertheless, in 1960 a 150-foot extension of the Vittoria Dock provided three berths at the *simple lineal quayage* on each side of the dock. *Specialized quayage* has been provided within the docks; and in many cases docks originally built for the largest vessels then in existence have found their later role as specialized terminals, for class of vessel, for trading route, or for cargo. Some examples are: the Princes Dock (reconstructed in 1868 and 1949), for the Irish Sea mail boats; the southern docks, dominated by the West African trade; Hornby Dock, for timber; and Bidston Dock, for iron ore. Outside the docks there are the specialized terminals for cattle (Woodside and Wallasey Landing Stages); and for oil at Dingle and, most spectacularly of all, at Tranmere, opened in 1960.

The lay-out of the Port of Liverpool before the coming of the docks closely resembles the model of *Anyport*, complete with the Strand, Water Street as the transverse track, and the Tower[29] as the proximate strong-point. The docks also get progressively larger away from the port nucleus. But *Anyport* has a situation at the estuary head occupied by Runcorn and Widnes on the Mersey. Because of the shallow nature of the Upper Basin (see Chapter 12), Liverpool grew as a port much nearer the sea and not on an estuarine flood-plain. Like Dover, Liverpool had to be a water-encroaching port, its docks parallel to the shore until development of Birkenhead impounded water in Wallasey Pool transverse to the shore of the Narrows—a fundamental difference in the lay-outs at Liverpool and Birkenhead. It may be argued that the oil terminal occupies a different site from that suggested for *Anyport* in that it is upstream of the port nucleus. Yet this oil terminal serves the Stanlow oil

Mersey Docks and Harbour Board
PLATE XVI LIVERPOOL PORT NUCLEUS
Looking north-north-west, as far as Salisbury Dock, beyond the Clarence Generating Station. Note the sharp boundary between the dark windowless warehouses, north of the Royal Liver Building (centre), and the buildings of Liverpool's central business district, *cf.* Fig. 79.

depot and refinery within the Port of Manchester, and indeed has contributed to the decline in usefulness of Manchester's Queen Elizabeth II Oil Dock. Just as the title of the Manchester *Ship Canal* Company emphasizes that port's complete dependence on the canal, so the title *Mersey Docks* and Harbour Board emphasizes the dominance of the impounded water on which the Port of Liverpool depends. Nothing was more impressive than to travel the whole length of Liverpool Docks by that most original 'longitudinal' route, the Liverpool Overhead Railway, closed in 1956.[30] As on a flickering film, dock after dock flashed by, each different in its scene of port activity, relentlessly building up an unrivalled panorama six miles long, past forty docks. The port is certainly more public than anywhere else in Britain, with large passenger ships sailing right to the heart of the conurbation.

After the Old Dock was filled in, a new Custom House was built on its site in 1828–39.[31] This was damaged beyond repair by bombs in 1941, and the Custom House is now in the Cunard Building, exactly opposite the site it occupied in the *primitive* port before the nineteenth century. At Birkenhead the nucleus has always been close to the Woodside Peninsula. And below, supplementing the work of the ferries, two tunnels cut in the Keuper Sandstone link these port foci precisely. The Queensway road tunnel even uses the line of the transverse track of the *primitive* Port of Liverpool, below Dale Street, as if to drive home the fact that the nucleus of the port has remained close to where it was first established.

The Port of Liverpool in 1860

As a pendant to the story of Liverpool port development it might be useful to have a brief picture of what the port looked like one hundred years ago, as a contrast to the modern scene to be described in the chapters that follow. Thomas Baines in his *The Port and Town of Liverpool* (Liverpool, 1860) gives a remarkably comprehensive picture of the port lay-out and functions at that time. A few details from this book are summarized below.

One hundred years ago the Liverpool Docks extended from Canada Dock to Brunswick Dock on the south, with some very small docks further south on the undeveloped dock estate. At Birkenhead the dock walls were being erected around the Great Float, the Low Water Basin (which was to become Alfred Dock) was still in course of completion, and the Morpeth Dock was being enlarged, all consequent on being taken over by the Board.

'In erecting the sea wall, in front of the Liverpool Docks, great difficulties had to be overcome, in obtaining a solid foundation. The foundation in front of Princes Dock, in the narrowest part of the river, and that in which the currents are strongest, had to be laid on great balks of timber, sunk to a depth which could be reached only twice in the year, and then only for a few days, namely, at the vernal and autumnal equinoxes, when the tides ebb to the lowest point of the whole year. At one of those periods, in the month of March, 1817, the low water workings were entirely prevented by the tempestuousness of the weather, and nothing could be done, at that part of the foundation, until the end of September and the beginning of October.'[32]

In 1860 each dock at Liverpool was entered via a tidal basin or half-tide dock, and in the docks themselves there were no branch docks, nor vestibule docks for turning. The biggest paddle-wheel ships entered Canada Dock, opened in the previous year, 1859, because it was equipped with the widest dock entrance. Coburg Dock had been 'built for the accommodation of the great ocean steamers [only the year before, 1858], but these have now chiefly removed to the Huskisson and the Canada Docks.'[33] Timber trade was largely handled at Huskisson and Canada Docks, and wide quays had been built there for that purpose. The trade to the U.S.A. and Canada had become of greatest importance at this time, being the leading trade at all the northern docks except at Nelson, Clarence, and Princes.[34] Nelson Dock dealt with the Mediterranean trade and imports from 'the coasts of Europe from Gibraltar to Elsineur [sic]'.[35] Clarence Dock retained its original role as a base for steamers, but by this time it had been downgraded to 'steamers in the coasting trade'. The Princes Dock had also lost the largest ships in the American trade, and now dealt with the other chief trade of the port, the East India and China trade, sharing the imports with Albert Dock, 'its dock warehouses giving great advantage for that trade'.[36] The same trade used Wapping Dock and for the same reason. The North American trade also predominated in the southern docks, Queen's, Coburg, and Brunswick. Salthouse Dock was a 'favourite dock for East India and China trade, loading vessels'.[37] The only other export trade specifically mentioned was that of coal from the high-level railway serving the east quays of Wellington and Bramley-Moore Docks. Apart from Clarence Dock, Trafalgar and Canning Docks had also been downgraded to the coasting trade; while the Duke [of Bridgewater]'s Dock and Manchester Dock [near the Pierhead, filled in by Mersey Road Tunnel excavators, 1930] dealt with the river trade. A century ago the tonnage of imports was about half that of the exports; today the position is nearly reversed. Meat, fruit, ores, and animal feeding stuffs which are imported in great quantities today were hardly represented at all in the trade of 1860. Grain imports have increased enormously, though cotton shows a decline. Coal and salt were then important export cargoes; very little is handled now compared with a wide range of manufactured goods for export.[38] Although the first dock had been built in 1715, some 140 years before Baines wrote his book, he was justified in declaring:

'. . . the docks, as they now stand, have been constructed or entirely re-modelled during the last thirty years. . . . [and] A dock of four acres, large enough to receive 100 small vessels, and yielding a revenue of £600 a year, was the germ, from which the present docks and dock estate of the River Mersey have sprung.'[39]

REFERENCES

1. G. Chandler, *Liverpool*, London: Batsford, 1957, 97.
2. T. C. Barker, 'Lancashire Coal and Cheshire Salt and the Rise of Liverpool', *Transactions of the Historic Society of Lancashire and Cheshire*, 103 (1951), 83–101, 99–100; C. N. Parkinson, *The Rise of the Port of Liverpool* [until 1793], Liverpool: University Press, 1952, 57–9; and F. J. Routledge, 'History of Liverpool to 1700', *A Scientific Survey of Merseyside*, Published for the British Association, Liverpool: University Press, 1953, 94–106, 105–6.
3. *Liverpool Town Books*, August 16, 1611, Picton Reference Library, Liverpool; and G. Chandler, *op. cit.*, 279.
4. T. C. Barker, *loc. cit.*, 100.
5. F. J. Routledge, *loc. cit.*, 105; and C. N. Parkinson, *op. cit.*, 58.
6. *Ibid.*, 59.
7. F. J. Routledge, *loc. cit.*, 106.
8. E. H. Rideout, *The Custom House Liverpool*, Liverpool: Elly, 1928, gives details of earlier Custom Houses. See also R. C. Jarvis, *Custom Letter-Books of the Port of Liverpool 1711–1813*, Manchester: Chetham Society, 1954.
9. E. Ekwall, *Place-names of Lancashire*, Chetham Society, 1922, 116–17.
10. All the Mersey anchorages are on the west side of the Narrows, see J. E. Allison, *The Mersey Estuary*, Liverpool: University Press, 1949, 11–34.
11. *New and Exact Survey of the River Dee and Chester Water.*
12. Picton Reference Library, Liverpool, G. Chandler, *op. cit.*, 85.
13. D. Defoe, *Tour through England and Wales*, 1724–6, quoted by C. N. Parkinson, *op. cit.*, 84.
14. For the part played by Sir Thomas Johnson of Liverpool, see C. N. Parkinson, *op. cit.*, 68–83.
15. H. Peet, 'Thomas Steers', *Transactions of the Historic Society of Lancashire and Cheshire*, 82 (1930), 163–242 gives an account of what is known of Steers's life; and of George Sorocold, Appendix M, p. 239.
16. *An Act for Making a Convenient Dock or Bason at Leverpole, for the Security of All Ships Trading to and From the Said Port of Leverpole.* 8 Anne c. 12.
17. *Op. cit.*, 81.
18. *Ibid.*, 144.
19. Built partially on the site of the Herculaneum Pottery. Other docks are named after Royal and historical personages, battles, suburbs of Liverpool, and officials of the port authority.
20. F. E. Hyde, B. B. Parkinson, and S. Marriner, 'The Cotton Broker and the Rise of the Liverpool Cotton Market', *Economic History Review*, 8 (1956), 75–83, 76.
21. *British Waterways: The Leeds and Liverpool Canal: a Detailed Itinerary and Sectional Plans*, London: Pyramid, 1959, 80; and H. F. Killick, 'Notes on the Early History of the Leeds and Liverpool Canal', *Journal of the Bradford Historical and Antiquarian Society*, Part 2 (1897), 169–238.
22. G. S. Veitch, *The Struggle for the Liverpool and Manchester Railway*, Liverpool: Daily Post, 1930, 21–3.
23. Sir Rex Hodges, 'The Dock-System of the Port of Liverpool', *Merseyside: A Scientific Survey, op. cit.* 164–9.

24. G. F. Lyster, *On the Physical and Engineering Features of the River Mersey and the Port of Liverpool*, Paper read to the British Association Meeting at Liverpool, 1896, Picton Reference Library, Liverpool, H387/1/LY5,560.

25. The summary is based on information in J. A. Picton, *Memorials of Liverpool*, 2 vols., London: Longmans, 1873, I, 573 *et seq.*; P. Sulley, *History of Ancient and Modern Birkenhead*, London: Murphy, 1907, 56–77, 153 *et seq.*: B. D. White, *A History of the Corporation of Liverpool, 1835–1914*, Liverpool: University Press, 1951, 67–78; P. J. Emery, *Wallasey Pool: the Birth Pangs of a Port*, Unpublished thesis, M.A., University of Liverpool, 1959; and E. C. Woods, *The Intended Ship Canal Between the Rivers Mersey and Dee*, Unpublished MS, Wallasey Central Library, 1959.

26. For further details see P. J. Emery, *op. cit.*, 40–56; see also J. Ellacott, 'Description of the Low Water Basin at Birkenhead', *Minutes of Proceedings of the Institution of Civil Engineers*, 28 (1868–9), 518–35.

27. P. Sulley, *op. cit.*, 308.

28. *Ibid.*, 316.

29. Controlled by the Stanley family whereas the other powerful Liverpool family, the Molyneux, controlled Liverpool Castle, 1235–1725, of which no trace remains.

30. C. E. Box, *Liverpool Overhead Railway 1893–1956*, London: Railway World, 1959. This first overhead electric railway in the world, at an average of sixteen feet above ground, had to be closed because the viaduct had come to the end of its working life. It was estimated that £2 million was needed to put it in order at a time when annual receipts were £160,000, and traffic had fallen due to competition from motor omnibuses.

31. E. H. Rideout, *op. cit.*; and H. J. Muir, *Liverpool Custom Houses: Ancient and Modern* [Privately printed], 1947, Picton Reference Library, Liverpool, H337, MU1.

32. T. Baines, *op. cit.*, 64.

33. *Ibid.*, 104.

34. G. Chandler, *Liverpool Shipping: A Short History*, London: Phoenix, 1960 explains this importance, 103–36.

35. T. Baines, *op. cit.*, 87.

36. *Ibid.*, 99.

37. *Ibid.*, 97.

38. *Business in Great Waters*, Mersey Dock and Harbour Board, 1958, 13–15.

39. T. Baines, *op. cit.*, 62–3.

FURTHER REFERENCES

Allison, J. E. *The Geographical Growth of Birkenhead.* Unpublished thesis, M.A., University of Liverpool, 1939–40.

——. 'The Development of Merseyside and the Port of Liverpool', *Town Planning Review*, 24 (1953), 52–76.

Chandler, G. and E. Saxon. *Liverpool under James I.* Liverpool: Brown, Picton, and Hornby Libraries.

Gibson Martin, W. A. *A Century of Liverpool's Commerce.* Liverpool: Chamber of Commerce, 1950.

Hyde, F. E. 'The Expansion of Liverpool's Carrying Trade with the Far East and Australia 1860–1914', *Transactions of the Royal Historical Society*, 6, 5th Series (1956), 139–60.

Jones, D. C. (ed.). *The Social Survey of Liverpool.* 3 vols. Liverpool: University Press, 1934.

McIntyre, W. R. S. *Birkenhead: Yesterday and Today.* Liverpool: Philip, 1948.

Poole, B. *The Commerce of Liverpool.* London: Longmans, 1854.

Rees, H. 'Evolution of Mersey Estuarine Settlements', *Economic Geography*, 21 (1945), 97–103.

Roxby, P. M. 'Aspects of the Development of Merseyside', *Geography*, 16 (1927), 91–100.

Smith, W. *Physical Survey of Merseyside.* Liverpool: University Press, 1946.

Thompson, F. L. *Merseyside Plan 1944.* H.M.S.O., 1945.

Walford, C. *A Review of the Causes which Have Contributed to the Commercial Greatness of Liverpool.* London: Clowes, 1883.

Webster, T. *The Port and Docks of Birkenhead.* London: Chapman and Hall, 1848.

——. *Minutes of the Evidence and of Proceedings on the Liverpool and Birkenhead Dock Bills in the Sessions of 1848–52 and 1855–6.* 2 vols. London: King 1857.

Woods, E. C. and P. C. Brown. *The Rise and Progress of Wallasey.* Wallasey: Corporation, 1960.

and

Chandler, G. *Liverpool.* London: Batsford, 1957, for more complete bibliography of historical works.

Chapter 12

THE MERSEY AS LIVERPOOL'S WATER SITE

THE Mersey enters the sea in Liverpool Bay, which is bestrewn by the sand that chokes the Dee estuary and strangled the Port of Chester. Yet the Mersey estuary provides the approaches and the water site of the Liverpool Docks, Bromborough Dock, and the two earliest Garston Docks; it also provides the approaches to Birkenhead Docks and the Manchester Ship Canal—making it one of the world's busiest waterways. The Port of Liverpool in its widest sense is not merely the dock systems of Liverpool and Birkenhead, but includes the waterway between, and far upstream, and well out to sea. The Board is the pilotage authority for the Liverpool Pilotage District, which includes the River Mersey upstream to the entrance to the Manchester Ship Canal and extends as far as lines joining the Isles of Anglesey and Man to the Cumberland coast. The seaward boundary of Liverpool's water site most clearly begins at the Bar Lightship, where all ships converge towards the buoyed entrance channel. A vessel passing this lightship is certainly within the Port of Liverpool, yet she is still twelve sea miles north-west of the nearest dock. From Liverpool Bay, or the *Outer Estuary*, the flood-tide sweeps through the venturi-like passage of *The Narrows* and largely spends itself in filling the opportune reservoir of the *Upper Basin*. From this natural Great Pent (*vide* Dover in 1581), the ebb-stream flushes through the Narrows and is trained between the lurking sand-banks in Liverpool Bay. Everything interlocks. The Upper Basin is vital to the sea approaches. This explains Liverpool's vigorous opposition in the late nineteenth century when Manchester wished to erect training walls confining the Mersey through the Basin (Fig. 70); and why J. A. Cashin felt it necessary to go as far east as Runcorn railway bridge before the point was reached beyond which the river was not considered to play an important part in the regime of the *sea* channels in Liverpool Bay.[1]

The Upper Basin

The extent of the Upper Basin results from the position of the present high-water mark at the end of a series of sea-level oscillations in post-glacial times. The bordering land is low-lying, and it has been shown that a rise of mean sea-level of 50 feet would triple the area of the Upper Basin,[2] while a rise of only 25 feet would extend it over the Mersey flood-plain for some seven miles east of Runcorn. Eighty-five per cent of the 36 square miles of the Basin, occupied by the Stanlow and Dungeon Banks, is uncovered at L.W.O.S.T., the remainder consisting of narrow anastomotic channels with two or three feet of water trickling through them. At high tide the Upper Basin is an impressive sheet of water, and at springs vessels drawing $11\frac{1}{2}$ feet can reach Warrington, seven miles east of Runcorn. The sailing channel varies widely. It is faintly ironic that in the Upper Basin of the Mersey (O.E. Mæres-ea), which means 'boundary river', the Ordnance Survey writes: 'The boundary between Cheshire and Lancashire is not determined in the River Mersey', because of the instability of channels and banks. Since 1892, the channel to Widnes has rarely been on the Cheshire or southern side of a median line between high-water marks. This is in such striking contrast to the positions of the channel between 1829–84 (Fig. 70) that it has been fairly inferred that works in connection with the Manchester Ship Canal, 1887–94 and the first dredging of the Bar in the Outer Estuary were the cause of this change of regime.[3] The engineers to the Mersey Docks and Harbour Board have always contended that the movement of the channel across the greater part of the Upper Basin is vital. This movement contributes to the instability of the banks, facilitating their erosion, and thereby maintains the capacity of the Upper Basin as a reservoir or cistern of water, which on the ebb would sluice the channel in Liverpool Bay. This idea was put forward at least as early as 1822.[4] Since 1881 the Board has made a quinquennial survey of the cubic capacity of the Upper Basin and would view any marked decrease with concern. The capacity of the basin has in fact decreased by about eight per cent since the first reliable survey of 1851. In the Upper Basin the main ebb-channels are the Garston and Eastham channels leading from Garston Docks and the entrance to the Manchester Ship Canal. It is now known that material dredged from the seaward end of the Garston and Eastham Channels in the Pluckington Bank and Bromborough Dock areas enters from the sea and not from upstream. The flushing movement of land water is not completely effective since, being of a lower salinity and density than sea water, the ebb flow rides over a bottom layer of water moved in from the sea. And, as on the Thames, the estuary would benefit if all dredgings were removed from the system by being pumped ashore, rather than deposited in Liverpool Bay, even though the deposit ground is five miles north-west of the Queen's Channel training walls.[5] Ultimate conservancy authority was vested in the Mersey Conservancy Commission (established under an 1842 Act). The principal duties of conservancy, now vested in the Minister of Transport, are to preserve the Mersey navigation and to guard against encroachment on the tideway, which might tend to reduce the tidal capacity of the Upper Basin.

The Manchester Ship Canal Company and British Transport Docks (Garston) depend on the two principal channels from Eastham and Garston respectively, leading to the single channel which runs downstream through the Narrows. Both channels are buoyed by the Board. But the Manchester Ship Canal Company is responsible for depths in the Eastham Channel. Both the Eastham and Garston Channels have bars at their western ends and to that point on the Eastham Channel, Unilever Merseyside Ltd. dredge a short approach to their Bromborough Dock entrance. Elsewhere, in the Narrows and in Liverpool Bay, the Mersey Docks and Harbour Board maintain and buoy the channels.

The Narrows

Opposite Dingle Point, at the southern end of the Liverpool Docks, the Upper Basin has contracted from its maximum width of 16,000 feet to 7,000 feet. Here the Narrows begin, with a minimum width of only 2,500 feet opposite the Princes Landing Stage. The Liverpool Docks are on a 'water-encroaching' site, the river wall of the docks is about on the line of low water, except towards the south (see below). At two hours after high water in the Upper Basin the ebb gradient is about 10 inches per mile, increasing to the surprisingly large maximum of nearly 30 inches per mile. No wonder the ebb current through the Narrows is as fast as 5 knots—or even 7 knots at springs with a following wind. Much of the sand is scoured away, in places only 'stones and shell' are found on the bed, the only part of the entire estuary which is free of sand from shore to shore.[6] Low water soundings give depths of 40–50 feet and over. Unfortunately, the current swings towards the Birkenhead side in the Sloyne deep, giving slack water alongside the river wall of the southern docks of Liverpool. This is the site of Pluckington Bank extending southward from near the Pierhead. G. F. Lyster, the Board's engineer in the second half of the nineteenth century, attempted to overcome this inconvenience by avoiding it, taking the shoal in flank. The deep-water entrance to the southern docks at Liverpool is sited well to the south—the Brunswick Entrance, with intercommunication between other docks to the north. Even so, the channel to the Brunswick Entrance has to be dredged continually and most carefully watched. It is surveyed three times a week, possibly the most frequently surveyed dock entrance channel in the United Kingdom.

The origin of such a bottle-neck as the Narrows on a tidal estuary is a puzzle. Some authors have wished to make the Mersey a tributary of the Dee across the Wirral Peninsula as late as historic times, but this theory has been effectively countered.[7] There are three great difficulties in attempting to suggest how the Narrows came about, due to:

(1) the deposition of glacial Boulder Clay burying the pre-glacial channel of the Mersey cut in rock;

(2) the presence of a number of fault blocks of Keuper Sandstone, from the north-west corner of the Wirral Peninsula north-eastwards to Liverpool itself;[8]

(3) several post-glacial changes of sea-level (combined effect of eustatic changes of the sea and isostatic recovery of the land), though, certainly, the last movement has been a rise in sea-level.

Boulder Clay forms the Wirral watershed and wraps around the above-mentioned Keuper Sandstone blocks. From Dingle Point the shortest route to the sea in Hillhouse Coast[9] times (about 5,000 B.C.) may well have been between the Birkenhead and New Brighton fault blocks along the line of Wallasey Pool. This valley is the only one in the Liverpool–Birkenhead area not controlled by the north south-faulting. But another route from Dingle was possible, north-north-west along a line of faulting, and thus two exits may have been used concurrently, the Wallasey fault block forming an island between them. In this hypothesis the Narrows appears as a fault-guided valley. Being fault-guided, it may have been eroded down more quickly with the rejuvenation that followed the fall in sea-level after Hillhouse Coast times. Progressively, the Narrows took over from the Wallasey Pool outlet, leaving a forest growing up there (in the peat on the site of the present Wirral coast), with the Narrows submerged by the most recent rise in sea-level. The Fender river was diverted eastward into the Wallasey valley, the lower part of which was drowned, first to form Wallasey Pool, and later, water was artificially impounded there to form the Great Float of Birkenhead Docks. Once the Narrows took the whole of the tidal flow, this was confined between rock outcrops at Dingle, Tranmere, the sandstone of southern Liverpool, and the rocks of the New Brighton promontory. But even the Narrows has been exposed to recent wind and sea attack. Immediately north of the medieval site of Liverpool, blown sand is to be found on the very part of the shore that had receded under wave attack from the north-west across Liverpool Bay, creating the former Bootle Bay.[10] This embayment has now been largely masked by the building of larger docks north of Nelson Dock after 1848; but the bay outline is still partially reflected in the alignment of the river wall of the northern dock system on the Liverpool side. This whole section on the origin of the Narrows is speculative. It is based largely on a suggestion of R. Kay Gresswell[11] and does account for the alignment both of the Narrows and its tributaries.

Liverpool Bay or the Outer Estuary

It is in Liverpool Bay that the majority of the Mersey approach difficulties have been found. Before dredging began on the Bar in 1890, there was then a depth there of only 10–12 feet L.W.O.S.T. (19 feet L.W.O.N.T.), increased to 31 feet H.W.O.N.T. and 41 feet at H.W.O.S.T. The story of the evolution of the channels in Liverpool

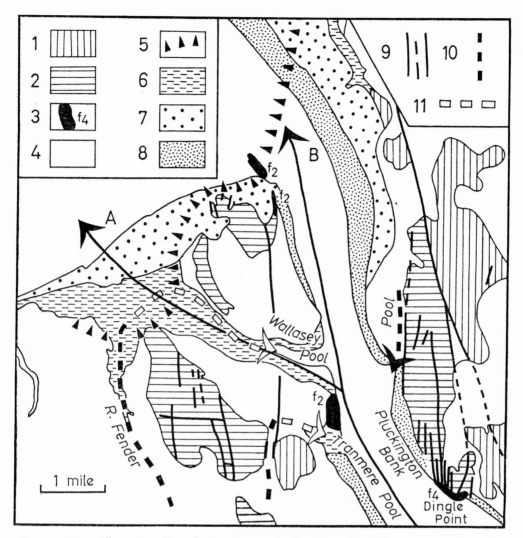

FIG. 74 Factors Illustrating a Hypothesis to Account for the Orientation of the Mersey Narrows and Wallasey Pool (Birkenhead Docks) and the Former Pool of Liverpool and Tranmere Pool

A. Outlet of Mersey via Wallasey Pool; B. Later outlet via the Narrows.
1. Bunter Pebble Beds, f_2; 2. Upper Bunter Sandstone, f_3 and Keuper Sandstone, f_4; 3. Outcrops of solid rock on the shore of the Narrows; 4. Glacial Boulder Clay; 5. Inferred position of the 'Hillhouse' coastline, *circa* 5,000, B.C.; 6. Present distribution of alluvium; 7. Present distribution of blown sand; 8. Dry at low water (docks omitted); 9. Faults; 10. Stream courses parallel to faults oriented to A; 11. Stream courses oriented to B.
The factors involved are A, B, 5, 9, 10, and 11.
Based in part on Crown Copyright Geological Survey Maps by permission of the Controller of H.M. Stationery Office.

Bay is complicated, but the development falls into four periods: the period of natural channels before Denham's survey, 1833; 1833–90; 1891–1909, the period of the first successful dredging of the Bar and channels; and 1909 to the present, with continued dredging, and training of the principal ebb- and flood-channels.

The first comprehensive survey of Liverpool Bay is that by Captain Greenville Collins in 1689. A constant feature on all charts from that survey until today is the Great Burbo Bank, lying athwart the line that bisects the right angle formed by the Wirral coastline and the coastline of Lancashire from the Narrows to Formby Point (Fig. 75). Gresswell showed that a diminution in the velocity of the ebb-stream issuing from the Narrows would lead to deposition of material, with the ebb bifurcating around the bank to form two ebb-channels[12]—shown on Collins's chart as the Rock and Formby Channels. On this chart the only approach for which landmarks were given was the Rock Channel, vessels being lightened if necessary in the Hyle Lake, a deep-water area off Hoylake on the north-west corner of the Wirral Peninsula. These three features, Great Burbo Bank, Rock Channel, and Crosby-Formby Channels appear on all the eighteenth- and early nineteenth-century charts, though variations in detail are great. The chief cause of variation in the channels was silting in the ebb-channels, with subsequent diversion and the mutual evasion of ebb- and flood-channels. Ebb-channels shoal towards the sea, while flood-channels shoal towards the land, and often there is a sill between them. The channels evade each other for two reasons: the ebb flows on after the flood has set in causing the latter to find a different path; ebb- and flood-channels are of different salinities, and there is often horizontal stratification between water moving in different directions at the ebb- and flood-channel boundary.[13] Modern illustration of this can be given. On the early flood, the water-level outside the Crosby West Training Bank is six inches higher than between the training banks where the ebb is still running;[14] and the 1960 chart shows mutual evasion between the untrained ebb- and flood-sections of the Formby Channel, with the sill between them dry at L.W.E.S.T.

On the 1813 chart two ebb-channels are shown, the Rock Channel and the South Channel, and each had a flood-channel associated with it.[15] One of these flood-channels, the Formby Channel, was actually used as a possible approach, and there was a pronounced bend where the sailing channel twisted across the bar between the Formby (flood) and South (ebb) channels (Fig. 75). Apart from silting in such channels, the dominant westerly winds, with a long fetch across the Irish Sea may, in free natural conditions, have caused banks to move eastward, blocking the existing channels and causing the main ebb- and flood-streams to break through somewhere else. In any event, the Rock and Formby Channels shoaled so considerably in the early nineteenth century that by 1833 the port was shut for four hours out of every twelve.[16] Lieutenant [later Admiral] H. M. Denham was called in to make an Admiralty survey and discovered that the ebb had indeed found a new exit, the New Channel. Naturally, it had a bar at its seaward end, and Denham attempted to dredge it.

> 'The most simple and economical means . . . is by towing, with a steamer, a flexible harrow, made of lengths of old chain cable, spiked at intervals and spread on a beam of African oak, towards the towing span, with their ends connected with a double saw-toothed scraper . . . cost £68.'[17]

This operation in 1838 and 1839 cost between £3,000 and £4,000, but probably had little effect on the estuary, since physical removal of the sand was to prove necessary to make any significant effect on the bar—and fifty more years were to pass before that operation was attempted.

Between 1833 and 1890 the ebb-stream twice broke through to the north in what might be regarded as a cyclic return to the position it occupied in 1813, and this might well have been attained eventually but for a later training revetment. The Victoria Channel broke through to the north of the New Channel about 1840, and the Queen's Channel took over from the Victoria Channel between 1851 and 1856 (Fig. 75).

In 1876 G. F. Lyster, engineer to the Board, had seen a suction dredger at work on the sandy bed of the River Loire clearing out the foundations for a bridge. His first attempt at using a centrifugal pump dredger in the Liverpool Docks was not a success because the material was too light, but it gave promise of success on the coarser material of the Bar.[18] Until 1885 no dredging alone, unaccompanied by permanent river works, had ever succeeded in making any permanent improvement across any river bar. Between 1885–7 Gedney's Channel, across a bar in New York harbour, was lowered 2 feet by dredging, to 26 feet L.W.O.S.T. This was a case of regulating the depth of the channel, by which the maximum depths obtaining in some places were extended along its entire length. Here was a spur to Liverpool. If New York, the other terminal of the transatlantic ferry, could accept vessels drawing up to 26 feet at all states of the tide, it meant that the Liverpool Bar alone might hold up the large fast liners coming into service, 'Ocean Greyhounds carrying a large number of impatient passengers.'[19] An attempt had to be made to emulate the success at New York. Whereas New York has a tidal range of 5 feet, the spring tide rose and fell 30 feet over the Liverpool Bar, and to admit vessels drawing 26 feet at all times no less than 17 feet of sand had to be removed from the Bar.

In 1891 the first successful dredging took place. Two hopper barges, built to carry dock dredgings out to sea, were fitted with centrifugal sand pumps. This device has been the key to deep channels in Liverpool Bay. Such pumps could become efficient only with the development of the steam turbine, and therefore not until after 1880. A centrifugal pump is in principle the reverse of a water turbine,

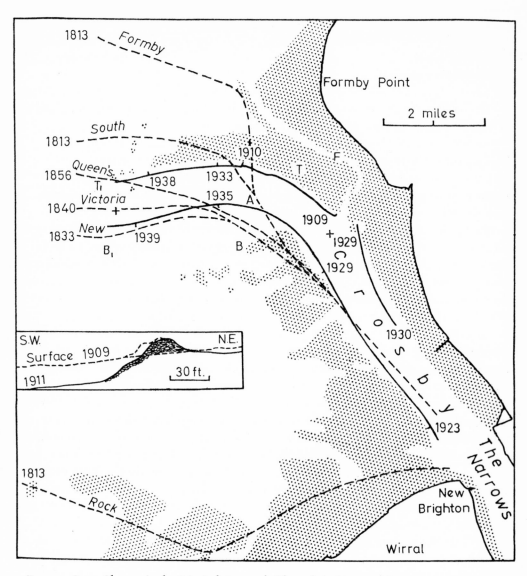

FIG. 75   Some Changes in the Principal Approach Channels in Liverpool Bay, 1813–1960: Inset—
Cross-sections of Taylor's Bank Revetment in 1909 and 1911

Names of channels are in sloping lettering. Twentieth-century dates adjoining barbs on the walls
indicate progressive construction of training banks, though only the Taylor's Bank Revetment and
Crosby Training Banks were built continuously between the dates indicated (see J. A. Cashin, *loc. cit.*
Fig. 12). The crosses in the present channel represent Crosby Light-vessel (to the east) and Formby
Light-vessel (to the west). The stippled areas dry out at L.W.E.S.T. For explanation of initial letters
of banks, etc., see Fig. 76.

Based on copies of charts kindly supplied by the Marine Surveyor and Water Bailiff, Mersey Docks
and Harbour Board.

and G. F. Lyster was quick to seize on the possibilities of the apparatus. Later, special sand pump dredgers were to be built embodying several patents of A. G. Lyster,[20] G. F. Lyster's son. Their first target was the coarse sand of the Bar, piled up between an ebb- and a flood-channel,

> 'with a long sloping foreshore on each side, stretching across the mouth of the main channel; in plan its form is that of an irregular curve, somewhat in the shape of a horseshoe with its convex side seaward, separating the deep water of the channel from that of the offing.'[21]

When dredging began, the approach to Liverpool was by a two-course channel: from the Bar Lightship to Crosby Lightship, the Queen's Channel; and from the Crosby Lightship to the Narrows, the Crosby Channel. The position of the dredged cut across the Bar was made in line with the Queen's Channel, in order not to produce another bend in the approach. A 3,000-ton dredger was at work in 1893. It was realized that deepening the two-course channels would help the cut across the Bar, so dredging of the rest of the Crosby Channel began in 1893 and of the Queen's Channel in 1894. By 1899 a minimum depth of 27 feet was achieved throughout the whole approach.

But the dredging had other less satisfactory results. Deepening the Crosby Channel caused it to take an increasing proportion of the ebb flow at the expense of the Rock Channel, which shoaled by an average of 3 feet during the period 1895–1905. (Since 1939 this channel has dried completely at low water springs.) In addition, the Queen's Channel received more flood water with the dredging of the Bar. Since strong flood- and ebb-channels are mutually evasive, an early result was the sharpening of the Crosby Bend. The increased ebb flow eroded Taylor's Bank on the outside of the bend while Askew Spit grew on the inside of the bend. Moreover, Askew Spit spread faster than the opposite bank was eroded, reducing the width of the channel at the bend from 2,700 feet in 1892 to 1,350 feet in 1906.

> 'The Navigation has thereby been rendered less easy, requiring Pilots and others to use great care when rounding this point. On the North East side of the Channel, Taylor's Bank has been eroded, but the erosion is not equal to the advance of Askew Spit.' [1906][22]

Though additional sand pump dredgers were brought into action, the radius of the curve continued to decrease. Further west, Taylor's Spit began to project into the channel, which after 1905 had ceased to be a simple two-course approach.

Fig. 76 shows the progressive changes in the shapes of Askew's Spit and Taylor's Spit, formed between the mutually evasive ebb- and flood-channels, with the channel gradually corrected by training walls and dredging. In view of the rapid deterioration of the Crosby Bend after 1905, A. G. Lyster advised the revetting of Taylor's Bank, since it was feared that a new channel might break through to the north as had twice happened since Denham's survey. In April 1909 Taylor's Bank revetment was begun—the first training wall in Liverpool Bay—and the result was anxiously awaited.

> '. . . the current, in sweeping around the curve, undermined the stone work, and gradually drew the stone down the face of the bank. Stone was continually supplied to the mound until the whole face of the bank was revetted with about 2 feet thickness of stone right down to the sea-bed . . . a diver could walk up quite comfortably all round the face of the bank.' [See Fig. 75, inset][23]

Two self-propelled steam hopper barges were used for the work, each carrying 650 tons of stone, and later the fleet was increased to a maximum of eleven of such vessels. The limestone was obtained from the Board's quarries at Llanddulas and Penmaenmawr, North Wales, a run of between 25 and 35 miles. The quantity of stone necessary to build the banks has varied between 18 and 80 tons per foot run. As there are now some fifteen miles of training walls, the magnitude of the work can be imagined.

> 'The normal method of dumping is to allow the hopper to drift sideways across the line, bow-on to the finished work, with just enough use of the engines to hold her parallel to the line of the bank. At the instant of crossing the line, marked by sighting poles on the finished bank, the doors are let go simultaneously.'[24]

Dumping from the fleet of hoppers began at about $1\frac{1}{2}$ hours before high water, so that all would be finished before the ebb began to run. The walls have remained remarkably stable, each piece fitting in with its neighbours mechanically. Later topping of the crest is necessary as the bank settles, and this process accounts for two-fifths of

FIG. 76 Changes in the Queen's and Crosby Channels in the Vicinity of the Crosby Bend, 1890–1960

Each rectangular chart extract measures 5 nautical miles east–west by 2 nautical miles north–south. The two- and three-fathom contours represent depths at L.W.E.S.T. Banks dry at L.W.E.S.T. are stippled. A, Askew Spit; B, Northern tip of Great Burbo Bank; B₁, Little Burbo Bank; F, Formby Channel; T, Taylor's Bank; T₁, Taylor's Spit. The position of black conical buoys (on the starboard hand when entering) and of red can boat beacons (on the port hand), marking the entrance channel, are indicated by larger dots; with two crosses representing the Formby Lightship to the west and the Crosby Lightship to the east. Taylor's Bank Revetment and later walls are shown by thicker lines.

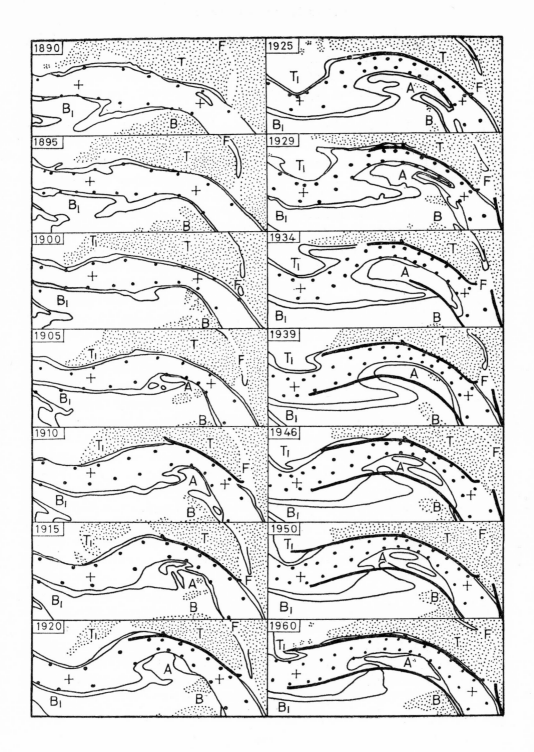

the total weight of stone dumped. The top of the walls runs from about −15 feet O.D. at the seaward end to −6 feet O.D. in the Crosby Channel. The greater part of the length of the walls is uncovered at low water since Liverpool Bay Datum is −14·54 feet O.D. at L.W.E.S.T. Any greater height would call for excessive maintenance.

In 1912 A. G. Lyster had proposed training the Crosby Channel to improve depths there so that dredging could be concentrated in Queen's Channel and across the Bar. The First World War postponed this scheme, but in 1922 Sir John Purser-Griffith endorsed the 1912 proposals, adding that a comprehensive scheme ought to be prepared with the aid of experimental tidal models. This was carried out with the aid of two models constructed in 1923 and 1930.[25] Work went on in Liverpool Bay, and actual results compared very favourably with predictions based on model experiments. It was decided not to make a bell-mouth at the seaward end of the walls, since this design would be an embarrassment if it were decided to extend them at a later date. Since 1929 the two- and three-fathom L.W.E.S.T. contours show the inter-digitation of the ebb- and flood-channels. Fig. 76 shows that in 1934, before the intensive dredging of Taylor's Spit began, the ebb-channel is pushing westward north of Taylor's Spit, while the interlocking flood-channel pushes eastward south of Askew Spit.

The alignment of the navigation channel crosses over from ebb- to flood-channels in passing between Taylor's Spit and Askew Spit which would possibly join up if dredging were relaxed. If there is anything like an incipient bar in Liverpool Bay, it is here. The Bar Lightship, two miles west-north-west, is named after a feature long since dredged away; and the Board might well pay itself the merited compliment of changing the name. One letter could be altered to assure all who enter Liverpool that there is no sill beneath them as they pass the *Bay* Lightship.

The actual pattern of the training walls in the Queen's Channel follows closely the lay-out recommended in a *Report* to the Board, April 1932, by Sir John Purser-Griffith, M. Wilson, H. A. Reed, and Sir Frederick Palmer, incorporating knowledge gained from experiments with the second Mersey model.[26] It was felt that the western half of Taylor's Bank Revetment, built after 1915, curved too far to the south. This directed the ebb-channel to the south, causing the flood-channel to be off-set further to the south to avoid the ebb and consequently to erode a blind channel *behind* Askew Spit. About 1,000 yards of the Taylor's Bank revetment was removed in 1932–3, and the wall was set back to the north, reducing the curvature. In addition, between 1935 and 1937, intensive dredging was undertaken on the eastern end of Taylor's Spit, 31 million tons of sand being removed. This had the results forecast on the model, even though all work had to cease in 1939. The ebb-channel impinged more directly on the face of Taylor's Spit and the flood-channel more directly on the face of Askew Spit. The happy effect of this had practical proof. Although the eastern end of Taylor's Spit reformed during the war, the second bout of intensive dredging there had to remove only 11 million tons to achieve the same effect as the pre-war operation.

The immensity of the comprehensive 30-year programme built upon the first revetment, Taylor's Bank 1909–10, from 1923 to 39 and since 1946 is largely hidden from view. The walls are almost finished. Only one hopper is now employed on dumping stone. But dredging of a patch halfway along the Crosby East Training Bank, of the edge of Askew Spit, and of the Queen's Channel must go on day and night, the dredgers manned by double crews. The training walls help to stabilize the position of the main approach in forcing a marriage between ebb- and flood-channels. But should the dredging once cease, the sand beyond the walls and within them would creep and grow—a myriad, circling, sliding fingers ready to seal the mouth of the Mersey as Liverpool's water site.

REFERENCES

1. J. A. Cashin, 'Engineering Works for the Improvement of the Estuary of the Mersey', *Journal of the Institution of Civil Engineers*, 32 (1949), 296–367, 511–7, 308; L. Leighton, *The River Mersey and the Port of Liverpool: Improvement of the Estuary by Dredging and Training Works*, paper read to the XVIIth International Navigational Congress, Lisbon, 1949; and J. E. Allison, *The Mersey Estuary*, Liverpool: University Press, 1949 are other valuable general references published in the same year.

2. R. Kay Gresswell, 'The Coast', *A Scientific Survey of Merseyside*, published for the British Association by the University Press of Liverpool, 1953, 49–52, Fig. 18.

3. C. Peel, in discussion on paper by J. A. Cashin, *loc. cit.*, 364; and author's comment, 515; and *Hydraulics Research, 1960; Report of the Hydraulics Research Board*, Published for the Department of Scientific and Industrial Research, H.M.S.O., 1961.

4. C. Peel [a former engineer to the Manchester Ship Canal Company] concurred with this, *ibid.*; and 'The Mersey Estuary', paper read to the Manchester and District Association of the Institution of Civil Engineers, February 24, 1926. See also evidence of Captain J. B. Eads on the Manchester Ship Canal Bill, 1884 [pp. 258–9 above]. This idea has been held since at least as early as 1822 when it was embodied in a *Report* of Whidbey, Chapman, and J. Rennie to the Trustees of the Docks and Harbour of Liverpool, May 25, 1822.

5. *Hydraulics Research 1959: Report of the Hydraulics Research Board*, Published for the Department of Scientific and Industrial Research, H.M.S.O., 1960; and *Ibid.*, 1961.

6. *Estuary of the Mersey: Report* [on Water Pollution], prepared by Department of Scientific and Industrial Research, London, H.M.S.O., 1938.

7. J. A. Steers, *The Coastline of England and Wales*, Cambridge: University Press, 1946, 109–11. 'The Mersey as a tributary of the Dee' idea seems to have developed from the fact that Ptolemy's map, *circa* 140 A.D., shows only two estuaries in the area where there are now three: those of the Dee, Mersey, and Ribble. See also R. Kay Gresswell, *Sandy Shores in South Lancashire: the Geomorphology of South-West Lancashire*, Liverpool: University Press, 1953, 148–9.

8. The presence of these miniature horsts of Keuper Sandstone so far west in the Wirral–Liverpool area is possibly due to the Welsh Massif protecting them from marine erosion during the high sea-level obtaining after glaciation, when dominant westerly winds impelled the sea against the coast more violently further to the north (the 'Hillhouse Coast' of R. Kay Gresswell).

9. R. Kay Gresswell, *op. cit.*, 11–29, and 150.

10. The wave attack may have been made possible by the former Beacon Gutter which reached the shore in the former Bootle Bay. This small stream may have eroded the foreshore on crossing it, allowing waves to attack the shore, much as in the case of the River Alt, immediately to the north. See *ibid.*, 87–97; R. Stewart-Brown, 'The Townfield of Liverpool 1207–1807', *Transactions of the Historic Society of Lancashire and Cheshire*, 68 (1916), 24–72; and W. Yates and G. Perry, *A Map of the Environs of Leverpool*, 1768.

11. R. Kay Gresswell, *op. cit.*, 150.

12. *Ibid.*, Fig. 39.

13. A. H. W. Robinson, 'Ebb-Flood Channel Systems in Sandy Bays and Estuaries', *Geography*, 45 (1960), 183–99.

14. R. A. Stephenson in discussion on J. A. Cashin, *loc. cit.*, 363 and 514.

15. Work on this section and on the diagrams which illustrate it was greatly assisted by a study of copies of charts of Liverpool Bay from 1689 to 1960 kindly made available by the Marine Surveyor and Water Bailiff of the Mersey Docks and Harbour Board. See also A. H. W. Robinson, 'The Submarine Morphology of Certain Port Approach Channel Systems', *Journal of the Institute of Navigation*, 9 (1956), 20–46, 33–9.

16. A. S. Mountfield, 'Admiral Denham and the Approaches to the Port of Liverpool', *Transactions of the Historic Society of Lancashire and Cheshire*, 105 (1953), 123–36, 123.

17. 'Report by Lieut. [later Admiral] Denham to the Dock Committee, Liverpool, October 4, 1838', *Sailing Directions from Point Lynas to Liverpool*, 1840, Appendix, 142–6, 144.

18. G. F. Lyster, *The Physical and Engineering Features of the River Mersey and Port of Liverpool*, paper read to the British Association at Liverpool, 1896, 10.

19. *Ibid.*, 9.

20. A. G. Lyster, *Dredging Operations on the Mersey Bar* [Paper read to the British Association 1895]; *Sand Pump Dredgers* [Paper read to Section II of the Engineering Conference, Institution of Civil Engineers, 1899]; and *Notes on Certain Improvements in Suction Dredgers Employed on the Mersey* [Reprint from *Annales de travaux publics de Belgique*, 5], all published in Liverpool: Reed, 1900. See also 'Sand-pump Dredging on the Mersey', *Engineering*, 79 (1905), 301–3, 464–6.

21. G. F. Lyster, *op. cit.*, 7.

22. *Report* by the Acting Conservator of the Mersey Conservancy Commission, 1906.

23. A. G. Lyster [Contribution to a discussion on a paper entitled 'The Rangoon River Training Works'], *Minutes of Proceedings of the Institution of Civil Engineers*, 202 (1917), 191–4, 192.

24. J. A. Cashin, *loc. cit.*, 330.

25. These models are described by J. A. Cashin, *loc. cit.*, see also J. Allen, *Scale Models in Hydraulic Engineering*, London: Longmans, 1947, 246–50.

26. J. Palmer in discussion on J. A. Cashin, *loc. cit.*, 358–9; and 512–13, Fig. 23.

FURTHER REFERENCE

Shoolbred, J. N. 'On the Changes in the Tidal Portion of the River Mersey and Its Estuary', *Minutes of the Proceedings of the Institution of Civil Engineers*, 46 (1875–6), 20–60.

Chapter 13

MERSEY DOCKS AND MERSEYSIDE

BECAUSE of the great tidal range of up to 31 feet, most of the port activities on the Mersey take place on impounded water at Liverpool and Birkenhead, but including the private dock at Bromborough, and the Garston Docks operated by British Transport Docks, all within the Customs Port of Liverpool. The approach channels of Garston, Bromborough, and the Manchester Ship Canal pass through the Upper Basin of the Mersey, and river traffic is increased by tankers using oil jetties on both shores and by vessels berthing at passenger landing stages. There is also a famous shipbuilding yard at Birkenhead. Yet the docks dominate the scene, and in them many berths are regularly occupied by the ships of one line. These lines, or their agents, are not leaseholders of the particular quay and shed, but on payment of a fee to the Board they can regard the berth and its installations as their Liverpool base. That part of the quay is then known as an 'appropriated berth'. While all the major shipping lines have appropriated berths, not all the berths in the docks are thus allocated. Lists of such berths, however, give an idea of the basic regular traffic of the particular group of docks, and together with the maps and air photographs provide an outline of the general functions and lay-outs of the docks. Some other points not covered by these means will be dealt with in the sections that follow.[1]

Liverpool Central Docks and the Port Nucleus

None of these docks now deals with deep-sea vessels (*cf.* 1860 p. 289), since none has a width of entrance lock of more than 60 feet, while a minimum of 80 feet is now required for deep-sea ships. Duke's Dock was built for the Duke of Bridgewater in 1776 to receive canal barges after their passage via the river from the Bridgewater Canal extension to Runcorn. Warehouses were built over a branch of the dock so that the barges could pass right into the store; the warehouses are still used for bagged grain. Albert Dock is surrounded by five-storey warehouses with the first and upper floors built flush with the quayside, supported on massive pillars, the whole bearing

TABLE 93

Liverpool Central Docks: Appropriated Berths
South to North

Short name of Shipping Line, etc.	Trading to	Berth
Guinness	Dublin	Salthouse, South End, East Side*
Coe	Larne & Coleraine	Salthouse, North End, East Side
Abel	Tugs and ships' ballast	Salthouse, North Side and North End, West Side
Coast Lines	Londonderry	Canning, North End, West Side
Coast Lines	Dublin	Princes, East Side*
Coast Lines	Belfast	Princes, West Side*

* With railway facilities

an extraordinary resemblance to the western St. Katharine Dock, London, built eighteen years earlier. There is no room for vehicle movement along the quays, and so all deliveries are made on the perimeter cobbled road. All kinds of cargo may be stored, though small cases are the rule, since the maximum safe load of the warehouse hoists is only one ton. As later docks were built, the Board did not compete with private warehouses, though tobacco, grain, and wool have always been stored on the dock estate; and warehouse stores are available on the upper floors of some transit sheds. In Salthouse Dock Guinness Stout in giant drums is unloaded by ships' gear and transferred to road or rail transport by fork-lift trucks. Princes Dock is used by the Irish passenger ships, but an even more important passenger terminal is the Princes Landing Stage, with its southward extension, the Georges Landing Stage, used by the Birkenhead and Wallasey river ferries. The southern berth of the Princes Landing Stage is used by the Isle of Man steamers. The combined floating stage is 2,534 feet long, secured by numerous booms and bridges, the main bridges being 110 feet long. The stage was opened in 1876, replacing a former landing-stage destroyed by fire. At all states of the tide the largest liners can tie up alongside. Two berths can be used at once at the northern end opposite the Riverside Station, and luggage and mails are also handled through this floating passenger terminal. In 1895 the Board opened the Riverside Railway Station, one of the very few private passenger railway stations in the United Kingdom. A single track curves from it across the northern end of the Princes Dock, and the platforms are within 70 yards of the ship's rail. It must be remembered that the Princes Dock and the station are on sites reclaimed from the Mersey (Fig. 71). This explains why, at such a short distance westward from solid ground, the stage projects into water 30 feet deep at all times, swept clear of silt by the rush of water where the estuary is at its narrowest.

The water was not run out of Georges Dock until 1900, although the development of the site had been discussed at least forty years earlier.[2] Three buildings

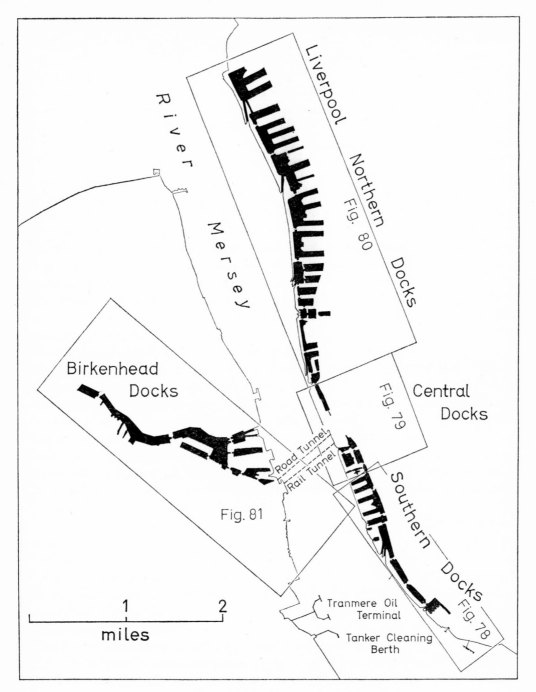

River

Mersey

Liverpool Northern Docks
Fig. 80

Birkenhead
Docks

Fig. 81

Road Tunnel
Rail Tunnel

Central
Docks
Fig. 79

Southern Docks
Fig. 78

Tranmere Oil
Terminal

Tanker Cleaning
Berth

1   2
miles

FIG. 77   The Docks of the Port of Liverpool: Location Diagram

were erected on what was once the foreshore of the *primitive* port (Fig. 71). From south to north these are the headquarters of the Board, built in 1907, the headquarters of the Cunard Steamship Company, and the Royal Liver Building. These buildings house more interests vital to the port than their names suggest: in the Cunard building is the present Custom House, curiously enough exactly opposite the foot of Water Street and the site it occupied in the *primitive* port. The headquarters building of the Royal Liver Friendly Society, with the mythical liver birds on its towers, also houses the offices of several shipping companies. Opposite, on the other side of the Strand, is the Tower Building, on the site of Liverpool's Tower, housing the offices of many more shipping companies. In the central business district of Liverpool there is a sharp contrast between the many-windowed, multi-storied office blocks and the much darker brick of the warehouses and their blind loopholes. South of Lord Street it is easy to draw a line between an area mainly with port functions to the west and other functions to the east. North of Lord Street the port district cannot be delimited by a line. As in the City of London, port functions are inextricably bound up with a whole financial complex of banks and assurance offices. This is a city office area deserted at night, the shops catering for office workers: men's hairdressers and outfitters, office furnishers, business lunch restaurants, and taverns.[3] The port district is approximately bounded by a line due north to the Exchange Station, east of which there is a merging with the outskirts of Liverpool's shopping centre across and astride the Pool, where cafés and restaurants are open all day on Saturday. The line does, however, leave the Fruit Exchange and fruit importers' area well to the east. From the Exchange Station south-westwards to St. Nicholas Church there is a knife-sharp boundary between the port offices area and the line of warehouses to the north. The air view shows this as clearly as it can be seen on the ground, culminating in a building in Chapel Street opposite the church which is part office block and part warehouse. This street remains a significant boundary of the port district today, just as it was once the northern boundary of the *primitive* port.

The Southern Docks

The chief entrance to the southern docks is the Brunswick Entrance, remodelled in 1898 and reconstructed in 1909 (two locks: 350 × 100 × 44 feet H.W.O.S.T.; and 240 × 79 × 44 feet H.W.O.S.T.). As explained in the previous chapter, the site was chosen to avoid the Pluckington Bank close to the river wall from Albert to Coburg Docks. The larger entrances to the Liverpool Docks all point upstream. In this way they are protected from the worst swells, coming from Liverpool Bay to the north-west. The small angle between the locks and river wall reduces the

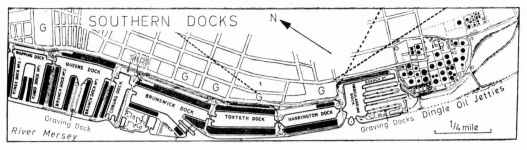

FIG. 78 Liverpool Southern Docks

G, Railway Goods Station
Figs. 78–81 are based on a Mersey Docks and Harbour Board drawing, by permission.

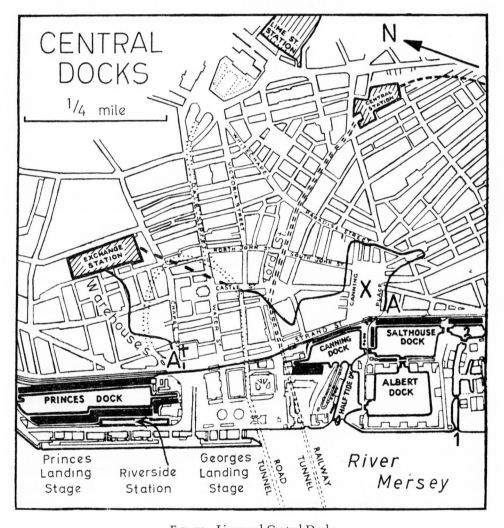

FIG. 79 Liverpool Central Docks

A − A₁, is a line enclosing an area with a predominant port function; X, is the site of the former
Pool and Old Dock, 1715–1826; 1, Duke's Dock; 2, Wapping Basin.

effect of the strong tide in the Narrows. The Langton and Gladstone Entrances make an even smaller angle with the river—only fourteen degrees—and this is still great enough to allow vessels to clear the river wall even with a strong nor'-wester.

TABLE 94

Liverpool Southern Docks: Appropriated Berths
North to South

Short Name of Shipping Line, etc.	Trading to	Berth
Swedish Lloyd ...	Baltic and Mediterranean	King's No. 1, East End, South Side
Kilkeel and Mersey ...	Channel Islands and France	Wapping Basin, East Side
Irish and Mersey ...	Kilkeel	Wapping Basin, East Side
Palm	West Africa	Queen's No. 2, East End, North Side
Booth	Brazil	Queen's No. 2, South Side
Limerick	Limerick	Queen's North End, East Side
British and Continental	Antwerp and Rotterdam outward	Queen's Dock Middle and South End, East Side
Currie	Hamburg and Bremen	Queen's No. 1, West End, South Side
United Steamship ...	} Copenhagen, Rotterdam, and Amsterdam inward	} Queen's No. 1, East End, South Side
British and Continental		
Liverpool Grain Storage Co. ...	Silo	Coburg, East Side
Isle of Man	Isle of Man	Coburg, North Side
Guinea Gulf	West Africa	Brunswick, North End, West Side
Elder Dempster ...	West Africa	Brunswick, South End, West Side
Liverpool Grain Storage Co. ...	Silo	Brunswick, North End, East Side
Harrison	West Indies, New Orleans, Mexico, South America, Calcutta	Brunswick, South End, East Side
Elder Dempster ...	West Africa	Toxteth, West Side
Booker	West Indies	Harrington, North End, West Side
Holland	Amsterdam	Harrington, Middle, West Side
Elder Dempster ...	West Africa	Harrington, South End, West Side

The table shows that deep-sea vessels are not normally encountered until the Queen's Dock is reached, and that thereafter ships trading to West Africa are predominant. These vessels, though voyaging deep-sea, are of shallow draught because of the depth restrictions off West African ports. Hence this traffic can be concentrated at the southern docks, which are shallower than the later northern docks. Three notable quayside buildings are: the Wapping Dock Warehouses, very similar to those of the Albert Dock and housing a wet bonded store for wines and spirits; and the grain silos of Brunswick and of Coburg Docks. The only open quay is at Harrington, East Side, where such cargoes as steel tubes and pipes may be dealt with. Elsewhere, transit sheds are the rule, and they have to be close to the quayside to allow room for roads up the peninsulas or along the river wall at Brunswick, Toxteth, and Harrington Docks. There are no quayside cranes at all, but in King's and Queen's Docks roof cranes have been added to supplement ships' gear. Because of their site the lift is restricted to a maximum of 30 cwt. There are no appropriated liner berths in the southernmost dock, Herculaneum, where the original casemates cut into the solid sandstone can still be seen. Designed as safe stores for oil and other inflammable liquids in barrels, their role has been taken over by the tanks of the Dingle Tank Farm immediately overhead. The Herculaneum Dock has four graving docks, about one-quarter of the Liverpool capacity, the other graving docks being sited parallel to dock peninsulas in the north. Export coal is handled at Herculaneum Dock by the simple method of lifting a 22-ton rail wagon by crane and tipping the coal through end-doors, but the method is only about one-quarter as rapid as that achieved by the most modern appliances.

The Northern Docks

Towards the north the solid foundation of Bunter Sandstone, some 18–20 feet below blue clay at the central docks, descends to as much as 38 feet below sand and blue clay at the Alexandra Dock in the former Bootle Bay.[4] The biggest development since the Second World War at the northern docks has been the construction of the Langton Entrance Lock, begun in 1949 and finished by 1962. This lock is 825 × 130 × 50 feet H.W.O.S.T. compared with the Gladstone Lock 1,070 × 130 × 50 feet H.W.O.S.T., giving altogether three deep-water entrances to the northern system. As a complementary work to the new lock, which lies athwart the former Canada Basin, the passage between Brocklebank and Canada Docks has been widened to 130 feet and deepened to practically 40 feet, and new berths have been constructed on the inner face of the river wall at Langton and Canada Docks. Since the bigger entrances are towards the north where the three-berth quays are to be found, it is not surprising that as a general rule, although there are exceptions, the bigger ships will be found towards the north also. But the table of appropriated berths allows another generalization, again with certain exceptions: in the northern docks the further north the berth, the further away is the overseas terminal of the line using it.

In the older docks three modern developments may be noted. There is the fine quay for the 'container' ships at Victoria Dock, east quay; adjacent are the liquid lard and edible oil tanks at Victoria Dock, south quay. Finally, Coast Lines have a fine row of five transit sheds on the river wall of Trafalgar Dock, with sliding shed doors 30 feet high for high-piling of goods on pallets by fork-lift trucks. At the north side of the Bramley-Moore Dock there is the High Level Coal Railway, where three

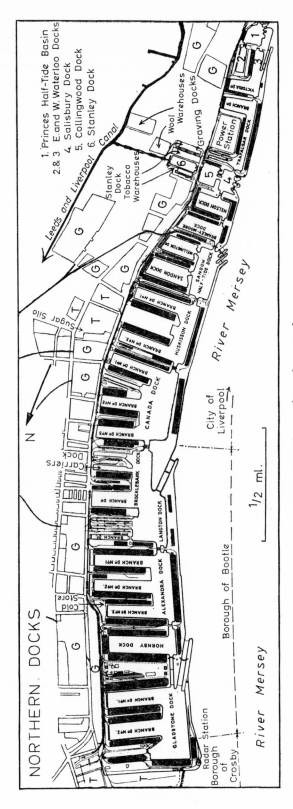

FIG. 80 Liverpool Northern Docks

G, Railway Goods Station; T, Timber Storage Ground.

TABLE 95

Liverpool Northern Docks: Appropriated Berths
South to North

Short Name of Shipping Line, etc.	Trading to	Berth
Clyde Shipping ...	Waterford	West Waterloo, East Side
	Containers to Belfast	Victoria, East Side
	Glasgow	Victoria, North Side
Coast	Belfast	Trafalgar, West Side
	Glasgow	Trafalgar Branch, East Side
Irish and Mersey ...	Kilkeel	Collingwood, South Side
Ellerman's Wilson and Stott	Scandinavia and the Baltic	Bramley-Moore, South Side
Sansinena	Cold Store	Sandon, South Side
Cunard	U.S.A.	Sandon, East Side
Cunard	U.S.A.	Huskisson No. 1, North and South Sides
Huskisson Transit Co.	Bulk and Bagged Sugar	Huskisson No. 3, North Side
Elder Dempster ...	West Africa	Canada No. 1, East End, South Side
Pacific Steam Nav. ...	South America	Canada No. 1, West End, South Side and North Side
MacAndrew	Mediterranean	Canada No. 3, West End, South Side
Ellerman and Papayanni	Mediterranean	Langton Branch, West End, North Side
Ellerman and ... Papayanni	Mediterranean	*Alexandra No. 1, South Side*
Moss Hutchinson ...	Mediterranean	Alexandra No. 1, West End, North Side
Liverpool Grain Storage and Transit Co.	Silo	Alexandra No. 1, East Side
	Silo	Alexandra No. 2, East Side
	Grain Discharge	Alexandra No. 2, East End, South Side
Sellers	Coastwise and Channel Islands	Alexandra No. 2, East End, North Side
Donaldson and Houston Houlder Lamport and Holt Pacific Steam Nav.	South America	Alexandra No. 3, South Side
Union Cold Storage	Cold Store	Alexandra No. 3, East Side
Clan	India and South Africa	*Alexandra No. 3, North Side*
Lamport and Holt ...	River Plate and Brazil	*Alexandra West Side*, South
Hall	East Indies	*Alexandra West Side*, Middle
Furness Withy and Johnston Warren ...	Boston	Hornby, East End, South Side
Furness Withy ...	Amsterdam, Levant, Newport News, and Norfolk, Virginia	Hornby West Side, and West End, South Side
Blue Funnel	China, Japan and Australia	*Gladstone No. 1, South Side*
Canadian Pacific ...	Canada	Gladstone No. 1, North Side
Blue Funnel	China, Japan and Australia	Gladstone No. 2, East End, South Side
United States	U.S.A.	Gladstone No. 2, East End, North Side
Federal Steam Nav. ...	Australia and New Zealand	Gladstone, North and West Sides

Simple Lineal Quayage (3 berths in one line) in italics

cranes can ship coal from end-door wagons at the rate of 200 tons an hour each. The first really large dock is the Sandon Dock, able to receive ships of up to 100-foot beam, the home of Cunard; but the first quayside cranes are not encountered until Huskisson Branch Dock No. 1. The middle branch of this dock was devastated when the s.s. *Malakand* with 1,000 tons of bombs and shells was set on fire and exploded May 2, 1941, the worst single 'incident' in Liverpool's wartime story.[5] The branch has been filled in to provide spacious road access and storage areas for the rebuilt sheds at the berths to north and south. At Huskisson Branch No. 3, north side, eight grab cranes unload sugar from bulk-carrying vessels in the 8,000-ton gross range carrying up to 10,000 tons of sugar. Since the refinery is not alongside, it was at first necessary to have a large fleet of lorries removing the sugar from 25-ton hoppers, until a 100,000-ton silo was built east of the dock road, and this has evened out the flow. It might be noted that there is no room for factories on the Liverpool Dock Estate, and the sugar refinery is some distance inland athwart the Leeds and Liverpool Canal. This was the axis of Liverpool's first industrial zone where coal from Lancashire met raw materials from the docks transhipped into canal lighters. H. Tate built his Love Lane refinery in 1872, and in 1929 absorbed the adjacent refinery of Fairrie and Co., which now manufactures Fairrie Wrapped cube sugar. Because of the difficulty of expanding the 18-acre site, development has been upwards, and with some 2,500 workers this is the largest single sugar refinery in the world.[6] Coal is still received via barges on the canal. The oilseed and cattle-cake trade is also sited close to the canal zone.

Despite the impressive range of docks and the ingenious provision of *simple lineal quayage*, the narrowness of the river wall and the peninsular lay-out certainly impose some restrictions on quay lay-out, as may be seen from Table 96 below.

TABLE 96

Quay Development Alexandra Dock, West Side[7]

What was Desired

Quay Margin	*Transit Shed*	*At Rear*
35 feet wide, with two sets of rails 3- and 5-ton cranes	Width 120 feet	Two rail lines and a wide roadway

What was done

Reduce to 20½ feet wide, with no rails because of sharp turns at either end	Reduce to 110 feet	Two rail lines, and narrow road, total 60½ feet

because total width available only 191 feet

At Alexandra No. 1, south side, because of the peninsular lay-out the quay margin had to be reduced even further, to 12½ feet. At import berths double-storied sheds are preferred with balconies for receiving cargo on the upper floor; at export berths single-storey sheds are the rule. The wide peninsula at Hornby Dock eases timber discharge, and there is another timber storage area north of the liner berths in Gladstone Dock. On the north-west corner of Gladstone Dock is the Port Radar Station, providing a port information service on the movement of vessels, the first in the world when established in 1948. Lastly, one may note the fourteen railway goods stations along the length of the docks. This great number is largely an inheritance from the many separate railway companies with termini on Merseyside in the nineteenth century. The original method of transfer was a first sorting on the dock estate and then movement by horse and cart to the adjacent goods stations, aided by the lack of gradient everywhere. This method has of course been replaced by motorized road transport, and nearly all berths now have direct rail access, but the nineteenth-century circumstances explain why the rail lay-out between quay and goods shed is not as close as at a railway-operated port.[8]

Birkenhead Docks

The reason for the lay-out of the Birkenhead Docks has been explained in previous chapters, and further development is difficult for the following reasons. The Morpeth and Egerton system of docks has been abandoned by liner traffic, and this began as long ago as 1900 when the City Line transferred its base in the Morpeth Dock to the West Float. The entrance was too narrow and passages are too awkwardly placed for large vessels, and so these docks are largely used as a laying-up ground for ferry-boats and small Admiralty vessels. The only entrance locks are those leading to Alfred Dock and they have rather small dimensions (North 480 × 99½ feet; South 600 × 80 feet). In consequence, while small vessels can be locked for eight hours on each tide, the longer ocean vessels entering the Float require the water in Alfred Dock to be lowered to meet the level of the incoming tide two to three hours before high water. This enables the largest vessels to enter the Float, but the procedure must be used with discretion because it is wasteful of water, and the water must not be allowed to escape into the Mersey faster than the pumps can replace it. Because of the built-up area to north and south, it is impossible to provide a second large entrance on a new site. This entrance restriction has certainly interfered with the extension of the Birkenhead estate at the Bidston end, for any quay extension throws additional burdens on the existing entrances.[9]

A striking feature of the appropriated berths is the lack of regular calls by liners trading to North America and West Africa, trades already flourishing at Liverpool before Birkenhead began. On the other hand, the grain trade developed particularly after the establishment of the first 'futures' contract in 1883, and so there are great groups of granaries on the north side of the East Float and the south side of the West Float, where there was more room than at Liverpool. Grain may of course arrive in the lower holds of vessels delivering general cargo to quays in Liverpool

TABLE 97

Birkenhead Docks: Appropriated Berths
East to West

Short Name of Shipping Line, etc.	*Trading to*	*Berth*
Anchor	India and Pakistan	East Float, East Side
Blue Funnel	China and Japan	East Float, Cathcart Street Wharf (South-east Side); also *Vittoria, South Side*
Clan	South Africa	*Vittoria, North Side*
Clan	India and South Africa	East Float, Vittoria Wharf, East End
Brocklebank, City	⎱ Calcutta	⎱ East Float, Vittoria Wharf, West
Harrison	⎰ East and South Africa	⎰ End
Rea (Stevedores) ...	Bulk discharge	East Float, Jetty (South-west Corner); also West Float, Wharf South Side
Henderson, Bibby ...	Rangoon	West Float, North Side

Then Westward

Hall, City	Karachi and Bombay	West Float, North Side

Then Westward

Harrison, Hall ...	East and South Africa	West Float, North Side
Rea (Stevedores) ...	Iron ore discharge	Bidston, North Side

Simple Lineal Quayage (3 berths in one line) in italics

Docks. It may then be transferred by floating suction plant to barges for transmission to a granary at Birkenhead. There are about 230 barges within the port, but used particularly in trading to Manchester. The West and East Floats were built to follow the original meanders of Wallasey Pool to save expense, but in 1960 the Vittoria Dock was lengthened to provide two splendid general cargo quays to north and south. The last two items about Birkenhead Docks that deserve special mention are at either end of the estate. With their own landing stages allowing vessels to berth at all states of the tide are the Woodside (1879) and Wallasey (1890) Lairages where accommodation is provided for 5,500 cattle, 5,200 sheep, and 1,800 pigs, together with chill rooms for over 2,000 carcasses. The first pens were designed for the transatlantic trade, but cattle from Ireland have predominated in this century,

318

Mersey Docks and Harbour Board

PLATE XVII ALEXANDRA AND GLADSTONE
DOCKS, LIVERPOOL
Looking north-north-east, *cf.* Fig. 80.

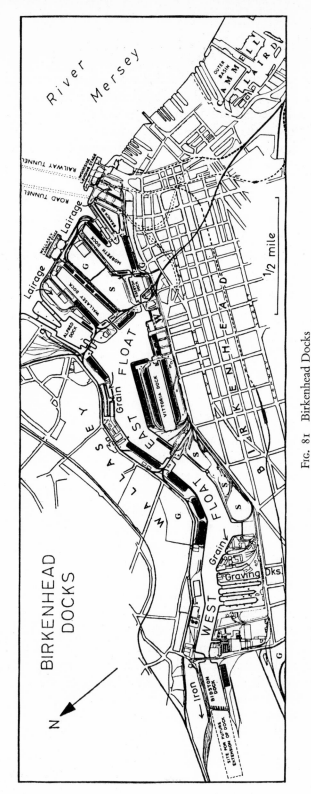

FIG. 81 Birkenhead Docks

G, Railway Goods Station; S, Railway Sidings; W, General Warehouses, south-east of East Float.

PLATE XVIII BIRKENHEAD DOCKS

Looking north-west along the axis of the former Wallasey Pool, with low ground evident from the Mersey, right foreground, across the Wirral peninsula to Liverpool Bay in the background, *cf*. Fig. 74. The prominent construction, right foreground, is one of the air shafts for the Mersey Road Tunnel. For details of the dock estate see Fig. 81.

particularly since 1912. In that year quarantine requirements restricted cattle trade to specific berths at ports, and Birkenhead had the great advantage over Liverpool in the ease with which it could provide quarantine isolation. Fewer than a third of the cattle are slaughtered at the dockside abattoir, and only about half the sheep. The rest are sent inland for fattening, particularly on the pastures of Cheshire. At the other end of the estate, on the north side of Bidston Dock, three 13-ton grabbing transporters can unload iron ore simultaneously from two ships of 8,000–10,000 tons deadweight for transmission to the Hawarden Bridge Steelworks at Shotton on the River Dee, a final crushing reminder of the rise of the Mersey and the death of the Dee for shipping. Behind the iron ore berth the land rises very quickly, and this is the best point on the estate to see that the Birkenhead Docks occupy a former valley.

South of Birkenhead and Garston Docks

Cammell Laird & Company Ltd. occupy a site on each side of the former exit of Tranmere Pool, which like Wallasey Pool has been impounded to form the ship builders' fitting-out basin with a 200-ton floating crane. Laird & Son began building ships in Wallasey Pool in 1824, and although William Laird was an early town planner in Birkenhead and a leading advocate of Birkenhead Docks, his greatest success came in the use of iron for shipbuilding, in which he was a pioneer.[10] In 1903, four years after the steel firm of John Brown & Company acquired the Clyde-bank Yard, Laird's amalgamated with the steel firm of Charles Cammell & Company of Sheffield, also steelmakers.[11] This amalgamation was responsible for the great development at Tranmere opposite Brunswick Dock on the Liverpool side. There are ten building berths, the longest 1,000 feet, seven graving docks, marine engineering works, and, since 1960, a tanker cleaning berth at Rock Ferry to the south. Previously, if a tanker after discharging her cargo was due for repair at the yard, she was bound by law to make a trip to an area 100 miles beyond British territorial waters to carry out gas-freeing and cleaning operations. (For recent shipbuilding output see under 'Birkenhead' in Table 10). South of the shipbuilding yard is the Tranmere Oil Terminal, opened in 1960, which can handle two tankers of 65,000 deadweight tons simultaneously even through a 30-foot range of tide. There is an intricate system of 16 booms, for should such a fully-laden vessel inadvertently knock the floating stages, there are 90,000 tons behind the blow.

Three miles south of Birkenhead is the private port of Bromborough Dock, built on the estuary of the River Dibbin known as Bromborough Pool. In 1889 production of soap started at Port Sunlight, the factory having been established on the site by William Lever, who realized its strategic value for transport by water as well as

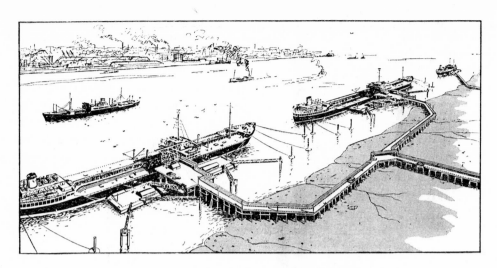

FIG. 82 Tranmere Oil Terminal on the Mersey

Looking south-east. The artist has shown two tankers of 65,000 tons deadweight moored to the two large floating stages, each capable of taking larger vessels on restricted draught. Further up the estuary a smaller tanker is moored to Cammell Laird's tanker cleaning berth. Reproduced by permission of the Mersey Docks and Harbour Board.

rail.[12] The site was far enough up river to be out of reach of the Liverpool Dock and Harbour Dues—on a ton of tallow these might have been as much as 4s. 10d. Using water transport in and out meant that Lever was in a good bargaining position with the railways. On this empty site he could buy land ahead of needs. The proximity of Bromborough Pool to the works implied that barges could discharge raw materials ferried across the River Mersey from ships in Liverpool direct to the Port Sunlight wharf. The opening of Bromborough Dock in 1931 enabled the Unilever group of companies and other tenants on the estate to receive raw materials direct by ship, and also resulted in Bromborough Pool being impounded to give permanent water access to the wharf of the Lever Brothers soap factory. The Dock can accept vessels up to 29 feet draught, 16,500 tons deadweight, the limiting factor being a beam of not more than 70 feet. Raw materials—groundnuts, palm kernels, copra (all to the southern quay silos) and whale oils, marine oils, and vegetable oils for tank storage can be received in large bulk quantities. The dry cargoes are largely destined for the works of the British Extracting Company for cattle cake and animal feeding stuffs after the oil has been extracted for margarine and soap manufacture. Price's (Bromborough) Ltd., makers of oleo-chemicals and fatty derivatives, take certain classes of oil by pipe-line direct from the Dock storage tanks, and receive other materials largely by road. The Dock is served by the estate private railway system, and oils for edible purposes are moved to the margarine works of Van den Berghs &

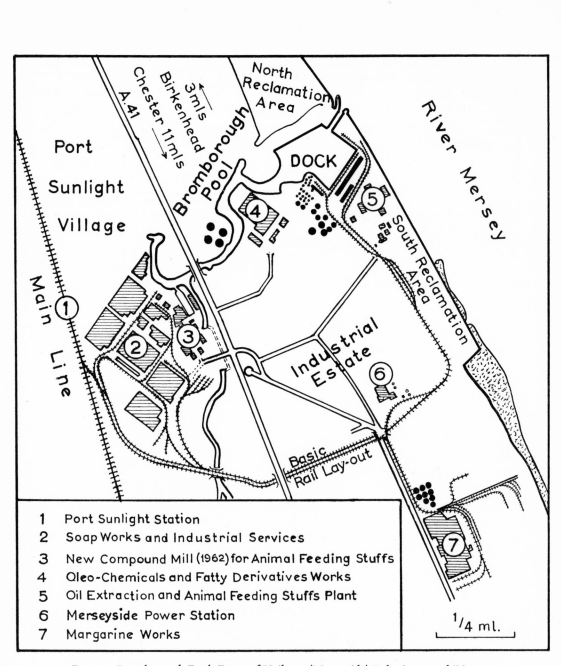

1   Port Sunlight Station
2   Soap Works and Industrial Services
3   New Compound Mill (1962) for Animal Feeding Stuffs
4   Oleo-Chemicals and Fatty Derivatives Works
5   Oil Extraction and Animal Feeding Stuffs Plant
6   Merseyside Power Station
7   Margarine Works

Fig. 83 Bromborough Dock Estate of Unilever (Merseyside) Ltd.: Annotated Diagram
Bromborough Dock is on a water-encroaching site reclaimed from the Mersey foreshore at the
former mouth of the now impounded Bromborough Pool.

Jurgens Ltd., by this means in lagged tank wagons. These four factories, together with Unilever Merseyside Ltd., who are responsible for operating the estate, the Dock, the Merseyside Power Station, and other services, employ some 10,000 people. Certain services are also supplied for some twenty or so other firms on the industrial estate. The Dock is used to a small extent for exports coastwise, but consignments of manufactured products for overseas are normally despatched in vessels from Liverpool or Birkenhead Docks, as they amount to only a small part of a vessel's total cargo, in complete contrast to the inward movements.

On the opposite shore facing Bromborough Dock are Garston Docks, developed by the London and North Western Railway Company.[13] The docks have always

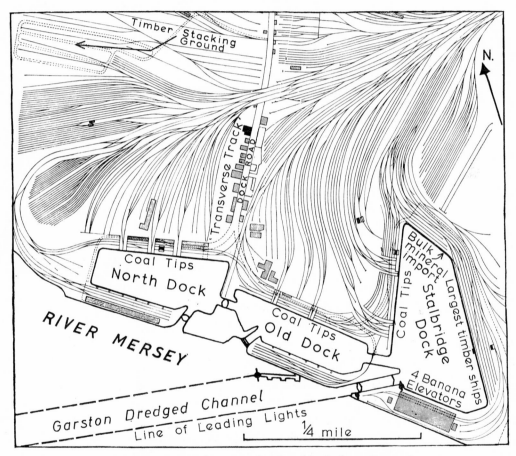

FIG. 84   Garston Docks: a Port Developed by Railway Companies

Maximum dimensions of vessels entering the channel and Stalbridge Dock are: 490 feet in length, 33 feet in draught, approximately 12,500 tons deadweight. All the buildings along Dock Road, south of the Dock Manager's Office (solid black) are connected with the port.

been important for coal export, particularly to Ireland, though nowadays Lancashire coal has been superseded by exports from the East Midland fields. Some of the coaling appliances in the Old Dock recall the counterbalanced wagon drops once in use on the Tyne (Fig. 7). Timber has become the chief import, for Garston can offer vast storage grounds adjacent to the docks of a size not to be found at Liverpool. Bananas transferred to steam-heated railway wagons are to be expected in a once railway-operated port. Leading to the docks is Dock Road, a wonderful example in miniature of a typical port 'transverse track' with all the offices and installations necessary to the docks' operation.

TABLE 98

Trade of Birkenhead within the Port of Liverpool, 1960
(Tons)

	Birkenhead	Liverpool
★ Imports (foreign and coastwise)	2,980,595	7,057,244
★ Exports (foreign and coastwise)	1,770,508	4,425,916

★ Excludes bulk petroleum and livestock.

TABLE 99

Thirty Most Valuable Foreign Trade Imports into Liverpool (incl.
Birkenhead, Bromborough, and Garston), 1960

	Value £ Million
Unwrought Copper	63·1
Raw Cotton	48·9
Raw Wool	39·9
Unbleached Woven Cotton Fabrics	32·2
Raw Rubber	30·0
Unmanufactured Tobacco	28·2
Unrefined Sugar	26·9
Sawn Softwood	20·0
Crude Petroleum	20·0
Wheat	18·1
Tin Ore	15·3
Live Cattle	12·2
Butter	11·9
Maize	10·9
Tea	10·5
Palm Oil	9·9
Canned Salmon	9·7
Chilled or Frozen Lamb	9·1
Organic Chemicals	8·9
Iron Ore	8·5
Metal Scrap	8·0
Lard	7·8
Soya Beans	7·2

Machine Tools	... ...	6·4
Raw Cocoa	... ...	6·0
Plastics	... ...	5·7
Ground Nuts	... ...)	5·3
Aluminium	... ...	5·1
Electric Machinery	... ...	5·1
Uncoated Iron and Steel Plates and Sheets	...	5·0

Total of all Imports ... 809·9 (18·7 per cent of total U.K. imports by value)

TABLE 100

Thirty Most Valuable Foreign Trade Exports from Liverpool (incl. Birkenhead, Bromborough, and Garston), 1960

	Value £ Million
Cars	36·7
Woven Cotton Fabrics	27·4
Tractors	22·4
Textile Machinery	22·0
Woven Woollen Fabrics	20·4
Road Vehicle Parts	18·4
Wool Tops	16·9
Railway Vehicles	15·0
Internal Combustion Engines (not for Road Vehicles and Tractors)	14·2
Iron and Steel Tubes and Pipes	13·9
Road Vehicle Chassis	12·9
Tools and Implements (excl. Machine Tools) ...	11·7
Plastics	11·4
Machine Tools	11·3
Glass and Glassware	11·0
Commercial Vehicles	10·9
Rubber Tyres and Tubes	10·9
Worked Copper	10·7
Medicinal Drugs	9·9
Whisky	9·8
Electric Switchgear	9·6
Cycles	9·0
Pottery Articles	8·4
Uncoated Iron and Steel Plates and Sheets ...	8·0
Dyeing Chemicals	7·2
Iron and Steel Bars and Rods	7·2
Electric Cables and Wires	7·1
Telegraphic Apparatus	6·8
Refined Petroleum	6·8
Internal Combustion Engines (for Road Vehicles and Tractors)	6·6

Total of all Exports ... 923·6 (27·8 per cent of total U.K. exports by value)

From the list of imports it is not hard to imagine where many of the cargoes will be landed: crude oil,[14] iron ore, cattle, vegetable oils, and raw sugar in particular are off-loaded at specialized berths. General cargoes are discharged at one of the appropriated liner berths, dependent on the country of origin, while part-cargoes of grain move to quayside warehouses or may be transhipped into barges by floating suction elevators. About one-fifth of the raw rubber is re-exported, by far the largest item in Liverpool's small trade in the export of imported merchandise (Raw Rubber, £11·7 million; Beer, £3·9 million; Cotton, £1·1 million; total, £26 million; year 1960). The chief warehouses for rubber are at Gladstone Dock, Liverpool's importance in this trade being explained by both its Far East cargo liner connections and its situation with regard to Britain's road vehicle industry. Nevertheless, the Rubber Exchange is in London, with samples dispatched each evening by rail from Liverpool for display in London before 10 a.m. next day.

The distance that goods penetrate inland depends on the nature of the commodity. As with London, the hinterland is not simple. While some imports are manufactured on Merseyside, others range over all Britain. A gallant attempt to define Liverpool's hinterland confirms these generalizations.[15] An export that must catch a particular Liverpool liner may travel from the ends of the Kingdom. Liverpool's drawing power for cargoes destined for North America, West Africa, and the Far East is greater than for northern Europe, where east coast ports may eat into its adjacent territory. A north-west to south-east axis across England has London at the other end, and the two busy estuaries in north-west and south-east England are by far the largest general cargo ports in the country. Some large-scale industrial firms have a large plant on each of the estuaries to give national and international coverage: Lever (soap); Van den Berghs & Jurgens (margarine); Bowater (newsprint); Shell (oil refining); Tate & Lyle (sugar refining); and Spillers and Rank (grain). Just as there is a 'City' of London helping to administer this vast complex of trade, so there is a 'City' of Liverpool, almost coincident with the medieval area of the town, providing exchanges for cotton, corn, fruit, dairy produce, and eggs. One interesting feature is the 'Newsroom', where business men meet on neutral ground to receive up-to-the minute news of terminal market prices. During the Second World War the premises were used by the Admiralty, with a most appropriate title—Headquarters of the Western Approaches. It will come as no surprise to learn that the Newsroom is situated only 250 yards along Water Street (the 'transverse track') leading from the port nucleus at Pierhead.

REFERENCES

1. For further details of ships and shipping lines see latest issues of *The Port of Liverpool*, Mersey Docks and Harbour Board; and *Port of Liverpool Official Monthly Sailing List and Shipping Guide*, Liverpool: Littlebury. Also *The Times Special Supplement on the Port of Liverpool*, February 10, 1958; H. M. Le

Fleming, *Ships of the Mersey and Manchester*, Southampton: Adlard Coles, 1959; and G. Chandler, *Liverpool Shipping: a Short History*, London: Phoenix, 1960.

2. B. D. White, *A History of the Corporation of Liverpool 1835–1914*, Liverpool: University Press, 1951, 77.

3. See the 'office blocks' on Fig. 48, W. Smith, 'The Urban Structure of Liverpool', *Merseyside: A Scientific Survey*, British Association: Liverpool University Press, 1953, 188–99, 193.

4. G. H. Morton, *The Geology of the Country Around Liverpool*, London: Philip, 2nd ed., 1891, Figs. 12–14.

5. *Port at War: Liverpool 1939–1945*, Mersey Docks and Harbour Board.

6. *Tate & Lyle Times*, 1956.

7. F. H. Cave, 'Post War Developments at Liverpool', *The Dock and Harbour Authority*, 37 (1956–7), 397–402, 397.

8. G. F. Lyster [in reply to discussion on] 'Recent Dock Extensions at Liverpool, with a General Description of the Mersey Dock Estate, the Port of Liverpool, and the River Mersey', *Minutes of the Proceedings of the Institution of Civil Engineers*, 100 (1890), 2–114, 80–1. See also J. A. Patmore, 'The Railway Network of Merseyside', *Transactions and Papers*, 29 (1961), Institute of British Geographers, 231–43.

9. K. J. Norris, *A Geographical Study of the Birkenhead Dock Estate*, Unpublished Dissertation, B.A., University of Liverpool, 1951.

10. P. Sulley, *History of Birkenhead: Ancient and Modern*, Liverpool: Murphy, 1907, 85–92; and *Shipbuilding in Lancashire and Merseyside*, Lancashire and Merseyside Industrial Development Association, Research Memorandum No. 4, 1954.

11. The firm still has close connections with the steel industry through its holdings in the English Steel Corporation Ltd., and owns half Metropolitan-Cammell Carriage & Wagon Company Ltd., railway vehicle builders. See also 'New Dry Dock at Birkenhead: Extensive Shipyard Modernization Scheme', *The Dock and Harbour Authority*, 42 (1962), 388–92.

12. This is covered in more detail in C. Wilson, *The History of Unilever*, 2 vols., London: Cassell, 1954, I, 34–8, II 277–8.

13. The first dock was constructed by the St. Helens Railway & Canal Company, later taken over by the London and North Western, and then by the London, Midland and Scottish. For further details see D. W. McKay, *The Growth and Development of Garston and Speke*, Unpublished B.A. thesis, University of Manchester, 1955.

14. Under-represented in the 1960 table of imports since the Tranmere Oil Terminal did not begin operations until June 8, 1960.

15. W. Smith, 'Merseyside and the Merseyside District', *A Scientific Survey of Merseyside, op. cit.*, 11–15. For an exhaustive analysis of the import trade, particularly between the wars, see G. C. Allen, F. E. Hyde, D. J. Morgan, and W. J. Corlett, *The Import Trade of the Port of Liverpool*, Liverpool: University Press, 1946; and *Merseyside*, Lancashire Industrial Development Association, Industrial Report No. 3, 1949, 25–33.

Chapter 14

ERAS IN THE DEVELOPMENT OF THE PORT OF LONDON

A VISITOR to London stands bewildered by the rising buildings and seeming confusion on the ground. He should see London from the air. All is then dwarfed except the river and the docks downstream, and the vast extent of the Port of London from the city to the sea is revealed. The port has spread along seventy miles of tidal estuary, with events of each successive era of development concentrated on different parts of the river and riverside. Great contrasts result, perhaps easier to demonstrate here than at less extensive sites where some modern constructions have obliterated the lines of former lay-outs. Armed once again with the apparatus of *Anyport*, and for the last time, there is hope of giving a brief yet perhaps useful account of the largest British port. Some may argue that *Anyport* was made too much like London in the first place. Against this it may be pointed out that a gigantic port that under-takes every possible kind of port function, except the loading of bulk raw materials, is easier to analyse than a smaller port where developments are more concentrated in space. In an attempt at successful abridgement[1] the eras must first be recognized, and some basic facts about the expansion of the port brought out. This will allow space in this and succeeding chapters to consider the two crises that have been surmounted and then give room to consider modern aspects of the port.

The Primitive Port and the First Marginal Quays

As there is still no archaeological evidence for a London before the Roman occupa-tion, it might be useful to consider the Thames from the Romans' point of view. Firstly, Roman Britain was at the end of a power axis stretching north-westward through Gaul. The Romans needed a base somewhere in south-east England whence they could control Lowland Britain, roughly of the same extent as their later civil districts, south-east of the line from the Rivers Tees to Exe. Secondly, they needed a port to supply their garrisons and colonists. St. Albans (*Verulamium*) and Colchester (*Camulodunum*) fulfilled the first requirement, but neither was capable of being a

TABLE 101

Eras and Epochs in the Development of the Port of London

Eras and Chief Areal Characteristics	*Present-day Symbols*
I *Primitive:* north bank of the Thames each side of the South-wark crossing (forerunner of Old London Bridge)	The line of Thames Street close to the present London Bridge
Era ended when construction of the semi-circular Roman Wall gives protection to a wider riverfront from the River Fleet (west) to the south-east Roman bastion [later the Norman Wardrobe Tower] *circa* A.D. 200	
II *Marginal Quay Extension:* landing-places at intervals along the whole length of the Roman river wall, including estuary of the Walbrook (Dowgate)	The complete line of Thames Street
Era ended by the use of artificial inlets in the bank, particularly one furthest from the bridge-head, Ethelredshithe (Queenhithe), first written reference, A.D. 899[2]	
III *Marginal Quay Elaboration:* line of riverfront extended by artificial embayments, notably at Queenhithe and Bil-lingsgate; with quays downstream of the bridge becoming more important, especially after 1558	Queenhithe[3] is the only hithe now remaining; site of the Custom House between London Bridge and the Tower
Era ended by the opening of the West India Docks, 1802	
IV *Dock Elaboration:* docks with tidal basins and complicated quay patterns	Docks opened before 1886, such as India and Millwall, Surrey, and London and St. Katharine Dock Systems
Era ended when King George V Entrance Lock opened (800 ft. long) 1921	
V *Simple Lineal Quayage:* straight quays in impounded docks over 1,500 feet long accessible via a lock over 750 feet long	Royal Docks and Tilbury Docks
VI *Specialized Quayage:* quays and jetties of progressively larger scale downstream	*e.g.* the largest private jetty on the Thames, Ford Motor Company Ltd., Dagenham; and oil terminals in Sea Reach

large port close to the imperial line of power. Dover and Richborough were ports on the Channel, but from a coastal site south of the Thames it was difficult to make roads fan out in all directions to the frontiers. This is argument after the fact. But two circumstances throw light on the Romans' planning. There is no evidence to suppose that they set out deliberately to build a 'new town'. In other parts of the Empire and Britain they actually preferred to adapt existing native towns where possible. Secondly, the Saxons who came later had at first little use for London.[4] Whereas the Romans' prime consideration was that of keeping lines open with the continent and the Imperial City, the first Saxons were settlers and farmers interested in the land for its own sake, cutting all ties with their continental homeland. When ports were not required, London languished, to be inhabited by a 'few decivilized sub-Roman Londoners'.[5]

Granted that there was a necessity for a Roman base on the Thames, why was the actual site of London chosen? Many writers have discussed this. One advantage possessed by the Southwark crossing was dry gravel approaches on both sides of the river. A gravel remnant of the 'Flood-Plain Terrace' approaches close to the South-wark shore. On the north there is a river bluff leading to the top of the 'Taplow Terrace'.[6] These gravel areas gave a firm approach to a ferry or a bridge. Down-stream the marshy alluvium of the flood-plain is always to be found at least on one side of the river, sometimes as much as a mile and a half wide. The northern bridge-head possessed the largest spread of gravel and outgrew the southern suburb at Southwark ('south work', *i.e.* fort of the city and bridge). Like *Anyport*, the *primitive* port on the Thames was sited at the estuary head, and tidal limits may well have been at Southwark in Roman times,[7] the ebb and flood providing free motive power down and up the estuary. Bridgehead and estuary head, and land and water site advantages were thus combined at the site of Londinium.

The *primitive* port must have been on the north side close to the crossing. Whether the Romans erected a bridge is not known for certain,[8] but a wooden bridge certainly spanned the river in Saxon times,[9] and was equipped with a drawbridge like its stone successor. When the Roman land walls were complete at the end of the second century, *marginal quay extension* could be protected along the whole line of the present Thames Street, from the south-east bastion to the River Fleet. Later Baynard's Castle and the Tower of Montfichet[10] to the west, and the Norman Tower to the east gave protection where the walls met the river upstream and downstream respectively. The Norman Tower became the most important stronghold, since it was at the more vulnerable site which raiders from the east would first encounter. Not only were quays extended along the riverfront,[11] but land was reclaimed from the river south of Thames Street. If the reclamation was made piecemeal, embayments, called hithes, occurred in the frontage. At places like Puddle Dock, Broken Wharf, Queenhithe, the later Dowgate, and Billingsgate ships could be hauled ashore on to the mud, the sides of the hithes being piled with timber to prevent the quays slipping forward. Originally, Dowgate was much larger, being the estuary of the Walbrook, and was contracted by Thameside reclamation before Elizabethan times. The era of *marginal quay elaboration* on the north bank lasted for the incredibly long period of 900 years, and during all that time the port hardly grew in area. Though Sufferance Wharves were to be developed on the south bank, the quays on the north bank downstream of the bridge discharged most of the trade. In spite of the fact that the port was physically enlarged very little in this long span of time, its character changed greatly through the enormous increase in its trade. It is possible to pick out only a few historical headlines to emphasize the changes within the port.[12]

These changes can be illustrated by a comparison of the fortunes of three of the most important hithes: Dowgate (formerly the estuary of the Walbrook) and Queenhithe, both upstream of London Bridge; and Billingsgate, downstream of the bridge. If the establishment of the *primitive* port was derived from the continental outlook of the Roman occupying power, port development ceased after the Roman withdrawal, only to begin again with increasing visits by 'foreigners', culminating in the proselytizing mission from Rome carried out by St. Augustine in A.D. 604. By this time, wrote the Venerable Bede—and in this context the famous quotation has added significance—London had become:

'. . . the mart of *many nations*, resorting to it by sea and land.'[13] [Italics added]

Among these foreigners, the most important traders were the German (later Hanseatic) merchants who are referred to in the laws of King Ethelred, 978–1016, as:

'the Emperor's men, who came in their own ships.'[14]

The focus of German activities was close to the estuary of the Walbrook,[15] at Dowgate. As recently as 1959, 1,000 sherds were found in silt lying over gravel containing Roman pottery, just east of the original Walbrook estuary on the former foreshore of the Thames. All the pottery was contemporaneous, and it is suggested that it was a German ship's cargo which was broken in transit and thrown overboard on arrival. The pottery dates from the first half of the twelfth century and is of the Pingsdorf type, suggesting the existence of a flourishing Rhineland traffic at that date.[16] The German merchants had legal privileges granted by the Crown and later erected a depot, called the Steelyard, on the reclaimed Thames foreshore east of the Walbrook.[17]

Several factors, however, contributed to the eventual decline of Dowgate as an important hithe. It was upstream of Old London Bridge, built in stone between 1176 and 1209. Although the bridge was equipped with a drawbridge, it caused tedious delays to vessels wishing to sail upstream. In 1464 there were complaints of the 'slackness of drawing up London Bridge',[18] and in 1481 because of the weight of houses upon the bridge, it was ordained by the Common Council of the City that the drawbridge should be raised only in times of real necessity and not for the ordinary passage of vessels.[19] In 1551 the King seized the liberty of the Steelyard, and in 1597 Elizabeth deprived the foreign merchants of their privileged position, though many of them stayed on without their former security of tenure.

The first plan of London in 1543 shows that the Dowgate estuary of the Walbrook had been largely built over as a result of Thameside reclamation (see above). Queenhithe had become the chief hithe upstream of the bridge, and such foreign vessels as penetrated above the bridge before the fifteenth century would probably have used this hithe rather than the shrunken Dowgate. Queenhithe first appears in a Charter of King Alfred, A.D. 899, as Æderedys Hyde—Ethelred's Hithe. Previously, in A.D. 886,

> 'Alfred occupied London, and all the English people submitted to him, except those who were in captivity to the Danes; and he then entrusted the city to ealdorman [Earl of Mercia] Ethelred to rule.'[20]

Ethelred was Alfred's son-in-law,[21] and it is deduced that the King must have given him land on the western side of the Walbrook. The evidence for this comes a little later. Now, Alfred's Charter of A.D. 899 states that the King, his daughter, and Ethelred met at Chelsea, and

> '. . . King Alfred granted two plots [literally, but probably not actually, *jugera*, acres] in the place that is called Æderedys Hyde; one to Plegmund, Archbishop of Canterbury . . .; the other to Werefrid [Bishop of Worcester] . . . There is however a public way from the river Thames dividing these two plots, stretching towards the north. But both properties extend up to the wall, [former quay-line along Thames Street?] and outside the wall there are moorings for vessels as far as the width of the properties within the wall. . . .'[22]

This charter contains the first reference to Ethelredshithe, and it is to be noticed that the Archbishop and the Bishop received land *in the place* that is called Ethelredshithe. That this was an extensive soke (forerunner of a city ward) on the west side of the Walbrook, fronting on the Thames, may be safely deduced because that was the position of the later soke of Queenhithe, a name which replaced Ethelredshithe.[23] Indeed, the rights of Queenhithe were to be described in the early fourteenth century as extending from Dowgate (estuary of the Walbrook) to the soke of the Archbishop of Canterbury,[24] which strongly suggests that the Charter of A.D. 899 dispensed land on the western side of the soke of Ethelredshithe. This soke was no doubt named after the landing-place built between A.D. 886, when Ethelred became governor of London, and A.D. 899, the date of Alfred's charter. Ethelredshithe came into the possession of the Queen during the twelfth century in the reign of Henry I. A charter of Henry II specifically makes the link between the two names by referring to *'Ripa Reginae quae appelatur Athereshethe'*.[25] Transferred by the King to the City of London in 1245, Queenhithe continued as a chief market for imported food,

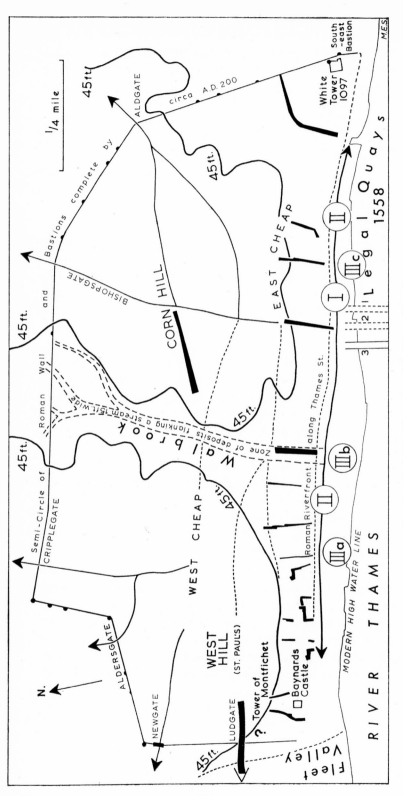

FIG. 85 Early Development of the Port of London

I—Site of the *Primitive Port and Port Nucleus*.
II—*Marginal Quay Extension*, when Roman Wall complete.
III—*Marginal Quay Elaboration*.

IIIa, Queenhithe; IIIb, Dowgate, estuary of the Walbrook; IIc, Billingsgate; and others.

Roads filled in as thick black lines represent the sites of present streets in the City of London bearing the name '-hill', with the present 45-foot contour inserted. The original surface is about fifteen feet below the artificial 'made ground'. By Norman times the principal streets parallel to the waterfront were: Thames Street; East Cheap and its westward prolongation; and West Cheap and its eastward prolongation. Principal streets transverse to the port are shown with an arrowhead, leaving the city by gates in the wall.

1—Wooden Bridge (Saxon, possibly originally Roman);
2—Old London Bridge (1176–1832);
3—The present London Bridge (1831– to date).

notably corn and fish.[26] No doubt Queenhithe was a bigger harbour than Dowgate, but Billingsgate, downstream of the bridge, was better sited than either of them. Sixteenth- and early seventeenth-century plans[27] all show the larger ships at the port moored downstream of the bridge at Billingsgate[28] or more particularly in the river, here called the Pool. As early as 1464

> '. . . it was ordained, that . . . if the vessel being great, comming with salt from the Bay, and could not come to these Keyes, then the same to be conueyed by lighters . . .'[29]

This is perhaps the earliest reference to the fact that the largest ships when heavily laden could not tie up alongside quays that dried out.

Thus wharves upstream of the bridge became less important for direct ocean-going trade just at the time when for other reasons the foreigners' influence in the port, based on Dowgate and Queenhithe, was being curtailed. The port was no longer merely along the line of the riverfront between the ends of the City wall. The bridge caused the port focus to be inclined slightly downstream where the bigger ships anchored. No wonder the Custom House was established in 1382 at Wool Wharf midway between the London Bridge and the Tower, a position which it has occupied ever since.[30] Two pieces of evidence support this initial change of emphasis downstream. When in the first year of her reign a commission of Elizabeth appointed Legal Quays,[31] where all dutiable cargo had to be landed, these were sited exclusively downstream of the bridge, between it and the City boundary at the Tower.[32] And of those wharves mentioned by John Stow in 1603 as lying upstream of the bridge nearly all were specialized landing places, indicating that their cargoes had been first sorted into lighters which braved the rapids beneath the narrow arches of the bridge as they transferred cargoes from ships moored in the Pool downstream. By this time Thames Street was undoubtedly the longitudinal street serving the port. The chief transverse route inland was from the bridge northwards, via Fish Street Hill and Gracechurch Street to Bishopsgate, crossing an important east-west route, via Leadenhall Street and Cornhill at the carfax[33] upon the summit of the city's eastern hill.

Apart from changes within the port outside events in the second half of the sixteenth century combined to stimulate the trade of the port. Sir Thomas Gresham (1519?–79) was appointed Royal [or financial] Agent at Antwerp in 1551. This port was London's superior in north-west Europe both in financial resources and in *entrepôt* trade. Gresham became very familiar with the monetary system at Antwerp and contemplated establishing a bourse at London. In 1566 he was obliged to leave Antwerp because of an insurrection against the Spaniards, and in 1568 at his own expense he opened a bourse in London which became the Royal Exchange two years

Port of London Authority

PLATE XIX LONDON AND ST. KATHARINE DOCKS

Looking south-west up-river, *cf*. Fig. 95. The river is here lined by multi-storey warehouses, typical of the Pool of London, see Table 120.

later on the occasion of the Queen's visit. When Antwerp was sacked by the Spaniards in 1576, London was thus in a position to become a banker to Europe. Moreover, many English trading companies received charters in the second half of the sixteenth century.[34] The defeat of the Armada in 1588 allowed England to rise to a commanding position at sea and to build an empire founded on sea communications. No wonder that the trade of the imperial port expanded continuously. Nevertheless, the port itself hardly expanded at all for a further 200 years.

The First Crisis and Its Resolution, 1793–1802

In 1796 Liverpool opened its sixth commercial dock. London had none. The port was still in the *marginal quay elaboration* era that had begun in Saxon times. Lest this appear too fanciful, here is part of a plan submitted on behalf of the Corporation of the City of London in 1796:

> 'The Legal Quays which are at present 1464 feet in extent, are by five Transverse Docks [*i.e.* jetties] to be extended to 4150 feet.'[35]

Although this plan also included two small docks downstream, this was essentially a scheme to retain the most important traffic within the City boundary at the Tower. The nub of the matter was that despite a threefold increase by value in the trade at the port during the eighteenth century alone[36]

> '. . . the legal Quays . . . are not of greater extent than they were in the Year 1666, [rebuilt after the Great Fire] . . . that the Remedy hitherto afforded has been by granting Sufferances to land at private Wharfs which are, in the very increased . . . Commerce of the Port found inadequate to its complete Accommodation . . .
> That as early as the Beginning of this Century, the Inconveniences arising from the confined Limits of the Wharfs, were experienced, and from Time to Time Plans have been proposed for their Remedy, but have not been carried into Effect, either from Interference with the Limits of the Tower, or from Informality in the Proceedings.' [From a *Memorial of the Committee of Merchants* . . . July 14, 1795][37]

London did have two small non-commercial docks downstream; at Blackwall, south of the present East India Dock; and at Rotherhithe, on a site now occupied by the Greenland Dock of the Surrey Commercial Dock System. Both these docks were

Y

Port of London Authority
PLATE XX SURREY COMMERCIAL DOCKS
Looking south-west up-river, *cf.* Fig. 96, with concrete runways, for mobile cranes piling timber, prominent in the docks. Timber wharves and single-storey premises line Limehouse Reach foreground in contrast to the Pool, background, see Table 120.

FIG. 86 Old London Bridge and the Legal Quays, *circa* 1630

Looking north-east. This extract from an engraving by Matthew Merian shows shipping in the Pool downstream of the bridge, moored near the Legal Quays between the north end of the bridge and the Tower. While the artist has shown ships crowded into Billingsgate Hithe (centre), there are none depicted upstream of the bridge. From *Neuwe Archontologia Cosmica*, . . . Durch Johann Ludwig Gottfried, Franckfurt-am-Mayn, 1638, reprinted by the London Topographical Society, May 24, 1922, showing the bridge before 1632, when the houses on its northern spans were burned down.

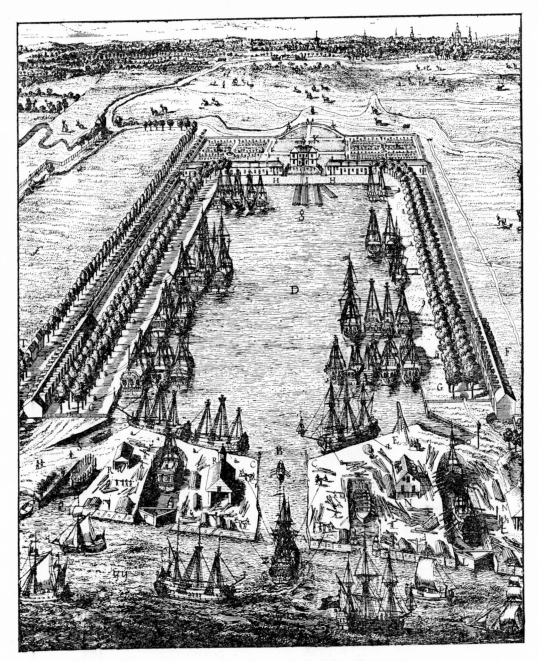

FIG. 87 The Howland Great Wet Dock

Looking west–north–west towards London, with St. Paul's three and a half miles away. The Dock, surrounded by trees as wind-breaks was used for ship refitting and not for commerce, since its quays were not
designated 'legal quays'. The site is now occupied by the Greenland Dock, Surrey Commercial Dock
System. From part of a view dated 1717, drawn by T. Badslade and engraved by T. Kip.

for fitting-out and repair, and neither was designated as a legal quay. The former, the first wet dock in Britain, is mentioned by Pepys:

'. . . we took barge and went to Blackwall and viewed the dock [Shipyard] and the new Wet dock, which is newly made there . . .' January 15, 1661.[38]

It was probably built by Sir Henry Johnson (?–1683), who had purchased the shipyard from the East India Company in 1652.[39] The second wet dock was much larger: 1,070 feet long, 500 feet wide, and 17 feet deep. This was probably excavated between 1696, when the venture received an enabling Act,[40] and 1703, when its usefulness was demonstrated. In that year a great storm wreaked havoc on ships in the open river while those in the dock remained safe. This Howland Great Wet Dock was a venture of the powerful Russell family, and the engineers they most probably employed were later to be responsible for Liverpool's first wet dock opened in 1715 (see page 281).[41]

Complaints against the port were not confined to the congestion at the Legal Quays. A host of vessels crowded the river; there were very long delays in discharging ships; and an enormous conspiracy of criminals was tempted by the rich plunder that such floating and sitting targets provided. The 1796 *Report* abounds in vivid evidence about these interlocking defects. Three quotations from the evidence must suffice here to illustrate the following summary of the position.

The Legal Quays were choked. Along a mere 1,400 feet of quayage most of the port's trade was supposed to be carried out. The quays were also used for markets in spirits, oils, and fruit; wines were landed at one wharf, but gauged at another. Amid the press of unloading cargoes and tallying, a clutter of hand-carts jostled the goods away to warehouses behind the quays; and the nine narrow lanes leading north from Thames Street swarmed with imports, exports, and any who had business with the port. Warehouses at the Legal Quays could store 32,000 hogsheads of sugar.[42] Sometimes the annual import was above 100,000 hogsheads arriving within three months of the year. Goods were damaged as they lay on open wharves or in barges used as floating warehouses. Revenue Officers were far too few, and although Sufferance Wharves were established as a relief as early as 1663, this sufferance to land cargo was temporary, and a separate sufferance had to be made out not only for each cargo but for each consignee. In addition, merchants were reluctant to have their cargoes landed 'remote from the seat of business',[43] with pilferage even more likely. It was estimated that more than two-thirds of London's trade was carried on at the Legal Quays, with only 38 customs landing waiters: while the Sufferance Wharves discharged the remainder with but 8 landing waiters available.[44] A contemporary witness emphasizes the chaos:

338

FIG. 88 The Legal Quays and the Crowded Pool, 1757

Looking east. On the extreme left is the façade of the east wing of the Custom House (1718–1814). From an engraving by L. P. Boitard.

'The Causes of this Complaint are, the present narrow State of the Quays—the Want of Water to remove the Craft [*i.e.* lighters grounding]—the Detention of Goods by Landing Waiters for port Entries . . . the Clashing and Interference of the Import and Export Branches—the Coasting Business [also] being carried on at the legal Quays—the occasional Want of Warehouse Room—the quaying of Ships at one Wharf and landing the Cargoes at other places—and the Narrowness of Thames Street and the Avenues thereto . . .'[45]

Because of the delays ships were crowded together in the Pool for weeks at a time before lighters carried away their cargoes. Vessels sheered and ranged together in the open tideway, some grounding on their anchors at the ebb because they were forced to lie in dangerous places. There was accommodation for 545 ships in the Pool, but as many as 775 were commonly found there, with sometimes as many as another 1,000 vessels thronging Limehouse Reach towards the lower Pool.[46] A Trinity House Pilot reports:

'I have been delayed by the crowded state of the River six or seven Days at Deptford, and could not get higher—last November when the Jamaica Fleet came in, most of the ships were obliged to stop five or six days at Deptford on Account of the crowded state of the Pool.'[47]

And all the time the number of ships using the port was increasing, and so was their average size.

TABLE 102

Vessels Entered Inwards at the Port of London in the Eighteenth Century[48]

Year	Number of Coastwise Vessels	Average Tonnage per Vessel	Number of Vessels from Foreign Ports	Average Tonnage of Vessel
1700	5,562	50	—	—
1702	—	—	1,335	118
1750	6,396	80	—	—
1751	—	—	1,682	139
1795	11,964	100	2,832	205

At every delay plunderers seized upon the valuable cargoes so ill-protected, even with the connivance of ships' masters and Revenue Officers. Among the ships and on the quays peculation was rampant.

'. . . Revenue Officers generally come on board West India Ships provided, for this Purpose [of Plunder], with large Bladders, with wooden, horn, or ivory

Mouths, in order to receive their Proportion agreed upon of Rum or other Liquors; . . . The Extent of this Practice, during my Time might amount sometimes to Five, and sometimes to Seven Puncheons of Rum out of about One Hundred and Twenty, out of One Ship in One Voyage. . . . Smuggling and Plunderage is carried on in the quickest Manner that possibly can be, and in the various Parts of the Ship, from the Ports and Cabin Windows, so that it is impossible altogether to prevent it.'[49]

P. Colquhoun, founder of the Thames Marine Police, estimated that of the 36,000 men working in the port a quarter were given to major plunder or petty pilfering. And ever-hovering in their punts and bum-boats were the professionals: 100 river pirates; 200 night-plunderers of barges; 200 'light-horsemen'—night-plunderers of ships; 550 receivers;[50] and 200 mudlarks scavenged greedily along the shore.

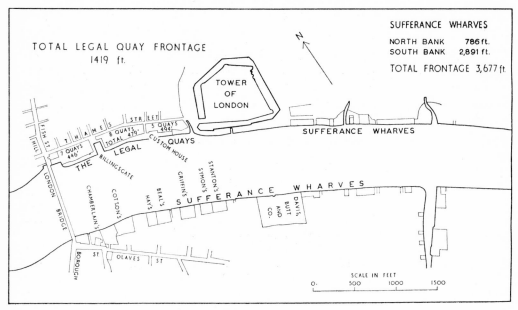

FIG. 89   The Port of London, 1789
Based on a plan in Appendix (Uu) 2 of the *Report* (1796), *op. cit.*

The 1796 *Report* gives a clear impression that the brunt of the port's difficulties was being borne by the West India merchants. In 1797 trade from the East Indies (today's India and Pakistan) and the West Indies accounted for 44 per cent of London's total imports, about half each by value. East Indiamen discharged in Blackwall Reach, where the East India Dock is to be found today. Goods were then conveyed to fortress-like town warehouses of the East India Company (the present Cutler

Street Warehouses) under armed guard by the employees of this powerful and well-organized Company. The West India trade, on the other hand, was not centralized. Its rum and sugar, being of lower value per unit of weight, needed larger fleets of shipping than the East India trade. But it was not until William Vaughan became the merchants' spokesman in 1793 that the question of removing much of the trade from the river into the security of wet docks became actively debated.

TABLE 103

A Comparative Statement of the Charges upon Imports via London's Legal Quays and the Docks of Liverpool, c. 1795
(based on *Report*, 1796, *op. cit.*, Appendix O)

	Land Waiters	Lighter-age	Wharf-age	Landing Housing Weighing	Cooper-age	Ware-house Rent per Week	Cartage	Total Charge
On a Hogshead of Sugar, 16 cwt.								
London	3*d.*	1*s.* 4*d.*	6*d.*	1*s.* 7*d.*	1*s.* 6*d.*	4*d.*	1*s.* 9*d.*	7*s.* 3*d.*
Liverpool	8*d.*	—	—	8*d.*	1*s.* 0*d.*	3*d.*	9*d.*	3*s.* 4*d.*
							Difference	3*s.* 11*d.*★
On a Bag of Cotton, 3 cwt.								
London	3*d.*	6*d.*	6*d.*	10*d.*	—	1*d.*	6*d.*	2*s.* 8*d.*
Liverpool	3*d.*	—	—	3*d.*	—	¾*d.*	2*d.*	8¾*d.*
							Difference	1*s.* 11¼*d.*★
On a Hogshead of Coffee, 7 cwt.								
London	1*s.* 3*d.*	1*s.* 0*d.*	6*d.*	1*s.* 6*d.*	1*s.* 0*d.*	4*d.*	1*s.* 3*d.*	6*s.* 10*d.*
Liverpool	4*d.*	—	—	6*d.*	6*d.*	2*d.*	6*d.*	2*s.* 0*d.*
							Difference	4*s.* 10*d.*★
On a Barrel of Ashes, 3 cwt.								
London	5*d.*	3*d.*	2*d.*	6*d.*	6*d.*	½*d.*	—	1*s.* 10½*d.*
Liverpool	2*d.*	—	—	5*d.*	1*d.*	½*d.*	—	8½*d.*
							Difference	1*s.* 2*d.*★

★ 'When Business is done at Sufferance Wharves, for Want of Room at Legal Quays the Difference of Charges is still more considerable from extra Fees paid the Revenue Officers for attendance there.'

William Vaughan published his first historic tract, *On Wet Docks, Quays, and Warehouses for the Port of London with Hints Respecting Trade*, in 1793.[51] It is dated just six days before an important meeting of the West India Merchants at the Marine Society's Office on December 20. There is no doubt that Vaughan was the prime mover in focusing the clamour for reform into a discerning plea for wet docks. Though neither merchant nor mariner, he was certainly the spokesman for both the London merchants and the merchants in the West India trade from 1793 until December 1797, when the latter became wedded to a separate scheme, but also one founded upon commercial wet docks. Vaughan, 1752–1850, the son of a London merchant, was elected a director of the Royal Exchange Assurance Corporation in 1783. His interest in docks appears to have developed out of his rather unusual education at Warrington Academy.

'My studies were much directed to geography, history, travels, and voyages of discovery. I took great interest in accounts of shipwrecks and other disasters at sea. I also saw and heard a great deal respecting canals, docks, manufactures, commerce, and population; and as small beginnings often lead to greater efforts, I was in 1791, induced to join with some friends in endeavouring to procure a good collection of the history and plans of the canals of this country . . .'[52]

Vaughan was also a member of a society for the improvement of naval architecture which conducted experiments at the Greenland (formerly Great Howland) Dock. This helps to explain how such an epoch-making tract as that of 1793 came to be written. After pointing to docks at Liverpool, Hull, Le Havre, Ostend, and Cherbourg, he suggested sites for docks at London, which all materialized during his lifetime.

The advantages for docks were in speed of discharge, cutting down by half the average time of 30 days, and in security against plunder. The promoters of docks were not concerned with any embarrassment from the tide or any lack of depth of water in the river, except where too many ships crowded together and where some were forced to anchor at unauthorized places in shallow water. Here is Vaughan before the 1796 Committee beginning his answer to the question,

'What, in your Opinion, are the means of Relief? . . . The greater security against Accidents, Plunder, and Smuggling, will be Dispatch in landing a Ship's Cargo immediately on her Arrival, with as few intermediate Transhipments as possible. Nothing short of wet Docks will give Accommodation and Security, and lessen the Risques and Expenses to the Merchant, and give Increase and Security to Revenue than by taking out of the River the most valuable Ships and

Cargoes that employ the most Hands to inspect and watch, and to leave the River free to those Trades that are the most bulky and least valuable . . . accompanied with the fewest Risques and Temptations . . .'[53]

The 1796 *Report* not surprisingly pronounced the port 'incompetent to the great purposes of its extended commerce',[54] but the Committee merely paraded the eight plans put before it. In 1797 there was no time in the Parliamentary session to approve a Bill, and in 1798 the West India merchants proposed docks on the Isle of Dogs (germ of the present India Docks), and separated from the London merchants, who adhered to the original plan for docks at Wapping (germ of the present London Docks). No doubt the West India merchants became impatient at the delay in 1797. The City Corporation had seen which way the wind was blowing and allied itself to the West India Dock scheme which was to include a canal across the meander of the Isle of Dogs to shorten the distance to the Legal Quays within the City limits. In this co-operation between two former rivals may be seen the mediating hand of George Hibbert, West India merchant and City alderman, later first chairman of the West India Dock Company. Probably because of this lobbying combination, the *West India Dock Act* was passed quickly in 1799, while the *London Dock Act* had to wait until 1800.[55] The City Canal across the Isle of Dogs was a failure, largely because the associated docks removed from the river all the West India ships that formerly sailed upstream. The river was freed of many anchored vessels, so that sailing upstream was easier.[56] Steam power finally rendered the City Canal superfluous, and eventually it was made into the South West India Dock in 1829 and widened to its present dimensions in 1866–70.[57]

The era of *dock elaboration* in London was thus inaugurated by two rival dock companies, each endowed with 21-year monopolies in certain trades.[58] When these monopolies were reviewed by a *Select Committee on Foreign Trade* in 1823, they were not renewed. The stage was set for competition between various dock companies. While private initiative deserves the credit for establishing the docks, unrestricted competition later in the century became a handicap in the comprehensive planning of the dock facilities and port approaches. Painful amalgamations reduced as many as nine dock companies to three when the Port of London Authority (hereafter called the P.L.A.) was set up in 1909.[59] An opportunity to have established a unified port authority only seven years after the founding of the Mersey Docks and Harbour Board was clearly lost in 1864. But at Liverpool the stresses were external to the original port, the question of expansion on to the opposite shore, and the refusal of traders from other towns to look kindly on the Liverpool Town Dues. At London the stresses were internal until 1887. Dock companies competed with one another, even for a time over-providing the port with docks; and the river wharves competed with the dock companies. The strain was borne by the dock company shareholders who drew derisory dividends. Only gradually did it become apparent that there was insufficient revenue for deepening the river or saving the docks from bankruptcy.

TABLE 104

The Pedigree of the P.L.A.

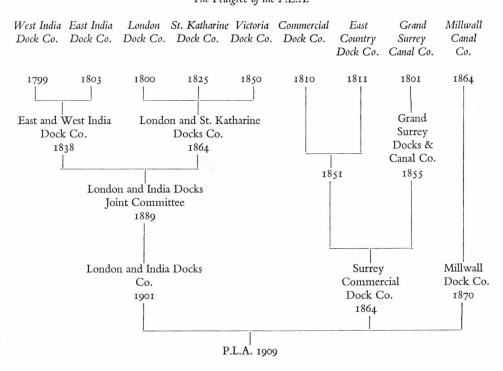

Dock Quay Perimeters, Elaborate and Simple

Until the opening by the London and St. Katharine Docks Company of the Royal Albert Dock in 1880, the quays of the docks were complicated in outline with included peninsulas. The quays of the India Docks were certainly long, but like others of their time they were designed to receive fleets of sailing vessels crowded into the docks through a tidal basin. The Victoria Dock, when opened in 1855, had eight jetties projecting from its north quay, and the south quay was interrupted by a Pontoon Dock where ships could be repaired. But the Royal Albert Dock of 1880 had long straight quays. At the same time the prefix 'Royal' was added to the Victoria Dock. So London had its first Royal Docks since Queen [Mathilda's] hithe, some 750 years before. The original Tilbury Docks, opened by the East and West India Dock

345

Company in 1886, had three branch docks, remarkably similar in lay-out to the Alexandra Docks at Liverpool opened five years earlier. Thus long quays of over 1,500 feet in one line existed at the West India, Royal Albert, and Tilbury Docks by 1886. However, another requirement for *simple lineal quayage* at *Anyport* was 26 feet at low water and an ability to receive a vessel 750 feet long. A 26-foot channel was made to Tilbury in 1888, but did not reach the Royal Docks until the twentieth

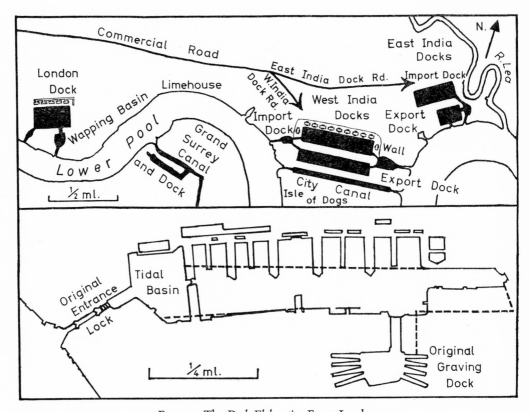

FIG. 90   The *Dock Elaboration* Era at London

Top: The Docks of London 1808
    The London Dock indicated is now the Western Dock, London Docks; and the dock and canal of the Grand Surrey Canal Company are now both part of the Surrey Commercial Dock System. The 'commercial roads' were completed in 1810.
Bottom: The Lay-out of the Royal Victoria Dock, 1855–1936
    The present quays are shown by pecked lines. There were transit sheds on the shorter jetties and multi-storey warehouses on the others; with transit sheds at the head of each branch dock, and a line of warehouses behind, of which those marked appear on the modern plan. W. J. Kingsbury, 'Description . . . of the Victoria (London) Docks *etc.*', *Minutes of the Proceedings of the Institution of Civil Engineers*, 18 (1858–9), 445–89, giving 'the greatest facilities for the trade that could be desired', A. Giles [in discussion], 470.

century. Tilbury's original entrance lock was however only 695 feet long. So the fifth era dates from the provision of the King George V 800-foot long entrance lock in 1921, opening to *simple lineal quayage* in both the King George V and the Royal Albert Docks. Further *simple lineal quayage* was available when the upper Tilbury Entrance Lock was opened in 1929; and when the jetties of the Royal Victoria Dock were swept away in favour of a quay three-quarters of a mile long in 1944. This provision of nearly six and a half miles of *simple lineal quayage* in the Royal and Tilbury Docks, arranged in lay-outs at least 1,500 feet long available to ships up to 700 feet long, is perhaps a novel way of assessing the results achieved by unified control of the docks and conservancy of the river. *Specialized quayage* has of course been provided within the docks originally designed exclusively as general cargo docks. But this type of quayage has developed in more marked fashion at industrial terminals on the riverside. Certainly, the key that unlocked the door to these two eras of development was the effective dredging of the river. For the moment the modern account of the docks must be postponed in order to describe the past and present river approaches.

REFERENCES

1. The standard history is Sir Joseph Broodbank, *History of the Port of London*, 2 vols., London: O'Connor, 1921. See also L. R. Jones, *The Geography of London River*, London: Methuen, 1931; and J. Bird, *The Geography of the Port of London*, London: Hutchinson, 1957.

2. A Charter of King Alfred, A.D. 899. Authorities: MS. Lambeth. 1212, p. 321; and R. Twysden, *Historiae Anglicanae*, X, A.D. 1652, p. 2218. Quoted in J. M. Kemble, *Codex Diplomaticus Aevi Saxonici*, V, 1847, Document 1074, pp. 141–2; and Sir Walter de Gray Birch, *Cartularium Saxonicum*, 2, London: Whiting, 1887, 220–1.

3. Modern Queenhithe occupies a site a little south of Saxon Queenhithe since the riverfront is now south of the old line because of reclamation from the river, and the northern part of old Queenhithe has been filled in.

4. The entrance phase of Saxon settlement, marked by early Saxon burial grounds, reveals no occupance of a site near London, S. W. Wooldridge, *The Geographer as Scientist*, London: Nelson, 1956, Chapter 12, Fig. 25.

5. R. E. M. [now Sir Mortimer] Wheeler, 'Introduction', *Report of the Royal Commission on Historical Monuments*, 3, *Roman London*, H.M.S.O., 1928, 67.

6. This name derives from the upstream continuation of the terrace where it was first named by H.M. Geological Survey.

7. Tidal limits are now at Teddington, nineteen miles upstream of the bridge (see the following chapter).

8. G. Parsloe, *Report of the Royal Commission on Historical Monuments, op. cit.*, Appendix V, 192–4.

9. *Ibid.*, 47.

10. H. A. Harben, *A Dictionary of London*, London: Jenkins, 1918 gives the history of these two strongholds, 55–6, 424–5.

11. It is not known whether the Romans completed a river wall. Certainly, it was never as massive as the land walls, and the line of 'wall' remnants along Thames Street may be the remnants of the Saxon quay line.

12. A selective bibliography for this long period is: E. Power and M. M. Postan, *Studies in English Trade in the Fifteenth Century*, London: Routledge, 1933; J. Stow, *A Survey of London, 1603*, 2 vols., edited by C. L. Kingsford, Oxford: Clarendon, 1908; R. A. Pelham, 'Medieval Foreign Trade: Eastern

Ports', *An Historical Geography of England before 1800*, edited by H. C. Darby, Cambridge: University Press, 1951, 298–329; and O. H. K. Spate, 'The Growth of London, A.D. 1660–1800', *Ibid.*, 529–47.

13. *Historia Ecclesiastica Gentis Anglorum*, J. A. Giles, editor, 1843; II, 3, 181. See also R. H. M. Dolley, 'Coin Hoards from the London Area as Evidence for the Pre-eminence of London in the later Saxon Period', *Transactions of the London and Middlesex Archaeological Society*, 20 (1960), 37–50, 45.

14. *Ancient Laws and Institutes of England*, edited by B. Thorpe, 2 vols., London, 1840, I, 300.

15. H. Ormsby, *London on the Thames*, London: Sifton, Praed, 1928, 103–4, makes a clever guess at the original site of their original 'Old Hall'.

16. G. C. Dunning, J. G. Hurst, J. N. L. Myres and F. Tischler, 'Anglo-Saxon Pottery: A Symposium', *Medieval Archaeology*, 3 (1959), 1–78, 73.

17. A site now occupied by Cannon Street Railway Station. For the legal bases of the Hanse privileges and the origin of the name Steelyard, see H. A. Harben, *op. cit.*, 550–1.

18. J. Stow, *op. cit.*, 362 original pagination.

19. *Calendars of the Letter Books of the City of London*, edited by R. R. Sharpe [Lettered A–L], London: Francis, 1912, L, 180.

20. *Anglo-Saxon Chronicle*, A.D. 886; and William of Malmesbury, *Gesta Regum Anglorum* (Rolls Series), I, 128.

21. Collated references as a biography of Ethelred appear in W. G. Searle, *Anglo-Saxon Bishops, Kings, and Nobles*, Cambridge: University Press, 1899, 390.

22. *Loc. cit.*, see footnote 2.

23. W. Page, *London: Its Origin and Early Development*, London: Constable, 1929, 131–3.

24. *Munimenta Gildhallae Londoniensis: Liber Albus, Liber Custumarum et Liber Horn*, edited by H. J. Riley, Vol. 2, London: Longmans, 1859, 241.

25. Dugdale's *Monasticon Anglicanum* (Caley, Ellis, Bandinel eds.), 1830, VI, 635.

26. The customs or trade of Queenhithe and Dowgate are set out in the *Munimenta Gildhallae Londoniensis*, *loc. cit.*, 237–41.

27. Wyngaerde, 1543; Agas *c.* 1561–70; Hoefnagel *c.* 1572–8; Ryther, 1608; Visscher, 1616; Merian, 1638 (see Fig. 86); Hollar, 1647. See also Sir Laurence Gomme, 'The Story of London Maps', *Geographical Journal*, 31 (1908), 489–509, 616–40; and *Maps of Old London*, edited by G. E. Mitton, London: Black, 1908.

28. For the reasons why Billingsgate, London's chief food importing port in the seventeenth century, is now London's riverside fish market receiving no fish via the Thames, see J. Bird, 'Billingsgate: a Central Metropolitan Market', *Geographical Journal*, 124 (1958), 464–75.

29. J. Stow, *op. cit.*, 362, original pagination.

30. The present Custom House (1814–17) is the fourth and occupies a site immediately to the west of the former Wool Wharf.

31. Under *An Act Limiting the Time for Laying on Land Merchandizes from Beyond the Seas and Touching Customs for Sweet Wines*, I Elizabeth, c. 11, 1558.

32. H. Phillips, *The Thames About 1750*, London: Collins 1951, 199–202, for details of the Legal Quays.

33. Carfax—there was a carfukes at Leadenhall in 1370. M. E. *carfoukes*, from late Latin *quadrifurcus*, see H. A. Harben, *op. cit.*, 123; *cf.* carfax at Exeter, Horsham, Oxford, *etc.*

34. Between 1553 and 1600 the Russia, Eastland [or North Sea] Turkey, African, Virginia, and East India Companies all received charters of establishment.

35. *Report from the Committee Appointed to Enquire into the Best Mode of Providing Sufficient Accommodation for the Increased Trade and Shipping of the Port of London*, May 13, 1796, Appendix Ee [from the accompanying plan]. This report contains vivid accounts of the state of the port at the end of the eighteenth century. For further summaries of it and extracts see Sir Joseph Broodbank, *op. cit.*; J. Bird (1957), *op. cit.*; and R. A. Heaton Page, *The Dock Companies in London 1796–1864*, Unpublished M.A. thesis, University of Sheffield, 1959.

36. *Report*, 1796, *op. cit.*, Appendix D. The Inspector General of Customs who provided the absolute values of trade for years from 1700–94, explained that they took into account changes in the value of money throughout the century, *ibid.*, iv.

37. *Ibid.*, Appendix A.
38. *The Diary of Samuel Pepys*, edited by H. B. Wheatley, London: Bell, 1904, I, 325–6. Pepys has another reference to the dock, September 22, 1665. See H. Green and R. Wigram, *Chronicles of Blackwall Yard*, London: Whitehead, Morris, and Lowe, 1881. This first dock was replaced by the Brunswick Dock in 1789, sited a little to the east; and this became incorporated in the East India Export Dock in 1806, sold by the P.L.A. in 1951 to provide a site for the present Brunswick Electricity Generating Station.
39. Sir William Foster, *John Company*, London: Lane, 1926, 148–50.
40. *An Act to enable Trustees to raise money for the making of A Wett Dock and Improveing the estate of the Marquesse and Marchionesse of Tavestock at Rodderith* [Rotherhithe] *in the County of Surrey*, 7 & 8 William III, c. 25, in 1696.
41. In 1695 Lord Tavistock, son of Lord William Russell, married Elizabeth Howland, heiress of Sir Giles Howland's property on the Thames at Rotherhithe, which was acquired by the Russell family as the bride's dowry.
42. *Report of a Meeting of West India Merchants at the Marine Society's Office*, December 20, 1793, Vaughan papers, see (Further References) below.
43. *Report*, 1796, *op. cit.*, xvi.
44. *Ibid.*, Appendix Mmm.
45. *Ibid.*, evidence of J. Tilstone, landing surveyor, 76. See also E. E. Hoon, 'The Organization of the Port of London', *The Organization of the English Customs System, 1696–1786*, London: Appleton-Century, 1938, 122–66.
46. *Report*, 1796, Appendix E, and p. 33.
47. *Ibid.*, evidence of E. Nicholls, 42.
48. *Ibid.*, compiled from Appendices G and H.
49. *Ibid.*, evidence of R. Walker, ship's officer in the Jamaica trade, 153–5.
50. Figures estimated by P. Colquohoun, *A Treatise on the Commerce and Police of the River Thames*, 1800, 198, who even ranged the receivers in twelve classes from 'Opulent receivers who trade on a large scale, 20' to 'Inferior receivers who deal with Lumpers [port labourers] &C, 25', 197. See also T. Fallon, *River Police*, London: Muller, 1956.
51. This tract appears in *Tracts on Docks and Commerce Printed between the Years 1793 and 1800 . . .* London: Smith, Elder, 1839.
52. *Ibid.*, [personal] Narrative, 7.
53. *Report*, 1796, *op. cit.*, 206.
54. *Ibid.*, xvi.
55. The Parliamentary timetable of these measures and an amplification of why the *West India Dock Act* was passed first are given by R. A. Heaton Page, *op. cit.*, 77–80.
56. W. M. Stern, 'The Isle of Dogs Canal: a Study in Early Public Investment', *Economic History Review*, 4 (1952), 359–71.
57. L. F. Vernon-Harcourt, 'Description of the New South Dock in the Isle of Dogs Forming Part of the West India Docks', *Minutes of Proceedings of the Institution of Civil Engineers*, 34 (1871–2), 157–80.
58. W. M. Stern, 'The First London Dock Boom and the Growth of the West India Docks', *Economica*, 19 (1952), 59–77.
59. For the reasons behind the amalgamation see Sir Joseph Broodbank, *op. cit.*; J. Bird (1957), *op. cit.*, 73–5; and R. A. Heaton Page, *op. cit.*, who collates much material from dock company minute books, together with the relevant reports and Acts up to 1864.

FURTHER GENERAL REFERENCES TO THE HISTORY OF THE PORT OF LONDON

Bryant, Sir Arthur. *Liquid History: to Commemorate Fifty Years, 1909–59*. Port of London Authority, 1960.
Capper, C. *The Port and Trade of London*. London: Smith, Elder, 1862.

Elmes, J. *A Scientific, Historical and Commercial Survey of the Harbour and Port of London*. London: Weale, 1838.

Millard, A. M. *The Import Trade of London, 1600–1640*. Unpublished thesis, Ph.D., University of London, 1956.

Owen, Sir David. *The Port of London: Yesterday and Today*. London: P.L.A.. 1927.

Pulling, A. *A Practical Treatise on the Laws, Customs, Usages and Regulations of the City and Port of London*. London: Butterworth, 1842.

Stewart, B. *The Library and the Picture Collection of the Port of London*. London: Richards, 1955.

Vaughan, William. The Vaughan papers are arranged in five folio volumes, consisting of letters, tables, MSS., and pamphlets: Vol. 1, London Dock Bill: Petitions for and Against; Vol. 2, Reports for the Improvement of the Port of London; Vol. 3, Commerce and Navigation of the Port of London; Vol. 4, Comparative Dock Rates: London and the Outports; Vol. 5, Tides, Imports, Exports; and Miscellaneous; Vols. 6 and 7 are two collections of Maps, Plans, Charts, Surveys, *etc.* [P.L.A. Library].

Williams, G. A. *Medieval London*. University of London: Athlone, 1963.

Note: The works on London which contain incidental and often important reference to the port are obviously far too numerous to mention. As a first step readers wishing to sample this rich source are directed to the London Subject Catalogue of the Guildhall Library, London, E.C.2. See also P. N. Newman, *The River Thames at London: an Historical Bibliography*. Unpublished thesis, Dip Lib. University of London, 1956 [Arranged in six subject sections with an alphabetical list of authors' names].

Chapter 15

THE THAMES CHANNELS

NORTH-WEST of London the Chalk of the Chiltern Hills dips south-eastwards; south of London the Chalk of the North Downs dips northwards. A major river might be expected to flow equidistant between these two areas of exposed Chalk, flowing north-eastwards to the sea. But the London Basin is not a simple structural gutter widening eastwards, and the lower Thames flows far to the south of any median line between the outcrops of the Chalk. There is no doubt that the Thames did once flow further to the north for there are geomorphological and geological records of its former courses;[1] among these are the Thames river terraces.[2] But glaciation diverted the river to the south until it now impinges on the Chalk of the North Downs at the southern bends of its meanders. Moreover, there has been an oscillating sea-level since Pleistocene times. When the sea rose the lower Thames was flooded as a marine gulf; when sea-level fell the river was able to erode its former flood-plain. In south-east England the sea-level is at present rising at about nine inches per century,[3] and the Thames is tidal for over seventy miles.

The width of the river has been narrowed artificially by embankments since Norman times, and there is evidence to suggest that the embanking was far advanced as early as the fourteenth century.[4] Further work in the lowest reach, Sea Reach, gave the River Thames the following characteristics by the middle of the seventeenth century. The river had been confined to its main tidal channel between embankments so that in plan it looks like any meandering river, until it is remembered that twice a day the river flow is opposed by a tide with a crest surging upstream of the City of London. Embankments were not built to one giant design. They were begun not with the idea of canalizing the river which was deep enough for most traffic until the second quarter of the nineteenth century. The purpose was to reclaim the tidal marshes of the estuarine flood-plain. As one landowner pushed his wall out longitudinally into the river, he had also to prevent water rushing in from either side by erecting transverse or 'counter' walls.[5] No doubt this piecemeal reclamation assisted the river to deepen its main channel by confining the ebb and flow within a narrower cross-section. Such deepening was largely confined to the river down-stream of Old London Bridge (1176–1834). This bridge had narrow arches and wide piers and acted as a weir, or (in geomorphological terms) a knickpoint, protecting the upper reaches from the full effects of erosion consequent upon embanking downstream.[6] Upon reclamation the saltings shrink into marshes and unless protected by secure embankments the river 'reclaims' its own flood-plain. In 1707, for example,

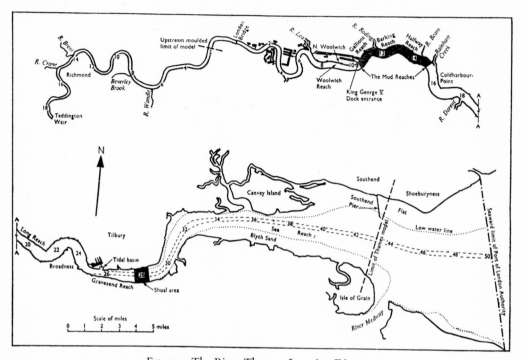

FIG. 91   The River Thames: Location Diagram

Figures in the river represent mileage upstream and downstream of London Bridge. Two areas of the river where siltation gives the greatest trouble are shown in solid black. Reproduced from Sir Claude C. Inglis and F. H. Allen, *loc. cit.*, Fig 1, by permission of the Institution of Civil Engineers.

occurred the Dagenham Breach when the river flooded 1,000 acres of former flood-plain. As recently as 1953, 40,000 acres of the Thames marshes were flooded as a result of a storm-induced tidal surge.[7]

The mean tidal range increases from about 14 feet at Southend to about 18 feet some forty miles westward at London Bridge, thereafter decreasing upstream. This is occasioned by the fact that tidal forces have to raise less water in cross-section as they proceed upstream. For example, while the maximum instantaneous discharge during the ebb or flood of a spring-tide is about 1,500,000 cusecs at Southend, the

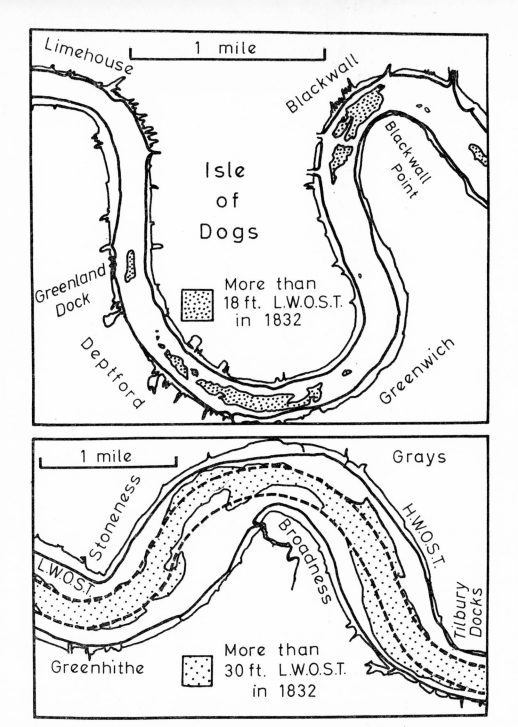

FIG. 92 Thames River Channels in 1832 at the Sharpest Bends in the River

Top: From Limehouse to Blackwall Point

In 1832 the ruling depth in these reaches was 10 feet, with 'holes' off Deptford and Blackwall, anchorages for vessels drawing 16–20 feet, either natural deeps at concavities or holes dredged by ballast-men. The present channel depth is 20 feet L.W.O.S.T. from Greenland Dock and 16 feet upstream.

Bottom: From Greenhithe to Tilbury

The modern channel, shown by pecked lines. 1,000 feet wide by 30 feet, L.W.O.S.T., is uniform in width with a regular curve around Broadness compared with the natural channel as it was in 1832.

See L. R. Jones, *op. cit.*, 30–9.

amount pouring through the cross-section at London Bridge is only 50,000 cusecs.[8] The progressive narrowing upstream is of course in great contrast to the cube relationship of the water capacity of the Narrows and the Upper Basin on the Mersey estuary. On the Thames, although the altitude of the river bed rises upstream, the high-water level is raised even further above O.D., and the former effect does not reduce the resultant tidal range until above London Bridge. The Southwark crossing thus retains its significance to the tidal regime, though in the earliest days of the port it probably marked the absolute tidal limits. Embanking, the post-Norman rise in sea-level, and the removal in 1834 of the weir formed by the foundations of Old London Bridge have all combined to push the tidal limits nineteen miles upstream of the present London Bridge.

TABLE 105

The Tide of the Thames[9]

	Richmond Lock	London Bridge	North Woolwich	Tilbury	Southend Pier
Miles from London Bridge, upstream (u) and downstream (d) ...	15·5u	—	9·6d	25·9d	43·2d
Tidal range (feet):					
Mean springs	15·1	21·4	21·0	19·0	16·7
Mean	13·0	18·1	17·7	15·8	13·8
Mean neaps	10·8	14·8	14·3	12·5	10·9
Average time of High Tide relative to London Bridge after (A) or before (B)	1 h. 01 m. A	—	26 m. B	51 m. B	1 h. 18 m. B

The Second Crisis, 1887–1909

Until 1857 the Corporation of the City of London was the conservator of the River Thames, under some six charters, the first dated 1197, and five Acts, the first dated 1394, although the crucial Act appears to have been 4 Henry VII c. 15, 1489.[10] Yet the Port and Navigation Committee of the Corporation was not required by statute to remove any shoals and indeed had no funds that it could legally apply for this purpose. Tonnage dues on vessels entering the Port of London were not even levied until 1799.[11] When a particularly bad shoal occurred, the Committee came to an arrangement with ballast-men for its removal. Such an unsatisfactory state of affairs was ended in 1857, when the Thames Conservancy Board was set up. At last some revenue was available for dredging, but the objective was limited: the removal of irregularities in the river to achieve a more even profile where the ruling depth was the one naturally provided. There was no attempt to create a new deeper sailing channel. As the draught of ships increased, complaints about the channels also increased, culminating in what was called by *The Times* a 'weighty and influential memorial' to the Thames Conservators. It was signed by representatives of 1½ million gross tons of shipping using the port, and dated January 26, 1887. The following is an extract:

'. . . During the last few years the tonnage trading to the Port of London has enormously increased. The tonnage of vessels entering inwards and outwards in 1871 was about 7,600,000 tons, while in 1885 it amounted to upwards of 12,000,000, being an increase of nearly 60 per cent. At the same time it is needless to inform you of the change which has taken place in the individual tonnage of ships, both steam and sail, and of the greater draft of water which merchant vessels generally require as compared with that which was necessary a few years ago. . . . conversion . . . from sail to steam renders any delay or risk in entering or leaving port doubly disadvantageous, inasmuch as steamships must be worked more rapidly and energetically than sailing vessels, while the value of the former and the cargoes they carry is relatively much greater. . . .

[If] . . . vessels . . . leaving Gravesend for the docks encounter unexpectedly a belt of fog . . . [they] are compelled to push on through the same at imminent risk [for fear of going aground on a falling tide] . . .

At the present time there are numerous patches in the river below the Albert Docks where there are not more than 18 ft. at low water, and, in fact, no vessel drawing more than that could venture to anchor between the Albert Dock and Purfleet, a distance of seven miles.'

Extract from *The Times* editorial:

'. . . In the Port of London it appears that little or nothing in comparison [with some other British estuaries] has yet been done. Is this to be attributed to supineness of the Board of Conservators, or to the *natural* superiority of the Thames as a mercantile port? We suspect that both causes have been in operation. The Tyne, for instance, is almost entirely an artificial port; so also is the Clyde above Greenock. The Thames by comparison is a natural port. But the development of modern shipping has now clearly outrun the natural capacities of the Thames. . . . a depth of 18 feet at low water is clearly not fitted for vessels which when fully loaded draw 25 feet or even more. . . .' [Italics added: both extracts from *The Times*, February 1, 1887]

Eventually, the Board of Trade set up the Lower Thames Navigation Commission under section 189 of the *Thames Conservancy Act*, 1894. There is no doubt that the letter to *The Times* had been an effective focus of agitation. A piece of evidence from the 1894 proceedings may be quoted which brings one of the complaints to life:

> 'Question. "Do you have reports of delays sent to your firm?" Answer [by A. S. Willians, shipping company director]. "Yes; time after time we have complained to the Trinity House about . . . [their] pilots anchoring there [at the Nore in the Outer Estuary], but they more or less defend their position by saying that they dare not go over the shallows which lie between the Nore and Gravesend until the tide has made to a certain extent; . . . and so they get up too late to come up to the Royal Albert Dock on that tide" . . .'[12]

The Thames Conservators stated that their programme was to provide an 18-foot channel for 10 miles downstream of London Bridge, thereafter a 22-foot channel for $6\frac{1}{2}$ miles, and finally a 24-foot channel out to sea. But the Commissioners in their *Report* concurred with the view of shipowners and others that a 30-foot channel ought to be provided as far upstream as Gravesend at least,[13] and shipowners wanted this extended if possible to the Royal Albert Dock, only $10\frac{1}{2}$ miles from London Bridge, although this part of the river was outside the Commission's terms of reference. The Thames Conservators did not accept this as mandatory and made no alteration to their stated programme. Here is the heart of the second crisis of the port: the contrast between what was clearly needed in the water approach and what was being done. To be fair to the Thames Conservators it must be pointed out that the revenue they had legally applicable to dredging was less than was to be available later. But that they could have done more in 1894 is shown by the fact that they did eventually propose in 1905, when they obtained a permissive Act, to dredge a 30-foot channel from Gravesend to the sea.

Five years earlier a Royal Commission on the port had been appointed. Now the limited finances of the dock companies at the end of the nineteenth century was referred to in the previous chapter. So it is no surprise to learn that the terms of reference of this Royal Commission began by coupling the question of the administration of the port with the question of the state of its water approaches. As a result of the Commission's *Report* in 1902 the P.L.A. was set up in 1909. Its first chief engineer, Sir Frederick Palmer, accepted the *Joint Engineers' Report to the Thames Conservancy, May 21, 1908*, which implied a programme of capital or creative dredging.

Dredging

TABLE 106

Shipping Channel Programme, 1908, and Present Channels, London Bridge to the Sea
All depths are L.W.O.S.T.

Programme (Recommendations of Joint Engineers' Report, 1908)	*Present Channels*
London Bridge to Greenland Dock: 400–500 ft. by 14–16 ft.	London Bridge to Tower Bridge: 300–350 ft. by 14 ft.
	Tower Bridge to Thames Tunnel, Wapping: 400 ft. by 14 ft.
	Thames Tunnel to Greenland Dock: 400–600 ft. by 16 ft.
Greenland Dock to Royal Albert Dock: 600 ft. by 20 ft.	Greenland Dock to King George V Dock: 450–600 ft. by 20 ft.
Royal Albert Dock to Coldharbour Point (between Erith Reach and Erith Rands): 600 ft. by 30 ft.	King George V Dock to Coldharbour Point: 600 ft. by 27 ft.
Coldharbour Point to Sea Reach Buoy No. 1: 1,000 ft. by 30 ft.	Coldharbour Point to Sea Reach Buoy No. 1: 1,000 ft. by 30 ft.

In the following table the annual rate of capital dredging necessary to achieve the present channels by 1927 is compared with previous dredging rates and with the rate of maintenance dredging necessary since.

TABLE 107

Material Dredged from the River Thames

	Material Dredged. Annual Average in Cubic Yards
By Thames Conservancy: 1878–1908	359,500[14]
By P.L.A. during Capital Dredging Programme: 1909–14; 1919–25	2,496,000[15]
By P.L.A. as Maintenance Dredging: 1928/9–1938/9; and 1947/8–1955/6	1,113,000[16]

The docks and Tilbury Tidal Basin have also to be dredged giving the following average pattern 1947–57:

TABLE 108

Average Annual Percentages of Total Dredging
(2,700,000 cubic yards per annum approx.)

From the River:
Lower Gravesend Reach and 'Mud Reaches' (Gallions, Barking, Halfway)	40
All other Reaches	5
Docks	40
Tilbury Tidal Basin	15

This cost the P.L.A. £879,043 in the year ended March 31, 1960, 4½ per cent of its total expenditure. Apart from the siltation one might expect in the still water of docks and the slack water of the Tilbury Tidal Basin, the table shows that nearly 90 per cent of the dredging in the Thames is concentrated in two areas (Fig. 91). But for these two areas the river channels are almost self-maintaining. In Lower Gravesend Reach there is a shoal area between miles 28 and 29 (from London Bridge). In this reach the cross-section of the river widens rapidly, the eastern end being slightly more than twice the width of the western end. The resultant loss of velocity causes silting on the ebb. The dredged channel is straight for navigational purposes whereas the river would tend to swing to the north, so that silting is worse towards the north bank. Beyond mile 29 the channel bends to enter Lower Hope Reach, and the shoaling becomes less marked.

Silting in the Mud Reaches between miles 10 and 15 has been more difficult to explain. The dredging plan of the *Joint Engineers' Report*, 1908, recommended a channel of 30 feet L.W.O.S.T. to the Royal Albert Dock. This uniform ruling depth from the sea to the Royal Docks took no account of the fact that in the natural regime an estuary bed rises landward. In practice it has been found that 27 feet or more could be obtained without maintenance dredging just downstream of the Mud Reaches, but that heavy siltation occurs if dredging is attempted below 27 feet within the Mud Reaches.

> 'In brief, the main causes of siltation in the Mud Reaches lie in the attempt to maintain greater depths of water than those dictated by regime in an area where the concentration of suspended solids is high.'[17]

The origin of these 'suspended solids' and the manner in which they reach the Mud Reaches were the targets of an eight-year programme of hydraulics research.[18] This was carried out with the aid of models in No. 8 Shed, Royal Victoria Dock. The largest model has a horizontal scale of 1:600 making its waterway 400 feet long and 44 feet wide at its seaward end.[19] This model has also been used to investigate Thameside flooding and the effect of a movable barrier in Long Reach.[20]

Until 1960 the policy was to dump practically all dredged material in Black Deep, a flood channel of the Outer Estuary. This dumping ground remained un-filled, and samples from the bed revealed clean sand. Where did the dumped spoil go? It has been calculated that material brought by the Thames and its tributaries, and by sewage and industrial effluents,[21] and the very small amount of dredgings formerly dumped within the river, accounted for only about half of the total material which accumulates in the estuary. The clear inference is that the other half must have entered from the seaward end, not only from material eroded from the Kent and Essex coastal flats but also from the spoil dumped in Black Deep. Sampling at mile 19 in Long Reach downstream of the Mud Reaches showed marked net land-ward movement of currents along the bed during spring tides with low Thames land flow conditions; the net movement was evenly balanced or even slightly sea-ward during neap tides. Upstream of the Mud Reaches, in Woolwich Reach at mile 9, sampling showed that for neap tides the net movement was zero and in-creased seawards for larger tides. This suggested that the landward bed drift extends only as far as the Mud Reaches, above which all net river movement in the bottom layer is seaward. This confirmed results obtained in the tidal model: that the Mud Reaches are situated in the area where the landward bed drift is tending to cease allowing rapid siltation to take place. It will be remembered that a similar zone of deposits drifted in from the sea is to be found in the Upper Basin of the Mersey. In the Thames the zone extends for 4½ miles (the Mud Reaches) because with high land flow the area of maximum deposition is pushed downstream. Under these conditions highly silt-laden water from the estuary is replaced by 'relatively clear silt-hungry water'[22] from the land which consequently scours the river bed. Radio-active tracers were injected in the bed of Gravesend Reach in the Thames;[23] hollow celluloid balls, filled with water so that their density was only slightly greater than the surrounding water, were also placed in the model's Gravesend Reach. The resultant concentrations of tracers in the Thames and balls in the model finishing up in the Mud Reaches and the shoal area of Gravesend Reach showed a remarkable correspondence.[24]

As a result of this research the P.L.A. decided to pump dredgings ashore, on to 294 acres of marsh at Rainham (mile 15), originally 7 feet below H.W.O.S.T. This area has been protected by embankments called bunds to form lagoons in which dredgings will settle after being pumped ashore.[25] The site should suffice until 1968 when the P.L.A. has another site available in Kent (opposite mile 32). Although the capital expense of new plant has been necessary, the round journey of up to 138 miles to Black Deep has been saved. In addition, the P.L.A. is consolidating riparian marshland it already owns. Disposal ashore may well cause a slight change of regime (balance between accretion and erosion), stabilizing the Mud Reaches at a depth closer to the 27-foot channel required. And all the time south-east England is sinking at about one inch per decade allowing more tidal water to enter the es-tuary to form a deeper channel. No spectacular decrease of mud in the Mud Reaches is likely to occur immediately. For some time it is expected that material dredged from the Mud Reaches will be replaced by fine material drifting landward, but in smaller quantities, it is hoped, than before. This fine material will have been eroded not from the spoil heap in Black Deep, but from the mud flats bordering the Outer Estuary.

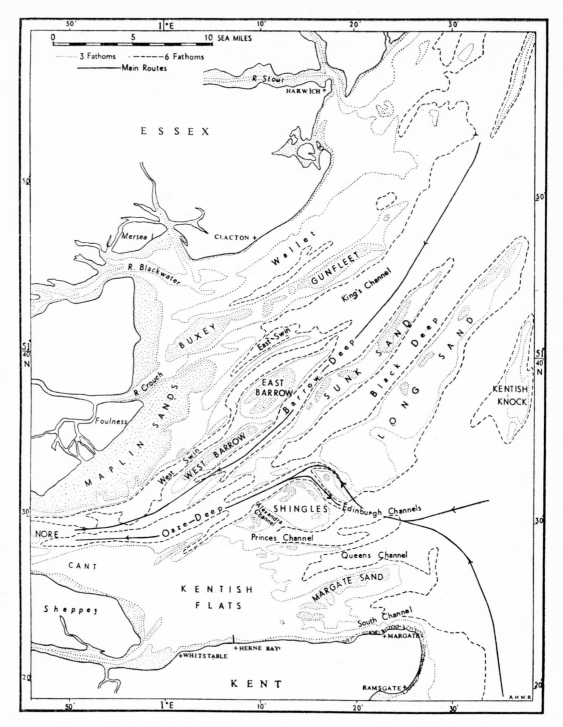

Fig. 93   The Outer Thames Estuary

After a diagram by A. H. W. Robinson (1951) *loc. cit.*, reproduced by permission of the Institute of Navigation, and based upon Admiralty Charts Nos. 1607 and 1975 by permission of the Controller of H.M. Stationery Office and of the Hydrographer of the Navy.

The Outer Estuary

Beyond the seaward limit of the P.L.A. in the Outer Estuary no dredging takes place. The natural channels have sufficed and are buoyed, like the river channels, by the Trinity House Authority. A. H. W. Robinson has pointed out[26] that the majority of the channels of the Outer Estuary are flood-channels formed by North Sea tidal streams: the Wallet, King's Channel, East Swin, Barrow Deep, and the above-mentioned Black Deep; with intervening narrow sandbanks aligned parallel to the Essex shore: Gunfleet; Barrow, Sunk, and Long Sands. The Maplin Sands are a fringing coastal flat. When the North Sea tide is on the turn, the English Channel tide enters the bell-mouth estuary and it has also cut flood-channels roughly parallel to the coast—this time east-west parallel to the Kent coast, with the Cant and Kentish Flats remaining as a counterpart of the Maplin Sands. These east-west flood-channels (1–5 in the table below), at increasing distances from the coast, were discovered and charted at successive periods.

TABLE 109

Successive Southern Approaches in the Outer Thames Estuary[27]

		Shown on Chart of
1. South Channel		1588
2. Queen [Elizabeth]'s Channel		1586
3. Prince's Channel		1775
4. Alexandra Channel		1862
5. [Duke of] Edinburgh['s] Channel		1886
[formerly Smuggler's Swatchway	pre	1828
Thomas's Channel		1828
Bullock's Channel		1844]

The last three channels (3–5) are swatchways cut by the English Channel tide across the Long Sand to debouch into the Oaze and Black Deeps.

The ebb-channels of the Rivers Thames and Medway are respectively the West Swin and the Oaze Deep. As in the Outer Estuary of the River Mersey, the crucial area is where the navigation channels have to cross the sills between the offset flood- and ebb-channels. Before the nineteenth century most vessels kept as close to shore as possible to obtain landmarks, but as ships' draught increased flood-channels further and further from the land had to be used. The sill for the approach from the North Sea between Barrow Deep (flood-channel) and the West Swin (ebb-channel) has 30 feet L.W.O.S.T. with little change of course. The story of the southern route is more complicated. In 1844 the Edinburgh Channel swatchway (then called Bullock's

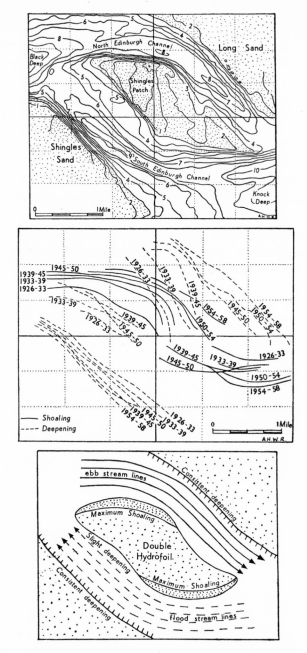

FIG. 94   The Edinburgh Channels in the Outer Estuary of the Thames

Top: The submarine configuration of the Edinburgh Channels in fathoms L.W.O.S.T.

Centre: Axes of significant belts of shoaling and deepening as indicated on isoballath maps constructed for varying intervals between 1926 and 1958

Bottom: The above axes interpreted in relation to Shingles Patch seen as a 'double hydrofoil'

All after A. H. W. Robinson (1960), *loc. cit.*, reproduced by permission from *Geography*, and the top diagram is also reproduced by permission of the Controller of H.M. Stationery Office and of the Hydrographer of the Navy.

Channel) was a simple flood-channel of the English Channel tide. But as this channel became wider a median shoal began to develop as the tidal flood-streams became unable to erode the whole cross-section. This accounts for the origin of the shoal called the Shingles Patch, separating two channels on either side; the South Edinburgh (flood) Channel and the North Edinburgh Channel, eroded by the ebb-stream from the Oaze Deep. At present inward bound vessels deep in the water, including the largest tankers, use the North Edinburgh Channel, 36 feet L.W.O.S.T., while outward-bound traffic uses the South Edinburgh Channel, 31 feet L.W.O.S.T. On the North Sea route (minimum 30 feet L.W.O.S.T.) vessels are either smaller, or laden with only part-cargo, and there is no traffic by large laden tankers.

A. H. W. Robinson has provided an isoballath map (showing areas of equal change of depth) for the area of interlocking channels around Shingles Patch for periods between 1926 and 1958. He has suggested that these changes can be understood if the Shingles Patch is considered to be a double hydrofoil shape facing the ebb-stream coming from the west and the flood-stream coming from the east. As in the case of an aerofoil in an air-stream, low pressure (shoaling) develops just beyond the leading edge on the convex surface with positive pressure (deepening) beyond the leading edge on the concave surface. There is also deepening along the edges of Long Sand and Shingles Sand to which the ebb- and flood-streams are deflected.[28]

The flood tidal crest sweeps on up the river. At low water a liner bound for the Royal Docks may be at Gravesend, sailing up on the young flood. Some two hours before high water she is off the King George V Entrance Lock, and is in the dock before the tidal crest sweeps by in the river outside. The tidal pulse spends itself eventually against Teddington Weir some two and a half hours after first entering from the Outer Estuary, and on the ebb the ships ride in deep water in the holes cut in the flood-plain of the river.

REFERENCES

1. See map in S. W. Wooldridge and H. C. K. Henderson, 'Some Aspects of the Physiography of the Eastern Part of the London Basin', *Transactions and Papers*, 21 (1955), Institute of British Geographers, 19–31, Fig. 2.

2. A comprehensive account of the evolution of the London Basin and the Thames drainage is to be found in S. W. Wooldridge and D. L. Linton, *Structure, Surface, and Drainage in South-east England*, London: Philip, 1955. See also W. B. R. King and K. P. Oakley, 'The Pleistocene Succession in the Lower Part of the Thames Valley', *Proceedings of the Prehistoric Society*, 2 (1936), 52–76.

3. Sir Claude C. Inglis and F. H. Allen, 'The Regimen of the Thames Estuary as Affected by Currents, Salinities, and River Flow', *Proceedings of the Institution of Civil Engineers*, 7 (1957), 827–78, 833.

4. J. Bird, *The Geography of the Port of London*, London: Hutchinson, 1957, 54–5, relying on Sir William Dugdale, *History of Imbanking and Draining*, 2nd edition, 1772, 59 and 74.

5. B. E. Cracknell, *The Alluvial Marshlands of the Lower Thames Estuary*, Unpublished thesis Ph.D.,

University of London, 1953, Fig. 4. See also Sir Cyril Kirkpatrick, 'The Tidal Thames', *Proceedings of the Institution of Civil Engineers*, 233 (1931–2), 2–34, 6–10; and B. Cunningham, *The Estuarial Embankments of the Tidal Thames*, Report to the 16th International Congress of Navigation, 1935. The traditional material used in the construction of embankments has been Kentish Ragstone covering a clay hearting, but interlocking concrete slabs are taking the place of ragstone, B. E. Cracknell, 'Kentish Ragstone', *P.L.A. Monthly*, 24 (1959), 18–20.

6. J. B. Redman, 'The River Thames', 49, *Minutes and Proceedings of the Institution of Civil Engineers*, (1876–7), 3–95, stated that Old London Bridge caused a 'step-down' in water upstream and downstream of up to 5 feet at low tide, 7. Also *Ibid.*, *loc. cit.*, 59 (1879–80), 286–8 and 72 (1882–3), 3–10. Erosion upstream caused by the removal of this 'weir' or 'knickpoint' in 1834 is believed to be still continuing, Sir Claude Inglis and F. H. Allen, *loc. cit.*, 857.

7. *Report of the Departmental Committee on Coastal Flooding*, Cmd. 9165, London: H.M.S.O., 1954; and H. Grieve, *The Great Tide: the Story of the 1953 Flood Disaster in Essex*, Essex County Council, 1959.

8. Sir Claude Inglis and F. H. Allen, *loc. cit.*, 830. 'Cusec' represents 'cubic foot per second'.

9. Based on data in *Ibid.*, 830, and supplied by the River Department of the P.L.A. The Richmond tidal range figures are approximate because low water levels so far upstream are largely dependent on the volume of land discharge of fresh water.

10. A. Pulling, *A Practical Treatise on the Laws, Customs, and Regulations of the City and Port of London*, London: Smith, Elder, 1844, 320–2, *et seq.*

11. *Minutes of Proceedings of the Lower Thames Navigation Commission*, 1894, 5.

12. *Ibid.*, 121.

13. *Report to the Board of Trade*, by J. Wolfe Barry, Sir George Nares, and G. F. Lyster [the Lower Thames Navigation Commission], March 25, 1896, 10.

14. Sir Cyril Kirkpatrick, *loc. cit.*, 13.

15. *Ibid.*, 15.

16. Sir Claude Inglis and F. H. Allen, *loc. cit.*, 867.

17. *Ibid.*, 834.

18. *Ibid.*, is a report on this programme.

19. F. H. Allen, 'The Thames Model Investigation', *The Dock and Harbour Authority*, 32 (1952), 373–8.

20. A Government Blue Book described as technically feasible a movable flood barrier in the Long Reach of the Thames costing between £13 million and £17 million. But navigational problems and extra flooding on the downstream side would 'require further study'. *Technical Possibilities of a Thames Flood Barrier*, London: H.M.S.O., Cmnd. 956, 1960.

21. B. A. Southgate, 'A Study of the Pollution of the Thames Estuary', *Journal of the Royal Society of Arts*, 107 (1959), 459–74. See also *Notes of Proceedings at a Conference on the Condition of Tidal Thames Water*, held at the Port of London Authority, Trinity Square, E.C.3, February 25, 1955 [Mimeographed].

22. Sir Claude Inglis and F. H. Allen, *loc. cit.*, 856.

23. F. H. Allen and J. Grindley, 'Radioactive Tracers in the Thames Estuary', *The Dock and Harbour Authority*, 37 (1957), 302–6.

24. Sir Claude Inglis and F. H. Allen, *loc. cit.*, 854, Fig. 20.

25. 'Disposal of Dredgings Ashore', *P.L.A. Monthly*, 25 (1960), 285–8.

26. This section on the Outer Estuary is based on the following works of A. H. W. Robinson, *The Thames Estuary: a Regional Hydrographic Study*, Unpublished thesis, M.Sc., University of London, 1952; 'The Changing Navigation Routes of the Thames Estuary', *Journal of the Institute of Navigation*, 4 (1951), 357–70; 'The Submarine Morphology of Certain Port Approach Systems', *Ibid.*, 9 (1956), 20–46; and 'Ebb-flood Channel Systems in Sandy Bays and Estuaries', *Geography*, 45 (1960), 183–99, 186–9.

27. E. C. Osborn, 'The Southern Approaches', *P.L.A. Monthly*, 23 (1958), 147–50; and L. R. Jones, *The Geography of London River*, London: Methuen, 1931, 123–8.

28. A. H. W. Robinson (1960), *loc. cit.*, 186–9. He is careful to point out that the 'double hydrofoil' in two dimensions cannot fully explain the complex three-dimensional form of Shingles Patch, 189.

FURTHER REFERENCES

Addison, W. *The Thames Estuary*. London: Hale, 1954.

Belloc, H. *The River of London*. London: Foulis, 1912.

Evans, H. Muir. *A Short History of the Thames Estuary*. London: Imray Laurie, 1937.

Linney, A. G. *Lure and Lore of London's River*. London: Sampson, Low, 1932.

Preddy, W. S. 'The Mixing and Movement of Water in the Estuary of the Thames', *Journal of the Marine Biological Association*, 33 (1954), 645–62.

Shankland, E. C. *A Contribution on the Hydrographic Research of the Yantlet Dredged Channel in Sea Reach*. London, 1940.

——. *The Thames Estuary and the Port of London: Channel Development by Dredging*. Paper read at the XVIIth International Navigational Congress, Lisbon, 1949.

Chapter 16

THE DOCK SYSTEMS OF LONDON

WITHIN London's five dock systems there are 197 berths and a total quayage nearly thirty-five miles long. But because the docks are split up into five separate systems, originally begun by rival dock companies in the nineteenth century, few people realize the magnitude of the installations. In addition, the docks are downstream of the city, excavated away from the walled-off river, and many Londoners never see a ship at all from one year to the next, in great contrast to Merseyside.

Perhaps the reader will forgive the length of the tables in this chapter. They are inserted to give an idea of the contrasting trading patterns of the dock systems, and this will enable the text to deal with some of the more important features, particularly stressing recent developments. The 'dock tour'[1] is preceded by an explanation of the background to the tables of shipping lines provided for each dock system. The following tables are headed '*Some* of the Shipping Lines and Services Operated' and '*Usual (not necessarily fixed)* Location for *mainly* Discharge (D) and Loading (L)'. These italicized hesitations are necessary because of the complexities involved in berthing cargo ships of all classes from all over the world alongside the quays available. Firstly, not all the shipping lines are listed, since in some cases visits by vessels to a particular dock system are irregular. In all cases, the berthing situation is fluid, and this is the reason for omitting actual berth numbers. Even where the P.L.A. and the shipping company have a long-term agreement over the use of a particular berth, the agreement is looked upon only as 'semi-permanent'. For such an 'appropriated berth', complete with cargo transit shed, the company pays an annual rent. Signs of such a semi-permanent occupation are the name of the line on the transit shed and the shipping company's branch office close by. But the P.L.A. retains the right to let the berth to other ships when the tenant's vessels are not on the quay, because the berths must be in use as continuously as possible. An 'allocated berth' in London is one allotted to ships of a conference group of liners where its constituent ships can load. But here, in contrast to an appropriated berth, the P.L.A. administers the adjacent transit shed, since it supervises the reception of cargoes for export, arranging

TABLE 110

Dimensions and Berthing Accommodation of London's Five Dock Systems

		London & St. Katharine Docks	Surrey Commercial Docks	India & Millwall Docks	Royal Victoria, Royal Albert, & King George V Docks	Tilbury Docks	Total
Dimensions:							
	Total area (acres)	125¼	381½	515	1,112	725	2,858¾
	Water area (acres) ...	45	136	155	235	104	675
Principal Entrance Lock	Length (feet)	350	550	584	800	1,000	—
	Width (feet)	60	80	80	100	110	—
	Depth (feet)★	28	35¼	35	45	45½	—
	Total length of Quay (miles)	4	8¾	8	10	4	34¾
Berths:						*and Cargo Jetty*	
	Deep Sea	13	20	33	46	19	131
	Short Sea	7	6	4	—	3	20
	Coastwise	4	—	2	—	—	6
	Timber	—	27	2	—	—	29
	Banana	—	—	—	1	—	1
	Chilled Meat	—	—	—	2	—	2
	Bulk Grain	—	—	2	4	—	6
	Passengers	—	—	—	—	2	2
	Total Berths	24	53	43	53	24	197

Note: The classification of the berths, timber, deep sea, short sea, coastwise, etc., is in general terms; many of the berths are interchangeable according to requirements.

The bulk grain berths are alongside tenants' flour mills, except for one berth at the Central Granary, Millwall Dock.

★Below Trinity High Water, a Port of London datum, approximately 11·4 feet above O.D.[2]

them in the shed sorted to marks (ports of destination) and delivers them to the ship's side. Despite the systems of appropiation and allocation, the berthing system remains flexible, and the following may help to explain some of the complexities in the choice of berth for a ship visiting the port and not proceeding to an appropriated berth.[3]

The precise time of the ship's arrival is not certain, since she may be delayed at the overseas port, by strike or breakdown, or by bad weather en route. The dimensions of the ship in relation to lock entrances impose limitations on the choice of dock system. Within the selected dock the choice of the berth may be affected by

2 A

the wish of the master to unload or load only part-cargo, and the nature of such cargo. It may need a specialized unloading appliance or heavy cranage. Quick unloading of perishable cargo is necessary, perhaps by mechanical apparatus, not available at every berth. Even if the whole cargo is to be unloaded overside into barges, a quayside transit shed may be necessary to help sort it out—the shed then acting as an extension to the ship's deck. The previous ship at the berth may be delayed for similar reasons to the incoming ship. And some of the previous ship's cargo may be shut-out, that is, left in the shed. Such cargo may be noxious to the incoming cargo; imagine if tea were to be stored under the same roof as onions! The type of export cargo might dictate the quay chosen. If the ship is loading explosives or steel pipes, these are normally delivered by rail truck; the chosen berth should have its own rail spur from the main track rather than a track which runs alongside adjacent berths causing the export cargo possibly to interfere with their working. If cars or bulky crates (containers) are being loaded, a large parking area adjacent to the shed is required. Such problems as these condition the choice of a ship's berth at all general cargo ports. But the difficulty of a jigsaw increases with the number of pieces and with the number of seemingly possible places that the difficult piece might fit.

The London and St. Katharine Docks

The chief characteristic of this dock system is that there is no regular deep-sea liner service operating. From the original Western Dock (1805) extensions have been made eastward via the Eastern Dock (1828), the Shadwell Old Basin (1831), and the Shadwell New Basin (1858). The Wapping Basin is the original tidal basin, leading from the original entrance lock which was finally closed in 1956. The St. Katharine Docks (1828–9) are physically separate, and although their small entrance lock has been rebuilt (1957–9), they now receive only barge traffic. This is a clue to the importance of this dock system. The site is too far upstream to accommodate big ships; the chief (eastern) entrance can receive vessels of only up to 330 feet in length and about 2,300 gross tons.[4] Half the goods entering these docks is carried in barges, having been unloaded from bigger ships in bigger docks downstream. The docks have many adjacent warehouses,[5] and the P.L.A. also inherited the Cutler Street Warehouses,[6] which the St. Katharine Dock Company purchased from the East India Company in 1836. A detailed tour around the Western Dock, London Docks, alone would cover some forty different types of storage accommodation, so that this account must necessarily be selective.

The north quay lay-out will give an idea of some of the functions. Upon the quayside the following notice is encountered:

'Persons going from one part of the dock to another should use the roadways and paths at the back of the sheds. There is no thoroughfare along the quays.'

TABLE III

London Docks: Some of the Shipping Lines and Services Operated
(arranged clockwise from the north-west corner of each dock)

Short Name of Shipping Line, etc.	Usual (not necessarily fixed) Location for mainly Discharge (D) and Loading (L)	Trading to
WESTERN DOCK, NORTH QUAY		
Ellerman; General Steam Nav.; MacAndrew }	D (4 berths)	Portugal, Spain
MacAndrew; Currie	L	⎰ Spain, North Africa, ⎱ Western Italy
WESTERN DOCK, EAST QUAY		
Currie	D/L	Western Italy
WESTERN DOCK, SOUTH QUAY		
Currie	D/L	Western Italy
Phoenix	D/L	Amsterdam
Bergen	D/L	Norway
Compagnie Nantaise	D/L	Charente
WESTERN DOCK, WEST QUAY AND JETTY		
Kirsten; Argo; General Steam Nav. }	D/L (3 berths)	Rhine
Clyde Shipping	D/L (2 berths)	Belfast
WAPPING BASIN, WEST QUAY		
Kirsten; Argo; General Steam Nav. }	D/L (see also Western Dock, West Quay)	Rhine
General Steam Nav.	D/L	Le Havre
EASTERN DOCK		
Bulk Wine Traffic	D (No. 22 Berth)	
General Steam Nav.	D/L (North-west Quay)	Western Italy
SHADWELL NEW BASIN, NORTH QUAY		
MacAndrew	L	Gibraltar, Spain, North Africa express
General Steam Nav.	L	Bordeaux
SHADWELL OLD BASIN		
Brussels S.S.	D/L	Belgium

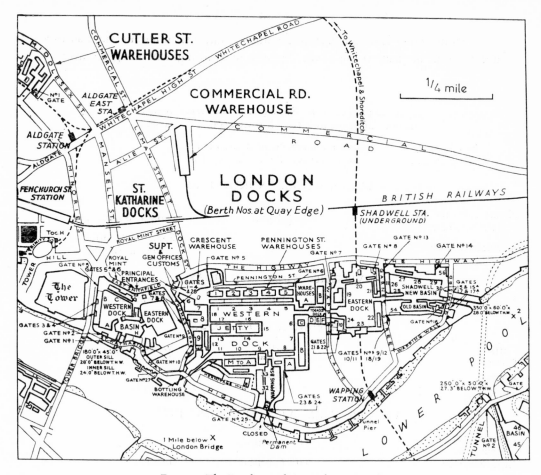

FIG. 95   The London and St. Katharine Docks
The head offices of the Port of London Authority are shown in solid black. Figs. 95–99 inclusive are based on a P.L.A. drawing by permission.

This is greatly in contrast to modern requirements for a quay, which usually specify up to 55 feet between quay edge and transit shed wall. But these transit sheds were built in 1912. They are used mainly for discharging fruit; Spitalfields Market is under a mile away. The dock lay-out was designed before the railway age, and, as in the Surrey Commercial Docks, the elaborate perimeters of such early docks have defeated all attempts to give them rail access. Five of the original 1805 four-storey warehouses are behind the north quay transit sheds: No. 1 is the chief rubber store for London; No. 2, essential (*i.e.* derived from essences) oils and drugs; No. 3, canned goods; No. 4, gums, waxes, and general goods; and No. 5 is a general warehouse. Behind is yet another line of single-storey Pennington Street Warehouses: Nos. 1 and 2 have been converted into staff canteens; in No. 3 wine examination is carried out, with casks delivered from vaults beneath the quay; Nos. 4 and 5 are cased wine stores, with some 20,000 cases of wine (40,000 gallons); and lastly, No. 6 is an iodine store. Other specialized warehouses are No. 10 Eastern Dock (tea and coffee), No. 11 Shadwell Basin (dried fruit); and St. Katharine A, B, G, and H (tea) and I (ivory). Perhaps the most important are the Crescent Warehouses with some 24 acres of storage space for 40,000 bales of wool, with a display floor illuminated by a north light. Every year buyers from the Wool Exchange visit the floor during the eight London wool sales, the only European spot wool sale where a merchant can make up deficiencies of almost any grade of wool, so wide is London's 'foreland' for this commodity. Beneath the north quay are 20 acres of the Crescent Vaults storing up to 60,000 casks of wines and spirits at a constant temperature of 13° C. At No. 22 Berth wine, notably vermouth, is unloaded by pumping either from 500-gallon stainless steel containers off-loaded into barges which come alongside the berth, or from the tanks of specially designed ships. Besides the increased speed of discharge, the 200,000-gallon capacity of the berth's tanks saves the cost of some 4,000 casks.[7]

An amazing range of services is provided by P.L.A. employees, apart from the discharge of cargo:[8] weighing, sampling, lotting, displaying, bottling wine; and blending and vatting (spirits). In the nineteenth century dock labour was among the cheapest available, and it was good economics to use dockers for these rather skilled processes. The P.L.A. inherited the system which tends to be self-perpetuating for two reasons. Experience in rather strange skills is learnt by a specialized labour force; and seller and buyer appreciate the impartial sampling and display by a neutral third party. In this way trust is built up, an important intangible where highly valuable commodities are in question,[9] and where wrong or careless handling could result in great damage to the trade.[10]

These docks are surrounded by built-up property and horizontal expansion is impossible. Moreover, the docks are split by three roads with bascule bridges leading to the first of the real dockland areas closest to the city. The term dockland may be reserved for those residential areas cut off between the water areas of docks and the backs of riverside wharves. Wapping is such an area, without a bus service or shopping centre though only a mile and a quarter from the Bank of England. No wonder the eighteenth-century merchants proudly called these docks the *London* Docks, though a familiar name in the port is the 'Town Docks' with their 'Up-town Warehouses'.

The Surrey Commercial Docks

This is the only dock system on the south side of the Thames, and it is dominated by the discharge of timber in docks north of Redriff Road. Compared with the

London and India Docks, these docks were developed by small companies which never achieved trading monopolies, and which did not gain the status of legal quays for their docks until late in the nineteenth century. But there was an important role for the docks to play in the importing of the less valuable commodities, like grain and timber. Grain is now imported to the silos and mills of later docks downstream, but timber has remained a Surrey speciality. It is not an easy cargo to handle because of the bulk of individual pieces. In timber importing the open quays upon which the timber is discharged act the role of transit shed, while the timber sheds and yards are really timber warehouses. Because the tracks of a quayside crane would quickly become clogged, ships' gear is used at timber berths for unloading. Many of the old directors of the Surrey Dock companies were also timber merchants. They had

TABLE 112

Surrey Commercial Docks: Some of the Shipping Lines and Services Operated
(arranged clockwise from the north-west corner of each dock)

Short Name of Shipping Line, etc.	Usual (not necessarily fixed) Location for mainly Discharge (D) and Loading (L)	Trading to
CANADA DOCK, SOUTH-EAST QUAY		
United Baltic Finland S.S.	} D/L (see Greenland Dock, South Quay)	
GREENLAND DOCK, NORTH QUAY		
Furness, Withy	D	Pacific Coast
Lykes	D/L	U.S.A. Gulf
GREENLAND DOCK, SOUTH QUAY		
United Baltic; Finland S.S.; State Steamship Lines (U.S.S.R.)	} D/L	{ Finland and joint Leningrad service
Scindia	D/L	India
Cunard	D/L	Great Lakes
Cunard	D/L (2 berths)★	U.S.A. and Canada
SOUTH DOCK, SOUTH QUAY		
Hamburg–London; Argo; General Steam Nav.	D/L	Hamburg
SOUTH DOCK, WEST QUAY		
General Steam Nav.	D/L	Dunkirk and Boulogne

★ Operated in conjunction with a berth on King George V, North Quay.

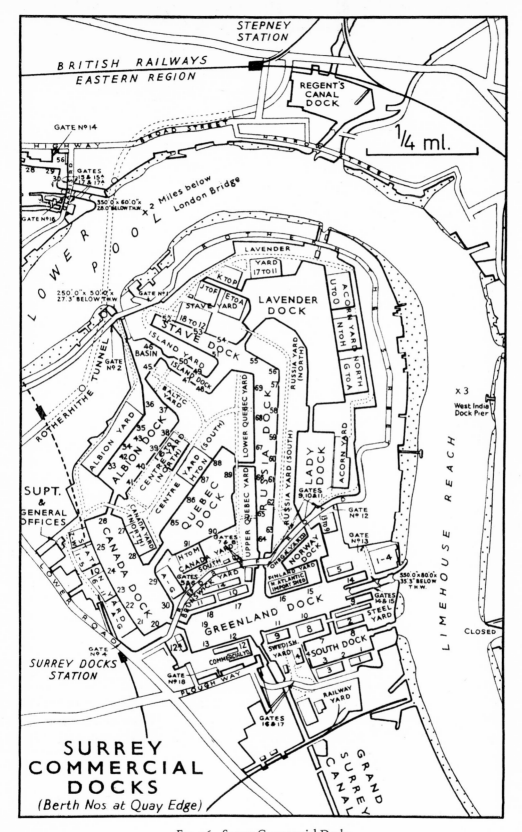

FIG. 96   Surrey Commercial Docks

a great say in the lay-out of the rather small docks with their yards and timber ponds and saw little need to provide the expensive quayside installations associated with general cargo. Until 1939 London timber merchants had little yard capacity of their own, and the P.L.A. provided much covered storage within these docks. In September 1940 incendiaries caused the loss of 176 timber sheds and seriously damaged 57 others. Fortunately, imported timber now reaches the consumer much more quickly, but even so about a fifth requires dock storage, and some, particularly hardwood, is brought by barge from ships in other dock systems. The remaining four-fifths are unloaded to barges, and there may be as many as 500 of these in the docks during the summer Baltic softwood season. The Surrey Entrance Lock is the main barge entrance. Island, Lavender, and Lady Docks are former timber ponds used only by barges, though floating Douglas Fir is stored in Lady Dock. Post-war timber sheds have been designed to suit some sixty mobile cranes which have largely replaced the pre-war hand-piling of timber. These cranes require access alleys fifteen feet wide between timber piles; but this loss of horizontal space is compensated by the greater height to which the cranes can pile. The modern timber shed must have a clear internal height of over thirty feet and wide areas between stanchions. The tubular steel shed at Acorn Yard South has 125 feet clear between roof supports. This shed also receives plywood imports, which have increased enormously in recent years. Taken by lighter from Baltic cargo liners discharging in the Greenland and Canada Docks, the plywood is unloaded by mobile crane at Acorn Yard South and piled by fork-lift truck in the shed to a height of 16 feet.

The general cargo berths south of Redriff Road result from the Commercial Dock Company's decision in 1893 to remodel the Greenland Dock. The entrance gave particular trouble since the Thames Buried Channel, the Thames Ballast Stratum, here lies over Thanet Sand instead of the more stable London Clay to the north.[11] The lock was finally opened in 1904 and transformed the Greenland Dock into a modern general cargo dock. Unfortunately, six exit cuts [12] restrict the longest continuous quay length to only 800 feet. Transit sheds between the Greenland and South Docks can receive goods ex-ship on the north and off-load them to lighters in the South Dock. This dock even has two warehouses on its south quay but can receive ships of up to only 240 feet in length because of the limitation of the Greenland-South Dock cutting. Ships can also penetrate north of Redriff Road by the other cuts. Russia Dock is only 19 feet deep, and so only very small vessels are handled there.[13] In 1926 the P.L.A. replaced three timber ponds by the Quebec Dock which has a shelving bank on its east side. While it might appear that the Canada,[14] Albion, and Quebec Docks could receive any vessel via the Greenland Entrance Lock, in practice the inter-dock cuttings have imposed limitations. This became an embarrassment a few years ago when British Columbia timber vessels of 10,000 tons gross were unable to navigate the Canada–Greenland cutting. These vessels added to the press of general cargo shipping in Greenland Dock, the only large general cargo dock. So the P.L.A. decided to deepen the 27-foot cutting to the Canada Dock by removing $4\frac{1}{2}$ feet from the bottom and raising the impounded water level by $1\frac{1}{2}$ feet. In addition, it was decided to raise the clearance of the bridge across the cutting so that it would not have to be lifted for the extensive barge traffic that interrupted the original bridge about ten times a day. This work took six years. If this seems a long time, it should be remembered that it had to be carried out with no interruption to the road or shipping at a busy part of the busiest dock in the system.[15] This scheme included a new general cargo berth at the south-east quay of Canada Dock.

The axes of development within these docks may be compared to two interlocking semi-circles: one is of general cargo via the Greenland, South and Canada Docks; and the second is storage of timber delivered by lighter via the Surrey Entrance, through Stave and Russia Yards with their adjacent docks, yards, and timber ponds. And outside the dock perimeter is the cut-off area of dockland housing, ribbon-like along Rotherhithe Street. One block of flats here sees timber in two directions, in Acorn Yard and in the complementary storage of timber at wharves on the riverside.

The India and Millwall Docks

Although this group of dock is classed as one system, the East India Dock (1806) has always been physically separate from the others; and the Millwall and India Docks were not connected until 1926. An outstanding characteristic of this dock system is that it combines features of docks upstream (warehousing) and downstream (deep-sea trading). Two of the original sugar warehouses[16] north of the Import Dock and the smallest entrance lock in the port (to the East India Dock) are in great contrast to transit sheds for mechanical handling at both import and export berths, and the bulk suction unloading in Millwall Dock (1868). Goods are brought here by barges off-loaded in docks downstream; and some cargoes are taken upstream by barge for warehousing in the Town Docks. Only the really big ships are missing, and the table shows the widespread trading connections of cargo liners in the 10,000 gross tonnage class.

In the 1790's H.M. Customs and Excise had insisted that import and export functions should be carried out in two separate docks before the West India merchants were allowed to make use of the first bonded dock warehouses in the country; and the table shows that these separate functions remain, although the trading links have vastly altered. Both Import and Export Docks have since been narrowed by 56 and 26 feet respectively so that 'false quays' could be built over the originally sloping masonry to give a vertical face and greater effective depth immediately alongside. The Import Dock false quay of 1912 provided room for the north

TABLE 113

India and Millwall Docks: Some of the Shipping Lines and Services Operated
(arranged clockwise from the north-west corner of each dock)

Short Name of Shipping Line, etc.	Usual (not necessarily fixed) Location for mainly Discharge (D) and Loading (L)	Trading to
WEST INDIA IMPORT DOCK, NORTH QUAY		
U.S. Lines	D/L (3 berths)	U.S.A. Gulf
WEST INDIA IMPORT DOCK, SOUTH QUAY		
Various, importing Green and Dried Fruits }	D (2 berths)	Mediterranean
Fred Olsen	D	Canary Islands
WEST INDIA EXPORT DOCK, NORTH QUAY		
Prince; Westcott and Laurance }	L (2 berths)	Mediterranean
Hamburg–Amerika	L	U.S.A. Gulf
Various	L	Mediterranean
SOUTH WEST INDIA DOCK, NORTH QUAY		
Ben	D	Far East
City	D	South Africa
Harrison (mainly)	L	South Africa and West Indies
SOUTH WEST INDIA DOCK, SOUTH QUAY		
Harrison	L	West Indies
Nippon Yusen Kaisha		
Osaka Shosen Kaisha		
Mitsui }	D/L	Far East
Lambert Bros.		
Westcott and Laurance	L	Mediterranean
MILLWALL INNER DOCK, EAST QUAY		
Swedish Lloyd; Svea; Wilson	D/L	Stockholm
Strick	L	Persian Gulf
Various	D/L	Mediterranean

376

MILLWALL OUTER DOCK, SOUTH QUAY

Yugoslav	L	Yugoslavia
McDougall's Flour Mill	D	
Timber Wharves Ltd.	D	

MILLWALL OUTER DOCK, NORTH QUAY

Swedish Lloyd; Svea; Wilson	D/L	Scandinavia
United Steamship	D/L	Denmark, Baltic

MILLWALL INNER DOCK, WEST QUAY

Saguenay	L (2 berths)	Mainly West Indies

EAST INDIA IMPORT DOCK, NORTH QUAY

Coast Lines	D/L	Dublin, Cork, Liverpool
Coast Lines	D/L	Kirkcaldy
Coast Lines	D/L	Jersey and Guernsey

EAST INDIA IMPORT DOCK, EAST QUAY

Nor-Med	D/L	Mediterranean

quay transit sheds. On the south side much wartime damage was done. Hardwood is still dealt with at the Wood Wharves in the south-east corner of the dock, but the Rum Quay was entirely burnt out, with rum now being handled at London Docks. The opportunity was seized to provide two fine sheds: Nos. 10 and 11 with three storeys, the upper floors staggered for the reception of cargoes on 15-foot verandahs, and the top floors acting as warehouses; and there is a third shed (two-storeys) at Canary Wharf, built in 1937. In South Dock, H shed was chosen as the first mechanized export berth in the port, using fork-lift trucks piling on pallets or loading trays (6 feet × 4½ feet) which can be stacked high in the shed. When delivered by truck to slings of the quayside crane, these are connected to the eyes welded at the corner of each pallet. Capital cost of mechanization is high, but loading times are cut by about 20 per cent and unloading times by as much as 40 per cent compared with working by manual gangs. Whereas the old sugar warehouses were designed for the manual piling of sugar only two hogsheads high, now most sugar comes in bulk. This is an example of how new shipping techniques can render obsolete quayside buildings of inflexible design. Berth L, South Dock, is often the scene of grab unloading of bulk sugar.[17]

The South West India Entrance Lock is now the chief lock for the system, although the lower lock is a useful secondary entrance, particularly for barges. Millwall Dock is still dominated by the grain trade to the 13-storey Central Granary and McDougall's Silo, both prominent landmarks to be seen all the way around the

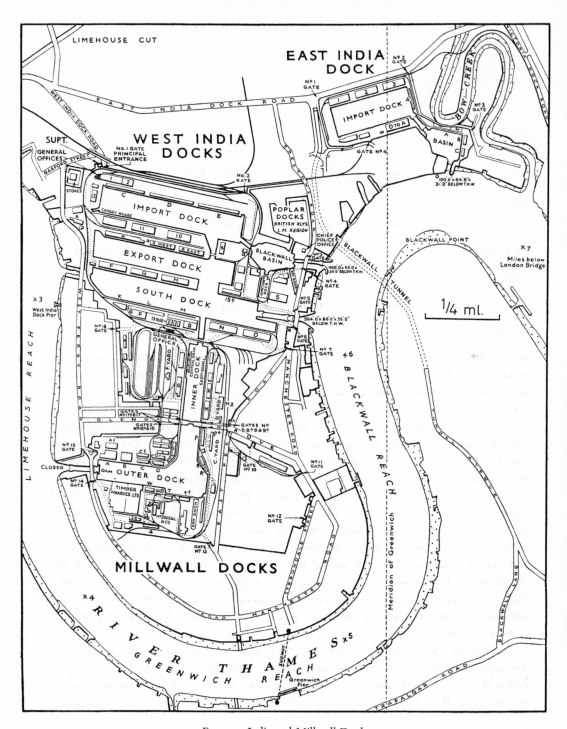

FIG. 97 India and Millwall Docks

river's great meander. This loop, unmistakable from the air, was no doubt largely responsible for the great damage sustained by these docks, and Millwall Dock in particular. The table of shipping lines shows that, in addition to the grain and timber trades, there is an important cargo liner traffic. New tubular steel transit sheds have been provided for mechanical handling (pallets and containers) for Scandinavian and West Indies trades. Dock reconstruction has allowed a better road lay-out to be planned after research had shown that no fewer than 8,000 road vehicles enter and leave this dock system every day.[18] The Millwall Entrance was also damaged by an air attack, but this has proved of little loss since the Millwall Dock is connected to the more convenient entrances downstream.

The name *East India* Dock and the coastwise and short-sea traffic actually carried on there is a contrast which illustrates *Anyport*'s practice of downgrading a dock in traffic importance in order to prolong its life.

Millwall to the east and Cubitt Town to the west of Millwall Dock are dockland suburbs on the Isle of Dogs. This was really a peninsula within a meander bend until the excavation of the City Canal, now the South West India Dock, really converted the peninsula into an island. These dockland communities are served by one main road, named West Ferry Road to the west and Manchester Road to the east. It is the longitudinal road serving the wharves on the river-front and can be traced back in its westward extensions continuously all the way to Thames Street, the longitudinal road of the medieval port.

The Royal Docks

Simple lineal quayage is the outstanding feature of all three docks in this group. Each has quays of three-quarters of a mile in one uninterrupted line, the north quay of the Royal Albert Dock being over a mile long in one line. That all the docks should be so well-equipped may be surprising, considering that the Royal Victoria Dock was opened as long ago as 1855, the Royal Albert Dock in 1880, and only the King George V Dock, opened in 1921, dates entirely from this century.[19] To achieve such lengths of *simple lineal quayage* for modern deep-sea vessels the P.L.A. has had to do much redevelopment. The King George V Entrance Lock allows vessels up to the 25,000 gross tons class of passenger/cargo liner regularly to enter the system.[20] In 1960 the Connaught Road cutting between the Royal Albert and Victoria Docks was widened from 80 feet to 100 feet along most of its length so that the largest Royal Mail Lines' ships of the 20,000 g.r.t. class could enter the Royal Victoria Dock.[21] The respective impounded depths of water in the docks are: King George V Dock, 38 feet; Royal Albert Dock, 34 feet; and Royal Victoria Dock, 31 feet.

By 1944 the Royal Victoria Dock had been modernized so that the present

TABLE 114

Royal Docks: Some of the Shipping Lines and Services Operated at Simple Lineal Quayage
(arranged clockwise from the north-west corner of each dock)

Short Name of Shipping Line, etc.	Usual (not necessarily fixed) Location for mainly Discharge (D) and Loading (L)	Trading to

ROYAL VICTORIA DOCK, NORTH QUAY

Royal Mail; Houlder	D	South America East Coast (meat)
Various	D	Mainly South America (meat and fruit)
Canadian Pacific	D/L	Canada
Blue Star	L	Australia
Ben	L	Far East
Blue Star	D	Australia and New Zealand
Blue Star	D	South America (meat)

ROYAL VICTORIA DOCK, SOUTH QUAY

U.S. Lines	D/L (2 berths)	U.S.A. East Coast
Four Flour Mills	D	
Royal Mail	D/L	West Indies, Central and South America, and West Coast, North America
Royal Mail	L (2 berths)	

ROYAL ALBERT DOCK, NORTH QUAY

Jamaica Banana Producers	D	West Indies
New Zealand Shipping	D (2 berths)	New Zealand
Conference Loading	L (2 berths)	New Zealand
Conference Loading	L	India
Conference Loading	L (2 berths)	East and South Africa
Conference Loading	L	India
Jamaica Banana Producers	L	West Indies

ROYAL ALBERT BASIN, NORTH QUAY

Conference Loading (including Houlder)	L	South America
Fell–Oranje	D/L	Great Lakes

ROYAL ALBERT BASIN, SOUTH QUAY

Holland–Persian Gulf	L	Persian Gulf

ROYAL ALBERT DOCK, SOUTH QUAY

Shaw Savill	D	Australia and New Zealand
Conference Loading	L	South Africa
Glen Line	D	Far East
British India	D	India

KING GEORGE V DOCK, NORTH QUAY

Glen	L	Far East
P. & O. and Orient★	D/L (2 berths)	India, Far East, Australia
Cunard★★	D/L	U.S.A. and Canada
Shaw Savill	D/L	Australia and New Zealand
Royal Mail★★★	D/L	West Indies, Central and South America and West Coast, North America

KING GEORGE V DOCK, SOUTH QUAY

P. & O. and Orient★	D/L	India, Far East, Australia
Shaw Savill	L	Australia
Port	D	Australia and New Zealand
Port	L	Australia
Union Castle	D	South Africa
Union Castle	L	South Africa
Glen	D	Far East

★ P. & O. and Orient Lines general cargo ships; their mail ships dock at Tilbury.

★★ Operated in conjunction with berths in Greenland Dock.

★★★ The larger Royal Mail vessels ('A' class) always load here, *Amazon*, *Aragon*, and *Arlanza*, each of 20,360 g.r.t.

splendid north quay replaced the original jetties and western tidal basin. Since it was the first London dock to be served by rail, it is appropriate that the name Royal Victoria Exchange Sidings is given to the railway lay-out north of the dock. These sidings serve the whole system and form the largest dockside marshalling yard in the country with capacity for 1,200 wagons. There are meat berths at either end of the north quay and five general cargo transit sheds with warehousing floors above, normally for tobacco. Tobacco is also to be found in the tobacco bonded warehouses north of the quay, and in the floors above transit sheds on the north quay of the King George V Dock. It is the chief commodity warehoused in the Royal Docks. On the south quay of the Royal Victoria Dock four lofty grain mills, owned and operated by tenants of the P.L.A., are fed direct by bulk grain ships. They are separated by the Pontoon Dock, a relic of the 1855 lay-out, the first dockside shiprepairing base in the port now giving access to a timber stockyard.

In 1960 the fine No. 4 Berth was opened, 1,290 feet long, to berth two ships of the United States Lines, and served by the largest dockside transit shed in the country. This was made necessary by the upsurge of traffic, particularly exports, on the north Atlantic route. The shed is 700 feet long by 200 feet wide, with doors 20 feet by 20 feet and a clear interior height of again 20 feet, with no interior supports whatever. These features make it easy for mobile cranes and fork-lift trucks to enter the shed; and, significantly, the possibility of container traffic was taken into account when designing the lay-out. The United States Lines originally wanted a two-storey shed with road access up a ramp to the first floor. But this design was rejected mainly on account of the additional expense of over £500,000. A first floor would have needed columnar supports on the ground floor 50 feet apart, and these would have interfered with any future development in large container traffic. The shed is not central on the two-berth quay because of the mills at the western end. The main discharging and loading berth is at the eastern end of the quay, and vessels dealing with part-cargoes are berthed at No. 4a at the western end. The imports are usually dealt with at the western end of the shed and the exports at the eastern end, but there is no fixed division between them, a flexible arrangement to match the changing volume of traffic. Some 200,000 tons of goods pass through this shed each year, and yet 70 per cent of the total imports are discharged to lighters which use another quay extending northwards from the eastern end of the No. 4 Berth as their marshalling area.[22]

The Royal Albert Dock has always had most of its cargoes in transit, and the only commodity in store is meat; Nos. 5, 6, and 7 Cold Stores have a combined capacity for 640,000 carcasses.[23] A long quay with single-storey transit sheds is ideal for the loading of general cargo exports, which is particularly important on Royal Albert Dock, North Quay, a visible 'front-line' in Britain's export trade battle. One disadvantage is that the average length of ships using the dock has outgrown the length of the original transit sheds of 300–350 feet, giving one and a half sheds per ship's berth. This inconvenience has been overcome by giving one large covered access between sheds Nos. 25 and 27 for road transport delivering to unloading platforms tail-board high. This is now a mechanized berth with fork-lift trucks and mobile cranes. But such road access causes interruption to rail services which, because of the lay-out of the docks, can be provided only from the west. This solution therefore cannot be repeated. Another method of remodelling the transit sheds has been to convert three into two as on the south side of the dock where No. 18 has been absorbed into larger Nos. 16 and 20. Finally, there is a banana-unloading berth to No. 35 shed, and a quarantine area for cattle south of the Basin, on a site very reminiscent of that at Birkenhead.

In the King George V Dock the berth at No. 5 is specially dredged for the largest vessels. Sheds in this dock are much longer, up to 550 feet. On the south side of the dock there are seven dolphins 32 feet from the quay against which ships berth, giving access to lighters between ship and quay.[24] This emphasizes the importance of lighterage in these docks where some 70 per cent of imported goods are discharged overside into barges. In addition the P.L.A. operates eight floating elevators, many of which can be seen delivering bulk grain to barge (or even bagging it first). The smallest entrance lock, Gallions Upper Entrance Lock,[25] is used mainly by barges, as is the original Royal Victoria Entrance Lock,[26] which was blocked off for use by ships when the road access to these docks was improved by the opening of Silvertown Way in 1934.[27] Between the Royal Docks and the

Port of London Authority

PLATE XXI WEST INDIA AND MILLWALL DOCKS

Looking north-west, *cf.* Fig. 97.

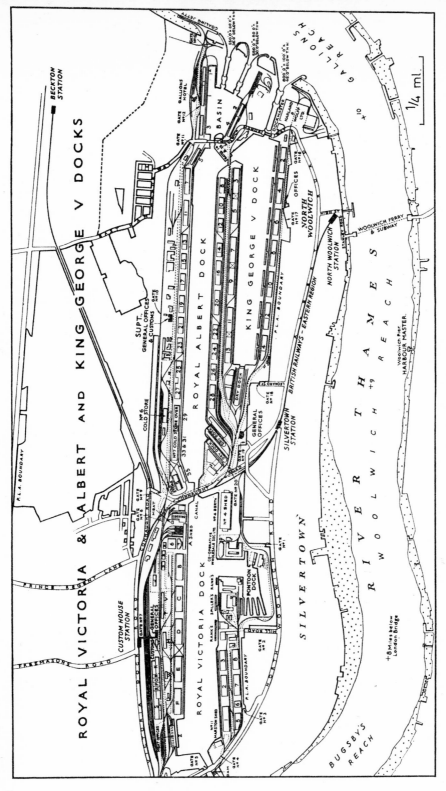

PLATE XXII ROYAL DOCKS

Looking east-north-east, downstream, *cf.* Fig. 98. Industrial
premises on the north bank of the River Thames are prominent,
with Woolwich Reach to right, and Beckton Gas Works and
Barking Generating Station, centre background at top.

riparian industrial frontages of Woolwich Reach is yet another cut-off dockland residential area, Silvertown[28] and North Woolwich.

Tilbury Docks

This dock system was opened in 1886 by the East and West India Dock Company as a rival to the Royal Albert Dock, which had been opened six years earlier by the London and St. Katharine Docks Company. Twenty-six miles downstream from London Bridge, the alluvium of the dock site has an average thickness of forty feet, twice as great as at the Royal Docks. While excavation in a flood-plain might seem entirely opposite from building a dock upon a reclaimed water site, at Tilbury the original works were dug behind the river wall used as a coffer-dam. The excavated spoil was then used to build up the quay areas twelve feet above the original level of the marshes which were six feet below the level of high water.[29] This is reminiscent of the method of constructing South Wales docks out into the Severn, and of building Southampton Old Docks out into Southampton Water. The original Tilbury layout consisted of the Tidal Basin, a 695-foot long entrance and a vestibule dock leading to three branch docks, with thirty-one berths for ships up to 400 feet long.

TABLE 115

Tilbury Docks: Some of the Shipping Lines and Services Operated
(arranged clockwise from the north-west and from the north-west corner of each dock)

Short Name of Shipping Line, etc.	Usual (not necessarily fixed) Location for mainly Discharge (D) and Loading (L)	Trading to
WEST BRANCH DOCK, EAST QUAY		
Clan	D	India
WEST BRANCH DOCK, WEST QUAY		
Atlantic Steam Nav.	D/L	Antwerp and Rotterdam
CENTRE BRANCH DOCK, EAST QUAY		
Clan	L (2 berths)	West Africa
CENTRE BRANCH DOCK, WEST QUAY		
Conference Discharge	D	West Africa
Bibby	D/L	Rangoon
EAST BRANCH DOCK, EAST QUAY		
Brocklebank	D	India
City	D (3 berths)	India

384

EAST BRANCH DOCK, WEST QUAY

Clan   D (2 berths)   India

MAIN DOCK, SOUTH QUAY

P. & O. and Orient   D/L (3 berths)   Australia (mail)

MAIN DOCK, WEST QUAY

Conference Discharge   D   West Africa

MAIN DOCK, NORTH-WEST QUAY
No. 1 Passenger Terminal

TIDAL BASIN, EAST QUAY

Cockerill   D/L   Ostend

CARGO JETTY

Various   D (2 berths: with latex discharge facilities at
                               lower berth)

Simple Lineal Quayage (3 berths in one line) in italic capitals

This lay-out was very similar to that of the Alexandra Docks, Liverpool, opened five years earlier, of only slightly smaller dimensions. The north-west to south-east orientation of the Tilbury Docks was a result of the shape of the site in the angle of a Thames meander lying to the south-west of the railway from London to Tilbury built in 1850.

The chief characteristics of Tilbury Docks have been that they deal with the largest ships and all cargoes are in transit. In this they are the antithesis of the London and St. Katharine Docks. Any goods for warehousing are taken by road, rail, and barge for up-town or up-river warehouses; the Commercial Road Depot (Fig. 95) is Tilbury's special London warehouse. Tilbury has not functioned as an outport of London—a role partly assumed by Southampton, Harwich, and Dover. Instead these docks have seen some of the largest developments of the P.L.A. in its unified control of Thameside docks: the extension of the Main Dock westward from 1912,[30] the western 1,000-foot long entrance lock, the longest in the port, 1929; the longest dry dock in the port, 750 feet; and the Floating Passenger Landing Stage in 1930.[31] This last installation has caused the passenger trade of the port largely to be concentrated at Tilbury; though passengers may be embarked or disembarked at other docks, the master of the vessel may well prefer to use this stage *en route* at any state of the tide and so save time. The largest ships using the port of the 20,000–30,000-ton class, 700 feet long, berth at the *simple lineal quayage* of the Main Dock. The sheds at these berths are 600 feet long, nearly twice as long as those of the Branch Docks, with 42½

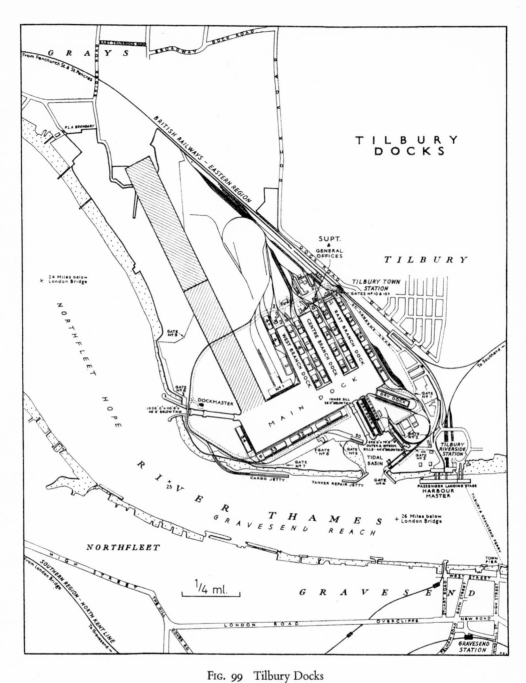

FIG. 99 Tilbury Docks

The diagonal ruling represents the provisional lay-out of a dock extension, to be started in 1963, possibly in two stages.

feet of water alongside the quays. To keep abreast of passenger/cargo liner development the P.L.A. opened a second passenger terminal, this time within the dock at No. 1 Berth, 842 feet long, in the construction of which the Main Dock was widened by cutting back the west quay of the West Branch Dock.[32] Lord Waverley, then chairman of the P.L.A. called this £1½ million development an 'act of faith' when the terminal was opened in 1957. Unfortunately, two new ships of the P. & O. and Orient Lines on the Europe–Australia–Pacific run, the *Canberra* and the *Oriana*, use Southampton, and the Tilbury terminal has not yet attracted the passenger traffic hoped for.

At the head of the West Branch Dock is a ramp for the stern-loading 'roll-on roll-off' vessels of the Transport Ferry Service. Following the early use of tank-landing vessels to supply British forces in Germany via Hamburg and Antwerp, the company now has a fleet of vehicle ferry vessels for the Tilbury–Antwerp/Rotterdam and Preston—Belfast/Larne services (see pages 112–13), designed to carry as many as 100 lorries, trailers, and containers across the sea. Road transport was hardly catered for at all in Tilbury Docks before 1939, but now accounts for about three-quarters of the goods brought by land, which has necessitated about two miles of road construction within the docks. The biggest defect in the design of Tilbury has proved to be the Tidal Basin, a mud trap (see pages 357–8). Its complete closure would rob the docks of the original (now secondary) entrance lock so useful for small vessels and barges. There is plenty of room for development to the north-west, and in 1961 a development project was announced for a long dock, 6,000 feet × 600 feet, west of No. 1 Berth, based on the original 1910 idea of Sir Frederick Palmer.[33] How glad the Mersey Docks and Harbour Board would be of the opportunity so to extend the Alexandra Docks! There is also room for a fourth 'Royal' dock north of the Royal Albert Dock, but the difficulty so far encountered of maintaining more than 27 feet through the 'Mud Reaches' has given Tilbury an advantage. In the seven-year £30 million modernization and development plan for P.L.A. docks from 1962, £20 million are devoted to radical extensions of the dock system at Tilbury.

Outside Tilbury Docks is 'Tilbury Town', originally laid out as a place where dock workers could live. It has suffered subsidence and flooding as a result of its site upon a flood-plain, and has always been secondary to Gravesend across the river, from which some 450 workers in Tilbury Docks commute each day.[34]

Port of London Administration

At the Royal Terrace Pier, Gravesend, is the pilot boarding station, and next door are the Port Health Authority and H.M. Customs in the Thames Navigation Service Building—the radar 'eyes' and V.H.F. radio 'ears' of the port operated by the P.L.A.

The Authority is a non-profit-making public trust of which ten members are appointed: one by the Admiralty, two by the Ministry of Transport, four by the London County Council, two by the City Corporation, and one by Trinity House; and another 18 members are elected by the payers of dues, wharfingers and owners of river craft. The Chairman and Vice-chairman may be drawn from outside the 28-strong membership. The Authority is responsible for the conservancy of the river, surveying and dredging the channels; for administering the docks; and for providing certain services within the docks, like dock towage, heavy lifts, reception of exports, and acting as master stevedores employing dock labour in only some of the docks. But river pilots are administered by the Corporation of Trinity House; the health authority is the Corporation of the City of London; and crime prevention in the river is the responsibility of Essex or Kent Constabularies, or Metropolitan Police, dependent upon the area. Within the docks responsibility for discharge remains with the shipowner, who may employ a private master stevedore, who in turn may obtain labour from the 30,000 dock workers in the Port of London registered with the National Dock Labour Board to add to the nucleus of permanent employed staff. Most important, the barges that deliver cargoes to and from riverside wharves, and the wharves themselves that may receive seagoing vessels, are all in private hands. Such divided control in the port resulted from the deliberations upon the Report of the Royal Commission of 1902 when the P.L.A. was constituted in 1909. Any comment on the port's efficiency should bear this in mind. Even many Londoners would be surprised to learn that only one-eighth of the total tonnage of goods entering and leaving the port actually passes over the dock quays.

TABLE 116

Tonnages of London's Imports and Exports 1958–60
For the two years ended March 31, 1960

(Annual total tonnages respectively, 52 million and 57·1 million)

Where handled:

River			69%
Docks { over quays	12·8% }	31%	
{ transferred into barges	18·2% }		

Nearly 70 per cent of the cargoes are finally landed or first discharged not in the dock systems described in this chapter, impressive as they may appear in size. The river itself is also a mighty port.

REFERENCES

1. A different form of 'dock tour' is given in J. Bird, *The Geography of the Port of London*, Hutchinson, 1957, 75–114, where the emphasis is placed on the functions of all the quayside buildings.
2. For further explanation and references see *ibid.*, 93.

3. The following section is largely based on L. M. Bates, 'Port of London: Berthing Ships in the Docks', *Lloyd's List and Shipping Gazette*, October 5, 1961, 4–6.

4. If the Shadwell New Basin is used as a lock, ships up to 2,500 gross tons can enter, *cf.* a similar arrangement via the Alfred Dock at Birkenhead.

5. The biggest gaps in both eastern docks of the London and St. Katharine Docks were caused by war damage.

6. Five stories high, covering five acres, they miraculously escaped damage during the war. Apart from being the world's chief market for carpets, they store all kinds of drugs, imported manufactured tobacco, and exotic goods like isinglass and ostrich feathers. Wines are bottled and vintage wines are stored in the basement of these historic buildings built in seven stages between 1769 and 1821. I am grateful to Mr. C. E. C. Townsend of the P.L.A. whose researches provide the evidence for such an early date.

7. 'New Bulk Wine Berth, London Dock', *P.L.A. Monthly*, 24 (1959), 314–17.

8. At other docks, except the India Docks, master stevedores or shipowners call upon labour from the National Dock Labour Board.

9. Perhaps the most valuable cargo dealt with on the Cutler Street Warehouses drug floors has been rauwolfia, a vegetable root, arriving in drums weighing a little more than a hundredweight, from which a nerve sedative is prepared, at £350 per pound.

10. Imagine the care necessary in No. 2 Warehouse London Dock when two-ounce samples must be taken from drums of aniseed or sassafras oil which are solid at 16° C. A special sampling pipette or valinche is kept for each of the fifty-odd types of essential oil.

11. Some generalized geological sections at the dock systems, with 'gravel' referring to the Thames Ballast stratum, the Buried Channel of the Thames, so useful as an aggregate or quay foundation when at the right depth:

    London and St. Katharine Docks: gravel at — 9 feet O.D. (13–17 feet thick) over London Clay;

    Surrey and Millwall Docks: gravel (variable thickness) over Reading, Woolwich, and Thanet Beds;

    East and West India Docks: gravel at — 3–16 feet O.D. (14–24 feet thick) over London Clay;

    Royal Docks, gravel at — 7 feet O.D. at western end to — 20 feet at the eastern end (20 feet thick) over London Clay except at eastern end where gravel over Chalk;

    Tilbury, gravel 8–30 feet thick over mud clay and peat in a submerged valley cut in the Chalk, a stratum which is encountered at about — 55 feet O.D. W. S. Shepherd-Barron, 'The Docks of London', *Proceedings of the Institution of Civil Engineers*, 3 (1954), 12–42, 15.

12. One of these exits leads to the Grand Surrey Canal, a project of the Grand Surrey Canal Company, 1801, to bring market-garden produce from south London to the centre. The canal never reached beyond Camberwell with a branch to Peckham, and is now used only as far as the 'Railway Yard' south of the South Dock by lighters taking timber for storage.

13. Norway Dock now has no commercial functions, being used as a P.L.A. engineering base.

14. When opened in 1876 this dock received vessels via the Surrey Entrance, half a mile away, until the Greenland Lock was opened in 1904.

15. D. E. Glover, E. Newton, and H. M. Dale, 'Port of London Authority: Development of Two Dock Areas', *Proceedings of the Institution of Civil Engineers*, 15 (1960), 411–34, 411–22.

16. Only 600 feet in length, remaining from the original line of warehouses (Fig. 90) nearly three-quarters of a mile long, the rest having been destroyed in September, 1940.

17. E. S. Tooth, 'Handling of Port Traffic', *Proceedings of the Institution of Civil Engineers*, 5 (1956), 276–301, 278–81.

18. 'Modernizing Millwall Docks', *P.L.A. Monthly*, 26 (1961), 173–6, 174.

19. A. Binns, 'The King George V Dock, London', *Minutes of Proceedings of the Institution of Civil Engineers*, 216 (1923), 372–420.

20. The largest vessel to enter the Royal Docks has been the *Mauretania*, 35,674 gross tons, which used the entrance lock once in 1939 and berthed in the Royal Albert Dock via the 100-foot wide cutting.

21. D. E. Glover, E. Newton, and H. M. Dale, *loc. cit.*, 422–32.

22. T. E. Cook, 'No. 4 Berth, Royal Victoria Docks, Port of London', *The Dock and Harbour Authority*, 42 (1961–2), 137–42, and D. E. Glover, E. Newton, and H. M. Dale, *loc. cit.*, 422–32.

23. The P.L.A. also has two subsidiary cold stores close to the Central Meat Markets, West Smithfield in the City of London.

24. Although barges were only 24 feet wide in 1921, the dolphins were placed 32 feet from the quay to allow for an increase of barge size and to bring the face of the dolphins clear of the 5:1 slope at the dock bottom. A. Binns, *loc. cit.*, 418.

25. The second ship entrance has been reconstructed and was reopened in 1956, J. A. Fisher, 'Reconstruction of the Gallions Lower Entrance Lock at the Royal Docks of the Port of London Authority', *Proceedings of the Institution of Civil Engineers*, 5 (1956), 136–69.

26. It is better that ships should enter the Royal Victoria Dock via the still water of the other docks. The original Victoria entrance always involved a difficult turn in the river.

27. D. Kennedy and H. E. Aldington, 'Royal Docks Approaches Improvement, London', *Journal of the Institution of Civil Engineers*, 2 (1935–6), 4–48.

28. Silvertown from Messrs. S. W. Silver and Co., a firm of Cornhill outfitters who in 1852, transferred their waterproofing works to this stretch of the riverfront.

29. J. F. Scott, 'The Construction and Equipment of the Tilbury Docks', *Minutes of Proceedings of the Institution of Civil Engineers*, 120 (1895), 276–88, 284.

30. F. M. G. Du Plat-Taylor, 'Extensions at Tilbury Docks 1912–17', *Minutes of the Proceedings of the Institution of Civil Engineers*, 215 (1923), 165–200.

31. F. W. Davis and W. Mackenzie, 'Major Improvement Works of the Port of London Authority, 1925–30', *Minutes of the Proceedings of the Institution of Civil Engineers*, 240 (1934–5), 258–340, 259–306.

32. C. Peel, A. J. Carmichael, and R. F. Smeardon, 'No. 1 Berth, Tilbury Dock', *Proceedings of the Institution of Civil Engineers*, 8 (1957), 331–62 and 10 (1958); and G. A. Wilson, 'A Passenger Cargo Terminal in the United Kingdom', *Bulletin of the Permanent International Association of Navigation Congresses*, 45 (1957 Vol. 1), 95–103.

33. The *Report of the Committee of Inquiry into the Major Ports of Great Britain*, London: H.M.S.O., Cmnd. 1824, 1962, para. 522, recommended that the major development of the Port of London should take place at Tilbury, and that the scheme should have high priority, subject only to a review of the comparative merits of Sheerness (see pp. 404–5).

34. R. F. Baker, *Influence of Transport and Other Factors on the Development of Thames-side since the Late Eighteenth Century*, University of London thesis, in preparation.

FURTHER REFERENCES
FOR THE PORT OF LONDON DOCKS

A list of engineering papers on the Port of London Docks is given in G. A. Wilson, 'Port of London Authority Engineering Works, 1952', *Proceedings of the Institution of Civil Engineers*, 2, part II (1953), 551–86, 584–6.

Binns, A. 'The Thames and Its Docks', *Transactions of the Institution of Engineers-in-Charge*, 42 (1936–7), 124–40.

——. 'Mainly Port of London', *Proceedings of the Institution of Mechanical Engineers*, 144 (1940), 50–3.

Ford, Sir Leslie. 'The Development of the Port of London', *Journal of the Royal Society of Arts*, 107 (1959), 821–35.

Griffin, J. *History of the Surrey Commercial Docks*. London: Smith and Ebbs, 1877.

Liddell, R. R. 'Improvements at the Royal Docks, Port of London Authority', *Journal of the Institution of Civil Engineers*, 10 (1938–9), 283–310 and volume 12, 363–6.

Ordman, N. N. B. 'The Port of London', *The Dock and Harbour Authority*, 33 (1952–3), 131–6, 170–2.

Smith, D. K. 'St. Katharine Docks', *Architectural Association Journal*, 73 (1958), 172–81.

Turner, S. 'The Port of London: Planning for the Future', *The Dock and Harbour Authority*, 43 (1962), 42–5.

Chapter 17

TRAFFIC AND TRADE OF THE TIDAL THAMES

WHILE the helicopter passenger sees the vastness of the docks, they remain hidden from those who sail upon the river, screened by the façade of riverside wharves. The Port of London depended on such marginal quays alone until 1802, but the coming of the docks has in no way diminished the absolute importance of the wharves. The 'port in the river' stretches along seventy miles of the estuary, embracing well over 600 riverside wharves,[1] and the connecting thread is the river itself. About half the wharves and jetties can receive sea-going vessels, and this proportion will increase as more are built downstream, and all of them can be served by the taxis of the port, the Thames barges or lighters.

Thames Lighterage

The use of small craft to transfer goods from sea-going vessels to riverside wharves has a long history in the Port of London. An early need for lighterage arose when ships could not moor alongside every quay, and it has been shown that Old London Bridge became a barrier to shipping movement upstream. In addition, as vessels became larger, their masters wished to avoid grounding and anchored in midstream, so that watermen were needed to ferry passengers and baggage to and from the shore while lightermen handled cargo transhipments. In 1603 John Stow noted that:

> '. . . there pertayneth to the Cities of *London*, *Westminster*, and Burrough of *Southwarke*, aboue the number as is supposed of 2000. Wherryes and other small boats, whereby 3000. poore men at the least bee set on worke and maintained.'[2]

In 1796 there were 3,419 barges and craft[3] of all types with 2,596 barges 'commonly in use' with an average tonnage of 33.

The Watermen's Company takes its foundation from an Act of 1556, and in 1700 the Watermen and Lightermen were incorporated in one company. The Court of the Watermen's Company is still the body that examines apprentices and issues watermen's licences. Literature about London up to the early nineteenth century is full of references to passenger travel on the Thames. But the building of further bridges and the coming of the railway and steamship eventually killed the watermen's passenger trade. On the other hand, lightermen have gone from strength to strength, their business increasing as the total trade of the port increased. The building of docks advanced rather than diminished their importance, because of the longer haul from downstream docks to upstream warehouses.

Free entry to the docks has always been a feature of Thames lighterage, provided the barges do not dock more than two tides before the vessel for which they are bound, or remain in dock for more than three tides after the completion of loading. This privilege derives from the 'free water clause', which has its original expression in the first commercial dock Act of 1799, the *West India Dock Act*, Section 138:

> 'Provided always and be it enacted that this Act shall not extend to charge with the said rate or duty of six shillings and eight pence per ton hereinbefore granted any lighters or craft entering into the said docks or basins to convey, deliver, discharge or receive ballast or goods to or from on board any ship or ships, vessel or vessels.'

The dock companies of the early nineteenth century could afford to allow this concession because their empowering Acts gave them monopolies of certain trades for a period of years. When these monopolies expired the 'free water clause' could not be rescinded. Many copies of the old Acts exist with the clause heavily underscored by some despairing dock director, all to no avail since the clause is still on the statute book as Section 68 of the *Port of London (Consolidation) Act*, 1920. Indeed, when the London and India Docks Joint Committee deposited a Bill in 1899 seeking powers to levy dues on barges, there was such an outcry that the Bill was rejected, and the resultant publicity led to the appointment of the Royal Commission, 1902, to look into the affairs of the port.

The only other major British port with a large lighterage fleet is Hull. As at London there are several private wharfingers along a river separate from the dock systems. At both ports the ebb- and flood-streams are not so powerful as to damage barges rising and falling at riverside wharves, as would happen in the Bristol Channel or on the Mersey, although there is a considerable barge traffic between Liverpool and Manchester. The approach channels at Hull and London are not too narrow for ships and barges to manoeuvre, as they are on the Clyde or Tyne. Lastly, if the general cargo quays are compact marginal quays as at Belfast and Newcastle, lighterage loses its *raison d'être*, which is to bind together a rather dispersed port by means of interior lines of water communication.

TABLE 117

London's Tug and Barge Fleet

		1936[4]	1961
Tugs:			
Steam		190	44
Motor		160	292
Total Tugs		350	336
Barges:			
Insulated		180	167
Tank		330	324
Canal		430	100
Sailing		430	3
Mechanically Propelled		70	211
Dumb		7,440	5,535
Miscellaneous		30	—
Total Barges		8,910	6,340
Total Craft (Tugs and Barges) ...		9,260	6,676

Motor tugs have displaced steam tugs for barge towing because diesel oil costs less than half the price of coal bunkers for a given output of power. Thirty of the forty-four steam tugs are of high power and engaged solely on attending the movement of large ships. It is likely that tugs reserved for towing will grow more powerful, able to haul a full load against the tide, and controlled by radio-telephone to speed operations and reduce the number of barges necessary. Although the number of dumb barges is lower than pre-war, the total carrying capacity is nearly 8 per cent greater because the average capacity is now 160 tons compared with 112 tons in 1936. Barges on the Regent's Canal are restricted to 95 tons maximum. Whereas a humble 200-ton dumb barge cost £1,000 in 1938, such a vessel now costs £5,000, an increase which may be compared with that of road transport vehicles:

TABLE 118

Relative Costs of Barges Versus Lorries[5]
Cost in £s per Ton Carrying Capacity

	1938	1959	Increase
5-ton Lorry	65	210	3x
200-ton Thames Dumb Barge	5	25	5x

This helps to explain why the lighters have lost small parcel traffic; any load under five tons is more economically hauled by road transport.

Since dumb barges generally last at least thirty years, the incidence of replacement costs can become masked when rates are quoted which do not take them fully into account. As for shipping, a 40 per cent allowance is made for barge replacements by the Inland Revenue authorities. Most of the Thames barges are 'dumb', without an engine, thereby qualifying under the free water clause. But an engine on each barge would not be economical, for the barge is moving for about only one-fifth of its working life: the master lighterman allows two days for loading, one day for transit, and two days for unloading. Awaiting loading or discharging in docks or in the river, the barges may nevertheless be performing a useful function as 'floating warehouses', much cheaper than using a ship for such a purpose and perhaps relieving congestion ashore. The Thames barge is punt-shaped, the keel slopes upward at each end at about 35-40 degrees. These are the swims that make the lighter more easily controllable when towed by a tug. The swims act also as protective bumpers, and the budget, or fixed rudder, is worked down the centre of the after swim as a continuation of the keel plate. If it projected beyond it might be damaged; while a fixed rudder is necessary if the lighter is to maintain a straight course when being towed. Self-propelled barges are stem-headed with projecting rudders to give better response to the helm. Dumb barges are now generally made of welded steel, of a higher strength specification than craft that are not required to bump aground twice a day. Flat bottoms allow the barges to sit on the mud. At some wharves there are 'barge beds', made by placing chalk on fascines of brushwood bound together to form a mattress to prevent the material sinking into the river mud. The angle of these beds for flat-bottomed barges is 1:60, and because the angle of repose of fluid mud is 1:75, the beds are self-cleansing. They have a width of 20 feet for every rank of barges to berth alongside (see frontispiece).

There are about 130 master lightermen, or lighterage firms, since the industry has grown up to suit the traffic offering, and not as a general transport facility attracting customers. It seems likely that the higher replacement costs may cause horizontal amalgamation within the industry to increase capital resources. For some time large industrial firms in specific trades have operated their own lighter fleets, and some lighterage firms are connected with shore interests within the port. One anomaly is that lightermen employed in the 'quay goods' traffic (originally 'Legal Quay goods' or general cargo), as distinct from those handling 'rough goods' (*e.g.* coal, ballast, refuse), are employed nominally on a daily basis, since they are regarded as part of the dock labour pool. In practice, they rarely leave the service of one lighterage firm, but it is still required that each lighter be attended by one lighterman even if six barges, the maximum permitted, are united behind one tug. The fact that such a tug can move 900 tons of merchandise, perhaps helped by the tide, on London's least congested main street, is an indication that the industry itself is not an anachronism. Fig. 100 shows the flexibility of discharge for import cargo when cargo is being discharged by ships' gear to barges lying outside a vessel. If ships are berthed against a dummy or raft, or against the dolphins of King George V Dock south quay, barges can penetrate between the ship and the dock quay wall as well. Were the free water clause to be abandoned and dues levied on lighters, lighterage rates

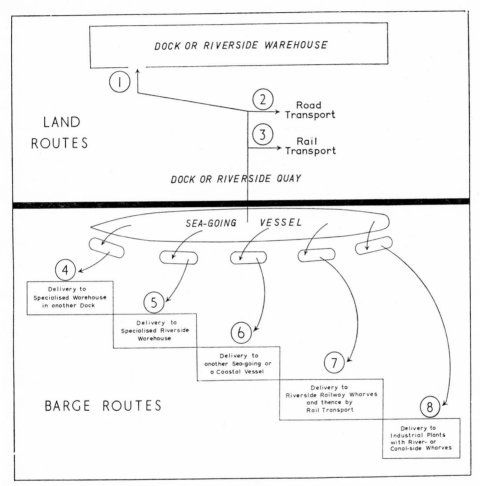

FIG. 100   Extra Routes Provided by London Lighterage: Schematic Diagram

would be increased. More goods would then have to be handled over the quays leading to slower discharge and loading. The port might well lose shipping traffic because of this, and the loss of shipping dues might far outweigh the small increase gained by levying upon lighters. The tug and barge fleet enables the port to use intensively many reaches of the tidal Thames and helps to siphon off to riverside wharves the causes of congestion—the simultaneous arrival within a dock quay length of only 700 feet of fifteen thousand tons of packaged goods for hundreds of different destinations. An idea of the tremendous barge traffic within the docks is given in Table 119.

TABLE 119

Number of Barges Entered Inwards at P.L.A. Docks
(Year Ended March 31, 1961)

Dock System			Light	Loaded	Total
London and St. Katharine Docks	...	...	2,781	2,715	5,496
India and Millwall Docks ...	...	... ...	11,300	5,957	17,257
Surrey Commercial Docks	...	... ...	14,356	3,800	18,156
Royal Docks	...	... ...	17,384	9,340	26,724
Tilbury Docks	...	... ...	8,866	3,081	11,947

The Riverside

If the tidal Thames be considered as a west-east diameter across the circular shape of London's continuously built-up area, with an eastward extension beyond the 'circle', it is obvious that different sites along the riverside will have different space relationships with the functional zones of London, in particular with City markets and the industries of Greater London. This is one of the factors producing different patterns of riverside activity. On the tidal Thames there are twenty-eight fixed bridges from London Bridge upstream and these form another differentiating factor since they prevent navigation by high-decked sea-going vessels. Other causes of differences in riverside functions are connected with the physical nature of the sites. Depth of water alongside normally increases downstream, but approaches from the shipping channel are usually easier to maintain on the outside concave bend of a meander. Eastwards the available flood-plain sites widen, though in irregular fashion, with progressively less competition from housing, docks, and industries established before 1914. As one voyages downstream, the relative weighting of all these factors is undergoing subtle changes. At Queenhithe a wharf is right at the centre of the City's waterfront, close to the City commodity markets at a central point for distribution, but there are only fourteen feet of water alongside at high tide and the barge beds dry out completely at low tide (see frontispiece). No ships can be received because of the three fixed bridges downstream. At the other extreme, 33 miles downstream of London Bridge, there are the oil jetties in Sea Reach stretching out into 42 feet at low water capable of receiving tankers up to 65,000 tons deadweight.[6]

The pattern of activity has been summarized below and in Fig. 101:

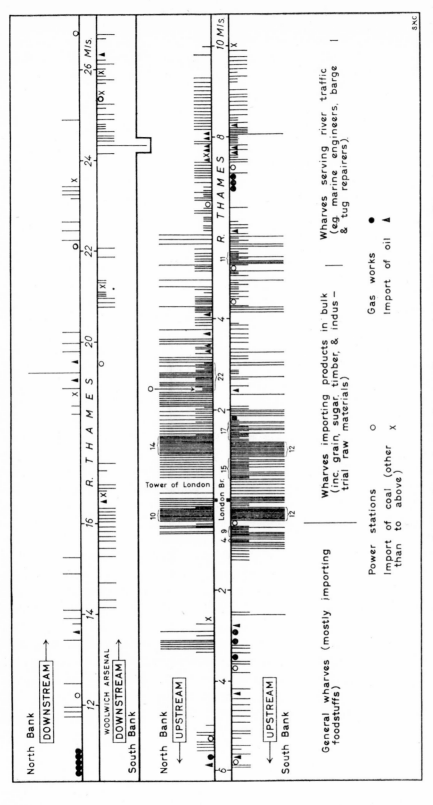

FIG. 101 River Thames Wharves shown Schematically According to Seven Types of Functions

Mileage along the river is measured upstream and downstream of London Bridge. Wharves serving refrigerated premises are classed as general wharves; wharves operated by British Railways are classified as wharves dealing with goods in bulk. Exports are not considered; the only wharves dealing with exports exclusively are those operated by local authorities for the disposal of refuse by barge. The diagram represents wharves with the same function by the same symbol irrespective of great variation in size and capacity for berthing barges and ships.

TABLE 120

Patterns of Thameside Wharves and Jetties

	Location	
	North (or left) Bank	South (or right) Bank
Nature of Pattern	Mileage above London Bridge	
I *The Upper Tidal Thames:* widely spaced bulk* wharves, with wharves serving public utilities	14–2½	7½–2½
II *City Riverfront and Pool of London, with Bankside:* general wharves, with some bulk wharves	¾–bridge	1¼–bridge
	Mileage below London Bridge	
	bridge—2¾	bridge—2
III *The Isle of Dogs Meander:* bulk wharves, with general wharves interspersed	2¾–6¾	2–6¾
IV *Bugsby's and Woolwich Reaches:* bulk wharves, with wharves serving river traffic ...	6¾–10	6¾–10¼
V *Lower Thameside:* widely spaced bulk wharves and wharves serving public utilities, with wide intervals alternately on each bank of the river	10¼–32½	10¼–32½
VI *Sea Reach:* oil discharge, including the Isle of Grain jetties on the River Medway ...	32½–50	32½–50

* 'Bulk' refers to goods landed in bulk (including grain, sugar, timber, fuels, and industrial raw materials); 'general' wharves deal with general cargo in packaged form or as separate parcels (predominantly foodstuffs).

In the account below figures in brackets represent mileage upstream and downstream from London Bridge, on the north or south bank (N or S).[7]

The *Upper Tidal Thames* has sets of wharves serving six gas-works and four serving electricity generating stations, and these public utilities stand out amid the one-storey lay-out of the bulk-handling riverside wharves. Coal is brought by colliers—'flat-irons', of flat profile with telescopic masts and rectractable funnels, or with no funnels at all if diesel-driven. Several wharves receive oil brought by barges or by self-propelled 'flat-iron' tanker, able to penetrate beneath the bridges. West London depots distribute oil over much of south-east England by road tanker. There are other depots for cement and building materials, perhaps a present-day example of using the river as far as possible for a good 'take-off' for inland distribution. There are some riverside industries: milling, chemicals, brewing, distilling, and paint manufacture, although they are hardly continuous enough to warrant description as a zone of manufacturing industry. While railway-operated wharves, and one or two others, export cased goods by barge bound for the docks, the only wharves dealing with exports alone are those operated by borough councils in order to get rid of house refuse by barge, tipped on Hornchurch and Bowers Gifford Marshes

PLATE XXIII   TILBURY DOCKS
Looking north-west, *cf.* Fig. 99.

($14\frac{1}{4}$ N and 35 N). Only one in eight of the riverside properties makes no use of the river at all, and this proportion is about the same all the way down to Woolwich ten miles downstream of London Bridge. But upstream of Westminster there are no public wharfingers dealing with general packaged cargo through multi-storey warehouses.[8]

The *City Riverfront and Pool of London, with Bankside* is where the Thames flows through the heart of London. In Westminster, at the embankments and Houses of Parliament, and at West Bankside (1–$2\frac{1}{2}$ above the Bridge), riverside wharves have been superseded by the functions of government and by thoroughfares. But opposite Fleet Street on the south bank (1 S) there are cold stores, and warehouses for paper brought by road or barge from mills downstream. On the City riverfront there are many multi-storey warehouses built flush with the quayside, handling cargoes very valuable for their weight; many of these require bonded accommodation. The original London Dock and West India Dock warehouses have the distinction of being named in the important warehousing Act of 1803, 43 Geo III c.132 (Sections 1 and 2), Section 10 of which provided for the extension of bonding privileges to other ports. Bonding is a device whereby a merchant enters into a bond that goods placed in H.M. Customs approved warehouses, with private and Crown locks upon them, shall not have the duty paid until the goods are removed for internal use. This practice began with Acts in 1685, and an Act in 1832 gave H.M. Customs wide discretion in appointing sufferance wharves with certain bonded privileges. In British ports this method has been preferred to the erection of foreign-trade zones or free ports. This is because of the number of interests within British ports, which would make it difficult for them all to be fairly represented. A more serious difficulty is that of finding a suitable isolated site where all classes of shipping could be received. The dispersed linear pattern of many of the large British general cargo ports is a disadvantage in this respect.

All kinds of food, including refrigerated and quick-frozen commodities, are imported to these wharves on the river immediately upstream and downstream of London Bridge: furs, rubber, essential oils, vegetable oils, wines and spirits, and beer are some of the cargoes handled. Immediately downstream of London Bridge the wharves are equipped with very long-jibbed cranes. These are able to carry produce to the loop-holes of four- and five-storey warehouses, and they can plumb a barge lying outside a ship, which has sailed to the wharf through the bascules of Tower Bridge. During his lunch-hour the pale-faced London office worker can lean on the downstream parapet of London Bridge and watch Canary Island produce being unloaded to New Fresh Wharf below from vessels up to 500 feet long and delivered to a ten-storey warehouse. Vessels up to 8,000 g.r.t. berth between Tower and London Bridges. On the south bank are the premises of Hay's Wharf stretching from west of London Bridge as far downstream as Tower Bridge.

Port of London Authority

PLATE XXIV THE UPPER POOL OF LONDON

Looking west-north-west upstream. The premises of the Proprietors of Hay's Wharf Ltd. line the far bank from Tower Bridge to beyond the next bridge, London Bridge. Opposite, adjacent to London Bridge, are the white premises of New Fresh Wharf Ltd.; Billingsgate Market; the Custom House, with a river frontage marked by a line of trees; and in the bottom right corner are the Tower of London and the Western Dock, St. Katharine Docks.

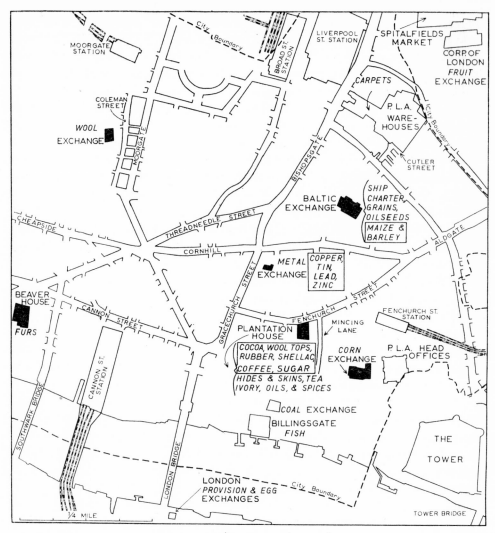

FIG. 102 London Commodity Markets

Markets which are held in private rooms under the auspices of the respective trade associations are shown in solid black. The names of commodities appearing inside a rectangle are those for which a 'futures' market exists.

The history of this firm[9] is an epitome of the three strands that need to be woven together for a successful public wharfinger enterprise. They may be personified in the nineteenth-century wharf owner, John Humphery, who wished to rebuild Hay's Wharf (one of the 1789 Sufferance Wharves, Fig. 89) after the Tooley Street fire of 1861;[10] Hugh Colin Smith, a financier; and Arthur Magniac, a member of a firm of merchant venturers with a fleet of tea clippers. Wharfinger, financier, and merchant styled themselves the Proprietors of Hay's Wharf in 1862 and so successful has the firm been in its century of existence that it operates eight steamer berths between London and Tower Bridges and is able to receive about 20 vessels per week up to 420 feet long, each carrying up to 2,000 tons of cargo, with regular sailings every week from Denmark and the Netherlands. Apart from these direct shipments, all London's Australian and New Zealand dairy produce is handled by this firm brought by barge—with white-painted decking to denote refrigerated cargoes. Four cool and four cold stores are operated, and there is even a large wine and spirit store in cellars formed by the arches supporting London Bridge railway station.[11] Hay's Wharf has thus expanded south of the longitudinal road serving the southern river front, Tooley Street (formerly St. Olave's Street), a counterpart of Thames Street. Practically every large London provision importer has premises in Tooley Street as a tenant of Hay's Wharf, and the London Provision Exchange has the splendid address of No. 1 London Bridge. Similar wharfinger premises are found for two miles downstream of London Bridge on the south side, and a little further on the north bank, because the south bank becomes dominated by timber wharves near the Surrey Docks. South of London Dock the riverside wharfingers, like the extensions of Hay's Wharf, have expanded their premises across the longitudinal road with connections by overhead ways and conveyors. Apart from Stepney Power Station, the only interruption is the Regent's Canal Dock, with its six steamer berths operated by British Transport Docks at the entrance to the canal link from the Pool of London to the Midlands via the Grand Union Canal (Figs. 96 and 106).[12]

The change to the next pattern of riverside wharves around the *Isle of Dogs Meander* (within which the West India and Millwall Docks are sited) is betrayed by the position of the longitudinal road around the meander, further back from the river than High Street, Wapping and Thames Street upstream. The wharves are one-storey, with great piles of sawn hardwood and softwood, some left to season in the open air. Builders' materials storage, and metal stockists are also typical, as are barge-repairers and barge-builders particularly in Blackwall Reach (5–6) where the river is slightly wider for launching. To the river passenger the most notable change from upstream is the low profile of the riverside premises. This is very apparent on a windy day as one emerges from the windbreaks of the multi-storey warehouses on both sides of the Pool.

Between Blackwall and Bugsby's Reaches, Bow Creek, the tidal portion of the River Lee Navigation, enters the Thames (6¾ N). Nearly one-seventh of the £6 million development plan of British Waterways, begun in 1956, has been spent on this navigation. Between the Thames and Enfield the waterway, with mechanized locks, carries some 2 million tons a year, including 750,000 tons of coal, 500,000 tons of bulk liquids, and 750,000 tons of other traffic, in which timber and non-ferrous metals predominate.

In *Bugsby's and Woolwich Reaches* ($6\frac{3}{4}$–$10\frac{1}{4}$) wharves receiving goods in bulk predominate, but unlike the premises with these functions upstream, these wharves serve many riverside factories: sugar refineries; paint, soap, chemicals, and cable works; and flour and oilseed mills. Most wharves are supplied by barge, but of course direct shipment is possible from larger vessels than those which can reach the Pool. Vessels carrying 8,000 tons of raw sugar in bulk can berth alongside the Plaistow Refinery ($7\frac{1}{2}$ N), and vessels with 11,000 tons will in future serve the Thames Refinery, at Silvertown (9 N). Silos capable of holding 80,000 tons of raw sugar are necessary to accommodate the fluctuations in availability of imported raw sugars.

Beyond the entrances to the Royal Docks ($10\frac{1}{4}$ N), a fifth pattern of riverside development is seen. Units served by riverside wharves and jetties are much larger. The biggest gas works, generating stations, and factories are to be found on Lower Thameside ($10\frac{1}{4}$–$32\frac{1}{2}$). One of the first to see the value of this part of the river was Henry Ford. In 1930 he wrote:

'We picked out the Dagenham site because it has water, rail and motor transport, and we can therefore put into it everything that we have learned at the River Rouge [Detroit] about the economic handling of materials.'[13]

The factory (14 N) was built upon 22,000 concrete piles and began working in 1931, with its own wharf, 1,800 feet long, capable of receiving vessels of 10,500 tons deadweight, the largest private wharf on the Thames. It is equipped with two transporter cranes delivering iron ore via a conveyor to the only blast furnace in southern England.[14] From the western end of the same wharf the manufactured iron ore in the form of road vehicles and tractors can be exported direct by ship, or delivered to barges lying inside the wharf. Since 1954 the modernization and expansion programme at Dagenham and associated factories has cost over £140 million, and the target has been the production of 2,500 vehicles *a day*, produced by 55,000 employees.

Other large industries on Lower Thameside include paper mills and cement works. The great newsprint mill at Northfleet ($25\frac{1}{4}$ S) is a counterpart in its national situation to the mill on the Manchester Ship Canal. Cement works quarry the Chalk adjacent to tide-water on the south bank where the Thames bites into the dip-foot zone of the North Downs (21–$24\frac{1}{2}$ S); and they have been established also on the north bank adjacent to the Purfleet Chalk inlier (20–$23\frac{1}{2}$ N). One-third of Britain's cement is produced on the banks of the Thames and its tributaries the Medway and the Swale (confluence with the Thames, 44 S). Industrial estates at Dagenham Dock ($13\frac{3}{4}$ N)[15] and West Thurrock (22 N) have fostered industrial development on Thameside marshes by firms unable to face all the capital charges of consolidating the land, providing primary services, building a factory, and providing a jetty. In 1952 the author wrote:

'Such a migration of industry downstream appears as a recent systematic development of general cargo ports situated at estuary heads . . . it must be remembered that in any evolution of this kind Greater London is likely to show the first and more remarkable symptoms because it is the largest among general cargo ports and possesses the greatest population. . . . [This will] enable the Thames marshes . . . to play an increasingly important role in the nation's economy as the industrial development of Lower Thameside proceeds.'[16]

In the succeeding ten years this trend has continued, and has indeed become even more marked if the oil installations of Sea Reach ($32\frac{1}{2}$–50) are included. The great modernization and expansion programme of the Ford project has been mentioned, doubling production since 1954. Four more large generating stations have been built, and major rebuilding and expansion of the Northfleet newsprint mill has been carried out. Planning authority has been given for the working of the greater part of the reserves of Chalk and clay stated by the cement industry to be required for the securing of its future operations.[17] A fertilizer factory at Stanford-le-Hope (32 N) and a phosphoric acid plant at Mucking ($31\frac{3}{4}$ N) must be added. There is the increased oil storage and gas-freeing plant at Purfleet, where tankers of 32,000 tons deadweight can also discharge oil and other bulk liquids ($19\frac{1}{2}$ N), just below the upstream limit for petroleum unloading by sea-going tankers at Crayford Ness (18 S).[18] There remains plenty of room, with, however, one disadvantage. Industries employing very large numbers would create heavy demands for housing in the eastern part of London's Green Belt, through which the Lower Thames flows. But available industrial sites are large, up to a mile wide—even $1\frac{1}{2}$ miles wide—on the marshes of a former flood-plain, with water supply augmented from the new Essex Hanningfield Reservoir or from wells in the Kentish Chalk. The river disposes of effluent and provides an approach channel with 27–30 feet depths at low water. In view of the strategic situation of this area relative to the European Common Market, and with the dramatic improvement in communications (the opening of the Dartford–Purfleet tunnel in 1963), the Board of Trade in issuing Industrial Development Certificates is looking carefully for the right developments. Lower Thameside can supply wide tide-water sites for more very big industries: further oil refineries, steel works (with a large supply of scrap close at hand), petro-chemicals (plastics), all with vast markets on either side of the southern North Sea for immediate customers. Developments will come from industries vitally dependent on tide-water, or large-scale, requiring wide sites, with a high capital investment per employee. Other areas of the country where similar developments are taking place are: Southampton Water, Belfast

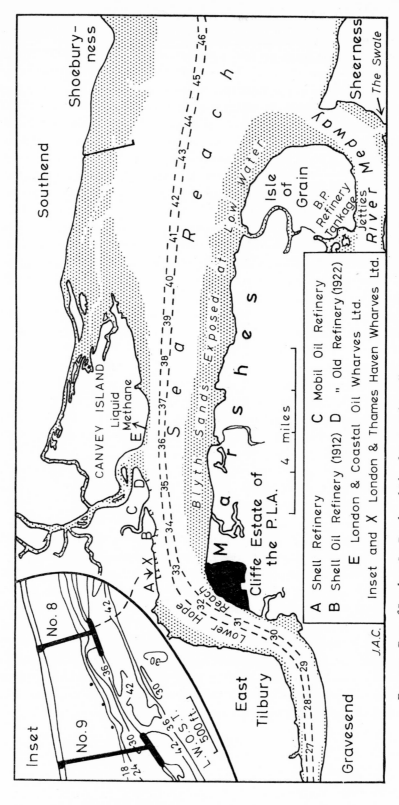

FIG. 103 Port of London: Sea Reach and Isle of Grain Oil Installations: Inset—Deep-water Jetties at Thameshaven.

The pockets of deep water shown on the inset, over 40 feet L.W.O.S.T., are believed to have been formed by vessels of the nineteenth century grabbing ballast. Alternatively, they may be due to helical eddies of the ebb—or flood—streams on a concave shore, *cf.* the 'holes' opposite Blackwall Point, in 1832 (Fig. 92).

Lough, Bristol's Severnside, Tees-side, and north and south Humberside. Lower Thameside with Sea Reach frontages may well prove to have the greatest scope of all (see the empty areas from the Cliffe Estate to Sheerness inclusive on Fig. 103).

In the ten years since 1952 even more spectacular developments have taken place in the Sea Reach oil installations, in which the Isle of Grain sites may be included. The Mobil Oil Company's refinery has been completed ($34\frac{1}{2}$ N), while the Shell refinery has been expanded, adding an associated petro-chemicals plant producing ammonia ($32\frac{1}{2}$ N). Tankers of up to 60,000 tons deadweight berth at one of the two deep-water jetties of the London and Thames Haven Oil Wharves Ltd. (33 N— Fig. 103, inset), who claim to be the largest public oil wharfingers in the world, with premises covering 400 acres of former estuarine marshland. From 1964 ships will discharge liquid petroleum gases at a terminal on Canvey Island ($36\frac{1}{2}$ N).[19] Two vessels carrying liquid methane from the Sahara can account for one-tenth of the country's gas requirements via an 18-inch pipeline from Canvey. On the opposite shore the second stage of development at the British Petroleum Kent Refinery on the Isle of Grain has been completed (opposite 44 S). The reason for this development on the southern side of the Isle of Grain, actually fronting on the River Medway, is the presence of the Blyth Sands on the southern side of Sea Reach. This area should not be written off; it may be possible to provide 'island jetties' on the edge of Blyth Sands connected to the shore by pipeline or conveyor. Another project is an island oil terminal in the Queen's Channel of the Outer Estuary. In any case, the Cliffe Estate of the P.L.A. at Lower Hope Point (32 S) is close to tide-water. And the consolidation of this area of marshland will be accelerated if the P.L.A's programme of pumping dredgings ashore takes place on the Cliffe marshes during the next decade.

Trade of the Port of London

The cross-section of trade in the docks and the river revealed in Tables 121 and 122 points to the range of London's commerce. Only the bulk loading into ships of raw materials and fuel is missing. For imports London appears as the first port for most items of food; and the exports comprise products of factories in all parts of Britain. A quick sidelight on this vast import traffic may be gained by noting the main commodities where London does not lead or where the traffic is shared with other ports of almost equal ranking. Much raw wool goes to the northern mills via Liverpool and Hull instead of by coaster to Goole, transhipped at London; but the importance of the London wool sales for the continental buyer remains. Liverpool is the chief port for imported raw rubber, and is almost as important as London for imported grain. Liverpool and Bristol normally exceed London in tobacco imports;

and London and Liverpool dominate the vegetable oil trade between them. London is poorly represented in the trades of imported tin and cotton.

The heaviest import into London is not recorded in the table below since it arrives coastwise—sea coal.[20] Much of this historic trade, dating from the thirteenth century is now carried on by the fleets of colliers belonging to the Central Electricity Generating Board (with additional chartered vessels), the North Thames Gas Board,

TABLE 121

Thirty Most Valuable Foreign Trade Imports into London (incl. Leigh, Queenborough, and Rochford), 1960

	Value £ Million
Crude Petroleum	127·2
Tea	92·8
Chilled or Frozen Beef	56·6
Butter	55·8
Chilled or Frozen Lamb	47·1
Bacon	39·3
Sawn Softwood	37·7
Raw Wool	37·5
Unrefined Sugar	36·7
Wood Pulp	35·9
Uncoated Iron and Steel Plates and Sheets ...	29·1
Unwrought Copper	27·9
Wheat	27·2
Raw Rubber	23·7
Motor Spirit	20·6
Newsprint	19·0
Plywood	18·2
Cheese	17·1
Organic Chemicals	13·9
Plastics	12·8
Wine	12·7
Sawn Timber (not Coniferous)	12·4
Fuel Oil	12·3
Undressed Fur Skins	12·1
Canned Beef	12·0
Gas Oil	11·1
Unmanufactured Tobacco	10·6
Canned Salmon	10·4
Coffee	9·3
Maize	9·2
Total of all Imports ...	1,523·4

(35·3 per cent of total U.K. imports by value)

TABLE 122

Thirty Most Valuable Foreign Trade Exports from London (incl. Leigh, Queenborough, and Rochford), 1960

	Value £ Million
Cars	122·2
Road Vehicle Chassis	51·1
Road Vehicle Parts	45·8
Tractors	37·5
Commercial Vehicles	23·7
Valves and Cathode Ray Tubes	19·7
Printed Matter	17·4
Copper and Copper Alloys	17·1
Iron and Steel Tubes and Pipes	16·0
Refined Sugar	15·9
Plastics	15·5
Internal Combustion Engines (for road vehicles)	14·8
Gas Oil	14·2
Internal Combustion Engines (not for road vehicles or aircraft)	12·3
Drugs (excl. antibiotics)	11·8
Motor Spirit	11·8
Machine Tools	11·6
Aircraft Engines	11·4
Rubber Tyres and Tubes	11·4
Fuel Oil	11·2
Tractor Parts	11·1
Electric Cables	11·1
Lubricating Oil	10·2
Aircraft and Parts	9·5
Whisky	9·3
Textile Machinery	8·9
Telegraphic Apparatus	8·9
Woven Woollen Fabrics	8·8
Office Machinery	8·3
Cigarettes	8·2
Total of all Exports ...	1,212·4

(36·3 per cent of total U.K. exports by value)

TABLE 123

The Collier Fleets of Public Utilities Trading to London

	Down-river Ships	Average Deadweight tonnage	Up-★ river Ships	Average Deadweight tonnage
Central Electricity Generating Board	12	4,276	14	2,648
North Thames Gas Board	9	4,460	10	2,636
South Eastern Gas Board	3	4,208	10	2,814

★ Flat-irons or flatties of low superstructure able to navigate beneath fixed Thames Bridges.

and the South Eastern Gas Board, which together account for about two-thirds of the total, see Table 123.

TABLE 124

Shipments of Coal to London 1956–8 inclusive
Thousand Tons

From		1956	1957	1958
Bristol Channel Ports	...	725	614	351
North-eastern Ports	...	12,932	12,885	11,971
Humber Ports ...	...	3,637	3,568	2,352
East Scotland Ports ...	...	549	758	719
Overseas	...	2,012	1,090	479
Total ...		19,855	18,915	15,872

There are nine gas-works and twenty electric power generating stations on the river. The largest gas-works, at Beckton (11 N), carbonizes an average of 4,500 tons of coal every day, while the largest generating stations burn about 3,000 tons during a winter day, although three of the stations are partially oil-fired and one wholly oil-fired, at Belvedere (15½ S).[21] Coal is also transhipped from 'down-river colliers'

TABLE 125

Fifteen Most Valuable Foreign Trade Exports of Imported
Merchandise from London (incl. Leigh, Queenborough, and
Rochford), 1960

	Value £ Million
Raw Rubber	11·0
Undressed Fur Skins	8·0
Tea	7·2
Raw Wool and Wool Tops	4·5
Bristles and Dried Animal Products (excl. Hair and Skins)	3·5
Copper	1·6
Hand-made Carpets	1·3
Essential Oils and Perfume Materials	·9
Spices	·8
Organic Chemicals	·7
Wine	·7
Undressed Leather	·5
Gums and Resins	·5
Rum	·5
Coffee	·5
Total of all Exports of Imported Merchandise	57·3

(51·2 per cent of total U.K. re-exports by value)

into 200- to 300-ton dumb barges which are towed upstream to public utilities at Brentford (14 N) and Kingston (20 S), above London Bridge.

In the export trade the riverside wharves play a part completely subservient to the docks. A few cargoes are shipped by lighters from riverside wharves to load into a vessel in one of the dock systems; but the dockside berths for export by general cargo liners are the magnets for land traffic. The re-export trade has declined since the growth of shipments against firm orders or indents. Shippers send goods *on consignment* less frequently, and this has contributed to the decline of international produce markets at ports in consuming centres. But several commodities are still influenced by the attraction of London markets, so that certain goods coming into the port are subsequently re-exported, their ownership having changed hands on the floor of a City market (see Table 125).

Many of the items that appear in this list are represented in one of the London Commodity Markets, either in an 'actuals' market, or in a 'futures' market, where buyers and sellers deal in goods which are deliverable at some future date. This is a sensitive form of insurance, helping to reduce price fluctuations and so regulate and encourage trade.[22] To this extent the City markets are linked with the *raison d'être* of the Port of London.

These markets are all sited within a mile of the *primitive* port close to Billingsgate and London Bridge. But the Port of London, which has always been the largest in the kingdom, has now spread far and wide, to every reach of the tidal river. Yet there is no lack of room for port expansion, particularly downstream. Golden opportunities await this national asset, for surely the nearest approach to a river of gold lies in the worth to the nation of the tidal Thames.

REFERENCES

1. For a list see *Report by Docks and Inland Waterways Executive on Review of Trade Harbours, 1948–50*, British Transport Commission, 1951, 37.

2. J. Stow, *A Survey of London, 1603*, 2 vols. edited by C. L. Kingsford, Oxford: Clarendon, 1908, 12, original pagination.

3. *Report from the Committee Appointed to Enquire into the Best Mode of Providing Sufficient Accommodation for the Increased Trade and Shipping of the Port of London*, May 13, 1796, Appendix Ss. 'Craft' has always been used in the Port of London for small vessels plying within the port and now is defined as comprising tugs and barges, *Port of London (Consolidation) Act*, 1920, Section 197. The terms lighter and barge are now synonymous.

4. C. L. Wheble, *The London Lighterage Trade: Its History, Organization, and Economics*, Unpublished thesis, M.Sc.(Econ.), University of London, 1939, 244, reduced to the nearest ten.

5. P. S. Henman, *Lighters and Lighterage with Special Reference to the Port of London*, paper read to the Humberside section of the Institute of Transport, November 19, 1957.

6. The vessel, *Olympic Challenger*, did not however arrive fully loaded.

7. J. Bird, *The Geography of the Port of London*, London: Hutchinson, 1957, 128–57; and *ibid.*, 'Contrasted Scenes in the Port of London', *A Geography of London*, Philip, in press, give more details. For a description of the riverside from London Bridge to the Royal Docks see J. Grosvenor, *The Port of*

London, Staples, 1957, 78–101; and for a riverside tour with legal observations see G. J. D. Tull, *Some Observations from a Legal Point of View about the River Thames in the Port of London*, P.L.A., 1956.

8. There are half a dozen wharves dealing with general cargo in order to by-pass congestion in central London, but they are not public wharfingers with multi-storey warehouses.

9. A. Ellis, *Three Hundred Years on London River: the Hay's Wharf Story 1651–1951*, London: Bodley Head, 1952.

10. 'This calamity is regarded as the greatest peacetime fire since the Fire of London 1666', and as a result the London Wharf and Warehouse Committee was set up by the insurance companies to exercise supervision over all public storage warehouses in the Port of London, J. W. Mills, 'The London Wharf and Warehouse Committee', *P.L.A. Monthly*, 36 (1961), 216–19.

11. The railway tracks and station have to be well above the street so that the trains can cross the river at bridge level.

12. H. Spencer, *London's Canal*, Putnam, 1961.

13. H. Ford and S. Crowther, *Moving Forward*, New York: Doubleday, 1930, 257.

14. H. J. Deane, 'The Jetty Works of the Ford Motor Company at Dagenham', *Minutes of Proceedings of the Institution of Civil Engineers*, 234 (1931–2), 312–56.

15. L. T. C. Rolt, 'Samuel Williams & Sons Ltd. 1855–1955' [Owners of the Dagenham Dock Estate], *A Company's Story in Its Setting*, London: Williams, 1955, 41–86.

16. J. Bird, 'The Industrial Development of Lower Thameside', *Geography*, 37 (1952), 89–96, 96. See also W. M. Spooner, *Geographical Aspects of the Paper and Cement Industries in the Gravesend–Dartford Area of North-west Kent*, Unpublished thesis, M.A., University of London, 1954.

17. A. Coleman, 'Landscape and Planning in Relation to the Cement Industry of Thames-side', *Town Planning Review*, 25 (1954), 216–30, gives the circumstances leading to these decisions.

18. B. E. Cracknell, 'The Lower Thames and Medway Petroleum Industry', *Geography*, 37 (1952), 79–88, gives a concise history of the oil trade.

19. B. E. Cracknell, *Canvey Island*, Leicester: University Press, 1958, gives an historical account of land reclamation in this area.

20. E. Fraser-Stephen, *Two Centuries in the London Coal Trade: the Story of Charringtons*, London, Privately Printed 1952; R. C. Estall, 'The London Coal Trade', *Geography*, 43 (1958), 75–85; and R. Smith, *Sea-Coal for London: History of the Coal Factors in the London Market*, London: Longmans, 1961.

21. For a national summary of power generation see J. R. James, S. F. Scott, and E. C. Willatts, 'Land Use and the Changing Power Industry in England and Wales', *Geographical Journal*, 127 (1961), 287–309.

22. B. S. Yamey, 'Futures Trading in Cocoa, Rubber and Wool Tops', *The Three Banks Review*, 23 (1954), 28–41; *ibid.*, 'The Metal Exchange', *The Three Banks Review*, 30 (1956), 21–39; and *Exchanges and Commodity Markets*, Swiss Bank Corporation, 1955.

FURTHER REFERENCES

[The] *Book of the City*, edited by Ian Norrie. London: High Hill 1961.

Commercial Guide to the River Thames (Directory of Wharves and Shipping Services). London: Pyramid Press, current issue.

Ferris, P. *The City*. London: Gollancz, 1960.

Hobson, Sir Oscar. *How the City Works*. News Chronicle: 1955.

London Wharves and Docks [Directory]. London: Temple Press, 1954.

Port of London Guide. London: Wheatland Journals, current issue.

[*The Times*] *Port of London Supplement*, March 16, 1959.

River Thames Wharf Directory. London: Gaselee, 1954.

Taylor, C. P. 'Deep-water Jetty at Bevan's Cement Works, Northfleet', *Minutes and Proceedings of the Institution of Civil Engineers*, 226 (1927–8), 290–341.

Williamson, J. 'Jetty and Pump-House Works at Barking Power Station', *Ibid.*, 135–52.

CONCLUSION

Chapter 18

THE PORTS IN PERSPECTIVE

IN SUMMING up this survey of major British seaports several propositions will be put forward each followed by some paragraphs of explanation leading to the next proposition. Those who may read this chapter in the distant future will have the opportunity of comparing actual developments at British ports with some of the points made here. But since the discussion is organized under the heads of separate premises, one is tempted to hope that the failure of one bulkhead will not necessarily sink the whole ship.[1]

Port Hinterlands[2]

There is no general pattern of exclusive port hinterlands in Great Britain.

Exclusive port hinterlands might be expected in lands of fairly simple economy with only a few products, with compact consuming areas separated by great distances, and with short regular coastlines facing different seas. None of these conditions obtains in Great Britain. There are several other complicating factors. Because of the high cost of a ship's time, the shipowner[3] prefers to call at as few ports as possible, and this, incidentally, has the additional advantage of cutting down the port charges he pays. He is also interested in those ports where there are regular return cargoes. A liner company is usually obliged to have a cargo superintendent's office ashore, and the company will not maintain such shore organizations at more ports than necessary. Liner conferences specify rates between certain ports only and not between all those that are available. Thus a really large vessel will go to a major port relying on inland transport to collect and distribute high-priced cargoes, while low-priced raw materials and bulk fuels can be redistributed by inland waterways and coastwise traffic.[4] In the first years of the St. Lawrence Seaway owners of large ships complained of the necessity of 'hopping from port to port like any coastal steamer' in order to fill their holds. Another attraction at a major port is the large dry dock and shiprepair facilities. All this tends to the conclusion that large ports have an advantage simply because they are large. There is another complication to the hinterland conception. If the return cargo is ideal bottom stowage, such as steel manufactures or tinplate, this may attract a large liner traffic seeking export cargo irrespective of the import hinterland.

The problem of drawing hinterland boundaries might appear simpler if only one type of cargo were considered. For heavy cargoes of low value per unit of weight, the exercise is of little use, since the high cost of land transport results in very restricted hinterlands. For example, steel works using large quantities of imported ore should be as close as possible to iron ore discharging berths. If the cargo is of very high value for its weight, one port may serve the whole kingdom. Eighty per cent

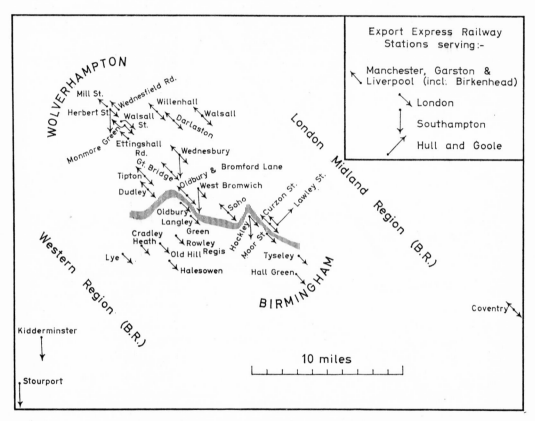

FIG. 104   British Railways Export Express Services in the West Midlands

Wagon-loads of export traffic are assured of next-day arrival at the ports indicated. The boundary (vertical ruling) indicates the southern limit of export express stations serving Manchester and Mersey-side ports *in the West Midlands only*. Among the rest of the total of 330 express services operated, London draws from as far north as Newcastle; and Liverpool is served from as far south as Tilbury on the Thames.

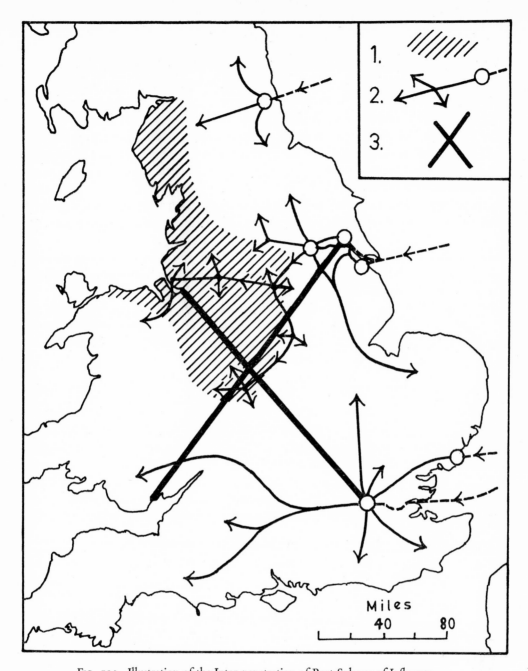

FIG. 105 Illustration of the Inter-penetration of Port Spheres of Influence

1. Area within which there are distribution centres served by importers of fruit at Liverpool, *A Scientific Survey of Merseyside*, edited by W. Smith, Liverpool: University Press, 1953, Fig. 8, p. 11.
2. An 'east-coast commodity'—general directions followed by road transport carrying dairy produce of a large Danish concern, via Newcastle, Humber ports, Harwich, and London (and Leith for all Scotland).
3. Lines joining (a) rough mid-point of the Ports of Liverpool and Manchester (Runcorn) to London; and (b) rough mid-point of Ports of Bristol and South Wales (Cardiff) to rough mid-point of Humber ports (Hull).

Where these lines cross is the centre of greatest competition between British ports due to actual distance.

of the nation's tea enters via London; the attraction of highly skilled sampling and blending and, above all, the nearby City market help to channel the trade. A high-value perishable commodity like bananas might hold out some hope for the hinterland definer. There are only two firms bringing bananas to only six British ports, London, Southampton, Avonmouth, Barry, Garston, and Preston. Since the product is perishable, it might be thought that the hinterlands would be restricted. In practice, this is not so. Ships arrive irregularly, yet continuity of supply has to be arranged nation-wide, and different areas of the country prefer different types of banana. Since no large railway station is more than twenty-four hours distant from any of the six ports, bananas may go from each of the ports to every part of the country, and about seven special banana trains run every day of the year. On the other hand, if the imported commodity comes from Europe (notably Danish dairy produce, and Scandinavian timber), then east coast ports are obviously at an advantage and will have a hinterland that may stretch right across Britain (Fig. 105). This circumstance helps east coast Scottish ports to live alongside the major Scottish port of Glasgow, which for many commodities, imports and exports, is the port for all Scotland, just as the major port of Belfast dominates the trade of Northern Ireland.

In England and Wales, however, there is obviously an area in the Midlands where actual distances are roughly equal to ports on four different estuaries: the Mersey (including the Manchester Ship Canal), the Humber, the Thames, and the Severn. In practice, the choice of port to be used will be made by the shipping or forwarding agent, who may have trading links with a particular port. If an export cargo is for northern Europe, Hull obviously stands a good chance; but if the cargo is for South Africa all actual distances in England may be ignored and Southampton will be chosen. The sailing of the right ship at the right time to the right overseas port is a potent factor cutting across any hinterlands based on actual distances. Some heavy cargoes destined for the Midlands need to travel by inland waterway. And it

---

FIG. 106   Inland Waterways of England and Wales

The classification is that of the *Report of the Committee of Inquiry into Inland Waterways* [the Bowes Committee], H.M.S.O., Cmnd. 486, 1958, Para. 92:

  Class A Canals, 380 miles in length, currently earning a surplus over working expenses;
  Class B Canals, 935 miles in length, mainly narrow canals, are worth restoring to enable the largest craft built for use on them to navigate safely.

The Dee, Nene, Thames, and Warwickshire Avon; and the lower reaches of the Bristol Avon, Trent, and Witham have been shown on the map in the Class B category, though not so included by the Committee. There are also many B class canals on the Birmingham Canal System within the small rectangle placed on the map.

The Class A canals focus on four estuaries serving major ports; while Class B canals focus on the West Midlands (with only one other east–west connection—the Leeds and Liverpool Canal); and the whole forms a St. Andrew's cross, an **X** pattern. Reproduced from a map in the *Report, vide supra*, by permission of the Controller of H.M. Stationery Office.

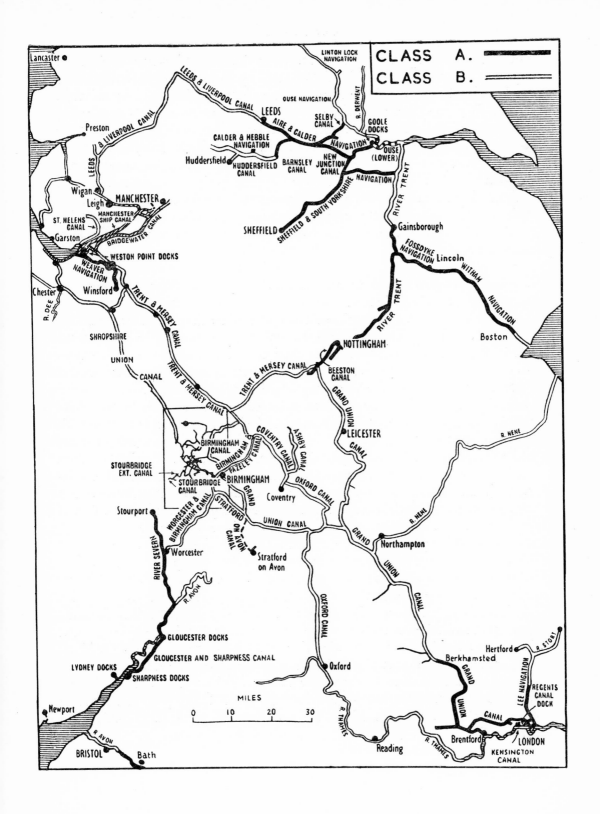

CLASS A.

CLASS B.

Lancaster

Preston

LINTON LOCK
NAVIGATION

LEEDS & LIVERPOOL CANAL

OUSE NAVIGATION

R. DERWENT

LEEDS

AIRE & CALDER

SELBY
CANAL

GOOLE
DOCKS

LEEDS & LIVERPOOL CANAL

CALDER & HEBBLE
NAVIGATION

NAVIGATION

OUSE
(LOWER)

Huddersfield

HUDDERSFIELD
CANAL

BARNSLEY
CANAL

NEW
JUNCTION
CANAL

RIVER TRENT

Wigan

Leigh

MANCHESTER

SHEFFIELD & SOUTH YORKSHIRE NAVIGATION

Gainsborough

ST. HELENS
CANAL

MANCHESTER
SHIP CANAL

SHEFFIELD

FOSSDYKE
NAVIGATION

Lincoln

WITHAM

Garston

BRIDGEWATER CANAL

WEAVER
NAVIGATION

WESTON POINT DOCKS

RIVER TRENT

NAVIGATION

Chester

R. DEE

Winsford

TRENT & MERSEY CANAL

Boston

SHROPSHIRE

UNION

CANAL

TRENT & MERSEY CANAL

TRENT & MERSEY CANAL

NOTTINGHAM

BEESTON
CANAL

GRAND UNION

Leicester

R. NENE

CANAL

BIRMINGHAM
CANAL

COVENTRY CANAL

ASHBY CANAL

STOURBRIDGE
EXT. CANAL

BIRMINGHAM CANAL

FAZELEY CANAL

BIRMINGHAM

GRAND

OXFORD CANAL

Coventry

STOURBRIDGE
CANAL

STRATFORD ON AVON CANAL

UNION CANAL

R. NENE

GRAND

Stourport

WORCESTER & BIRMINGHAM CANAL

Stratford
on Avon

Northampton

UNION

Worcester

RIVER SEVERN

R. AVON

CANAL

GLOUCESTER DOCKS

OXFORD CANAL

Hertford

R. STORT

LYDNEY DOCKS

GLOUCESTER AND SHARPNESS CANAL

Berkhamsted

LEE NAVIGATION

SHARPNESS DOCKS

Oxford

GRAND

REGENTS
CANAL
DOCK

MILES

0   10   20   30

Newport

R. AVON

R. THAMES

UNION

CANAL

LONDON

Brentford

BRISTOL

Bath

Reading

R. THAMES

KENSINGTON
CANAL

is interesting to compare the general St. Andrew's cross (**X**) pattern of the most important inland navigations with the **X** made by drawing straight lines from the rough mid-points of the four above-mentioned estuaries (*cf.* Figs. 105 and 106). Of these four estuaries, two are already occupied by giant ports, while the Humber and Severn seem to offer opportunities for further port developments to render less ill-matched the pairs of east and west coast terminals of the **X**. Humber ports will benefit if European trade increases markedly. On the other coast, if Bristol and Newport were to be administered by one authority, with one set of port charges, further liner traffic might be attracted. Swansea would remain as a large port because of the attraction of its tinplate exports for bottom cargo, while other South Wales ports would continue their tendency to become specialized terminals for local industries.

Complaints of congestion at British ports have mainly referred to delays to the export of manufactured goods brought by road.

As much as 30–35 per cent of export cargoes destined for a vessel arrives on the last day for receiving cargo.[5] The *Third Report of the Ports Efficiency Committee* (H.M.S.O., 1956) recommended more extensive use of rail transport for export cargoes. As a result in November, 1956, British Railways introduced the Export Express Service giving assured next-day arrival at specified ports for wagon-load traffic. This was subsequently extended to cover 10 ports and nearly 330 inland centres.[6] Concentration depots have been established for export consignments which do not make up a full wagon-load. It is significant that five of these seven depots are in the East and West Midlands (Birmingham 3, Stoke 1, Leicester 1). The others are at Manchester (serving Liverpool) and Bristol (serving London and Southampton). This really does reveal the fallacy of the hinterland conception and emphasizes in particular Bristol's difficulty in competing for export cargo. One in every ten of the national total of exporting manufacturers now uses this service, accounting for ten per cent of the total tonnage of British exports. In the East and West Midlands the proportions rise: over two-fifths of the exporting firms use the service in those areas. The Export Express rail traffic is segregated into consignments under one ton, making use of the concentration depots, and into loads over five tons, which are beyond the normal capacity of a standard road lorry. Manufacturing concerns of small size generally use more road transport than large-scale industries. The exporters of iron and steel and of chemicals are on a very large scale; whereas there are very many exporters of such finished goods as woven textiles. The following table illustrates the contrast between road and rail export traffic to Glasgow and Tees-side (exports of large-scale industry) compared with ports concentrating on exports of wide ranges of finished manufactured goods, like London and Liverpool.

TABLE 126

*Export Traffic to Ports by Road and Rail According to Area of Origin, Type
of Consignment, and Receiving Port, 1960*

| | *Proportion of Exports (by weight)* ★ | | |
	Sent by Rail		*Sent by Road*
From Chamber of Commerce Area of:			
Tees-side	84	(21)★	16
Glasgow	62	(19)	38
Manchester	21	(8)	79
West Riding	20	(11)	80
Midlands	17	(10)	83
Iron and Steel Consignments:		(35)	
Under 1 ton	34		66
1–2 tons	—		100
2–5 tons	—		100
Over 5 tons	88		12
Cotton and Piece Goods, Worsted and Piece Goods, Cloth, Lace, etc. Consignments:		(3)	
Under 1 ton	29		71
1–2 tons	6		94
2–5 tons	2		98
Over 5 tons	—		100
Received at:			
Middlesbrough	92	(12)	8
Glasgow	63	(14)	37
Liverpool	34	(18)	66
Birkenhead	31	(12)	69
London	23	(11)	77

★ Total tonnage in the sample used to draw up this table amounted to
about 10 per cent of the national exports; figures in brackets represent a percentage of this sample.

The Development of Major Ports

*Major ports show patterns of lay-out which are comparable in their different stages of devel-
opment during well-defined eras.*

Based on this premise was the idea of comparing actual ports with the hypothetical 'highest common factor' pattern of port development at *Anyport*. There is one
main reason why major ports should show similar features of lay-out, arranged in
many different ways, even if they grew up independently upon widely different sites.
All major ports serve the same world fleet of shipping, or similar cross-sections of
it, with the result that they have the same incentives to provide terminals of similar
dimensions and capacities. Each new era of port development is ushered in by a

growth of shipping trade or a technical innovation in the carriage of goods by sea. The ship designer has a much easier task than the port engineer. The former has merely to create a vessel that will float safely and voyage economically per ton-mile, while the port engineer must cope with all the difficulties of those complicated physical sites where land and water meet. For these reasons the naval architect makes demands which the port engineer struggles to fulfil. The working life of a ship may be no more than 25 years, whereas a large port installation may last, at the very least, four times as long. Moreover, the innovations in ship design can be a reality within twelve months; it may be as much as five or even ten years after the initial decision before a very large port development starts to earn revenue.

'In the case of ports and especially a great tidal port like Liverpool, much expenditure must be devoted to such works as docks and entrances, which are among the strongest and most enduring of man's labours and, therefore, take a considerable time to build and develop. One often feels in such matters balanced on a razor edge between too early a start with a consequent undue burden on the generation concerned or delaying too long with a hindrance to the next generation.' [M. Arnet Robinson, Chairman of the Mersey Docks and Harbour Board, November 24, 1960]

Port installations must be so designed that they can be adapted to ever-changing ship types and methods of cargo-handling.

One of the first to recognize this was Sir Frederick Palmer (1862–1934).[7] He saw the value of long straight quays—*simple lineal quayage*—which he recommended at Calcutta (1906) and London (1910), at which ports he was chief engineer, and also at Southampton (New Docks) and Glasgow (King George V Dock), where he was consultant engineer. A justification of Sir Frederick's foresight in this matter is that the Tilbury Dock Extension to be started in 1963 may well be built largely on the plan he outlined in 1910. Apart from the ability to berth the longest and the shortest liners together at one quay if necessary, Sir Frederick saw the enormous advantage of *simple lineal quayage* that lies in its capability of being constructed in instalments, later stages of the scheme being adapted to later demands of ship designers if the whole work takes many years.

The naval architect is, of course, not altogether free to design as he choses. The bigger his vessel and the larger her draught, the smaller is the number of terminals that can accommodate her. Port approaches cannot be deepened indefinitely; cost of dredging increases approximately in a ratio between the square and cube of the draught. Fortunately, because of the ease of unloading liquid cargo (oil) and its transport by land (pipeline), it has been possible to take oil-discharging berths to deep water wherever that might be, in a formerly isolated ria (Milford Haven), or in a fiord (Loch Long), or even where the tidal range is too great for other complete cargoes to be discharged from large vessels (Tranmere Oil Terminal). A further development may be the discharge of crude oil to artificial islands in British estuaries with submarine pipelines to refineries and depots. Much greater difficulty has been found in berthing the really large grain- and ore-carriers of 40,000 tons deadweight. British grain interests have preferred to extend existing premises rather than build giant silos adjacent to water over 30 feet deep. Heavy quayside equipment is necessary for unloading iron ore, and it is not easy to transport this cargo cheaply on land. These circumstances have rendered impossible the use of light jetty structures in isolated deep-water sites. Since no British port can as yet accommodate the largest ore-carriers, which are most economic between distant terminals, this is a major current defect of British ports (see footnotes 46 and 47, page 233).

The Port of the Future

The port of the future will contain much of the existing lay-out adapted to new uses, and new lay-outs and installations suited to new types of ship and new methods of cargo handling.

For some time ports are likely to continue in an era of *specialized quayage*. One development would be the 'liquefaction' of some dry cargoes so that they could be unloaded and transported on land by pumps and pipes. 'General' cargo becomes specialized cargo when it is put into containers. This would convert the thousands of miscellaneous packages of a ship's manifest into standardized shapes. The container is already a very important feature of coastwise general cargo traffic, which indeed could hardly survive without it. In 1960 the first transatlantic container service from British ports began, and several deep-sea vessels advertise that they will accept such cargo. The transit shed at No. 4 Berth, Royal Victoria Dock, was so designed as to be ready for the development of such traffic across the Atlantic. There are great difficulties involved where general cargo from numerous shippers must be collected for a deep-sea vessel. The problem is to ensure that containers can always be filled and that concentration depots can effectively provide for less-than-container loads. Customs examination of cargo is made more difficult, and this implies an urgent need for sympathetic co-operation by H.M. Customs in the working of new methods. Can the container size be standardized? Who shall own the container? If the container is filled by the shipper away from the port area, how can the shipowner be sure of exactly what cargo he is carrying? Is there a balanced trade or will empty containers pile up at one end of a long route? How can the straight sides of containers be best fitted into the sides of a ship which are curved for seaworthiness and fuel economy? There is a great incentive to solve these problems because the use of containers causes enormous savings in stevedoring costs. The following table was compiled from conditions in 1960, combining data from a variety of sources in the U.S. (not the results of any one company).

TABLE 127

Estimated Cargo Handling Costs (in $1,000) for a Fleet Carrying 675,000 Tons per Year[8]

	Conventional Ship	Container Ship*			
Container Cargo Percentage by Direct Shipment ...　...　...　...　...	0	0	20	50	100
Container Cargo Percentage Filled on Quayside ...　...　...　...　...	0	100	80	50	0
Annual Cargo Handling Costs:					
Stevedoring　...　...　...　...	13,200	1,400	1,400	1,400	1,400
Filling and Emptying Containers on Quayside　...　...　...　...	0	4,300	3,450	2,150	0
Container Handling in Terminals　...	0	80	80	80	80
Claims　...　...　...　...　...	430	0	0	0	0
Total Cargo Handling Costs ...　...	13,630	5,780	4,930	3,630	1,480

* 600 17 ft. × 8 ft. × 8 ft. containers carried.

The cargo-handling costs for a ship carrying all her cargo in containers are estimated to be only one-ninth of those for a conventional vessel.[9] Even if this estimate were 100 per cent over-optimistic, the savings would still be enormous if the traffic could be so organized. The spread of container traffic depends on solving organizational and management problems rather than upon overcoming any technical difficulties of loading, unloading, and transport. But it must be admitted that the more heterogeneous the cargo consignments and the more numerous their destinations, the greater is the organizational problem.

The authors of a paper entitled 'The Port of the Future' wrote:

'In describing the historical development of shipping and ports over the last five centuries in the introduction of this paper, it was the authors' intention to convey the continuum theory of growth. . . . [A] port contains remnants of the past as well as harbingers of the future.'[10]

and they recognized the present use of containers in coastwise traffic as a pointer to the future of deep-sea ports.

Amid all these problems the port authority and its chief engineer must tread a difficult path. At present, a shed some 700 feet long, running parallel to the quayside and some fifty feet from it, served by quayside cranes,[11] is considered suitable for general cargo traffic carried deep-sea.[12] But traffic in containers filled at inland centres might need wide, open storage areas for weatherproof general cargo. In that case, the transit sheds for conventional cargo might be required to be at right-angles to the quay to give room for container stevedoring.[13] It might assist the port of the future if transit sheds could be designed so that they could be moved to a different lay-out without great cost, especially if stern-loading or loading by conveyor through the side-ports of a ship become common.[14]

When planning port extensions it is now necessary to reserve sites that are large enough. Empty sites which are large, relatively flat, and have access to deep water have become extremely precious in the United Kingdom. If a large project is designed to be carried out in working instalments, it can if necessary be modified by future requirements. James Walker realized this principle as long ago as 1830 (pp. 102–3) Undoubtedly, the quays or sea terminals of the future will need much more space adjacent to them than has been provided in the past, not only for large-scale industry but also for the increased mechanical equipment used for the delivery and dispatch of cargoes.

Dock Labour, Port Administration, and Finance

The incidence of strikes should grow less as mechanization of cargo-handling increases, with the decline hastened if it proves possible to place more workers on a permanent basis of employment.

In a world-wide survey C. Kerr and A. Siegel have shown that among workers over the whole range of employment, dock workers share with seamen and miners the greatest propensities for strike action.[15] These authors concluded that these three classes of workers had the following features in common. The labour force is in 'isolated masses', a 'race apart', detached from the employer as well as from the community. The possibility of protest by leaving to take up another job is reduced because these three industries do not in general equip a worker with skills easily transferred into other industries. Thirdly, there is little occupational stratification so that the workers tend to be closely-knit communities where grievances can quickly spread 'horizontally'. Fourthly, the work is often relatively unpleasant and physically demanding, and this encourages the recruitment of tough and forceful workers. The strike-prone industry is therefore one that segregates large numbers of persons who have relatively unpleasant jobs of a similar character. From this it will be seen that increased mechanization of cargo-handling attacks 'strike-proneness' in three ways: it will give workers differential skills causing a stratification within the labour force; these skills will be of use if the worker wishes to transfer to another industry; and mechanization will take much of the physical effort out of dock work. It is significant that men permanently employed at specialized terminals by industrial firms rarely go on strike. Unfortunately, among many dock workers there is still a great fear of unemployment, and this has slowed down the general introduction of mechanical equipment.

The National Dock Labour Scheme, 1947, was a brave attempt to deal with one of the greatest difficulties facing employment of men in ports—the irregularity of the work-load due to seasonal rises and falls and the daily fluctuations due to the irregular arrivals of ships.[16] The Scheme does provide for the employment of men on a weekly basis, but this practice has spread only slowly, so that a joint working-party of employers and unions was set up in September 1961 in an attempt to speed the change-over. It has been asserted that the participation of trade union officials on the Board of Management of the National Dock Labour Board compromises the standing of these leaders in the eyes of the men they represent.[17] 'Unofficial' strikes by dock workers have certainly plagued British ports, particularly London. It is worth noticing that the term 'dock worker' has replaced that of 'docker' in official reports. Unfortunately, the general British public still thinks of the word 'docker' as having pejorative undertones, because there is a general failure to appreciate that as mechanized cargo-handling spreads, more and more dock workers are becoming really skilled men. Instead of learning the job merely by watching others, dock chargemen need to be trained in complicated skills; and the first move in this direction

TABLE 128

Dock Workers[18]

	Census of Average Port Employment in the London area	Number Entered on Register of Dock Workers in the London area	National Total on Register of Dock Workers
1921	34,000[a]	—	—
1924	31,000[a]	—	—
1925	—	55,000[a]	—
1931	26,000[a]	36,000[a]	—
1938	—	43,000[b]	130,000[c]
1949	—	26,798[d]	74,850[d]
1955	—	31,448[d]	80,577[d]
1961	—	27,789[d]	68,660[d]

[a]*New Survey of London Life and Labour*, London: King, 1931, Vol. ii, 399–402.

[b]D. L. Munby, *Industry and Planning in Stepney*, Oxford: University Press, 1951, 316.

[c]A. H. J. Bown, 'Ports and Shipping Turn-Round: Causes of Delay and Suggested Remedies', *The Dock and Harbour Authority*, 33 (1953), 264.

[d]Registered labour force at the last week of the year, National Dock Labour Board Statistical Officer.

was made at Bristol in 1962. The introduction of a dock workers' apprentice scheme would enable the industry to recruit trainee workers under the age of twenty-one.[19] Perhaps the biggest defect of the present port labour position is the fact that at many ports only one shift is worked, with overtime. Many other links in the transport chain work twenty-four hours as a matter of course, and it is surely not unreasonable to expect ports to operate a two-shift system more extensively, even if this requires a great deal of long-term planning.[20] Unions are not likely to throw away their rule-books without substantial inducements. That such a bargain can be worked out is shown by the Pacific Coast Waterfront Agreement, October 18, 1960, in which employers of port labour paid $27½ million for complete labour co-operation in manning new cargo-handling methods during a 5½-year period.[21] Nevertheless, Table 128 shows that British ports have been able to deal with the traffic increases since 1938 using a much smaller registered labour force, with a higher percentage regularly employed.[22]

The authorities administering and operating major British ports need not have uniform constitutions, but they should at least be comparable in style.

Major ports of the United Kingdom are administered by public trusts; a municipality (Bristol); by a company, partly municipal and partly private (Manchester); by a nationalized undertaking (like Humber Ports or Swansea); and by British Railways (Harwich). Some dock authorities are also the conservancy authority for river approaches; others are not. The Clyde Navigation Trust, despite its name, does not control the whole of the Clyde Estuary. These different styles grew up independently to suit local conditions at ports once widely separated, in some cases before the railway network was complete. Even in the last century some ports came to be looked on as a public trust, at which the profit motive should be excluded. The smaller private investor long ago realized the smallness of the dividends to be obtained by investing in dock companies. Large industrial undertakings, however, have invested enormous sums in specialized terminals, for oil refineries and steel works in particular, though in many cases the port authority is charged with maintaining the general approach channels to them.

'My personal leaning is towards getting the users of the facilities to provide them, wherever they have sufficient traffic . . . to keep these facilities reasonably fully employed. . . . So long as ports are run, as I think they should be, as non-profit making concerns . . . [o]nly in this way can we get invested in the port risk capital which is prepared to wait some years for development to mature.' [Viscount Simon, Chairman of the P.L.A. in an address to the Institute of Transport, November 13, 1961]

If the public trust is the right solution for the two largest British ports, it seems fair to argue that a similar style of authority should be introduced at other major ports so that each would be on the same footing in the search for capital and in the bearing of responsibility. Where a major port is based on estuarial approaches, it seems right that the port authority should contain or be amalgamated with the conservancy authority.

Ports should not be considered as entirely outside the realm of state aid.

Port public trusts can borrow from the public only with Government consent and only by means of Port Stock carrying fixed rates of interest. They cannot raise share capital or adjust dividends. Ports would be helped considerably if the assessment basis of Profits Tax were altered (where profits are allowed to be made); or if an increase were granted in the investment allowance for expenditure on dock develop-

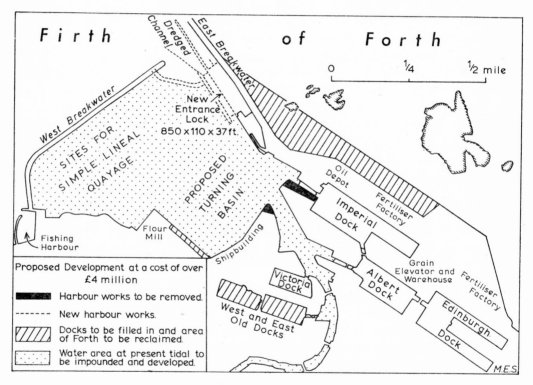

FIG. 107   Finance and Future Development: The Port of Leith

The 1961 plan of the Leith Harbour and Dock Commission would equip the port with *simple lineal quayage*, for the first time, via a lock, 850 feet long, impounding the Western Harbour. This would raise the status of this Scottish east coast port; but the cost is beyond the resources of the Commissioners and would need state financial assistance.

424

ment. The argument for some form of Government assistance is not unreasonable when one considers that the users of ports keep open many of the major port approaches by constant dredging, and thus have created and maintained national assets. At Rotterdam and Hamburg this work is a charge on the national exchequer, and in the United States it is carried out by the army. This is a differential burden added to that carried by many British ports in respect of the need to provide impounded docks because of the higher tidal ranges compared with ranges at ports overseas. The question of capital investment in ports is a national issue. Underdeveloped ports are a severe handicap to exporting industries and do not attract large tide-water plants operated by firms with international share capital.

Port Research—A Standing Committee

Port research involves continuous collection and analysis of data from home and overseas.
Shipowners desire the latest and best ocean terminals, but the port operator will want to know who will pay for the facility. The time has surely gone when a port builds vast new installations in the hope of attracting traffic. Close liaison between shipowners and port authority is necessary to ensure agreement on the design of new berths. But new techniques in port installations are liable to be invented at any of the major ports of the world, and one port authority cannot reasonably be expected to be familiar with all such activities, even with the aid of the excellent journals and international organizations that already exist. The fact that the Rochdale Committee was set up in 1961 to inquire into all aspects of major British ports proves that the industry itself has not been able to maintain the necessary research organization. But when the Rochdale Committee has published its report, port developments will not cease. What is needed is an organization of similar standing to the Rochdale Committee permanently in being,[23] perhaps taking over the following functions (including those of the Ports Efficiency Committee):

(1) To collect data world-wide on port and shipping developments and to set up a port and shipping library.
(2) To investigate all complaints of delays at ports. (For example, since congestion of export traffic is still largely caused by the fact that one-third of export cargo arrives on the last day for cargo reception, a comprehensive survey of exporters' practices seems called for.)
(3) To act as adviser to the Minister of Transport when Parliamentary Bills are deposited seeking powers to extend ports.
(4) To advise on the design of port installations in the light of experience of port developments all over the world.

Such a committee would have a precedent in the Inland Waterways Redevelopment Committee (the Parham Committee),[24] set up as a result of the Bowes Report on Inland Waterways.[25]

It might be argued that ports would resent yet another body interfering with their affairs. But the Rochdale Committee has been welcomed,[26] since it is realized that the Government will pay careful attention to the Committee's findings. If the 'standing Rochdale Committee' were to come into existence, the Government could at once give it importance in the eyes of the port industry by giving full weight to its recommendations. Without continuous research and the stimulus of comparative port studies an individual port authority may play too safe:

'. . . safe decisions may be preferred to bold ones, since a mistake will be evident while the potential results of an opportunity not grasped may never be known.'[27]

The cost of such a research body would be a small price to pay for a contribution towards the increased efficiency of the major seaports of the United Kingdom.

REFERENCES

1. The MS of this book was submitted as evidence to the Committee of Inquiry into the Major Ports of Great Britain, 1962. This chapter, with other material, is summarized in J. Bird, 'British Ports: Some Points for Debate: Present Problems and Future Planning', *The Dock and Harbour Authority*, 43 (1962), 61–5.
2. For the evolution of the English meaning of the word 'hinterland', see *A Glossary of Geographical Terms*, edited by L. D. Stamp, London: Longmans, 1961, 235–6.
3. In practice very often a 'liner conference'. There are about 40 conferences operating from British ports, wherein a number of shipping companies agree on fixed rates between ports within their zone of operations. The contract system is where a shipper sends an agreed number of consignments by the same conference group; and under the deferred rebate system the shipper receives a rebate, up to 10 per cent, after a specified number of shipments. Liner companies defend this practice as eliminating cut-throat competition and enabling them to provide expensive shore organizations and regular sailings by even more expensive ships. There is no inducement to send cargoes by specific lines of the conference, though each line may be restricted to a certain number of sailings per month. As 'common carriers' liner companies must accept all cargo they have room for, and this renders possible regular shipments of vast tonnages of cargoes in very small lots. Liner conferences are now becoming enmeshed with the nationalist desires of newly-independent countries, see 'The Crisis at Sea', *The Times*, January 3 and 4, 1962.
4. P. Ford and D. Bound, *Coastwise Shipping and the Small Port*, Oxford: Blackwell, 1951. Eighty per cent of the cargoes of coastwise shipping is sea coal; see R. C. Estall, 'The London Coal Trade', *Geography*, 43 (1958), 75–85; also H. Rees, 'Coastwise Shipping of the British Isles: Its Structure and Routes', *Modern Transport*, 76 (1955), July–December issues. *The Atlas of Britain*, Oxford University Press, in press, will contain a map showing routes of coastwise shipping in 1960. For the difficulties facing coastwise shipping see *The Guardian*, December 31, 1959.
5. Evidence of the London Chamber of Commerce to the Rochdale Committee, August 4, 1961.
6. British Railways 'Green Arrow' service from any station provides, for a small fee, a transit on the best available service; point-to-point telegrams ensure that the registered wagon is kept under notice

throughout its journey and next-day delivery to ports is achieved in many cases. This part of the text and the table are based on *Transport Services to the United Kingdom Ports: Report of Users' Survey by the Association of British Chambers of Commerce Conducted in Conjunction with the British Transport Commission*, December, 1960.

7. J. Bird, 'Centenary of a Great Port Engineer', *The Guardian*, January 26, 1962.

8. Based on D. C. MacMillan and T. B. Westfall, 'Competitive General Cargo Ships', *The [American] Society of Naval Architects and Marine Engineers*, presented at Annual Meeting, November 18, 1960, Table 10.

9. The cost of the containers would probably be more than offset by the savings in vessel turn-round time, involving less shipping for the same flow of cargo.

10. Paper presented to the International Cargo Handling Coordination Association Technical Conference, New York, 1961, p. 13; G. Chernowitz, P. Engelmann, R. P. Holubowicz, D. C. MacMillan, and D. T. Mallet were contributory authors.

11. A useful summary of the relative merits of ships' gear and quayside cranes is found in E. S. Tooth, 'The Ships' Gear and Quay Cranes Controversy', *The Dock and Harbour Authority*, 39 (1958), 77–80.

12. This is the lay-out at No. 4 Berth, Royal Victoria Dock, opened 1960. R. F. Biddle, 'Port Facilities and their Operation at Southampton', *The Dock and Harbour Authority*, 28 (1947), 27–8, comes to similar conclusions.

13. Interesting points about containers and British ports are to be found in S. A. Finnis, 'The Handling of Freight Traffic Between Ship and Shore', *The Dock and Harbour Authority*, 41 (1960), 252–5, and editorial notes, *ibid.*, 247–8.

14. The passenger liner *Canberra* is equipped with a cargo transporter operating through side ports.

15. 'The Interindustry Propensity to Strike—an International Comparison', *Industrial Conflict*, A. Kornhauser, R. Dubin, A. M. Ross, eds. New York: McGraw-Hill, 1954, 189–212; see also A. M. Ross and P. T. Hartman, *Changing Patterns of Industrial Conflict*, New York: Wiley, 1960.

16. *The Dock Workers (Regulation of Employment) Order* (S.R. & O. 1189), 1947. For a concise history of port labour in the United Kingdom see A. H. J. Bown, C. A. Dove, and E. S. Tooth, *Port Administration and Operation*, London: Chapman and Hall, 1960, Chapter VII.

17. Evidence of the London Chamber of Commerce to the Rochdale Committee, August 4, 1961.

18. For the distinction between 'dock worker' and other trades and professions in the docks see A. H. J. Bown, C. A. Dove, and E. S. Tooth, *op. cit.*, 249–50. Inclusion of all such workers in the table would about double the figures.

19. Evidence of the Association of British Chambers of Commerce to the Rochdale Committee, November 20, 1961. Pilot training of dock workers at London and Liverpool began in 1962.

20. The difficulties are set out in 'United Kingdom Ports and Shift Working', *The Dock and Harbour Authority*, 39 (1958), 45–7; but the author concludes that despite a great rise in labour and maintenance costs these would be less than the cost of keeping a ship idle in port.

21. W. L. Horvitz and P. Lancaster, *Pacific Coast Waterfront Mechanization and Modernization: the Collective Bargaining Approach*, paper read at the Conference of the International Cargo Handling Coordination Association, New York, September 1961.

22. For a brief summary of this point see K. G. J. C. Knowles, *Strikes—a Study in Industrial Conflict*, Oxford: Blackwell, 1954, 174–6.

23. In evidence to the Rochdale Committee, the U.K. National Committee of the International Cargo Handling Coordination Association went even further and proposed a National Port Planning Authority drawing resources where necessary from the Exchequer, and similar views were expressed by the Federation of British Industries and by the British Shippers' Council.

24. Cmnd. 676, H.M.S.O., 1959.

25. Cmnd. 486, H.M.S.O., 1958.

26. Indeed the River Wear Commissioners complained of the omission of Sunderland from the Rochdale inquiry. This part was, however, briefly considered in the *Report*.

27. D. Morse, Director-General of the I.L.O. at June 1961 Conference on the management of large-scale industries.

SELECTED FURTHER REFERENCES PUBLISHED
SINCE 1953

Appendices to the *Bulletin* of the Permanent International Association of Navigation Congresses contain a Bibliography on Port and Shipping Subjects, begun [for a trial period] January 1961, arranged under the following main headings: 1, General Information; 2, Basic and Applied Sciences; 3, Natural Aspects of Waters; 4, Technical Aspects of Waters; 5, Waterways and Harbours; 6, Construction, Execution, and Maintenance; 7, Transport; 8, Water Transport; 9, Miscellaneous.

Baudez, L. *Economie portuaire.* Antwerp: Lloyd Anversois, 1961.

Bown, A. H. J. *Port Economics.* London: Dock and Harbour Authority, 1953.

Bremen World Shipping Yearbook. (G. A. Theel Author and Editor). Bremen: Institute for Shipping Research. [Various editions, contains a bibliography and an international list of periodicals.]

Camu, P. 'Notes on Port Studies', *The Canadian Geographer,* 6 (1955), 51–9.

Cargo Handling. Monthly.

Celerier, P. *Les ports maritimes.* Paris: Presse Universitaires, 1957.

Course, A. G. and R. B. Oram, *Glossary of Cargo Handling Terms.* London: Brown, Son, and Ferguson, 1961.

Dock and Harbour Authority [The]. Monthly.

Fugl-Meyer, H. *The Modern Port: Its Facilities and Cargo Handling Problems.* Copenhagen: Danish Technical Press, 1955.

Hammond, R. *Introduction to Dock and Harbour Engineering.* London: Nelson, 1958.

Journal of Commerce and Shipping Gazette. Liverpool. Daily.

Lloyd's List and Shipping Gazette. Daily.

Morgan, F. W. *Ports and Harbours.* 2nd ed. London: Hutchinson, 1958 [with references and bibliography].

Port Dues and Charges Throughout the World. London: Philip. [Current Edition.]

Port of London Authority Monthly. [*P.L.A. Monthly.*]

Ports of the World. (ed. D. Maxwell.) London: Shipping World. [Directory] Yearly.

Report by the British National Committee of the Permanent International Association of Navigational Congresses. 'Depths to be Provided in Seaport Entrance Channels and Berths'. Excerpt from *Bulletin* 42 (1955).

Report of the Committee of Inquiry into the Major Ports of Great Britain. [The Rochdale Committee] London: H.M.S.O., Cmnd. 1824, 1962.

Svendsen, A. S. *Sea Transport and Shipping Economics.* Bremen: Institute for Shipping Research, 1958 [with references and bibliography].

Syren [The] *and Shipping.* Weekly.

Thorburn, T. *Supply and Demand of Water Transport.* Stockholm: Business Research Institute.

Tooth, E. S. *Some Modern Trends in Cargo Handling.* Port of London Authority, 1955.

Transport and Communications Review (1948–55). Department of Economic Affairs, United Nations World Bibliography of Ports, beginning with Europe III (1950), 68–81.

Weigend, G. C. 'Some Elements in the Study of Port Geography', *Geographical Review,* 48 (1958), 185–200.

World Ports. Washington. Monthly.

APPENDIX

REPORT OF THE COMMITTEE OF INQUIRY INTO THE MAJOR PORTS OF GREAT BRITAIN [THE ROCHDALE COMMITTEE]: SUMMARY OF MAIN CONCLUSIONS

This *Report*⋆ was published on September 26, 1962. The following is an extract entitled 'Summary of Main Conclusions', consisting of paras. 630–59:

The Adequacy of the Major Ports

630.   There is a lack of comprehensive statistical information about the port industry.

(Chapter 1)

631.   A large measure of concentration of port activities has already taken place. Fifteen major ports handle about 70 per cent. of Britain's imports and exports and their share of coastal traffic is almost as high. The main changes in the transport of goods by sea since before World War II have occurred in the field of bulk cargoes. There has been a steep decline in coal exports and a large increase in petroleum imports. Competition from air transport has had a significant effect on the proportion of passengers travelling by sea but passenger traffic is not a very important part of the activities of most major ports.

(Chapters 2 and 3)

632.   The growth of population and industry and changes in their location, the increase of trade with the Continent, which joining the Common Market would intensify, continued growth of the size of ships and the possible further decline of coastal shipping are among the factors which will affect the ports in varying degrees in future years. The construction of a Channel link should not have a great effect on the major ports but the influence of changes in technology could be profound.

(Chapter 4)

633.   Britain's major ports have benefited considerably from foresight exercised in the past and they have many achievements to their credit since the end of World War II. Nevertheless, there is excessive obsolescent capacity. In the light of forecasts which suggest that Britain's foreign trade might be doubled by 1980 there is a need for a properly planned programme of port development. This must be accompanied by increased efficiency and productivity. Selected existing major ports can be developed to meet most foreseeable national requirements and, except possibly for the requirements of specialized trades, e.g. oil and ore, there is in general no need to develop completely new ports. The major ports to be developed will be found on the main estuaries which already dominate the country's

⋆ London: H.M.S.O., Cmnd. 1824, 1962. Fifteen ports were selected as major, for various reasons: Bristol, Cardiff, Glasgow, Grangemouth, Hull, Immingham, Leith, Liverpool, London, Manchester, Middlesbrough, Newcastle, Newport, Southampton and Swansea; Belfast, Dover and Harwich are not included, for various reasons, paras. 4–6.

foreign trade. Within these main estuaries there is a need to concentrate ownership and operation of port and related undertakings. (Chapter 5)

Port Control, Organization and Management

634. The operating of ports is a complex business but there are often too many different authorities and employers in port areas. There is scope for combining port authority, conservancy and pilotage functions in single bodies and for reducing the number of employers. In general, cargo handling should be carried out by a small number of large employers, one of whom should be the port authority itself. The possibility of leasing berths to shipowners and stevedoring companies should be explored. (Chapter 6)

635. There should be changes in the constitutions of independent port trusts so as to extend, where necessary, their permitted activities, improve their financial arrangements and revise the size and composition of their Boards. Regular rates and dues payers should not have majority representation. (Chapter 7)

636. There is a fundamental need for the commercial viability of individual ports to be clearly recognized as the overriding condition of their continued existence. The publicly owned ports have achieved a great deal but there are strong arguments in favour of creating a number of new independent port authorities, generally on an estuarial grouping basis, in which the main British Transport docks and certain existing independent ports should be incorporated. Appropriate scheme-making powers should be vested in the Minister of Transport. An inevitable consequence would be the eventual disappearance of the new British Transport Docks Board. (Chapters 7 and 8)

637. There is no lack of enthusiasm among port authorities' principal officers and their staffs but the time has come to review methods of management and recruitment.
(Chapter 9)

638. It is most important that Customs procedures should be flexible. (Chapter 10)

639. There is an urgent need for some central machinery to co-ordinate and supervise the execution of plans for the development of the docks and harbours of Great Britain on a national basis. A non-operational National Ports Authority should accordingly be established with statutory powers to control capital investment, to exercise a limited supervision over port charges, to prepare schemes for the amalgamation of port undertakings and to promote port efficiency in general. The Authority should be financed, at least in its early years, out of public funds. (Chapter 11)

Finance

640. Ports should be regarded as commercial undertakings. (Chapter 12)
The present financial condition of the major ports is generally unsatisfactory and a comprehensive overhaul of their financial and accounting arrangements is needed. (Chapter 13)

641. The present system of statutory control of certain port charges serves no useful purpose and should be abandoned. In its place a limited supervision of charges should be exercised by the National Ports Authority. Port charges do not at present fully cover

costs assessed on a commercial basis and should be increased. They are unnecessarily complicated and there is room for a considerable degree of simplification and standardization. There is a wide variation in charges made for similar shipments at different British ports and the main near Continental ports (which are generally less expensive than British ports); the reasons for this should be investigated. (Chapter 14)

642. Capital investment by the major ports since the war has been relatively small; there has been an increase in such expenditure since 1949 but with one or two notable exceptions it has been devoted to minor works; work in hand or programmed follows a simliar pattern. (Chapter 15)

643. Government financial assistance for ports would not in general be desirable though there may be cases where Government loans, at normal interest rates, would be justified and a very limited number of cases where entirely exceptional circumstances would justify Government grants. It is not desirable that the Government should undertake the cost of dredging or conservancy work at ports. Ports should be subject to the same taxation and rating arrangements as industry generally and there is no justification for special reliefs; the basis of assessment for rates should, however, be reviewed. (Chapter 16)

644. Port authorities' arrangements for management accounting should be improved. (Chapter 17)

Access, Working Space and Local Planning

645. The seaward approaches to ports must be maintained at a high level of efficiency. Port authorities should seek to reduce the cost of dredging by all possible means. (Chapter 18)

646. In planning for the construction or improvement of docks, quays, sheds, handling facilities and internal transport services, port authorities should take a long-term view of the trend of port and shipping developments. (Chapter 19)

647. The inland transport system is a critical factor in port efficiency. The history of recent years has been dominated by the shift from rail to road transport. Arrangements for the delivery of exports to, and the collection of imports from, the docks must be improved. Road improvement schemes involving the main ports on the major estuaries should be given special consideration on grounds of national importance. (Chapter 20)

648. There should be full co-operation between local planning authorities, port authorities, the responsible Government Departments and the National Ports Authority to ensure that the best possible use can be made of sites with port potential. (Chapter 21)

Plant and Equipment

649. A good deal of progress has been made in recent years but there is still room for improvement in the mechanization of general cargo handling. The cost of introducing modern equipment should be more than counter-balanced by its consequential advantages. (Chapter 22)

650. It is vital that British ports should keep abreast of the latest developments in cargo-handling, especially containers. A wide-ranging programme of research and development is needed and a Port Industry Research Association should be established. This Association should be financed mainly by a levy on the industry. (Chapter 23)

651. There is a serious lack of facilities for dealing with heavy indivisible loads at some major ports and the problem of providing additional facilities and of meeting their cost should be studied. (Chapter 24)

Port Labour

652. The only practical approach to the solution of the problem of dock labour is de-casualization within the context of the Dock Labour Scheme. The general principles laid down as a basis for decasualization by the National Joint Council for the Port Transport Industry are sound. It must be accompanied by a reduction in the number of port employers, by increased flexibility in the deployment of labour and by greater use of mechanical aids (Chapters 25–27)

653. Useful progress has been made with the provision of training schemes and amenities for dock workers but further progress is needed. The age structure of the industry should be gradually improved. (Chapter 28)

Important Trades

654. There should be no difficulty in providing adequate terminal facilities for the import of petroleum in the foreseeable future. The industry itself, in co-operation with the port authorities and the National Ports Authority, can be relied on to expand existing terminals and develop new ones in accordance with its own and the country's needs. (Chapter 29)

655. Most British ore ports do not cater economically for the iron and steel industry's import requirements, which are likely to increase in the future. A suitable development programme must be undertaken. Ore terminal development should in the main be financed and undertaken by the steel industry itself. (Chapter 30)

656. The limitations of many major ports prevent large grain-carriers from being used and other difficulties lead to relatively high discharge costs and low discharge speeds. Principal grain ports should be improved where appropriate to accommodate large grain-carrying ships and the efficiency of grain handling should be increased by the improvement of unloading facilities and by steps to speed the movement of grain through ports' storage facilities. The cost of port improvements carried out for the benefit of the grain trade should be met directly or indirectly by the trade itself. (Chapter 31)

657. The timber trade is important and complex. The seasonal nature of the trade and the difficulties of handling timber present problems which need to be studied. The timber trade itself might assume responsibility for operating timber berths in the main timber ports. (Chapter 32)

658. The volume of coal passing through British ports has decreased greatly in recent decades but it is still an important cargo, especially for some ports. It is important that coal

handling machinery should be kept up-to-date at those ports which still have a considerable coal trade. Arrangements might be considered for enabling the National Coal Board to lease and operate berths at coal ports. (Chapter 33)

Reorganization and Development of Ports

659. Schemes for the amalgamation of port and related undertakings should be implemented in most of the main estuaries of Britain. An early start on suitable schemes for providing additional deep water dry cargo berths is essential. The cost will not be prohibitive and will be spread over several years. Highest priority should be given to development on the Thames and at Southampton. (Chapters 34–44)

The *Report* is concluded by a SUMMARY OF 141 RECOMMENDATIONS (arranged as paras. 660 and 661) and by 14 appendices.

INDEX

Major references are indicated by bold–face numerals; *n*. refers to the number of a footnote reference. Details of such footnote references are included only when the items in question are not indexed where the footnote numbers occur in the text.

Note: names of shipping lines, industrial firms, *etc.*, are often abbreviated.

434

438